Lecture Notes in Artificial Intelligence (LNAI)

Lecture Notes in Artificial Intelligence

Subseries of Lecture Notes in Computer Science
Edited by J. Siekmann

Lecture Notes in Computer Science

Edited by G. Goos and J. Hartmanis

Editorial

Artificial Intelligence has become a major discipline under the roof of Computer Science. This is also reflected by a growing number of titles devoted to this fast developing field to be published in our Lecture Notes in Computer Science. To make these volumes immediately visible we have decided to distinguish them by a special cover as Lecture Notes in Artificial Intelligence, constituting a subseries of the Lecture Notes in Computer Science. This subseries is edited by an Editorial Board of experts from all areas of AI, chaired by Jörg Siekmann, who are looking forward to consider further AI monographs and proceedings of high scientific quality for publication.

We hope that the constitution of this subseries will be well accepted by the audience of the Lecture Notes in Computer Science, and we feel confident that the subseries will be recognized as an outstanding opportunity for publication by authors and editors of the AI community.

Editors and publisher

Lecture Notes in
Artificial Intelligence

Edited by J. Siekmann

Subseries of Lecture Notes in Computer Science

475

P. Schroeder-Heister (Ed.)

Extensions of
Logic Programming

International Workshop
Tübingen, FRG, December 8–10, 1989
Proceedings

Springer-Verlag

Berlin Heidelberg New York London
Paris Tokyo Hong Kong Barcelona

Volume Editor

Peter Schroeder-Heister
Seminar für natürlich-sprachliche Systeme, Universität Tübingen
Biesingerstraße 10, W-7400 Tübingen, FRG

CR Subject Classification (1987): I.2.3

ISBN 3-540-53590-X Springer-Verlag Berlin Heidelberg New York
ISBN 0-387-53590-X Springer-Verlag New York Berlin Heidelberg

© Springer-Verlag Berlin Heidelberg 1991
Printed in Germany

Printing and binding: Druckhaus Beltz, Hemsbach/Bergstr.
2145/3140-543210 – Printed on acid-free paper

Preface

This volume contains papers presented at an international workshop on extensions of logic programming, which was held at the Institute for Natural-Language Systems (Seminar für natürlich-sprachliche Systeme SNS) of the University of Tübingen on December 8-10, 1989.

Several recent extensions of definite Horn clause programming, especially those with a proof-theoretic background, have much in common. One common thread is a new emphasis on hypothetical reasoning, which is typically inspired by Gentzen-style sequent or natural deduction systems. This is not only of theoretical significance, but also bears upon computational issues. It was one purpose of the workshop to bring some of these recent developments together.

In concentrating on the proof-theoretic approach, however, other extensions of logic programming (such as constraint logic programming) had regrettably to be omitted, or could only be touched upon.

The papers in this volume are mainly concerned with the theoretical foundations, implementation and/or applications of proof-theoretically motivated extensions of logic programming. Since most of them cover several or all of these areas, they have simply been arranged in alphabetical order.

I would like to thank the authors and reviewers for meeting the deadlines. Special thanks are due to Franz Guenthner for his support. Finally, I would like to thank Jörg Siekmann and Springer-Verlag for the quick decision to accept these proceedings for the Lecture Notes series.

Tübingen, October 1990   Peter Schroeder-Heister

Contents

Logic Programming with Sequent Systems

A Linear Logic Approach

Jean-Marc Andreoli   *Remo Pareschi*

European Computer-Industry Research Center,
Arabellastrasse 17, D-8000 Munich 81, West Germany
jeanmarc@ecrc.de   remo@ecrc.de

Abstract

The computational interest of SLD-resolution comes from its goal oriented strategy. One step of the computation consists in replacing the current goal (deterministically selected within the resolvent) by the body of a Horn clause (non deterministically selected in the program). This leads to a purely sequential computational model, where the whole computation is represented as a sequence of resolvents. We propose here an extension of Prolog in which the program clauses have multiple heads and which, at the same time, processes multiple current goals in parallel. The resulting computational model is well adapted to the implementation of concurrent systems, especially reactive systems where the computation is viewed as a perpetual interaction between the user(s) and the system. The natural framework for the description of our extension of Prolog is Linear Logic. However, we show here that the sequent system of propositional Classical Logic already contains the necessary tools for our purpose, especially the cut rule together with a Cut normalisation theorem. Further normalisation procedures (concerning the structural rules — Contraction, Weakening and Exchange — and directly inspired by Linear Logic) are required in Classical Logic to obtain the operational system that we propose.

1 Introduction

In a computational perspective, a (semi-)decision procedure for a given logic can be used as a theorem prover which yields "yes/no" answers to questions of the form: "is such formula valid?" (or, equivalently, "is such formula inconsistent?"). However, answers of this kind are clearly not enough for practical purposes; indeed, to go from theorem provers to logic programming languages, *how* a query has been solved must also be taken into account.

Take for instance Prolog, which is based on a semi-decision procedure (SLD resolution) for Horn clauses. By staying within this restricted subset of logic, it is possible to feed back information on how a set of formulae has been found inconsistent in terms of a *definite answer substitution* for the variables of one of the formulae (the initial goal). Thus, definite answer substitutions provide a well-defined notion of output of a logic program. On the other hand, the Horn restriction lays heavy bonds on the expressiveness of the language; much research has been lately devoted to finding ways to loosen it, still maintaining an appropriate characterization of the computational semantics of a logic programming language.

Our proposal here is twofold:

(*i*) we propose to replace the notion of answer substitutions with a more general one: *proofs as answers*.

(*ii*) we define a proof-oriented logic programming language which identifies a meaningful subclass of proofs.

The main motivation for point (*i*) comes from the distinction between *transformational* and *reactive* systems [9]. In fact, answer substitutions give us an appropriate operational semantics only for *transformational* logic programming languages like Prolog; that is, languages which, given a certain input, will compute a certain output and then terminate. But an important part in what is going on in the logic programming world is now also played by *concurrent* logic programming languages [11]. These should rather be viewed as *reactive* systems, in that they allow continuous interaction with the environment by exploiting the use of potentially perpetual, user-suspendable/resumable proof processes. Processes of this kind can be naturally identified with objects whose internal state is given by the values of the arguments occurring in their associated predicates (each argument corresponding to a "slot" of the object); thus, concurrent logic programming languages open a path in the direction of object-oriented programming. With such a style of programming, answer substitutions no longer play much of a role; rather, the (user-controlled) proofs themselves are the real output of a concurrent logic program.

Under the light of point (*i*), liberating logic programming from the expressive bonds imposed by Horn logic acquires a different meaning: in fact, now the emphasis is on proofs, and not on substitutions — hence point (*ii*). Therefore, the central question is the following: given the assumptions above, what makes a proof meaningful? Again, the answer is two-fold.

− From the point of view of reactive logic programming systems, we want to maintain the capability of implementing objects with a state as proof processes, but without the artificial restrictions coming from Horn logic syntax. Indeed, we have shown in [3, 2, 4] that the possibility of proving in the same *single* process *multiple* goals, precluded in Horn logic, paves the way to a finer-grained form of concurrency endowed with powerful knowledge-structuring capabilities (in terms of concepts like inheritance, modularity etc.); this enables us to go from simple *object-based* programming to full-fledged *object-oriented* programming as in procedural languages like Simula and Smalltalk, without giving up the declarative reading of programs which is the key feature of logic programming languages.

— On the other hand, from the point of view of transformational logic programming systems, we would like to see the idea of proofs as answers as simply extending that of definite answer substitutions; thus, we want answer substitutions to be extractable from proofs whenever this is needed.

To accomplish these requirements, we recast here logic programming under an entirely proof-theoretic perspective using Gentzen-style sequent systems. Our starting point is going to be full-blown Classical Logic — that is, the non-constructive logic *par excellence*. Our claim is that if we maintain a strictly operational standpoint, identifying the different roles played by hypotheses and conclusions in the course of a proof, then Classical Logic has in itself the full potentialities for a goal-driven style of programming. The key result over which our claim rests is an extended version of the fundamental theorem of proof theory, namely the "Gentzen Hauptsatz".

From a foundational point of view, we take the position that, in spite of its "non-constructivism", Classical Logic is endowed with expressive capabilities which are particularly useful for the reactive style of logic programming; in particular, the possibility of working with multiple conclusions (missing instead in Intuitionistic Logic) is quite handy for a structured representation of logical processes, as mentioned above. On the other hand, the notion of change of state as available in Prolog is not directly adaptable to full-blown Classical Logic; this is connected to the fact that classical reasoning (not different in this from intuitionistic reasoning) views computational resources as being *permanent*, so that once we consume a formula during the computation we still have available an exact copy of it, and the overall state of the proof process remains untouched (this state of affairs is directly reflected in the use of the structural rule of *contraction* in sequent systems for Classical and Intuitionistic Logic). However, we show that each proof satisfying a slight restriction on the form of its hypotheses can be factored out in such a way that a part of it corresponds to the overall allocation of the resources (that is, to the storing, for each formula, of a given number of needed copies), while in the remaining part we actually consume what has been allocated. Within this second half of the proof, it makes sense again to talk of change of state; furthermore, far from being non-constructive, subproofs of this kind lead to an improved notion of algorithm, characterized by a form of "temporary storage" of intermediate values, thus giving more flexibility to programs written in the transformational style of logic programming.

But we also tackle the problem of how all these features can be expressed in the logic itself, rather than being stated at the metalevel. In other words, we address the following questions: can we modify Classical Logic to make the optimal use of hypotheses and conclusions follow from the vocabulary and the inferential machinery of the logic itself? Can we generate directly the proofs of the paragraph above, instead of extracting them as subproofs of other proofs? We show that both these questions can be positively answered by shifting from Classical to Linear Logic [6, 8, 7], a logic specifically conceived to deal not only with truth but also with the complementary notion of "action". Our intent is indeed completely along the line of Girard's proposal to use Linear Logic to give full constructive content to Classical Logic [6].

The paper is organized as follows. Section 2 introduces the notion of proof as answer. Section 3 illustrates the problems involed with proof search algorithms, and shows how a general result from proof theory (the "Gentzen Hauptsatz") can be used to solve some of these problems. Section 4 proposes an extension of Prolog which lifts the restriction to Horn clauses while still keeping tractable. Section 5 shows how Linear Logic can be used as the framework for a fully satisfactory implementation of such an extension. Finally, in Section 6 we briefly summarize the main contents of the paper.

2 Proofs

2.1 Logic and Computation

We start by introducing the notion of proof within Classical Logic. We take all formulae to be into negation normal form (nnf). We shall deal only with propositional formulae; this is enough for the computational purposes we have in view. To begin with, we shall provide a reconstruction of Prolog within propositional logic.

The class, denoted by F, of propositional formulae in nnf is generated from atomic formulae, denoted by X, by the following grammar:

$$F = X \mid X^\perp \mid F \vee F \mid F \wedge F$$

$X^\perp$ denotes the negation of the atom X. $\vee$ and $\wedge$ are logical connectives for, respectively, disjunction and conjunction. The duality operator (borrowed from [6]), which, for all atoms X, produces a dual $X^\perp$, can be extended to the set of all formulae in terms of the following inductive definition:

$$(X^\perp)^\perp = X \qquad (F \vee G)^\perp = F^\perp \wedge G^\perp \qquad (F \wedge G)^\perp = F^\perp \vee G^\perp$$

The duality thus defined is an idempotent operator, i.e. for all formulae F, $F^{\perp\perp} = F$. In fact, $F^\perp$ is equivalent to the negation of F (by application of the De Morgan laws).

The complexity of a formula F is a positive integer $\mu(F)$ inductively defined as follows:

$$\mu(X) = \mu(X^\perp) = 1 \qquad \mu(F \vee G) = \mu(F \wedge G) = 1 + \mu(F) + \mu(G)$$

Notice that $\mu(F^\perp) = \mu(F)$.

A Boolean valuation is a map v from the set of atoms into the Boolean algebra $\{0, 1\}$. It can be inductively extended to the set of all formulae in the usual way:

$$v(X^\perp) = \neg v(X) \qquad v(F \vee G) = v(F) \mathbb{W} v(G) \qquad v(F \wedge G) = v(F) \mathbb{M} v(G)$$

$\neg, \mathbb{W}, \mathbb{M}$ are the Boolean operations for, respectively, negation, disjunction and conjunction. A formula is valid if its truth value is 1 in all Boolean valuations.

Several algorithms are available to decide validity of propositional formulae; for example, the truth table method provides one such decision procedure, yielding "yes/no" answers. But how can we get the more informative kind of answers which are needed for computational purposes? We consider here two solutions to this problem: substitutions as answers, and proofs as answers.

Substitutions as Answers The problem of the validity of a single formula is decidable in propositional logic, since the truth value of a formula in a Boolean valuation depends only on truth values of the finite number of atoms that it contains. This result cannot be extended to the problem of logical consequence. A formula F is a logical consequence of a set of formulae $\mathcal{F}$ if F is true in each Boolean valuation where all the elements of $\mathcal{F}$ are true. If $\mathcal{F}$ is infinite, then logical consequence is undecidable. However, semi-decision procedures are still available.

An infinite object is of no computational use if it cannot be given a finite representation. Therefore, we assume that atoms range over an infinite (free) algebra of terms built from a finite signature of constants and constructors.

Definition 1. Let $\mathcal{V}$ be a set of variables.

- An *open* term is built from $\mathcal{V}$ and the constants and constructors in the signature.
- An *open* formula is built from open terms and logical connectives.

Open terms and formulae supply us with the blueprint to produce an infinity of ground terms and formulae. In fact, with a finite set $\mathcal{E}$ of such open syntactic entities, we can represent the infinite set $[\mathcal{E}]$ of all the ground instances of the elements of $\mathcal{E}$, obtained by consistently replacing, in each of them, each occurrence of a variable with a ground term. Thus, we manipulate variables by substituting ground terms for them; nonetheless we remain within the boundaries of propositional logic, since we do not make use of quantifiers.

A query is here a pair $\langle \mathcal{F}, F \rangle$ where $\mathcal{F}$ is a (finite) set of open formulae and F is an open formula. A definite answer substitution is a ground substitution σ for the variables in F such that $\sigma.F$ is a logical consequence of $[\mathcal{F}]$. Clearly, a definite answer substitution obtained via a semi-decision procedure for logical consequence is much more informative than the simple "yes/no" answer of a decision procedure for validity.

Prolog typically relies on definite answer substitutions by exploiting the method of propositional resolution as a semi-decision procedure for a subclass of formulae — the Horn clauses. A substitution is built incrementally via the various unifications performed at resolution time; once this process is through, the given substitution can be returned as an answer to the query. But the restriction to Horn logic bans all possibilities to express disjunctive or negative information, as in the following example:

$$\langle \{p(a) \vee p(b)\} \; ; \; p(a) \vee p(X) \rangle$$

Notice that, although this query contains a disjunctive formula which Prolog cannot handle, still it can be solved only in terms of the definite answer substitution $X = b$.

Several extensions to Prolog have been proposed to tackle this problem, most of which centered on the idea of substitutions as answers. We ourselves are going to propose yet another one, centered however on the more general notion of proof, so as to encompass both reactive and transformational logic programming.

Proofs as Answers Resolution trees are but a restricted form of proofs. Natural deduction provides a more general form, quite well-suited for the fragment of logic based on conjunction and implication. However, the full system (including disjunction and negation) is less satisfactory (as shown in [8]). Therefore, we prefer to use Gentzen-style sequent systems, which manipulate disjunctions of formulae (the sequents) instead of single formulae. A sequent system similar to the one adopted here is described in detail in [5].

Definition 2. A sequent in Classical Logic is a finite set of formulae.

Let us stress the fact that, with this definition, sequents are sets and not lists (ordered or not); therefore, it does not make sense to talk of multiple occurences of the same formula inside a sequent. This is completely consistent with the disjunctive interpretation given to sequents, since disjunction in Classical Logic is associative, commutative and idempotent. As we shall see later on, shifting from Classical to Linear Logic will precisely imply viewing sequents as multisets rather than as sets — or, in other words, giving up the idempotency of classical disjunction.

Proofs are built from the inference system Σ_c defined in terms of a number of inference figures of the following form:

$$[R] \frac{\vdash E_1 \cdots \vdash E_n}{\vdash E}$$

$[R]$ is just a label, for reference purpose. $E, E_1, \ldots, E_n$ $(n \geq 0)$ are symbolic expressions denoting sequents. E is called the conclusion of the figure while $E_1, \ldots, E_n$ are the premises. The inference figures are split in three groups

– The *Identity* $[I]$ and *Cut* $[\bowtie]$ rules

$$[I] \frac{}{\vdash F, F^\perp} \qquad [\bowtie] \frac{\vdash \Gamma, F \quad \vdash \Delta, F^\perp}{\vdash \Gamma, \Delta}$$

– The *logical* rules

$$[\vee] \frac{\vdash \Gamma, F, G}{\vdash \Gamma, F \vee G} \qquad [\wedge] \frac{\vdash \Gamma, F \quad \vdash \Gamma, G}{\vdash \Gamma, F \wedge G}$$

– The structural rule of *Weakening* $[<]$

$$[<] \frac{\vdash \Gamma}{\vdash \Gamma, F}$$

In the figures above, the letters $\Gamma, \Delta \ldots$ denote sets of formulae, and the letters $F, G, \ldots$ denote single formulae. The union of two sets Γ and Δ is written Γ, Δ, even when they have non-empty intersection.

Beside Weakening, which says that not all the formulae in a sequent need to be used in the course of proving the sequent valid, two other structural rules are normally assumed in sequent systems for Classical Logic: *Contraction* and *Exchange*, which permit, respectively, to use any formula an unbounded number of times and to access formulae regardless of their order. Here, these rules are implicit in the fact that sequents are defined as sets — that is, as unordered collections where multiple occurrences of the same element reduce to single membership of the given element.

Definition 3. A proof is a tree structure obtained by plugging together instances of the inference figures.

Two instances of inference figures can be plugged together whenever the conclusion of the first is the same as one of the premises of the second. The *conclusion* of a proof is the root of the tree. Among the leaves of the tree, we must distinguish between

- *logical axioms*, which are instances of inference figures without premises (e.g. the Identity);
- *proper axioms*, or *hypotheses* of the proof, which are arbitrary sequents.

The depth of a proof Π is a non-negative integer, denoted $\omega(\Pi)$, inductively defined as follows:

- If Π is reduced to a single proper axiom, then

$$\omega(\Pi) = 0$$

- Otherwise, Π has the following form

$$[R] \frac{\overbrace{\bigvee}^{\Pi_1} \vdash \Gamma_1 \quad \cdots \quad \overbrace{\bigvee}^{\Pi_n} \vdash \Gamma_n}{\vdash \Gamma}$$

where $\Pi_1, \ldots, \Pi_n$ $(n \geq 0)$ are proofs. Then

$$\omega(\Pi) = 1 + \max\{\omega(\Pi_k)\}_{k=1\ldots n}$$

Clearly, a proof corresponding to a proper axiom has depth 0 while a proof corresponding to a logical axiom has depth 1. Fig. 1 contains two proofs in Σ_c, one, of depth 3, having as conclusion the empty sequent, and the other, of depth 2, having as conclusion the sequent whose only element is the atom a. The proof trees are pictured as growing up from their roots.

$$[M] \cfrac{[M] \cfrac{[M] \cfrac{\vdash a^\perp \quad \vdash a, b^\perp, c^\perp}{\vdash b^\perp, c^\perp} \quad \vdash b}{\vdash c^\perp} \quad \vdash c}{\vdash}$$

$$[M] \cfrac{\vdash a, (b \land c)^\perp \quad [\land] \cfrac{\vdash b \quad \vdash c}{\vdash b \land c}}{\vdash a}$$

Fig. 1. Two proofs in Σ_c

2.2 Semantic Justification

According to the disjunctive interpretation of the sequents, the truth value of a sequent in a Boolean valuation is taken to be the maximum ($\mathbb{W}$ in the Boolean algebra) of the truth values of its elements. To keep consistent, the empty sequent is given the truth value 0 (false).

Definition 4. Let $\mathcal{H}$ be a set of sequents and Γ be a sequent.

- Γ is a logical consequence of $\mathcal{H}$ if Γ is true in any Boolean valuation where all the elements of $\mathcal{H}$ are true.
- Γ is valid if it is a logical consequence of $\emptyset$.
- Γ derives from $\mathcal{H}$ (in Σ_c) if Γ is the conclusion of a proof (in Σ_c) whose hypotheses all belong to $\mathcal{H}$.
- Γ is derivable (in Σ_c) if it derives from $\emptyset$.

The semantic justification for the inference system Σ_c is given by the following result, of which we omit the lengthy but elementary proof.

Theorem 5. *The inference system Σ_c is sound and complete with respect to the Boolean semantics for Classical Logic.*

In other words, a sequent Γ is a logical consequence of a set of sequents $\mathcal{H}$ if and only if Γ derives (in Σ_c) from $\mathcal{H}$.

2.3 Proof Search

Definition 6. A query is a pair $\langle \mathcal{H}; \Gamma \rangle$ where $\mathcal{H}$ is a set of sequents and Γ is a sequent. An answer to a query $\langle \mathcal{H}; \Gamma \rangle$ is a proof, whose conclusion is Γ and whose hypotheses belong to $\mathcal{H}$.

Theorem 5 in the previous section shows that a query $\langle \mathcal{H}; \Gamma \rangle$ has an answer if and only if Γ is a logical consequence of $\mathcal{H}$. But the system Σ_c provides an effective procedure to compute all the answers to a query. Two kinds of algorithms can be devised, depending on their "orientation":

— forwardchaining algorithms, which, starting from the hypotheses, work their way towards the conclusion.

— backchaining algorithms, which, starting from the conclusion, try to go back to the hypotheses.

The distinction between these two kinds of algorithms may seem stronger than what it really is; for a conclusion can be made into a "distinguished" hypothesis, and thus we may have a forwardchaining algorithm which somehow simulates a backchaining one. This is typically the case with Prolog viewed in terms of resolution. In fact, resolution can be reconstructed from within sequent systems as a forwardchaining algorithm, which aims at reaching the empty sequent as the conclusion. The algorithm proceeds forward by generating, at each step, a new resolvent using the Cut rule between a proper axiom and the current resolvent, and successfully terminates when the empty resolvent is obtained. On the other hand, we can also look at Prolog from a backchaining standpoint, viewing it as a mechanism for building and searching AND-trees; in this case, the root of the tree is given by the initial goal, and the Cut implements backchaining instead of forwardchaining. Indeed, the two proofs in Fig. 1 illustrate these two different ways of looking at Prolog in querying a with respect to the program

```
a :- b, c.
b.
c.
```

The first of such proofs is in the resolution style, while the second one is of the backchaining kind.

In this paper, we focus on the second class of algorithms, since they generalize better to the full use of logical connectives we have in mind. Let us start by formalizing a backchaining procedure as follows. Given a query $\langle \mathcal{H}; \Gamma \rangle$, we incrementally build a proof Π, initially corresponding to a single node labelled with Γ. An open node is a leaf of Π labelled with a proper axiom (hypothesis) which does not belong to $\mathcal{H}$.

Algorithm $\mathcal{A}$
Loop
1. Choose an open node, labelled with a sequent Δ.
2. Choose an instance of an inference figure whose conclusion is Δ.
3. Expand the selected node in Π with the selected inference figure.
End Loop

This algorithm yields a solution whenever Π has no open nodes left. Π itself is then an answer to the query.

3 Logic Programming with Sequent Systems

Algorithm $\mathcal{A}$ can be used as the basis for a programming language based on logic, returning proofs as answers. The choices at steps 1 and 2 can be searched sequentially or in parallel. But, in both cases, we cannot dodge the issue of defining a tractable strategy for these choices. Indeed, the inference system Σ_c contains deep internal symmetries which lead to redundant proofs, and make a blind strategy totally inefficient.

3.1 Proof Search Strategy

Proof Redundancies We have seen in Sec. 2 that the Cut rule [⋈] plays the fundamental role of enacting causal dependencies during the computation: this holds both for forwardchaining and backchaining algorithms — in either case, the Cut rule implements the chaining, whatever its direction may be. But this rule implies two kinds of redundancies in the proofs:

(i) Some combinations of inference figures are purely cyclic:

$$[⋈] \dfrac{[\vee]\dfrac{\overset{\pi}{\widehat{\bigvee}}}{\vdash \Gamma, F, G}}{\vdash \Gamma, F \vee G} \quad [\wedge]\dfrac{[I<]\dfrac{}{\vdash F^\perp, F, G} \quad [I<]\dfrac{}{\vdash G^\perp, F, G}}{\vdash F^\perp \wedge G^\perp, F, G} \equiv \vdash \overset{\pi}{\widehat{\bigvee}} \Gamma, F, G$$

More precisely, we have
- $[I<], [\wedge]$ and $[⋈]$ cancel $[\vee]$
- $[I<], [\vee]$ and $[⋈]$ cancel $[\wedge]$

(ii) Some combinations of inference figures permute:

$$[⋈] \dfrac{[⋈]\dfrac{\vdash \Gamma_1, F \quad \vdash \Gamma_2, F^\perp, G}{\vdash \Gamma_1, \Gamma_2, G} \quad \vdash \Gamma_3, G^\perp}{\vdash \Gamma_1, \Gamma_2, \Gamma_3} \equiv [⋈] \dfrac{\vdash \Gamma_1, F \quad [⋈]\dfrac{\vdash \Gamma_2, F^\perp, G \quad \vdash}{\vdash \Gamma_2, \Gamma_3, F}}{\vdash \Gamma_1, \Gamma_2, \Gamma_3}$$

Thus, applications of the Cut rule can always be permuted. Another important case of permutation, involving only logical rules, will be discussed later on.[1]

Properties (i)-(ii) have two troublesome consequences from a computational point of view:

— because of (i), in searching a proof care must be taken to detect loops triggered off by cyclic combinations of inference figures
— because of (ii), the search strategy must also avoid generating two proofs which are equal up to permutations of inference figures.

Trying to cope with these problems by generating and then filtering out redundant proofs and subproofs seems quite hopeless. In fact, under such an approach, (i) would be handled within algorithm $\mathcal{A}$ by checking, at each step of the computation, whether the current open node is labeled by the same sequent as a

---

[1] For early proof-theoretic results on the problem of permutations of inference rules in sequent systems see also [10].

previous node on the same branch, in which case a loop is detected; this is practically unfeasible, albeit theoretically sound. But, as for (ii), we cannot even achieve theoretical soundness, without heavily committing ourselves to a particular mode of execution of the algorithm: for comparison of two generated proofs is possible only if such proofs are *temporally* generated one after the other, which makes sense within a sequential context, but is instead quite meaningless from the standpoint of parallel processing.

What we want is rather a strategy which relieves us from the burden of producing *all* the answer proofs for the query, under the assumption that generating only a *subclass* of proofs will suffice, since the remaining ones can be obtained from these via certain well-defined transformations. The rest of this paper is devoted to the definition of such transformations. They will be described in terms of a sequence of inference systems, each providing a further degree of computational specialization. For each of them, we give the transformation mapping each proof in Σ_c into an equivalent proof in the specialized system. These systems are more computation-oriented than Σ_c, while still being equivalent to it, and avoid, to a certain extent, the problems of proof redundancies mentioned above.

The Case of the Cut Rule The proof search algorithm $\mathcal{A}$ involves two choices: the choice of an open node to expand, and the choice of an inference figure to apply to it. The first choice can be made in a purely deterministic fashion, since, ultimately, all the open nodes must be expanded. Once this choice is made, of the four possibilities for the second choice the following three are at a certain extent controlled by the sequent Γ labelling the selected node:

- to apply one of the logical rules $[\vee]$, $[\wedge]$, a formula in Γ must be selected as the principal formula
- to apply the Weakening rule $[<]$, a formula must be cancelled from Γ
- to apply the Identity rule $[I]$, Γ must consist of a pair of dual formulae

But in the fourth case, involving an application of the Cut rule $[\bowtie]$, Γ has no control whatsoever: for a Cut can always be made whatever the structure of Γ, and the choice of the cut formula is in no way influenced by Γ.

Thus, the Cut is the culprit for several problems: cycles, permutations and a high degree of non-determinism. To salvage the situation, there is a famous result known as the "Gentzen Hauptsatz", which licences a strong restriction in the use of the Cut rule. In its basic form this theorem states that the Cut rule can be completely eliminated from proof without hypotheses. For proofs containing hypotheses, which is the case here, an extended version of the theorem states that the occurences of the Cut rule can be reduced to a certain normal form. The main idea of this Cut reduction theorem is that Cuts can be *sequentialized*, so that they always occur in a sequence starting from a hypothesis.

3.2 Cut Reduction

Let $\mathcal{H}$ be a set of sequents. The inference system $\Sigma_c[\mathcal{H}]$ contains the same rules as Σ_c except for the Cut, which is replaced by the following normalized Cut rule:

for each sequent Γ in $\mathcal{H}$ let Ω be the set of atoms in Γ and $F_1, \ldots, F_n$ be the other formulae of Γ.

$$[\bowtie] \frac{\{\vdash \Gamma_k, F_k^\perp\}_{k=1\ldots n}}{\vdash \Omega, \Gamma_1, \ldots, \Gamma_n}$$

This rule is but a compact notation for a normalized sequence of binary Cuts starting from the sequent $\Omega, \Gamma_1, \ldots, \Gamma_n$ in $\mathcal{H}$:

$$[\bowtie] \frac{[\bowtie] \cfrac{\vdots}{\cfrac{\vdash \Omega, F_1, \ldots, F_n \qquad \cfrac{\vdots}{\vdash \Gamma_1, F_1^\perp}}{\cfrac{\vdash \Omega, \Gamma_1, F_2, \ldots, F_n}{\cfrac{\ddots}{\vdash \Omega, \Gamma_1, \ldots, \Gamma_{n-1}, F_n}} \qquad \cfrac{\vdots}{\vdash \Gamma_n, F_n^\perp}}}{\vdash \Omega, \Gamma_1, \ldots, \Gamma_n}$$

But the normalized Cut rule contains a further restriction: the cut formulae $F_1, \ldots, F_n$ of the sequence must be exactly *all* the formulae in the initial sequent which are *not* atoms (they may be dual of atoms or complex formulae).

Important remark: the elements of $\mathcal{H}$ are themselves derivable in $\Sigma_c[\mathcal{H}]$ by application of the normalized Cut

$$[\bowtie] \frac{\{[I] \frac{}{\vdash F_k, F_k^\perp}\}_{k=1\ldots n}}{\vdash \Omega, F_1, \ldots, F_n}$$

Henceforth, in the system $\Sigma_c[\mathcal{H}]$, we take proofs to be proofs without proper axioms (hypotheses); in fact each instance of a normalized Cut in $\Sigma_c[\mathcal{H}]$ contains implicitly within itself an hypothesis from $\mathcal{H}$ — in other words, the elements of $\mathcal{H}$ are "hardwired" in the inference figures of $\Sigma_c[\mathcal{H}]$.

Theorem 7 (Cut Reduction). *Let $\mathcal{H}$ be a set of sequents and Γ be a sequent. Γ derives from $\mathcal{H}$ in Σ_c if and only if Γ is derivable in $\Sigma_c[\mathcal{H}]$.*

The soundness of $\Sigma_c[\mathcal{H}]$ is obvious since each occurence of the normalized Cut rule can be replaced by a (reduced) sequence of binary Cuts. To prove completeness, we have only to prove that each binary Cut rule can be eliminated using only the normalized Cut rule. In other words, we have to show that

Proposition. *For any formula R, if Γ, R and $\Delta, R^\perp$ are derivable in $\Sigma_c[\mathcal{H}]$ then so is Γ, Δ.*

Proof. Henceforth, we take derivable to mean derivable in $\Sigma_c[\mathcal{H}]$. Let $\mathcal{R}(m, n)$ be the following predicate for $m, n \geq 0$:

If
- R is a formula of complexity at most m
- Π_1 and Π_2 are proofs (without hypotheses) in $\Sigma_c[\mathcal{H}]$ the conclusions of which are, respectively Γ, R and $\Delta, R^\perp$

− The sum of the depths of Π_1 and Π_2 does not exceed n

Then Γ, Δ is derivable.

We only need to prove $\mathcal{R}(m, n)$ for all m, n, which can be done via double induction.

− If $m = 0$:

No formula has a null complexity. Therefore, $\forall n \; \mathcal{R}(0, n)$ is true.

− If $\forall n \; \mathcal{R}(m, n)$ is true:

Let $\mathcal{R}'(n)$ be the property $\mathcal{R}(m+1, n)$. We only need to prove $\mathcal{R}'(n)$ for all n, i.e. $\forall n \; \mathcal{R}(m+1, n)$. This can be done by induction. Let R be a formula of complexity $m+1$ and Π_1, Π_2 be proofs in $\Sigma_c[\mathcal{H}]$ the conclusion of which are Γ, R and $\Delta, R^{\perp}$.

- If $n = 0$:

    Π_1, Π_2 must contain each at least one inference figure and therefore have non-null depth. Hence $\mathcal{R}'(0)$ is true.

- If $\mathcal{R}'(n)$ is true and the sum of the depths of Π_1 and Π_2 is $n+1$:

    1. If R is in Γ, then $\Gamma = \Gamma, R$ which is derivable by Π_1. By weakening, Γ, Δ is derivable. Henceforth, we assume that $R \notin \Gamma$ and $R^{\perp} \notin \Delta$.

    2. If Π_1 is reduced to the Identity rule $[I]$, then $\Gamma = R^{\perp}$ and $\Gamma, \Delta = \Delta, R^{\perp}$ is derivable by Π_2. Henceforth we assume that neither Π_1 nor Π_2 are the Identity rule.

    3. If Π_1 ends with an instance of Weakening which introduces R

    $$[<] \frac{\vdash \Gamma}{\vdash \Gamma, R}$$

    then Γ is derivable and, by weakening, so is Γ, Δ. Henceforth we assume that neither Π_1 nor Π_2 ends with an instance of Weakening which introduces R or $R^{\perp}$, respectively.

    4. If Π_1 ends with a logical rule or a Weakening inside Γ, for example

    $$\Pi_1 = [\vee] \; \frac{\overbrace{\vdash \Gamma', F, G, R}^{\pi_1'}}{\vdash \Gamma', F \vee G, R}$$

    where $\Gamma = \Gamma', F \vee G$, then Π_1' and Π_2 are two proofs of, respectively, Γ', F, G, R and $\Delta, R^{\perp}$. The sum of their depths cannot exceed n. Since $\mathcal{R}'(n)$ is assumed, Γ', F, G, Δ is derivable, and so is Γ, Δ with the further step

    $$[\vee] \; \frac{\vdash \Gamma', F, G, \Delta}{\vdash \Gamma', F \vee G, \Delta}$$

    Henceforth, we assume that neither Π_1 nor Π_2 ends with a Weakening or a logical rule inside Γ or Δ, respectively. At this point, Π_1, Π_2 may only end with a logical rule on R or $R^{\perp}$, respectively, or with the normalized Cut rule.

5. If R is an atom then $R^\perp$ is atomic, hence Π_2 cannot end with a logical rule on $R^\perp$. Therefore Π_2 ends with the normalized Cut rule and $R^\perp$ is not an atom. This case is symetric to the one considered next.

6. If R is not an atom and Π_1 ends with an instance of the normalized Cut rule

$$\Pi_1 = [\bowtie] \; \frac{\overset{\pi_1^k}{\overset{\bigvee}{\{\vdash \Gamma_k, F_k^\perp\}_{k=1\ldots p}}}}{\vdash \Omega, \Gamma_1, \ldots, \Gamma_p}$$

where $\Gamma, R = \Omega, \Gamma_1, \ldots, \Gamma_p$, and $\Omega, F_1, \ldots, F_p$ is in $\mathcal{H}$, then, for all $k = 1 \ldots p$ let $\Gamma_k' = \Gamma_k \setminus \{R\}$.

(a) If $R \notin \Gamma_k$ then $\Gamma_k' = \Gamma_k$ hence $\Gamma_k', F_k^\perp$ is derivable and, by weakening, so is $\Gamma_k', \Delta, F_k^\perp$.

(b) If $R \in \Gamma_k$ then $\Gamma_k = \Gamma_k', R$. Therefore Π_1^k and Π_2 are two proofs of, respectively, $\Gamma_k', R, F_k^\perp$ and $\Delta, R^\perp$. The sum of their depths cannot exceed n. Since $\mathcal{R}'(n)$ is assumed, $\Gamma_k', \Delta, F_k^\perp$ is derivable.

In both cases, $\Gamma_k', \Delta, F_k^\perp$ is derivable, and so is $\Omega, \Gamma_1', \ldots, \Gamma_p', \Delta$, with the further step

$$[\bowtie] \; \frac{\{\vdash \Gamma_k', \Delta, F_k^\perp\}_{k=1\ldots p}}{\vdash \Omega, \Gamma_1', \ldots, \Gamma_p', \Delta}$$

Since R is not an atom and Ω contains only atoms, R is not in Ω, nor, by construction, in $\Gamma_1', \ldots, \Gamma_p', \Gamma$. Now $\Gamma, R = \Omega, \Gamma_1, \ldots, \Gamma_p = \Omega, \Gamma_1', \ldots, \Gamma_p', R$. Therefore $\Gamma = \Omega, \Gamma_1', \ldots, \Gamma_p'$ and hence, Γ, Δ is derivable.

7. Finally, if Π_1 ends with a logical rule on R, we may symetrically assume that Π_2 ends with a logical rule on $R^\perp$. Let us take, for instance, $R = R_a \vee R_b$. The possible endings for Π_1 are

$$[\vee] \; \frac{\vdash \Gamma, R_a, R_b}{\vdash \Gamma, R} \quad \text{or} \quad [\vee] \; \frac{\vdash \Gamma, R, R_a, R_b}{\vdash \Gamma, R}$$

Similarly, Π_2 may end with

$$[\wedge] \; \frac{\vdash \Gamma, R_a^\perp \quad \vdash \Delta, R_b^\perp}{\vdash \Delta, R^\perp} \quad \text{or} \quad [\wedge] \; \frac{\vdash \Gamma, R^\perp, R_a^\perp \quad \vdash \Delta, R^\perp, R_b^\perp}{\vdash \Delta, R^\perp}$$

Let us consider the following case (the others are similar and even simpler):

$$\Pi_1 = [\vee] \; \frac{\overset{\pi_1'}{\overset{\bigvee}{\vdash \Gamma, R, R_a, R_b}}}{\vdash \Gamma, R} \quad \text{and} \quad \Pi_2 = [\wedge] \; \frac{\overset{\pi_{2a}}{\overset{\bigvee}{\vdash \Delta, R^\perp, R_a^\perp}} \quad \overset{\pi_{2b}}{\overset{\bigvee}{\vdash \Delta, R^\perp, R_b^\perp}}}{\vdash \Delta, R^\perp}$$

Π_1' and Π_2 are two proofs of, respectively, Γ', R_a, R_b, R and $\Delta, R^{\perp}$. The sum of their depth cannot exceed n. Since $\mathcal{R}'(n)$ is assumed, the sequent Γ, R_a, R_b, Δ is derivable. The same reasoning applies to proofs Π_1, Π_{2a} and Π_1, Π_{2b}, therefore the sequents $\Gamma, \Delta, R_a^{\perp}$ and $\Gamma, \Delta, R_b^{\perp}$ are derivable. But R_a and R_b are of complexity at most m. Since $\forall p\, \mathcal{R}(m, p)$ is assumed, Γ, Δ is derivable.

Thus, in all cases, Γ, Δ is derivable. Hence $\mathcal{R}'(n+1)$ is true.

Thus, $\forall n\, \mathcal{R}(m+1, n)$ is true

□

4 Prolog Revisited and Extended

The main insight behind the Cut reduction theorem above is that a proof in a sequent system for full-blown Classical Logic can be decomposed in essentially two parts: one having to do with the use of the logical rules over the formulae being queried, the other concerning the proper axioms involved in the proof — the only place where the Cut plays a part. This feature of Cut-reduced proofs can be usefully exploited by a theorem prover to implement goal-directed search, since the query formulae themselves control the access to the axioms. From this point of view, it is not unreasonable to think of full-blown Classical Logic as of a feasible logic programming language. We want therefore to revisit and then extend Prolog in terms of this fundamental insight provided by the Cut-reduction theorem.

4.1 Standard Prolog

The operational mechanism of standard Prolog can be viewed as the proof search algorithm $\mathcal{A}$ restricted to Cut-reduced proofs and to a certain class of queries (Horn clauses).

Definition 8. A Prolog goal is a formula containing no negative atomic formula. A standard Prolog axiom (i.e. a Prolog program clause) is a sequent of one of the two following forms:

- a rule: $G^{\perp}, X$ also written $X :\text{-} G$ where G is a goal and X is an atom.
- a fact: X where X is an atom.

Let $\mathcal{P}$ be a set of rules. The operational mechanism of standard Prolog can be described in terms of the following inference system, to which we refer as $\Sigma_p[\mathcal{P}]$

- Logical rules

$$[\vee_1]\ \frac{\vdash_p G_1}{\vdash_p G_1 \vee G_2} \qquad [\vee_2]\ \frac{\vdash_p G_2}{\vdash_p G_1 \vee G_2} \qquad [\wedge]\ \frac{\vdash_p G_1 \quad \vdash_p G_2}{\vdash_p G_1 \wedge G_2}$$

– Cut rule (two forms)

$$[\bowtie] \; \frac{\vdash_p G}{\vdash_p X}$$

where $X :\text{-} G$ is a rule in $\mathcal{P}$.

$$[\bowtie] \; \frac{}{\vdash_p X}$$

where X is a fact in $\mathcal{P}$.

In fact, the system $\Sigma_p[\mathcal{P}]$ is a specialization of $\Sigma_c[\mathcal{P}]$ that takes into account the syntactic restriction on the form of Prolog axioms. This is formally captured by the following theorem.

Theorem 9. *Let $\mathcal{P}$ be a set of Prolog axioms and G be a Prolog goal. G is derivable $\Sigma_c[\mathcal{P}]$ if and only if G is derivable in $\Sigma_p[\mathcal{P}]$.*

Proof. Soundness (the "if" part of the theorem) poses no special problem. Notice that the rules

$$[\vee_1] \; \frac{\vdash_p G_1}{\vdash_p G_1 \vee G_2} \quad \text{and} \quad [\vee_2] \; \frac{\vdash_p G_2}{\vdash_p G_1 \vee G_2}$$

can be mapped in $\Sigma_c[\mathcal{P}]$ as

$$[\vee] \; \frac{[<] \; \dfrac{\vdash G_1}{\vdash G_1, G_2}}{\vdash G_1 \vee G_2} \quad \text{and} \quad [\vee] \; \frac{[<] \; \dfrac{\vdash G_2}{\vdash G_1, G_2}}{\vdash G_1 \vee G_2}$$

For completeness (the "only if" part of theorem), let $\mathcal{R}(n)$ be the following predicate for $n \geq 0$.

If Π is a proof in $\Sigma_c[\mathcal{P}]$ of depth at most n, and its conclusion contains only goals, then one of them is derivable in $\Sigma_p[\mathcal{P}]$.

We only need to prove $\mathcal{R}(n)$ for all n, which can be done by induction.

– If $n = 0$:
a proof in $\Sigma_c[\mathcal{P}]$ must contain at least one inference figure and therefore its depth cannot be null. Therefore $\mathcal{R}(0)$ is true.
– If $\mathcal{R}(n)$ is true and Π has depth $n + 1$:
  1. If Π ends with the logical rule $[\wedge]$

$$[\wedge] \; \frac{\overbrace{\vdash \Gamma, F}^{\Pi_1} \quad \overbrace{\vdash \Gamma, G}^{\Pi_2}}{\vdash \Gamma, F \wedge G}$$

then Γ contains only goals and $F \wedge G$ is a goal. Hence so are F and G and therefore the conclusions of Π_1, Π_2 contain only goals. But the depths of Π_1, Π_2 are at most n. Since $\mathcal{R}(n)$ is assumed, there exist two goals, respectively in Γ, F and Γ, G, which are derivable in $\Sigma_p[\mathcal{P}]$. If none of these two goals is in Γ then they must be F and G, and, with the further step

$$[\wedge] \ \frac{\vdash_p F \quad \vdash_p G}{\vdash_p F \wedge G}$$

we obtain that $F \wedge G$ is derivable in $\Sigma_p[\mathcal{P}]$. In any case, we have a goal in $\Gamma, F \wedge G$ which is derivable in $\Sigma_p[\mathcal{P}]$.

2. If Π ends with the logical rule $[\vee]$

$$[\vee] \ \frac{\vdash \Gamma, F, G}{\vdash \Gamma, F \vee G}$$

then Γ contains only goals and $F \vee G$ is a goal. Hence so are F and G and therefore, as in case 1, there exists a goal in Γ, F, G which is derivable in $\Sigma_p[\mathcal{P}]$. If it is not in Γ, then it must be either F or G (F for example) and, with the further step

$$[\vee_1] \ \frac{\vdash_p F}{\vdash_p F \vee G}$$

we obtain that $F \vee G$ is derivable in $\Sigma_p[\mathcal{P}]$. In any case, we have a goal in $\Gamma, F \vee G$ which is derivable in $\Sigma_p[\mathcal{P}]$.

3. If Π ends with the Weakening rule $[<]$

$$[<] \ \frac{\vdash \Gamma}{\vdash \Gamma, F}$$

then Γ contains only goals and, as in case 1, there exists a goal in Γ (a fortiori in Γ, F) which is derivable in $\Sigma_p[\mathcal{P}]$.

4. Π cannot be reduced to the Identity rule $[I]$

$$[I] \ \frac{}{\vdash F, F^{\perp}}$$

since a formula and its dual cannot both be goals.

5. If Π ends with the normalized Cut rule $[\bowtie]$ using a Prolog rule

$$[\bowtie] \ \frac{\vdash \Gamma, G}{\vdash \Gamma, X}$$

where $X, G^{\perp}$ is in $\mathcal{P}$, then, as in case 1, there exists a goal in Γ, G which is derivable in $\Sigma_p[\mathcal{P}]$. If it is not in Γ, then it must be G and, with the further step

$$[\bowtie] \ \frac{\vdash_p G}{\vdash_p X}$$

we obtain that X is derivable in $\Sigma_p[\mathcal{P}]$. In any case, we have a goal in Γ, X which is derivable in $\Sigma_p[\mathcal{P}]$.

6. If Π ends with the normalized Cut rule [⋈] using a Prolog fact

$$[\bowtie] \; \frac{}{\vdash X}$$

where X is in $\mathcal{P}$, then X is derivable in $\Sigma_p[\mathcal{P}]$ by

$$[\bowtie] \; \frac{}{\vdash_p X}$$

Thus $\mathcal{R}(n+1)$ is true.

□

4.2 Extended Prolog

In order to extend Prolog, let us consider how the Horn restriction licences the passage from $\Sigma_c[\mathcal{P}]$ to $\Sigma_p[\mathcal{P}]$. The main property of axioms in standard Prolog is that whenever Γ is derivable in $\Sigma_c[\mathcal{P}]$ then one goal in Γ is derivable in $\Sigma_p[\mathcal{P}]$. This property explains why, at any time, in $\Sigma_p[\mathcal{P}]$ there is always only one single goal involved at each node of the proof; consequently, two cases may occur during the proof search:

(i) if the current goal is an atom, then backchaining (i.e. use of the Cut) must be triggered.

(ii) if the current goal is not atomic, then the logical rule corresponding to its topmost functor must be triggered.

Thus, the syntactic restriction of axioms as in standard Prolog reduces considerably the non-determinism in the process of searching proofs. However, the toll to pay for this operational advantage is a severe loss of expressiveness of the proofs themselves. In particular, the possibility of dealing with multiple goals, as in full-blown Classical Logic, would add to the usual AND-concurrency of Prolog a complementary form of OR-concurrency, where we can view a proof process as given by several interacting components, capable of cooperating on a certain task and then taking separate paths again. This kind of OR-concurrency is indeed exploited for the purpose of knowledge structuring in the object-oriented logic programming language "Linear Objects", described in [3, 4]. In the same paper, it is also shown that such an extension of Horn logic provides an improved notion of algorithm, by exploiting multiple goals as a form of "temporary storage" for saving intermediate values which may be needed again in the course of the computation; a typical example is given by the problem of computing Fibonacci numbers, where we always use twice a given computed subvalue.

Replacing Sets with Multisets We could introduce our extension of Prolog directly as a restriction of the full-blown Cut-reduced system for Classical Logic $\Sigma_c[\mathcal{H}]$. However, the way this system was presented makes it unsuitable for a realistic operational implementation. In fact, let us observe that, although Cut-reduction eliminates many loops and proof redundancies, one major problem in applying the proof search algorithm $\mathcal{A}$ to $\Sigma_c[\mathcal{H}]$ still remains. It lies in the structure of the sequents, which are sets. Indeed, suppose that this algorithm selects, at one step of the computation, an open node in the proof labelled with the sequent $a, b \lor c$. It can then apply to it the logical rule $[\lor]$ in the two following ways:

$$[\lor] \frac{\vdash a, b, c}{\vdash a, b \lor c} \quad \text{or} \quad [\lor] \frac{\vdash a, b \lor c, b, c}{\vdash a, b \lor c}$$

The trouble with the second possibility is that the logical rule $[\lor]$ can again be applied to the premise, and this can be repeated forever. To avoid this problem, one solution is to view sequents as multisets instead of sets. Thus a multiset will contain all the instances of a formula needed to prove a sequent valid, each copy being consumed in the course of the proof as soon as it gets used by an inference figure. This corresponds to the idea of allocating beforehand the resources needed for a proof; of course, in general it will not be possible to know in advance how *many* resources are needed, but this can be obviated by retrying the proof with incrementally increased resources until we succeed. Notice that, within this setting, it makes sense to talk of state of the proof, corresponding to its current amount of available resources; this is important for object-oriented applications, which crucially rely on the notion of current state of the computation.

On the other hand, we cannot just translate the system $\Sigma_c[\mathcal{H}]$ simply by replacing sets with multisets and set union with multiset union. This would be sound but not complete. However, for the restricted system we have in mind, switching from sets to multisets is possible while still obtaining a completeness result. We start therefore by introducing our Extended Prolog directly in terms of multisets, and we prove then its soundness and completeness (modulo expansion of the initial goal) with respect to $\Sigma_c[\mathcal{H}]$.

Definition 10. An Extended Prolog axiom is a multiset of formulae of one of the following forms.

- An Extended Prolog rule: $G^{\perp}, X_1, \ldots, X_r$ also written $X_1, \ldots, X_r :\!\!- G$ where G is a goal and $X_1, \ldots, X_r$ are atoms ($r \geq 1$).
- An Extended Prolog fact: $X_1, \ldots, X_r$ where $X_1, \ldots, X_r$ are atoms ($r \geq 1$).

Let $\mathcal{P}$ be a set of Extended Prolog axioms. The inference system $\Sigma_P[\mathcal{P}]$ is defined as follows:

- Logical rules

$$[\lor] \frac{\vdash_P \gamma, G_1, G_2}{\vdash_P \gamma, G_1 \lor G_2} \qquad [\land] \frac{\vdash_P \gamma, G_1 \quad \vdash_P \gamma, G_2}{\vdash_P \gamma, G_1 \land G_2}$$

- Extended Prolog Cut rule (two forms)

$$[\bowtie] \frac{\vdash_P \gamma, G}{\vdash_P \gamma, X_1, \ldots, X_r}$$

where $X_1, \ldots, X_r :\!\!- G$ is an Extended Prolog rule in $\mathcal{P}$

$$[\bowtie] \frac{}{\vdash_P \gamma, X_1, \ldots, X_r}$$

where $X_1, \ldots, X_r$ is an Extended Prolog fact in $\mathcal{P}$

Notice that here, γ denotes a *multiset* of *goals* and γ, δ denotes the *multiset* union of γ and δ. For any multiset ϕ of formulae, we take $\overline{\phi}$ to be the set of its element. Conversely, for any set Φ of formulae, we take an *expansion* of Φ to be any multiset ϕ such that $\overline{\phi} = \Phi$.

In fact, the system $\Sigma_P[\mathcal{P}]$ is a specialization of $\Sigma_c[\mathcal{P}]$ that takes into account the syntactic restriction on the form of the Extended Prolog axioms.

Theorem 11. *Let $\mathcal{P}$ be a set of Extended Prolog axioms.*

- *Let γ be a multiset of goals. If γ is derivable in $\Sigma_P[\mathcal{P}]$ then $\overline{\gamma}$ is derivable in $\Sigma_c[\overline{\mathcal{P}}]$.*
- *Let Γ be a set of goals. If Γ is derivable in $\Sigma_c[\overline{\mathcal{P}}]$ then there exists an expansion of Γ which is derivable in $\Sigma_P[\mathcal{P}]$.*

where $\overline{\mathcal{P}}$ is the set of sequent defined as $\overline{\mathcal{P}} = \{\overline{\phi} \ / \ \phi \in \mathcal{P}\}$.

Proof. Soundness poses no special problem. Notice that the rule

$$[\bowtie] \ \frac{}{\vdash \gamma, X_1, \ldots, X_r}$$

where $X_1, \ldots, X_r$ is an Extended Prolog fact in $\mathcal{P}$ can be mapped in $\Sigma_c[\overline{\mathcal{P}}]$ as

$$[< \cdots] \ \frac{[\bowtie] \ \dfrac{}{\vdash X_1, \ldots, X_r}}{\vdash \overline{\gamma}, X_1, \ldots, X_r}$$

For completeness, we first state that the Weakening rule is still valid in $\Sigma_P[\mathcal{P}]$, although it has not been declared as a primitive rule:

Let γ, δ be multisets of goals. If γ is derivable in $\Sigma_P[\mathcal{P}]$ then so is γ, δ.

This result can be easily proved by induction on the depth of the proofs in $\Sigma_P[\mathcal{P}]$.

Now, let $\mathcal{R}(n)$ be the following predicate for $n \geq 0$.

If Π is a proof in $\Sigma_c[\overline{\mathcal{P}}]$ of depth at most n, and its conclusion contains only goals, then an expansion of this conclusion is derivable in $\Sigma_P[\mathcal{P}]$.

We only need to prove $\mathcal{R}(n)$ for all n, which can be done by induction.

- If $n = 0$:
  A proof in $\Sigma_c[\overline{\mathcal{P}}]$ must contain at least one inference figure and therefore its depth cannot be null. Therefore $\mathcal{R}(0)$ is true.
- If $\mathcal{R}(n)$ holds and Π has depth $n + 1$:
  1. If Π ends with the logical rule $[\lor]$

$$\Pi = [\lor] \ \frac{\overbrace{\bigvee}^{\Pi'} \quad \vdash \Gamma, F, G}{\vdash \Gamma, F \lor G}$$

then Γ contains only goals and $F \vee G$ is a goal. Hence so are F and G and therefore the conclusion of Π' contains only goals. But the depth of Π' is at most n. Since $\mathcal{R}(n)$ is assumed, there exists an expansion γ of Γ, F, G which is derivable in $\Sigma_P[\mathcal{P}]$.

(a) If both $F, G \in \Gamma$, then γ is an expansion of Γ hence $\gamma, F \vee G$ is an expansion of $\Gamma, F \vee G$. Since γ is derivable in $\Sigma_P[\mathcal{P}]$, so is $\gamma, F \vee G$, by weakening.

(b) If $F \in \Gamma$ and $G \notin \Gamma$, then $\gamma = \gamma', (G)^m$ with $m \geq 1$ and γ' is an expansion of Γ. Since $\gamma', (G)^m$ is derivable in $\Sigma_P[\mathcal{P}]$, so is $\gamma', (F)^m, (G)^m$ by weakening, and therefore so is $\gamma', (F \vee G)^m$ with m further steps using the logical rule $[\vee]$. Furthermore, $\gamma', (F \vee G)^m$ is an expansions of $\Gamma, F \vee G$.

(c) If $F \notin \Gamma$ and $G \in \Gamma$ the same reasoning holds.

Let's now assume that $F, G \notin \Gamma$ so that $\gamma = \gamma', (F)^p, (G)^q$ with $p, q \geq 1$ and γ' is an expansion of Γ. Let $m = \max(p, q)$. Since $\gamma', (F)^p, (G)^q$ is derivable in $\Sigma_P[\mathcal{P}]$, so is $\gamma', (F)^m, (G)^m$ by weakening, and therefore so is $\gamma', (F \vee G)^m$ with m further steps using the logical rule $[\vee]$. Furthermore, $\gamma', (F \vee G)^m$ is an expansion of $\Gamma, F \vee G$. In any case, we have found an expansion of $\Gamma, F \vee G$ which is derivable in $\Sigma_P[\mathcal{P}]$.

2. If Π ends with the logical rule $[\wedge]$

$$[\wedge]\ \frac{\vdash \Gamma, F \quad \vdash \Gamma, G}{\vdash \Gamma, F \wedge G}$$

then Γ contains only goals and $F \wedge G$ is a goal. Hence, so are F and G and therefore, as in case 1, there exists an expansion γ of Γ, F and δ of Γ, G which are derivable in $\Sigma_P[\mathcal{P}]$.

(a) If $F \in \Gamma$ then γ is an expansion of Γ, hence $\gamma, F \wedge G$ is an expansion of $\Gamma, F \wedge G$. Since γ is derivable in $\Sigma_P[\mathcal{P}]$, so is $\gamma, F \wedge G$, by weakening.

(b) If $G \in \Gamma$ the same reasoning holds.

Let's now assume that $F, G \notin \Gamma$ so that $\gamma = \gamma', (F)^p$ and $\delta = \delta', (G)^q$ with $p, q \geq 1$ and γ' and δ' are expansions of Γ. Let $m = p + q - 1$ and k be an integer between 0 and m

- if $0 \leq k < p$ then $m - k \geq q$ and, since $\delta', (G)^q$ is derivable in $\Sigma_P[\mathcal{P}]$, so is $\gamma', \delta', (F)^k, (G)^{m-k}$ by weakening.
- if $k > p$ then, since $\gamma', (F)^p$ is derivable in $\Sigma_P[\mathcal{P}]$, so is $\gamma', \delta', (F)^k, (G)^{m-k}$ by weakening.

Thus, for all $k = 0, \ldots, m$, $\gamma', \delta', (F)^k, (G)^{m-k}$ is derivable in $\Sigma_P[\mathcal{P}]$ and therefore, so is $\gamma', \delta', (F \wedge G)^m$ with $2^m - 1$ further steps using the logical rule $[\wedge]$. Furthermore $\gamma', \delta', (F \wedge G)^m$ is an expansion of $\Gamma, F \wedge G$. In any case, we have found an expansion of $\Gamma, F \wedge G$ which is derivable in $\Sigma_P[\mathcal{P}]$.

3. If Π ends with the Weakening rule $[<]$

$$[<]\ \frac{\vdash \Gamma}{\vdash \Gamma, F}$$

then Γ contains only goals and, as in case 1, there exists an expansion γ of Γ which is derivable in $\Sigma_P[\mathcal{P}]$. Hence, so is γ, F which is an expansion of Γ, F.

4. Π cannot be reduced to the Identity rule $[I]$

$$[I] \ \frac{}{\vdash F, F^\perp}$$

since a formula and its dual cannot both be goals.

5. If Π ends with the normalized Cut rule $[\bowtie]$ using an Extended Prolog fact

$$[\bowtie] \ \frac{}{\vdash X_1, \ldots, X_r}$$

where $X_1, \ldots, X_r$ is in $\mathcal{P}$ then $X_1, \ldots, X_r$ is derivable in $\Sigma_P[\mathcal{P}]$ by the Extended Prolog Cut rule.

6. If Π ends with the normalized Cut rule $[\bowtie]$ using an Extended Prolog rule

$$[\bowtie] \ \frac{\vdash \Gamma, G}{\vdash \Gamma, X_1, \ldots, X_r}$$

where $X_1, \ldots, X_r :- G$ is in $\mathcal{P}$, then, as in case 1, there exists an expansion γ of Γ, G which is derivable in $\Sigma_P[\mathcal{P}]$. If $G \in \Gamma$, then γ is an expansion of Γ hence $\gamma, X_1, \ldots, X_r$ is an expansion of $\Gamma, X_1, \ldots, X_r$. Since γ is derivable in $\Sigma_P[\mathcal{P}]$, so is $\gamma, X_1, \ldots, X_r$, by weakening. Let's now assume that $G \notin \Gamma$, so that $\gamma = \gamma', (G)^m$ with $m \geq 1$ and γ' is an expansion of Γ. Since $\gamma', (G)^m$ is derivable in $\Sigma_P[\mathcal{P}]$, then so is $\gamma', (X_1)^m, \ldots, (X_r)^m$ with m further steps using the Extended Prolog Cut rule $[\bowtie]$. In any case, we have found an expansion of $\Gamma, X_1, \ldots, X_r$ which is derivable in $\Sigma_P[\mathcal{P}]$.

Thus $\mathcal{R}(n+1)$ is true.

$\square$

Eliminating Permutations of Inference Figures The inference system Σ_P is much more adapted for using the proof search algorithm $\mathcal{A}$ than the general system Σ_c. Indeed, permutations and loops due to the unrestricted use of the Cut rule are now eliminated via Cut-reduction. Furthermore, loops due to the set structure of classical sequents are also eliminated by using multisets. We now achieve a fully operational system by forbidding, to a certain extent, the permutation of the inference figures, as for instance in

$$[\wedge] \ \frac{[\vee] \ \dfrac{\vdash \gamma, F, H, K}{\vdash \gamma, F, H \vee K} \quad [\vee] \ \dfrac{\vdash \gamma, G, H, K}{\vdash \gamma, G, H \vee K}}{\vdash \gamma, F \wedge G, H \vee K} \equiv [\vee] \ \frac{[\wedge] \ \dfrac{\vdash \gamma, F, H, K \quad \vdash \gamma, G, H, K}{\vdash \gamma, F \wedge G, H, K}}{\vdash \gamma, F \wedge G, H \vee K}$$

This is obtained as in the system Σ_P' below, of which we show soundness and completeness with respect to Σ_P.

Let $\mathcal{P}$ be a set of Extended Prolog axioms. The inference system $\Sigma_P'[\mathcal{P}]$ is defined as follows:

– Logical rules

$$[\lor] \frac{\vdash_P C : L, G_1, G_2}{\vdash_P C : L, G_1 \lor G_2} \qquad [\land] \frac{\vdash_P C : L, G_1 \quad \vdash_P C : L, G_2}{\vdash_P C : L, G_1 \land G_2}$$

– Exchange rule

$$[E] \frac{\vdash_P C, X : L}{\vdash_P C : L, X}$$

where X is an atom.

– Operational Cut rule (two forms)

$$[\bowtie] \frac{\vdash_P C : G}{\vdash_P C, X_1, \ldots, X_r :}$$

where $X_1, \ldots, X_r :\text{-} G$ is an Extended Prolog rule in $\mathcal{P}$

$$[\bowtie] \frac{}{\vdash_P C, X_1, \ldots, X_r :}$$

where $X_1, \ldots, X_r$ is an Extended Prolog fact in $\mathcal{P}$

Notice here that the sequents are split in two fields $C : L$ (separated by a semi-colon). C denotes a multiset of atoms while L denotes an *ordered* list of goals. L, G denotes a list the last element of which is G and the rest is L.

In fact, the system $\Sigma'_P[\mathcal{P}]$ is a direct reformulation of $\Sigma_P[\mathcal{P}]$ which reduces the degree of non-determinism, by showing that the logical rules can be deterministically applied as soon as a non-atomic formula appears and that the Cut rule can be triggered only when the sequent is fully decomposed into atoms. This system corresponds exactly to the object-oriented logic programming language of "Linear Objects" described in [3, 4].

Theorem 12. *Let $\mathcal{P}$ be a set of Extended Prolog axioms. Let C be a multiset of atoms and L be a list of goals. C, L is derivable in $\Sigma_P[\mathcal{P}]$ if and only if $C : L$ is derivable in $\Sigma'_P[\mathcal{P}]$.*

Proof. Soundness poses no special problem. Notice that the Exchange rule

$$[E] \frac{\vdash_P C : L, X}{\vdash_P C, X : L}$$

disappears when mapped to $\Sigma_P[\mathcal{P}]$ since its premiss and its conclusion are the same, when mapped to multisets. For completeness, we first state that the following properties hold in $\Sigma'_P[\mathcal{P}]$:

1. If $C : L, G_1, M$ and $C : L, G_2, M$ are derivable, then so is $C : L, G_1 \land G_2, M$.
2. If $C : L, G_1, G_2, M$ is derivable, then so is $C : L, G_1 \lor G_2, M$.
3. If $C : L, X, M$ is derivable, then so is $C, X : L, M$.

These results are shown by simple induction on the complexity of the list M and pose no problem. Using these properties, we can show, by induction on the complexity of the list M, N that if $C : L, G, M, N$ is derivable in $\Sigma'_P[\mathcal{P}]$ then so is $C : L, M, G, N$. Thus, derivability is preserved by transposition inside the second field of the sequents and, hence, by any permutation. In other words

If L and L' are lists of goals equal up to the order of their elements, then $C : L$ is derivable if and only if $C : L'$ is derivable.

Let's write $L \equiv L'$ when L and L' differ only by the order of their elements. We also need the following lemmas:

1. For each Extended Prolog rule $X_1, \ldots, X_r, G^\perp$ in $\mathcal{P}$, if $C : G, L$ is derivable then so is $C, X_1, \ldots, X_s : X_{s+1}, \ldots, X_r, L$ for any $s = 1 \ldots r$.
2. For each Extended Prolog fact $X_1, \ldots, X_r$ in $\mathcal{P}, C, X_1, \ldots, X_s : X_{s+1}, \ldots, X_r, L$ is derivable for any $s = 1 \ldots r$.

Again, these properties are shown by induction on the complexity of list L and pose no problem.

Let $\mathcal{R}(n)$ be the following predicate for $n \geq 0$.

If Π is a proof in $\Sigma_P[\mathcal{P}]$ of depth at most n and of conlusion C, L then $C : L$ is derivable in $\Sigma'_P[\mathcal{P}]$.

We only need to prove $\mathcal{R}(n)$ for all n, which can be done by induction.

- If $n = 0$:
  A proof in $\Sigma_P[\mathcal{P}]$ must contain at least one inference figure and hence its depth cannot be null. Therefore $\mathcal{R}(0)$ is true.
- If $\mathcal{R}(n)$ holds and Π has depth $n + 1$:
  1. If Π ends with a logical rule ($[\vee]$ for example) then the principal formula must be in L since C contains only atoms:

$$\Pi = [\vee] \; \frac{\overbrace{\vee}^{\Pi'} \quad \vdash_P C, L', G_1, G_2}{\vdash_P C, L', G_1 \vee G_2}$$

  where $L \equiv L', G_1 \vee G_2$. But the depth of Π' is at most n. Since $\mathcal{R}(n)$ is assumed, $C : L', G_1, G_2$ is derivable in $\Sigma'_P[\mathcal{P}]$ and so is $C : L', G_1 \vee G_2$ using the further step

$$[\vee] \; \frac{\vdash_P C : L', G_1, G_2}{\vdash_P C : L', G_1 \vee G_2}$$

  Since $L \equiv L', G_1 \vee G_2$, the sequent $C : L$ is derivable in $\Sigma'_P[\mathcal{P}]$.
  2. If Π ends with the Extended Prolog Cut rule $[\bowtie]$

$$[\bowtie] \; \frac{\vdash C', G, L'}{\vdash_P C', X_1, \ldots, X_r, L'}$$

  where $X_1, \ldots, X_r, G^\perp$ is an Extended Prolog rule in $\mathcal{P}$, then there is $s \in \{1 \ldots r\}$ such that $C = C', X_1, \ldots, X_s$ and $L \equiv L', X_{s+1}, \ldots, X_r$. As in case 1, $C' : G, L'$ is derivable in $\Sigma'_P[\mathcal{P}]$ and hence, so is $C', X_1, \ldots, X_s : X_{s+1}, \ldots, X_r, L'$ by application of a lemma stated above. Since $L \equiv L', X_{s+1}, \ldots, X_r$, the sequent $C : L$ is derivable in $\Sigma'_P[\mathcal{P}]$.

3. If Π is the Extended Prolog Cut rule [⋈]

$$[⋈] \ \overline{\vdash_P C', X_1, \ldots, X_r, L'}$$

where $X_1, \ldots, X_r$ is an Extended Prolog fact in $\mathcal{P}$, then there is $s \in \{1 \ldots r\}$ such that $C = C', X_1, \ldots, X_s$ and $L \equiv L', X_{s+1}, \ldots, X_r$. The sequent $C', X_1, \ldots, X_s : X_{s+1}, \ldots, X_r, L'$ is derivable in $\Sigma'_P[\mathcal{P}]$ by application of a lemma proved above. Since $L \equiv L', X_{s+1}, \ldots, X_r$, the sequent $C : L$ is derivable in $\Sigma'_P[\mathcal{P}]$.

Thus $\mathcal{R}(n + 1)$ is true.

$\square$

5 Linear Logic

5.1 Eliminating the Hypotheses

The system Σ'_P can be used as a theorem prover for full-blown Classical Logic. Indeed, it can be shown that the derivability of any classical formula F is equivalent to the derivability of a goal from a set of Extended Prolog axioms, computed from F. One way to achieve this is by converting $F^\perp$ to clauses (not only Horn clauses) in the usual way.

- The set of clauses containing at least one head is obviously a set $\mathcal{P}$ of Extended Prolog axioms.
- The set of clauses with an empty head is a conjunction of disjunctions of negative literals. Hence, its dual is a disjunction of conjunctions of positive literals, i.e. a goal G.

The derivability of F is equivalent to the inconsistency of the set of clauses associated with $F^\perp$, i.e. of $\mathcal{P}, G^\perp$, which is equivalent to the derivability of G from $\mathcal{P}$. (Notice that this transformation is in no way unique nor optimal.) Then, to show that G derives from $\mathcal{P}$ in Σ_c, it is enough to show that an expansion G^n of G is derivable in $\Sigma'_P[\mathcal{P}]$ (this is the combined result of Theorems 7, 11, and 12). This can be achieved by enumerating each value for n, starting from 1. Thus, this method provides a general semi-decision procedure for Classical Logic. It extends the atom-driven strategy of Prolog to general clauses and is therefore more suited for computational purposes than unrestricted resolution.

Let us apply this technique to the following simple example

$$F = (a \wedge (a \supset b)) \supset b$$

From $F^\perp$ (put into nnf), we obtain three clauses

$$a \ ; \ a^\perp, b \ ; \ b^\perp$$

which lead to

$$\mathcal{P} = \{a \ ; \ b :- a\} \quad \text{and} \quad G = b$$

Here, $\mathcal{P}$ is a set of standard Prolog axioms. Let us now consider a variant F_1 of F where we use the dual of the atom a, denoted a^* and considered an atom itself, instead of a. We have

$$F_1 = (a^{*\perp} \wedge (a^{*\perp} \supset b)) \supset b$$

which leads to

$$\mathcal{P}_1 = \{a^*, b\} \quad \text{and} \quad G_1 = a^* \vee b$$

Now $\mathcal{P}_1$ contains a single Extended Prolog fact. The formula a which appeared as a fact in the program $\mathcal{P}$ is mapped here into the subformula a^* of the goal G_1. We can also consider a variant F_2 of F which uses both atoms a and a^* (and, by analogy, b and b^*) by just stating that they are duals (i.e by including the hypothesis $a \vee a^*$)

$$F_2 = ((a \vee a^*) \wedge (b \vee b^*)) \supset ((a^{*\perp} \wedge (a \supset b^{*\perp})) \supset b)$$

which leads to

$$\mathcal{P}_2 = \{a^*, a \;\; ; \;\; b^*, b\} \quad \text{and} \quad G_2 = a^* \vee (a \wedge b^*) \vee b$$

In this case, all the formulae which appeared as axioms in $\mathcal{P}$ have been mapped to subformulae of the goal G_2.

These simple manipulations show that the distinction between the "conclusion" part of the query and the "hypotheses" part is not so clearcut. However, it is crucial for the Cut reduction procedure, which relies on a special treatement of the hypotheses. Hence, this procedure, and the subsequent extension of Prolog, loses one important feature of the usual refutation-based Prolog, namely that axioms and goals are treated at the same level (in usual Prolog, they are all input clauses for resolution refutation). This feature is interesting from a computational point of view, since it blurs the distinction between programs and data, which is one of the most important motivation when designing object-oriented programming languages.

There is, a priori, a general method to map any query into a query without hypotheses. For each sequent $\Gamma = F_1, \ldots, F_n$, let $\widehat{\Gamma}$ be the formula $F_1 \vee \cdots \vee F_n$ (which is semantically equivalent to Γ).

Theorem 13. *Let $\mathcal{H}$ be a set of sequents and Γ be a sequent. Any answer proof for the query $\langle \mathcal{H}; \Gamma \rangle$ can be mapped into a proof without proper axioms of $\{\widehat{\Delta}^\perp\}_{\Delta \in \mathcal{H}}, \Gamma$ and vice-versa.*

Proof. – Let $\mathcal{H}$ be $\{\Gamma_1, \ldots, \Gamma_n\}$. Given a proof Π of $\widehat{\Gamma_1}^{\perp}, \ldots, \widehat{\Gamma_n}^{\perp}, \Gamma$, we can build the proof Π'

$$
\Pi' = [\bowtie]\; \cfrac{
  [\bowtie]\; \cfrac{
    \overset{\displaystyle \Pi}{\overbrace{\displaystyle \bigvee}}\;\;\;\;\;\;\;\;\;\;\; [\vee \cdots]\; \cfrac{\vdash \Gamma_1}{\vdash \widehat{\Gamma_1}}
  }{
    \cfrac{\vdash \Gamma, \widehat{\Gamma_1}^{\perp}, \ldots, \widehat{\Gamma_n}^{\perp}}{\vdash \Gamma, \widehat{\Gamma_2}^{\perp}, \ldots, \widehat{\Gamma_n}^{\perp}}
  }
  \;\;\; \ddots \;\;\; \vdash \Gamma, \widehat{\Gamma_n}^{\perp} \;\;\;\;\;\; [\vee \cdots]\; \cfrac{\vdash \Gamma_n}{\vdash \widehat{\Gamma_n}}
}{\vdash \Gamma}
$$

Clearly, Π' is an answer proof for the query $\langle \mathcal{H}; \Gamma \rangle$. Notice that it is not in Cut reduced form.

– The converse property can be easily shown by induction on the depth of the proofs and poses no special problem.

$\square$

Given the considerations above, we want to address the following question: is it possible to deal directly with a hypothesis-free query, without converting it first back to a query where hypotheses and conclusions are separate? The answer is yes; however, if we want to achieve the same kind of normalization as that provided by the Cut reduction theorem, leading to a form of goal-driven computation as in the system Σ'_P, then we need some new syntactic tools, not available in Classical Logic, and provided instead by Linear Logic. Indeed, if we stay within Classical Logic, then the Cut reduction theorem "degenerates" into full Cut elimination in the case of hypotheses-free proofs, which leaves us bereft of the operational interpretation that we have previously given to it.

5.2 A Search Strategy Controlled by the Syntax

Let us consider a sequent $\sigma = a, b, F, G$ in the set $\mathcal{H}$ of hypotheses of a query. An answer proof for this query might therefore contain the normalized sequence of Cuts associated with the sequent σ, as in the following example:

$$
\Pi = [\bowtie]\; \cfrac{
  [\bowtie]\; \cfrac{\overset{\displaystyle \Pi_1}{\overbrace{\displaystyle \bigvee}} \;\;\; \vdash a, b, F, G \;\;\; \vdash \Gamma, F^{\perp}}{\vdash a, b, \Gamma, G} \;\;\; \overset{\displaystyle \Pi_2}{\overbrace{\displaystyle \bigvee}} \;\;\; \vdash \Delta, G^{\perp}
}{\vdash a, b, \Gamma, \Delta}
$$

According to Theorem 13, Π_1 and Π_2 can be mapped into hypotheses-free proofs Π'_1 and Π'_2 of, respectively, $\Gamma, F^{\perp}, \widehat{\mathcal{H}}^{\perp}$ and $\Delta, G^{\perp}, \widehat{\mathcal{H}}^{\perp}$. Proof Π itself is then mapped into the hypotheses-free proof

$$\Pi' = [\wedge'] \;\cfrac{[\wedge']\;\cfrac{[\wedge']\;\cfrac{\overset{\pi'_1}{\overbrace{\vee}}}{\vdash \Gamma, F^\perp, \widehat{\mathcal{H}}^\perp}\quad\overset{\pi'_2}{\overbrace{\vee}}\;\vdash \Delta, G^\perp, \widehat{\mathcal{H}}^\perp}{\vdash F^\perp \wedge G^\perp, \Gamma, \Delta, \widehat{\mathcal{H}}^\perp}}{\vdash b^\perp \wedge F^\perp \wedge G^\perp, b, \Gamma, \Delta, \widehat{\mathcal{H}}^\perp}}{\vdash a^\perp \wedge b^\perp \wedge F^\perp \wedge G^\perp, a, b, \Gamma, \Delta, \widehat{\mathcal{H}}^\perp}$$

where $[\wedge']$ stands for the following combination of inference rules $[\wedge]$ and $[<]$:

$$[\wedge]\;\cfrac{\vdash \Gamma, F \quad \vdash \Delta, G}{\vdash \Gamma, \Delta, F \wedge G} \equiv [\wedge]\;\cfrac{[<]\;\cfrac{\vdash \Gamma, F}{\vdash \Gamma, \Delta, F}\quad [<]\;\cfrac{\vdash \Delta, G}{\vdash \Gamma, \Delta, G}}{\vdash \Gamma, \Delta, F \wedge G}$$

Π' is indeed a hypothesis free proof of $a, b, \Gamma, \Delta, \widehat{\mathcal{H}}^\perp$ since $a^\perp \wedge b^\perp \wedge F^\perp \wedge G^\perp$ is precisely $\widehat{\sigma}^\perp$, which is in $\widehat{\mathcal{H}}^\perp$. The problem with proof Π' is that it contains occurences of the Weakening rule, hidden inside $[\wedge']$. We therefore lose here one basic feature of the system Σ'_P, namely that all the occurences of Weakening can be "pushed" upward to the leaves of the proof tree. Furthermore, it is hard to justify via a normalization procedure the specific treatment applied to formula $\widehat{\sigma}^\perp$ in Π' since nothing makes it different from the other formulae in the conclusion.

To deal with this problems, Linear Logic introduces new connectives, which permit an explicit control on the use of the different inference figures. First, Linear Logic deals directly with sequents as multisets of formulae instead of sets. The classical rules of Contraction and Weakening are still allowed, but they are explicitly controlled by a special connective, the modality "why-not", written here ?.

$$[<]\;\cfrac{\vdash \Gamma}{\vdash \Gamma, ?F} \quad \text{and} \quad [>]\;\cfrac{\vdash \Gamma, ?F, ?F}{\vdash \Gamma, ?F}$$

Furthermore, the connective $\wedge$ is mapped into two different connectives $\&$ and $\otimes$, depending on the intended inference $([\wedge] \text{ or } [\wedge'])$.

$$[\otimes]\;\cfrac{\vdash \Gamma, F \quad \vdash \Delta, G}{\vdash \Gamma, \Delta, F \otimes G} \quad \text{and} \quad [\&]\;\cfrac{\vdash \Gamma, F \quad \vdash \Gamma, G}{\vdash \Gamma, F \& G}$$

The connective $\vee$ also has two linear forms, @ and $\oplus$, defined as follows:

$$[@]\;\cfrac{\vdash \Gamma, F, G}{\vdash \Gamma, F @ G} \quad \text{and} \quad [\oplus_1]\;\cfrac{\vdash \Gamma, F}{\vdash \Gamma, F \oplus G} \quad \text{and} \quad [\oplus_2]\;\cfrac{\vdash \Gamma, G}{\vdash \Gamma, F \oplus G}$$

In this way, the control information is expressed within the syntax of the language itself, and not at the metalevel, by earmarking one sequent as the conclusion and other sequents as hypotheses.

Let us consider, for example, a classical sequent (which corresponds to an Extended P¡rolog rule) $\sigma = a, b, (c \wedge d)^\perp$ as belonging to the the set of hypotheses of a query. In Classical Logic, $\hat{\sigma}^\perp$ is the formula $a^\perp \wedge b^\perp \wedge c \wedge d$, for which it is hard to capture the intended difference in the treatement of the different occurences of $\wedge$ (the first two should be handled by $[\wedge']$ while the last should be handled by $[\wedge]$). In Linear Logic, this form of control is easily captured by the formula

$$?(a^\perp \otimes b^\perp \otimes (c\&d))$$

Here, the modality ? is needed, since a hypothesis can be used several times (and therefore may need to be duplicated using the Contraction rule). Furthermore, the connective $\otimes$ is used where $[\wedge']$ is intended and $\&$ where $[\wedge]$ is intended. In this way, we can completely reconstruct the control information expressed in Classical Logic by postulating σ as a hypothesis of the query.

In the previous sections, we have shown that the Cut rule, together with the proper normalization procedure (Cut reduction), provides the tools for defining a tractable proof search strategy for full Classical Logic. The linear connectives provide an alternative tool for a finer-grained form of control of the proof search for Linear Logic, but a normalization procedure is still required. One such procedure, called "focusing", is described in detail in [1]. It captures the basic idea of Cut reduction as expressed in this paper, i.e. that of a goal-driven strategy, without any restriction on the syntax of the formulae.

6 Conclusion

In this paper, we have shown that the goal-driven search of proofs, which makes Prolog computationally attractive, does *not* rely on the syntactical restriction to Horn clauses. Rather, it is the resolution-based approach to Prolog which makes this restriction necessary, since full clausal resolution is hardly capable of being goal-driven. On the other hand, the sequent-based approach taken here is endowed with such a capability; in fact, we have presented an extension of Prolog, which is equivalent to full-blown Classical Logic, and is based on sequent style proofs. In this extension, the rules can have multiple heads, connected by the disjunction operator interpreted in a concurrent way. Correspondingly, we have dropped the Prolog restriction which requires the current goal to be unique: multiple disjunctive goals are allowed, and can be treated in a concurrent way. Our extension of Prolog can in fact be characterized in terms of a new form of concurrency, called in [4] *OR*-concurrency, where the synchronisation takes place at the level of the proof process itself, which is complementary with the usual *AND*-concurrency found in concurrent logic programming languages [11], where the synchronization takes place at the unification level.

There are two main points in our analysis of Classical Logic as a computation system:

(i) we formalize a computation as being the process of searching a proof, for example in the sequent system of propositional logic, which we show to be sufficient for computational use

(ii) we also define a computationally *meaningful* subclass of proofs, shown to be complete, using a slightly modified version of the Cut reduction theorem

Some syntactic restrictions on the formulae are then needed to obtain an operational system. But, unlike the restriction to Horn clauses, they do not alter the expressive power of the language.

However, this extension of Prolog pays the price of a too sharp separation between "hypotheses" and "conclusions" in a query, analogous to the one between "programs" and "data" in computation. Many attempts have been made to blur (as much as possible) this distinction, especially in the field of object-oriented programming. Linear Logic gives us the syntactic tools to remedy this situation by introducing finer-grained connectives than those of Classical Logic, thus allowing a syntactically explicit form of control over the process of searching a proof.

Acknowledgements

We are grateful to Peter Schroeder-Heister and an anonymous referee for helpful comments, and to Gerard Comyn and Alexander Herold for their encouragement and support.

References

1. J.M. Andreoli. *Proposition pour une Synthèse des Paradigmes de la Programmation Logique et de la Programmation par Objets*. PhD thesis, Université Paris VI, Paris, France, 1990.
2. J.M. Andreoli and R. Pareschi. Formulae as active representation of data. In *Actes du 9eme Séminaire sur la Programmation en Logique*, Trégastel, France, 1990.
3. J.M. Andreoli and R. Pareschi. Linear objects: Logical processes with built-in inheritance. In *Proc. of the 7th International Conference on Logic Programming*, Jerusalem, Israel, 1990.
4. J.M. Andreoli and R. Pareschi. LO and behold! concurrent structured processes. In *Proc. of OOPSLA '90*, Ottawa, Canada, 1990. To appear.
5. J. Gallier. *Logic for Computer Science*. Harper & Row, New-York, 1986.
6. J.Y. Girard. Linear logic. *Theoretical Computer Science*, 50(1), 1987.
7. J.Y. Girard. Towards a geometry of interaction. In *Categories in Computer Science and Logic*, Boulder, Colorado, 1987.
8. J.Y. Girard, Y. Lafont, and P. Taylor. *Proofs and Types*. Cambridge University Press, 1989.
9. D. Harel and A. Pnueli. On the developpement of reactive systems. In K.R. Apt, editor, *Logic and Models of Concurrent Systems*. Springer Verlag, 1985.
10. S. C. Kleene. Permutability of inferences in gentzen's calculi lk and lj. *Memoirs of the American Mathematical Society*, (10), 1952.
11. E. Shapiro. The family of concurrent logic programming languages. Technical report, The Weizmann Institute of Science, Rehovot, Israel, 1989.

Predicates as Parameters in Logic Programming
A Set-Theoretic Basis

James H. Andrews

Edinburgh University, Department of Computer Science

1 Introduction

One important motivation for adding "higher order" features to logic programming (as in Lambda Prolog, for instance) is the need to allow programs to manipulate such things as formulae, predicates, and programs themselves in the same way as they manipulate object level terms. We can achieve a limited form of this by allowing predicate names to be passed as parameters to other predicates. In this paper, I give a simple extension to pure logic programming which allows us to pass predicate names as parameters, and I give a formal justification for the extension.

The extension is based on a variant of Gilmore's first order set theory NaD-SetI [Gil86]. NaDSetI is part of a nominalistic approach to resolving the set-theoretic paradoxes, which differs from the type-theoretic approach at a very basic, philosophical level. It thus addresses some of the same issues as higher order logic was developed to address, although it is only first order. In this respect it is like Chen, Kifer and Warren's HiLog [CKW89], which has a higher order syntax and a first order semantics.

The main differences between first order logic and the logic described here (called G) are: predicate names are considered to be terms; a new class of "abstracted set" terms (terms of the form $\{x \mid A\}$) is defined; a new class of set membership formulae (of the form $s \in t$) is defined; and predicate application formulae $P(t_1, \ldots, t_n)$ are re-interpreted as membership formulae $\langle t_1, \ldots, t_n \rangle \in P$. Equality between terms in G, including predicate names, is intensional: two sets are considered unequal if their "names" are different, even if they have the same members. This weak equality seems to still be powerful enough to allow us to program a wide variety of tasks for which higher order features are needed.

The standard logic programming interpreter can be extended, in a way I will describe, to handle the extra features of G. The resultant logic programming language is less powerful than Lambda Prolog, the language which first demonstrated that truly higher order features could be added to logic programming in an elegant and useful way. However, the language is not hampered by some of the problems of Lambda Prolog (such as the undecidability of higher order unifiability), and still manages to achieve some of the same power.

The organisation of the paper is as follows. Section 2 defines the logic, G, and its model theory, and gives a sound and complete proof system for it. Section 3 gives a nondeterministic operational semantics for G, and proves it sound and complete with respect to the proof system, thus justifying our view of G as a logic programming language. Section 4 discusses some of the computational strengths and weaknesses of the system, comparing it in particular with Lambda Prolog. Finally, Section 5 summarises and suggests future research directions.

2 Description of the Logic

G is a generalisation of first order logic. However, it is not a extension of first order logic in the formal sense, because in addition to adding new terms and formulae, G re-interprets some of the old terms and formulae.

2.1 Syntax and Informal Semantics

We assume that we are given a set of variables (x and y, possibly subscripted, being metavariables ranging over this set), a set of function symbols (f, g), and a set of predicate symbols (P, Q). From these we can define the terms and formulae of G, in much the same way as with a first order theory.

Terms. We will use the metavariables s and t to stand for arbitrary terms of G. Terms are those expressions recognised by the following pseudo-BNF syntax:

$$t ::= \ x \ | \ f(t_1, \ldots, t_n) \ | \ \langle t_1, \ldots, t_n \rangle \ | \ P \ | \ \{x \mid A\}$$

The significance of these classes of terms, in informal language, is as follows.

- x: the variables.
- $f(t_1, \ldots, t_n)$, where the t_i's are terms: these are just like the terms of the corresponding first-order language, except of course that they may contain predicate names and set abstraction terms.
- $\langle t_1, \ldots, t_n \rangle$: tuples of n terms. The tupling construct is treated as just one kind of function symbol application.
- P: the predicate names. Predicate names can appear in any term, and are intended to represent sets of closed terms; the exact set denoted is defined by a program.
- $\{x \mid A\}$, where A is a formula: set abstraction terms. These are intended to represent "the set of all x's such that A holds".

As in first order logic, the terms are the objects of the theory: quantified variables range over the closed terms, and any term can be tested for equality with another term, passed as a parameter, and so on. But closed terms in G are also intended to represent sets of closed terms; that is, they are intended to have additional significance when they appear on the right-hand side of the $\in$ symbol. I will expand on this point when we discuss set membership formulae, below.

Goal formulae. We will use the metavariables **A**, **B**, and **C** to stand for arbitrary goal formulae. Goal formulae are those expressions recognised by the following pseudo-BNF syntax:

$$\mathbf{A} ::= \quad s = t \mid s \in t \mid t(s_1, \ldots, s_n) \mid \mathbf{B\&C} \mid \mathbf{B \vee C} \mid \exists x\, \mathbf{B}$$

These formulae are intended to be read as follows.

- $s = t$: intensional identity between s and t. Any term is equal to itself, but for instance **P** is never equal to **Q** even if **P** and **Q** have the same extensions.
- $s \in t$: set membership. The meaning of such a formula depends on the form of t. Formulae of the form $s \in \mathbf{P}$ are atomic formulae representing *a priori* knowledge, as given by a model and constrained by a program. Formulae $s \in \{x|\mathbf{A}\}$ are *not* considered to be atomic, but hold only if $\mathbf{A}[x := s]$ holds. Formulae $s \in t$ are false if t is a function application or tuple; that is, function application terms represent the empty set.
- $t(s_1, \ldots, s_n)$: this is just an abbreviation for $\langle s_1, \ldots, s_n \rangle \in t$, mainly so that we can continue to write $\mathbf{P}(s_1, \ldots, s_n)$ for a predicate application.
- $\mathbf{B\&C}, \mathbf{B \vee C}, \exists x\, \mathbf{B}$: these have the usual logical significance.

We do not use the other connectives because we can completely characterise pure Prolog-style logic programming with only these connectives. I will usually abbreviate "goal formula" as just "formula" in the sequel.

Programs. A *predicate definition* of predicate **P** is an expression of the form

$$\mathbf{P}(x_1, \ldots, x_n) \leftrightarrow \mathbf{A}$$

in which the free variables of **A** (the *body* of the predicate) are all among $\{x_1, \ldots, x_n\}$. A *program* is a finite set of predicate definitions in which the names of all predicates being defined are distinct. I will sometimes write $\mathbf{A}(x_1, \ldots, x_n)$ and then $\mathbf{A}(t_1, \ldots, t_n)$ close to one another, to indicate a predicate body with free variables $x_1, \ldots, x_n$, and then the body with those variables replaced by $t_1, \ldots, t_n$.

Examples. Let us write [ ] and [_|_] for the empty list constant and the binary list-formation function, respectively. The standard "Append" predicate for appending two lists to make another can then be written as:

$Append(x, y, z) \leftrightarrow$
$\quad (x = [\,] \;\&\; y = z) \vee$
$\quad \exists xh \exists xt \exists zt(x = [xh|xt] \;\&\; Append(xt, y, zt) \;\&\; z = [xh|zt])$

The LISP function "map" takes a function and a list, and returns a list which is the image of the argument list in the function. The definition of the analogue of this function in G is:

$Map(p, x, y) \leftrightarrow$
$\quad (x = [\,] \;\&\; y = [\,]) \vee$
$\quad \exists xh \exists xt \exists yh \exists yt(x = [xh|xt] \;\&\; p(xh, yh) \;\&\; Map(p, xt, yt) \;\&\; y = [yh|yt])$

Programs act as the assumptions which we work from to prove the satisfiability of goal formulae. It would therefore suffice to give definitions with a simple implication ← instead of the bi-implication ↔; the other direction of the bi-implication is included mainly to emphasise that there is a single unique definition for each predicate in a program.

We will always be proving satisfiability with respect to the models of a program. A program therefore specifies, via the model theory, the set associated with each predicate it defines.

2.2 Model Theory

The logical semantics of G are almost as simple as the semantics of Horn clause logic. Briefly and informally, a *base* represents one assignment of *a priori* truth to a set of predicate application formulae; a *model* of a given program is defined much as it would be in first order logic.

Definition 1. A *base* is a set B of sentences (closed formulae) of the form $s \in P$.

Definition 2. The semantic consequence relation $\models$ between a base and a sentence holds just in the following cases:

1. If A is in B, then $B \models A$;
2. $B \models t = t$;
3. If $B \models A[x := s]$, then $B \models (s \in \{x \mid A\})$;
4. If $B \models B$ and $B \models C$, then $B \models (B \& C)$;
5. If either $B \models B$ or $B \models C$, then $B \models (B \vee C)$;
6. If there is a t such that $B \models B[x := t]$, then $B \models \exists x B$.

The relation $B \models A$ is read as "B satisfies A".

Definition 3. A base B is a *model* of a program Π if, whenever $P(x_1, \ldots, x_n) \leftrightarrow A(x_1, \ldots, x_n)$ is in Π and $B \models A(t_1, \ldots, t_n)$, we have that $P(t_1, \ldots, t_n)$ is in B.

Theorem 4. B_Π, *the intersection of all models of* Π, *is also a model of* Π; *it is therefore the least model of* Π.

Proof. B_Π contains all sentences found in all models of Π. We can prove by induction on the structure of A that if B_Π satisfies $A(t_1, \ldots, t_n)$ then every model of Π satisfies it. $P(t_1, \ldots, t_n)$ is therefore in every model of Π, and therefore in B_Π.

To prove the completeness of the proof system, it will also be convenient to have a characterisation of the least model in terms of closure operators.

Definition 5. $succ_\Pi(B)$, the Π-*successor of* B, is the least set such that:

1. If A is in B, then A is in $succ_\Pi(B)$;

2. If $P(x_1, \ldots, x_n) \leftrightarrow A(x_1, \ldots, x_n)$ is in Π, and $\mathcal{B} \models A(t_1, \ldots, t_n)$, then $P(t_1, \ldots, t_n)$ is in $succ_\Pi(\mathcal{B})$.

Theorem 6. $\mathcal{B}_\Pi = \bigcup_{k=0}^\infty succ_\Pi^k(\emptyset)$.

Proof. We can prove, by induction on k, that every member of every $succ_\Pi^k(\emptyset)$ must be in every model of Π. We can also prove that the union of all of them is a model; it must therefore be the least model.

This last theorem, a very weak form of the Knaster-Tarski fixpoint theorem, is all we need to prove completeness of the proof system for G. It is equivalent to saying that the least model is the least fixpoint of the associated transformation on the lattice of bases under set inclusion.

2.3 Proof Theory

Associated with each program Π there is a sound proof system Gnd_Π which is complete for all closed formulae. In general, the exact form of the program will be unimportant, and we will drop the subscript Π.

Definition 7. A formula A is *valid* with respect to a program Π if every model of Π satisfies every closed instance of A.

Proof. From the theorems in the last section.

$$=: \quad \overline{t = t} \qquad\qquad \&: \quad \frac{B \quad C}{B\&C}$$

$$\vee,1: \quad \frac{B}{B \vee C} \qquad\qquad \vee,2: \quad \frac{C}{B \vee C}$$

$$\exists: \quad \frac{B[x := t]}{\exists x(B)} \qquad\qquad P: \quad \frac{A(t_1, \ldots, t_n)}{P(t_1, \ldots, t_n)}$$

where Π contains the definition
$$(P(x_1, \ldots, x_n) \leftrightarrow A(x_1, \ldots, x_n))$$

$$\in: \quad \frac{A[x := s]}{s \in \{x | A\}}$$

Fig. 1. The proof system Gnd.

The rules of the system Gnd are as listed in Figure 1. The formal statements of the soundness and completeness results for G are as follows.

Theorem 8 (Soundness of Gnd). *If* **A** *is derivable in* Gnd_Π, *then* **A** *is valid with respect to* Π.

Proof. By induction on the structure of Gnd derivations. Every instance of a formula of the form $\mathbf{t} = \mathbf{t}$ is satisfied by every model of Π; the soundness of the other rules follows from the definition of the consequence relation and the model of a program.

The converse completeness theorem is not true: there are valid formulae which are not derivable in Gnd. An example of such a formula is $Append(x, [\ ], x)$, where *Append* is the predicate given above for appending two lists. Every closed instance of this formula is derivable, so (by the soundness theorem) every closed instance of it is valid; so the formula itself is valid. Nevertheless, the formula itself has no derivation; in fact, the logic is powerful enough to have no complete proof system. However, Gnd is complete for closed formulae.

Lemma 9. *(1) For every* $k \geq 0$, *if all members of* $succ_\Pi^k(\emptyset)$ *are derivable, then all* **A** *such that* $succ_\Pi^k(\emptyset) \models \mathbf{A}$ *are derivable. (2) For every* $k \geq 0$, *all* **A** *such that* $succ_\Pi^k(\emptyset) \models \mathbf{A}$ *are derivable.*

Proof. (1) By induction on the structure of **A**, with cases on the rules for the $\models$ relation. (2) By induction on k, by the definition of model.

Theorem 10 (Completeness of Gnd). *If* **A** *is closed and valid with respect to* Π, *then* **A** *is derivable in* Gnd_Π.

Proof. Since **A** is closed, it is valid iff it is satisfied by all models, and therefore iff it is satisfied by the least model. But if it is satisfied by the least model, then (by the theorems in the last section) there must be some k such that $succ_\Pi^k(\emptyset) \models \mathbf{A}$; so by the last lemma, **A** is derivable.

See Figure 2 for an example of a derivation in Gnd.

2.4 Comparison with NaDSetI

System G is based on Gilmore's NaDSetI [Gil86], but is not identical to it. I should say a few words here about how and why it is different from NaDSetI.

The differences between G and NaDSetI are mainly to make G fit in more easily with the logic programming paradigm. G is NaDSetI with the addition of non-nullary function symbols and tuples, and with a restricted version of set abstraction terms and a restricted set of connectives.

In NaDSetI, Gilmore starts with the empty set $\{\mathbf{x} \mid \mathbf{x} \neq \mathbf{x}\}$ and builds up the integers and pairs from it by Frege's method. We could have extended this method to define tuples and non-nullary function symbols, but this seems an unnecessary inconvenience in the context of logic programming, where we use function applications everywhere to build data structures. Of course, once we add function applications, we must give some meaning to formulae expressing

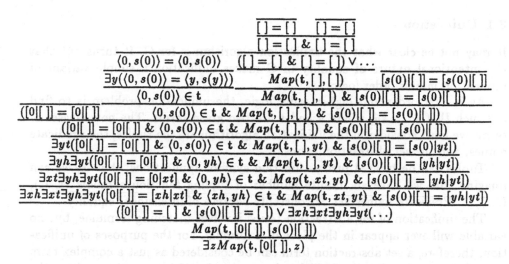

Fig. 2. Derivation of $\exists z Map(\{x \mid \exists y(x = \langle y, s(y)\rangle)\}, [0|[\,]\,], z)$. t stands for the set abstraction term $\{x \mid \exists y(x = \langle y, s(y)\rangle)\}$.

membership in those terms; I have chosen to say that function applications have no members (ie. that they denote the empty set), since it seems the most philosophically and technically natural option.

Set abstraction terms with arbitrary abstracted terms are allowed in NaDSetI – that is, set abstraction terms of the form $\{t \mid A\}$ rather than just $\{x \mid A\}$. This gives NaDSet extra power in the case of one rule in the left-hand side of its sequent calculus, but would give us no extra power in the simplified context of the logic programming connectives. We can achieve the effect of such a set abstraction term with a term of the form $\{x \mid \exists y_1 \ldots \exists y_n(x = t\&A)\}$, where $y_1 \ldots y_n$ are the free variables of t.

Finally, G has only "goal" formulae with the three connectives &, $\vee$, and $\exists$, rather than the full first order formulae given by NaDSet. This is, of course, because these are essentially the only forms of formulae that can be handled by simple pure Prolog-style logic programming interpreters. The restriction to goal formulae allows the simplification of the model theory, as presented above.

3 Operational Semantics

We can show that G can be seen as a useful logic programming language by giving an operational ("procedural") semantics for it, and showing that the semantics is sound and complete in some useful sense. This section presents such an operational semantics, called Glp. Glp is very similar to the conventional SLD-resolution strategy (for instance, it is nondeterministic in the same ways as SLD-resolution), but needs certain additional rules to handle the extra features of G.

3.1 Unification

It may not be clear what the unification algorithm is for G. It turns out that the intensional nature of equality in G makes unification a simple variant of unification in first order logic.

As in first order and higher order logic, the unification problem is to find a θ such that $s\theta = t\theta$, where s and t are two given terms. The new classes of terms we must consider in the unification algorithm are the tuples, the predicate names, and the set abstraction terms.

Tuples can be treated just as function symbol applications; that is, we can imagine that we have an infinite number of tupling function symbols $\langle\rangle$, $\langle\_\rangle$, $\langle\_,\_\rangle$, ... Predicate names act as constants because of intensional equality.

The unification of set abstraction terms involves matching formulae, but no variable will ever appear in the place of a formula. For the purposes of unification, therefore, a set abstraction term can be considered as just a complex term constructor, and unification still involves only identifying locations where the terms differ and constructing substitutions of terms for variables.

3.2 The Operational Semantics Glp

The operational semantics essentially takes the form of an abstract machine which keeps track of the current substitution and the current stack of subgoals. Like SLD-resolution, it is nondeterministic; the machine is able to make more than one transition at any particular time.

Definition 11. A *goal stack* is just a sequence of formulae. We will generally use α, possibly subscripted, to stand for an arbitrary goal stack. We will write the concatenation of two goal stacks α_1 and α_2 as α_1, α_2.

A *closure* is an expression $(\theta : \alpha)$, where α is a goal stack and θ is a substitution. (In practice, θ will be some syntactic representation of a substitution on a finite number of variables.)

ϵ will represent the empty goal stack.

There will be one operational semantics, called Glp_Π, corresponding to each program Π. (Again, we will usually drop the subscript.) Glp is a rewriting system which consists of a definition of a "start state" for a query, rules for a binary relation $\overset{\text{Glp}}{\Rightarrow}$ between closures, and a definition of which closures are to be considered "success states". The substitution in a closure represents the information which has been built up so far about a possible solution, and its goal stack represents the set of subgoals which remain to be processed. We can therefore think of a closure $(\theta : A_1, \ldots, A_n)$ as being a request to find a satisfying substitution for the formula $(A_1\theta \& \ldots \& A_n\theta)$.

Start states. The start state of the system, for a particular query A, is the closure $(() : A)$, where $()$ is the empty substitution; that is, a closure with no information about a solution and a single formula in the goal stack.

Rewriting rules.

1. **&:** $(\theta : \alpha_1, (\mathbf{B}\&\mathbf{C}), \alpha_2) \overset{\mathrm{Glp}}{\Rightarrow} (\theta : \alpha_1, \mathbf{B}, \mathbf{C}, \alpha_2)$

2. **∨, 1:** $(\theta : \alpha_1, (\mathbf{B} \vee \mathbf{C}), \alpha_2) \overset{\mathrm{Glp}}{\Rightarrow} (\theta : \alpha_1, \mathbf{B}, \alpha_2)$

3. **∨, 2:** $(\theta : \alpha_1, (\mathbf{B} \vee \mathbf{C}), \alpha_2) \overset{\mathrm{Glp}}{\Rightarrow} (\theta : \alpha_1, \mathbf{C}, \alpha_2)$

4. **∃:** $(\theta : \alpha_1, (\exists \mathbf{x}\mathbf{B}), \alpha_2) \overset{\mathrm{Glp}}{\Rightarrow} (\theta : \alpha_1, \mathbf{B}[\mathbf{x} := \mathbf{x}'], \alpha_2)$
   where $\mathbf{x}'$ is some variable not appearing free to the left of the arrow

5. **Defined predicates:** $(\theta : \alpha_1, \mathbf{P}(\mathbf{t}_1, \ldots, \mathbf{t}_n), \alpha_2) \overset{\mathrm{Glp}}{\Rightarrow} (\theta : \alpha_1, \mathbf{A}(\mathbf{t}_1, \ldots, \mathbf{t}_n), \alpha_2)$
   where Π contains the definition $(\mathbf{P}(\mathbf{x}_1, \ldots, \mathbf{x}_n) \leftrightarrow \mathbf{A}(\mathbf{x}_1, \ldots, \mathbf{x}_n))$

6. **Unification:** $(\theta : \alpha_1, \mathbf{s} = \mathbf{t}, \alpha_2) \overset{\mathrm{Glp}}{\Rightarrow} (\theta\theta' : \alpha_1, \alpha_2)$
   where θ' is the mgu of $\mathbf{s}\theta$ and $\mathbf{t}\theta$

7. **Instantiation:** $(\theta : \alpha_1, \mathbf{s} \in \mathbf{t}, \alpha_2) \overset{\mathrm{Glp}}{\Rightarrow} (\theta : \alpha_1, \mathbf{s}\theta \in \mathbf{t}\theta, \alpha_2)$

8. **Splitting:** $(\theta : \alpha_1, \mathbf{x} \in \mathbf{P}, \alpha_2) \overset{\mathrm{Glp}}{\Rightarrow} (\theta : \alpha_1, \mathbf{x} = \langle \mathbf{x}_1, \ldots, \mathbf{x}_n \rangle, \mathbf{x} \in \mathbf{P}, \alpha_2)$
   where $\mathbf{x}_1, \ldots, \mathbf{x}_n$ are variables not appearing to the left of the arrow, and
   where $\mathbf{P}$ is of arity n in Π

9. **Abstracted sets:** $(\theta : \alpha_1, \mathbf{s} \in \{\mathbf{x} \mid \mathbf{A}\}, \alpha_2) \overset{\mathrm{Glp}}{\Rightarrow} (\theta : \alpha_1, \mathbf{A}[\mathbf{x} := \mathbf{s}], \alpha_2)$

Success states. The success states of Glp are the closures $(\theta : \mathbf{A}_1, \ldots, \mathbf{A}_n)$ where each $\mathbf{A}_i$ is a formula of the form $\mathbf{s} \in \mathbf{x}$ such that $\mathbf{x}\theta \equiv \mathbf{x}$. θ, as the soundness theorem will show, can be used to derive a satisfying substitution for the query in the start state of the computation.

We say that a closure C *succeeds* (*with substitution* θ) if $C \overset{\mathrm{Glp}}{\Rightarrow} C'$, where C' is a success state (whose substitution is θ).

Remarks. The essence of the SLD-resolution method of processing queries is that we defer decisions about the witnesses for existentially quantified variables until we have complete information (obtained from unifications) about the kind of values they are required to have. The operational semantics Glp captures this idea in the form of a transition system acting in different ways on different connectives. (See Figure 3 for a computation of the query formula whose existential closure is derived in Figure 2.)

The transition rules 1-3 and 9 break down subgoal formulae into their constituent subformulae in a manner consistent with our interpretation of a closure $(\theta : \mathbf{A}_1, \ldots, \mathbf{A}_n)$ as the formula $(\mathbf{A}_1\theta \& \ldots \& \mathbf{A}_n\theta)$. The existential quantifier rule (4) simply renames the quantified variable to avoid name clash; the defined predicate rule (5) expands the predicate application formula in the same manner that the proof system Gnd does. The unification rule (6) essentially stores the new information about the variables in the substitution. The Instantiation and Splitting rules are present mostly for technical reasons; they allow us to put formulae on the goal stack into the proper form for processing by the other rules, and contribute to the completeness of the system.

There are essentially two sources of nondeterminism in the operational semantics, corresponding to the two sources of nondeterminism in SLD-resolution:

$(() : Map(t, [0|[ ]], z))$

(5) $\overset{\text{Glp}}{\Rightarrow} (() : ([0|[ ]] = [ ] \ \& \ z = [ ]) \vee \exists xh \exists xt \exists yh \exists yt(\ldots))$

(3) $\overset{\text{Glp}}{\Rightarrow} (() : \exists xh \exists xt \exists yh \exists yt(\ldots))$

(4) $\overset{\text{Glp*}}{\Rightarrow} (() : [0|[ ]] = [xh|xt] \ \& \ \langle xh, yh \rangle \in t \ \& \ Map(t, xt, yt) \ \& \ z = [yh|yt])$

(1) $\overset{\text{Glp*}}{\Rightarrow} (() : [0|[ ]] = [xh|xt], \langle xh, yh \rangle \in t, Map(t, xt, yt), z = [yh|yt])$

(6) $\overset{\text{Glp*}}{\Rightarrow} ([xh := 0, xt := [ ], z := [yh|yt]] : \langle xh, yh \rangle \in t, Map(t, xt, yt))$

(9) $\overset{\text{Glp}}{\Rightarrow} ([xh := 0, xt := [ ], z := [yh|yt]] : \exists y(\langle xh, yh \rangle = \langle y, s(y) \rangle), Map(t, xt, yt))$

(4) $\overset{\text{Glp}}{\Rightarrow} ([xh := 0, xt := [ ], z := [yh|yt]] : \langle xh, yh \rangle = \langle y, s(y) \rangle, Map(t, xt, yt))$

(6) $\overset{\text{Glp}}{\Rightarrow} ([xh := 0, xt := [ ], z := [s(0)|yt], yh := s(0), y = 0] : Map(t, xt, yt))$

(5) $\overset{\text{Glp}}{\Rightarrow} ([xh := 0, xt := [ ], z := [s(0)|yt], yh := s(0), y = 0] : (xt = [ ] \ \& \ yt = [ ]) \vee \ldots)$

(2) $\overset{\text{Glp}}{\Rightarrow} ([xh := 0, xt := [ ], z := [s(0)|yt], yh := s(0), y = 0] : xt = [ ] \ \& \ yt = [ ]))$

(1) $\overset{\text{Glp}}{\Rightarrow} ([xh := 0, xt := [ ], z := [s(0)|yt], yh := s(0), y = 0] : xt = [ ], yt = [ ]))$

(6) $\overset{\text{Glp*}}{\Rightarrow} ([xh := 0, xt := [ ], z := [s(0)|[ ]], yh := s(0), y = 0, yt := [ ]] :)$

Fig. 3. Computation of the query $Map(\{x \mid \exists y(x = \langle y, s(y) \rangle)\}, [0|[ ]], z)$. t stands for the set abstraction term $\{x \mid \exists y(x = \langle y, s(y) \rangle)\}$. Numbers on the left indicate which computation rule is used next, and $\overset{\text{Glp*}}{\Rightarrow}$ indicates more than one application of the same rule.

the choice of which subgoal in the goal stack to consider, and the choice of which $\vee$ rule to take when the subgoal is a disjunction. It will turn out that there is a deterministic rule that we can use for choosing a subgoal, under which the operational semantics remains complete; however, there must be some form of parallelism in choosing the $\vee$ rule. This situation corresponds exactly to the fact that, in SLD-resolution, a left-to-right computation rule is complete, but only a fair search rule can be complete.

3.3 Soundness

The soundness and completeness of the operational semantics will be proved in an entirely syntactic manner, by referring to the sound and complete proof system Gnd rather than to the semantics of G. This proof-theoretic approach to proving these fundamental theorems has been explored for Horn clause logic programming in [HS84, HSH88, And89].

The version of soundness that Glp has is that if a goal succeeds, then it is satisfiable. This is a corollary of a more powerful theorem which constructs, from a successful computation of a query, a substitution which satisfies the query.

Theorem 12. *If* $(\theta : A_1, \ldots, A_n)$ *succeeds with substitution* $\theta\rho$, *then there is a* ρ' *such that* $\vdash A_i(\theta\rho\rho')$ *for all* $1 \le i \le n$.

Proof. By induction on the length of the Glp-computation. The substitution ρ' is really important only in the base case, where it serves to instantiate any variables appearing on the right-hand side of $\in$ which are left uninstantiated by the computation.

When the length is 0, we have a success state already, which is of the form

$$(\theta : s_1 \in x_1, \ldots, s_n \in x_n)$$

(Note that in this case, ρ is the empty substitution.) Let ρ' be the substitution $[x_1 := r, \ldots, x_n := r]$, where r is the term $\{y | y = y\}$ (the "universe" set). $(\theta\rho')$ will then be a satisfying substitution for each of the formulae in the closure.

In the case that the length of the Glp-computation is greater than 0, we have one subcase for each possible first step in the computation.

Cases &, $\vee_1$, $\vee_2$, Defined predicates, Instantiation, Abstracted set membership: follows fairly directly from the induction hypothesis.

Case $\exists$: the computation has the form

$$(\theta : \alpha_1, \exists x \ B, \alpha_2) \overset{\text{Glp}}{\Rightarrow} (\theta : \alpha_1, B[x := x'], \alpha_2) \overset{\text{Glp}}{\Rightarrow} (\theta\rho : \alpha)$$

By the induction hypothesis, there is a ρ' with the required properties for each of the α_1 and α_2 formulae, and such that $\vdash B[x := x']\theta\rho\rho'$. Now take t to be $x'(\theta\rho\rho')$; then $B[x := t](\theta\rho\rho')$ is equivalent to $B[x := x'](\theta\rho\rho')$, But then we have a derivation ending in the step

$$\frac{B[x := x'](\theta\rho\rho')}{(\exists x \ B)(\theta\rho\rho')}$$

ρ' therefore also has the required property for $\exists x \ B$ as well.

Case Unification: the computation has the form

$$(\theta : \alpha_1, s = t, \alpha_2) \overset{\text{Glp}}{\Rightarrow} (\theta\theta' : \alpha_1, \alpha_2) \overset{\text{Glp}}{\Rightarrow} (\theta\theta'\sigma : \alpha)$$

where $\rho \equiv \theta'\sigma$. By the induction hypothesis, there is a ρ' such that $\vdash A_i\theta\theta'\sigma\rho'$, for all the A_i's in α_1 and α_2. But from the definition of unifier, we have that $s\theta\theta'$ and $t\theta\theta'$ are identical. So clearly $\vdash (s = t)\theta\theta'\sigma\rho'$ as well.

Case Splitting: we are just adding one formula to the closure, so clearly if the new closure has satisfying substitutions then so does the old one.

Corollary 13 (Soundness of Glp). *If $(() : A)$ succeeds then there is a substitution σ such that $\vdash A\sigma$.*

Proof. Take θ to be $()$, and say that the closure succeeds with substitution ρ. Then the previous theorem states that there is a ρ' such that $\vdash A\rho\rho'$; therefore take σ to be $\rho\rho'$.

3.4 Completeness

The converse of the soundness theorem holds as well: if a query is satisfiable, then it will succeed. However, the stronger inductive theorem used to prove this theorem has a different flavour from that used to prove soundness. The soundness theorem tells us how to construct one satisfying substitution from the substitution with which the computation ends. The completeness theorem, however, does not tell us the final substitution of the computation. It merely tells us that a successful computation exists, and that the final substitution will be more general than the given satisfying substitution. (Of course, we can find out what this final substitution is by running the computation.)

Another way of viewing these two theorems is in what they say about the mapping from derivations to computations. There will be at least as many derivations of instances of A as there are computations of A, and there may in fact be more. Soundness tells us how to get *one* such derivation from the computation, and completeness tells us that given a derivation a computation *exists*; but a single computation may be the one corresponding to many derivations.

The completeness theorem will essentially prove the completeness not of Glp, but of a version of Glp equipped with a strategy for selecting subgoals. This strategy will "suspend" formulae of the form $s \in x$ which cannot be currently instantiated.

Definition 14. A subgoal A_i in a closure $(\theta : \alpha)$ is called a *suspended subgoal* just in case $A_i\theta$ is of the form $s \in x$.

The strategy will repeatedly select the first unsuspended subgoal in the goal stack, and then try to re-activate suspended subgoals after each unification. The only nondeterminism in this restricted interpreter is therefore in the choice of which $\vee$ rule to apply. It should be clear that if even Glp with this restricted strategy is complete, the unrestricted, nondeterministic version of Glp is also complete.

Theorem 15. *Assume that, for given $A_1, \ldots, A_n$ and substitutions θ, ρ, we have that $\vdash A_i\theta\rho$ for all $1 \le i \le n$. Then there are ρ', ρ'' such that $A_i\theta\rho'\rho'' \equiv A_i\theta\rho$ for all $1 \le i \le n$, and such that $(\theta : A_1, \ldots, A_n)$ succeeds with substitution $\theta\rho'$.*

Proof. The point of the theorem is that given a starting θ and subgoals A_i, if there is a solution ρ then the operational semantics will find a solution ρ' which is at least as general as ρ. The proof is by strong induction on the total number of rule applications in all the derivations of the $A_i\theta\rho$'s.

When this total is 0, we have that $n = 0$; but then $(\theta : \epsilon)$ is a success state, so we can take ρ' to be () and ρ'' to be ρ.

Now consider the case that the total number of rule applications is greater than 0. If all the $A_i's$ are suspended subgoals, then the closure succeeds already; ρ' is the empty substitution and ρ'' is ρ.

If not all the A_i's are suspended, let A_i be the first of $A_1, \ldots, A_n$ which is not suspended. We have subcases on the rule used at the base of the derivation of $A_i\theta\rho$.

Case $=$: the derivation consists of a single axiom, $s\theta\rho = t\theta\rho$, where the two terms are identical. We therefore have that $s\theta$ and $t\theta$ are unifiable; let their mgu be θ'. We have the computation

$$(\theta : \alpha_1, A_i, \alpha_2) \overset{\text{Glp}}{\Rightarrow} (\theta\theta' : \alpha_1, \alpha_2)$$

But by the properties of mgu, there is a θ'' such that $\theta'\theta'' \equiv \rho$. By assumption, $\vdash A_1(\theta\theta')\theta'' \cdots \vdash A_n(\theta\theta')\theta''$, and so by the induction hypothesis there are σ', σ'' such that $A_i\theta\theta'\sigma'\sigma'' \equiv A_i\theta\theta'\theta''$, and such that $(\theta\theta' : \alpha_1, \alpha_2)$ succeeds with substitution $(\theta\theta')\sigma'$. Taking ρ' to be $(\theta'\sigma')$ and ρ'' to be σ'', we have the result.

Cases $\&$, $\vee1$, $\vee2$: follows fairly directly from the induction hypothesis, using the appropriate rules from the operational semantics.

Case $\exists$: the last step in the Gnd-derivation of $A_i\theta\rho$ looks like this:

$$\frac{B[x := t]\theta\rho}{(\exists x\ B)\theta\rho}$$

We therefore have that $\vdash (B[x := x'])\theta[x' := t\theta]\rho$, for any new x'. But if we choose x' to be not in any of the A_i's, then by assumption we also have that $\vdash A_i\theta([x' := t\theta]\rho)$ for all $1 \le i \le n$. So by the induction hypothesis, we have that there is some ρ', ρ'' such that $A_i\theta\rho'\rho'' \equiv A_i\theta([x' := t\theta]\rho)$, and such that $(\theta : \alpha_1, B[x := x'], \alpha_2)$ succeeds with substitution $\theta\rho'$. Since $(\theta : \alpha_1, \exists x\ B, \alpha_2) \overset{\text{Glp}}{\Rightarrow} (\theta : \alpha_1, B[x := x'], \alpha_2)$, the result follows.

Cases P, Abst: If A_i is of the form $s \in x$, we can first perform one Instantiation step – which, because we have selected the first active formula, will instantiate x. If it is of the form $x \in P$, we can then perform one Splitting step. Then the result follows fairly directly from the induction hypothesis, by the Defined Predicate or Abstracted Sets rule, respectively.

Corollary 16 (Completeness of Glp). *If $\vdash A\sigma$, then $(() : A)$ succeeds.*

Proof. Take θ to be the empty substitution, and ρ to be σ. Then the previous theorem states that $(() : A)$ succeeds.

We can summarise the Soundness and Completeness results in the following way.

Corollary 17. *For all goal formulae A, the closure $(() : A)$ succeeds in Glp iff there is a substitution σ such that $\vdash A\sigma$.*

4 Computational Strength of G

G is more powerful than regular Prolog, but it is unclear how much more computational expressiveness it gives us. We need to examine the computational strength of G, particularly in comparison to that of regular Prolog and Lambda Prolog.

4.1 Predicates as Parameters with Intensional Identity

The main extension to Prolog-style logic programming in G is the treatment of predicate names as closed terms. This is a fairly weak extension, and the use of intensional identity instead of some form of extensional identity is especially weak; for instance, $\{x \mid B\&C\}$ and $\{x \mid C\&B\}$ are not even identical, and a predicate name is not identical to anything but itself.

However, this intensional identity is sufficient for storing predicate names in data structures, and for passing them as parameters – common uses of higher order features in programming. For example, in G we can write common "metaprogramming" predicates such as Map (section 2.1). The presence of set abstraction terms means that we can also compose set terms "on the fly" and pass them to predicates which are expecting predicates as parameters. For instance, we could pass the set term $\{x \mid \exists y \exists z \exists w (x = \langle y, z \rangle \& Reverse(y, w) \& Flatten(w, z))\}$ as the first parameter to Map and expect it to behave sensibly.

4.2 Extensions and Variations

G is not a very useful programming language as it stands, since it is only slightly more powerful, and somewhat less syntactically convenient, than Prolog. Aside from syntactic sugar (such as implicit existential quantification for unquantified local variables), we can identify a few areas in which G could be improved as a programming language.

Universal Quantification and Iterated Implication. Following Miller et al. [MN86a], we should be able to add universal quantification and iterated implication to goal formulae. This would make goal formulae into G's equivalent of hereditary Harrop formulae. Universal quantification and iterated implication are useful in themselves; however, as Miller points out [Mil89], these two features in combination with the treatment of predicate names as terms give us the power to make local predicate definitions and perform other important operations having to do with scoping.

The implementation of Lambda Prolog-style universal quantification requires an infinite number of constants unused by programs. The analogue of this for G would be an infinite number of predicate names unused by programs, because predicate names act like closed terms under equality, and only predicate names can appear meaningfully on the right-hand side of $\in$. I have not pursued this line of development here, mainly because I wanted to present the basic idea of NaDSet-based logic programming in as simple a context as possible.

Sequentiality and Variable Modes. One practical problem with the operational semantics Glp is that subgoals are sometimes suspended and later reactivated. This would make it difficult for a programmer to follow the execution trace of a program, particularly if this happens by accident.

The problem of suspending and re-activating is a theoretical one, too. We can characterise Glp logically, but it would be very difficult to characterise a *sequential* version of Glp (a version in which "or"s are executed sequentially by failure and backtracking). Even the sequential version of normal Prolog is difficult to give a logical characterisation for [And90], and these difficulties would be compounded when the execution sequence jumps back and forth between all the subgoals.

One way of alleviating these problems would be to add variable mode declarations to the language (or to infer variable modes automatically [DW83]), and to insist that all variables which appear on the right-hand side of $\in$ be "input" mode. This would make the language less powerful, but not much less useful. As there would be no suspending and re-activating of subgoals (because the only subgoals which are suspended are of the form $t \in x$, where x is uninstantiated), the problems of characterising sequentiality should be no worse than with sequential Prolog.

4.3 Comparison with Lambda Prolog

Lambda Prolog [MN86a] was the first language to show that higher order logic could be used as the basis of a practical programming language. It is a very powerful language, but for a number of reasons it seems difficult to say whether G is more or less useful than Lambda Prolog.

The main area in which Lambda Prolog is more expressive than G is that it is possible to quantify over function symbols and define functions of the typed lambda calculus. So if we have reasons to program a particular notion as a function rather than as a predicate, Lambda Prolog is a better language to use.

Some uses of function application, however, can be replaced by uses of set membership formulae. The notion of membership in an abstracted set in G and the notion of lambda-term application in higher order logic are similar: $s \in \{x \mid A(x)\}$ and $(\lambda x.A(x))s$ are both semantically equivalent to $A(s)$. But this identification does not work completely in either direction.

In higher order logic, a formula can be applied to another to produce a formula, for instance $(\lambda X.(X \& B))A \leftrightarrow A \& B$. The corresponding thing is impossible in G, where a term can only be "applied" to another term to produce a formula. Higher order logic approaches therefore allow expressions not allowed in G.

But conversely, terms like $\{x \mid x \in x\}$, which are allowed in G, have corresponding lambda-terms like $\lambda x.(xx)$, which cannot be assigned a type and thus cannot appear in Lambda Prolog programs. (This is because typed lambda calculi have their ultimate origin in Russell's method of stratifying sets to avoid the set-theoretic paradoxes, whereas NaDSet results from Gilmore's completely different method of resolving those paradoxes.) Taking an example from [MN86b], the goal $\exists x Map(x, [a, b], [c, d])$, which fails in Lambda Prolog, succeeds in Glp with the substitution $[x := \{y \mid y = \langle a, c \rangle \lor y = \langle b, d \rangle\}]$. So neither system can claim to be strictly more expressive, in the sense of allowing more kinds of formulae, than the other.

From the programmer's point of view, perhaps the ultimate test would be whether the kinds of programs that we want higher order features for can be written in both languages. Examples of problems more easily handled by one or the other could of course be constructed. However, it seems, for instance, that all the examples in [MN86b] which do not involve universal quantification or implication (see above) can also be programmed naturally in G.

It may therefore transpire that G with the addition of universal quantification and iterated implication can be used for many of the applications of Lambda Prolog. On the other hand, we may find that the extra features of Lambda Prolog (functions, beta-equality, etc.) can offset such problems as the undecidability of unifiability of lambda-terms. We need more practical experience with G and Lambda Prolog to be able to make these judgments.

4.4 Comparison with HiLog

Chen, Kifer and Warren's HiLog [CKW89] offers a similar presentation of a language with "higher order syntax but first order semantics". The main differences between HiLog and G seem to be that HiLog eliminates the separation between term and formula by giving functional and relational denotations to all symbols, and that G has abstracted set terms.

The identification of term and formula means that in HiLog a term can be passed to a predicate and then "evaluated" as a formula, giving the Prolog "call" predicate a reasonable semantics, and (as in Lambda Prolog) allowing a wider range of higher order features. However, this would seem to complicate the operational semantics of the language, and it is not yet clear what an efficient operational semantics for a HiLog logic programming language would look like.

The presence of abstracted set terms in G serves a similar purpose to lambda-terms in Lambda Prolog, and the absence of such constructs in HiLog naturally means it is less powerful in this respect. The goal $\exists x Map(x, [a, b], [c, d])$, cited above as satisfiable in G and not in Lambda Prolog, is also in general an unsatisfiable HiLog query (no instance of it appears in the least model of a program, unless it happens to contain a predicate with the appropriate properties).

So as with Lambda Prolog, it seems that there are tradeoffs between the features of G and HiLog that make it difficult to judge one or the other as superior in all respects.

5 Summary and Future Work

I have presented a simple extension to first order logic programming which allows us to do useful metaprogramming tasks in a natural way. I have given model-theoretic and proof-theoretic foundations for this approach, and given a sound and complete operational semantics.

The system could be extended in several ways; perhaps the most important of these is the addition of universal quantification and implication, as suggested in Section 4.2. This would allow local predicate definitions and other useful and natural programming constructs.

The operational semantics Glp is sound and complete with respect to the proof system Gnd. As with all such systems, we can therefore use Gnd as the basis of a system for proving useful correctness and termination properties of logic programs [And89].

Finally, we need to know more about the relative strengths and weaknesses of G as compared to other logic programming systems such as Lambda Prolog and HiLog. Needles to say, an implementation of G would assist us in this.

6 Acknowledgements

My thanks to Paul Gilmore for discussing NaDSet with me at great length, and to Dale Miller, the other participants of this Workshop, and an anonymous reviewer, for helpful comments and suggestions.

References

[And89]   James H. Andrews. Proof-theoretic characterisations of logic programming. In *Proceedings of the 14th International Symposium on the Mathematical Foundations of Computer Science*, volume 379 of *Lecture Notes in Computer Science*, pages 145–154, Porąbka-Kozubnik, Poland, August-September 1989. Springer.

[And90]   James H. Andrews. The logical structure of sequential prolog. Technical Report LFCS-90-110, Laboratory for the Foundations of Computer Science, University of Edinburgh, Edinburgh, Scotland, April 1990.

[CKW89] Weidong Chen, Michael Kifer, and David S. Warren. HiLog: A first-order semantics of higher-order logic programming constructs. In *Proceedings of the North American Conference on Logic Programming*, Cleveland, Ohio, October 1989.

[DW83]   Saumya K. Debray and David S. Warren. Automatic mode inference for Prolog programs. In *Proceedings of 1986 Symposium on Logic Programming*, pages 78–88, Salt Lake City, Utah, September 1983.

[Gil86]   Paul C. Gilmore. Natural deduction based set theories: A new resolution of the old paradoxes. *Journal of Symbolic Logic*, 51(2):393–411, June 1986.

[HS84]   Masami Hagiya and Takafumi Sakurai. Foundation of logic programming based on inductive definition. *New Generation Computing*, 2:59–77, 1984.

[HSH88]   Lars Hallnäs and Peter Schroeder-Heister. A proof-theoretic approach to logic programming. Technical Report R88005, Swedish Institute of Computer Science, 1988.

[Mil89]   Dale A Miller. Lexical scoping as universal quantification. In *Proceedings of the Sixth International Logic Programming Conference*, pages 268–283, Lisbon, Portugal, June 1989.

[MN86a] Dale A. Miller and Gopalan Nadathur. Higher-order logic programming. In *Proceedings of the Third International Logic Programming Conference*, Imperial College, London, July 1986.

[MN86b] Dale A. Miller and Gopalan Nadathur. Some uses of higher-order logic in computational linguistics. In *Proceedings of the 24th Annual Meeting of the Association for Computational Linguistics*, pages 247–255, 1986.

A Survey of GCLA:
A Definitional Approach to Logic Programming

Martin Aronsson Lars-Henrik Eriksson Lars Hallnäs Per Kreuger
Knowledge Based Systems Laboratory, Swedish Institute of Computer Science
Box 1263, S-164 28 KISTA, Sweden
email: martin@sics.se

1. Introduction

GCLA (Generalized Horn Clause Language) is the kernel of a programming language belonging to the family of extensions of pure Horn clause languages.

GCLA is based on the idea of viewing the declarative part of a program as a definition rather than a set of formulas in some given formal language like first order logic. One consequence of this approach is that each program in a natural way will generate its own logic, i.e. a mode of reasoning that is intrinsic to the program as a definition.

A GCLA program consists of two parts: a declarative part which is a definition presenting declarative knowledge about a domain and a procedural part setting up the machinery for proof search in the local logic generated by the definition. So the first part gives the meaning of propositions, defines functions etc., while the second part specializes the built-in procedures for proving propositions or computing expressions.

The general idea is that these two parts form the natural components of an algorithmic presentation of a domain. Since we are striving towards greater flexibility and generality we want both parts to be explicit as parts in the written program. We want the programmer to have better tools for explicit control over the procedural part. We also think that the declarative and procedural parts should not be mixed, as in the case of Prolog programs, but instead be expressed separately.

This bears close resemblance to Kowalski's idea [Kow79]: "An algorithm can be regarded as consisting of a logic component, which specifies the knowledge to be used in solving problems, and a control component, which determines the problem-solving strategies by means of which that knowledge is used."

Programming languages today do not meet this requirement. For example, imperative languages (e.g. C, Pascal) do have a good control facility, but the logical part is very poor.

A pure logic program written in a logic programming language has a logical reading, but as the control is added, i.e. mixed with the logic program, the resulting program becomes more similar to an imperative program. A programmer writing programs in e.g. Prolog often tends to think something like "If I call that predicate, this variable will be instantiated to something like this, and then I have to call this predicate, and there I have to check that the variable X is bound...". This is hardly in the spirit of declarative programming. Many functional languages have similar problems.

The partition of a GCLA program into two different parts fulfils the requirement above, and gives us the freedom to change and develop the different parts one by one without affecting each other. This is a great advantage, since good program development often start with developing a (more or less executable) specification, which is then refined. This specification, on the other hand, does not tell the programmer how to find good strategies for proving things about the domain. As development proceeds, the programmer learns heuristics and general rules for making inferences, and this knowledge is then coded in the procedural part, which thus becomes more and more efficient without destroying the declarative (logical) part.

The paper is organized as follows: section 2 gives the theoretical background to GCLA, i.e. the theory of partial inductive definitions. In section 3 we present an operational semantics for a version of GCLA, called GCLA I, which consists mainly of the declarative part of programs. In section 4 we generalize the operational semantics by introducing a mechanism for controlling execution, turning GCLA I into GCLA II.

2. Theoretical Background

This section summarizes the basic features of the theory of partial inductive definitions [Hal87], which is the basis for the declarative semantics of GCLA [HS-H88].

The use of (ordinary) inductive definitions in logic programming has been proposed earlier by Hagiya and Sakurai [HS84]. In contrast to our work, they did not use inductive definitions as the basis for a programming language, but rather as a logic for reasoning about Prolog programs.

The declarative semantics of GCLA I is based on viewing a program as a *definition*. This can be seen as the basic idea of *declarative* programming languages. You could say that the declarative content of a program *is* a definition. A Prolog program is a definition of a set of predicates, a functional program is a definition of a set of functions and so on.

The notion of a definition considered here is more general than in the case of Prolog which among other things means that it will cover first order function definitions in a direct manner.

2.1. Partial inductive definitions

We start with a given universe $\mathcal{U}$ of atoms. The elements of $\mathcal{U}$ will be denoted by a, b, c,... A definition will then be viewed as a system of definitional clauses (equations) that define atoms in terms of certain conditions.

$$\left\{ \begin{array}{l} a = A \\ b = B \\ \quad ... \end{array} \right.$$

2.1.1. Conditions (over $\mathcal{U}$)

- $\top$ is a *condition* (over $\mathcal{U}$)
- $\bot$ is a *condition* (over $\mathcal{U}$)
- Each atom (in $\mathcal{U}$) is a *condition* (over $\mathcal{U}$)
- If C_i $(i \in I)$ is a condition (over $\mathcal{U}$), then $(C_i)_{i \in I}$ is a *condition* (over $\mathcal{U}$), where I is a given index set.
- If C and C' are conditions (over $\mathcal{U}$), then $C \rightarrow C'$ is a *condition* (over $\mathcal{U}$)

Conditions will be denoted by $A, B, C,...$ Let $Cond(\mathcal{U})$ stand for the set of conditions over $\mathcal{U}$. Finite sets of conditions will be denoted by $\Delta, \Gamma, \Sigma,...$

2.1.2. Definitional clauses (over $\mathcal{U}$)

If a is an atom (in $\mathcal{U}$) and A is a condition (over $\mathcal{U}$), then $a = A$ is a *definitional clause* (over $\mathcal{U}$).

Here we use the equality symbol to write definitional clauses as equations. In the programming syntax used in sections 3 and 4, we will instead use the symbol <=. This symbol is also used throughout in several earlier papers about GCLA and partial inductive definitions.

2.1.3. Definitions (Partial inductive definitions over $\mathcal{U}$)

A *definition* (over $\mathcal{U}$) is a set of definitional clauses (over $\mathcal{U}$). We denote definitions by $\mathcal{D},\ldots$

Let $Dom(\mathcal{D}) = \{a \mid (a = A) \in \mathcal{D}\}$ and $\overline{\mathcal{D}} = \mathcal{D} \cup \{a = \perp \mid a \notin Dom(\mathcal{D})\}$. *Definiens* of an atom a (relative to given definition $\mathcal{D}$) is then

$$D(a) = \{A \mid (a = A) \in \overline{\mathcal{D}}\}$$

2.1.4. Local D-consequence

The logical interpretation of a definition $\mathcal{D}$ will be given in terms of a derived notion of $\mathcal{D}$-*consequence* $\vdash_{\mathcal{D}}$:

Assume $\vdash$ is a relation between finite sets of conditions and conditions. Expressions of the form $\Gamma \vdash C$ will as usual be called *sequents*. Let $Seq(\mathcal{U})$ denote the set of sequents over $\mathcal{U}$. Let Γ, C be short for $\Gamma \cup \{C\}$. We say that $\vdash$ is a *condition relation* if $\vdash$ has the following closure properties:

$(\top)$ $\qquad\qquad\qquad \Gamma \vdash \top$

$(\perp)$ $\qquad\qquad\qquad \Gamma, \perp \vdash C$

$(\vdash ())$ $\qquad\qquad \dfrac{\{\Gamma \vdash C_i \mid i \in I\}}{\Gamma \vdash (C_i)_{i \in I}}$

$(() \vdash)$ $\qquad\qquad \dfrac{\Gamma, C_i \vdash C}{\Gamma, (C_i)_{i \in I} \vdash C} \quad (i \in I)$

$(\vdash \rightarrow)$ $\qquad\qquad \dfrac{\Gamma, C \vdash C'}{\Gamma \vdash C \rightarrow C'}$

$(\rightarrow \vdash)$ $\qquad\qquad \dfrac{\Gamma \vdash C \qquad \Gamma, C' \vdash C''}{\Gamma, C \rightarrow C' \vdash C''}$

A condition relation $\vdash$ is _D-closed_ if it also satisfies:

$$(\vdash \mathcal{D}) \qquad \frac{\Gamma \vdash A}{\Gamma \vdash a} \quad (A \in D(a))$$

$$(\mathcal{D} \vdash) \qquad \frac{\{\Gamma, A \vdash C \mid A \in D(a)\}}{\Gamma, a \vdash C}$$

$\vdash$ is _reflexive_ (I) if $\Gamma, a \vdash a$ holds for all a and Γ.

In the sequel, the symbol $\top$ will generally be omitted to the left of the turnstile.

Let $\vdash_{\mathcal{D}}$ be the smallest $\mathcal{D}$-closed reflexive condition relation. We say that a condition C is _true_ in $\mathcal{D}$ if $\vdash_{\mathcal{D}} C$ and _false_ in $\mathcal{D}$ if $C \vdash_{\mathcal{D}} \bot$. The property _defined by_ $\mathcal{D}$ is

$$Def(\mathcal{D}) = \{a \mid \vdash_{\mathcal{D}} a\}.$$

So $\mathcal{D}$ defines the set of atoms true in the local logic generated by $\mathcal{D}$.

The operational semantics of GCLA I will be based on rules corresponding to each of the closure properties defining $\vdash_{\mathcal{D}}$.

We may think of the closure properties defining $\vdash_{\mathcal{D}}$ as properties characterizing a notion of logical consequence. This notion is a _local_ one, since it depends on $\mathcal{D}$ in a non trivial way. We cannot a priori have a global reading of conditions that depend on atoms defined by a given definition. So the intended meaning of the clause $a = A$ is that a holds in $\mathcal{D}$, if A holds in $\mathcal{D}$. One can think of this in terms of A being _true_ in $\mathcal{D}$, which means:

$$\vdash_{\mathcal{D}} a \ \textit{iff} \ \vdash_{\mathcal{D}} A \quad \text{for some } A \in D(a)$$
$$\vdash_{\mathcal{D}} C \rightarrow C' \ \textit{iff} \ C \vdash_{\mathcal{D}} C'$$
$$\vdash_{\mathcal{D}} (C_i)_{i \in I} \ \textit{iff} \ \vdash_{\mathcal{D}} C_i \quad \text{for all } i \in I$$

This also gives a connection between viewing $\mathcal{D}$ as a "model" and viewing it as a set of "logical laws".

Note that the definition of $\vdash_{\mathcal{D}}$ is elementary, i.e. a monotone inductive definition. It is precisely this combination of an elementary and local interpretation that makes it possible to combine reasonable computational properties with expressive power in a simple manner. This is quite analogous to the partial recursive functions.

2.2. Definitions as type systems for lambda terms

For the benefit of readers familiar with the theory of functional programming, we will show how a Curry-Howard interpretation of partial inductive definitions can be done. Through such an interpretation, we get the *computational* counterpart to the *logical* constructions we use to introduce and explain the local logic $\vdash_{\mathcal{D}}$ generated by a definition $\mathcal{D}$.

From the definition of $\vdash_{\mathcal{D}}$ we may construct a system of natural deduction for $\mathcal{D}$ in the obvious way. Given such a system we can use the Curry-Howard interpretation of propositions as types to interpret a definition as a type system for lambda terms. In this way we get both a *logical* interpretation of simply typed lambda calculus extended with abstract data types and a *computational* interpretation of the local logic of a definition. An interpretation along these lines has been carried out in detail in [FS90].

2.2.1. Types and terms

Let $\mathcal{D}$ be a given definition. In order to carry out the Curry-Howard interpretation we give each clause in $\mathcal{D}$ a name c and write $a = c(A)$ to indicate that the clause $a = A$ is given the name c.

$$(\top) \qquad\qquad \top : \top$$

$$(\bot) \qquad\qquad \frac{e : \bot}{\bot(e) : C}$$

$$(Assumption\text{-}variable) \quad x : A$$

$$(()I\text{-}vector) \qquad \frac{\{c_i : C_i \mid (i \in I)\}}{(c_i)_{i \in I} : (C_i)_{i \in I}}$$

$$(()E\text{-}projection) \qquad \frac{c : (C_i)_{i \in I}}{c.j : C_j} \quad (j \in I)$$

$$(\to I\text{-}abstraction) \qquad \frac{f(x) : B[x : A]}{\lambda x.f(x) : A \to B}$$

$$(\to E\text{-}application) \qquad \frac{f : A \to B \qquad e : A}{Ap(f,e) : B}$$

$$(DI\text{-}a\text{:}construction) \qquad \frac{e : A}{c(e) : a} \quad c(A) \in D(a)$$

$$(DE\text{-}a : case) \qquad \frac{e:a \quad \{f_c(x):C[x:A] \mid c(A) \in D(a)\}}{E(e, f_c \ldots):C}$$

2.2.2. Computation rules

$$(c_i)_{i \in I}.j \qquad \Rightarrow c_j$$

$$Ap(\lambda xa, b) \qquad \Rightarrow a[b/x]$$

$$E(c(e), f_{c'} \ldots) \qquad \Rightarrow f_c(e)$$

So we see that the introduction of an atom a, given a definition $\mathcal{D}$, will correspond to building up a canonical object of the type a while elimination of an atom a will correspond to a *case* construction for the definiens of a. What matters from the computational point of view is the structure of the definition. Take the natural numbers as an example:

$$N = 0(\top)$$
$$N = s(N)$$

This definition is *logically* trivial, but gives precisely the structure of the natural numbers. So this computational interpretation of a definition is an intensional interpretation which focus on the structure of a particular presentation of a property.

3. Syntax and Semantics of GCLA I

This section defines the syntax and semantics of GCLA I, which is the basis for GCLA II. But first we have to introduce the notion of a variable, since the theory of partial inductive definitions does not have this concept.

The usage of variables are essentially the same in GCLA and in Prolog, but their meaning are quite different. In Prolog, variables in clauses correspond to universally quantified variables in first order predicate logic and variables in goals as existentially quantified variables. In GCLA variables have no such logical meaning, they are best seen as a meta-logical device.

In a clause, the variables stand for arbitrary ground terms. The declarative meaning of a clause is the same as the set of clauses obtained by substituting every possible ground term (of the Herbrand universe) for the variables in the clause. Clauses containing variables are to be regarded as shorthand notation for such sets of ground clauses.

In a goal with variables, the variables are placeholders that will be substituted by some term, "bound", during execution. The case where execution succeeds without any term being substituted for a variable, should be interpreted in such a way that the goal holds when any ground term is substituted for the variable in question.

In Prolog, this meta-logical reading of variables coincides with the logical reading - the "Lifting lemma" in Lloyd [Llo87] is an example of this. This interpretation of variables in GCLA is the key to the connection between the declarative and operational semantics and must be kept in mind.

For a more complete and detailed treatment of the semantics of generalized Horn clauses, see [HS-H88].

This section defines the syntax of the declarative part of a GCLA program, together with the default set of rules used in the GCLA I version of the language. We also give some small examples of code. The font Courier will be used for code, and *italic Courier* will be used for metalevel objects.

3.1. Syntax

i) Variables
  - A *variable* is a string beginning with an upper case letter or the character "_".

ii) Functors and constants
  - A *functor* is a string beginning with a lower case letter, which can be applied to some number of arguments. Some special symbols, e.g. "->", are also used as infix functors.
  - A *constant* is a functor with no arguments.

  Some functors are reserved, i.e. "->", ",", "def", "rem" (see *conditions* below)

iii) Terms
  - Each variable is a *term*.
  - If t_1 ... t_n are terms, and f is an n-ary functor, then $f(t_1, ..., t_n)$ is a *term*.

  We will also call a non-variable term $f(t_1, ..., t_n)$ an *atom*.

iv) Guards
  We assume that there is a given set of special propositional functions $g_1, ..., g_n$ called *guards*. These guards restricts the applicability of a clause.

v)   Conditions
- Each term is a *condition*
- If $C_1, ..., C_n$, C are conditions, then $(C_1, ..., C_n \rightarrow C)$ is a *condition*.
- If R is a clause and C is a condition, then $\text{def}(R, C)$ is a *condition*.
- If R is a clause and C is a condition, then $\text{rem}(R, C)$ is a *condition*.

vi)   Clauses
- If $C_1, ..., C_n$ are conditions, $g_1, ..., g_m$ guards and t is a term, then
  $t \mathrel{<=} [g_1, ..., g_m], C_1, ..., C_n$ is a *clause*. We will refer to t as the *head* of the
  clause, and $C_1, ..., C_n$ as the *body* of the clause.

  $t \mathrel{<=} C_1, ..., C_n$ will be short for the clause $t \mathrel{<=} [], C_1, ..., C_n$
  t will be short for the clause $t \mathrel{<=} []$

vii)   Sequents
- If $C_1, ..., C_n$, C are conditions, then $C_1, ..., C_n \mathrel{\backslash-} C$ is a *sequent*.

We call $C_1, ..., C_n$ the *antecedent* and C the *consequent* of the sequent.

viii)   Definition
- A *definition* $\mathcal{D}$ is a finite list (ordered set) of clauses, each ended with a ".".

3.2. Operational semantics

The operational semantics given here is a static one that corresponds to the declarative semantics given in section 2. As we shall see later, this inference mechanism is too general in some applications, where a possibility to guide the execution is essential. It could also be that this framework does not correspond to the intention of how a specific definition should be used.

Sequents are written $C_1, ..., C_n \mathrel{\backslash-} C$, where $n \geq 0$. The symbols Δ and Γ are used to represent 0 or more arbitrary conditions. The conditions in the antecedent are ordered, and can not be duplicated freely, that is, there is no general contraction rule. When there are more than one condition in the antecedent, the conditions are considered from left to right.

A substitution is a set of bindings $\{X_1/t_1, ..., X_n/t_n\}$ where each X_i is a variable and each t_i is a term. If t is a term and σ a substitution, then $t\sigma$ denotes the term obtained from t by simultaneously substituting each occurrence in t of every X_i by the corresponding t_i. $\theta\sigma$ denotes the composition of the substitutions θ and σ. $mgu(t_1, t_2)$ denotes the most general unifier of t_1 and t_2.

A guard is interpreted as a built-in propositional function, which evaluates to *true* or *false*.

When executing a program, we give a sequent $C_1, ..., C_n \setminus- C$ as a query to the program and try to find substitutions σ such that certain sequents $C_1\sigma, ..., C_n\sigma \setminus- C\sigma$ holds according to the given definition. Intuitively this means that we are looking for substitutions σ such that $C\sigma$ "follows from" the antecedent $C_1\sigma ... C_n\sigma$ in the logic defined by the definition $\mathcal{D}$.

The rules will be stated here as deduction rules working on a *context*, with premises, conclusion and a proviso where needed. A context consists of a list of sequents, a substitution and a definition $\mathcal{D}$. By using a list of sequents, it is possible to write the rules with only one premise, making the inference rules correspond to state transitions. The list of sequents corresponds to the goal stack of unsolved goals in the actual implementation.

The state is defined by a triple,

$$\Sigma \qquad \langle \theta, \mathcal{D} \rangle$$

where Σ is a list of sequents, θ a substitution and $\mathcal{D}$ the current definition.

The rules are of the form

$$\frac{\Sigma' \qquad\qquad \langle \theta', \mathcal{D}' \rangle}{\Sigma \qquad\qquad \langle \theta, \mathcal{D} \rangle}$$

Lists of sequents are built up using the concatenation operator ".". The empty list will be denoted by $\varnothing$.

To see if a certain sequent s holds according to the current definition $\mathcal{D}$, $s.\varnothing$ is put at the bottom, and we then try to find a proof working upwards.

The relation between the rules presented below and the declarative semantics given in 2.1 is investigated in [HS-H88].

i) *Initial context*

The initial contexts are the axioms of the operational semantics. They contain an empty list of sequents, so no inference rules are applicable to them;

$$\varnothing \qquad\qquad \langle \theta, \mathcal{D} \rangle$$

for any θ and $\mathcal{D}$. Since we carry out a proof backwards, from the bottommost list of sequents to the topmost one, this is the point where the resulting substitution θ is presented, as the answer of the execution.

ii) *Initial-sequent* or *axiom*

$$\frac{\Sigma\sigma}{(\Delta, C, \Gamma \setminus - C').\Sigma} \qquad\qquad \frac{\langle \theta\sigma, \mathcal{D} \rangle}{\langle \theta, \mathcal{D} \rangle}$$

where $\sigma = mgu(C, C')$.

iii) *Arrow-right*

$$\frac{(A_1, ..., A_n, \Gamma \setminus - C).\Sigma}{(\Gamma \setminus - (A_1, ..., A_n \rightarrow C)).\Sigma} \qquad\qquad \frac{\langle \theta, \mathcal{D} \rangle}{\langle \theta, \mathcal{D} \rangle}$$

iv) *Arrow-left*

$$\frac{(\Delta, \Gamma \setminus - A_1). ... .(\Delta, \Gamma \setminus - A_n).(\Delta, C, \Gamma \setminus - C').\Sigma}{(\Delta, (A_1, ..., A_n \rightarrow C), \Gamma \setminus - C').\Sigma} \qquad\qquad \frac{\langle \theta, \mathcal{D} \rangle}{\langle \theta, \mathcal{D} \rangle}$$

v) *Definition-right*

$$\frac{(\Gamma\sigma \setminus - A_1\sigma). ... .(\Gamma\sigma \setminus - A_n\sigma).\Sigma\sigma}{(\Gamma \setminus - C').\Sigma} \qquad\qquad \frac{\langle \theta\sigma, \mathcal{D} \rangle}{\langle \theta, \mathcal{D} \rangle}$$

where some $(C \leftarrow [y_1, ..., y_m], A_1, ..., A_n) \in \mathcal{D}$, $\sigma = mgu(C, C')$ and the $g_1\sigma, ...,$ $g_m\sigma$ are all *true*.

Operationally, this rule corresponds to ordinary SLD-resolution in Prolog.

vi) *Definition-left*

$$\frac{((\Delta, A_{11}, ..., A_{1n_1}, \Gamma \backslash - C'). \, ... \, .(\Delta, A_{k1}, ..., A_{kn_k}, \Gamma \backslash - C').\Sigma)\sigma \qquad \langle \theta\sigma, \mathcal{D} \rangle}{(\Delta, C, \Gamma \backslash - C').\Sigma \qquad \qquad \langle \theta, \mathcal{D} \rangle}$$

where σ is a <u>c-sufficient substitution</u> computed as explained below. The clauses C_i $<=$ $[g_{i1}, ..., g_{im_i}], A_{i1}, ..., A_{in_i}$ are all the clauses in $\mathcal{D}$ such that $C_i\sigma = C\sigma$ and $g_{i1}\sigma,...,g_{im_i}\sigma$ are all *true*.

The algorithm for computing C-sufficient substitution is based on the algorithm for calculating the most general unifier of two terms.

Let $C_1,..., C_n$ be some permutation of the heads of all definitional clauses in $\mathcal{D}$ and let

$$mgu'(C,C') = \begin{cases} mgu(C,C') & \text{if } mgu(C,C') \text{ exists} \\ \varnothing & \text{otherwise} \end{cases}$$

Then define

$$\sigma_0 \quad = \varnothing$$
$$\sigma_{m+1} = \sigma_m mgu'(C\sigma_m, C_{m+1})$$
$$\sigma \quad = \sigma_n$$

Note that this algorithm considers all heads of the definition $\mathcal{D}$. Those heads that are not applicable will be rejected by the condition $C_i\sigma = C\sigma$ in the inference rule.

The permutation of the heads is needed since different orderings of the clauses can result in different unifiers, meaning that there could be several ways to reduce a condition in the antecedent with the rule *definition-left*.

There is a condition on the A_i:s in the premises for the rule *definition-left* above, namely that they do not introduce any new variables, i.e. the A_i:s should not contain any variables that do not also occur in their corresponding clause heads C_i. This condition could be removed by introducing quantification in derivations (see [Eri90]). Currently the check is omitted, relying on the programmer to be conscious about this condition.

The algorithm above is incomplete in the sense that it does not always calculate all possible σ. This has to do with the fact that in this algorithm only the heads of the clauses in $\mathcal{D}$ are taken into account from which $C\sigma$ can be obtained by substitution, and not other possible $C\sigma$ (for example, such σ that makes $C\sigma$ be without a definition in $\mathcal{D}$). This restriction, however, makes the algorithm simple and efficient.

The two definition rules (*definition-right* and *definition-left*) are the "interface" to the definition $\mathcal{D}$, the declarative knowledge. Using these two rules it is possible to draw conclusions based on the domain knowledge.

With the rules above there is no possibility of changing the definition. We can *reason* about it, *assume* things about it during the execution by adding conditions to the antecedent, but not *extend* or *remove* anything from the definition.

The def and rem rules are used to alter the definition. They are local in the sense that the effect of their actions are undone upon backtracking or success of the execution.

By altering the definition we actually change the logic with which we reason. When using def or rem, we reason on basis of the fact that something really has changed in our world. When we add a condition to the antecedent, we *assume* that something holds, or is defined, in the current world. An analogue is that using def and rem corresponds to learning new knowledge; we have actually noted that something has changed in the world, and alter our knowledge to be in accordance with it.

vii) Def-right

$$\frac{(\Gamma \setminus - C).\Sigma}{(\Gamma \setminus - \text{def}(R, C)).\Sigma} \qquad \frac{\langle \theta, \mathcal{D} \cup \{R\}\rangle}{\langle \theta, \mathcal{D}\rangle}$$

viii) Def-left

$$\frac{(\Delta, C, \Gamma \setminus - C').\Sigma}{(\Delta, \text{def}(R, C), G \setminus - C').\Sigma} \qquad \frac{\langle \theta, \mathcal{D} \cup \{R\}\rangle}{\langle \theta, \mathcal{D}\rangle}$$

ix) Rem-right

$$\frac{(\Gamma \setminus - C).\Sigma}{(\Gamma \setminus - \text{rem}(R, C)).\Sigma} \qquad \frac{\langle \theta, \mathcal{D} \setminus \{R\}\rangle}{\langle \theta, \mathcal{D}\rangle}$$

x) Rem-left

$$\frac{(\Delta, C, \Gamma \setminus - C').\Sigma}{(\Delta, \text{rem}(R, C), \Gamma \setminus - C').\Sigma} \qquad \frac{\langle \theta, \mathcal{D} \setminus \{R\}\rangle}{\langle \theta, \mathcal{D}\rangle}$$

When removing clauses using the rem rules, clauses will be considered equal if they are variable renaming variants of each other (equal modulo variable renaming), so 0 or more clauses are removed. These rules always succeed.

Also note that the def and rem rules are written so that the sequents in Σ are also affected by their effects. An alternative formulation would be to just let the effect of these rules be local to the current sequent, and not affect the context in which Σ will be executed.

3.3. Examples of definitions

The examples in this section both demonstrate programs and some queries, which are executed with the rules defined in section 3.2. Some of the examples use control primitives. These primitives will only be used in this section. A more general system for control will be introduced in the section 4.

The primitives used in this section are listed below.

&axiom(X)

This primitive, or annotation, constrains the term x to be used only by the rule *initial-sequent*.

var(X),nonvar(X),neq(X,Y)

These primitives are used in guards. var(X) is true if x is a variable, nonvar(X) is true if x is currently not a free variable, neq(X,Y) is true if x and Y is not equal.

:- setglobal(Variable, Value)

This primitive call to the system sets a global parameter to a given value. It is used to alter the way GCLA executes a goal. The most common variables and their values are listed below.

- execution_order   list of axiom, right, left

  This parameter determines the order in which rules are applied to a sequent. The default value is [axiom,right,left]. The list is searched from left to right, so in the default case the rule *initial-sequent* is tried first, then a rule to the right of the turnstile, and lastly a condition in the antecedent and a corresponding rule to the left of the turnstile. right represents all the rules to the right of the turnstile, left represents all the rules to the left of the turnstile, and axiom is the rule *initial-sequent*.

- functor   total

  Declaring a functor in this way should be understood as adding a circular clause p <= p.to the current definition. This can be seen as defining p without giving any information that can be used to show how it holds. The effect of this is that when the term p occurs as a member of the antecedent, and there is no clause that defines p, p will not be used for reduction by the rule *definition-left*, since that would be pointless. With the closed world assumption, this would be "opening p".

Some terms are system defined to be declared total. These terms are the constant [] (i.e. the empty list), lists and numbers.

For each example of a definition in this section we will first give the code, then the queries and their answer substitutions. When several answers can be obtained by backtracking, we write ";" after the last substitution. We will use "..." under a substitution to indicate that there are more, possibly identical, substitutions.

3.3.1. Default reasoning

Consider the definition D_1, where an elephant is grey if it is not an albino elephant. We have an elephant clyde and an albino elephant karo. All albino elephants are of course elephants.

```
grey(X) <= elephant(X), (albino_elephant(X) -> false).

elephant(clyde).
elephant(X) <= albino_elephant(X).

albino_elephant(karo).
```

Below is a deduction of the query "Which elephant is grey", \- grey(Y). The deduction is performed from the bottom to the top, and when there are no more sequents to be proven, the answer substitution is presented.

"Present Y = clyde"	
∅	$\langle\{Y/clyde\}, D_1\rangle$
albino_elephant(Y) \- false.∅	$\langle\{Y/clyde\}, D_1\rangle$
\- (albino_elephant(Y) -> false).∅	$\langle\{Y/clyde\}, D_1\rangle$
(\- elephant(Y)).(\- (albino_elephant(Y)->false)).∅	$\langle∅, D_1\rangle$
\- grey(Y).∅	$\langle∅, D_1\rangle$

The first step (the bottommost) is an instance of the rule *definition-right*, the second step is also an instance of *definition-right*, where Y is bound to clyde. The third step is the rule *arrow-right* and the last step is performed by the rule *definition-left*. The last step is interesting, since it has a condition in the antecedent, which does not have any clauses in D_1 defining it. Therefore the step has no premises (the assumed term albino_elephant(clyde) "is absurd" with respect to the definition D_1; c.f. the definition of ⊥ in section 2).

In fact, this is generally how negation is accomplished in GCLA. It is just an instance of hypothetical reasoning, and any term which does not have a definition is treated as false, and therefore absurd with respect to the current definition. It is more general than negation as failure, since variables in "negative" queries can be bound during execution. The next deduction is an example of a negative query, grey(Y) \- false, which instantiates Y to karo.

"Present Y = karo"	
elephant(Y),false \-false.Ø	$\langle\{Y/karo\}, D_1\rangle$
(elephant(Y) \- albino_elephant(Y)).(elephant(Y),false\-false).Ø	$\langle\emptyset, D_1\rangle$
(elephant(Y),(albino_elephant(Y)->false) \- false).Ø	$\langle\emptyset, D_1\rangle$
grey(Y) \- false.Ø	$\langle\emptyset, D_1\rangle$
\- grey(Y)->false.Ø	$\langle\emptyset, D_1\rangle$

3.3.2. A definition for type checking

This definition shows how GCLA could be used for type checking of terms in the lambda calculus. The coding is straightforward, with one clause for function abstraction and one clause for application. The lambda term $\lambda x \lambda y.xy$ is coded as lambda(x,lambda(y,ap(x,y))), types are constructed using the --> functor (to distinguish them from GCLA conditions of the form c-->c'), and queries are of the form \- type(Term,Type).

```
:- setglobal(type,total).

type(lambda(X,T),(Alfa --> Beta)) <=
     (type(X,Alfa) -> type(T,Beta)).
type(ap(T,R),Beta) <=
     type(T,(Alfa --> Beta)),type(R,Alfa).
```

Here are some examples of queries and their answer substitutions:

```
\- type(lambda(x,lambda(y,y)),T).

    T = _358-->(_774-->_774)

\- type(lambda(x,lambda(y,ap(x,y))),T).

    T = (_804-->_805)-->(_804-->_805)

\- type(lambda(x,lambda(y,ap(x,ap(x,y)))),T).

    T = (_834-->_834)-->(_834-->_834)
```

```
\- type(lambda(x,lambda(y,ap(x,ap(x,ap(x,y)))))),T).

    T = (_864-->_864)-->(_864-->_864)
```

A query which uses the same name for two bound variables has two solutions, since we have no scope rules:

```
\- type(lambda(x,lambda(x,x)),T).

    T = _362-->(_776-->_776) ;
    T = _362-->(_776-->_362) ;
    no
```

3.3.3. A toy expert system

This example shows how a simple expert system can be implemented in GCLA. It also shows how hypothetical reasoning is accomplished in GCLA.

The definition is formulated as ordinary if-then rules forming the logic in which GCLA reasons. The way we formulate our queries determine how the system interprets and computes the answers. The knowledge of diseases is expressed as rules where each known disease is described in terms of different symptoms.

```
:- setglobal(temp,total).
:- setglobal(symptom,total).

disease(plague) <=
     temp(high),
     symptom(perspire).
disease(pneumonia) <=
     temp(high),
     symptom(chill).
disease(cold) <=
     temp(normal),
     symptom(cough).
```

As can be seen, this definition has no atomic facts. It just contains the rules describing the relation between symptoms, temperature and diseases. The queries should give the atomic facts when they are needed, depending on the type of query. For example, a query about which disease a specific set of symptoms corresponds to is

```
symptom(perspire),temp(high) \- disease(K).

    K = plague;
    no
```

Another query is

```
symptom(Symp),temp(high) \- disease(K).

    Symp = perspire, K = plague ;
    Symp = chill, K = pneumonia;
    no
```

where we ask for a disease which follows from high temperature and (possibly) a symptom to fill in. In this query we have partial knowledge about the world and want to derive additional information. By backtracking we can list the solutions possible with this information.

Still another type of query is

```
    disease(plague) \- temp(T).

        T = high
```

where we assume that someone has the plague, and want to know what temperature he would have.

3.3.4. A functional definition: append

As mentioned before, one can write functional definitions in GCLA. It is in fact also just an instance of hypothetical reasoning, where the expression is added to the antecedent, and the result is given as the consequent. The expression is then reduced to its canonical value by repeated application of definition-left and the arrow rules, and that value is bound to the consequent by the rule *initial-sequent*. Since GCLA has first order unification and first order variables, it is also possible to do simple equation solving by replacing arguments with variables, which become bound during execution.

Below is the definition of the function `append` (which, in this case, is a true function of two arguments, and not a relation between three arguments). The execution order is altered by setting the global variable `execution_order` to [left, right, axiom] in order to first try to reduce a condition in the antecedent, then, if that is not possible, try a rule to the right of the turnstile and finally to try the rule *initial-sequent*. This gives us eager evaluation, as can be seen in the examples below.

The first two clauses defines the termination case and the recursive case respectively. The term in the second argument is not evaluated until it becomes free in the body of the first clause.

The third clause handles the case when the first argument x is not in canonical form, i.e. x should be evaluated to a list or to []. This new value is then used as the first argument instead of the old value. This is a version of a substitution schema, which substitutes the first argument with its computed value.

The clause for cons is also a substitution schema. Since the value of the evaluation of the two arguments of cons is in canonical form, the result of cons is also in canonical form, hence the &axiom annotation of the answer to prevent looping. In this particular case this annotation is actually not needed, since lists are always looked upon as canonical values. We include it since that gives this clause the general structure of a substitution schema.

It is interesting that the &axiom annotation much behaves as quote in Lisp, i.e. its argument is seen as data. In Lisp this means that evaluation of a quoted term is the term itself, and in GCLA the &axiom annotation means that its argument may be used just by the rule *initial-sequent*. In the functional case this means that unification of an expression and the result variable is the only way to use the &axiom-annotated term.

In a sense it is in the substitution schemas that execution takes place. It is there the arguments are evaluated and given their values. The same idea of substitution schemas can be found in [GH88], although they are considering term rewriting systems for ML languages with pattern matching, and not full first order unification.

```
append([],X) <= X.
append([F|R],X) <= cons(F,append(R,X)).
append(X,Y) <= [neq(X,[_|_]),neq(X,[])],
        ((X -> Z) -> append(Z,Y)).

cons(X,Y) <= ((X -> Z), (Y -> W) -> &axiom([Z|W])).

:- setglobal(execution_order,[left,right,axiom]).
```

As a first query, consider append([1],[2]) \- x. (We have here constrained the rules *definition-left* and *definition-right* not to be applicable to a variable). x will be bound to [1,2]. The deduction is presented below (we substitute variables directly in expressions).

$$\frac{\text{"present X = [1,2]"}}{(\&\text{axiom}([1,2])\backslash-X).\varnothing}$$

$$\frac{([2]\backslash-W_1).(\&\text{axiom}([1|W_1])\backslash-X).\varnothing}{(\text{append}([],[2])\backslash-W_1).(\&\text{axiom}([1|W_1])\backslash-X).\varnothing}$$

$$\frac{(\backslash-(\text{append}([],[2])->W_1)).(\&\text{axiom}([1|W_1])\backslash-X).\varnothing}{(1\backslash-Z_1).(\backslash-(\text{append}([],[2])->W_1)).(\&\text{axiom}([Z_1|W_1])\backslash-X).\varnothing}$$

$$\frac{(\backslash-(1->Z_1)).(\backslash-(\text{append}([],[2])->W_1)).(\&\text{axiom}([Z_1|W_1])\backslash-X).\varnothing}{(((1 -> Z_1),(\text{append}([],[2]) -> W_1) -> \&\text{axiom}([Z_1|W_1]))\ \backslash- X).\varnothing}$$

$$\frac{(\text{cons}(1,\text{append}([],[2]))\ \backslash- X).\varnothing}{(\text{append}([1],[2])\ \backslash- X).\varnothing}$$

As can be seen, the substitution schema for cons is used to evaluate the number 1 and for evaluating the expression append([],[2]).

Another possible query is append(append([1],[2]),[3]) \- x, which binds x to [1,2,3]. Here the substitution schema for append (the third clause in the definition) is used to evaluate append([1],[2]) to [1,2].

It is also possible to do some equation solving by changing the instantiation pattern in the query. For instance, the query append([1],X) \- [1,2] gives as an answer substitution X = [2]. Below are these question and some other possible queries listed.

```
append([1],[2]) \- X.

    X = [1,2] ;
    X = [1|append([],[2])] ;
    X = cons(1,append([],[2])) ;
    X = append([1],[2]) ;
    no


append(append([1],[2]),[3]) \- X.

    X = [1,2,3] ;
    X = [1,2|append([],[3])] ;
    X = [1|cons(2,append([],[3]))] ;
    ...


append([1],X) \- [1,2].

    X = [2] ;
    no
```

```
append(X,[2]) \- [1,2].

    X = 1 ;
    ...(Looping on the second clause, with longer and longer
            lists)

append(X,Y) \- [1,2].

    X = [], Y = [1,2] ;
    X = [1], Y = [2] ;
    X = [1,2], Y = [] ;
    ... (Looping for the same reasons as above)
```

As can be seen in the first query, we get a trace of the steps taken to reach a canonical result. This means that if we change the ordering of the rules, by changing the value of the global variable execution_order, it is possible to get other evaluation strategies. For example, the value [axiom,left,right] gives lazy evaluation, with backtracking as the "engine" for evaluating expressions:

```
append([1],[2]) \- X.

    X = append([1],[2]) ;
    X = cons(1,append([],[2])) ;
    X = [1|append([],[2])] ;
    X = [1,2] ;
    no
```

3.3.5. Case analysis

One way of understanding the *definition-left* rule is to think of it as case analysis (c.f. section 2.2 and [FS90]). That is, to eliminate a term in the antecedent, every possible case of that term must give the same consequent. For example, if we eliminate $\sqrt{4}$, we have to consider both 2 and -2. The definition for the square example is (we assume that "*" is defined somewhere else; also see the examples *functional append* for the explanation of how functional definitions are written and executed):

```
root(X) <= (Y * Y -> &axiom(X)) -> pos_neg(Y).
pos_neg(Z) <= Z.
pos_neg(Z) <= -Z.
```

The query root(4) \- x will fail, since x can not be bound to both 2 and -2 (see the definition of *definition-left*). But the query root(4) \- or(X,Y), where or(X,Y) is the disjunction of x and y, will succeed with the answer substitutions x = 2, y = -2 (or, equivalently, x = -2, y = 2).

3.3.6. Quicksort

This definition makes use of the append definition above. It demonstrates a mixture of relational and functional programming, since qsort and append are seen as functions, while split is seen as a relation. We assume that the relations "<" and ">" on numbers are predefined.

```
qsort([]) <= [].
qsort([F|R]) <=
      (split(F,R,L,G) ->
        append(qsort(L),cons(F,qsort(G)))).

append([],F) <= F.
append([F|R],X) <= cons(F,append(R,X)).
append(X,Y) <= [neq(X,[_|_]),neq(X,[])],
      ((X -> Z) -> append(Z,Y)).

split(_,[],[],[]).
split(E,[F|R],[F|Z],X) <= E > F,split(E,R,Z,X).
split(E,[F|R],Z,[F|X]) <= E < F,split(E,R,Z,X).

cons(X,Y) <= ((X -> Z), (Y -> W) -> [Z|W]).

:- setglobal(execution_order,[left,right,axiom]).
```

One possible query, and its answer substitution, is

```
qsort([2,1,4,3]) \- X.

      X = [1,2,3,4]
```

As before, by changing the value of the variable execution_order, lazy evaluation can be accomplished.

3.3.7. Simulation of communicating processes

In Prolog programming, and especially in parallel Prolog programming (for example GHC, Parlog etc), the literals in a body can be seen as different processes, communicating through their shared variables. By using annotation strategies for variables the processes can be suspended and resumed as the variable instantiation changes. There is also a way of achieving this in many Prolog implementations, using the built-in predicate `freeze`, which suspends a goal until a certain variable becomes instantiated.

By using the antecedent as the "machine state", where some terms in the antecedent are seen as processes, it is possible to simulate several processes communicating with each other through their shared variables, or, as we shall see in the next example, by using the rule *initial-sequent*. If the function determining the choice of the condition in the antecedent can be freely defined by the user (see section 4), this function can be seen as a scheduler, scheduling the different processes.

The example below shows how two processes, a producer and a consumer, interacts with each other through a stream (a list). The order of the conditions in the antecedent is crucial, since the opposite order would make the producer being chosen first in each step, and the consumer would starve, i.e. never be chosen.

We assume that `write` and `nl` are system defined procedures, which writes its argument on the terminal and moves to a new line on the terminal respectively. Here we make use of the possibility to declare circular clauses by the `setglobal` primitive.

```
produce([item(X)|R],X) <=
      ((X + 1 -> X1) -> produce(R,X1)).

consume([item(X)|R]) <= [nonvar(X)],
      (write(X),nl -> consume(R)).


:- setglobal(consume,total).
:- setglobal(produce,total).
```

A simple query to this definition is

```
consume(X),produce(X,1) \- false.
    1
    1+1
    1+1+1
    1+1+1+1
    ...
```

and x is a potentially infinite list, successively instantiated to `[item(1),item(1+1),...`

In this example, the clause for `consume` is guarded by the expression `nonvar(X)`. This has the effect of not permitting the clause to be used in a context where x would be uninstantiated. Since `consume` is declared total, there is an implied circular clause

```
consume(A) <= consume(A)
```

The effect of this is that as long as x is uninstantiated, all attempts to use consume would return to the same state! The GCLA implementation recognizes this and avoids using consume altogether, effectively freezing conditions using it.

In the next example we shall see how processes can communicate without a specific variable working as a stream.

3.3.8. Object oriented programming

It is possible to achieve a kind of object oriented programming in GCLA, using terms in the antecedent to hold objects and classes, and sending messages using the *initial-sequent* rule, or by using a stream, as in the producer-consumer definition above. Each of these two possibilities have their own field of application. A stream should be used where the ordering of the messages are of importance. The message passing by the *initial-sequent* rule is used when the ordering of the messages is not important, and where the message can be forgotten as soon as the action of the message is performed. In GCLA II, it should be possible to remove this distinction between a stream and the usage of the rule *initial-sequent*, in favour of also using *initial-sequent* where the ordering of the messages matters.

In this example we have the class ship, and the subclass sailing_ship. Each ship has a length, weight, and name. A sailing ship has in addition a sail area, and that area can be changed during execution.

The methods for length, weight and name are implemented in the class ship, and the sailing ships can pass these messages to the class ship, while methods for sail area are specific to sailing ships. Every sailing ship instance has an internal state, consisting of its length, weight, name and its sail area.
The definition is listed below.

```
ship(weight(W),N,W,L) <= susp_object(R,ship(R,N1,W1,L1)).
ship(name(N),N,W,L) <= susp_object(R,ship(R,N1,W1,L1)).
ship(length(L),N,W,L) <= susp_object(R,ship(R,N1,W1,L1)).
ship(new_sailship(S,MaxS),N,W,L) <=
     susp_object(S,sailing_ship(S,N,W,L,0,MaxS)),
     susp_object(R,ship(R,N1,W1,L1)).
ship([],N,W,L).
```

```
sailing_ship([max_sailarea(MaxS)|R],N,W,L,S,MaxS) <=
     susp_object(R,sailing_ship(R,N,W,L,S,MaxS)).
sailing_ship([current_sailarea(S)|R],N,W,L,S,MaxS) <=
     susp_object(R,sailing_ship(R,N,W,L,S,MaxS)).
sailing_ship([change_sailarea(S1)|R],N,W,L,S,MaxS) <=
     (S1 >= 0, S1 =< MaxS ->
      susp_object(R,sailing_ship(R,N,W,L,S1,MaxS))).
sailing_ship([],N,W,L,S,MaxS).
sailing_ship([F|R],N,W,L,S,MaxS) <=
     [nonvar(F),neq(F,max_sailarea(_)),
      neq(F,current_sailarea(_)),
      neq(F,change_sailarea(_))],
     (susp_object(F,ship(Y,N,W,L)) ->
      susp_object(R,sailing_ship(R,N,W,L,S,MaxS))).

susp_object(X,Y) <= [nonvar(X)],Y.
:- setglobal(susp_object,total).

answer(X) <= [nonvar(X)].

A = A.

:- setglobal(execution_order,[axiom,left,right]).
:- setglobal(sailing_ship,total).
:- setglobal(ship,total).
```

The clause susp_object has much the same behaviour as the Prolog predicate *freeze*, that is, it suspends the execution of its term until some variable has been instantiated. However, there is one major difference: with this coding we can still reach the suspended object and see and alter (i.e. unify) its internal state, without keeping track of the frozen variable.

The first argument to ship is the command to perform, and the other three arguments are used to pass information from the inquiring object; the first is used for passing the name, the second the weight, and the third the length. The message passing to ship should be by the rule *initial-sequent*, and as can be seen, the message is forgotten as soon as the action is performed, by introducing a new variable R in the body.

The sailing ships has the same structure, but the first argument is a stream, since the order of the messages to them matters (see the last query in this section), and they have in addition a sail area and a maximum sail area. The last clause of sailing_ship is where the inheritance is implemented. All the queries that cannot be answered here are passed to the ship class.

The "living" objects occur to the left of the turnstile, and the questions to the objects are put to the right. For example, here we have an instance of the class `sailing_ship`, called *Fia*, to which we send a message asking for its current sail area:

```
susp_object(X,sailing_ship(X,fia,3600,8,0,45)) \-
    X = [current_sailarea(S)|R], answer(S).
```

This query binds S to 0. The message is passed through the variable X (by instantiation) to the object, and the term `answer(S)` is fulfilled when the variable S has been instantiated to something. As a matter of fact, the object does not perform the action (in this case, finds the name of itself) until it is asked for the answer of the question. This is much the same as the consumer-producer coding in the example before.

The query

```
susp_object(X,sailing_ship(X,fia,3600,8,0,45)) \-
    X = [name(N)|_],answer(N).
```

will fail, since there is no class `ship` in this query.

If we instead pose the query

```
susp_object(Z,ship(Z,A,B,C)),
susp_object(X,sailing_ship(X,fia,3600,8,0,45)) \-
    X = [name(N)|_],answer(N).
```

the query will succeed with N bound to `fia`, since now the class `sailing_ship` can ask the class `ship` about the name. When the sailing ship asks the class `ship`, this is an example of a question which is asked through the rule *initial-sequent*, and no stream is used.

The `ship` class can also create a new sailing ship. The creation of a new object is simple, the body of a clause just consists of two or more terms, as in the fourth clause of `ship` above. In the query below a new sailing ship called `olga` is created, and then asked to change its current sail area to 25, and lastly we ask `olga` about its current sail area:

```
susp_object(Z,ship(Z,A,B,C)) \-
    &axiom(susp_object(_,ship(new_sailship(G,45),olga,4000,9))),
    G = [change_sailarea(25),current_sailarea(Area)|R],
    answer(Area).
```

`Area` will be instantiated to 25, which is the current sail area after we have changed its sail area from 0 to 25. Here it is essential that `olga`'s message variable is implemented as a stream, since we want the last question, the one about its current sail area, to be performed *after* the action `change_sailarea(25)` has been fulfilled.

This example shows how a kind of object oriented programming can be done in GCLA, although we do not claim that it *is* "real" object oriented programming. There are, however, several other interesting extensions within this approach. If we combine this approach with for example relational programming and/or functional programming, what is the resulting system? For example, a "split" of the state to the left of the turnstile by an application of the rule *definition-right* results in the same state of the objects being copied into two identical states, which thereafter could perform (depending on their internal structure) different actions and end up in total, different states.

We have not considered all these possibilities yet, but are looking forward to examine these topics in more detail.

The same technique as this example has been used to implement a simulation of an operating system, with system processes and user processes interacting with each other.

4. GCLA II - The issue of control

4.1 Introduction

4.1.1. The need for control

The generality and expressive power of GCLA gives the programmer the freedom to express his problems in a multitude of ways. He may, when formalizing his domain, choose a functional approach, a relational approach or any combination thereof. He may want to treat antecedents in the goals as representations of process states, and application of the axiom rule as process communication etc.

This freedom and generality has a price, however, and that is the efficiency of his programs. In fact, many intuitively correct GCLA programs will not even terminate lacking a heuristic in the way search for proofs is conducted. Other programs may terminate with trivial, redundant or otherwise unwanted answers. Still others may get caught in enumerating infinite sets of unwanted solutions and thus never produce the desired solutions

From this tradeoff between expressive power of the language, and complexity of the execution mechanism rises the the issue of control. With a language like GCLA control issues become central. Some problems that arise in connection with control in GCLA are:

- How do we direct the search in an optimal manner?
- How do we exclude unwanted solutions from our answer substitutions?
- How do we manage exponential growth in our search spaces, and infinite branches in our search trees.

In GCLA I, we had ad hoc solutions to some of these problems. We could manage the global behaviour of the interpreter by various parameters. However, this compromised the simplicity and elegance inherent in the theoretical foundations of GCLA programming. GCLA II is an attempt to construct a uniform framework for managing control issues in the definitional approach to programming.

4.1.2. A definitional approach to control

Most control issues in GCLA arise in connection with the choice of the inference rule used to prove a certain sequent. This is a fundamental difference between GCLA and resolution based systems, e.g. Prolog, that use only one rule of inference. The situation in GCLA is more similar to that of providing tactics for (semi-)automatic theorem provers like LCF (see e.g. [Pau83]).

Of course GCLA could also be used as a basis for a system for theorem proving, but as such it has two major drawbacks: there is currently no natural way to include user interaction in semi-automated proof construction and GCLA is not a complete system. The theory of partial inductive definitions *has* been used as basis for a semi-automatic proof editor. One of the authors of this paper is currently involved in work with such a system.

In GCLA the order in which rules are tried may affect both termination and the order in which answers are presented. In addition certain programming methodologies (notably functional programming) require repeated application of certain sequences of rules in order to become efficient.

Given a specified part of the sequent to operate on, a rule is a partial function from sets of sequents to sequents. I.e. from the premises to the conclusion in a derivation. These functions can be inductively defined. In fact the inference rules of GCLA can be expressed in a subset of GCLA.

With each rule function we associate a particular set of conditions for the rule to be applicable, sometimes called *provisos* or side conditions. If the provisos are not fulfilled for a set of premises, we may regard the function as undefined for that particular set of premises.

As proof search is conducted "backwards", from conclusion to premises, it is actually the inverses of these rule functions that are interesting in the context of proof search. Proof search can be regarded as the process of constructing a functional expression consisting of repeated applications of rule functions, where each functor in the expression is the name of a rule and the arguments are the representation of the proofs of the premises. Such an expression codes the structure of the proof. We will call such a functional expression a *proof term*.

Now, how can proof terms be utilized to exercise control over the possible inferences in a proof search? If we allow the provisos to constrain the structure of a partially instantiated proof term (i.e. a proviso that is a relation between the way the premises are proved and the consequence of the rule application),we achieve explicit control over the proof search. But how is this possibility to be utilized in an economical fashion?

In general, we do not want to write a specialized set of rules for each problem giving us a specialized interpreter for that particular problem, although in some cases we *do* want to do just that (c.f. partial evaluation). In most cases we would instead like to associate certain classes of sequents with sets of rule sequences, i.e. sets of partially instantiated proof terms.

In a loose sense we can think of this association as a kind of typing of the sequents by sets of proofs represented as partially instantiated proof terms[1]. This can be accomplished by giving an inductive definition of a "types" relation, ":", between sequents and sets of proof terms. If we then let the rule functions of GCLA be parameterized by this typing we get a flexible language in which to express control information. The control information would then be completely separate from the original definition,while preserving a declarative reading of the definition, i.e. in the spirit of Kowalski's classical paper: "Algorithm = Logic + Control" [Kow79].

We are now in a position to distinguish the main parts of the execution model of GCLA II.

There is a *definition*, that corresponds to the definition of GCLA I. There is a set of *rule definitions* that is relatively fixed, and that can be expressed in a restricted syntax. In addition there is a set of *proviso definitions* used to determine when a certain rule is applicable in a proof. Among the proviso definitions is an association of proof terms with sequents posed as queries to the definition. This part of the proviso definition is called the *typing* of the program.

A GCLA II program consists of all these parts, although most of the rule definitions are generally provided as primitives by the system and only referred to in the typing. The system also provides a set of primitive functions and relations that can be used in the construction of rule definitions, provisos in general and the ":" relation in particular.

4.1.3. An example

Assume that we want to prove the sequent

```
plus(s(0),s(0)) \- Y
```

---

[1]It is quite possible that this loose connection with the formulas as types concept can be formalized to give a deeper interpretation of the association between control and logic in GCLA. However, we have not yet looked into this possibility enough to give an account of it here.

where \- is the sequent constructor, plus is defined by

```
plus(0,Y) <= Y.
plus(s(X),Y) <= s(plus(X,Y)).
```

and s has the definition

```
s(X) <= (X -> Y) -> s(Y).
```

This is an example of a functional program in GCLA. In the absence of rules guiding the search, the axiom rule could be used to get the substitution

$$\{<Y, plus(s(0),s(0))>\}$$

e.g., which of course is correct, but trivial (c.f. the discussion of lazy v.s. eager evaluation in section 3.2.).

Instead we would like to somehow put the antecedent in normal form before applying the axiom rule to export the relevant binding. This can be accomplished by always executing the substitution schema s(X) <= (X -> Y) -> s(Y) by a particular sequence of rules and trying rules to the left before the axiom rule.

Now if a completely instantiated proof term is a representation of a path in the search tree of the sequent plus(s(0),s(0)) \- z, GCLA II will try to construct such a term adhering to the constraints set up by the rule definitions and the provisos of the program. The process of finding such an expression can be thought of as trying to find a proof for the meta level sequent:

```
R0 ⊢ (plus(s(0),s(0)) \- z),
```

where R0 is a variable to be instantiated to a proof term by a successful search for a proof of plus(s(0),s(0)) \- z.

Each step in a proof of this goal consists of finding a rule function that, when applied to a suitable set of premises, has the sequent to the right of ⊢ as its value. This is repeated until no more premises remains. The possible alternatives for such a function is given by the typing of the sequent, and by additional provisos in the definition of the chosen rule definition. A proof of the above goal not only gives a proof of the sequent to the right of ⊢ but also an instantiation of R0 to a completely instantiated proof term which can be used for e.g. debugging or explanation.

The derivation of this goal we in most cases would like to see is

```
        ─────────────────────── I
        R6 ⊢ (s(0) \- s(0))
      ─────────────────────────── D⊢
      R5 ⊢ (plus(0,s(0)) \- s(0))
    ───────────────────────────────── ⊢→        ─────────────────────────── I
    R3 ⊢ (\-(plus(0,s(0)) -> s(0)))              R4 ⊢ (s(s(0)) \- s(s(0)))
  ──────────────────────────────────────────────────────────────────────── →⊢
      R2 ⊢ (plus(0,s(0)) -> s(0)) -> s(s(0)) \- s(s(0))
  ──────────────────────────────────────────────────────────────────────── D⊢
      R1 ⊢ (s(plus(0,s(0))) \- s(s(0)))
  ──────────────────────────────────────────────────────────────────────── D⊢
      R0 ⊢ (plus(s(0),s(0)) \- s(s(0)))
```

This type of derivation is very common, and the basis for using GCLA as a functional language. It is also a good example of the type of search behaviour we would like to associate with certain classes of sequents.

The proof of `plus(s(0),s(0)) \- z` gives the following substitution for R0:

```
        d_left(plus(s(0),s(0)),
              d_left(s(plus(0,s(0))),
                    arrow_left((plus(0,s(0)) -> s(0) -> s(s(0))),
                          arrow_right((plus(0,s(0)) -> s(0)),
                                d_left(plus(0,s(0)),
                                      axiom(s(0)))),
                          axiom(s(s(0)))))),
```

or, equivalently, given this term, the structure of the proof is completely determined. The first argument of each rule constructor is the condition on which it operates. The proof functions are actually determined only when this term is given, though the rules defined in the rule definition are generally parameterized by the term. The following arguments are the proof terms representing the proofs of the premises of the rule application.

In the general case we would like to always see terms defined by substitution schemata (like the definition of s above) occurring to the left of \-, treated by a sequence of rule applications similar to this one. Given the framework sketched above this association could be made by specifying for each sequent of this kind that it should be proved by a sequence of rules represented by a suitable partially instantiated proof term. A simplified form of the proviso clause corresponding to this statement is:

```
Sequent : d_left(…, arrow_left(arrow_right(…,_), axiom(…))) <=
     atom(hd(anteced(Sequent)), s/1)².
```

Another way to handle this is to give a rule definition that corresponds to this sequence of rules. As this is such a common case that could be a good idea. In fact, a rule of this kind is supplied by the system in the current implementation. We will return to a similar example in more detail later.

---

²The last argument of atom is a notation for the name and arity of a functor occurring in the definition. See definition of the atom function in section 3.3.1.*iv*.

4.2. GCLA II - A framework for definitional programming

A GCLA II program consists of three parts with well defined interfaces. The definition $\mathcal{D}$ is the declarative part of our program, while the rule definition $\mathcal{R}$ and the proviso definition $\mathcal{P}$ gives a procedural interpretation of $\mathcal{D}$. As both $\mathcal{R}$ and $\mathcal{P}$ are also inductive definitions we can give a declarative reading of these as well. It should be noted also that $\mathcal{R}$ and $\mathcal{P}$ are really part of the same definition. They are separated in this presentation only to clarify their relationship to the definition $\mathcal{D}$.

The following description of GCLA II is a presentation of the execution model and not a final version of how the language will actually look to the programmer. The syntax used for the proviso definitions in particular is rather detailed. This may give the interested reader insights into the actual workings of the model, but of course, in an actual implementation a more concise notation will be used. We are currently working on the design of such a notation.

It should also be noted here that the control we achieve by adding a typing to the definition is in no way dependent on the fact that the rules of the inference mechanism can be (re-) defined by the user. The reason we took such an approach was to achieve maximum flexibility when developing the system. It is quite possible that this flexibility must later be compromised to achieve realistic implementations.

In section 3.3.1 the different components of a GCLA II program are described in detail. In section 3.3.2 an informal operational semantics is given. This gives a procedural interpretation of the program as a whole. This must be sound with respect to the declarative reading the definition. The soundness is of course also dependent on the exact definitions used for the rules in the set $\mathcal{R}$. Finally in section 3.3.3 of this chapter we give a series of examples and comparisons with the procedural behaviour of GCLA I .

4.2.1.   The structure of a GCLA II program

A GCLA II program consists of the following parts:

i)   A set $\mathcal{D}$ of clauses that constitutes the *definition*.

The definition constitutes our formalization of the problem domain, and in general contains a minimum of control information. It would not be correct to call the definition a specification, but it may in many cases be quite close to a specification. This is because other parts of the program contains control information that guarantees that the definition will be used in an efficient manner. The intention is that the definition by itself has a purely declarative interpretation while a procedural interpretation is obtained only by putting it in the context of the rest of the program.

The *concrete syntax* of a definition is given as:

Definition	::=	*DefClause* .	*DefClause* . *Definition*
DefClause	::=	*Atom* <= *Cond*	*Atom* <= *Guard*, *Cond*
Atom	::=	*Name*	*Name* (*Term*, ..., *Term*)
Name	::=	"Non capitalized alphanumeric string that is not a *Constr*"
Term	::=	*Atom*	*Var*
Var	::=	"Capitalized alphanumeric string"
Cond	::=	*Term*	*Constr*	*Constr* (*Cond*, ..., *Cond*) "possibly infix"
Constr	::=	true	false	->	,	`	def	...
Guard	::=	[*Term* ≠ *Term*, ..., *Term* ≠ *Term*]

while the corresponding *abstract syntax* on which the rules and proviso parts of the program operates is slightly different.

DefClause	::=	*Atom* <= *CondList*
CondList	::=	[]	[*Cond*	*CondList*]
Atom	::=	*Name*	*Name* (*Term*, ..., *Term*)
Name	::=	"Non capitalized alphanumeric string that is not a *Constr*"
Term	::=	*Atom*	*Var*
Var	::=	"Capitalized alphanumeric string"
Cond	::=	*Term*	*Constr*	*Constr* (*Cond*, ..., *Cond*) "possibly infix"
Constr	::=	false	->	,	`	def	etc

The main difference is that the bodies of clauses are treated as list which gives a more convenient formulation of the rules *definition-right* and *definition-left*. A second difference is that the *Guards* are not part of the representation of clauses, but are used as constraints on unification in the predefined provisos (i.e. clause and definiens) that constitute the interface between the $\mathcal{D}$ and $\mathcal{R}$ and $\mathcal{P}$ respectively. These are described below.

Sequents are used as queries to the definition $\mathcal{D}$.

The concrete syntax of sequents is given as:

Seq	::=	*Cond* \- *Cond*	\- *Cond*.

Again the abstract syntax is slightly different:

Seq	::=	*CondList* \- *Cond*
CondList	::=	[]	[*Cond*	*CondList*]

In the abstract syntax the antecedent is regarded as a possibly empty sequence of conditions, rather than as a single (or empty) condition.

Sequents are treated by the system as a primitive data type with an associated set of accessor and constructor functions. This set consists of the following functions:

- `seq` : *CondList, Cond → Seq*;
  where `seq(A,C)` = A `\-` C, i.e. a sequent constructor.
- `anteced` : *Seq → CondList*;
  where `anteced(A \- C)` = A
- `conseq` : *Seq → Cond*;
  where `conseq(A, C)` = C

ii) A set $\mathcal{R}$ of rule clauses of the following restricted form that constitutes the *rule definition*:

$$Rule <= Proviso \rightarrow (Premises \rightarrow Seq),$$

where *Proviso* is a conjunction $(P_1, ..., P_n)$ of conditions for the rule to be applicable and *Premises* a conjunction of premises on which the truth of *Seq* depends (according to the defined rule). The premises has the general form $(Rule_i \rightarrow Seq_i)$. The actual premises are of course the Seq_i. The $Rule_i$ associated with each Seq_i is a constraint on how Seq_i is to be proved. This constraint is generally obtained from the "∴" proviso by instantiating the $Rule_i$ to a partially instantiated proof term, but it could also be inherent in *Rule* itself.

Formally:

RuleDef   ::=   *RuleClause . | RuleClause . RuleDef*
RuleClause ::=   *Rule <= Proviso -> (Premises -> Seq)*
Rule   ::=   *Var | Name (Term, Rule, ..., Rule)*
Proviso   ::=   true | false *| Term | Proviso, Proviso | Proviso -> Term*
Premises   ::=   true | *(Rule -> Seq),...,(Rule -> Seq)*

As rules conceptually are functions a functional expression should never become absurd. The rule definition as given should be thought of as containing an additional clause for every *Rule* defined in $\mathcal{D}$:

$$Rule(\_,...) <= Guard, Rule(\_,...),$$

where *Guard* guarantees that this clause is used only when no other clause is applicable. This should be interpreted as opening the closed world inherent in inductive definitions. As all the rules have this property it is not necessary to actually write these clauses in the rule definition but the soundness of the operational semantics depend on the fact that we think of them as part of the rule definition.

A complete set of rule definitions for GCLA II is given in an appendix

iii) A set $\mathcal{P}$ of proviso clauses defines a set of provisos used to restrict the applicability of the rules. $\mathcal{P}$ constitutes the *proviso definition*. There is no syntactical restriction on the proviso definitions. But as all inferences of provisos are performed in runtime we strongly recommend that the proviso definitions are kept to an efficiently executable subset of GCLA. One such subset that allows efficient execution of functions and Prolog-like inferences is currently implemented and seems fairly adequate for most of the cases we have encountered.

The syntax of a proviso definition is given by:

ProDef   ::=   *ProClause*. | *ProClause*. *ProDef*
ProClause ::=   *Atom* <= *Proviso* | *Atom* <= *Guard, Proviso*

Among the atoms defined by the proviso definition is one with the functor ":", relating sequents with rules from $\mathcal{R}$. This relation may or may not be utilized by an individual rule definition to deduce the rule sequences to associate with the sequents occurring in the premise arguments of the rule function.

A set of proviso relations and functions are provided as primitives of the system. First among these are the set of accessor and constructor functions on the representation of the sequents described above in connection with the representation of sequents.

- seq : *CondList, Cond* → *Seq*;
  where seq(A,C) = A \- C
- anteced : *Seq* → *CondList*;
  where anteced(A \- C) = A
- conseq : *Seq* → *Cond*;
  where conseq(A, C) = C

In addition to these, there is a set of functions and recognizers on lists of conditions:

- hd : *CondList* → *Cond*;
  returns the first element of a list
- tl : *CondList* → *CondList*;
  returns a list consisting of all but first element of the original list
- cons : *Cond, CondList* → *CondList*;
  constructs a new list from an element and a list
- null : *List* → *Bool*;

true of an empty list, *false* otherwise

- consp : *List → Bool*;
  true of a non-empty list, *false* otherwise

Atoms and constructed conditions from sequents are also regarded as primitive types. The following predicates and functions relate these primitive objects with their parts.

- atom : *Cond, Name/Arity → Bool*;
  atom(*Cond, Name/Arity*) is *true* if *Cond* is an *Atom* with functor *Name* and arity *Arity*, *false* otherwise
- c_cond : *Cond, Constr/Arity → Bool*;
  c_cond(*Cond, Constr/Arity*) is *true* if *Cond* is a constructed condition with constructor *Constr* and arity *Arity*, *false* otherwise
- term : *Cond, Name/Arity → Bool*;
  term(*Cond, Name/Arity*) is *true* if *Cond* is either an *Atom* with functor *Name* and arity *Arity*, or a variable, and *Name/Arity* is equal to var/0, *false* otherwise.
- arg : *Int,Cond → Cond*;
  returns the *i*:th argument of either a constructed condition or an *Atom*, arg is undefined for variable conditions.

In addition to these, three primitive provisos are provided by the system that affects the global variable binding environment, and that acts as interfaces between the rules and proviso parts of the program, $\mathcal{R}$ and $\mathcal{P}$, the one hand, and the definition $\mathcal{D}$ on the other:

- unify(*Term₁,Term₂*) is true if *Term₁* and *Term₂* are unifiable. As a side effect, the two terms are unified, and the resulting substitution is applied to the global environment. If the terms are not unifiable the proviso is false.

- clause(*Atom,CondList*) is true if a clause *Atom′* <= *CondList* is part of the definition $\mathcal{D}$, and *Atom* and *Atom′* are unifiable. If they are, the unifying substitution σ is applied to the global binding environment. This corresponds to the operation *Cond* ∈ *D*(*Atomσξ*) in the theory of partial inductive definitions for some grounding substitution ξ. clause will produce all such *CondList*s and substitutions σ upon backtracking. If no such clause exists the condition is false.

- definiens(*Atom,Defs*) is true if there exists a *Atom*-sufficient substitution σ such that *Defs* is an ordered list of *CondList*s that constitutes a finite representation of the set

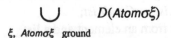

$$\bigcup_{\xi, \; Atom\sigma\xi \; \text{ground}} D(Atom\sigma\xi)$$

in the theory of partial inductive definitions (See section 2.1.) for the given definition $\mathcal{D}$. If it is, σ is applied to the global binding environment. `definiens` will produce all such substitutions σ with their corresponding lists of *CondLists* upon backtracking. If no such substitution exists, `Defs` is defined to be the empty list. Thus, this condition is always true, but may produce the representation of an empty set as a substitution for `Defs`. This corresponds to the case where `Atom` lacks a definition in $\mathcal{D}$.

As we already mentioned, the syntax used for proviso definition in this presentation is most probably not the one a user would like to see. In the actual programming language we imagine that the user would give specifications that in combinations with implicit default behaviour would be translated into something like what we have presented above. For example: we would like the user to be able to give the typing only for those sequents that should be proved by other methods than some standard ones. We are also considering the possibility of allowing several named typings, giving a concept of type modules that can be defined hierarchically. This would also give us possibility to dynamically change control strategy during execution of our programs without coding the current strategy in the sequents.

4.2.2.   An informal operational Semantics for GCLA II

GCLA II will execute a program consisting of the above four parts in the following manner.

Given a sequent, s, GCLA II will find a rule R from $\mathcal{R}$ associated with that sequent according to the proviso definition $\mathcal{P}$. If there are more than one rule applicable to a given sequent, the set of rules will be enumerated upon backtracking.

From these two components GCLA II forms a *goal*, i.e. a sequent of the following form.

$$R \vdash S$$

This goal will then be used as a query to the rule definition and proviso definition parts of the program in the following manner. A specialized version of a GCLA I interpreter is used to perform a sequence of operations on the given goal. These operations corresponds to the rules *definition-left*, *arrow-left*, *arrow-right* and *axiom* in GCLA I. Each step in the evaluation of the goal corresponds to the following fragment of a derivation.

$$\frac{\dfrac{\begin{array}{c}\vdots\\ \dfrac{R_1 \vdash S_1}{\vdash R_1 \to S_1}\vdash\to\end{array} \quad \cdots \quad \begin{array}{c}\vdots\\ \dfrac{R_n \vdash S_n}{\vdash R_n \to S_n}\vdash\to\end{array}}{\dfrac{\dfrac{\vdots}{\vdash Proviso} \quad \dfrac{\vdash (R_1 \to S_1,\, ...,\, R_n \to S_n)}{((R_1 \to S_1,\, ...,\, R_n \to S_n) \to S') \vdash S}}{\dfrac{Proviso \to ((R_1 \to S_1,\, ...,\, R_n \to S_n) \to S') \vdash S}{R \vdash S}\,\mathcal{D}\vdash}\to\vdash}\,,\,\vdash\,\dfrac{S' \vdash S}{}I}{}$$

where the definition of R is

$$R <= Proviso \to ((R_1 \to S_1,\, ...,\, R_n \to S_n) \to S')$$

First *definition-left* is used to get the definition of R from $\mathcal{R}$. Then *axiom* is applied to the goal $S' \vdash S$ after two successive applications of *arrow-left*. After that the goal $\vdash Proviso$ is proved in order to determine if the rule is applicable, and in order to check/instantiate the R_i used to prove the S_i. If $Proviso$ is provable, the execution continues with the aim of proving each of the new goals, $R_i \vdash S_i$. The provisos will provide the information needed to construct each new goal. E.g. the R_i in each new goal $R_i \vdash S_i$ is generally obtained from the ":" relation in the proviso definition. The ":" relation will in general provide alternative R_{i_j} for each goal $R_{i_j} \vdash S_i$ upon backtracking.

Other provisos like `clause` and `definiens` also provide multiple answers and will enumerate alternative ways to prove the original goal upon backtracking.

4.3. Examples and comparisons

The following examples illustrate the kind of control information we are able to express in GCLA II.

4.3.1. Elephant example

As an example of how GCLA II can restrict the search space in complex domains, consider the elephant example. The elephant example is not really a complex domain in itself, but the treatment given to it here illustrates one way GCLA II can be used to restrict the complexity of problem domains.

If the definition part of the program is:

```
grey(E) <=
  elephant(E),
  (albino_elephant(E) -> false).
```

```
elephant(clyde) <= true.
elephant(fido) <= true.
elephant(E) <=
  albino_elephant(E).

albino_elephant(karo) <= true.
```

The query

```
grey(karo) \- false
```

results in a moderate explosion in the number of (redundant) solutions. The default search behaviour of GCLA I results in 38 solutions. For the more interesting query:

```
grey(E) \- false
```

GCLA I gives us 6 identical solutions (i.e. E = karo). Obviously this behaviour is unsatisfactory. The redundancy is inherent in the problem formulation, but intuitively we would expect much fewer redundant answers.

One source of redundancy here is the constant false. In GCLA I this constant is treated no different from any other atom that lacks a definition. This is in the nature of inductive definitions, and in the general case gives us just the kind of closed world behaviour we would expect. However, as false is an atom it can occur in applications of the *axiom* rule, even though this will always give redundant solutions. If an undefined atom occurs in the antecedent, the *definition-left* rule will always succeed. If the consequent is that same atom, the *axiom* rule will succeed as well. In general, if the atom is 0-ary (or any ground atom) these two possible derivations will generate redundant solutions.

Of course we could utilize this knowledge to introduce a heuristic into a GCLA interpreter, but GCLA II gives us a general mechanism to handle this kind of heuristic.

If we associate a typing with the above definition, i.e. a set of rules or rule sequences associated with each type of sequent that is likely to occur in our derivations, we can get the desired behaviour from our GCLA II interpreter.

One such typing could be[3]:

```
Seq : `c_right(Constr,conseq(Seq),_) <=
    dif_constr(conseq(Seq),`false/0),
    c_cond(conseq(Seq),Constr).
```

---

[3]The quotes occurring in the proviso are used to separate data from functions in functional GCLA programs. The use of these quotes is part of a general methodology for using GCLA as a functional language but will not be described further in this context.

```
Seq : `d_right(conseq(Seq),_) <=
   atom(conseq(Seq),_).
Seq : `c_left(Constr,Cond,_) <=
   c_cond(conseq(Seq),`false/0),
   member(Cond,anteced(Seq)),
   c_cond(Cond,Constr).
Seq : `d_left(Cond,_) <=
   c_cond(conseq(Seq),`false/0),
   member(Cond,anteced(Seq)),
   atom(Cond,_).
```

This would be part of the proviso definition of a program. The functor being defined is
":". The conditions occurring in the bodies of the clauses must of course also be defined
in the proviso part of the program. Intuitively their meaning is:

- `dif_constr` is true if its first argument is a constructed condition and the constructor
  and arity of that condition is different from the ones occurring as its second argument.

- `member` defines a left to right traversal of its second argument generated on
  backtracking.

The procedural interpretation of this typing should be:

- The first clause of the above typing states that if the consequent of `Seq` is a constructor
  (other than `false`), we should apply the *constructor-right* rule to a suitable set of
  premises to obtain the `Seq`. The *constructor-right* rule is a generalization of the *arrow-
  right* and *conjunction-right* rules (i.e. handling the constructors '->' and ', '). The
  conjunction-right rule is not part of the linear calculus of partial inductive definitions,
  but is made explicit here in order to gain control over the order in which subgoals are
  executed. It is of course a parallel to the ⊢() rule in the theory of partial inductive
  definitions.

- The second clause states that if the consequent of `Seq` instead is an atom we shall instead
  apply the *definition-right* rule.

- The third and fourth clauses accomplishes the analog of this on each condition in the
  antecedent. However, in each case where the antecedent is either a constructed
  condition with `Constr` different from `false`, or an *Atom*, we would generate a choice
  point in the selection of rule to proceed with (as the interpreter will backtrack over the
  clauses in the proviso definition).

For this problem these alternatives will not contribute to different answer-substitutions,
and the two derivations with their roots at the choice point will be trivial variants of each
other. We can avoid this redundancy by ensuring that the *constructor-left*, and the

definition-left rules are never utilized unless the the consequent actually is the constructor
`false`.

The condition `c_cond(conseq(Seq),`false/0)` occurring in the last two clauses of the
typing ensures precisely this.

It turns out we never have to use the axiom rule for this particular problem, so we simply
exclude any clauses defining the use of the axiom rule. Excluding the axiom rule applied
to the constant `false` cuts the number of redundant answers to the query

```
grey(karo) \- false
```

from 38 to 19. Not using it at all reduces these further to 14, while the restriction on the
application of the *definition-left* and *constructor-left* rule (stated in the third and fourth
clauses) cuts these 14 to 6.

For the query

```
grey(E) \- false
```

GCLA I gives 6 identical substitutions. If we choose not to utilize the axiom rule we cut
the number of solutions to 3, while the other restrictions discussed above do not improve
the situation further for this particular query.

It would be feasible to further restrict the search space for queries of this type, but that
would involve defining an alternative selection function for choosing a condition from the
antecedent - instead of the member relation occurring in the above proviso - and that
would lead us too far at this point.

4.3.2. Append example

As we saw in the "plus" example above, the functional programming methodology of
GCLA requires that the search tree is traversed in a certain order for the solutions in
canonical form to be found first. In addition we may want to exclude the other solutions,
that, although theoretically correct, are counterintuitive when the definitions are regarded
as defining first order functions.

As an example consider the definition of the append function on lists:

```
%% The function append

append([],ListExpr) <= ListExpr.
append([Hd|Tl],ListExpr) <= cons(Hd,append(Tl,ListExpr)).
append(ListExpr1,ListExpr2) <=
   [neq(ListExpr1,[]),neq(ListExpr1,[_|_])],
   ((ListExpr1 -> List) -> append(List,ListExpr2)).

%% Substitution Schema

cons(HdExpr,TlExpr) <=    % Substitution schema for lists
   (HdExpr -> Hd), (TlExpr -> Tl) -> [Hd|Tl].

%% Objects in canonical form are not absurd

[] <= [], [].              % first list in body is
[Hd|Tl] <= [],[Hd|Tl].     % an empty guard
```

The intended meaning of each clause is:

- append of an empty list in canonical form, and a list expression has as its value the value of that same list expression.

- append of a non empty list in canonical form, and a list expression has as its value the result of applying the cons function to the first element of the canonical list, and the value of applying append to the rest of the canonical list and the list expression occurring as the second argument of the original call.

- append of a list expression that is not in canonical form, and an other list expression has as its value the value of applying append to the *value* of the list expression occurring as its first argument, and the list expression occurring as its second argument.

- cons of a list element expression, and a list expression has as its value the value a list with a first element that is the value of the first argument of cons, and where the rest of the list is the result of evaluating the second argument of cons.

- The last two clauses state that objects in canonical form are not absurd. I.e. their truth values are unknown, or irrelevant. With an appropriate typing of the program (as the one given below), these two clauses can be disregarded, as the *definition-left* rule can be prevented from operating on canonical terms when they occur in the antecedent. Without a typing all additional constants that can occur in queries must also be defined in an analogous manner.

Now, if we would try to use this definition with the default execution mechanism of GCLA I we would be quickly discouraged.

E.g. the query

```
append([a,b],[c,d]) \- X.
```

would result in the following set of answer substitutions

```
X = append([a,b],[c,d]);
X = cons(a,append([b],[c,d]));
X = [a|append([b],[c,d])];
X = [a|cons(b,append([],[c,d]))];
X = [a,b|append([],[c,d])];
X = [a,b,c,d];
no,
```

in that order. Obviously the last solution is the one we are looking for, while the other ones are in a sense correct, but should perhaps occur after the last one, if at all (assuming eager evaluation is the desired behaviour).

The order of the solutions can be reversed simply by stating that the *definition-left* rule should always be tried before the *axiom* rule. If we would like to completely exclude all solutions but the one in canonical form we would have to place restrictions on when and how the *axiom* rule may be applied. The necessity of the last two clauses in the definition can be avoided by stating that objects in canonical form should only be handled by the *axiom* rule.

A typing of the above definition that accomplishes this is

```
Seq : `c_right(Constr,conseq(Seq),_) <=
    c_cond(conseq(Seq),Constr).
Seq : `c_left(Constr,Cond,_) <=
    member(Cond,anteced(Seq)),
    c_cond(Cond,Constr).
Seq : `d_left(Cond,_) <=
    member(Cond,anteced(Seq)),
    atom(Cond,`append/2).
Seq : `subst(Cond,_) <=
    member(Cond,anteced(Seq)),
    atom(Cond,`cons/2).
Seq : `axiom(Term,_) <=
    member(Term,anteced(Seq))
    dif_term(Term,`append/2),
    dif_term(Term,`cons/2).
```

The first two clauses simply take care of the constructors '->' and ','. The third clause states that the append function occurring in the antecedent shall always be executed by the *definition-left* rule. The fourth clause states that the cons function shall be executed by a specialized rule called *subst*. The fifth clause guarantees that all other terms are regarded as being in canonical form.

The *subst* rule is a rule occurring in the rule definition part of the program. It performs in one step the inferences normally computed by a sequence of rule applications i.e. *definition-left*, *arrow-left*, and then *axiom* on one of the resulting sequents (the rightmost one in the derivation below). It then continues the proof search in the normal manner by utilizing the proviso definition of the program. In our example the application of the *subst* rule corresponds to the following derivation:

$$
\vdots
$$

$$
\cfrac{\cfrac{\ \backslash -\ (\text{HdExpr} \to \text{Hd}, \text{TlExpr} \to \text{Tl}) \qquad \cfrac{([\text{Hd}|\text{Tl}])\ \backslash -\ \text{X}}{}\ ^{I}}{(\text{HdExpr} \to \text{Hd}, \text{TlExpr} \to \text{Tl}) \to ([\text{Hd}|\text{Tl}])\backslash -\ \text{X}}{\to}\vdash}{\text{cons}(\text{HdExpr}, \text{TlExpr})\ \backslash -\ \text{X}}\ \mathcal{D}\vdash
$$

The *subst* rule is defined in the rule definition part of the program as:

```
subst(Atom,Rule) <=
atom(Atom,_)
clause(Atom,Def),
unify(arg(2,hd(Def)),conseq(Seq))
-> ((type(seq(`[],arg(1,hd(Def))),Rule) ->
       seq(`[],arg(1,hd(Def))))
     -> Seq).
```

The same effect could be achieved by instead in the proviso definition giving the type clause

```
Seq : `d_left(Cond,
               [`c_left(`('->'/2),hd(Def),
                        [_,`axiom(arg(2,hd(Def)),
                         [])])]) <=
clause(Cond,Def),
member(Cond,anteced(Seq)),
atom(Cond,`cons/2).
```

for cons, but as functional programming is such a common case and this operation is performed over and over again, it is a better idea to use a specialized rule. In the current implementation the *subst* rule is provided as a primitive by the system.

The *Provisos* part of the *subst* rule definition is

```
atom(Atom,_)
clause(Atom,Def),
unify(arg(2,hd(Def)),conseq(Seq)),
```

For the rule to be applicable all of these must be fulfilled. atom simply checks that Atom really is an *Atom*. clause is used here instead of definiens (which is the essential part of the *definition-left* rule) because a substitution schema always consist of only one clause, and with a singleton as a body. *arrow-left* is performed by accessing the arguments of the constructed condition. The third condition is the axiom unification.

Note that the axiom unification here is done before the premises are proved, which reverses the order in which these steps are normally performed. This gives us termination in some cases where we would otherwise loop. This behaviour is *not* captured by the alternative typing given above.

The *Premises* part of the rule definition states that the first argument of the arrow-construction in the definition of atom should be proved by the sequence of rules obtained from the typing of the program. In general this will be an instance of the *c-right* rule. Note the type function applied to the premise sequent. This function is defined in the proviso definition and returns the type of its first argument as its value, *and* as its second argument. It is defined in terms of the " : " relation.

In the case of cons and the typing given above, the following sequence of rules will be performed after the application of the *subst* rule:

```
c_right(`(',`/2),((HdExpr -> Hd), (TlExpr -> Tl)),
     [c_right(`('->'/2),(HdExpr -> Hd),_),
      c_right(`('->'/2),(TlExpr -> Tl),_)].
```

giving a derivation for every occurrence of a cons expression in the antecedent with the following general structure

$$
\cfrac{
\cfrac{
\cfrac{\vdots}{
\cfrac{\text{HdExpr } \backslash- \text{ Hd}}{\backslash- \text{ HdExpr } -> \text{ Hd}} \vdash\to
}
\quad
\cfrac{\vdots}{
\cfrac{\text{TlExpr } \backslash- \text{ Tl}}{\backslash- \text{ TlExpr } -> \text{ Tl}} \vdash\to
}
}{\backslash- \text{ (HdExpr } -> \text{ Hd, TlExpr } -> \text{ Tl)}} ,\vdash \quad \cfrac{}{[\text{Hd}|\text{Tl}] \ \backslash- \ X} I \to\vdash
}{
\cfrac{\big((\text{HdExpr } -> \text{ Hd, TlExpr } -> \text{ Tl}) -> [\text{Hd}|\text{Tl}]\big)\backslash- \ X}{\text{cons}(\text{HdExpr,TlExpr}) \ \backslash- \ X} \mathcal{D}\vdash
}
$$

The append and cons definitions together with the above proviso and rule definitions gives exactly the procedural behaviour we would like to see. The definition gives the declarative content of the program, while the typing associated with the definition gives a procedure that computes the intended answer substitutions in a reasonably efficient way.

E.g. the query

```
append([a,b],[c,d]) \- X
```

now gives only the desired solution

```
X = [a,b,c,d],
```

while the query

```
append(X,Y) \- [a,b,c],
```

gives us the following sequence of substitutions on backtracking:

```
X = []
Y = [a,b,c];

X = [a]
Y = [b,c];

X = [a,b]
Y = [c];

X = [a,b,c]
Y = [];
no.
```

The *subst* rule above is an example of a complex type of rule, that can be defined to perform specialized types of inferences. The process of defining rules is not a trivial one, but in general a major programming task that requires intimate knowledge of the abstract syntax of GCLA II, and the semantics of the language. In addition, each new rule definition introduced must be proved sound with respect to the declarative semantics of the definition $\mathcal{D}$. If not, soundness of the inference mechanism cannot be guaranteed.

The majority of problems however, can be solved by giving trivial reformulations of the default rules, or simply by giving a typing of the program. Very few problems require the user to write complex specialized rules. Still, in cases where efficiency is important this possibility may become essential.

The construction of a typing for a program is far from trivial in itself. If we consider what we are actually doing, the effort spent on this part of the program becomes more understandable. The definition is generally quite close to a specification of the program, while the complete program defines an efficient procedure to make inferences from this definition. Constructing a typing, and possibly some rules is then analogous to program synthesis/transformation. As long as the rules introduced are sound, the extensions introduced to the program preserve the declarative meaning of the definition. Transforming a high level program or a specification into an efficient program preserving its declarative meaning is never a trivial task.

5. Conclusions and Related Work

Through the years, Prolog has proven to be a good comprise between logical expressiveness and computational power. The key to this is Horn clause logic combined with SLD resolution. Several attempts to extend Prolog have been proposed, for example Miller's lambda-Prolog [Mil89], Gabbay and Reyle's N-PROLOG [GR84], Naish's NU-Prolog [Nai86], Contextual-Prolog [MP89], metaProlog [Bow85] among others. They all try to extend Prolog within the logical approach, while our attempt is to take a more proof-theoretic approach.

All the examples presented have been executed in the two interpreters defining GCLA I and GCLA II. The interpreter for GCLA I [Aro89a] is implemented in Prolog, and is available from SICS. An abstract machine, which is an extension of the WAM [War83], has also been constructed [Aro89b]. The interpreter for GCLA II is an experimental one, but we hope to both build a more stable interpreter for GCLA II, and to incorporate the extensions compared with GCLA I into the abstract machine, giving a complete, efficient GCLA system.

On the theoretical side, GCLA like formalisms has been used as a basis for a framework for formal program development [EH88], and work on finite representation in the theory of partial inductive definitions [Eri90].

6. References

[Aro89a] M. Aronsson, *The GCLA User's Manual*, Technical Report SICS T89012, Swedish Institute of Computer Science, 1989.

[Aro89b] M. Aronsson, *GAM, An Abstract Machine for GCLA*, Research Report SICS R89002, Swedish Institute of Computer Science, 1989.

[Aro90] M. Aronsson, L-H. Eriksson, A. Gäredal, L. Hallnäs, P. Olin, *The Programming Language GCLA: A Definitional Approach to Logic Programming*, New Generation Computing 7(4), pp. 381-404, 1990.

[Bow85] K. A. Bowen, *Meta-Level Programming and Knowledge Representation*, New Generation Computing, 3(4), pp. 359 - 383, 1985.

[EH88]   L.-H. Eriksson, L. Hallnäs, *A Programming Calculus Based on Partial Inductive Definitions*, Research Report SICS R88013, Swedish Institute of Computer Science.

[Eri90]   L.-H. Eriksson, *A Finite Version of the Calculus of Partial Inductive Definitions*, SICS Research Report in preparation.

[FS90]   Fredholm D, Serafimovski S, *Partial inductive Definitions as Typesystems for Lambda Terms*, in Proceedings of the Workshop on Programming Logic, Chalmers University of Technology, 1990.

[GH88]   J.R.W. Glauert, K. Hammond, *Implementing Pattern-Matching Functional Languages using Dactl*, Internal Report, University of East Anglia, 1988.

[GR84]   D.M. Gabbay, U.Reyle, *N-PROLOG: An Extension of Prolog with Hypothetical Implications: I*, Journal of Logic Programming, 1(4), pp. 319-355,1984.

[Hal87]   L. Hallnäs, *Partial Inductive Definitions*, In A. Avron et.al., editor, Workshop on General Logic, Report ECS-LFCS-88-52. Department of Computer Science, University of Edinburgh, 1987. Also published as Research Report SICS R86005C by the Swedish Institute of Computer Science, 1988. A revised version to appear in Theoretical Computer Science.

[HS84]   M. Hagiya, T. Sakurai, *Foundation of Logic Programming Based on Inductive Definition*, New Generation Computing, 2(1), pp. 59-77, 1984.

[HS-H88]   L. Hallnäs, P. Schroeder-Heister, *A Proof-Theoretic Approach to Logic Programming*, Research Report SICS R88005, Swedish Institute of Computer Science, 1988. A revised version to appear in the Journal of Logic and Computation, 1990.

[Kow79]   R. Kowalski, *Algorithm = Logic + Control*, Communications of the ACM 22(7), pp. 424 - 436, 1979.

[Llo87]   J.W. Lloyd, *Foundations of Logic Programming*, Springer Verlag, 1987.

[Mil89]   D. Miller, *A Logical Analysis of Modules in Logic Programming*, Journal of Logic Programming 6(1-2), pp. 79 - 108, 1989.

[MP89]   L. Monteiro, A. Porto, *Contextual Logic Programming*, in Proceedings of 6th ICLP, Lisbon, Portugal, The MIT Press, 1989.

[Nai86]   L. Naish, *Negation and Quantifiers in NU-Prolog*, In Proceedings of the Third International Conference on Logic Programming, pp. 624-634, Springer Verlag Berlin, 1986.

[Pau83]   L. Paulson, *Tactics and Tacticals in Cambridge LCF* Tech. Report No 39, Computer Laboratory, University of Cambridge.

[War83]   D.H.D Warren, *An Abstract Prolog Instruction Set*, Technical Note 309, SRI International, October 1983.

Appendix

```
%%%%%%%%%%%%%%%%%%%%%%%%%%%%%%%
%%%    Rules definitions    %%%
%%%%%%%%%%%%%%%%%%%%%%%%%%%%%%%
```

```
%%%%%%%%%%%%%%
% Subst Rule %
%%%%%%%%%%%%%%

%% Definition of subst(Rule) a rule that in one step performs:
%% first P Left, arrow Left, Axiom, and then Arrow Right
%% followed by Rule
%% This operation is used to evaluate substitution schemata
%% in functional programs

subst(Atom,Rule) <=      % There must be only one clause defining Atom
  atom(Atom,_),          % for this rule to be sound
  clause(Atom,Def),      % hd(Def) == ((X1 -> Y1), ... (Xn -> Yn) -> Z)
  unify(arg(2,hd(Def)),conseq(Seq)),   % arg(2,hd(Def)) == Z
  (seq(` [],arg(1,hd(Def))) -> Seq1)
  -> ((type(` Seq1,Rule) -> ` Seq1)  -> Seq).


%%%%%%%%%%%%%%
% Axiom rule %
%%%%%%%%%%%%%%

axiom(Term,[]) <=
  term(Term,_),
  unify(Term,conseq(Seq))
  -> (true -> Seq).


%%%%%%%%%%%%%%%%%%%%%%%%%%%%
% Definition right rule %
%%%%%%%%%%%%%%%%%%%%%%%%%%%%

d_right(Atom,Rules) <=
  atom(Atom,_),          % Check just in case
  clause(Atom,CondList)
  -> ((` conj_right(CondList,Atom,Rules) -> Seq) -> Seq).
```

```
conj_right(CondList,Atom,[]) <=
  null(CondList) -> (true -> Seq).
conj_right(Conds,Atom,[Rule|Rules]) <=
  consp(Conds),
  (seq(anteced(Seq),hd(Conds)) -> Seq1)
  -> ((type(` Seq1,Rule) -> ` Seq1),
       (` conj_right(tl(Conds),Atom,Rules) -> Seq)
       -> Seq).



%%%%%%%%%%%%%%%%%%%%%%%%%%%%%
% Constructor right rule %
%%%%%%%%%%%%%%%%%%%%%%%%%%%%%

c_right(`(true/0),Cond,[]) <=
  c_cond(Cond,`(true/0))
  -> (true -> Seq).

c_right(`('->'/2),Cond,[Rule1]) <=    % Arrow expression
  c_cond(Cond,`('->'/2)),           % Check just in case
  (seq(cons(arg(1,Cond),anteced(Seq)),arg(2,Cond)) -> Seq1)
  -> ((type(` Seq1,Rule1) -> ` Seq1) -> Seq).

%  Traverse a conjunction occurring to the right in left to right order

c_right(`(','/2),Conj,[Rule1,Rule2]) <=    % Conjunction
  c_cond(Conj,`(','/2)),                  % Check just in case
  (seq(anteced(Seq),arg(1,Conj)) -> Seq1),
  (seq(anteced(Seq),arg(2,Conj)) -> Seq2)
  -> ((type(` Seq1,Rule1) -> ` Seq1),
       (type(` Seq2,Rule2) -> ` Seq2)
       -> Seq).



%%%%%%%%%%%%%%%%%%%%%%%%%%%%
% Definition left rule %
%%%%%%%%%%%%%%%%%%%%%%%%%%%%

d_left(Atom,Rules) <=
  atom(Atom,_),            % Check just in case
  definiens(Atom,Def)
  -> ((` conj_left(Def,Atom,Rules) -> Seq) -> Seq).

conj_left(Def,Atom,[]) <=
  null(Def) -> (true -> Seq).
```

```
conj_left(Def,Atom,[Rule|Rules]) <=
  consp(Def),
  (seq(replace(Atom,hd(Def),anteced(Seq)),conseq(Seq)) -> Seq1)
  -> ((type(` Seq1,Rule) -> ` Seq1),
       (` conj_left(tl(Def),Atom,Rules) -> Seq)
       -> Seq).


%%%%%%%%%%%%%%%%%%%%%%%%%%%%%%
% Constructor left rules %
%%%%%%%%%%%%%%%%%%%%%%%%%%%%%%

c_left(`(false/0),Cond,[]) <=
  true
  -> (true -> Seq).

c_left(`('->'/2),Conj,[Rule1,Rule2]) <=
  (seq(remove(Conj,anteced(Seq)),arg(1,Conj)) -> Seq1),
  (seq(replace(Conj,list(arg(2,Conj)),anteced(Seq)),conseq(Seq))
   -> Seq2)
  -> ((type(` Seq1,Rule1) -> ` Seq1),
       (type(` Seq2,Rule2) -> ` Seq2)
       -> Seq).

c_left(`(','/2),Conj,[Rule1]) <=
  c_cond(Conj,`(','/2)),
  (seq(inplace(Conj,arg(1,Conj),arg(2,Conj),anteced(Seq)),conseq(Seq))
   -> Seq1)
  -> ((type(` Seq1,Rule1) -> ` Seq1) -> Seq).
```

Some Applications of Gentzen's Proof Theory in Automated Deduction

MICHAEL BEESON
MATHEMATICS AND COMPUTER SCIENCE
SAN JOSE STATE UNIVERSITY
SAN JOSE, CALIFORNIA 95192, USA

Reasoning and problem-solving programs must eventually allow the full use of quantifiers and sets, and have strong enough control methods to use them without combinatorial explosion.[1]

J. McCarthy

Abstract

We show that Prolog is intimately connected with Gentzen's cut-free sequent calculus G , analyzing Prolog computations as the construction of certain cut-free derivations. We introduce a theorem-proving program GENTZEN based on Gentzen's sequent calculus, which incorporates some features of Prolog's computation procedure. We show that GENTZEN has the following properties: (1) It is (non-deterministically) sound and complete for first-order intuitionistic predicate calculus; (2) Its successful computations coincide with those of Prolog on the Horn clause fragment (both deterministically and non-deterministically). The proofs of (1) and (2) contain a new proof of the completeness of (non-deterministic) Prolog for Horn clause logic, based on our analysis of Prolog in terms of Gentzen sequents instead of on resolution. GENTZEN has been implemented and tested on examples including some proofs by induction in number theory, an example constructed by J. McCarthy to show the limitations of Prolog, and "Schubert's Steamroller." An extension of GENTZEN also provides a decision procedure for intuitionistic propositional calculus (but at some cost in efficiency).

TABLE OF CONTENTS

---

[1] McCarthy [1987], p. 1032.

1. Introduction

Prolog is a programming language in which the underlying computation mechanism is logical deduction. The language uses a subset of the first-order predicate calculus called Horn clauses. These may be defined as formulae $A_1, \ldots, A_n \to B$, where the A_i and B are atomic. The deduction process used by Prolog has been explained in the literature as a form of resolution (Lloyd [1984]). It is one of our purposes here to give an alternate, and we believe more useful, explanation of Prolog's deduction process, in terms of the classical proof theoretic results of G. Gentzen. Acquaintance with the systems of Gentzen (see Kleene pp. 452-501) is presumed.

Our second purpose is to extend Prolog to the full intuitionistic first-order predicate calculus, without sacrificing efficiency.[2] Note that this is a *stronger* result than completeness for classical logic: we can define classical logic within intuitionistic logic, simply by expressing $\exists$ and $\vee$ in terms of $\forall$, $\wedge$, and $\neg$. Intuitionistic logic is *more general* than classical logic. The (family of) program(s) we provide for extending Prolog to intuitionistic predicate calculus is called GENTZEN in honor of the proof theorist G. Gentzen, whose ideas have illuminated proof theory for half a century and may yet help in automated deduction.

Both Prolog and GENTZEN are described by algorithms which can be interpreted either non-deterministically or deterministically. All known metamathematical results about Prolog apply only to the non-deterministic version, while it is the deterministic version that executes in practice. In this paper, we prove corresponding metamathematical results for the non-deterministic version of GENTZEN.

The deterministic version of Prolog makes sacrifices of both soundness and completeness for speed. GENTZEN makes similar sacrifices, but we also show how to make these trade-offs explicit: if you are willing to accept a slower GENTZEN, you can come much closer to completeness with deterministic GENTZEN.

If the simpler versions of GENTZEN are run deterministically under Prolog, they work very well on many interesting examples. However, on examples require complicated search, such as Schubert's Steamroller, they fail rather miserably. The control structure provided in these simple versions for the use of the rules is simply inadequate. There are, however, a wide variety of possibilities for deterministic versions of GENTZEN. We believe that the framework provided by non-deterministic GENTZEN provides a unifying conceptual apparatus into which one can translate and compare various approaches to automated deduction. We have, for example, discovered simple control structures for the use of GENTZEN's rules which permit very rapid solution of the Steamroller and other such problems. This will be taken up in a later paper.

The main results of this paper can be summarized as follows:

- The completeness of (non-deterministic) Prolog for Horn clause logic is a consequence of the proof theory of a Gentzen sequent calculus.[3] A Prolog computation uses

---

[2] Of course, one can construct examples where even Prolog requires exponential time for backtracking. We are discussing *practical* efficiency, not theoretical efficiency.

[3] More precisely, of the completeness of Gentzen's cut-free rules, which can be directly proved without the cut-elimination theorem, (or via the cut-elimination); and of an additional not-quite-trivial "Permutation Lemma".

backtracking and unification to construct a Gentzen derivation of a sequent representing the program and goal.

- GENTZEN's computations on sequents representing Prolog programs and queries exactly parallel Prolog's computations. This is true both deterministically and non-deterministically.
- Non-deterministic GENTZEN is complete for intuitionistic predicate calculus.
- If deterministic GENTZEN terminates, it decides whether the input is provable in intuitionistic predicate calculus; incompleteness only can result from infinite regress.
- GENTZEN has been implemented and tested, and can rapidly prove several test problems, including some proofs by induction in number theory and an example which J. McCarthy invented to show the limitations of Prolog. It can also do many independence proofs by terminating with failure.
- If certain "redundancy checks" are added to GENTZEN, it runs somewhat slower, but then provides a decision procedure for intuitionistic propositional calculus, thus improving on Prolog even on the propositional fragment.

The analysis of Prolog given here answers two questions which haunted the author for several years after he began programming in Prolog:

- Why is it that Prolog seems so "constructive", yet resolution is non-constructive?
- What is the true source of Prolog's efficiency?

The answers to these questions are clear and short, so we give them here, even though you may have to read the paper to understand them fully: Prolog is constructive because its computation method is essentially the construction of a proof in an intuitionistic sequent calculus. The source of its efficiency is threefold: (1) Use only cut-free intuitionistic proofs; (2) Use unification to calculate the terms required at the rules $\Rightarrow \exists$ and $\forall \Rightarrow$; and (3) never go up the right branch of a left implication; use left implication only if the right premise is an axiom.

Having understood Prolog in terms of Gentzen sequents, we were able to generalize Prolog's computation method to the full intuitionistic predicate calculus. We think we have thus contributed some answers to the following two general questions:

- How can logic programming be extended to first-order predicate calculus?
- What general logical principles (as opposed to domain-specific knowledge) can guide the construction of improved automated theorem-provers?

Namely, the same three principles just mentioned, with (3) modified to permit going up the right branch of a left implication only if all other proof methods fail.

GENTZEN bridges the gap between logic programming and automatic theorem proving. If you add the clause `derive(( Gamma => A)):- call(A)` to the top of the program listing for GENTZEN, an attempt to prove A can call on Prolog's built-in procedures, so that what you have is an extension of Prolog to full first-order predicate calculus, but able to access all the non-logical features of Prolog at the same time.

Although GENTZEN can be viewed as an extension of Prolog, we think in addition that the framework of GENTZEN is a good skeleton on which to build a general-purpose mathematical theorem prover. Personally we find Prolog adequate as a programming language, and our interest in GENTZEN is rather from the perspective of automated deduction. GENTZEN makes theorem-proving look like logic programming: In order to get a proof, you pay attention to the order in which you list your axioms, thus controlling the execution of the prover. There is a trade-off between efficiency and completeness. Since GENTZEN is non-deterministically complete, there are no obvious theoretical limits to its deterministic abilities. For example, if you were willing to pay the price of replacing its Prolog-like search strategy by "depth-first iterative deepening", you could achieve deterministic completeness. Bledsoe [1984] (p. 93) says:

> Experience so far has shown that complete procedures tend to be weak, in the sense that they take too long to prove easy theorems (or cannot prove them at all) ...

With GENTZEN's basic architecture, we can have either a fast incomplete prover or a slower complete prover, and we can explore many possible intermediate versions. The version presented here is the fast incomplete version, which we show is still more than adequate as a useful extension of Prolog to problems involving quantifiers.

The completeness of non-deterministic GENTZEN makes deterministic GENTZEN "partially complete": when it terminates, it decides provability of the input, so it can be used for independence proofs. (Note that this means independence from intuitionistic axiom systems, which is often rather difficult to prove.)

Finally, we would like to mention a widespread misconception: that intuitionistic logic is esoteric and not useful for mainstream mathematics. This is really two misconceptions: one, that using intuitionistic logic involves rejecting classical logic. This is not the case, as explained above. Rather, it involves *refining* classical logic to keep track of extra information (about algorithms) provided in the proof. The other misconception is related: that constructive methods can't be powerful in mathematics. On the contrary, the more information you keep track of (without getting lost) the better off you are. We think this principle should apply in automated deduction algorithms as well as to people, and so we think more work should be done on proving theorems constructively by machine. We hope GENTZEN will contribute to this program. We have purposely not considered versions of GENTZEN based on classical sequent calculi, believing that restriction to the intuitionistic rules should improve performance.[4]

We are under no illusions that four pages of Prolog code make a general purpose theorem prover. Rather, we think GENTZEN offers a particularly fruitful underlying architecture for a theorem-prover. There are natural places to integrate the following into GENTZEN: type theory, equality reasoning using symbolic computation, semantic methods, symbolic computation, control of expansion or non-expansion of definitions.[5] Whether or not our hopes for the power of theorem-provers based on GENTZEN's architecture will be borne out remains to be seen; the proof of the pudding lies in actually building such theorem-provers and using them to prove theorems. It is thus not the point of this paper to discuss "real control structures and efficiency in a practical sense", in the words of a referee. On the contrary, the purpose of this paper is to

---

[4] When considering devices to improve completeness at the expense of efficiency, the classical sequent calculi should be reconsidered.

[5] See also the work of N. Shankar, described in Section 11, for an improvement to GENTZEN's purely logical search algorithm.

exhibit a unified theoretical framework based on the sequent calculus, in which one can understand both Prolog and general-purpose theorem-provers, and in which one has the flexibility to use the logical form of both goals and axioms to specify control structures.

Prerequisites to this paper are an acquaintance with Gentzen's logical systems and an acquaintance with unification, up through the concept of "most general unifier". For background on Gentzen, see Kleene [1952], pp. 481-501. For background on unification, see Lloyd [1984]. Familiarity with Prolog will be required to actually read the program of GENTZEN, but in theory it is not required to read the paper.

A detailed comparison of our work with that of Bledsoe, Bowen, Boyer and Moore, Constable, Feferman, Felty, Hayashi, Lifschitz, McCarty, Miller, Paulson, Shankar, Stickel, and others is given in the last section of the paper.

2. Proof-theoretic Preliminaries

Matters of Notation

The basic reference we use for sequent calculi is Kleene [1952]. We have, however, changed the notation for sequents slightly, writing $\to$ for implication and $\Rightarrow$ for the separator between the left part (antecedent) and the right part (succedent) of a sequent.

We have also adopted a different typography for proof trees than is traditional. Instead of drawing tree diagrams growing upwards from goal to axioms, our trees grow left-to-right, with indentation being used instead of horizontal bars to indicate passage to subtrees. For example, the rule $\to\Rightarrow$ is written in traditional notation as

$$\frac{A \to B, \Gamma \Rightarrow A \qquad B, A \to B, \Gamma \Rightarrow \Theta}{A \to B, \Gamma \Rightarrow \Theta}$$

and in our notation as

$$A \to B, \Gamma \Rightarrow \Theta$$
$$A \to B, \Gamma \Rightarrow A$$
$$B, A \to B, \Gamma \Rightarrow \Theta$$

This notation is similar to that used in the "proof refinement logic" of NuPrl (Constable *et. al.* [1986]). It is much more convenient to write or typeset than the traditional notation. However, it is almost impossible to break the habit of visualizing proof trees with the axioms at the top and the conclusions at the bottom; so we will retain the informal meaning of 'above' as meaning nearer the leaves of the tree (the axioms) and 'below' as meaning nearer the root, even though 'above' means 'to the right and below on the page' in the newer notation.

Let me remind the reader that there are several different Gentzen sequent calculi. G3 (Kleene [1052], p. 481) is the one designed to provide a decision procedure for intuitionistic propositional calculus. In this calculus, as you work up the tree from the goal, you do not discard formulae; this enables a bound (in the propositional case) on the size of the proof tree.

G1 (Kleene [1952], p. 442) does not provide a propositional decision procedure, because there is a rule that permits dropping duplicated hypotheses. When that rule is used in reverse, you lose control over the possible size of the proof. On the other hand, the rule $\rightarrow\Rightarrow$ in **G1** is closer to Prolog than **G3**.

Note: In Kleene [1952], **G1** and **G3** contain the cut rule. We use these letters instead to stand for the corresponding *cut-free* systems. *All systems in this paper are cut-free.*

In a Gentzen sequent $\Gamma \Rightarrow \Delta$, usually Γ and Δ are finite sets (or lists) of formulae. The difference between intuitionistic and classical Gentzen calculi is only that in the intuitionistic calculus, the succedent Δ is allowed to contain at most one formula (it may be empty). If we permit the atomic formula **false** to stand for the empty sequent in the succedent, we can assume Δ always contains exactly one formula, in which case we may as well write sequents in the form $\Gamma \Rightarrow \Theta$, where Θ is a formula and Γ is a finite set of formulae.[6] The calculus **G3** as formulated in Kleene in effect treats Γ as a set, i.e. duplicates and order are ignored, while **G1** treats Γ as a list. The treatment as a set is more convenient for our purposes, even though ultimately sets must be represented as lists for an implementation.

The Sequent Calculi G4 and G

In order to explain Prolog, we found it necessary to develop a hybrid version of Gentzen's calculus incorporating some of the features of **G1** and some of the features of **G3**. **G3** differs from **G1** by carrying more formulae from conclusion to hypothesis. For our purposes, the definition of **G3** was "overkill". It isn't necessary to carry quite so many formulae to the hypothesis.[7] Our system **G** is an extension of **G3**. It is similar to **G3**, but permits carrying fewer formulae to the hypothesis under certain circumstances. This is accomplished by giving **G** a different rule $\rightarrow\Rightarrow$ (and also $\wedge\Rightarrow$ and $\vee\Rightarrow$) than **G3**. A related system is **G4**, which *requires* the omission of premisses whenever **G** *permits* it. We shall refer to a **G4** derivation as a *strict* **G** derivation.

In rule $\rightarrow\Rightarrow$, the question is whether the principal formula $A \rightarrow B$ is to occur in the premise(s) as well as the conclusion of the rule. In **G3** it does, in **G1** it does not. Our system **G** adopts the following rule: In case $A- > B$ is obtained by a substitution from the matrix of a universally quantified member of Γ (the rest of the antecedent), then it may be omitted from the premise of the rule. Otherwise, it shall occur. The universally quantified member of Γ may have several universal quantifiers. Here are the two rules for comparison:

(G3)
$$A \rightarrow B, \Gamma \Rightarrow C$$
$$A \rightarrow B, \Gamma \Rightarrow A$$
$$B, A \rightarrow B, \Gamma \Rightarrow C$$

---

[6] Unless **false** is specified "by the user" in listing the axioms (the formulae of the antecedent), it can never occur except in the succedent, where it can be interpreted as the empty list. However, if the user is permitted to use **false**, as seems natural, an argument which we have not given is required to show that the rules of the system handle it correctly. To stay strictly in the scope of proved metatheorems, **false** should not be used in axioms; use $\neg$ instead.

[7] In fact, there is a version of $\mathrm{GENTZEN}$ based on each of these calculi. It is only the **G** and **G4** versions, however, which exactly imitate Prolog. The others work in a slightly less efficient way. In fact, on certain computations the **G3** version suffers practical problems due to Prolog's lack of an "occurs check" in unification, which the **G** and **G4** versions do not seem to. However, on all the examples in this paper, all of these versions run more or less equally well.

That rule applies in **G** too; but when $A \to B$ is obtained by a substitution from the matrix of a universally quantified member of Γ, the following rule can be applied instead:

(G)
$$A \to B, \Gamma \Rightarrow C$$
$$\Gamma \Rightarrow A$$
$$B, \Gamma \Rightarrow C$$

The rules $\wedge \Rightarrow$ and $\vee \Rightarrow$ are also changed in **G**. In **G3**, the rule $\wedge \Rightarrow$ causes branching: there are two rules with the same conclusion. There is no reason (except possibly symmetry with rule $\Rightarrow \vee$) for this; we can just take this one rule instead:

$$A \wedge B, \Gamma \Rightarrow C$$
$$A, B, \Gamma \Rightarrow C$$

Similarly, in rule $\vee \Rightarrow$, there is no reason to carry $A \vee B$ from conclusion to premise, as either disjunct is stronger. Just take this rule instead:

$$A \vee B, \Gamma \Rightarrow C$$
$$A, \Gamma \Rightarrow C$$
$$B, \Gamma \Rightarrow C$$

A similar variation is made in the rules $\wedge \Rightarrow$ and $\vee \Rightarrow$.

G also admits a more general syntax than the Gentzen calculi described in Kleene [1952]. In particular, we admit formulas $\forall x A$ and $\exists x A$ where x is not a single variable, but a list of variables. In this case, however, we require that the list x be in alphabetical order.[8] There are obvious generalizations of the quantifier rules to list quantifiers. In the case of rule $\forall \Rightarrow$, adding the generalized rule is not just a matter of abbreviation: if we were to "strip off" the quantifiers one at a time (using the rule of **G3** in reverse) we would get a lot of extra formulas in the antecedent. It is important to be able to strip them all off at once.

For reference, here are the rules exactly:

Rules of G

(axiom)
$$C, \Gamma \Rightarrow C$$

$(\Rightarrow \to)$
$$\Gamma \Rightarrow A \to B$$
$$A, \Gamma \Rightarrow B$$

---

[8] Kleene is not specific about which symbols are legal variables, specifying only that there is a fixed list of variables. We specify that the variables are any legal Prolog atoms (except `false` and `true`), and that the order on the variables is the lexicographical order determined by the Prolog system's ordering predicate. Requiring quantified lists to be in order is done for the sake of efficiency.

$(\Rightarrow \wedge)$
$$\frac{\Gamma \Rightarrow A \wedge B}{\Gamma \Rightarrow A}$$
$$\Gamma \Rightarrow B$$

$(\Rightarrow \vee)$
$$\frac{\Gamma \Rightarrow A \vee B}{\Gamma \Rightarrow A}$$

$(\Rightarrow \vee)$
$$\frac{\Gamma \Rightarrow A \vee B}{\Gamma \Rightarrow B}$$

$(\Rightarrow \neg)$
$$\frac{\Gamma \Rightarrow \neg A}{A, \Gamma \Rightarrow \mathtt{false}}$$

$(\rightarrow \Rightarrow)$
$$\frac{A \rightarrow B, \Gamma \Rightarrow C}{(A \rightarrow B), \Gamma \Rightarrow A}$$
$$B, (A \rightarrow B), \Gamma \Rightarrow C$$

where the formulae in parentheses may be omitted if $A \rightarrow B$ is a substitution instance of the matrix of a universally quantified formula in Γ.

$(\wedge \Rightarrow)$
$$\frac{A \wedge B, \Gamma \Rightarrow C}{A, B, \Gamma \Rightarrow C}$$

$(\vee \Rightarrow)$
$$\frac{A \vee B, \Gamma \Rightarrow C}{A, \Gamma \Rightarrow C}$$
$$B, \Gamma \Rightarrow C$$

$(\neg \Rightarrow)$
$$\frac{\neg A, \Gamma \Rightarrow C}{\neg A, \Gamma \Rightarrow A}$$

$(\Rightarrow \forall)$
$$\frac{\Gamma \Rightarrow \forall x A}{\Gamma \Rightarrow A[y/x]} \quad (y \text{ not free in } \Gamma, \forall x A)$$

$(\exists \Rightarrow)$
$$\frac{\exists x A, \Gamma \Rightarrow C}{A[y/x], \Gamma \Rightarrow C} \quad (y \text{ not free in } \Gamma, C)$$

$(\forall \Rightarrow)$
$$\forall x A, \Gamma \Rightarrow C$$
$$A[t/x], \forall x A, \Gamma \Rightarrow C$$

$(\Rightarrow \exists)$
$$\Gamma \Rightarrow \exists x A$$
$$\Gamma \Rightarrow A[t/x]$$

LEMMA. *Every derivation in* **G** *can be converted to a derivation in* **G3** *(first replacing list quantifiers by iterated quantifiers). Conversely, every derivation in* **G3** *can be converted to a strict* **G** *derivation. Consequently, the cut-elimination theorem holds for* **G** *and* **G4** *as well as for* **G3**.

PROOF: ($\Rightarrow$) By induction on the length of derivations in **G**. Suppose the last inference is by rule $\rightarrow \Rightarrow$, and we are in the case where the principal formula is omitted from the hypothesis. Then by inserting some extra applications of rule $\forall \Rightarrow$, we can recover the omitted formula; indeed it was this possibility that determined the cases in which we could afford to omit the formula.

Suppose that the last inference is by rule $\wedge \Rightarrow$; let the last two lines of the derivation be

$(\wedge \Rightarrow)$
$$A \wedge B, \Gamma \Rightarrow C$$
$$A, B, \Gamma \Rightarrow C$$

By induction hypothesis, there is a **G3** derivation of $A, B, \Gamma \Rightarrow C$. Thus all we need to know is that **G3** is closed under the $\wedge \Rightarrow$ rule of **G**. We can prove this directly with two applications of cut elimination: start with a derivation of $A \wedge B \Rightarrow A$ and one of $A, B, \Gamma \Rightarrow C$. Apply cut-elimination with cut-formula A, to get $A \wedge B, B, \Gamma \Rightarrow C$. Take a derivation of $A \wedge B \Rightarrow B$, and use B for a cut-formula, getting $A \wedge B, \Gamma \Rightarrow C$.

Suppose the last inference is by rule $\vee \Rightarrow$; let the last two lines of the derivation be

$(\vee \Rightarrow)$
$$A \vee B, \Gamma \Rightarrow C$$
$$A, \Gamma \Rightarrow C$$
$$B, \Gamma \Rightarrow C$$

By induction hypothesis, there are **G3** derivations of the premises (so again all we really need is the closure of **G3** under this rule, which is the same as the $\vee \Rightarrow$ rule of **G1**). Just add $A \vee B$ to the antecedent of every sequent in the derivations of the premises. The derivation will remain a derivation, unless there are free variables in $A \vee B$ that cause a violation of the "restriction on variables" above this point. This problem can be avoided by renaming eigenvariables in the derivation of $A, \Gamma \Rightarrow C$ to avoid the free variables of B, and vice-versa renaming eivenvariables in the derivation of $B, \Gamma \Rightarrow C$ to avoid the free variables of A.

Suppose that the last inference is by rule $\forall \Rightarrow$, applied to a list quantifier. If we had used the $\forall \Rightarrow$ rule of **G3** several times (one quantifier at a time) (proceeding backwards from the root), we would have produced a sequent just like the hypothesis of this inference, except with some extra formulae in the antecedent. We can add these formulae to the antecedents of every formula above this point in the proof tree. The free variables of these intermediate formulae already occur in the antecedent, so no inferences are invalidated by violations of the "restriction on variables" due to these added formulae in the antecedents.

($\Rightarrow$) By induction on **G3** derivations. Suppose the last inference of the given **G3** derivation is by rule $\rightarrow\Rightarrow$ in the case where the principal formula is not dropped in the hypothesis. Then the deduction is already in **G3**. In the case where the principal formula is dropped, we copy the principal formula to the antecedents everywhere above, first renaming eigenvariables if necessary to avoid violating the restriction on variables. Similarly, if the last inference is by rule $\wedge\Rightarrow$ or rule $\vee\Rightarrow$, we copy the principal formula to the antecedents above. ∎.

Substitutions and Unification

A *substitution* is a (partial) map from terms to variables which commutes with all function symbols. Lower-case Greek letters are used to denote substitutions. They are written on the right in algebraic notation: $t\theta$ instead of $\theta(t)$. Juxtaposition of symbols for substitutions indicates composition. We write $\theta \geq \delta$ ("θ is more general than δ") if for some μ we have $\theta\mu = \delta$. Note μ might be the identity. We regard all substitutions as defined everywhere, extending them to be the identity where they are not explicitly defined. Substitutions determined by their action on a finite number of variables can be indicated by a list of equations such as $x = a^2, y = a^3$. Similarly, if θ is a substitution satisfying $x\theta = x$, we denote by $\theta, x = t$ the new substitution which agrees with θ except at x, and takes x to the value t. This is not a "union" since we regard all substitutions as defined everywhere.

Note that substitutions can be applied to formulas as well as to terms, the difference being that formulas may contain bound variables. In this case the application of a substitution θ to a formula (or other expression with bound variables) is presumed not to affect the bound variables, even if θ has a non-trivial action on those bound variables.

A substitution θ is said to *unify* terms t and s if $t\theta$ and $s\theta$ are identical. A *most general unifier* of t and s is a unifier more general than any other unifier. The most general unifier is unique up to renamings of variables.

The Permutation Lemma

Note: The reader is invited to postpone reading the rest of this section until it is clear why it is needed.

We shall make use of the "permutation lemmas" about Gentzen's calculus. These lemmas, familiar (at least in outline) to experts in proof theory but less well-known than the material in Kleene's book, show how the order of application of Gentzen's rules can be changed, so that one may assume that a cut-free proof of a given sequent ends with a certain rule. This restructuring of the proof tree cannot be done arbitrarily; there are certain restrictions on the form of the formulae involved.

Kleene [1952a] contains a thorough analysis of the possibilities for such "permutations" of the inference rules. Since there are on the order of ten rules, there are on the order of 100 cases to consider— a number which is doubled when you realize that some permutations are permissible classically, but not intuitionistically. Each individual case is simple: you can work them out yourself in a few lines by writing out the last two lines of a derivation and then trying to reverse the order of the last two rules. Many cases are obviously permutable, for example if one rule affects only the antecedent and the other only the succedent. However, it is not the case that any two rules permute.

Remark (examples of non-permutable pairs of rules): The permutation of certain pairs is blocked by the "restriction on variables". An example of this kind of non-permutable inference is given by the proof of the sequent $\forall x A \Rightarrow \exists y A[y/x]$, which must have the $\forall \Rightarrow$ inference last. In classical logic, this is the only block to the permutation of inferences. In intuitionistic logic, there are others: for example the sequent $A \vee (B \vee C) \Rightarrow (A \vee B) \vee C$ can only be proved by opening up the left side first.

In this paper we need only certain cases of Kleene's Permutation Lemma (Lemma 7 of Kleene [1952a]). We need those cases, however, not (only) for the system **G1** treated in Kleene [1952a] but also for the systems **G3**, **G4**, and **G**. In the interest of a complete and self-contained presentation, we therefore give the proof of the cases we need.

PERMUTATION LEMMA. *(Kleene [1952a])* **G** *derivations (***G3** *derivations; strict* **G** *derivations) can be transformed so as to permute the order of applications of the rules* $\rightarrow \Rightarrow$, $\forall \Rightarrow$, *and* $\Rightarrow \exists$, *and we can permute* $\forall$*seq below* $\Rightarrow \wedge$. *(except of course in the case when the principal formula of the first inference is a subformula of the principal formula of the second one).*

This includes permuting two applications of $\rightarrow \Rightarrow$. *When two applications of the* $\rightarrow \Rightarrow$ *rule are permuted, the principal formulae of the inferences are the same before and after the transformation.*

In addition, we can permute $\forall$*seq below* $\Rightarrow \wedge$.[9]

PROOF: Consider for example the permutation of the rules $\forall \Rightarrow$ and $\rightarrow \Rightarrow$. To bring $\rightarrow \Rightarrow$ 'below' $\forall \Rightarrow$ we transform the deduction steps[10]

$$\forall x A, C \rightarrow D, \Gamma \Rightarrow Q$$
$$A[t/x], \forall x A, C \rightarrow D, \Gamma \Rightarrow Q$$
$$A[t/x], \forall x A, (C \rightarrow D), \Gamma \Rightarrow C$$
$$D, (C \rightarrow D), A[t/x], \forall x A, \Gamma \Rightarrow Q$$

into the steps

$$\forall x A, C \rightarrow D, \Gamma \Rightarrow Q$$
$$\forall x A, (C \rightarrow D), \Gamma \Rightarrow C$$
$$A[t/x], \forall x A, (C \rightarrow D), \Gamma \Rightarrow C$$
$$\forall x A, D, (C \rightarrow D), \Gamma \Rightarrow Q$$
$$A[t/x], \forall x A, D, (C \rightarrow D, \Gamma \Rightarrow Q$$

---

[9] The *principal formula* of an inference is the one whose connective is introduced by the inference.
[10] where the parentheses around $(C \rightarrow D)$ indicate that this formula may possibly be omitted at the indicated location, if it is obtained by substitution from a matrix of a universally quantified member of $\Gamma, \forall x A$. If we consider only **G3** derivations, no such omissions are allowed. If we consider *strict* **G** derivations, they will occur whenever allowed. In cases in which some possible omissions are not made, some inferences by $\forall \Rightarrow$ may have to be inserted in the exhibited transformed derivations, so that the same formula is either omitted or not throughout a given exhibited piece of a derivation.

Next consider the reverse transformation, in which we desire to bring an application of $\forall \Rightarrow$ below an application of $\rightarrow\Rightarrow$. The derivation we start with thus contains:

$$\forall x A, C \rightarrow D, \Gamma \Rightarrow Q$$
$$\forall x A, D, (C \rightarrow D), \Gamma, \Rightarrow Q$$
$$A[t/x], \forall x A, D, (C \rightarrow D), \Gamma \Rightarrow Q$$
$$\forall x A, (C \rightarrow D), \Gamma \Rightarrow C$$
$$A[s/x], \forall x A, (C \rightarrow D), \Gamma \Rightarrow C$$

Note that this is not quite the reverse of the preceding situation since two instances of A are used, i.e. s may not be the same term as t. The calculus **G** does not permit simply padding the antecedent with more hypotheses as you go up the tree. However, extra hypotheses can be introduced by an extra application of $\forall \Rightarrow$, resulting in the intermediate tranformation

$$\forall x A, C \rightarrow D, \Gamma \Rightarrow Q$$
$$\forall x A, D, (C \rightarrow D), \Gamma, \Rightarrow Q$$
$$A[t/x], \forall x A, D, (C \rightarrow D), \Gamma \Rightarrow Q$$
$$A[s/x], A[t/x], \forall x A, D, (C \rightarrow D), \Gamma \Rightarrow Q$$
$$\forall x A, (C \rightarrow D), \Gamma \Rightarrow C$$
$$A[s/x], \forall x A, (C \rightarrow D), \Gamma \Rightarrow C$$
$$A[t/x], A[s/x], \forall x A, (C \rightarrow D), \Gamma \Rightarrow C$$

The extra instances of A on the 'top' two lines can be carried 'upwards' in the antecedents of preceding lines until they reach an axiom. The final transformation is then

$$\forall x A, C \rightarrow D, \Gamma \Rightarrow Q$$
$$A[t/x], \forall x A, (C \rightarrow D), \Gamma \Rightarrow Q$$
$$A[t/x], A[s/x], \forall x A, (C \rightarrow D), \Gamma \Rightarrow Q$$
$$A[s/x], A[t/x], \forall x A, D, (C \rightarrow D), \Gamma \Rightarrow Q$$
$$A[t/x], A[s/x], \forall x A, (C \rightarrow D), \Gamma \Rightarrow C$$

Next we show the permutability of rule $\rightarrow\Rightarrow$ and rule $\Rightarrow \exists$. Suppose we are given a derivation containing

$$A \rightarrow B, \Gamma \Rightarrow \exists x C$$
$$A \rightarrow B, \Gamma \Rightarrow C[t/x]$$
$$(A \rightarrow B), \Gamma \Rightarrow A$$
$$B, (A \rightarrow B), \Gamma \Rightarrow C[t/x]$$

It can be transformed to

$$A \to B, \Gamma \Rightarrow \exists x C$$
$$(A \to B), \Gamma \Rightarrow A$$
$$B, (A \to B), \Gamma \Rightarrow \exists x C$$
$$B, (A \to B), \Gamma \Rightarrow C[t/x]$$

and this transformation is reversible, so that rules $\Rightarrow \exists$ and $\to \Rightarrow$ commute.

Rules $\Rightarrow \exists$ and $\forall \Rightarrow$ affect opposite sides of the $\Rightarrow$ sign, and hence obviously commute.

It remains to permute two different applications of $\to \Rightarrow$. There are two cases, according as the 'higher' application is on the right branch or the left branch of the 'lower' application. We take the right branch case first. Suppose given:

(*)
$$A \to B, C \to D, \Gamma \Rightarrow Q$$
$$(A \to B), C \to D, \Gamma \Rightarrow A$$
$$B, (A \to B), C \to D, \Gamma \Rightarrow Q$$
$$B, (A \to B), (C \to D), \Gamma \Rightarrow C$$
$$D, B, (A \to B), (C \to D), \Gamma \Rightarrow Q$$

We transform this to

$$A \to B, C \to D, \Gamma \Rightarrow Q$$
$$A \to B, (C \to D), \Gamma \Rightarrow C$$
$$(A \to B), (C \to D), \Gamma \Rightarrow A$$
$$B, (A \to B), (C \to D), \Gamma \Rightarrow C$$
$$D, A \to B, (C \to D), \Gamma \Rightarrow Q$$
(*)
$$D, (A \to B), (C \to D), \Gamma \Rightarrow A$$
$$B, D, (A \to B), (C \to D), \Gamma \Rightarrow Q$$

Of the four 'top' nodes in this (partial) derivation, three are 'top' nodes in the given derivation (so we can graft on the subtrees at those nodes). The fourth node, tagged (*), is like the tagged node in the given derivation, except it has the extra formula D in the antecedent. We can graft on the subtree 'above' the tagged node in the given derivation, provided we write D in the antecedent of every formula in that subtree. (This will not affect the validity of any inference, including the axioms at leaves, since D is already a subformula of the antecedent, so its free variables cannot cause any violation of the restriction on variables.)

This transformation, unlike the others we have constructed, may increase the number of applications of $\to \Rightarrow$, as the implication which is moved 'upwards' has to be opened up twice, and a subtree of the old derivation has to be duplicated in the new.

Finally we consider the case of permuting an application of $\to\Rightarrow$ with another application on the left branch of the first. Suppose given:

$$A \to B, C \to D, \Gamma \Rightarrow Q$$
$$(A \to B), C \to D, \Gamma \Rightarrow A$$
$$(A \to B), (C \to D), \Gamma \Rightarrow C$$
$$D, (A \to B), (C \to D), \Gamma \Rightarrow A$$
$$B, (A \to B), C \to D, \Gamma \Rightarrow Q$$

We transform this to

$$A \to B, C \to D, \Gamma \Rightarrow Q$$
$$A \to B, (C \to D), \Gamma \Rightarrow C$$
$$D, A \to B, (C \to D), \Gamma \Rightarrow Q$$
$$D, (A \to B), (C \to D), \Gamma \Rightarrow A$$
$$B, D, (A \to B), (C \to D), \Gamma \Rightarrow Q$$

whose 'top' nodes are the same as those of the given derivation.

Now there is only one more permutation to consider: permuting $\forall \Rightarrow$ below $\Rightarrow \wedge$. Suppose given a derivation ending

$$\forall x P, \Gamma \Rightarrow A \wedge B$$
$$\forall x P, \Gamma \Rightarrow A$$
$$P[t/x], \forall x P, \Gamma \Rightarrow A$$

(*)
$$\forall x P, \Gamma \Rightarrow B$$

We transform this to

$$\forall x P, \Gamma \Rightarrow A \wedge B$$
$$P[t/x], \forall x P, \Gamma \Rightarrow A \wedge B$$
$$P[t/x], \forall x P, \Gamma \Rightarrow A$$

(*)
$$P[t/x], \forall x P, \Gamma \Rightarrow B$$

Note that the starred line isn't exactly the same; there is an extra formula $P[t/x]$ in the succedent of the transformed derivation. We will have to copy this formula to the succedent of every sequent 'above' the starred line (that is, nearer the axioms) in the original derivation. In so doing, we won't violate any conditions on variables, since the condition on variables is satisfied in the original derivation. ∎

3. Explaining Prolog by Gentzen Sequents

We view Prolog's deduction algorithm as the construction of a formal derivation in an intuitionistic sequent calculus. The Prolog program, a finite list of clauses, constitutes the antecedent of a sequent, and the query constitutes the succedent.

The clauses in the program go in the antecedent as implications, while the goal is existentially quantified in the succedent:[11]

$$(\forall x)(Hyp_1 -> P_1), (\forall y)(Hyp_2 -> P_2), \ldots => (\exists z)Goal$$

Note that since "the scope of a Prolog variable is the clause in which it occurs", the clauses are universally quantified in the antecedent. Here the quantifier $\exists z$ is short for a finite sequence of quantifiers over every variable free in $Goal$, and similarly for the universal quantifiers on the left.

To make matters as clear as possible: the above sequent is the expression as a Gentzen sequent of a Prolog program (given by the antecedent) together with a query. Normally a user of Prolog would enter the clauses in the form P_n :- Hyp_n, and Hyp_n would be a conjunction of atomic formulae. The system understands the universal quantifiers implicitly. These clauses would be put in a program file and consulted, after which the query $Goal$ would be typed to the Prolog interpreter prompt. The existential quantifier(s) are also understood implicitly by the Prolog system. When we refer to "clauses" in this paper, we will be speaking of implications in the antecedent of a sequent; the usual form of clauses in connection with resolution will not be mentioned. (We do count a clause with no "body", i.e. a universally quantified atomic formula in the antecedent counts as a "clause".)

The following definitions make the above considerations precise:

DEFINITION. A "Prolog clause" is a formula of one of the forms $\forall x(Con)$ or $\forall x(Hyp \Longrightarrow Con)$, where Con is atomic, and Hyp is either atomic or a conjunction of (possibly many) atomic formulae. The universal quantifier need not actually occur.

DEFINITION. A Prolog sequent is a sequent whose succedent is either atomic, a conjunction of atomic formulae, or an existentially quantified atomic formula, and whose antecedent contains (only) Prolog clauses as just defined.

A closed Prolog sequent corresponds to a Prolog program and query. Prolog sequents with free variables may arise in the course of Prolog's computations, as we shall see below.

Prolog's deduction algorithm tries to unify $Goal$ with the "head" P_n of one of the clauses in the antecedent. Let us suppose for notational simplicity that $Goal$ unifies with P_1. The deduction step which unifies $Goal$ with $P1$ involves the most general unifier θ of $Goal$ and P_1. Suppose for the moment that we are in the simplest case, in which $Goal\theta$ has no free variables. Prolog's computation in this case is represented by the following incomplete **G** proof

$$\forall x(Hyp_1 \to P_1), \forall y(Hyp_2 \to P_2), \ldots => \exists z Goal$$
$$\forall x(Hyp_1 \to P_1), \forall y(Hyp_2 \to P_2), \ldots => Goal\theta$$
$$Hyp_1\theta \to P_1\theta, \forall x(Hyp_1 \to P_1), (\forall y)(Hyp_2 \to P_2), \ldots => Goal\theta$$
$$\forall x(Hyp_1 \to P_1), \ldots \Rightarrow Hyp_1\theta$$
$$P_1\theta, \forall x(Hyp_1 \to P_1), \ldots \Rightarrow Goal\theta$$

---

[11] This is one important place where our treatment differs from Bowen [1980]. He puts the program clauses as separate sequents, and considers them as "sequent axioms", thus treating Prolog deductions as applications of the cut rule instead of constructions of cut-free derivations.

The last sequent is an axiom, since $P_1\theta$ is the same formula as $Goal\theta$ (that's what it means that θ unifies $Goal$ and P_1), so that formula occurs on both sides of $\Rightarrow$. The computation will continue in an attempt to construct a proof of the previous sequent. The last inference is by rule $\rightarrow\Rightarrow$; compare it with the list of rules to see why.

Note that we have allowed conjunction in the succedent; the main reason for doing so is that such formulae will arise in derivations anyway, when a "clause" containing a conjunction is "opened up". It is customary to extend Prolog to allow disjunction in the query and the heads of the clauses, but these are easily reduced to formulae of the above form by the introduction of new predicate letters. Alternately, one can easily extend the description of Prolog's algorithm in terms of Gentzen sequents to this somewhat larger fragment. We shall not take the space to do so, since we shall extend the algorithm to all of first-order predicate calculus later in the paper.

Non-deterministic versus deterministic Prolog. Implementations of Prolog search for a proof of the goal in a deterministic manner. By a *non-deterministic Prolog deduction* we mean a deduction as described above in which the choice of clause $Hyp_n \rightarrow P_n$ can be made at will (non-deterministically). In practice, an implementation of Prolog chooses the leftmost clause whose head will unify with the goal; and it is possible that the search regresses infinitely along this branch, while another choice would have succeeded in producing a proof. All known metamathematical results on the semantics of Prolog refer to non-deterministic proofs, as will the results of this paper. Nevertheless, our implementation of the algorithm described here, like Prolog, makes a deterministic choice. Experiments show that, like Prolog, it still works.

Note that in the case of Horn clause syntax, the succedent is always atomic or atomic preceded by $\exists$; so it can unify only with conclusions of the clauses, i.e. with formulae P_n, where $\forall x_n(Hyp_n \rightarrow Con_n)$ is one of the "clauses" of the Prolog program represented by the antecedent, or possibly with formulae generated from some P_n by applying some other substitution (lower down the proof tree). These formulae P_n are positive in the antecedent, so actual Prolog deductions fit the formal definition just given. Moreover, restricted to Horn clause syntax, Prolog deductions as just defined clearly correspond to (non-deterministic) Prolog deductions as informally defined above.

More generally, if $Goal\theta$ does still contain free variables, the Prolog computation algorithm constructs a cut-free (**G**) proof, but it does not do it line-by-line. Instead, the terms needed in the hypotheses of the $\forall \Rightarrow$ and $\Rightarrow \exists$ rules are constructed gradually, only being settled on after the computation has progressed some lines above the application of the rule in question.

PROLOG EXPLAINED BY GENTZEN PROOFS, USING PROLOG FOR THE EXPLANATION

We give here the fragment of our theorem-prover which is needed for the derivation of Prolog sequents. This Prolog program defines the predicate derive($\Gamma \Rightarrow A$) which succeeds if the system can construct a Gentzen proof (in **G**) of $\Gamma \Rightarrow A$. We write $\forall x A$ in Prolog as all(x, A). The predicate prove(A) is defined to mean, "find a derivation of the sequent $\Rightarrow A$ (with empty antecedent)". Sequents are represented in Prolog using the infix operator $\Rightarrow$, where the antecedent is a list of formulae and the succedent a single formula (with false representing the empty succedent). Logical variables ("object variables") are represented as Prolog atoms. Prolog variables (beginning with upper-case letters) range over object terms.

The Prolog Program

```
% construct a strict G derivation of a Prolog sequent
  axiom((Gamma ⇒ A)):- member(A,Gamma).
  derive(( Gamma => T=T )).
          %this accounts for Prolog's treatment of equality
  derive(( Gamma => C )):-                    %rule -> =>
    memberandrest( (A->B), Gamma,Delta),
        %Delta is what's in Gamma besides (A->B)
    A \== C,    %prevent an obviously redundant proof
    axiom(( [B|Gamma] => C )),
    derive((Delta => A)).
  derive(( Gamma => and(A,B)):-               %rule => &
    derive(( Gamma => A )),
    derive(( Gamma => B )).
  derive((Gamma => B)) :-   %rule all => (list quantifier)
    member(all([X|Rest],A),Gamma),
    findall(_,member(_,[X|Rest]),NewVarList),
    list_fsubst(NewVarList,[X|Rest],A,NewA),
    not fmember(NewA,Gamma),
    derive(( [NewA|Gamma] => B )).
  derive((Gamma => B)) :-   %rule all => (single quantifier)
    member(all(X,A),Gamma),
    fsubst(_,X,A,NewA),
    not fmember2(NewA,Gamma),
        %don't make multiple instances of same clause
    derive(( [NewA|Gamma] => B )).
```

The predicates fmember, fmember2, fsubst, and memberandrest are not printed here, for lack of space. The program can still be understood by means of the following descriptions of these predicates:

fmember(A,L) generates members A of a given list L, or tests whether A belongs to L, but without unification: thus A and L can contain Prolog variables which will be treated like atoms. fmember2 is similar, but it does not distinguish terms that differ only be renaming of Prolog variables. Similarly, fsubst(New,Old,Term,Ans) substitutes New for Old in Term obtaining Ans, but treating Prolog variables as atoms (not subject to unification). They are distinguished from the more ordinary member and subst by the prefix f for "free variables". list_subst takes a list of items New to be substituted respectively for the members of a list of items Old and uses fsubst to carry out the substitutitions. The line using findall in the rule for a list quantifier just generates a list of new Prolog variables of the right length. The predicate memberandrest(Mem,List,Rest) generates members Mem of List, instantiating Rest to List with (the occurrence in question of) Mem deleted.

The main theorem explaining Prolog in terms of Gentzen sequents can now be stated:

THEOREM 1. *(1) Let $\Gamma \Rightarrow \exists x A$ be a Prolog sequent representing a Prolog program Γ and goal A. Then the goal A succeeds with program Γ if and only if the goal* derive($\Gamma \Rightarrow \exists x A$) *succeeds with the program listed above.*

(2)If we give the program the query derive($\Gamma \Rightarrow A[X/x]$), *in which the succedent contains Prolog variables (which range over terms), then the Prolog interpreter will supply an instantiating term such that $\Gamma \Rightarrow A[t/x]$ is provable in* **G**.

This is two theorems: one when "succeed" is interpreted non-deterministically, and another when it has the deterministic interpretation given by an actual interpreter.

Remark: While derive is obviously sound, it is not obviously complete, since it requires the right branch of an application of rule $\rightarrow \Rightarrow$ to be an axiom already. The issue of completeness is addressed in the next section.

PROOF: (1) follows from (2). We prove (2) by induction on the length of Prolog computations from the given program. Suppose then that $\Gamma \Rightarrow A$ is a closed Prolog sequent, and suppose that Prolog's computation of the query A relative to program Γ begins by unifying A with the head P of a member $\forall x(H \rightarrow P)$ of Γ. For simplicity let us assume that the members of Γ have at most one universal quantifier. Evidently the program above will begin by applying the clause of derive corresponding to rule $\forall \Rightarrow$ with this same member of Γ as principal formula of the inference. That will result in an attempt to derive the sequent $H\theta \rightarrow P\theta, \Gamma \Rightarrow A\theta$, where θ is the most general unifier of A and P. Then rule $\rightarrow \Rightarrow$ will be applied, resulting in an attempt to derive $\Gamma \Rightarrow H\theta$. Note that the formula $H\theta \rightarrow P\theta$ has been dropped from the antecedent in accordance with the rules of **G**.

If H is a conjunction, an application of the clause labelled "rule => &" will reduce to the case H is atomic, so that $\Gamma \Rightarrow H\theta$ is again a Prolog sequent. Now the Prolog computation proceeds as specified by the Prolog sequent $\Gamma \Rightarrow H\theta$. By hypothesis, this Prolog computation succeeds; so by induction hypothesis, the attempt to derive this sequent also succeeds. But then the original call to derive succeeds. ∎

EXPLANATION OF PROLOG BY GENTZEN PROOFS, NOT USING PROLOG

The remainder of this section serves two purposes: it introduces the technical tool of "extended" Gentzen sequents and derivations, and it uses that tool to explain Prolog in terms of Gentzen sequents, in a way not dependent on a prior understanding of Prolog.

To see how Prolog works in terms of Gentzen sequents, let us consider an example. Consider the Prolog sequent (program and goal) given by

$$\alpha(2), \forall u(\alpha(u) \rightarrow \beta(u^2)), \forall x(\beta(x) \rightarrow \gamma(x^3)) \Rightarrow \exists z \gamma(z) \tag{1}$$

Prolog tries to construct a proof whose last inference is by the $\Rightarrow \exists$ rule; for this it needs a term t so that $\gamma[t/z]$ can be put in the succedent. For reasons that will be clear in a minute, we prefer to place the emphasis on the substitution η such that $t = \eta x$. At first we cannot determine t, we can only place a constraint upon η: by unifying $\gamma(z)$ with the head of one of the clauses in the succedent, we can see that ηx should have the form $(x\theta)^3$, where θ is a substitution to be determined.

We then consider the sequent

$$\alpha(2), \forall u(\alpha(u) \rightarrow \beta(u^2)), \forall x(\beta(x) \rightarrow \gamma(x^3)) \Rightarrow \gamma((x\theta)^3) \tag{2}$$

and open up the $\forall$ on the left with the $\forall \Rightarrow$ rule (working in what would traditionally be the upwards direction of a proof, i.e. towards the axioms):

$$\beta(x\theta) \rightarrow \gamma((x\theta)^3), \alpha(2), \forall u(\alpha(u) \rightarrow \beta(u^2)), \forall x(\beta(x) \rightarrow \gamma(x^3)) \Rightarrow \gamma((x\theta)^3) \qquad (3)$$

Next we use the $\rightarrow\Rightarrow$ rule (in reverse) to open up the first formula. The two sequents which occur above the line of this inference are:

$$\alpha(2), \forall u(\alpha(u) \rightarrow \beta(u^2)), \forall x(\beta(x) \rightarrow \gamma(x^3)) \Rightarrow \beta(x\theta) \qquad (4)$$

and

$$\gamma((x\theta)^3), \alpha(2), \forall u(\alpha(u) \rightarrow \beta(u^2)), \forall x(\beta(x) \rightarrow \gamma(x^3)) \Rightarrow \gamma((x\theta)^3) \qquad (5)$$

The last sequent (5) is an axiom; not by accident, as that was how we chose the term $t = (x\theta)^3$ in the first place.

The sequent (4) is analyzed as follows: Prolog tries to unify the succedent formula with the head of one of the clauses. The only possibility in this case is to unify $\beta(u^2)$ with $\beta(x\theta)$. Hence we impose a constraint on θ: it must satisfy $x\theta = (u^2)\delta$ for some substitution δ. (If the variable u had occurred in the succedent, we should have renamed it first.) Introducing a symbol for this unknown substitution δ, we work upwards in the proof using the rule $\forall \Rightarrow$:

$$\alpha(u\delta) \rightarrow \beta((u\delta)^2), \beta(x\theta) \rightarrow \gamma((x\theta)^3), \alpha(2),$$
$$((6)) \qquad \forall u(\alpha(u) \rightarrow \beta(u^2)), \forall x(\beta(x) \rightarrow \gamma(x^3)) \Rightarrow \beta(x\theta)$$

Now we can use the rule $\rightarrow\Rightarrow$ as before, generating the following two sequents:

$$\beta(x\theta) \rightarrow \gamma((x\theta)^3), \alpha(2), \forall u(\alpha(u) \rightarrow \beta(u^2)), \forall x(\beta(x) \rightarrow \gamma(x^3)) \Rightarrow \alpha(u\delta) \qquad (7)$$

$$\beta((u\delta)^2), \beta(x\theta) \rightarrow \gamma((x\theta)^3), \alpha(2), \forall u(\alpha(u) \rightarrow \beta(u^2)), \forall x(\beta(x) \rightarrow \gamma(x^3)) \Rightarrow \beta(x\theta) \qquad (8)$$

As before, the last sequent (8) is an axiom by our choice of (constraint upon) δ. We must continue from the sequent (7), by unifying the succedent with the head of a clause in the antecedent. The only possibility is the clause $\alpha(2)$. If $\alpha(u\delta)$ is to unify with this, we must have $u\delta = 2$. This determines $x\theta = (u\delta)^2 = 2^2$, and hence $\eta x = (x\theta)^3 = (2^2)^3$. Substituting these values for the symbols $\eta, \theta,$ and δ, we find that a **G** proof has been constructed:

Example 1.

$$\alpha(2), \forall u(\alpha(u) \rightarrow \beta(u^2)), \forall x(\beta(x) \rightarrow \gamma(x^3)) \Rightarrow \exists z\gamma(z)$$
$$\alpha(2), \forall u(\alpha(u) \rightarrow \beta(u^2)), \forall x(\beta(x) \rightarrow \gamma(x^3)) \Rightarrow \gamma((2^2)^3)$$
$$\beta(2^2) \rightarrow \gamma((2^2)^3), \alpha(2), \forall u(\alpha(u) \rightarrow \beta(u^2)), \forall x(\beta(x) \rightarrow \gamma(x^3)) \Rightarrow \gamma((2^2)^3)$$
$$\alpha(2), \forall u(\alpha(u) \rightarrow \beta(u^2)), \forall x(\beta(x) \rightarrow \gamma(x^3)) \Rightarrow \beta(2^2)$$
$$\gamma((2^2)^3), \alpha(2), \forall u(\alpha(u) \rightarrow \beta(u^2)), \forall x(\beta(x) \rightarrow \gamma(x^3)) \Rightarrow \gamma((2^2)^3)$$
$$\alpha(2) \rightarrow \beta(2^2), \beta(2^2) \rightarrow \gamma((2^2)^3), \alpha(2), \forall u(\alpha(u) \rightarrow \beta(u^2)), \forall x(\beta(x) \rightarrow \gamma(x^3)) \Rightarrow \beta(2$$
$$\beta(2^2) \rightarrow \gamma((2^2)^3), \alpha(2), \forall u(\alpha(u) \rightarrow \beta(u^2)), \forall x(\beta(x) \rightarrow \gamma(x^3)) \Rightarrow \alpha(2)$$
$$\beta(2^2), \beta(2^2) \rightarrow \gamma((2^2)^3), \alpha(2), \forall u(\alpha(u) \rightarrow \beta(u^2)), \forall x(\beta(x) \rightarrow \gamma(x^3)) \Rightarrow \beta(2^2)$$

This example shows how the Prolog deduction algorithm can be regarded as constructing (or attempting to construct) a G proof of a sequent representing the program and query. The algorithm itself can be precisely specified as a systematic attempt to proceed from the given sequent to axioms by applying the rules of inference, leaving symbols for unknown substitutions to be determined, and simultaneously building up a system of equational constraints on these symbols for substitutions. The algorithm terminates successfully if axioms are reached. When that happens, the system of equational constraints is certainly solvable, since its form is just a chain of substitutions.

We next define a more precise notation for this process. Instead of permitting symbols for substitutions in the derivation itself, we write the symbols for substitutions outside the formula on each line,

$$\Gamma \Rightarrow A \quad : \theta$$

This notation will be precisely defined. In order to explain Prolog in terms of Gentzen sequents, which is the purpose of this section, we need only the first four clauses of the following definition; the rest are needed only to generalize this explanation to our theorem-prover (GENTZEN) for the entire intuitionistic predicate calculus.

We shall need an alphabet of variables distinct from the "object variables" of our logical language. The object variables have been defined as Prolog atoms (other than true and false), i.e. they all begin with lower-case letters. By a "Prolog variable" we mean a syntactic object specified by the same syntax as Prolog usually accepts for variables, i.e. a word beginning with an upper-case letter.[12]

DEFINITION. *(Extended Formulae). These are just ordinary formulae in which Prolog variables are allowed to occur free.*

DEFINITION. *(Extended Sequents). These are expressions of the form $\Gamma \Rightarrow A \quad : \theta$, where Γ is a finite set of extended formulae, A is an extended formula, and θ is a substitution. The substitution θ must act non-trivially only on Prolog variables.*

Note that the substitutions occurring in extended sequents will in general act non-trivially on variables which do not occur in the formula part of the extended sequent. Expressions of the form $\Gamma \Rightarrow A \quad : \theta$ will always stand for extended sequents.

DEFINITION. *(Extended G Derivations). The following clauses define the notion* $\vdash \Gamma \Rightarrow A \quad : \theta$

Indentation is used for 'if' just as in specifying rules of inference. Certain premises of rules $\rightarrow \Rightarrow$, $\vee \Rightarrow$, and $\wedge \Rightarrow$ are parenthesized, with a similar meaning as in the specification of the rules of G . Namely, the premise $A \rightarrow B$ can be omitted if $A\theta \rightarrow B\theta$ is a substitution instance of the matrix of a universally quantified formula in $\Gamma\theta$.

(axiom) $\qquad\qquad\qquad B, \Gamma \Rightarrow A \quad : \theta \quad$ if $B\theta = A\theta$

---

[12] Calling them "Prolog variables" is suggestive of the implementation of derive used in this paper, where actual Prolog variables are used for "Prolog variables". However, this is not the case in some other implementations; the only point is to distinguish a kind of variable distinct from the object variables of the language.

$(\rightarrow\Rightarrow)$ $\qquad\qquad\qquad A \rightarrow B, \Gamma \Rightarrow C \quad : \theta$

$$(A \rightarrow B), \Gamma \Rightarrow A \quad : \theta$$
$$B, (A \rightarrow B), \Gamma \Rightarrow C \quad : \theta$$

$(\Rightarrow \exists)$ $\qquad\qquad \Gamma \Rightarrow \exists x A \quad : \theta$

$\qquad\qquad\qquad \Gamma \Rightarrow A[X/x] \quad : \theta$ (where X is a Prolog variable)

$(\forall \Rightarrow)$ $\qquad\qquad \forall x A, \Gamma \Rightarrow C \quad \theta$

$\qquad\qquad\qquad A[X/x], \Gamma \Rightarrow C \quad : \theta$ (where X is a Prolog variable)

$(\Rightarrow \forall)$ $\qquad\qquad\qquad \Gamma \Rightarrow \forall x A \quad : \theta$

$\qquad\qquad\qquad\qquad \Gamma \Rightarrow A \quad : \theta$ ($x\theta$ not free in $\Gamma\theta$)

$(\exists \Rightarrow)$ $\qquad\qquad\qquad \exists x A, \Gamma \Rightarrow B \quad : \theta$

$\qquad\qquad\qquad\qquad A, \Gamma \Rightarrow B \quad : \theta$ ($x\theta$ not free in $\Gamma\theta$)

The remaining clauses of the definition are exactly the same as the propositional rules of inference, but with $: \theta$ written beside each formula.

Example 2: The extended derivation corresponding to Example 1 above is as follows: (When the page is not wide enough to place the annotations on the same line as the formulae, they are placed on the next line.)

$\alpha(2), \forall u(\alpha(u) \rightarrow \beta(u^2)), \forall x(\beta(x) \rightarrow \gamma(x^3)) \Rightarrow \exists z \gamma(z) \quad : Z = (2^2)^3, X = 2^2, U = 2$

$\quad \alpha(2), \forall u(\alpha(u) \rightarrow \beta(u^2)), \forall x(\beta(x) \rightarrow \gamma(x^3)) \Rightarrow \gamma(Z) \quad : Z = (2^2)^3, X = 2^2, U = 2$

$\quad\quad \beta(X) \rightarrow \gamma(X^3), \alpha(2), \forall u(\alpha(u) \rightarrow \beta(u^2)), \forall x(\beta(x) \rightarrow \gamma(x^3)) \Rightarrow \gamma(Z)$
$\quad\quad\quad : Z = (2^2)^3, X = 2^2, U = 2$

$\quad\quad\quad \alpha(2), \forall u(\alpha(u) \rightarrow \beta(u^2)), \forall x(\beta(x) \rightarrow \gamma(x^3)) \Rightarrow \beta(X) \quad : Z = (2^2)^3, X = 2^2, U = 2$

$\quad\quad\quad \gamma(X^3), \alpha(2), \forall u(\alpha(u) \rightarrow \beta(u^2)), \forall x(\beta(x) \rightarrow \gamma(x^3)) \Rightarrow \gamma(Z)$
$\quad\quad\quad\quad : Z = (2^2)^3, X = 2^2, U = 2$

$\quad\quad\quad\quad \alpha(U) \rightarrow \beta(U^2), \beta(X) \rightarrow \gamma(X^3), \alpha(2), \forall u(\alpha(u) \rightarrow \beta(u^2)), \forall x(\beta(x) \rightarrow \gamma(x^3)) \Rightarrow \beta(X)$
$\quad\quad\quad\quad\quad : Z = (2^2)^3, X = 2^2, U = 2$

$\quad\quad\quad\quad \beta(X) \rightarrow \gamma(X^3), \alpha(2), \forall u(\alpha(u) \rightarrow \beta(u^2)), \forall x(\beta(x) \rightarrow \gamma(x^3)) \Rightarrow \alpha(U)$
$\quad\quad\quad\quad\quad : Z = (2^2)^3, X = 2^2, U = 2$

$\quad\quad\quad\quad \beta(U^2), \beta(X) \rightarrow \gamma(X^3), \alpha(2), \forall u(\alpha(u) \rightarrow \beta(u^2)), \forall x(\beta(x) \rightarrow \gamma(x^3)) \Rightarrow \beta(x)$
$\quad\quad\quad\quad\quad : Z = (2^2)^3, X = 2^2, U = 2$

Note that an extended derivation gives rise to an actual **G** derivation if we carry out the substitutions indicated on each line.

LEMMA. *If* $\vdash \Gamma \Rightarrow C \quad : \theta$, *then there is a* **G** *derivation of* $\Gamma\theta \Rightarrow C\theta$.

PROOF: Induction on the length of the extended derivation of $\Gamma \Rightarrow C \quad : \theta$. ∎

We are now in a position to explain in terms of Gentzen sequents what Prolog "really" does:

DEFINITION. *An extended derivation is called a "Prolog derivation" if it satisfies the following conditions at each application of rule* $\rightarrow\Rightarrow$, *and if* θ *cannot be replaced in the derivation by any more general substitution:*

$(\rightarrow\Rightarrow)$
$$A \rightarrow B, \Gamma \Rightarrow C \quad : \theta$$
$$A \rightarrow B, \Gamma \Rightarrow A \quad : \theta$$
$$B, A \rightarrow B, \Gamma \Rightarrow C \quad : \theta$$

Then θ *is required to unify* C *with* B. *That is, the right premise of the inference is required to be a logical axiom.*

The following "Observation" codifies the sense in which "what Prolog does is compute extended **G** derivations":

OBSERVATION 1. *A Prolog computation with program* Γ *and query* $A[X/x]$ *constructs a substitution* θ *and a Prolog* **G** *derivation of* $\Gamma \Rightarrow A[X/x] \quad : \theta$.

One who has understood the definitions and who knows Prolog will recognize the truth of this "Observation". It is difficult to "prove" it, since it depends on a precise definition of "Prolog computation". We could take the definition in Lloyd [1984] in terms of SLD resolution, in which case the Observation would be a Theorem, but we feel that extended **G** derivations are closer to what Prolog interpreters actually do than SLD resolution. We therefore omit any formal definition and corresponding proof. The reader who is not familiar with Prolog may take the "Observation" simply as an "Explanation": this is what Prolog does.

For a theorem with essentially the same content, we refer to Theorem 1 above.

In this section, we are interested only in derivations of Prolog sequents. In that case, the antecedent contains only formulas $\forall x(Hyp \rightarrow Con)$ or $\forall x(Con)$, where Con is atomic, and the succedent is always atomic or an existentially quantified atomic formula, so the above condition amounts to requiring that the goal unify with the head of a clause in the program. Thus the unification steps allowed by the above definition are just those permitted by Prolog. In other words, we have the converse of Observation 1:

OBSERVATION 2. *Any Prolog derivation of an extended Prolog sequent* $\Gamma \Rightarrow Goal \quad : \theta$ *corresponds to a (non-deterministic) Prolog computation proving* $Goal$, *with answer substitution* θ, *from the program* Γ.

Like Observation 1, this theorem could be "proved" if we accept some other concept as the definition of "Prolog computation", but we prefer to let it stand as an intuitively clear characterization of the notion, as we feel it is closer to what Prolog computation systems actually do than the notion of SLD resolution.

We summarize, somewhat less formally, the main result:

Prolog computations correspond to the construction of cut-free extended derivations from the root up, in which process, at each application of rule $\to\Rightarrow$, the right premise is already an axiom on the basis of the substitution constructed so far.

4. Completeness of Prolog

The completeness of Prolog deductions for the Horn clause fragment of logic is the fundamental result on the semantics of Prolog. See Lloyd [1981] (Chapters 1 and 2) for the standard proof, in terms of Herbrand models and resolution. Here we give an alternate proof, which is informative because it shows that the fundamental result on semantics of Prolog depends on proof-theoretical properties of Gentzen calculi.

At first, the author thought that the completeness of Prolog would boil down to just the cut-elimination theorem in the Horn-clause fragment. This was not quite the case: Prolog deductions have the important restriction that the right premise of an inference by rule $\to\Rightarrow$ must be an axiom. We must not only rely on cut-elimination, but also on the Permutation Lemma to show that proofs satisfying this restriction are complete.

The reader should now glance at the statement of the theorem near the end of this section, before continuing in logical fashion to read the lemmas leading up to it.

We begin with a lemma that shows it doesn't matter whether we use classical or intuitionistic logic in Horn clause deductions:

LEMMA. *A Prolog sequent has a proof in intuitionistic* **G1** *if and only if it has a proof in classical* **G1**.

PROOF: Suppose we have a Prolog program Γ (regarded as a set of G formulae) and suppose the sequent $\Gamma \Rightarrow \exists x A$ is provable in classical **G1**. Here A is atomic and we assume $\exists x A$ possibly abbreviates several existential quantifiers; but for notational simplicity we shall write only one.

The only propositional connectives in the sequent are $\to$, which occurs only in the antecedent and is not iterated, and $\&$, which occurs only in the left part of implications in the antecedent, and possibly in the succedent. It follows that the **G1** proof in question uses only quantifier rules, the rule $\to\Rightarrow$, and the rule $\Rightarrow\&$. None of these rules introduces two formulae on the right as we go up the tree: that is done only by the classical rule

$$\frac{\neg A, \Gamma \Rightarrow \Theta, A}{\neg A, \Gamma \Rightarrow \Theta}$$

Consequently the proof is actually in intuitionistic **G3**. (Remember the only difference between intuitionistic and classical sequent calculi is the restriction to one formula in the succedent in the intuitionistic calculi.)[13] ∎

The essence of the problem is now clear:

(1) An arbitrary **G** proof can introduce unknown substitutions at rules $\forall \Rightarrow$ and $\to \exists$. Prolog, on the other hand, admits only substitutions produced by certain specified unifications. Are these specifications general enough to produce a proof of every sequent that has some **G** proof?

---

[13] Note that Gödel's double-negation interpretation is not sufficient to establish the connection between classical and intuitionistic proofs here: it would leave double negations on the prime formulae.

(2) An arbitrary **G** proof can use both branches of applications of rule $\rightarrow\Rightarrow$, while a Prolog derivation can use only the left branch. Can the use of the right branch be avoided?

The answer to both questions is yes. To some extent they can be answered separately; we first address (2).

LEMMA. *Let* $\Gamma \Rightarrow Goal$ *be a Prolog sequent derivable in* **G**. *Then it has a* **G**-*derivation in which at every application of rule* $\rightarrow\Rightarrow$, *the right branch is an axiom.*

PROOF: First, by Gentzen's cut-elimination theorem, we may find a cut-free derivation of the given sequent. In this derivation, the existential quantifier in the succedent (if any) must be introduced after all applications of rule $\rightarrow\Rightarrow$, since no existential quantifiers occur in the antecedent. We may use the Permutation Lemma to bring applications of $\Rightarrow \exists$ to the root of the tree. Then, again by the Permutation Lemma, we may bring all applications of $\forall \Rightarrow$ towards the root of the tree until there are no applications of other rules except $\Rightarrow \exists$ below them. At some points in the derivation, as we move "up" the tree (towards the axioms), an application of $\rightarrow\Rightarrow$ may create a conjunction in the succedent. If this happens, we may assume (by the Permutation Lemma) that the conjunction is immediately broken up by (enough applications of) rule $\Rightarrow \wedge$ until the succedents are atomic.

We now give an algorithm based on the Permutation Lemma for transforming the given derivation from the form explained so far to a derivation of the desired form.

Case 1: If the last inference is by rule $\Rightarrow \exists$, $\forall \Rightarrow$, or $\Rightarrow \wedge$, just apply the algorithm to transform the derivations of the premise(s) of the last inference.

Case 2: If the last inference is an application of rule $\rightarrow\Rightarrow$, then by the form required of the input, the only rules used in the derivation are $\rightarrow\Rightarrow$ and $\Rightarrow \wedge$, and $\Rightarrow \wedge$ is used only to break up conjunctions in the premises of an application of $\rightarrow\Rightarrow$. Let the sequent derived have atomic succedent D. Trace upwards (towards the axioms), taking the right branch at all applications of $\rightarrow\Rightarrow$, so that D is always the succedent, and the rule of inference is always $\rightarrow\Rightarrow$, until we reach an axiom $D, \Delta \Rightarrow D$ at the right branch of a certain inference by $\rightarrow\Rightarrow$. Then use the Permutation Lemma (that is, the algorithm implicit in its proof) to permute that inference with all the others we have traced through to find it, until it becomes the last inference. We then have a derivation of the form

$$A \rightarrow D, \Delta \Rightarrow D$$
$$(A \rightarrow D), \Delta \Rightarrow A$$
$$D, \Delta \Rightarrow D$$

Apply the algorithm recursively to the sequent $(A \rightarrow D), \Delta \Rightarrow A$ occurring on the left branch. The resulting derivation is tacked on to the derivation fragment shown, producing the output derivation.

This defines an algorithm: but does it converge? Yes, because applications of the permutation lemma to permute two $\rightarrow\Rightarrow$ inferences do not increase the depth of the proof tree (though they may increase the total number of lines in the proof). It follows inductively that the algorithm being defined here does not increase the depth of the proof tree. Since the recursive calls are made on shorter trees, they terminate by induction hypothesis. Hence the algorithm terminates.

It still remains to prove that the transformed derivation is a Prolog derivation. We prove this by induction as follows: If the input is an axiom, so is the output. If the last inference is by $\Rightarrow \exists$, $\Rightarrow \wedge$, then the transformed derivation has the same last rule, and the subtrees are all Prolog derivations by induction hypothesis. If the last inference is by $\rightarrow\Rightarrow$, then the last inference of the output derivation is a right-branch-an-axiom application of $\rightarrow\Rightarrow$, by the above construction, and all the subtrees are Prolog derivations by induction hypothesis. ∎

MAIN LEMMA. *Let $\Gamma \Rightarrow Goal$ be a Prolog sequent derivable in* **G**. *Then there is a substitution θ and a Prolog derivation of $\Gamma \Rightarrow Goal \quad : \theta$.*

PROOF: By the preceding lemma, there is a **G** derivation of $\Gamma \Rightarrow Goal$ in which at every application of rule $\rightarrow\Rightarrow$, the right branch is an axiom. We show how to convert such a derivation into an equivalent extended derivation. We do not proceed from the axioms to the root, since we wouldn't have any idea what substitution to annotate the axioms with. Instead, we must start from the root sequent, and proceed 'up' the tree. As we do this, we shall annotate each line with a substitution. When we pass a quantifier rule $\forall \Rightarrow$ or $\Rightarrow \exists$, so that $A[t/x]$ occurs where $\exists x A$ or $\forall x A$ did one line before, we replace $A[t/x]$ by $A[X/x]$, where X is a new Prolog variable, and annotate with $\theta, X = t$, where θ is the annotation on the conclusion of this inference. At the same time we copy the equation $X = t$ to the annotation space of all nodes we have already passed along that branch from the root.[14] When we pass an inference by $\rightarrow\Rightarrow$, we simply copy the annotation θ already given to the conclusion to both premises (restricting the domain if necessary– one branch may not mention all the variables in the domain of θ, so on that branch we should not put θ but rather θ restricted to the variables occurring in that premise.) Continuing in this way, we will eventually reach the axioms. The result is an extended derivation. ∎

THEOREM 2. *(Prolog Completeness Theorem) Prolog deductions are complete for the Horn-clause fragment of (classical) predicate logic. That is, every valid Prolog sequent $\Gamma \Rightarrow Goal$ has a Prolog deduction. Still more precisely: for some substitution θ, there is a Prolog deduction of $\Gamma \Rightarrow Goal \quad : \theta$.*

PROOF: Suppose $\Gamma \Rightarrow \exists x A$ is a valid Prolog sequent. By the completeness of Gentzen's cut-free (classical) system **G1**, $\Gamma \Rightarrow \exists x A$ has a derivation in classical **G1**.[15] By the

---

[14] Thus the answer substitution returned will be defined on some Prolog variables that are not in the original query. This feature of GENTZEN generalizes Prolog; in a normal Prolog query we really use Prolog variables, not existentially bound object variables, and of course explicit $\forall$ never occurs. The mechanism we have defined in the text does not provide an explicit bookkeeping mechanism to explain the meaning of the "extra" variables on which the answer substitution is defined; you will have to examine the extended derivation produced.

[15] The completeness of **G1** can be proved directly as is done for a similar system in Schütte [1977] (p. 28), or derived from Gentzen's cut-elimination theorem, the equivalence of **G1** plus the cut-rule with Hilbert-style axiomatizations, and the completeness theorem for Hilbert-style axiomatizations. The direct proof is easy and does not involve the machinery of the cut-elimination theorem, which is really a separate matter.

Lemma, it has an intuitionistic **G1** proof. By the equivalence of **G** and **G1**, it has a **G** proof. By the Main Lemma, it has a Prolog deduction. ∎

Define $\Gamma \Rightarrow Goal \quad : \theta$ to be valid if $\Gamma\theta \Rightarrow Goal\theta$ is valid. (For this to make sense, θ must eliminate all Prolog variables.) One can strengthen the statement of the completeness theorem, as suggested to me by P. Schroeder-Heister:

THEOREM. *(Extended Completeness Theorem) Suppose* $\Gamma \Rightarrow Goal \quad : \theta$ *is valid. Then there is a substitution* ψ *agreeing with* θ *on Prolog variables occurring in* $\Gamma \Rightarrow Goal$ *and a Prolog derivation of* $\Gamma \Rightarrow Goal \quad : \psi$.

PROOF: By the previous theorem there is a Prolog derivation of $\Gamma\theta \Rightarrow Goal\theta \quad : \mu$ for some substitution μ. Taking ψ to be the composition of θ and μ, we claim that there is a Prolog derivation of $\Gamma \Rightarrow Goal \quad : \psi$. This "lifting lemma" about Prolog derivations can be proved by induction on the length of the Prolog derivation of $\Gamma\theta \Rightarrow Goal\theta$. Consider the induction step: Given a derivation with last step

$$(\rightarrow\Rightarrow) \qquad \begin{array}{ll} A\mu \rightarrow B\mu, \Gamma\mu \Rightarrow C\mu & : \theta \\ A\mu \rightarrow B\mu, \Gamma \Rightarrow A\mu & : \theta \\ B\mu, A\mu \rightarrow B\mu, \Gamma \Rightarrow C\mu & : \theta \end{array}$$

where by hypothesis $C\mu\theta = B\mu\theta$, we can transform the derivations of the hypotheses using the induction hypotheses, to obtain a derivation terminating as follows:

$$(\rightarrow\Rightarrow) \qquad \begin{array}{ll} A \rightarrow B, \Gamma \Rightarrow C & : \mu\theta \\ A \rightarrow B, \Gamma \Rightarrow A & : \mu\theta \\ B, A \rightarrow B, \Gamma \Rightarrow C & : \mu\theta \end{array}$$

This still meets the condition required to be a Prolog derivation, namely $C\mu\theta = B\mu\theta$. ∎

5. *The Program* GENTZEN

In this section we exhibit a simple version of a Prolog program we call GENTZEN for a theorem-prover for the full intuitionistic predicate calculus. Like any Prolog program, GENTZEN determines a non-deterministic algorithm, as well as a deterministic algorithm that will be executed when the program is run. The emphasis in this paper is on non-deterministic GENTZEN. Questions of efficiency and completeness of non-deterministic GENTZEN will be taken up briefly in Section 9 and continued in another paper.

This program has the following properties:

• Restricted to Prolog sequents, GENTZEN's computations coincide with Prolog's deduction algorithm.

• GENTZEN can be applied to any sequent.

- It is sound: only intuitionistically valid formulae can be derived by GENTZEN, even non-deterministically.

- It is (non-deterministically) complete for intuitionistic predicate calculus: if a sequent has a **G** proof, the (nondeterministic version of) the algorithm will find it eventually. In other words, if GENTZEN terminates with failure, the sequent has no **G** proof.

- On input $\Gamma \Rightarrow \exists x A$, if there is a term t such that $\Gamma \Rightarrow A[t/x]$ is derivable, non-deterministic GENTZEN can find one. (It can also derive such formulae in case no such term t exists.)

Deterministic GENTZEN, like Prolog, is not complete. GENTZEN is really a family of programs, some of which include more "redundancy checks" than others. The role of redundancy checks is to prevent infinite loops in the deterministic execution of GENTZEN; they are irrelevant to non-deterministic GENTZEN. In general, the more redundancy checks, the slower GENTZEN runs, though of course there are efficient and inefficient ways of implementing a given redundancy check. These issues are discussed in Section 9. The program listed here contains no redundancy checks at all (except the obvious checks for cognate sequents one immediately above the other).

GENTZEN generalizes the Prolog program given for Horn clause logic in Section 3, so the reader is invited to study that much shorter program first. Before listing the program, we provide some information about its design.

The main predicate of the program is `derive(($\Gamma \Rightarrow A$))`, which constructs a derivation of the sequent $\Gamma \Rightarrow A$. If A contains Prolog variables X, these will be instantiated to object terms t and a **G** derivation of $\Gamma \Rightarrow A[t/X]$ will be constructed. The derivation trees themselves are not visible to the user; they are constructed only internally by Prolog.[16]

The predicate `prove(A)` means to derive the sequent $\Gamma \Rightarrow A$, where the axioms Γ are specified in an input file that has been consulted (see below); or if there is no such file, then it means to derive the sequent $\Rightarrow A$ with empty antecedent.

It is now time to raise the question: in which sequent calculus does GENTZEN construct a derivation? In fact there is a version of GENTZEN based on **G3**, a version based on **G**, and a version based on **G4**. The non-deterministic versions of these all turn out to be complete. The deterministic versions all solve all the examples in this paper. The **G3** version has the simplest program (because you don't have to worrry about when to delete hypotheses); but it is the **G4** version (or the **G** version) which imitate successful Prolog computations exactly. The labels drop in the program below are used to implement the omitting of formulae in the premise of rule $\to \Rightarrow$. You should ignore them at first reading.

---

[16] Of course, if you want to see them explicitly, it is easy to add another argument to `derive`; in fact our first program did so. But you gain efficiency by leaving the proof-trees internal.

Logical Notation in Prolog

GENTZEN uses the Prolog notation (A,B) for $A \wedge B$, and (A;B) for $A \vee B$.[17] Implication is written A -> B.[18] Negation is written neg(A) to distinguish it from Prolog's negation by failure, not(A). Object variables (which can be quantified) are represented by Prolog atoms (except true and false). $\forall x A$ is written all(x,A) and $\exists x A$ is written exists(x,A). As mentioned previously, we allow a more general syntax in which one may quantify over a list of variables all at once. The notation for this is, for example, all([x,y,z],(a(x,y) -> b(z))). The list of object variables is required to be in lexicographic order, as defined by the Prolog system's primitive ordering of terms.

For reasons to be explained in the section on proofs by induction, we also allow λ-abstraction on formulas; the syntax is explained in that section, and the clauses of the program mentioning lambda and ap should be ignored for now.

Treatment of Variables

We distinguish *Prolog variables* (written as identifiers beginning with an uppercase letter) from *object variables* (treated as Prolog atoms, i.e. beginning with a lower-case letter). Prolog variables should be thought of as ranging over terms of the object language (or sometimes, over other syntactic categories such as variables or even formulae). That is, they serve as what logicians call "meta-variables".

If the formula A contains any Prolog variables in the syntactic position of a term, the program attempts to instantiate them by terms. For example, the query:

$$\text{prove((a(0) -> a(X)))}$$

will succeed and return X=0. The query

$$\text{prove((a(0) -> exists(x,a(x))))}$$

will succeed, but will return only yes. The query

$$\text{prove((exists(x,a(x)) -> exists(x,a(x))))}$$

will succeed, returning yes, but the query

$$\text{prove((exists(x,a(x)) -> a(X)))}$$

will fail, because there is no term t such that $\exists x a(x) \Rightarrow a(t)$ is provable. Thus in practice, if you want an "instantiating term" t for a sequent $\Gamma \Rightarrow \exists x A$, you must first ask with a Prolog variable for x. If there is an instantiating term t, you will get it. If you then want to know whether the sequent is derivable (without an instantiating term),

---

[17]We could have used A∨B and A ∧ B or even A & B; and we could have made the prover accept all these notations, but at a price in efficiency.

[18]Unfortunately the operator declarations are such that extra parentheses are required when formulae formed with binary operators are used as arguments: we need prove((A -> B)), not just prove(A->B).

you ask again, this time with an explicit existential quantifier and an object variable. (Of course this double query method could be automated.)

Treatment of Axioms

Most problems in automated deduction involve a given set of axioms Γ, and a desired conclusion A. We then desire a derivation of the sequent $\Gamma \Rightarrow A$. As a matter of convenience, we want to enter the axioms Γ in a text file, and type only the desired conclusion A directly to GENTZEN. This is done by means of the predicate `axiom` of two arguments. The first argument is an (optional) name of the axiom. The second argument is the axiom itself.

Axioms should be *closed* formulae, i.e. should have no free variables, either object variables or Prolog variables. If you put a Prolog variable X in an axiom $B(X)$, and ask for a proof of $B(X) \Rightarrow A$, you are in effect asking if there is a term t such that $B[t/x] \Rightarrow A$ is provable. This may or may not be the case, but it is a different question from asking if $\forall x B(x) \Rightarrow A$ is provable.

The key to Prolog's efficiency, generalized

Note particularly the crux of the algorithm in the treatment of the rules $\Rightarrow \exists$ and $\forall \Rightarrow$, where Prolog variables are introduced for the instantiating term. When the computation reaches the `axiom` rule, unification will instantiate these variables, producing the desired terms efficiently. Note also the treatment of rule $\forall \Rightarrow$, in which we check whether the right branch is an axiom, and if it is not, we select another rule to apply, rather than go 'up' the right branch further. Only if all else fails do we go up the right branch. This corresponds to Prolog's selection of a clause whose head unifies with the goal, and causes the program to exactly imitate Prolog's computation on Horn clause input. In the case of more general input, it often causes the quick and efficient selection of the correct axiom to use at the next step. As much as unification, this restriction on the search for a proof-tree is the key to Prolog's efficiency:

Don't look up the right branch of $\rightarrow \Rightarrow$ unless nothing else works.

Avoiding infinite regress

Kleene [1952], pp. 482, uses Gentzen's system **G3** to give a decision method for intuitionistic propositional calculus. The point of using **G3** (**G** would also do) instead of the system **G1** is that as we work 'upwards' in constructing a proof tree, no new copies of formulas already present are introduced by 'thinning' as in **G1**. This lets us bound the size of the (possible) proof tree. However, even in **G** it is possible that "loops" can occur in this process. For example, consider the sequent $a \rightarrow b, b \rightarrow a, a \Rightarrow a$. Prolog will loop on this example: to avoid the loop, you must write the input in a different order, for example $a, a \rightarrow b, b \rightarrow a \Rightarrow a$. GENTZEN will not loop on this particular example, as it checks for axioms before using $\rightarrow \Rightarrow$, but even this example illustrates the fact that infinite regress is possible in the process of constructing proof trees in **G**.

If one wants only 'parlor algorithms', it is easy to avoid loops by stopping whenever a 'redundancy' is created, i.e. a formula is generated that already occurs 'below' (on the same branch). However, it is difficult to check for redundancies efficiently. In the case of Prolog, it would change a linear algorithm to $O(n \log n)$ at best. So Prolog omits "loop checks"; and following this lead, we present here a version of GENTZEN with no redundancy checks. This leaves it up to the user of GENTZEN (like the user of Prolog) to avoid infinite regress by choosing a suitable ordering of the axioms before presenting them to GENTZEN.

See Section 9 for further discussion.

Can I run GENTZEN on my machine?

The program runs in Arity Prolog, version 5.0x, on the IBM AT. It is written in standard Clocksin and Mellish Prolog, except for the operators == and \==. The operator X == Y tests whether X and Y are identical terms, even if they contain free variables, without instantiating any of the free variables in those terms. The operator X \==Y is its negation. So the program should run in any Prolog supporting these operators. Perhaps one should also worry about the relative precedences of the logical operators, which may vary between implementations of Prolog for all the author knows.

We present below a version of GENTZEN based on the system G3 instead of on G. For simplicity, we present the version with absolutely no redundancy checks, and no attempt at controlling the search for a derivation except the one needed to explain Prolog. This simple version, however, is included in entirety. If you are a Prolog programmer, you can supply the utilities described in Section 3, and then run the program whose main part is listed below. You can verify for yourself that it solves the examples given in later sections. Just consult your axiom file and give the query prove(*Goal*). Anyone seriously interested in running GENTZEN should request source code for this and more complicated (but more efficient) versions of GENTZEN from the author, as the version presented here is really just a toy (albeit a working toy) whose purpose is to demonstrate the principles on which GENTZEN is based.

We list here only the main predicates **prove** and **derive**. A short description of some of the utility predicates used has been given already in Section 3. The predicate **pieces** is declaratively identical to append, but is used to break a given list into pieces (in different ways on backtracking) rather than to append two given lists.

GENTZEN Partial Program Listing

```
% direct implementation of Gentzen sequents
% without explicit proof trees */
% No redundancy checks at all, for speed and simplicity
% No control of search beyond the
% (right-branch of -> => an axiom) principle
% Author:  M. Beeson
% last edited 6.27.88
% original date of this version 5.18.88
% similar program with explicit proof-terms and equality, 9.30.87
  :- op(1160, xfx, =>).
%infix, non-associative, binds looser than ',' and ';'.
  prove(A):-
    findall(B, axiom(Name,B) ,Gamma),
    derive(( Gamma => A)).
  axiom((Gamma => A)):-             % A = false is legal
    member(X,Gamma), unify(X,A).
```

```prolog
% for finitely axiomatized theories, "member(A,Gamma)" would suffice;
% but this allows unification to select an instance of an axiom schema
derive(( Gamma => A )):- axiom((Gamma => A)).
derive(( Gamma => T=T )).
        %this accounts for Prolog's treatment of equality
derive(( Gamma =>  A->B )):-          %rule => ->
    derive(( [A|Gamma] => B )).
derive(( Gamma => (A,B) )):-          %rule  => &
    derive(( Gamma => A )),
    derive(( Gamma => B )).
derive(( Gamma => (A;B) )):-          %rule => ';'
    derive(( Gamma => A )).
derive(( Gamma => (A;B) )):-          %rule => ';'
    derive(( Gamma => B )).
derive(( Gamma => neg(A))):-          %rule => neg
    derive(( [A|Gamma] => false )).
derive(( Gamma => C )):-              %rule & =>
    pieces(First,[(A,B) | Rest],Gamma),
    append(First,[A,B|Gamma],Delta),
    derive(( Delta => C )).
derive(( Gamma => C )):-              %rule ';'=>
    pieces(First,[(A;B)|Rest], Gamma ),
    not(fmember(A,Gamma)),            %prevent cognates on left branch
    not(fmember(B,Gamma)),            %prevent cognates on right branch
    append( First, [A|Rest], LeftHyp),
    derive(( [A|Gamma] => C )),
    append( First, [B|Rest], RightHyp),
    derive(( [B|Gamma] => C )).
```

Taking the right branch first as the following clause specifies is important when using this clause to instantiate a schema as in proofs by induction. On the other hand, one of the keys to the efficiency of GENTZEN is the use of axiom in the next clause instead of derive.

```prolog
derive(( Gamma => C )):-              %rule -> =>
    memberandrest( drop(A->B), Gamma,Delta),
            %drop A->B, it came from (all =>)
    A \== C,                %prevent an obviously redundant proof
    axiom(( [B] => C )),        %[B] instead of [B|Gamma] is ok
    not(fmember(B,Gamma)),
            %prevent redundant proofs (cognates on right branch)
    derive((Delta => A).
derive(( Gamma => C )):-              %rule -> =>
    member( (A->B), Gamma),     %don't drop this occurrence of A->B
    A \== C,                %prevent an obviously redundant proof
    axiom(( [B] => C )),        %[B] instead of [B|Gamma] is ok
    not(fmember(B,Gamma)),
```

```
                    %prevent redundant proofs (cognates on right branch)
    derive((Gamma => A).
 derive(( Gamma => C )):-                        %rule  neg=>
   member(neg(A),Gamma),
   A \== C,                                      %prevent immediate redundancy
   derive((  Gamma => A )).
 derive(( Gamma => all([X|Rest],A) )):- %rule => all (list quantifier)
   gensymlist([X|Rest],x,Varlist),
           %make a list of new object variables
   list_fsubst(Varlist,X,A,AofVar),
   derive(( Gamma => AofVar )),
   not (member(Var,Varlist),fcontains([all([X|Rest],A)|Gamma],Var)).
        % restriction on variables
 derive(( Gamma => all(X,A) )):-  %rule => all (ordinary quantifier)
   gensym(x,Var),
   fsubst(Var,X,A,AofVar),
   derive((  Gamma => AofVar )),
   not fcontains([all(X,A)|Gamma],Var). % restriction on variables
 derive((  Gamma => C  )):-            %rule  exists => (list quantifier)
   member( exists([X|Rest],A), Gamma),
   gensymlist([X|Rest],x,Varlist),
           %make a list of new object variables
   list_fsubst(Varlist,X,A,AofVar),
   derive(( [AofVar|Gamma] => C )),
   not (member(Var,Varlist), fcontains([C|Gamma],Var)).
        % restriction on variables
 derive((  Gamma => C )):-      %rule  exists => (ordinary quantifier)
   member( exists(X,A), Gamma),
   gensym(x,Var),
   fsubst(Var,X,A,AofVar),
   derive(( [AofVar|Gamma] => C )),
   not fcontains([C|Gamma],Var). % restriction on variables
                   %rule => exist (list quantifier)
 derive((Gamma => exists([X|Rest],A))):-
   findall(_,member(_,[X|Rest]),NewVarList), %generate new variables
   list_fsubst(NewVarList,[X|Rest],A,NewA),
   derive(( Gamma => NewA )).
                   %rule => exists (ordinary quantifier)
 derive(( Gamma => exists(X,A) )):-
   fsubst(_,X,A,NewA),
   derive((Gamma => NewA )).
 derive((Gamma => B)) :-                %rule all => (list quantifier)
   member(all([X|Rest],A),Gamma),
   findall(_,member(_,[X|Rest]),NewVarList), %generate new variables
   list_fsubst(NewVarList,[X|Rest],A,NewA),
   not fmember2(NewA,Gamma),
```

```
    ((functor(NewA,'->',_),
          derive(( [drop(NewA)|Gamma] => B ))
       );                    %label implications with 'drop'
     derive(([NewA|Gamma] => B))
  ).
  derive((Gamma => B)) :-    %rule all => (ordinary quantifier)
     member(all(X,A),Gamma),
     fsubst(_,X,A,NewA),
     not fmember2(NewA,Gamma),
     ((functor(NewA,'->',_),
          derive(( [drop(NewA)|Gamma] => B ))
       );                    %label implications with 'drop'
     derive(([NewA|Gamma] => B))
  ).
  derive( (Gamma => ap(lambda(X,A),T) )):-
     fsubst(T,X,A,AofT),
     derive((Gamma => AofT)).
  derive((Gamma => A)):-
     pieces(Firstpart,[ap(lambda(X,A),T)|Rest], Gamma),
     fsubst(T,X,A,AofT),
     append(Firstpart,[AofT|Rest],Delta),
               %replace ap(lambda(X,A),T) by AofT
     derive(( Delta => A )).
  derive(( Gamma => C )):-   %rule -> =>, going up right branch further
     memberandrest( drop(A->B), Gamma,Delta),
     A \== C,                              %prevent immediate redundancy
     not(fmember(B,Gamma)),
        %prevent immediate redundancy on right branch
     derive(( [B|Delta] => C )), %Not just "axiom" but "derive" now
     derive((Delta => A)).
  derive(( Gamma => C )):-   %rule -> =>, going up right branch further
     member( (A->B), Gamma),
     A \== C,                              %prevent immediate redundancy
     not(fmember(B,Gamma)),
        %prevent immediate redundancy on right branch
     derive(( [B|Gamma] => C )), %Not just "axiom" but "derive" now
     derive((Gamma => A)).
```

Note: In the above program, gensym is supposed to generate new variables. If your axioms contain variables such as x17, you should run gensym enough times first to be sure that the variables it generates will indeed be new. In practice it's simpler to avoid using such variables in the axioms.

6. McCarthy's sterilization example

John McCarthy has given the following example to illustrate the shortcomings of Prolog.[19] We will show that GENTZEN works the problem nicely. In order to help the reader understand how GENTZEN works, we will trace the execution of GENTZEN on this example.

(sterile1)
$$\forall \; \texttt{container}(\; \forall \; \texttt{bug} \; (\texttt{in(bug,container)} \rightarrow \texttt{dead(bug)})$$
$$\rightarrow \texttt{sterile(container)}$$

(heat1)
$$\forall \; \texttt{bug}(\; \exists \; \texttt{container} \; (\; \texttt{heated(container)} \land \texttt{in(bug,container)})$$
$$\rightarrow \texttt{heated(bug)})$$

(heat2)
$$\forall \; \texttt{bug}(\; \texttt{heated(bug)} \rightarrow \texttt{dead(bug)})$$

(sterile2)
$$\forall \; \texttt{container} \; (\texttt{sterile(container)}$$
$$\rightarrow \forall \; \texttt{bug} \; (\texttt{in(bug,container)} \rightarrow \texttt{dead(bug)}))$$

(special)
$$\texttt{heated(dish1)}$$

McCarthy points out that Prolog cannot represent this simple logic problem, let alone solve it, as it isn't formulated in Horn clause logic.

We shall show how GENTZEN solves this problem. The initial goal given to the program is prove(sterile(dish1)). First, the rule $\forall \Rightarrow$ is used to open up sterile1, replacing the bound variable container with a Prolog variable. Then rule $\rightarrow\Rightarrow$ applies, since the goal matches the "head" of sterile1. This generates the new goal $\forall$ bug (in(bug,dish1) $\rightarrow$ dead(bug). Next GENTZEN uses $\forall \Rightarrow$ to open up the other universal axioms (and also the one which has already been used once), replacing the bound variables by Prolog variables. But none of the implications thus created can be used yet, so we reach the clause for $\Rightarrow \forall$. A new variable name x1 is generated and we get the goal to prove in(x1,dish1) $\rightarrow$ dead(x1). Then rule $\Rightarrow\rightarrow$ moves in(x1,dish1) to the antecedent, and we have to prove dead(x1). Finally the goal matches the head

[19]See McCarthy [1987] where the problem is informally stated and the unsuccessful attempt to formalize it in Prolog is discussed. The axioms given here were written down by L. T. McCarty in a talk. Similar axioms (omitting sterile2 and coalescing heat1 and heat2) are in Miller [1988], p. 65; McCarty's work and Miller's work are discussed in Section 11.

of an implication in the antecedent, namely the one obtained by opening up `heat2`. Rule $\rightarrow\Rightarrow$ generates the new goal of proving `heated(x1)`. This matches the head of the implication obtained from `heat1`, and generates the new goal of showing that `x1` is in some heated container. Now rule $\Rightarrow\exists$ comes into play, replacing `container` with a Prolog variable and setting up the goal `heated(Container)`, `in(x1,Container)`. Then $\vee\Rightarrow$ calls for proving `heated(Container)`. That goal, however, unifies with the axiom `heated(dish1)`, so `Container` is instantiated to `dish1`, leaving the goal `in(x1,dish1)` to work on. That formula, however, is in the antecedent, so the clause for `axiom` applies. GENTZEN now exits from all these recursive calls, back to the rule $\Rightarrow\forall$, where it still has to check the restriction on variables: indeed, $x1$ is not free in the antecedent at that point. That completes the proof.

It is interesting to note that the order of the axioms is important: if we put the axiom `heated(dish1)` last, then an infinite regress results. The system tries to prove `dish1` is heated by finding a container x such that `dish1` is in x and x is heated. This it will try to do by trying to find a container y such that x is in y and y is heated, and so on. This phenomenon is familiar from Prolog. In this case, it reflects a failure of the axioms to express all the information of the informal problem: we should have used a typed system with types bug and `container`, or at least unary predicates bug and *container*, and made sure that $in(x,y)$ holds only when x is a bug and y is a container. Similarly, the axioms above permit the deduction of `dead(dish1)`, which is surely not intuitive! The role of types will be discussed more in another section.

In the version of GENTZEN listed in Section 5, with no redundancy checks, it is important that the axiom "sterile2" come *after* "heat2". Otherwise GENTZEN tries to prove `dish1` is sterile by showing all bugs in it are dead, and then tries to prove that by showing it is sterile, entering a loop. One intermediate version of GENTZEN has redundancy checks only on rule $\forall\Rightarrow$. This version doesn't care where you put "sterile2", but it still must have "special" last. Its speed is intermediate between the version with no redundancy checks and full redundancy check.

7. *Completeness of Non-deterministic* GENTZEN

The program listing of GENTZEN, like any Prolog program, describes a non-deterministic algorithm, as well as a deterministic algorithm determined by the actual execution under Prolog. Just as all known metatheorems about Prolog concern the non-deterministic version, so our completeness theorem concerns non-deterministic GENTZEN. As in the case of Prolog, in the case of the actual running prover, it matters in what order you state your antecedent formulae.[20]

---

[20] The classic example is the logic program for `member`, which has two clauses:

$$\text{member(A,[A|X]).}$$

$$\text{member(A,[B|X]):- member(A,X).}$$

Putting these clauses in the other order produces infinite regress in the computations generated by the query `member(a,X)`. This is equally true whether the clauses are given to Prolog or to GENTZEN as listed in this paper.

Note: In the theorems of this section, "GENTZEN" refers to the non-deterministic algorithm defined either by the listing of `derive` in Section 5, or by the similar but simpler programs based on **G3** or even **G1**, or by any more elaborate version of the program which improves on that listing's deterministic efficiency while retaining non-deterministic equivalence.[21] The general plan in developing GENTZEN as a practical theorem prover is to make modifications for efficiency which still preserve non-deterministic equivalence to the prototype `derive` studied here.

THEOREM 3. *(Soundness and Completeness of non-deterministic GENTZEN) Let $\Gamma \Rightarrow A$ be a closed, intuitionistically valid sequent. Then GENTZEN answers the query* prove($\Gamma \Rightarrow A$) *by constructing a* **G** *derivation of the sequent.*

If the sequent is allowed to contain free variables $x = x_1, \ldots, x_n$, and if $X = X_1, \ldots, X_n$ are corresponding Prolog variables, then GENTZEN answers the query prove($\Gamma[X/x] \Rightarrow A[X/x]$) *by constructing terms t and a derivation of $\Gamma[t/x] \Rightarrow A[t/x]$, if it is possible to find such terms.*

Any answer to either of the above queries (for a sequent not containing equality) implies the construction of appropriate derivations, so GENTZEN is sound.

COROLLARY. *(Classical Completeness) Let $\Gamma \Rightarrow A$ be a closed, classically valid sequent, in which every atomic formula is doubly negated and in which $\vee$ and $\exists$ have been replaced by the classical equivalents not involving these connectives. Then GENTZEN constructs a* **G3** *derivation of $\Gamma \Rightarrow A$.*

PROOF OF COROLLARY: This follows from the theorem by Gödel's double-negation interpretation (Kleene [1952], p. 495, Theorem 60(d)). ∎

PROOF OF THEOREM: The soundness of GENTZEN is proved by a straightforward induction on the length of (non-deterministic) Prolog computations of `derive`(Γ,A). There is one induction step corresponding to each clause in the program for `derive`.

Turning to the completeness, let $\Gamma \Rightarrow A$ be an intuitionistically valid sequent. By the completeness of Gentzen's cut-free rules (which can be proved either directly or using the cut-elimination theorem), there is an irredundant derivation of $\Gamma \Rightarrow A$.[22] It thus suffices to proceed by induction on the length of irredundant derivations, showing that every sequent with an irredundant derivation is proved by (non-deterministic) GENTZEN. We shall carry out the proof for the version of GENTZEN based on **G3**; the proof for the version based on **G** is only slightly more complicated, but we have given the program listing only for the version based on **G3**. Using the notion of *extended derivation* introduced in Section 3, we prove more: if there is an irredundant extended derivation of $\Gamma \Rightarrow A \quad : \theta$, where the variables free in the extended sequent are Prolog variables, and θ is the identity on variables not contained in $\Gamma \Rightarrow A$, then there is a Prolog computation of the query `derive`($\Gamma \Rightarrow A$) such that the substitution produced

---

[21] Two versions of `derive` are non-deterministically equivalent, if they determine the same derivable formulae when the Prolog clauses are interpreted as the clauses of an inductive definition of "derivable".

[22] The notion of *redundant derivation* is defined in Kleene [1952], p. 482: it means that no two sequents on the same branch are *cognate*, i.e. have the same set of formulae in the antecedent and the same succudent. Evidently every derivation can be shortened to an irredundant derivation, since the rules of G3 are construed to treat the antecedents as sets of formulae. An irredundant extended derivation is one whose associated derivation (obtained by applying the substitution at each line) is irredundant).

by Prolog is more general than θ. This statement implies both parts of the completeness theorem.

If you seriously intend to follow the proof, you should read it with a copy of the program for GENTZEN at hand, as we will not repeat every clause when it is needed.

Basis case: $\Gamma \Rightarrow A$: θ is an axiom in case there is a member B of Γ such that $A\theta = B\theta$. In this case the predicate axiom$((\ \Gamma \Rightarrow A\ ))$ will succeed, in view of its definition, with a unifying substitution more general than θ, since Prolog finds the most general unifier.

There is one induction step for each rule of **G3**.

Rule $\Rightarrow \exists$: Suppose the last rule in the given **G3** derivation is rule $\Rightarrow \exists$. Then the last two lines of the derivation look like:

$$\Gamma \Rightarrow \exists x A \quad : \theta, x = X\theta$$
$$\Gamma \Rightarrow A[X/x] \quad : \theta$$

where we may suppose x does not occur elsewhere in the sequent, and θ does not act on x. Then by induction hypothesis, the query derive$(\Gamma \Rightarrow$ A[X/x]$)$ succeeds with substitution more general than θ. Expressed more precisely, the right-hand side of the clause of GENTZEN for this rule succeeds. (Assuming, as we shall, that fsubst meets the specification given for it in the comments of the program.) Hence, the query derive$(\Gamma \Rightarrow$ exists(x,A) succeeds with substitution more general than θ.

All the rules involving list quantifiers are handled similarly to the cases of individual quantifiers, and will not be written out explicitly.

Rule $\forall \Rightarrow$: In this case we may assume the last two lines of the given derivation are of the form

$$\forall x A, \Delta \Rightarrow B \quad : \theta, x = X\theta$$
$$A[X/x], \Delta \Rightarrow B \quad : \theta$$

where x doesn't occur elsewhere, and θ does not act on x.

The program works differently according to whether A is an implication or not; it labels implications with the prefix drop. It would be non-deterministically equivalent to the listing in Section 5 just to have two clauses, one applying to the case A is an implication, and the other the ordinary clause modelled on **G3**.[23] Since more clauses only make it easier to find proofs, we can for this proof just forget about the part of this clause involving drop. (After having checked its soundness.)

Note that since order is disregarded in the antecedent in the rules of **G**, the formula $\forall x A$ could actually be interspersed somewhere in Δ. The first line of the relevant clause of GENTZEN can choose (non-deterministically) this member of the antecedent (deterministically, it might choose a previous one!). The next line, involving fsubst, makes sure the variable is new, i.e. "x doesn't occur elsewhere". The next line rejects the derivation if the newly generated formula for the antecedent is already present; in that case the derivation would be redundant. Since we have assumed we have an

---

[23]Deterministically, that way of writing the program would give preference to cases of $\forall \Rightarrow$ in which the matrix is an implication, instead of just taking the leftmost formula $\forall x A$ in the antecedent.

irredundant derivation, this line will also succeed. By induction hypothesis, the last line succeeds with substitution more general than θ, completing this case.[24]

Rule $\Rightarrow \forall$: In this case, we may assume the last two lines of the derivation are of the form

$$\Gamma \Rightarrow \forall x A \quad : \theta$$
$$\Gamma \Rightarrow A \quad : \theta$$

where x does not occur free in Γ. Let x_{17} be the new variable produced by gensym(x,Var). Renaming the free occurrences of the variable x in the derivation 'above' the root to be x_{17}, we obtain an irredundant derivation of $\Gamma \Rightarrow A[x_{17}/x] \quad : \theta$. Hence the call to derive in this clause of GENTZEN will succeed, by induction hypothesis. The last line of the clause is not fcontains(Γ, x_{17}). Since Γ did not contain x free, it does not contain x_{17} at all. Hence this line succeeds, completing this case.

Rule $\exists \Rightarrow$: In this case, we may assume the last line of the given irredundant extended derivation is

$$\exists x A, \Delta \Rightarrow B \quad : \theta$$
$$A, \Delta \Rightarrow B \quad : \theta$$

where x does not occur free in Δ or B, and (as in the case of rule $\forall \Rightarrow$) the formula $\exists x A$ may actually be interspersed in Δ. Non-deterministically, the first line of the relevant clause of GENTZEN can choose this member of the antecedent. Let x_{27} be the variable produced by the call to gensym in the second line of this clause; as above, rename the free occurrences of x above the root by x_{27}. Then x_{27} does not occur at all in Γ or B. By induction hypothesis, the recursive call to derive in this clause succeeds, with a substitution more general than θ. The last two lines will succeed since x_{27} doesn't occur in Γ or B, completing this case.

Rule $\rightarrow \Rightarrow$: The last lines of the given derivation are

$$A \rightarrow B, \Delta \Rightarrow C \quad : \theta$$
$$(A \rightarrow B), \Delta \Rightarrow A \quad : \theta$$
$$B, (A \rightarrow B), \Delta \Rightarrow C \quad : \theta$$

Of course the formula $A \rightarrow B$ in the antecedent might be interspersed in Δ; and as indicated by parentheses, it may even not occur in the premises. There are two clauses for this rule in the listing in Section 5, the first one checking for the case in which $A \rightarrow B$ has been labelled with drop when introduced by rule $\forall \Rightarrow$. Non-deterministically, we are free to ignore that clause; the second one suffices. We are assuming we have derivations of the premises; if the premises actually omit the parenthesized $A \rightarrow B$, we can add it back to the antecedents of all formulae above this point, if necessary renaming some bound variables above this point to avoid violating the restrictions on variables. Hence

---

[24] The line involving fmember prevents certain infinite regresses in the deterministic version.

we may assume that we have derivations of the premises with $A \to B$ *not* omitted; that is, that this inference follows the pattern of **G3**.

There are two cases, according as whether the 'right' (second) premise is an axiom or not. Let us first take the case in which it is, i.e. in which $C\theta = B\theta$, or possibly θ unifies C with some member of Δ. In the latter case, we would have found a successful computation of `derive` already under the clause calling `axiom` directly, so we may assume $C\theta = B\theta$. Now consider the computation by Prolog according to the first clause of GENTZEN for rule $\to \Rightarrow$. The first line (call to `member`) we may suppose has selected $A \to B$ from Γ, leaving Δ as the set of remaining formulae in the antecedent. If $A == C$, then we have a redundant[25] proof, since the left premise would be cognate to the root. Since by hypothesis the given derivation is irredundant, the second line `A \== C` succeeds. Since we have assumed $C\theta = B\theta$, the third line succeeds. Since the given proof is irredundant, the line `not fmember(B,`Γ`)` succeeds, for if B belongs to Γ then the right premise is cognate to the root. Finally, by induction hypothesis the last line, `derive((`$\Gamma \Rightarrow A$`))`, succeeds with a substitution more general than θ, completing this case of this rule.

Now consider the second case of rule $\to \Rightarrow$, in which the right premise is not an axiom. This case corresponds to the second group of clauses of GENTZEN for this rule. (For efficiency's sake this clause is placed at the end of `derive`, but that is irrelevant to the present proof, which is about non-deterministic GENTZEN.) As above we may ignore the clause involving `drop` and assume that $A \to B$ is not omitted. The first line of this clause chooses a principal formula for the inference. The next two lines, which check for cognates on the left and right branch respectively, work as before. By induction hypothesis, the recursive call to `derive(([B|`Γ`]` $\Rightarrow C$`))` succeeds, producing a Prolog computation of `derive(([B|Gamma]` $\Rightarrow$ `C))` with a substitution θ_1 more general than θ. Using the definition of "more general", we can write $\theta = \theta_1 \delta$ for some substitution δ. Applying the substitution θ_1 to the given derivation of $\Gamma \Rightarrow A \quad : \theta$, we obtain a **G3** derivation of $\Gamma \theta_1 \Rightarrow A \quad : \delta$. Applying the induction hypothesis to this derivation, we see that the Prolog computation of `derive((`$\Gamma\theta_1 \Rightarrow A\theta_1$`))` will succeed with a substitution η more general than δ; thus $\delta = \eta\gamma$ for some substitution γ, so $\theta = \theta_1\delta = \theta_1\eta\gamma$. The substitution with which the computation of `derive((`$\Gamma \Rightarrow C$`))` has progressed so far is $\theta_1\eta$, which is thus more general than θ. This completes the argument for this rule.

The cases corresponding to the other propositional rules are comparatively simple and are left to the reader to verify by inspection. ∎

8. GENTZEN *Extends Prolog*

In this section, "GENTZEN" will be used generically to refer to versions either without redundancy checks, as in Section 5, or with redundancy checks. However, in this section we consider both deterministic and non-deterministic GENTZEN. When deterministic GENTZEN is considered, it is important that we consider a version somewhat more complicated than the listing exhibited in Section 5. That listing does not behave quite like Prolog, because it first instantiates a clause, and then retains the

---

[25]It might *become* redundant later, after a unification, even if this condition is not satisfied; but we have no way of checking for that now.

instantiated clause after it is used, which Prolog does not. To imitate Prolog, we must discard implications which result from instantiated clauses: we must actually omit the premises that **G** allows us to omit.

This version of GENTZEN is implemented by making the following changes to the listing in Section 5: (1) when rule $\forall \Rightarrow$ is used (in reverse) the new instance added to the antecedent is labelled with the functor drop. That is, the formula $\mathrm{drop}(A)$ is added to Γ rather than just A. (2) An extra clause for rules $\rightarrow \Rightarrow$ is added to the program, just before the clause in Section 5, which checks for formulae $\mathrm{drop}(A \rightarrow B)$; it then takes such a formula for the principal formula of the inference, and "drops" the formula $\mathrm{drop}(A \rightarrow B)$ from the antecedent, in accordance with the rules of **G**. (3) Similar clauses are added for rules $\wedge \Rightarrow$ and $\vee \Rightarrow$. The use of the functor drop saves repeated checking whether candidate principal formulae are substitution instances of other formulae in the antecedent. The resulting derivation will be in **G4** provided "droppable" formulae were not included among the axioms; if they were, however, some optional "drops" will be missed, and the derivation will be only in **G**.

We will prove that this version of GENTZEN imitates successful Prolog computations. This should be more or less obvious to the reader by now, although we give a proof below. The theorem, however, concerns only the *result* of the computation (that is, the answer substitution); while actually somewhat more is true: Not only does GENTZEN have the same *result* as Prolog, but the *computation process* is substantially identical. There is one difference, however: GENTZEN uses atomic clauses P first, rather than treating them as implications true $\rightarrow P$. If you want GENTZEN to *exactly* imitate Prolog, you have to write your atomic clauses as implications this way.[26] No doubt GENTZEN is slowed down slightly by the process of checking the program for atomic clauses instead of simply proceeding left-to-right.

Another point which may not be obvious is that the theorem only concerns *successful* Prolog computations. GENTZEN does not always imitate Prolog on *unsuccessful* computations: sometimes it terminates when Prolog goes into a loop. There are some invalid Prolog sequents on which Prolog does not terminate, even though they are purely propositional. For example, the sequent $a \rightarrow b, b \rightarrow a \Rightarrow a$. GENTZEN terminates and says no on such inputs. In this sense, GENTZEN *properly* extends Prolog: it improves on Prolog even in the propositional fragment. Similarly, there are *valid* Prolog sequents on which Prolog does not terminate (because the clauses are in the wrong order), such as $a \rightarrow b, b \rightarrow a, a \Rightarrow a$. GENTZEN terminates successfully on this example, so deterministic GENTZEN improves upon Prolog, even on the *valid* propositional fragment. See Section 9 for further discussion.

THEOREM 4. *(Extension of Prolog) Non-deterministic GENTZEN extends non-deterministic Prolog. More precisely: Let the Prolog sequent $\Gamma \Rightarrow A$ correspond to the query A to the logic program Γ. Suppose Prolog answers* yes *with answer substitution θ for the Prolog variables in A (if any). Then GENTZEN answers* yes *with the same answer substitution to the query* derive$(\Gamma \Rightarrow A)$.

*Moreover, deterministic GENTZEN (based on **G4** and running under Prolog) extends actual Prolog. That is, if $\Gamma \Rightarrow A$ is a Prolog sequent, and actual Prolog returns an answer substitution θ to the query A under the program Γ, then deterministic*

---

[26] Prolog actually represents them as implications true $\rightarrow P$ in just this way in its internal database.

GENTZEN *constructs an extended* **G4** *derivation of* $\Gamma \Rightarrow A$: θ. *This remains true for versions of* GENTZEN *including (various) redundancy checks.*

PROOF: First we consider non-deterministic GENTZEN. We use the tool of extended **G** derivations introduced in the proof of completeness of Prolog.

Suppose the Prolog sequent $\Gamma \Rightarrow A$ corresponds to a successful query A to the (non-deterministic) logic program Γ. Note that Γ has no Prolog variables, though A may. Then (by Observation 1) there is an extended **G** derivation of $\Gamma \Rightarrow A$: θ, where θ is the answer substitution produced by Prolog. Removing any redundancies from this derivation, we may assume we have an irredundant extended **G** derivation of $\Gamma \Rightarrow A$: θ. By the completeness of GENTZEN, the query derive($\Gamma \Rightarrow A$) succeeds, with the Prolog variables X of A instantiated by means of a substitution more δ more general than θ. By the soundness of GENTZEN, there is an extended **G** derivation of $\Gamma \Rightarrow A$: δ. Then by the completeness of Prolog, there is a Prolog computation answering the query A to program Γ by a substitution more η more general than δ, and hence more general than θ. But Prolog produces most general unifiers: hence $\eta = \theta$. Hence $\delta = \theta$ too. This completes the proof for non-deterministic GENTZEN.

Now consider the case of deterministic GENTZEN. To understand what has to be proved, consider what has been proved already in Section 4. There we considered a variant of GENTZEN obtained from the full **G4**-based GENTZEN by

(1) deleting from the program for derive all clauses except those corresponding to rules $\rightarrow \Rightarrow$, $\forall \Rightarrow$, and $\Rightarrow \exists$; and

(2) deleting the label drop from implications everywhere, i.e. in rules $\forall \Rightarrow$ where they are introduced and in rule $\rightarrow \Rightarrow$ where they are dropped.

(3) deleting the second group of clauses corresponding to rule $\rightarrow \Rightarrow$ (for going up the right branch), and retaining only the first clause of the two for going up the left branch; and

(4) in case of versions of GENTZEN with redundancy checks, deleting all redundancy checks.

We proved in Theorem 2 that this program corresponds to Prolog. Evidently in case the input is a Prolog sequent, only clauses corresponding to rules $\rightarrow \Rightarrow$, $\forall \Rightarrow$, and $\Rightarrow \exists$ can be used, so (1) is no problem.

(2) is no problem either: every implication has to have originated in a Prolog clause, and so got labelled with drop when it first appeared. Since every implication is labelled, we may as well drop the labels.

Since we only have to prove that GENTZEN succeeds when Prolog does, it does no harm whatever to add more clauses to derive at the end of the program; these can only result in GENTZEN succeeding when it otherwise would not. Hence (3) makes no difference, since the clause in question comes at the end of the program for derive.

Finally, consider (4). Adding a redundancy check can only improve GENTZEN's performance: no computations which succeeded without a redundancy check will fail when a redundancy check is included. Hence (4) makes no difference.

We have now proved that GENTZEN will succeed at least on those inputs for which the program in Section 4 succeeds; but by Theorem 2 this includes all cases in which Prolog succeeds. ∎

Remark: There are a number of more elaborate versions of GENTZEN not discussed in this paper; but they all work the same on the Prolog fragment, so the theorem applies to them all.

9. Deterministic GENTZEN as a Theorem Prover

Deterministic GENTZEN is incomplete. This section contains a preliminary discussion of the factors leading to this incompleteness, and of the tradeoff of incompleteness for efficiency. We describe an extension of GENTZEN that provides a decision method for intuitionistic propositional calculus.

We intend to show in the future by demonstration that control structures can be introduced into the framework provided by non-deterministic GENTZEN which produce a very efficient practical theorem-prover. A full discussion of these problems, let alone their solutions, is beyond the scope of this paper.

Using GENTZEN for independence proofs

GENTZEN attempts to generate a **G** derivation of the 'goal' sequent given it as input, by using the rules of **G** in reverse, proceeding 'upwards' from the goal, and relying on Prolog's unification to later determine the terms needed at rules $\Rightarrow \exists$ and $\forall \Rightarrow$. Non-deterministic GENTZEN can make "choices" about which rule to use next. Deterministic GENTZEN specifies the order of rules to be tried. However, Prolog's backtracking will eventually try all the rules, so long as GENTZEN does not go into infinite regress. More specifically, suppose we have completed a partial (extended) derivation up to a certain sequent $\Gamma \Rightarrow A$. We then choose a rule, generate its premises (possibly containing new Prolog variables), and try to complete the derivations of these premises. If we succeed, fine. If we fail, a new rule will be tried. The only danger to the completeness of deterministic GENTZEN is thus the possibility of infinite regress in the attempt to complete the derivation of one of the premises. The following theorem makes this precise:

THEOREM 5. *If deterministic GENTZEN terminates with answer no when asked to derive $\Gamma \Rightarrow A$, then $\Gamma \Rightarrow A$ is underivable in intuitionistic predicate calculus.*

PROOF: Suppose GENTZEN answers no to the query derive($\Gamma \Rightarrow A$). There are no cuts or non-logical predicates in the clauses for derive. Hence, if GENTZEN terminates with failure, every branch of the search tree has been explored, so any solution that might be found by non-deterministic GENTZEN would have been found. Hence non-deterministic GENTZEN also fails on this query. By the completeness of non-deterministic GENTZEN, $\Gamma \Rightarrow A$ is underivable in **G** . ∎

Example. GENTZEN returns no when asked to derive the sequent $\forall x(\ a \vee b(x)) \Rightarrow a \vee \forall x b(x)$. This sequent is therefore underivable. Compare Theorem 58(b), p. 487 of Kleene [1952]; GENTZEN proves this independence result and others like it automatically, by essentially the same proofs given in Kleene.

Causes of Infinite Regress

Remember that we are dealing with extended sequents, i.e. sequents that may contain Prolog variables and labeled with a substitution affecting those variables (and possibly some of the bound variables). Such a sequent $\Gamma \Rightarrow A \quad : \theta$ is called "valid" if there is a substitution δ refining θ (i.e. $\delta \geq \theta$) such that $\Gamma\delta \Rightarrow A\delta$ is valid.

There are two possible cases to distinguish: Case 1, the premise in question is not valid. Because there is no decision procedure for predicate calculus, infinite regress on at least some invalid sequents is absolutely inevitable.[27] Case 2, the premise in question is valid. Then we can distinguish three possible causes of infinite regress. First of all, a valid goal can generate an invalid subgoal, as in the case of a theorem $A \vee B$ where B is valid but A is invalid. If A causes infinite regress, then so will $A \vee$ true. Second, there can be infinite regress due to a loop: the same formula is generated again and again. This is a "redundancy" in Kleene's sense. We will discuss methods of eliminating this possibility below. The third cause is infinite regress without loops, as in the search for a proof of member(a,X) when the clauses for member are given in the "wrong" order.

Some Examples

We shall now give some examples to show that GENTZEN can go into loops and regresses in various ways, just like Prolog. Lest the reader form an ill opinion of GENTZEN at first acquaintance, we hasten to point out that this is not a bad thing: it is the price we pay for getting speedy performance most of the time, just as in Prolog. Just as Californians get used to earthquakes, Prolog programmers get used to occasional loops and regresses, and learn how to write programs that don't get out of hand. We want to use GENTZEN the same way.

Let us take Case 1 first. Is it possible to generate an invalid premise from a valid conclusion by the reverse application of one of the (extended) **G** rules? Yes, e.g. by rule $\Rightarrow \exists$ in case $\Gamma \Rightarrow \exists x A$ is provable but for all terms t, $\Gamma \Rightarrow A[t/x]$ is not. Also it is possible by a purely propositional rule: The valid sequent $\neg A \rightarrow \neg A$ can be derived from the invalid sequent $\neg A \rightarrow A$ by rule $\Rightarrow \neg$. Thus the possibility exists to improve GENTZEN by adding modules which check for invalidity, e.g. by semantic methods.[28]

Now consider Case 2. How can we save GENTZEN from infinite regress on valid formulæ? First consider some examples where (deterministic) Prolog loops: $a \rightarrow b, b \rightarrow a, a \Rightarrow b$. In the attempt to prove b, the first clause $a \rightarrow b$ leads to an attempt to prove a. The third clause (which would settle the matter) is never reached, because the second clause is used first and leads to the new goal b, which is a previous goal and so leads to a loop. We call this example *loop(2)*. Similarly, one can construct *loop(n)*. For example, *loop(3)* is $a \rightarrow b, b \rightarrow c, c \rightarrow a, a \Rightarrow b$. Note that GENTZEN will succeed on all these examples, because it tries the **axiom** rule before the rule $\rightarrow\Rightarrow$.

However, GENTZEN (as presented in Section 5) does not escape the Prolog phenomenon of loops. Something similar happens with the classical example of member, where if the definition of member is given with the two clauses in reverse order, the computation of member(a,X) will diverge, generating as first subgoal X = [_|Y], member(a,Y). GENTZEN duplicates Prolog's behavior on this example. We recommend

---

[27]In fact, it is possible to write a program which would take a theorem-proving program P as input, and produce as output a formula on which P would go into infinite regress.

[28]In the dawn of automatic theorem-proving, Gelernter used such a method for geometry: Does this premise hold in the diagram? Since that time there have been other uses of semantic methods. The use of Gentzen sequents provides a clear opportunity for integrating semantic methods into an otherwise purely syntactic prover.

that the (serious) reader hand-simulate GENTZEN on this example, to see that cognate (extended) sequents do result one immediately above the other, but that they are not seen to be cognate when first generated, only after another unification takes place later 'up' the branch. Hence GENTZEN's checks for immediate redundancies do not find these cognates, permitting the computation to diverge like Prolog.

Loops can sometimes occur that involve quantifier inferences, although above we gave an examples of propositional looping and quantifier regress. For example, if the two clauses sterile1 and sterile2 are placed at the top in McCarthy's sterilization example (Section 6), then the attempt to prove dish1 is sterile leads to an attempt to prove all bugs in it are dead, which leads to another attempt to prove it is sterile.

Moreover, such loops can occur of arbitrary length. For example, if we were to introduce another predicate clean and replace the axioms for sterile by three looping axioms saying that sterile(x) implies all bugs in x are dead, which in turn implies clean(x), which in turn implies sterile(x), McCarthy's example would fail. Similarly, we can hide loops of any given length inside universal quantifiers.

Redundancy Checks

It is easy to supply GENTZEN with a full redundancy check. All we have to do is add another parameter to derive, so that derive(Avoidlist,Sequent) constructs a G derivation of Sequent which does not contain any sequent in the input list of sequents Avoidlist. Then we define prove(Sequent):- derive(Sequent,[]) (in the case of no axioms), and modify the clauses of derive so that the current goal is added to the front of Avoidlist. This algorithm has been implemented, and of course it eliminates the examples of incompleteness given under Case 2 above.

Such a scheme will be expensive, however: it will cost $O(d)$, where d is the depth of the proof tree so far constructed, at each step. This will turn a linear algorithm into a quadratic algorithm, in case the input is restricted to Prolog sequents.

By keeping the list of formulae on the current branch in a sorted array, so access time is independent of the length, we can reduce the cost to $O(\log d)$ at each step. That will give an algorithm with speed $O(d \log d)$ on Prolog sequent input. This algorithm cannot be implemented in Clocksin-and-Mellish Prolog, which does not support arrays or constant-access-time lists in any form. A similar scheme using B-trees could be implemented in Arity Prolog, but this has not yet been done. While doing this, we may as well keep a record of goals attempted (successfully or not) so as to prevent duplication of effort.

There may well be interesting programs intermediate between GENTZEN as listed and the version with full redundancy check. One such possibility is suggested by the "tortoise and hare" technique for loop-checking in Prolog. See the discussion of van Gelder's work in Section 11.

Propositional Decision Procedure

THEOREM 6. *Deterministic GENTZEN with full redundancy check provides a decision procedure for intuitionistic propositional calculus.*

Remark: The theorem implies that we can decide if an arbitrary sequent can be proved by propositional axioms alone, even if the sequent contains function symbols and quantifiers.

PROOF: As proved in Kleene [1952], p. 485, there is a bound on the depth of any branch of a partially constructed proof tree, since the sequents on the branch are all subformulae of the root, and a propositional formula has only finitely many subformulae. Hence infinite regress is impossible, and GENTZEN must eventually (by Prolog's backtracking) examine all possible ways of constructing an irredundant proof, finally either finding one or proving by its failure after a finite time that no irredundant proof exists. ∎

Remark: With the $O(n^2)$ implementation of full redundancy check, the sterilization example in the next section runs about six times slower than with no redundancy check. But: it runs no matter how you order the axioms.

Question: Implementing a full redundancy check makes the worst-case speed of the propositional decision procedure $O(\log n2^n)$, where n is the length of the input formula. One may think the exponential makes the log hardly worth worrying about; but all the same there is a theoretical question whether it can be eliminated. Does anyone know a decision procedure for propositional intuitionistic calculus which is faster than $O(\log n2^n)$? Is the validity problem for intuitionistic propositional calculus in Co-NP?

GENTZEN as a Theorem Prover

In addition to redundancy checks, we have made other improvements to GENTZEN, which for reasons of simplicity we have not included in the listing in Section 5. The general plan in improving GENTZEN's performance is to make restrictions on the application or order of application of the (reverse) rules, in such a way that the completeness of non-deterministic GENTZEN is not affected, but the performance of deterministic GENTZEN is improved. We have had considerable success in determining the proper control structures: for example, Schubert's Steamroller[29] can be solved by essentially the most efficient sequence of deductions, except for some duplicated derivations. (This takes 85 seconds in interpreted Prolog on an IBM AT; allowing a factor of 10 for compilation and a factor of three or four for the slow hardware, this is approximately state-of-the-art.) See Section 11 for a comparison with SATCHMO. The control structures involved will be sketched below.

The essence of the difficulties in using GENTZEN as it stands in section 5 can be seen by trying it on a problem like Schubert's Steamroller, in which there is a lot of branching in the proof construction process. Since GENTZEN proceeds depth-first, when confronted with several possible ways to proceed, it chooses the first and then fights to the death to prove the theorem that way, never stopping to consider that another choice might be much easier. Others have met the same fundamental problem, and tried to solve it by limiting the resources to be expended on a given branch, for example by "iterative bounded depth-first search", etc. Our idea is instead to limit the *means* which can be applied. We define derive1 which (1) uses only the minimal-logic form of rule ¬ ⇒, (2) only the right-branch-an-axiom case of rule → ⇒, and (3) does not use rule ∨ ⇒. When faced with a choice, we use only derive1 before going on. When derive1 finally fails, we use another case of rule → ⇒: this time we require the *left* branch to be an axiom; and we also use ∨ ⇒. When these two rules can do no more, we start over with derive1, and so on. Only if all else fails do we use the full

---

[29] This is a standard "benchmark" problem for theorem provers. See Stickel [1986].

intuitionistic $\neg \Rightarrow$ or $\rightarrow \Rightarrow$. These rules almost always lead us down the garden path, except on examples concocted specifically to need them.

The Steamroller problem seems intuitively to be solved by a combination of backwards and forwards reasoning. It seems that the backwards reasoning corresponds to the right-branch-an-axiom case of $\rightarrow \Rightarrow$, and the forwards reasoning is the left-branch-an-axiom (or conjunction of axioms) case. GENTZEN (in this version) uses Prolog-style backwards reasoning till it does no more, then reasons forward to generate new facts that can be used for another round of backward reasoning, and so on.

Types in GENTZEN

We have also extended GENTZEN (in theory, but not yet in implementation) to various type theories. Analogues of the theorems proved here for first-order logic also can be proved in some of these situations; certainly they are without complication as long as the language does not include some form of λ-calculus, e.g. in a simple many-sorted predicate logic. We view the extensions to type theory as vital for a practical proof-checker or proof-finder, but a description of this work is beyond the scope of this paper. See Constable *et. al.* [1986], Feferman [1985], Huet [1987], and Martin-Löf [1984] for descriptions of the kinds of type theories to which GENTZEN can be extended, and Paulson [1986] for a type-theoretic theorem-prover based on natural deduction.

Equality in GENTZEN

As presented here, GENTZEN has no more ability to do equality reasoning than Prolog does. However, one can add clauses to derive with the head derive((Gamma => X=Y)), which embed in GENTZEN the equality reasoning mechanisms of your choice. That is, the framework of GENTZEN permits the natural integration of logical theorem-proving with, for example, rewrite rule techniques or even symbolic computation in the style of MACSYMA. These matters are also beyond the scope of this paper.

Using the Prolog Database to Store the Antecedent

One would like not to have to use an extra predicate prove to give GENTZEN a goal; one would like to type it directly to the Prolog prompt, and generally mix quantifiers and implications at will into Prolog programs. One needs the source code to Prolog to arrange that; but one may try to do it by using the Prolog database to store the antecedent formulae. Since this paper was first written, there have been several experimental versions of GENTZEN, testing different ways of storing the antecedent. In practical theorem-proving, the antecedent will be very long, including all the non-logical axioms and previously-proved theorems. The antecedent must, for efficiency, be stored in a fixed location rather than passed as a parameter to each call to the theorem-prover. Another aim of these experimental versions is to take as much advantage of the compiled inference supplied by the underlying Prolog as possible. A desideratum is that Prolog sequents ought to be derivable in GENTZEN as fast as they are when expressed directly in Prolog (at least, when GENTZEN is not using an occurs check). The program MATHPERT, designed for learning calculus, trigonometry, and algebra, incorporates one of these versions of GENTZEN to handle the logical aspects of calculus. For more information on the application of GENTZEN to calculus (but not on implementation details), see Beeson [1989].

10. Automating proofs by induction with GENTZEN

If Prolog variables are used in places where formulas belong while stating axioms, the program is not confused. In fact, it sometimes works beautifully: the unification step at rule **axiom** selects the appropriate instance of an axiom schema. Thus Prolog variables can be used not only to range over terms, but also to range over formulas. We have made use of this feature of GENTZEN to automate some proofs by induction in number theory.

The first problem is to state the axiom schemata of induction in Prolog using Prolog variables for formulae. Note that the usual method of stating the axiom of induction is not in this form, since it mentions substitution. It is for this reason that we have introduced λ-abstraction into the syntax of first-order logic (following Church and Aczel).[30] We introduce a primitive application operator **ap**, and allow $\mathbf{ap}(\lambda x. A, t)$ to be a formula whenever A is a formula and t is a term, and specify that to derive such a formula is the same as to derive $A[t/x]$, we obviously obtain a conservative extension of the usual formulation of first-order logic. This extension of notation is accepted by GENTZEN. We then can state the schema of mathematical induction as

$$\mathbf{ap}(\lambda x. A, 0) \wedge \forall x(A \to \mathbf{ap}(\lambda x. A, \mathbf{s}(x))) \to \forall x A$$

in which we can understand A as a Prolog variable. (In Prolog syntax, we write $\lambda x. A$ as $\mathtt{lambda}(x, A)$, and we write $\forall x A$ as $\mathtt{all}(x, A)$.)

We can now write down the axioms of Peano arithmetic (except the equality axioms) in a finite list, with one entry for the axiom of induction. Equality is a distraction to the point of this section, which can be made sufficiently well using only the single equality axiom $x = x$. This axiom is enough to illustrate proofs by induction. For example, in intuitionistic number theory the decidability of equality $x = y \vee \neg x = y$ has to be proved by a double induction, first proving $x = 0 \vee \neg x = 0$ by induction on x, then proceeding by induction on y. GENTZEN succeeds nicely in automatically generating the required instances of induction and finding this proof (which is rather tricky for advanced undergraduates) automatically.

To some extent, our success with induction is pure good fortune. Not every axiom schema can be treated in this way. For example of one that cannot, consider the axiom schema of the law of the excluded middle $A \vee \neg A$. You can ask GENTZEN to derive $\neg\neg a \to a$ from this axiom schema; but unfortunately it can't do it. The unification part of GENTZEN settles too soon on an instance of the schema, and never can find the right one.

11. Relations to the Literature

We have certainly not worked in a vacuum; many of the ideas in this paper are "in the air". There are a number of connections of this with the work of others. As we found out only after writing GENTZEN, Felty and Shankar have written quite similar

---

[30] Church and Aczel were following Frege, who regarded a formula $A(x)$ as a propositional function. The quantifier $\forall$ then is a functional which applies to functions. What we usually write $\forall x A$ is really $\forall(\lambda x. A)$.

programs; the main ideas of using Gentzen sequents for a theorem prover and using Prolog's unification to find the terms needed, had already been anticipated by Bowen and found by Felty and Miller; the idea of using **G3** instead of **G1** was found more of less simultaneously by Shankar (but not by Felty and Miller); so perhaps the only really new ideas in this paper are (1) the explanation of Prolog in terms of Gentzen sequents, and (2) the rule *don't go up the right branch of a left implication unless all else fails*. The former suggested the latter, which seems to be the final key, after the other ideas mentioned, to an efficient extension of logic programming to all of first-order logic. In this section, we try to trace the connections with the work of others (given in alphabetical order). Apologies in advance to those whose work we may have omitted or mis-described.

Bledsoe

Bledsoe and his associates have implemented a theorem prover based on "natural deduction"; but more precisely, I believe it is actually based on a sequent calculus, using the cut rule only for the use of lemmas. They have added a number of other techniques to the prover, notably rewrite rules, variable shielding, and inequality chaining. I do not know how the search strategy used compares with that of GENTZEN.

Bowen

K. Bowen [1980] gives an explanation of Prolog in terms of Gentzen sequents. His work, like ours, uses unification to construct the terms needed by the rules $\forall \Rightarrow$ and $\Rightarrow \exists$. This is the main point of similarity.

However, his analysis differs from ours in several essential points. First of all, he does not analyze Prolog in terms of cut-free derivations, but in terms of derivations using only the cut-rule. He considers Gentzen derivations from "sequent axioms", and instead of considering the Prolog program as the antecedent of a sequent and the query as the succudent, he considers the query as a sequent and the program as a set of sequent axioms. Prolog's computation is then mimicked by the cut rule. This analysis does not permit a useful generalization to first-order logic.

Bowen does, however, give an algorithm for generating Gentzen proofs of an input sequent. The second main point of difference between Bowen's work and GENTZEN is that his algorithm (he calls it "reverse2") proceeds to generate *all* branches of a (prospective) proof tree, upwards from the goal sequent. The essential restriction that the exploration of the right premise of rule $\rightarrow\Rightarrow$ is not made in Bowen's work. His algorithm proceeds in breadth-first fashion, developing all branches simultaneously. This prevents the construction of later ("right-hand") branches from benefitting from unifications made deep in the left-hand branch. GENTZEN, by contrast, proceeds depth-first, like Prolog.

Moreover, Bowen's algorithm seems to depend on the idea stated in his Lemma (p. 9) that the rules of Gentzen's calculus are arbitrarily permutable. As we have seen in Section 2, this is not the case. Bowen's algorithm is thus in need of a more precise definition; as it now stands it will generate false "proofs" and fail to prove many valid sequents. In particular, this algorithm has surely never been implemented and tested.

A relatively minor point is that Bowen uses **G1** instead of **G3** or a hybrid system like **G** , and thus cannot obtain a decision procedure for propositional calculus.

Boyer and Moore

Boyer and Moore's famous theorem-prover ([1979]) incorporates special heuristics for finding the right instance of mathematical induction needed to prove a given theorem. These techniques are more sophisticated than the unification-based choices made by GENTZEN. Like other "high-level" heuristics, these could be added to a GENTZEN-based theorem prover.

Feferman

Feferman [1975], [1979] (see also Beeson [1985]) has given theories which were originally presented as theories of operations and "classes", but which are in the present context more usefully thought of as type theories with variable types in which logic is not explicitly reduced to type theory. Feferman [1988] develops versions of the systems more explicitly suited to this viewpoint, and containing the polymorphic λ-calculus of Girard and Reynolds. GENTZEN can be extended to a theorem prover for this kind of system. There is one additional feature of the logic of these systems: they admit possibly undefined terms ("partial terms"). The necessary modifications to the logic are given in Beeson [1985], p. 97; it is not difficult to adapt GENTZEN to this logic.

Gabbay and Reyle

In their papers [1984] and especially [1989], Gabbay and Reyle describe a theorem-prover for intuitionistic logic which is based on a sequent calculus.

van Gelder

van Gelder [1987] has given an interesting method of "loop detection" in Prolog, known as the "tortoise and hare" technique. In our context this appears as a method for detecting certain kinds of redundant proofs in linear time, instead of time $O(d \log d)$ or $O(d^2)$ as in Section 9. The method does not detect all redundancies, and since it was developed in connection with Prolog, it is concerned only with redundancies involving the $\rightarrow \Rightarrow$ rule. Perhaps it can be generalized to a larger fragment of logic. In any case, it would be of interest to add such techniques to GENTZEN, producing fast-running versions with at least some redundancy checks.

Girard

Girard's influential book [1989] contains the explanation of Prolog in terms of the cut-rule discussed under Bowen, above.

Hällnas and Schroeder-Heister

Their technical report [1987] contains a proof-theoretical explanation of Prolog similar to Bowen's, discussed above.

Hayashi

Hayashi [1987] has built a proof-checker PX for a version of Feferman's systems, writing in LISP. The logic of PX is based on natural deduction, rather than on Gentzen systems. PX can handle the logic of partial terms discussed above. A proof-finder such as GENTZEN can be used in a proof-checker, to increase the "step-size" of the proofs that can be checked: the lines of the proof to be checked are given as successive goals to the proof-finder. It would be interesting to see if the algorithm of GENTZEN could increase the power of a proof-checker like PX; but this will in practice require re-writing a system like PX based on Gentzen sequents instead of natural deduction, and in Prolog instead of LISP.

Lifschitz

Lifschitz [1986] has given a characterization of circumscription in terms of logic programming (or, as he would put it, a characterization of logic programming in terms of circumscription). His work applied to the case when the circumscribing formula can be expressed in Horn clause logic extended to "stratified" occurrences of negation. Perhaps there is an extension of his theorem to more general cases if negation is not treated as negation-by-failure; this is a topic for further research.

Manthey and Bry

Manthey and Bry [1988] describe a theorem prover called SATCHMO. It works on the "clausal fragment": in sequent calculus terms, it works on sequents with atomic succudent, and whose antecedent formulae are either atomic, or implications whose left side is a conjunction of atomic formulae and whose right side is a disjunction of atomic formulae. Consequently quantifier rules never come into play. As discussed in Section 9, on this fragment we can implement GENTZEN to use the Prolog database to store the antecedent formulae. It then turns out that GENTZEN, with the control structure sketched in Section 9, exactly reproduces the action of SATCHMO. This is somewhat remarkable, as the creators of SATCHMO thought of SATCHMO's computations as a model-construction process; but proof theorists have long known that the proof of the completeness theorem is a process which either constructs a model or a cut-free proof, so you can view it either way. The proof-theoretic framework of GENTZEN permits a unified understanding of the two processes in SATCHMO, whose interaction was previously a bit mysterious (at least to the author). In particular, GENTZEN with the control structure described in Section 9 proves the Steamroller very rapidly, and by essentially the same process as SATCHMO.

McCarty

L. McCarty [1988] has given a semantics of Prolog in terms of partial Kripke models, and an extension of Prolog to a fragment of intuitionistic predicate calculus he calls "clausal intuitionistic logic", which generalizes Prolog by permitting negation and universally quantified implications in the "body" of a (generalized) clause. McCarty [1988a] gives a tableau proof procedure for this fragment. The procedure has a similar flavor to GENTZEN, in that there are two kinds of variables (McCarty writes $?x$ for what correspond to our Prolog variables), and bindings are determined later and propagated down. There is surely a close connection between this tableaux method and GENTZEN, but it works only for the fragment mentioned.

L. McCarty (not yet published) uses intuitionistic negation in combination with negation by failure to define a form of "default reasoning": a "default rule" is one of the form $B \wedge \text{not}(\neg A) \rightarrow A$. In words: B normally implies A, i.e. it does unless we have evidence that A is false. That is, A is true by default if the condition B holds and at present we can't refute A. Since GENTZEN provides efficient means to handle intuitionistic logic (including negation), it would be interesting to develop a default reasoning system based on GENTZEN's inference mechanisms and McCarty's ideas on default reasoning.

Miller et. al.

Miller *et. al.* [1987] define the "hereditary Harrop formulae". This fragment is essentially defined so that when analyzed as Gentzen sequents, the reverse proof process never leads to any connective other than $\forall$ or $\rightarrow$ in the antecedent. (Thus other connectives are barred from the left part of implications also in the succudent.) The language λ-prolog is a logic programming language based on the hereditary Harrop fragment of (higher-order) logic. In this language, the quantifiers are represented as a composition of functionals $\forall$ and $\exists$ with λ-abstraction, as described in Section 10 of this paper. For this restricted fragment, the proof process described on p. 64 of Miller [1988] is essentially that of GENTZEN, since the formulae and the proof process are so restricted that the process amounts to using only those cases of rule $\rightarrow\Rightarrow$ in which the right branch is an axiom. Miller says that this process is non-deterministically complete for the hereditary Harrop fragment of intuitionistic logic. This result (at least for first-order hereditary Harrop formulae) is a special case of the completeness of non-deterministic GENTZEN.[31]

Felty and Miller [1988] report on the implementation of theorem provers (for all of logic, not just the hereditary Harrop fragment) in λ-Prolog[32]

The implementation of Gentzen's calculus described in Felty and Miller [1988] is similar to the **G1** version of GENTZEN, but without the separation of the clauses for the rule $\rightarrow\Rightarrow$ into two cases, implementing the principle *don't go up the right branch of a left implication unless all else fails.* In fact, on p. 70, they admit "Another aspect of these theorem provers not yet considered is control." Then on p. 71, they mention the problem which led us to use **G3** or **G** instead of **G1**. Another minor difference is that they keep proof-terms explicit, rather than letting Prolog construct them only implicitly; this is a duplication (since Prolog constructs them internally anyway) and slows the prover down. (Of course, for proof *checking* you may need to keep the terms explicit.)

Nadathur

I have been told that Nadathur's Ph. D. thesis [1987] contains a proof of a theorem closely related to the "Main Lemma" of Section 4 of this paper. I have not yet seen the thesis.

NuPrl

---

[31] While neither is directly relevant to our work, we note that the fixed-point Kripke model semantics of Miller *et. al.* [1987] is extremely similar to McCarty [1988].

[32] They argue that ordinary Prolog is insufficient for writing theorem-provers, because of the difficulties of handling bound variables. They say that encoding formulas as first-order terms as GENTZEN does is "unnatural and spoils the elegance with logic programming offers". We disagree wholeheartedly; but we do agree that is (also) elegant to decompose quantification into a functional and λ-abstraction. Besides, from the point of view of efficiency, it is better to run a theorem prover written directly in Prolog than to run a theorem prover written in another language which itself is written in Prolog. Eliminate the middle-man. In my opinion, the main point of λ-prolog is the use of Huet's λ-calculus unification.

The rules of NuPrl (Constable *et. al.* [1986]) are best understood as an extension of Gentzen's **G1** (with cut) to a typed formalism as discussed above. The cut rule is NuPrl's *SEQUENCE* rule. In spite of a superficial similarity to natural deduction, the function type rules clearly mimic Gentzen's rules. NuPrl is designed primarily as a proof-checker, not as a proof-finder. However, the use of "tactics" permits the user to write proof-finding algorithms in the programming language ML. One such tactic, backchain_with (pp. 202-203), is billed as being similar to Prolog. However, it "first breaks down the conclusion and then tries to back through each hypothesis in turn until it succeeds". This tactic also misses the point of stopping exploration of the right premise of rule $\to \Rightarrow$. Clearly, however, a tactic could be written for NuPrl which implements the algorithm of GENTZEN.

Paulson

Paulson [1986] describes a theorem-prover *Isabelle* which is based on natural deduction, as opposed to a sequent calculus such as GENTZEN uses. He has used *Isabelle* to implement Martin-Löf's constructive type theory.

Shankar

N. Shankar at Stanford has written a theorem-prover in LISP based on Gentzen's **G3**. This work is extremely closely related to ours. His prover differs from GENTZEN in only four ways:

- It does not incorporate the key provision, "don't go up the right branch of left implication unless all else fails", from which GENTZEN derives its ability to generalize Prolog.
- It is written in LISP, not Prolog. This is inessential if one thinks of it as a theorem-prover, but it prevents adding one line (derive((Gamma => A)) :- call(A).) to convert it into a generalized logic-programming language.
- It does, however, improve upon GENTZEN by implementing an algorithm for early detection of violation of the "restriction on variables" at inferences by rules $\Rightarrow \forall$ and $\exists \Rightarrow$.

Here is a more complete explanation of the last point: Let P denote a node in the proof where a "restriction on variables" has to be met. The variable to be introduced must not occur in the terms in the rest of the formula, but those terms are still under construction and will not be settled upon until unification takes place at the axioms. GENTZEN does not check the restriction on variables until it has already constructed a candidate proof 'above' P, which will then be tested for whether it meets the restriction on variables. Shankar's prover, by contrast, labels every formula with a list of variables which must be avoided. Hence if there are several branches above P in a derivation, his prover can detect after the first branch that the restriction on variables will be violated, while GENTZEN does not detect it until later, when all recursive calls to derive have been completed and execution returns to the point P. Here is a concrete example where this happens:

$$\forall x(\mathsf{a} \vee (\mathsf{b}(x) \wedge \mathsf{c}(x))) \Rightarrow \mathsf{a} \vee \forall x(\mathsf{b}(x) \wedge \mathsf{c}(x))$$

This is an unprovable sequent, but Shankar's prover discovers that fact sooner than GENTZEN, as follows. When we attempt to prove this sequent, it soon becomes apparent that you must 'open up' the left side first. Then you drop the $\forall x$ on the left and replace x with a Prolog variable X. Then you use $\vee \Rightarrow$ and soon come to the goal

$$(b(X) \wedge c(X))) \Rightarrow \forall x (b(x) \wedge c(x))$$

Then you use $\Rightarrow \forall$ to introduce a new variable x_1 subject to the restriction that x_1 is not free in X. Then you try to verify that from the given antecedent, both $b(x_1)$ and $c(x_1)$ are provable. Shankar's prover will realize after attempting the first of these two that it is impossible to meet the restriction on variables, but GENTZEN doesn't realize it until both attempts have resulted in candidate proofs.

It is not difficult to add Shankar's idea to GENTZEN.

Stickel

Stickel [1986a, 1988] describes his "Prolog Technology Theorem Prover" (PTTP) which is "an extension of Prolog that is complete for the full first-order predicate calculus". PTTP differs from GENTZEN in that (1) it is not designed for intuitionistic logic; (2) it is not intended to provide an *explanation* of Prolog; (3) it is not based on sequent calculus. It is similar to GENTZEN in that as a practical theorem prover, it implements a Prolog-like depth-first search strategy. It incorporates two additional features which can easily be added to GENTZEN: iterative bounded depth-first search (to stop infinite regress), and unification with occurs check.

Thistlewaite, McRobbie, and Meyer

In their book [1988], they discuss the use of finite models to prune the search tree in propositional non-standard logics. The point is that if one had a fast way of detecting (some) non-theorems, one could save the effort of trying fruitlessly to construct that branch of a proof tree when a non-theorem is generated as a goal. The difficulty is that model-testing isn't fast; but these authors show that it is sometimes useful anyway.

References

Beeson, M. [1985], *Foundations of Constructive Mathematics*, Springer-Verlag, Berlin/ Heidelberg/ New York (1985).

Beeson, M. [1989], Logic and computation in MATHPERT: An expert system for learning mathematics, in: Kaltofen and Watt (eds.), *Computers and Mathematics '89*, pp. 202-214, Springer-Verlag, New York/ Heidelberg/ Berlin (1989).

Bishop, E. [1967], *Foundations of Constructive Analysis*, McGraw-Hill, New York (1967).

Bledsoe, W. W. [1984], Some automatic proofs in analysis, in: *Automated Theorem Proving: After 25 years*, ed. by W. W. Bledsoe and D. W. Loveland, A.M.S. Contemporary Mathematics series, vol. 29, Providence, R. I. (1984).

Bowen, K. [1980] Programming with Full First Order Logic (dissertation), School of Computer and Information Sciences, Syracuse University, November 1980.

Boyer, R., and Moore, J. [1979] *A Computational Logic*, Academic Press, New York (1979).

Clocksin and Mellish [ ], *Programming in Prolog*, Springer-Verlag, Berlin/ Heidelberg/ New York (1981).

Constable, R. L. [1986], *et. al.*, *Implementing Mathematics with the NuPrl Proof Development System*, Prentice-Hall, Englewood Cliffs, N. J. (1986).

Feferman, S. [1975], A language and axioms for explicit mathematics, in: *Algebra and Logic*, Lecture Notes in Mathematics **450** 87-139, Springer-Verlag, Berlin (1975).

Feferman, S. [1979], Constructive theories of functions and classes, in: Boffa, M., van Dalen, D., and McAloon, K. (eds.), *Logic Colloquium '78: Proceedings of the Logic Colloquium at Mons, 1978*, pp. 159-224, North-Holland, Amsterdam (1979).

Feferman, S. [1985] A theory of variable types, *Rev. Colombiana de Matemáticas*, XIX, 95-106.

Felty,A., and Miller, D. [1988] Specifying Theorem Provers in a Higher-Order Logic Programming Language, in: *Proceedings of the Ninth International Conference on Automated Deduction, Argonne Ill, May 1988*, pp. 61–80, Springer Lecture Notes in Computer Science **310**, Springer-Verlag, Berlin/ Heidelberg/ New York (1988).

Gabbay, D. M., and Reyle, U. [1984], N-Prolog: an extension of Prolog with hypothetical implication, Part I, *J. Logic Programming* **1** (1984) 319-355.

Gabbay, D. M., and Reyle, U. [1989], Computation with run time skolemisation (N-Prolog Part 3), to appear.

van Gelder, A. [1987], Efficient loop detection in Prolog using the tortoise-and-hare technique, *J. Logic Programming* **4** (23–32), 1987.

Girard, J. [1989] *Proofs and Types*, Cambridge University Press, New York (1989).

Hallnäs,L, and Schroeder-Heister, P., [1987] A proof-theoretic approach to logic programming, SICS R88005 Research Report ISSN 0283-3638, Swedish Institute of Computer Science, Box 1263, S-164 28 Kista, Sweden (1987).

Hayashi, S. [1988], *PX: A Computational Logic*, MIT Press, Cambridge, Mass. (1988).

Howe, D. [1988], Computational metatheory in Nuprl, in: *Proceedings of the Ninth International Conference on Automated Deduction, Argonne Ill, May 1988*, pp. 238–257, Springer Lecture Notes in Computer Science **310**, Springer-Verlag, Berlin/ Heidelberg/ New York (1988).

Huet,G. [1987] A uniform approach to type theory, INRIA Laboratory Research Report No. 795 (February 1988). An earlier version is more accessible:

Huet, G. [1986], Deduction and computation, in: *Fundamentals in Artificial Intelligence*, ed. by Bibel, W. and Jorrand, P., Lecture Notes in Computer Science **232**, Springer-Verlag, Berlin/ Heidelberg/ New York (1986).

Kleene, S. C. [1952], *Introduction to Metamathematics*, van Nostrand, Princeton, N. J. (1952).

Kleene, S. C. [1952a], Permutability of inferences in Gentzen's calculi LK and LJ, in: *Two Papers on the Predicate Calculus*, A.M.S. Memoirs **10** (1952), A. M. S., Providence, R. I.

Lifschitz, V. [1986], On the declarative semantics of logic programming with negation, in: *Proc. Workshop on Foundationsof Deductive Databases and Logic Programming*, *Washington, D.C., August, 1986*.

Lloyd, J. W. [1984], *Foundations of Logic Programming*, Springer-Verlag, Berlin/ Heidelberg/ New York (1984).

Manthey, R., and Bry, Francois [1988], SATCHMO: a theorem prover implemented in Prolog, in: *Proceedings of the Ninth International Conference on Automated Deduction, Argonne Ill, May 1988*, pp. 415–434, Springer Lecture Notes in Computer Science **310**, Springer-Verlag, Berlin/ Heidelberg/ New York (1988).

Martin-Löf, P. [1984], *Intuitionistic Type Theory*, Bibliopolis, Naples (1984).

McCarthy, J. [1987], Generality in artificial intelligence, *Communications of the ACM*, vol. **30**, no. 12, December, 1987, pp. 1029–1035.

McCarty, L. T., [1984], Programming directly in a nonmonotonic logic: extended abstract, in: *Proceedings, AAAI Nonmonotonic Reasoning Workshop*, New Paltz, N.Y, Oct 1984, pp. 325–336.

McCarty, L. T., [1988] Clausal intuitionistic logic I. Fixed-point semantics, *J. Logic Programming* **5**, 1–33 (1988).

McCarty, L. T., [1988a] Clausal intuitionistic logic II. Tableau proof procedures, *J. Logic Programming* (to appear).

Miller, D., Nadathur, G., and Scedrov, A. [1987], Hereditary Harrop Formulas and Uniform Proofs Systems, in: *Proceedings of the Symposium on Logic in Computer Science, Cornell University, June 1987*, pp. 98–105, IEEE Computer Society Press, Washington, D.C. (1987).

Miller, D., Nadathur, G., Pfenning, F., and Scedrov, A. [TA], Uniform Proofs as a Foundation for Logic Programming, to appear in *Annals of Pure and Applied Logic*, available as Report MS-CIS-89-36, Department of Computer and Information Science, University of Pennsylvania, Philadelphia, PA 19104.

Nadathur, G. [1987], *A Higher-Order Logic as the Basis for Logic Programming*, Ph. D. Thesis, University of Pennsylvania, 1987.

Paulson, L. C. [1986] Natural deduction as higher-order resolution, *J. Logic Programming* **3** 237-258.

Schütte, K. [1977], *Proof Theory*, Springer-Verlag, Berlin/Heidelberg/New York (1977).

Stickel, M. [1986] A Prolog technology theorem prover: implementation by an extended Prolog compiler, in: *Proc. 8th CADE*, Oxford, 1986, pp. 573-587, Lecture Notes in Computer Science **230**, Springer-Verlag, Berlin/ Heidelberg/ New York (1986). Longer version is to appear in *J. Automated Reasoning*.

Stickel, M. [1988] A Prolog technology theorem prover, in: *Proceedings of the Ninth International Conference on Automated Deduction, Argonne Ill, May 1988*, pp. 752–753, Springer Lecture Notes in Computer Science **310**, Springer-Verlag, Berlin/ Heidelberg/ New York (1988).

Thistlewaite, P.B., McRobbie, M.A., and Meyer, R.K., *Automated Theorem Proving in Non-Classical Logics*, Pitman, London, and Wiley, New York (1988).

A Logic Program for Transforming Sequent Proofs to Natural Deduction Proofs

Amy Felty

INRIA Sophia-Antipolis
2004, Route des Lucioles
06565 Valbonne Cedex, France

Abstract

In this paper, we show that an intuitionistic logic with second-order function quantification, called hh^2 here, can serve as a meta-language to directly and naturally specify both sequent calculi and natural deduction inference systems for first-order logic. For the intuitionistic subset of first-order logic, we present a set of hh^2 formulas which simultaneously specifies both kinds of inference systems and provides a direct and concise account of the correspondence between cut-free sequential proofs and normal natural deduction proofs. The logic of hh^2 can be implemented using such logic programming techniques as providing operational interpretations to the connectives and implementing unification on λ-terms. With respect to such an interpreter, our specification provides a description of how to convert a proof in one system to a proof in the other. The operation of converting a sequent proof to a natural deduction proof is functional in the sense that there is always one natural deduction proof corresponding to each sequent proof. Our specification, in fact, provides a direct implementation of the transformation in this direction.

1 Introduction

Intuitionistic logic with quantification at all function types has been proposed as a meta-language for the direct and natural specification of a wide range of logics [5, 12]. As illustrated by these papers, the second-order subset of this logic, called hh^2 here, is all that is required to suitably specify both sequent calculi and natural deduction for first-order logic. From these specifications, it is possible to obtain a description of goal-directed theorem proving and proof checking for these inference systems by providing simple operational interpretations for the connectives of hh^2.

The correspondence between cut-free sequential proofs and normal natural deduction proofs for first-order intuitionistic logic has been formalized in [16, 13]. (There, the formal relation between cut-elimination and proof normalization is also explored in detail.) In this paper, we show that it is possible to merge an hh^2 specification of a sequent system for first-order intuitionistic logic with one for natural deduction, resulting in a specification which demonstrates the correspondence between these two systems in a concise and natural manner. The operational interpretations of the connectives of hh^2 provide descriptions for simultaneous proof construction and proof checking in these two inference systems, as well as a description of how to convert a proof in one system to a proof in the other.

The transformation from sequent proofs to natural deduction proofs is "functional" since the relation between sequent proofs and natural deduction proofs is many to one, *i.e.*, there will always be exactly one normal natural deduction proof corresponding to each cut-free sequent proof. Our specification in fact provides a direct implementation of the transformation in this direction with respect to a deterministic logic programming interpreter which implements hh^2. Our specification cannot, however, serve directly as a program for the transformation in the other direction. More control information must be added in order to obtain a program that can transform a natural deduction proof to one of the possibly many sequent proofs to which it is related.

The logic of hh^2 is a sublanguage of *higher-order hereditary Harrop formulas* which serve as the foundation of the logic programming language λProlog [11]. In particular, it is the sublanguage with function quantification restricted to second-order and with no predicate quantification. Thus, an implementation of λProlog includes an interpreter for hh^2. The transformation from sequent proofs to natural deduction proofs has in fact been implemented and tested in λProlog.

In Sect. 2 we present the meta-logic hh^2 and an interpreter for it. In Sect. 3 we discuss the specification of a sequent system for first-order intuitionistic logic using this meta-logic. In Sect. 4 we will see that there are many options in specifying natural deduction. We first present a direct specification of the inference rules and then discuss alternatives, leading to a specification in which only normal proofs can be constructed and which can be merged directly with the sequent specification. Then, in Sect. 5 we demonstrate how these two specifications can be merged, and finally, in Sect. 6 we conclude.

2 The Meta-Logic and Language

The logic of hh^2 extends positive Horn clauses in essentially two ways. First, it replaces first-order terms with the more expressive simply-typed λ-terms. Second, it permits richer logical expressions in both goals and the bodies of program clauses. In particular, implication and second-order universal quantification over functions are permitted.

The types and terms of this language are essentially those of the simple theory of types [1]. We assume a fixed set of *primitive types*, which includes at least the symbol o, the type for propositions. *Function types* are constructed using the binary infix symbol $\rightarrow$; if τ and σ are types, then so is $\tau \rightarrow \sigma$. The type constructor $\rightarrow$ associates to the right. The *order* of a primitive type is 0 while the order of a function type $\tau_1 \rightarrow \cdots \rightarrow \tau_n \rightarrow \tau_0$ where τ_0 is primitive is one greater than the maximum order of $\tau_1, \ldots, \tau_n$.

For each type τ, we assume that there are denumerably many constants and variables of that type. A *signature* is a finite set of constants, such that for each constant c, the type of c has the form $\tau_1 \rightarrow \cdots \rightarrow \tau_n \rightarrow \tau_0$ where $n \geq 0$, τ_0 is primitive, and $\tau_1, \ldots, \tau_n$ do not contain o. If τ_0 is o, then c is a *predicate constant*. In this paper, the types of constants in signatures will always be of order 2 or less.

Simply typed λ-terms are built in the usual way using constants, variables, applications, and abstractions. Equality between λ-terms is taken to mean $\beta\eta$-convertible. We shall assume that the reader is familiar with the usual notions and properties of substitution and α, β, and η conversion for the simply typed λ-calculus. See [7] for a fuller discussion of these basic properties.

The logical connectives are defined by introducing suitable constants as in [1]. The constants $\wedge$ (conjunction) and $\supset$ (implication) are both of type $o \rightarrow o \rightarrow o$, and $\forall_\tau$ (universal quantification) is of type $(\tau \rightarrow o) \rightarrow o$, for all types τ not containing o. The expression $\forall_\tau (\lambda z\ t)$ is written simply as $\forall_\tau z\ t$. An *atomic formula* is of the form $(p t_1 \ldots t_n)$, where $n \geq 0$, p is a predicate constant of the type $\tau_1 \rightarrow \cdots \rightarrow \tau_n \rightarrow o$, and $t_1, \ldots, t_n$ are terms of the types $\tau_1, \ldots, \tau_n$, respectively. We write A to denote a syntactic variable for atomic formulas. We define two classes of *non-atomic formulas* called *goal formulas* and *definite clauses*. Let G be a syntactic variable for goal formulas and let D be a syntactic variable for definite clauses. These two classes are defined by the following mutual recursion.

$$G := A \mid G_1 \wedge G_2 \mid D \supset G \mid \forall_\tau x\ G$$
$$D := A \mid G \supset A \mid \forall_\tau x\ D$$

Here τ is a type of order 0 or 1 not containing o. We say that a formula has order n if in each of its subformulas of the form $\forall_\tau z\ t$, type τ has order strictly less than n. Thus all goal formulas and definite clauses are second-order. A *logic program* or just simply a *program* is a finite set, generally written as $\mathcal{P}$, of closed definite clauses. In definite clauses of the form $\forall_{\tau_1} x_1 \ldots \forall_{\tau_n} x_n\ (G_1 \wedge \cdots \wedge G_n \supset A)$, we call A the *head* and $G_1 \wedge \cdots \wedge G_n$ the *body*. The subformulas $G_1, \ldots, G_n$ are also called *subgoals*.

Based on properties shown for the full logic of higher-order hereditary Harrop formulas in [9], a sound and complete (with respect to intuitionistic logic) *non-deterministic* search procedure can be described using the following four search primitives.

AND: $G_1 \wedge G_2$ is provable from $\mathcal{P}$ if and only if both G_1 and G_2 are provable from $\mathcal{P}$.

GENERIC: $\forall_\tau x G$ is provable from $\mathcal{P}$ if and only if $[c/x]G$ is provable from $\mathcal{P}$ for some new constant c of type τ not in $\mathcal{P}$ or G.

AUGMENT: $D \supset G$ is provable from $\mathcal{P}$ if and only if G is provable from $\mathcal{P} \cup \{D\}$.

BACKCHAIN: The atomic formula A is provable from $\mathcal{P}$ if and only if there is either (1) a universal instance of a definite clause in $\mathcal{P}$ that is $\beta\eta$-convertible to A, or (2) a universal instance of the form $G \supset A$ such that G is provable from $\mathcal{P}$.

In order to implement a *deterministic* interpreter, it is necessary to make choices left unspecified in the high-level description above. We will make choices as in the λProlog language, many of which are similar to those made in Prolog. For example, logic variables are employed in the BACKCHAIN operation to create universal instances of definite clauses. As a result, second-order unification is necessary since logic variables for functions (with types of order one) can occur inside λ-terms. Also the equality of terms is not a simple syntactic check but a more complex check of $\beta\eta$-conversion. Second-order unification is not in general decidable. In λProlog, full higher-order unification is required and this issue is addressed by implementing a depth-first version of the unification search procedure described in [8]. (See [10, 9].) In this paper, the second-order unification problems that result from programs we present are all rather simple: it is easy to see, for example, that all such problems are decidable.

In the AUGMENT search operation, clauses get added to the program dynamically. Note that as a result, clauses may in fact contain logic variables. The GENERIC operation must be implemented so that the new constant c introduced for x, must not appear in the terms eventually instantiated for logic variables free in the goal or in the program when c is introduced.

Finally, we assume conjuncts are attempted in the order they are presented, and definite clauses are backchained over in the order they are listed in $\mathcal{P}$ using a depth-first search paradigm to handle failures.

In presenting example hh^2 formulas in this paper, we will adopt the syntax of the eLP [3] implementation of λProlog. Fortunately, very little of this syntax is needed here. In particular, a signature member, say f of type $a \rightarrow b \rightarrow c$, is represented as simply the line:

```
type   f        a -> b -> c.
```

Tokens with initial capital letters will denote either bound or free variables. All other tokens will denote constants. λ-abstraction is written using backslash \ as an infix operator. Universal quantification is written using the constant pi in conjunction with a λ-abstraction, *e.g.*, pi X\ represents universal quantification over variable X. We omit type subscripts for this quantifier. They can always be inferred from context. The symbols , and => represent $\wedge$ and $\supset$, respectively. The symbol :- denotes the converse of => and is used to write the top-level implication in definite clauses. We omit universal quantifiers at the top level in definite clauses, and assume implicit quantification over all free variables.

Consider a set of primitive types that includes the types a and a_l. Here, a_l is meant to represent the type for lists of elements of type a. Consider a signature which includes the following declarations:

```
type   nil_a    a_l.
type   ::_a      a -> a_l -> a_l.
type   memb_a   a -> a_l -> o.
```

where nil_a represents the empty list of elements of type a, ::_a is the cons operator for a-lists, and memb_a is a predicate which takes as arguments an element and a list of elements of type a. We will write ::_a using infix notation. The following hh^2 definite clauses axiomatize the membership relation for type a.

```
memb X (X ::_a L).
memb X (Y ::_a L) :- memb X L.
```

With respect to the deterministic interpreter described above, these formulas implement the standard program testing list membership as often written in Prolog. In this case, the program is restricted to lists of type a. In the programs in this paper, we will make use of such a membership predicate at two primitive types. We will omit type subscripts from the constants nil, ::, and memb since it will be clear from context which of the two is meant. In λProlog, these constants can be treated in a polymorphic fashion similar to their treatment in ML.

3 Specifying Sequent Calculi

Since we will be specifying first-order logic within the logic of hh^2, to avoid confusion we will refer to first-order logic as the *object-logic* to distinguish it from hh^2, the *meta-logic*. To represent first-order logic in hh^2, we introduce two primitive types: form for object-level formulas and tm for first-order terms. The new type form serves to distinguish formulas of the object-logic from formulas of the meta-logic (which have type o). Given these new primitive types, we introduce the following constants for the object-level connectives.

```
type    and      form -> form -> form.
type    or       form -> form -> form.
type    imp      form -> form -> form.
type    neg      form -> form.
type    forall   (tm -> form) -> form.
type    exists   (tm -> form) -> form.
type    false    form.
```

The constant and, for example, takes two formulas as arguments and constructs their conjunction. For readability, we write and, or, and imp using infix notation. By declaring forall and exists to take functional arguments, we have defined object-level binding of variables by quantifiers in terms of lambda abstraction, the meta-level binding operator, as is done in [1]. Thus, bound variables of the object-language are identified with bound variables of type tm at the meta-level. Meta-constants representing object-level constants, function symbols, propositions, and predicates can also be introduced and given appropriate types. For example, a constant p of type tm -> form represents an object-level unary predicate. Using these definitions, the first-order formula $\forall x \exists y (px \supset py)$, for instance, is represented by the λ-term below where X and Y are meta-variables of type tm.

```
(forall X\ (exists Y\ ((p X) imp (p Y))))
```

Figure 1 contains a complete set of inference rules for a sequent calculus for first-order intuitionistic logic. This inference system, which we call L_I, is a variant of the L system in [2]. In this system a sequent is written $\Gamma \longrightarrow A$ where Γ is a *set* of formulas, and A is a formula. Γ is called the *antecedent* of the sequent and A the *succedent*. Following convention, we write A, Γ to denote

$$\frac{\Gamma \longrightarrow A \qquad \Gamma \longrightarrow B}{\Gamma \longrightarrow A \wedge B} \wedge\text{-R} \qquad\qquad \frac{A, B, \Gamma \longrightarrow C}{A \wedge B, \Gamma \longrightarrow C} \wedge\text{-L}$$

$$\frac{\Gamma \longrightarrow A}{\Gamma \longrightarrow A \vee B} \vee\text{-R} \quad \frac{\Gamma \longrightarrow B}{\Gamma \longrightarrow A \vee B} \vee\text{-R} \qquad \frac{A, \Gamma \longrightarrow C \qquad B, \Gamma \longrightarrow C}{A \vee B, \Gamma \longrightarrow C} \vee\text{-L}$$

$$\frac{A, \Gamma \longrightarrow B}{\Gamma \longrightarrow A \supset B} \supset\text{-R} \qquad\qquad \frac{\Gamma \longrightarrow A \qquad B, \Gamma \longrightarrow C}{A \supset B, \Gamma \longrightarrow C} \supset\text{-L}$$

$$\frac{A, \Gamma \longrightarrow \perp}{\Gamma \longrightarrow \neg A} \neg\text{-R} \qquad\qquad \frac{\Gamma \longrightarrow A}{\neg A, \Gamma \longrightarrow \perp} \neg\text{-L}$$

$$\frac{\Gamma \longrightarrow [y/x]A}{\Gamma \longrightarrow \forall x A} \forall\text{-R} \qquad\qquad \frac{[t/x]A, \Gamma \longrightarrow C}{\forall x A, \Gamma \longrightarrow C} \forall\text{-L}$$

$$\frac{\Gamma \longrightarrow [t/x]A}{\Gamma \longrightarrow \exists x A} \exists\text{-R} \qquad\qquad \frac{[y/x]A, \Gamma \longrightarrow C}{\exists x A, \Gamma \longrightarrow C} \exists\text{-L}$$

$$\frac{\Gamma \longrightarrow \perp}{\Gamma \longrightarrow A} \perp\text{-R} \qquad\qquad \frac{\Gamma \longrightarrow A \qquad A, \Gamma \longrightarrow C}{\Gamma \longrightarrow C} \text{cut}$$

The $\forall$-R and $\exists$-L rules have the proviso that the variable y cannot appear free in the lower sequent.

Fig. 1. The L_I sequent calculus for first-order intuitionistic logic

the set $\Gamma \cup \{A\}$. An *initial* sequent has the form $\Gamma \longrightarrow A$ where $A \in \Gamma$. The L_I inference system differs from the sequent system originally given in [6] in that we consider sets instead of sequences of formulas as antecedents and allow a more general form of initial sequent. As a result, in our formulation there is no need for explicit structural rules in the antecedent. The $\perp$-R rule is as in the specification of sequent systems in [15], and corresponds to the usual rule for thinning on the right.

To represent sets of formulas in antecedents, we will use lists of elements of type form where the order and number of copies of each element is not significant. Thus we introduce the primitive type form_l. In addition, we introduce the primitive type seq for sequents and add the signature item --> of type form_l -> form -> seq. We will write --> as an infix operator whose antecedent is a list of formulas and succedent is a single formula.

Finally, we introduce the primitive type lprf for the type of sequent proofs. The basic relation between a sequent and its proofs will be represented as a binary predicate at the meta-level by the infix constant >- of type lprf -> seq -> o. Each inference rule of the sequent calculus will be expressed as a simple declarative fact about this relation. Operationally, with respect to the interpreter described in the previous section, >- can be viewed as the theorem proving predicate.

For illustration purposes, we present the specification of a small subset of the inference rules of L_I. The others can be specified similarly. In specifying these rules, there are often many choices in choosing a representation of sequent proofs. In this presentation, we simply choose one. For a more thorough discussion of the issues involved in specifying inference rules and proofs for this inference system and others in hh^2, see [5, 4].

First, consider the ∧-R inference rule in Fig. 1 which introduces a conjunction on the right side of the sequent. This rule has a natural rendering as the following definite clause.

```
(and_r Q1 Q2) >- (Gamma --> (A and B)) :- Q1 >- (Gamma --> A),
                                            Q2 >- (Gamma --> B).
```

This formula may be read as: if Q1 is a proof of (Gamma --> A) and Q2 is a proof of (Gamma --> B), then (and_r Q1 Q2) is a proof of (Gamma --> (A and B)). The constant and_r is a "proof constructor" which takes two proofs as arguments (the premises of the ∧-R rule) and builds a new proof (its conclusion). Its type is lprf -> lprf -> lprf.

The following clause specifies the ⊃-L rule and illustrates that introductions of logical constants into the antecedent of a sequent can be achieved similarly.

```
(imp_l (A imp B) Q1 Q2) >- (Gamma --> C) :- memb (A imp B) Gamma,
                                             Q1 >- (Gamma --> A),
                                             Q2 >- ((B::Gamma) --> C).
```

The main difference here is that the antecedent is a list instead of a single formula. We use the memb predicate (on type form) defined in Sect. 2 to choose an implication (A imp B) from the list Gamma. Note that the proof term in the head of the clause contains a record of the particular implication from Gamma to which the rule is applied.

We now consider the quantifier introduction rules. The declarative reading of the ∃-R inference rule is captured by the following definite clause.

```
(exists_r T Q) >- (Gamma --> (exists A)) :- Q >- (Gamma --> (A T)).
```

The existential formula of the conclusion of this rule is written (exists A) where the variable A has functional type tm -> form. Thus A is an abstraction over first-order terms and (A T) represents the formula that is obtained by substituting T for the bound variable in A. Declaratively, this clause reads: for first-order term T, if Q is a proof of (Gamma --> (A T)), then (exists_r T Q) is a proof of (Gamma --> (exists A)). Note that the proof term contains a record of the substitution term T. Operationally, the existential instance (A T) is obtained via the interpreter's operation of β-reduction. Thus β-conversion at the meta-level is used to specify substitution at the object-level.

Next, we consider the ∀-R rule, which has the additional proviso that y is not free in Γ or $\forall x A$. This proviso is handled by using a universal quantifier at the meta-level as in the following definite clause.

```
(forall_r Q) >- (Gamma  > (forall A)) :-
      pi Y\ ((Q Y) >- (Gamma --> (A Y))).
```

As in the previous clause, A has functional type. In this case, so does Q; it has type tm -> lprf, and thus the type of the constant forall_r is (tm -> lprf) -> lprf. Declaratively, this clause reads: if we have a function Q that maps arbitrary terms Y to proofs (Q Y) of the sequent (Gamma --> (A Y)), then (forall_r Q) is a proof of (Gamma --> (forall A)). Operationally, the GENERIC search operation is used to insert a new constant of type tm into the sequent. Since that constant will not be permitted to appear in Gamma or A the proviso will be satisfied.

As a final example, consider the cut rule which has the straightforward specification as the following formula.

```
(cut A Q1 Q2) >- (Gamma --> C) :- Q1 >- (Gamma --> A),
                                   Q2 >- ((A::Gamma) --> C).
```

A complete set of hh^2 formulas specifying the rules of L_I serves as a specification of a theorem prover for this inference system. To prove sequent (Gamma --> A), we start with a goal of the form (Q >- (Gamma --> A)) where Q is a logic variable to be filled in with a term representing a proof of (Gamma --> A). Note, though, that there may be multiple definite clauses that can be used in backchaining to prove a particular sequent, or a single clause that can be used repeatedly. For example, if there is an implication in Gamma, it will always be possible to backchain on the clause specifying the ⊃-L rule. Thus, this set of formulas cannot serve as an implementation with respect to a depth-first interpreter that backchains over definite clauses in a particular order. (See [5] for more on implementing theorem provers and controlling search in this setting.) On the other hand, when Q is a closed term in the original goal, this program behaves as a proof checker and is complete even with respect to the deterministic interpreter. The top-level constant of a proof term completely determines the unique definite clause to be used in backchaining at each step.

By Gentzen's cut-elimination result [6], L_I without the cut rule is a complete set of rules for first-order intuitionistic logic. Thus, by simply eliminating the formula for the cut rule, we obtain a set of hh^2 formulas which serves as a specification for both building and proof checking cut-free proofs.

4 Specifying Natural Deduction

Figure 2 presents the inference rules for natural deduction in intuitionistic logic as presented in [15], called N_I here. The premise of an elimination rule (E-rule) containing the connective for which the rule is named is called the *major premise*, and other premises are *minor premises*. The *discharge* of assumptions is indicated by parentheses. For example, in the ⊃-I rule, (A) indicates that occurrences of A at the leaves are discharged by the application of this rule. A formula occurrence B in a tree is said to *depend* on an assumption A if A occurs as a leaf and is not discharged by a rule application above B. A tree with root B constructed using these inference rules is a *deduction* of B from the set of formulas Γ if all assumptions on which B depends occur in Γ. Such a tree is a *proof* of B if Γ is empty.

$$\frac{A \qquad B}{A \wedge B} \wedge\text{-I} \qquad\qquad \frac{A \wedge B}{A} \wedge\text{-E} \qquad\qquad \frac{A \wedge B}{B} \wedge\text{-E}$$

$$\frac{A}{A \vee B} \vee\text{-I} \qquad \frac{B}{A \vee B} \vee\text{-I} \qquad \frac{A \vee B \quad \overset{(A)}{C} \quad \overset{(B)}{C}}{C} \vee\text{-E}$$

$$\frac{\overset{(A)}{\underset{B}{\vphantom{x}}}}{A \supset B} \supset\text{-I} \qquad\qquad \frac{A \qquad A \supset B}{B} \supset\text{-E}$$

$$\frac{\overset{(A)}{\underset{\bot}{\vphantom{x}}}}{\neg A} \neg\text{-I} \qquad\qquad \frac{A \qquad \neg A}{\bot} \neg\text{-E}$$

$$\frac{[y/x]A}{\forall x A} \forall\text{-I} \qquad\qquad \frac{\forall x A}{[t/x]A} \forall\text{-E}$$

$$\frac{[t/x]A}{\exists x A} \exists\text{-I} \qquad\qquad \frac{\exists x A \quad \overset{([y/x]A)}{B}}{B} \exists\text{-E}$$

$$\frac{\bot}{A} \bot_I$$

The ∀-I rule has the proviso that the variable y cannot appear free in $\forall x A$, or in any assumption on which $[y/x]A$ depends.

The ∃-E rule has the proviso that the variable y cannot appear free in $\exists x A$, in B, or in any assumption on which the upper occurrence of B depends.

Fig. 2. The N_I natural deduction inference system for first-order intuitionistic logic

The inference rules of natural deduction can be specified directly in the same manner as those for the L_I sequent system, where the conclusion of the rule corresponds to the head of the clause and the premises to the subgoals. In the next subsection, we discuss this specification. The corresponding notion to cut-free proofs in L_I is *normal* proofs [15] in N_I. To specify N_I so that only normal proofs are built is more complicated than simply adding or removing clauses, which was all that was required to eliminate the use of cut in sequent proofs. Here, it is a matter of specifying the rules in a different manner. In subsection 4.2, we present such a specification. In subsection 4.3, we discuss alternative ways to specify some of the inference rules retaining the property that only normal proofs are built. The alternatives we present are in fact those needed to be able to merge the N_I specification with the cut-free L_I specification. Finally, in subsection 4.4, we present an alternative way of handling assumptions so that assumptions in N_I correspond to antecedents of sequents in L_I. The result is a specification that can be merged directly with the one for L_I discussed in the previous section.

4.1 A Direct Specification

To represent natural deduction proofs, we introduce the new primitive type nprf. Here, the basic proof relation is between proofs and formulas (instead of sequents). We introduce the infix predicate # of type nprf -> form -> o for this relation. In the previous section, we adopted the convention of using variable names Q, Q1, Q2, etc., to represent sequent proofs. We use P, P1, P2, etc., here for natural deduction proofs. Several of the introduction rules (I-rules) for this system resemble rules that apply to succedents in the sequential system just considered. The ∧-I, ∃-I, and ∀-I rules correspond to examples given in the previous section and can be specified similarly as follows.

```
(and_i P1 P2) # (A and B) :- P1 # A, P2 # B.
(exists_i T P) # (exists A) :- P # (A T).
(forall_i P) # (forall A) :- pi Y\ ((P Y) # (A Y)).
```

Note that universal quantification is used to handle the proviso on the ∀-I rule in the same way that it is used for the ∀-R sequent rule.

In natural deduction, unlike sequential systems, we have the additional task of specifying the operation of discharging assumptions. Consider the implication introduction rule in Fig. 2. This rule can very naturally be specified as the definite clause below.

```
(imp_i P) # (A imp B) :- pi W\ ((W # A) => ((P W) # B)).
```

This clause represents the fact that if P is a "proof function" which maps an arbitrary proof W of formula A, to a proof (P W) of formula B, then (imp_i P) is a proof of (A imp B). Here, the proof of an implication is represented by a function from proofs to proofs. The constant imp_i has the type (nprf -> nprf) -> nprf. Notice that while sequential proofs only contain abstractions of type tm, natural deduction proofs may contain abstractions of both types tm and nprf.

Operationally, when backchaining on this clause, the GENERIC operation is used to choose a new object, say c, to replace W and play the role of a proof of the formula A. The AUGMENT goal is then used to add the assumption (c # A) to the current set of program clauses. This clause is then available to use in the search for a proof of B, i.e., in solving the goal ((P c) # B). The proof of B may contain instances of the proof of A (the constant c). The function P is the abstraction over this constant.

The elimination rules and ⊥-I can be specified similarly to the introduction rules. For example the following formulas specify the ∧-E and ∃-E rules.

```
(and_e1 B P) # A :- P # (A and B).
(and_e2 A P) # B :- P # (A and B).
(exists_e A P1 P2) # B :- P1 # (exists A),
   pi Y\ (pi W\ ((W # (A Y)) => ((P2 Y W) # B))).
```

The ∃-E rule contains both a proviso handled by a universal quantifier at the meta-level, and the discharge of an assumption, again handled by meta-level universal quantification and implication. Here, P2 is an abstraction over both the first-order term Y and the proof term W. Note that the proof terms in the heads of these clauses contain more than just the subproofs of the premises as arguments. For example, the missing conjunct in the conclusion of the ∧-E rules is included in the proof terms for these rules.

As for L_I, the set of hh^2 formulas resulting from the direct specification of the rules of N_I serves both as a specification of a theorem prover and as an implementation of a proof checker with respect to the deterministic interpreter. As before, in proof checking, the top-level constant of a proof term completely determines the unique definite clause to be used in backchaining at each step.

4.2 A Specification of N_I That Constructs Normal Proofs

Before discussing specifications of N_I that construct normal proofs, several definitions are required. We begin by defining the notion of normal N_I proofs as in [15]. The main condition for an N_I deduction to be normal is that it must contain no *maximal formula*, that is, a formula that is the conclusion of an I-rule or $\perp_I$ and the major premise of an E-rule, since such applications are redundant (as in the example in Fig. 3 (a)). For the fragment of N_I without the ∨ and ∃ connectives, this condition is taken as the definition of normal. With these connectives in the logic the condition must be made slightly stronger, and requires some further definitions. A *segment* in a deduction is defined to be a sequence of formula occurrences $A_1, \ldots, A_n$ such that the following hold.

1. A_1 is not the conclusion of an application of ∨-E or ∃-E.
2. For $i = 1, \ldots, n - 1$, A_i is a minor premise of an application of ∨-E or ∃-E.
3. A_n is not the minor premise of an application of ∨-E or ∃-E.

All occurrences in a segment are occurrences of the same formula. The deduction in Fig. 3 (b) contains a segment of length 3 of occurrences of $A \wedge B$. As in [15], we will say a segment is the premise of an application of a rule when its last formula is the premise of the rule. A *maximal segment* is a segment that begins with a conclusion of an application of an I-rule or $\perp_I$ and ends with a major premise of an E-rule. The segment of length 3 in Fig. 3 (b) is in fact maximal. Note that a maximal formula is a special case of a maximal segment. A *normal* deduction is then defined to be a deduction that contains no maximal segment. Figure 3 (c) contains a normal deduction of $r \supset s$ from $\{p \vee q, p \supset (r \supset s), q \supset (r \supset s)\}$.

Normal deductions can be characterized in terms of the form of certain sequences of formulas called paths. A *path* in a deduction is a sequence of occurrences $A_1, \ldots, A_n$ such that the following conditions hold.

1. A_1 is a leaf that is not discharged by an application of ∨-E or ∃-E.
2. For $i = 1, \ldots, n - 1$, A_i is not the minor premise of an application of $\supset$-E or ¬-E. If A_i is the major premise of an application of ∨-E or ∃-E, then A_{i+1} is an assumption discharged by this application. Otherwise, A_{i+1} is the conclusion of the rule for which A_i is a premise.
3. A_n is either the minor premise of $\supset$-E or ¬-E or the root of the deduction.

$$\dfrac{\dfrac{A \quad B}{A \wedge B} \wedge\text{-I}}{\dfrac{A \wedge B}{A} \wedge\text{-E}}$$

(a)

$$\dfrac{\exists x C \quad \dfrac{\dfrac{A \quad B}{A \wedge B} \wedge\text{-I}}{\dfrac{A \wedge B}{\exists y D} \quad \dfrac{A \wedge B}{A \wedge B} \exists\text{-E}}}{\dfrac{A \wedge B}{A} \wedge\text{-E}} \exists\text{-E}$$

(b)

$$\cfrac{r \qquad \cfrac{p \vee q \qquad \cfrac{p \quad \cfrac{p \supset (r \supset s) \,_{(1)}}{r \supset s \,_{(2)}} \supset\text{-E}}{\qquad} \qquad \cfrac{q \quad \dfrac{q \supset (r \supset s)}{r \supset s} \supset\text{-E}}{}}{r \supset s \,_{(2)}} \vee\text{-E}}{\cfrac{s \,_{(3)}}{r \supset s \,_{(4)}} \supset\text{-I}} \supset\text{-E}$$

(c)

Fig. 3. Maximal formulas, maximal segments, and paths in N_I deductions

A path of length 5 (containing 4 segments) in a normal deduction is indicated in Fig. 3 (c). Note that the second segment, indicated by the number (2), has length 2. The other paths in this deduction are:

1. a similar path starting with $q \supset (r \supset s)$
2. $p \vee q, p$
3. $p \vee q, q$
4. r.

We define an *E-path* to be a subsequence of a path such that each segment except the last is a major premise of an E-rule, and an *I-path* to be a subsequence of a path such that each segment except the first is a conclusion of an I-rule or $\perp_I$. We say that a deduction is an *E-deduction* if all paths containing the root are E-paths. Note that the subtree rooted at s in Fig. 3 (c) is an E-deduction.

In a normal deduction, each path contains a series of segments divided into two parts: an E-path followed by an I-path such that the last segment in the E-path called the *minimum segment* is also the first segment in the I-path. In Fig. 3 (c), the formula occurrence s is the minimum segment separating the E-paths and the I-paths of the two paths beginning with $p \supset (r \supset s)$ and $q \supset (r \supset s)$. The minor premises and conclusion of applications of $\vee$-E and $\exists$-E may appear in the E-path or I-path (or both) of all paths through them. In Fig. 3 (c), the middle premise and conclusion of $\vee$-E, for example, occur in the E-path of the indicated path. Note that an E-deduction is normal if and only if all deductions rooted at a minor premise of an application of $\supset$-E or $\neg$-E are normal.

The division of paths in normal deductions into E-paths and I-paths will be reflected in our specification. We will use two relations in specifying the definite clauses for the inference rules. The first one is the #e predicate used to relate a formula and a normal E-deduction. For the second, we continue to use #, but this time to relate a formula with a normal deduction. Both predicates have type nprf -> form -> o. Thus, in a provable formula of the form (P #e A), P represents a normal E-deduction of A, while in a provable formula of the form (P # A), P is a normal deduction of A. Operationally, the clauses for the #e relation will apply E-rules, and the clauses for the # relation will apply I-rules and join I-paths and E-paths at the minimum segment.

Using these two predicates, the introduction rules and $\perp_I$ can be specified exactly as in the direct specification, except that discharged assumptions are added as facts about the #e relation since they are one-node E-deductions. They may occur at the leaves in larger deductions and will always occur in the E-paths that pass through them. Thus, the ⊃-I rule, for instance, is now specified as follows.

```
(imp_i P) # (A imp B) :- pi W\ ((W #e A) => ((P W) # B)).
```

The elimination rules ∧-E, ⊃-E, ¬-E, and ∀-E are specified using the #e predicate since, in a normal deduction, both the major premise and conclusion of all applications of these rules are roots of normal E-deductions. For example, the clauses for the ∧-E rules now have the following form.

```
(and_e1 B P) #e A :- P #e (A and B).
(and_e2 A P) #e B :- P #e (A and B).
```

The ⊃-E rule, on the other hand, is represented by the following clause where the subgoal for the minor premise uses the # predicate.

```
(imp_e A P1 P2) #e B :- P1 # A, P2 #e (A imp B).
```

This reflects the fact that the subproof at the minor premise can be an arbitrary normal deduction. By the definition of path, the root of this subproof will always be the last formula occurrence in the paths through it. The ¬-E rule is similar.

∨-E and ∃-E are each specified by two definite clauses, the first corresponding to when the minor premises and conclusion occur in I-paths of paths through them, and the second when they occur in E-paths. The following two clauses are those for the ∨-E rule.

```
(or_e A B P P1 P2) # C :- P #e (A or B),
                  pi W\ ((W #e A) => ((P1 W) # C)),
                  pi W\ ((W #e B) => ((P2 W) # C)).

(or_e A B P P1 P2) #e C :- P #e (A or B),
                   pi W\ ((W #e A) => ((P1 W) #e C)),
                   pi W\ ((W #e D) => ((P2 W) #e C)).
```

Note that when the minor premises of this rule are the roots of arbitrary normal deductions, the conclusion is also at the root of an arbitrary normal deduction, as indicated by the use of the # relation to relate formula C to its various proofs in the head and body of the first of the two clauses above. On the other hand, when the minor premises of this rule are at the roots of normal E-deductions, as in the latter clause above, the conclusion is also the root of a normal E-deduction.

Finally, we must also add the clause P # A :- P #e A. This clause serves to join I-paths and E-paths at the minimum segment. Its declarative reading is that any normal E-deduction is a normal deduction.

4.3 Alternative Specifications for Constructing Normal Proofs

We now discuss several modifications that can be made to this specification. This presentation both illustrates alternative ways of specifying the rules of N_I so that only normal proofs get constructed and also brings us closer to a specification that corresponds to cut-free L_I.

In the specification discussed in the previous subsection, the ¬-E rule would have the following formulation, since it is similar to ⊃-E.

```
(neg_e A P1 P2) #e false :- P1 # A, P2 #e (neg A).
```

In a normal N_I deduction, any occurrence of ⊥ is always in the minimum segment of paths through it, since it cannot be the major premise of an E-rule or the conclusion of an I-rule. As a result, we have the option of modifying the above formula so that # instead of #e appears in the head of the clause. With this modification, it is still the case that P in a provable formula of the form (P #e A) represents an E-deduction of A, but now it is one that does not end in ¬-E. Operationally, the clauses for the # relation now build I-paths in a goal directed fashion, and possibly also add the last segment in the E-paths of paths through false. Clauses for #e will then add the remaining E-paths.

We can simplify the specification of the previous subsection if we consider the following refinement of normal deductions. We define an *E-segment* in a normal deduction to be a segment whose last occurrence is the conclusion of an application of ∨-E or ∃-E and the major premise of an E-rule. Note that maximal segments are a special case of E-segments. As pointed out to Prawitz by Martin-Löf [14], the definition of normal can be sharpened to require that normal deductions contain no E-segments or maximal formulas. We call such deductions *S-normal* deductions. In an S-normal deduction, every minor premise or conclusion of an application of ∨-E and ∃-E will appear either in the minimum segment (in which case it is both in the I-path and E-path) or only in the I-path of paths through it. The deduction below is a modification of the deduction in Fig. 3 (c) that meets the extra restriction on segments to make it S-normal.

$$
\cfrac{
  p \lor q
  \qquad
  \cfrac{
    \cfrac{
      r
      \qquad
      \cfrac{p \qquad p \supset (r \supset s)}{r \supset s}\text{ ⊃-E}
    }{s}\text{ ⊃-E}
  }{r \supset s}\text{ ⊃-I}
  \qquad
  \cfrac{
    \cfrac{
      r
      \qquad
      \cfrac{q \qquad q \supset (r \supset s)}{r \supset s}\text{ ⊃-E}
    }{s}\text{ ⊃-E}
  }{r \supset s}\text{ ⊃-I}
}{r \supset s}\text{ ∨-E}
$$

The specification for N_I that we will eventually merge with the specification for L_I is one that builds deductions in this sharpened normal form. In order to discuss this specification we refine some definitions given earlier. By an *E-path*, we will still mean a subsequence of a path such that each segment except the last is a major premise of an E-rule, but now we add the additional restriction that each segment must be of length 1. The definition of I-path remains the same. In an E-deduction, all paths containing the root must now meet the additional restriction on E-paths. With respect to this modified definition, each path in an S-normal deduction will still contain an E-path followed by an I-path, but now there may not be any overlap in these two parts. The minimum segment will always be in the I-path, but will not be in the E-path if it has length greater than 1.

Note that under these new definitions, the latter of the two clauses given for ∨-E in the previous subsection is no longer correct. Even when all three premises are E-deductions, the conclusion will not be, since the root will be in a segment of length greater than 1, and thus paths through it will not be E-paths. Hence, we must eliminate this clause and the similar one for ∃-E. The simple elimination of these two clauses is all that is required to obtain a specification that constructs only S-normal deductions. In the remainder of this paper, we use the term "normal" to mean "S-normal" since we now only consider deductions in S-normal form.

With the above modifications, the remaining clauses with #e in the head are those for ∧-E, ⊃-E, and ∨-E. These rules can also be modified. We illustrate using the ∧-E rules. The clauses in subsection 4.2 specifying the ∧-E rules can be replaced by the following clause with # in the head.

```
PC # C :- P #e (A and B),
          (((and_e1 B P) #e A) => (((and_e2 A P) #e B) => (PC # C))).
```

The declarative reading of this clause is as follows: PC is a proof of formula C if there is a normal E-deduction of conjunct (A and B) (whose proof is P), and from the assumptions that A and B are provable separately (with proofs (and_e1 B P) and (and_e2 A P) respectively) it can be shown that PC is a proof of C. Operationally, in attempting to find a normal deduction for any formula C, this clause will look for an E-deduction of a conjunction (A and B), apply both versions of the ∧-E rule to it to obtain two new E-deductions, add the new subproofs as atomic program clauses, and attempt to find a normal deduction for C in the environment extended with these new assumptions.

As stated and proved in [15], normal deductions have the *subformula property*, that is, every formula occurring in a normal deduction of A from Γ is a subformula of A or of some formula in Γ. In fact, every formula occurring in an E-path is a subformula of a formula in Γ, every formula occurring in an I-path is a subformula of A, and every formula occurring in a minimum segment is a subformula of both A and some formula in Γ. This property is reflected in the following operational description of our new specification. The clauses for the I-rules apply the rules in a backward direction so that the formulas in the subgoals (which correspond to the premises) are always subformulas of the formula in the head of the clause (the conclusion). In contrast, the clauses for ∧-E, ⊃-E, and ∨-E apply the rules in a forward direction from the assumptions so that the conclusion is always a subformula of the major premise. In applying E-rules, new E-deductions get built from existing E-deductions and are then added to the program as new facts about the #e relation.

Note that this program can no longer serve as a proof checker with respect to the deterministic interpreter. It is no longer the case that the top-level constant of a proof term completely determines the definite clause to be used in backchaining. In fact, clauses like the specification of ∧-E above can always be used in attempting to prove an atomic goal for the # predicate since any formula and proof term will be instances of the formula and proof in the head of the clause.

4.4 Explicit vs. Implicit Representation of Assumptions in Natural Deduction

In specifying N_I we showed that it was quite natural to specify the discharge of assumptions "implicitly" using universal quantification and implication at the meta-level. It is also possible to explicitly keep track of assumptions by storing them in a list, and make use of a membership predicate to extract individual elements in much the same way that antecedents were handled in the specification of L_I. For N_I, such assumption lists will contain pairs of formulas associated with their E-deductions. We will call such lists of pairs *contexts*. We can obtain an "explicit context" specification of N_I via a systematic modification of the definite clauses of any of the "implicit context" specifications discussed so far. We illustrate using the formulation in the previous subsection.

We continue to use #e and # for the basic relations between a formula and its deductions, but no longer as predicates; they will now have the type nprf -> form -> judg where judg is a new primitive type introduced to represent these basic judgments. Contexts will be lists of elements of type judg_l where judg_l is, of course, the primitive type introduced for lists of elements of type judg. We must modify each definite clause so that it has an extra argument for a context, which corresponds to the set of assumptions that exist at the time the rule is applied. We use the sequent arrow --> as our predicate, now used to form "judgment sequents." This predicate has type judg_l -> judg -> o and expresses the relation between a context and a single formula paired with a normal deduction or normal E-deduction.

For those clauses that do not involve the use of implication to add assumptions to the program, the modification simply requires adding a list and sequent arrow to form a judgment sequent in the head and subgoals of each clause. For example, the clause for ∧-I is rewritten as follows.

```
Gamma --> ((and_i P1 P2) # (A and B)) :- Gamma --> (P1 # A),
                                          Gamma --> (P2 # B).
```

The discharge of assumptions as in the ⊃-I rule is specified as below where the new assumption gets added to the context rather than the program.

```
Gamma --> ((imp_i P) # (A imp B)) :-
   pi W\ (((W #e A)::Gamma) --> ((P W) # B)).
```

All other formulas can be modified similarly. For example, the clause for ∧-E adds two assumptions to the context.

```
Gamma --> (PC # C) :- Gamma --> (P #e (A and B)),
  (((and_e1 B P) #e A)::((and_e2 B P) #e B)::Gamma) --> (PC # C).
```

The formula expressing the fact that a normal E-deduction is a normal deduction is replaced by the following clause.

```
Gamma --> (P # A) :- Gamma --> (P #e A).
```

As before, this clause operationally joins E-paths and I-paths at the minimum segment. Finally, we need the following clause for completing E-deductions.

```
Gamma --> (P #e A) :- memb (P #e A) Gamma.
```

Of course, the memb predicate here is at type judg. In previous implicit context specifications, we did not need an explicit clause for closing E-deductions. There, an E-deduction was closed by unifying an atomic goal formula of the form (P #e A) with an atomic clause of the program.

This completes the description of the systematic modification from implicit to explicit context specifications. We now discuss two final modifications that can be made to this particular specification of N_I.

Recall that in the specification in the previous subsection, all clauses have # as the predicate occurring in the head. Thus in the modified specification here, all clauses except for the one immediately above have # as the relation on the right of the sequent arrow in the head of the clause. Hence, whenever an atomic formula of the form (Gamma --> (P #e A)) succeeds, it must be the case that (P #e A) is in the context Gamma. We could in fact remove the clause above for closing E-deductions, and replace each subformula of the form (Gamma --> (P #e A)) with (memb (P #e A) Gamma) directly in the formulas specifying the inference rules. The formula for ∧-E would then be written as follows.

```
Gamma --> (PC # C) :- memb (P #e (A and B)) Gamma,
  (((and_e1 B P) #e A)::((and_e2 A P) #e B)::Gamma) --> (PC # C).
```

After making such a modification, the resulting set of formulas is such that only the # relation appears on the right, while only the #e relation appears on the left of the sequent arrow. Thus, we can distinguish normal E-deductions from arbitrary normal deductions simply by where they occur in judgment sequents. As a result, we no longer need two distinct relations. They can be merged into one. We do so here by simply eliminating the #e relation and adopting # as the single relation between a formula and a deduction. Using this formulation, the above clause for ∧-E becomes the following formula.

```
Gamma --> (PC # C) :- memb (P # (A and B)) Gamma,
  (((and_e1 B P) # A)::((and_e2 A P) # B)::Gamma) --> (PC # C).
```

The specification obtained by making similar modifications to all of the clauses is the one we will now directly merge with the L_I specification.

5 Transforming L_I Proofs to N_I Proofs

The first step in merging the specifications of L_I and N_I is to combine the data structures for sequents and judgments. We do so using the same constants as before, but now give them the following types.

```
type    #       nprf -> form -> judg.
type    -->     judg_l -> judg -> seq.
type    >-      lprf -> seq -> o.
```

As before # is used for the relation between a formula and N_I deduction. We also again use the sequent arrow for judgment sequents. Here the type seq replaces o since it will no longer serve as the top-level predicate. As in the specification of L_I, >- is the top-level predicate with the same type as before. Note, though, that the second argument is a judgment sequent in this case. An atomic formula now has the form (Q >- (Gamma --> (P # A))) where Gamma is a list of judgment pairs. If such a formula is provable, it will be the case that Q represents a cut-free L_I proof of the sequent whose antecedent contains the formulas in Gamma and whose succedent is A, and P represents a normal N_I deduction of A from the formulas in Gamma.

In the clauses in this specification, the L_I rules for introducing a connective on the right of the sequent will be simultaneously specified with the corresponding N_I introduction rule. Similarly, the rules for introducing a connective on the left in L_I will be specified with the corresponding elimination rule. Finally, the ⊥-R rule in L_I and the $\perp_I$ rule in N_I will be specified together. For example, the first formula below simultaneously specifies the ∧-R and ∧-I rules from L_I and N_I, respectively, while the second formula specifies both ∧-L and ∧-E.

```
(and_r Q1 Q2) >- (Gamma --> ((and_i P1 P2) # (A and B))) :-
    Q1 >- (Gamma --> (P1 # A)), Q2 >- (Gamma --> (P2 # B)).

(and_l (A and B) Q) >- (Gamma --> (PC # C)) :-
    memb (P # (A and B)) Gamma,
    Q >- ((((and_e1 B P) # A)::((and_e2 A P) # B)::Gamma) --> (PC # C)).
```

They are obtained by a straightforward merging of the corresponding formulas of the separate specifications. They illustrate how N_I proof terms are associated with formulas within a sequent on the right and left, respectively, while the L_I proof terms are associated with the entire sequent using the top-level relation.

The following clause simultaneously specifies ∀-R and ∀-I.

```
(forall_r Q) >- (Gamma --> ((forall_i P) # (forall A))) :-
    pi Y\ ((Q Y) >- (Gamma --> ((P Y) # (A Y)))).
```

This clause illustrates how universal quantification at the meta-level is used to handle simultaneously the provisos on both ∀-R and ∀-I. Note that both Q and P are abstractions over the variable Y.

As a final example, consider the formula below for ⊃-R and ⊃-I.

```
(imp_r Q) >- (Gamma --> ((imp_i P) # (A imp B))) :-
   pi W\ (Q >- (((W # A)::Gamma) --> ((P W) # B))).
```

Universal quantification is used to introduce a constant to replace the variable W and serve as a proof for hypothesis A. As before, the term P is an abstraction over this constant. It represents a function from proofs of A to proofs of B. Note, on the other hand that, as in the L_I specification, Q is not an abstraction.

The complete specification for L_I and N_I is given in Fig. 4. Operationally, this program can take on several roles. In a query of the form:

```
(Q >- (nil --> (P # A)))
```

where both Q and P are logic variables, the program behaves as a theorem prover, and simultaneously constructs proofs in both inference systems. If P is also specified, then the program acts as a proof transformer, transforming an N_I proof P to an L_I proof Q. Conversely, an L_I proof Q can be used to guide the construction of an N_I proof P. The program is complete with respect to the deterministic depth-first interpreter for this latter transformation, for the same reason that the L_I specification is complete as a proof checker. The constant at the head of the proof term Q uniquely determines which definite clause must be used at each step. The converse, however, is not true since as discussed in subsection 4.3, this formulation of the N_I rules cannot serve as a proof checker with respect to the deterministic interpreter because of the clauses for the ∧-E, ⊃-E, and ∀-E rules. If however, the depth-first search strategy of the interpreter were replaced by breadth-first search, the transformation in this direction would be achieved by this program.

Alternatively, we could modify the specification in Fig. 4 so that the transformation from N_I to L_I proofs works with respect to the depth-first interpreter. One simple approach involves taking into account the form of E-deductions in S-normal proofs. In such deductions, there is one path to the root that begins at an assumption and contains a sequence of applications of ∧-E, ⊃-E, ∀-E, possibly ending in an application of ¬-E. One or more of the sequent proofs to which such an E-deduction is related will contain a sequence of ∧-L, ⊃-L, and ∀-L rules occurring in reverse order to the corresponding I-rules in the natural deduction proof. It is straightforward to write a program to convert an E-deduction to such a corresponding "inverted" sequent proof. Then, a program to convert general N_I normal deductions to L_I proofs can be obtained by removing the clauses for the ∧-E, ⊃-E, and ∀-E rules from the clauses in Fig. 4 and modifying the remaining program to make use of such an inversion procedure for E-deductions.

6 Conclusion

The program we have presented provides both a declarative and an operational description of the correspondence between the sequent calculus and natural deduction for intuitionistic logic. An interesting next step would be to extend this approach to provide illustrations of other well-known proof-theoretical results. One obvious candidate is the correspondence between cut-elimination in sequent

```
(initial A) >- (Gamma --> (P # A)) :- memb (P # A) Gamma.

(and_r Q1 Q2) >- (Gamma --> ((and_i P1 P2) # (A and B))) :-
    Q1 >- (Gamma --> (P1 # A)), Q2 >- (Gamma --> (P2 # B)).

(or_r1 Q) >- (Gamma --> ((or_i1 P) # (A or B))) :-
    Q >- (Gamma --> (P # A)).

(or_r2 Q) >- (Gamma --> ((or_i2 P) # (A or B))) :-
    Q >- (Gamma --> (P # B)).

(imp_r Q) >- (Gamma --> ((imp_i P) # (A imp B))) :-
    pi W\ (Q >- (((W # A)::Gamma) --> ((P W) # B))).

(neg_r Q) >- (Gamma --> ((neg_i P) # (neg A))) :-
    pi W\ (Q >- (((W # A)::Gamma) --> ((P W) # false))).

(forall_r Q) >- (Gamma --> ((forall_i P) # (forall A))) :-
    pi Y\ ((Q Y) >- (Gamma --> ((P Y) # (A Y)))).

(exists_r T Q) >- (Gamma --> ((exists_i T P) # (exists A))) :-
    Q >- (Gamma --> (P # (A T))).

(false_r Q) >- (Gamma --> ((false_i P) # A)) :-
    Q >- (Gamma --> (P # false)).

(and_l (A and B) Q) >- (Gamma --> (PC # C)) :-
    memb (P # (A and B)) Gamma,
    Q >- (((((and_e1 B P) # A)::((and_e2 A P) # B)::Gamma) --> (PC # C)).

(imp_l (A imp B) Q1 Q2) >- (Gamma --> (PC # C)) :-
    memb (P2 # (A imp B)) Gamma, Q1 >- (Gamma --> (P1 # A)),
    Q2 >- ((((imp_e A P1 P2) # B)::Gamma) --> (PC # C)).

(forall_l (forall A) T Q) >- (Gamma --> (PC # C)) :-
    memb (P # (forall A)) Gamma,
    Q >- ((((forall_e A T P) # (A T))::Gamma) --> (PC # C)).

(neg_l (neg A) Q) >- (Gamma --> ((neg_e A P1 P2) # false)) :-
    memb (P2 # (neg A)) Gamma, Q >- (Gamma --> (P1 # A)).

(or_l (A or B) Q1 Q2) >- (Gamma --> ((or_e A B P P1 P2) # C)) :-
    memb (P # (A or B)) Gamma,
    pi W\ (Q1 >- (((W # A)::Gamma) --> ((P1 W) # C))),
    pi W\ (Q2 >- (((W # B)::Gamma) --> ((P2 W) # C))).

(exists_l (exists A) Q) >- (Gamma --> ((exists_e A P1 P2) # B)) :-
    memb (P1 # (exists A)) Gamma,
    pi Y\ (pi W\ ((Q Y) >- (((W # (A Y))::Gamma) --> ((P2 Y W) # B)))).
```

Fig. 4. Definite clauses for simultaneous specification of L_I and N_I

systems and proof normalization in natural deduction. Such a specification may provide a program that simultaneously performs both operations.

In Sect. 4.4, we illustrated how to convert the specification of Sect. 4.3, which uses meta-level implication for the discharge of assumptions, into a specification using explicit assumption lists. It is easy to see that this operation can be performed on any of the "implicit context" specifications of natural deduction presented here. In fact, this operation is not limited to an intuitionistic object-logic. Specifications of natural deduction for classical logic or higher-order logic, for example, could be similarly transformed. Any such explicit context specification can be viewed as a specification of a sequent style inference system for the same logic. In the case of N_I, the fact that the inference rules could be specified in such a way that the corresponding sequent system was exactly L_I without the cut rule is a result of the close correspondence between the two. The well-known sequent and natural deduction inference systems for classical logic, for example, cannot be so easily related in this way.

Acknowledgements

I am grateful to Dale Miller and Peter Schroeder-Heister for valuable discussions and comments related to this paper. This research was supported in part by grants ARO-DAA29-84-9-0027, ONR N00014-88-K-0633, NSF CCR-87-05596, DARPA N00014-85-K-0018, and ESPRIT Basic Research Action 3245.

References

1. Alonzo Church. A formulation of the simple theory of types. *Journal of Symbolic Logic*, 5:56–68, 1940.
2. Michael Dummett. *Elements of Intuitionism.* Clarendon Press, Oxford, 1977.
3. Conal Elliott and Frank Pfenning. eLP, a Common Lisp Implementation of λProlog. May 1989.
4. Amy Felty. *Specifying and Implementing Theorem Provers in a Higher-Order Logic Programming Language.* PhD thesis, University of Pennsylvania, August 1989.
5. Amy Felty and Dale Miller. Specifying theorem provers in a higher-order logic programming language. In *Ninth International Conference on Automated Deduction*, Argonne Ill., May 1988.
6. Gerhard Gentzen. Investigations into logical deductions, 1935. In M. E. Szabo, editor, *The Collected Papers of Gerhard Gentzen*, pages 68–131, North-Holland Publishing Co., Amsterdam, 1969.
7. J. Roger Hindley and Jonathan P. Seldin. *Introduction to Combinatory Logic and Lambda Calculus.* Cambridge University Press, 1986.
8. Gérard Huet. A unification algorithm for typed λ-calculus. *Theoretical Computer Science*, 1:27–57, 1975.
9. Dale Miller, Gopalan Nadathur, Frank Pfenning, and Andre Scedrov. Uniform proofs as a foundation for logic programming. To appear in the *Annals of Pure and Applied Logic.*

10. Gopalan Nadathur and Dale Miller. Higher-order horn clauses. April 1988. To appear in the *Journal of the ACM*.

11. Gopalan Nadathur and Dale Miller. An overview of λProlog. In K. Bowen and R. Kowalski, editors, *Fifth International Conference and Symposium on Logic Programming*, MIT Press, 1988.

12. Lawrence C. Paulson. The foundation of a generic theorem prover. *Journal of Automated Reasoning*, 5(3):363–397, September 1989.

13. Garrel Pottinger. Normalization as a homomorphic image of cut-elimination. *Annals of Mathematical Logic*, 12(3):223–357, 1977.

14. Dag Prawitz. Ideas and results in proof theory. In J.E. Fenstad, editor, *Proceedings of the Second Scandinavian Logic Symposium*, pages 235–307, North-Holland, Amsterdam, 1971.

15. Dag Prawitz. *Natural Deduction*. Almqvist & Wiksell, Uppsala, 1965.

16. J. I. Zucker. Cut-elimination and normalization. *Annals of Mathematical Logic*, 1(1):1–112, 1974.

MODAL PROVABILITY FOUNDATIONS for NEGATION BY FAILURE

D. M. GABBAY[1]

Department of Computing

Imperial College of Science, Technology and Medicine

180 Queen's Gate, London SW7 2BZ

1 Introduction and Discussion

This paper is a contribution to the foundation of negation by failure. It presents a view of negation by failure as a modal provability notion. Negation by failure is a central notion in Logic Programming and is used extensively in practice. There are various attempts at its foundations each with its own difficulties and limitations. We would like to present the modal point of view which, as far as we can see, resolves the main problems. The modal point of view also makes the connection with the notion of Modal Provability, which is a well known, well established area of pure logic. The results were first published in Gabbay 1986 and presented in Logic Colloquium 86.

Statement of the Problem:
Given a Prolog program P, built up from Horn clauses extended with negation by failure and given a goal G, the following three cases arise:

(1)   G succeeds from **P**. (We use the notation **P** ? G = 1).
(2)   G finitely fails from **P**. (We use the notation **P** ? G = 0).
(3)   The computation of G from **P** loops. (We use the notation **P** ? G = loop).

The computation we have in mind for (1) - (3) is a *modified* version of the known SLDNF resolution, which we denote by *Grounding*-SLDNF. The usual SLDNF resolution is the one defined precisely in John Lloyd's book. This has the property that if we come in the course of the computation across a non-grounded negative literal (of the form $\neg A(x)$), we stop there in a *flounder*. We are not given the option of grounding it in the usual SLDNF resolution. Our own computation, the G-SLDNF, understands the query $\neg A(x)$ as $\exists x \neg A(x)$ (*find an instantiation t for which A(t) fails*) and therefore allows the computation to ground the negative literal and continue.

We would like a systematic translation * of clauses and goals into a reasonable logical system L such that if P* is the translation of P and G* is the translation of G then the following holds:

(1*)   If G succeeds from P then $P* \vdash_L G*$

---

[1] This research was supported by the Science and Engineering Research Council under grant GR/D/5939.7 as part of the ALVEY project 'Pure Logic Language IKBS/170' and by the National Science Foundation under grant IST-8505586. I am grateful to L Terracini, John Shepherdson and to the two anonymous referees for valuable criticism. Also thanks to L Lazarte for reading earlier versions of the manuscript.

(2*)   If G finitely fails from P then P* ⊢_L (¬G)*.

(3*)   If G loops from P then neither P* ⊢_L G* nor P* ⊢_L (¬G)*.

Clark's Completion uses L = classical logic and P* = $Com(P)$ and $(¬G)*$ = ~G, where $Com(P)$ denotes the Clark completion of P. Conditions (1*), (2*) and (3*) hold for programs P containing no negation by failure symbols.

When ¬ is allowed to be present in the body of clauses in P, the above does not hold for the Clark completion. *There are well known examples.*

This paper essentially continues Clark's attempts in finding a suitable "completion" by presenting negation by failure as a modal provability notion. In fact, we use a variation of the modal logic of Solovay, originally introduced to study the properties of the Gödel provability   predicate of Peano Arithmetic, and show that ¬A can be read essentially as 'A is refutable from the (logical content of the) program'.
We now motivate our aproach by clarifying in our minds what exactly we are looking for, as a solution to the problem above. The minimal view is that we would accept *any* translation * into *any* logical system L, which formally satisfies (1*)-(3*) above. This will give some logical meaning to the compuation procedure. This is a minimal position because the intuitive meaning of the translation (if it has any at all) may not be compatible with the intuitions associated with the notion of failure. We get in this case, nothing more than a formal logical interpretation complete for the computational procedure.

We want to achieve more. We want to give a modal interpretation to the Horn clause computation and a modal provability interpretation to the notion of failure. We hope to get the translation right intuitively and conceptually and obtain (1*)-(3*) as a by-product, a corollary to the successful translation. This is certainly more satisfactory because it says what failure is in terms of modality. We further would like to use as little as possible any special properties of the Horn clause syntactical structure or computation. There are other computational disciplines around, various extensions of logic programming and the notion of finite failure is meaningful there. Can we present a translation which will be valid and good in a wide range of systems?

We thus have to find a suitable model logic L and a suitable translation * so that the pair (L,*) yield an intellectually satisfactory representation of the logic program and the computation.

Our starting point for a modal logic can be to take the modal logic of provability used by Solovay and Boolos to analyse the provability notions of Peano arithmetic. There is no strong argument, at this stage, for using this logic, beyond the fact that it is well known, and technically satisfactory (one is guaranteed a unique fixed point solutions to modal equations satisfying some simple conditions), and thus it can serve as a starting point. We are going, however, to keep an open mind and look for a possibly better logic, by possibly, though reluctantly, taking advantage of the special syntactical properties of the Horn clause logic program.

We now have to decide how we want to translate ¬a into the modal logic. We would like to follow the intuition of reading ¬a as 'a is unprovable from the (logical content of) the program'. We will analyse at a later stage formally what this means. Meanwhile we already have a choice to make. If 'success' means 'provable', not success (ie failure) means 'unprovable', then we might wish to take 'finite failure' as 'provably unprovable' or even 'provably not'.

In symbols:

a succeeds corresponds to $\Box$a

a fails corresponds to $\sim\Box$a

a finitely fails corresponds to $\Box\sim\Box$a or to $\Box\sim$a

Thus $\neg$a should be translated either as $\sim\Box$a or as $\Box\sim\Box$a, or as $\Box\sim$a.

The general schema of the translation is as follows: First we choose the modal logic L we are going to use. For example it may be Solovay's logic Pr or it may be S4. Having fixed the logic, we choose how to translate $\neg$a, where $\neg$ is negation by failure. Suppose the translation of $\neg$a is Not(a). Not(a) may be $\sim\Box$a or perhaps $\Box\sim\Box$a or perhaps $\Box\sim$ a or a variation. Although we are not giving an exact definition of Not, we do know of some of its properties, for example, $\vdash_L$ Not (a) $\rightarrow \sim\Box$a (ie it is inconsistent with $\Box$a).

Given a program P, it contains lots of negation by failure symbols "$\neg$" in it. We want to build a matrix E in the modal logic L which is associated with P and is obtained syntactically from P. The matrix will be of the form E(x) with a free *new* propositional variable x. E(x) is obtained from P by replacing in the program each $\neg$a by Not(x$\rightarrow$ a), and by possibly other additions. E(x) is a theory in the modal logic L. Exactly how we get it we will see later. Intuitively one can understand E(x) as the result of translating $\neg$a in the program by Not(x$\rightarrow$ a), where x is supposed to be the program itself.

We now *solve*, in the modal logic L, the equation x $\leftrightarrow$ E(x). If we choose a modal logic which always allows for a unique solution $x_0 = E(x_0)$, then this unique x_0 can be taken as the translation P* of P into the modal logic L, and we hope it will satisfy properties (1*)-(3*) mentioned above.

The above is the schema of steps of this entire paper. In order to show that the choice of L and E and Not is not ad-hoc, let us motivate them by doing a qualitative study of how they should behave, and narrowing down the possibilities and options open before us.

We thus start with an open mind about what L, E and Not should be. I must admit, however, that we have already made some decisions at this stage about our modal choices. We do want a *provability* reading of $\neg$ and not just any old translation into modal logic. Modal logic and especially temporal logic, is able to simulate the Horn clause comptation mechanism (our G-SLDNF resolution) and thus provide a satisfactory translation.

Since we are making here a key decision, we will make this point clear through an example. Consider the program

$\neg$b $\rightarrow$ a

a $\rightarrow$ b

The procedural steps are

1 **Success (a) if Success ($\neg$b)**
2 **Success ($\neg$b) if Failure (b)**
3 **Failure (b) if Failure (a)**
4 **Failure (a) if Failure ($\neg$b)**
5 **Failure ($\neg$b) if Success (b)**
6 **Success (b) if Success (a)**

We have completed a full cycle.

If N is the temporal modality Next, □ is read as *Always* and q true at time t means that q was obtained at step t of the compuation, then we can write the temporal translation

1   □ (N~b → a)

2   □(~Nb → N~b)

3   □ (~Na→ ~b)

4   □ (~N~b → ~a)

5   □ (Nb → ~~b)

6   Na → Nb

Here we translated

> **Success** (a) as a
> **Failure** (a) as ~a
> a if b as □ (Nb → a)

We probably need some axioms to make it right, e.g.

~Nq → N ~Nq

This is a metalevel approach, and as we said, we are not taking this approach.

Let us resume our qualitative study of the porovability approach. Our unknown **L, E** and **Not** should be able to give us the right answers to simple examples. So let us check some examples and see what properties of **L, E** and **Not** are needed.

We first consider the program P={a}. The translation **P*** of P should be such that (1*) should hold. Thus **P* ⊢$_L$** □a must hold. This will be achieved if

P* = □a.

Similarly, the program {a, a → b} must satisfy:

{a, a → b}* ⊢$_L$ □b ∧ □a.

To achieve that we must have **P*** ⊢ □(a → b)

We thus conclude intuitively that program clauses should be translated as provable assumptions. This means that E(x) (whatever it is going to be) must satisfy the Heuristic condition 1 below:

HC1: ⊢$_L$ E ↔ □E.

Consider now the following program and query:

P = {a → b} ? ¬a

¬a succeeds. We thus have to be able to have **P*** ⊢$_L$ Not(a).

This will never happen unless we put Not(a) into E (and hence into **P***). Thus we conclude Heuristic condition 2:

HC2:   E(x) must contain as conjuncts at least all formulas of the form **Not**(a), where a is not a head of any clause in **P**.

We now look again at P = {a' → b, a → b}? ¬b.

We intuitively know that $P^* \supseteq \{Not(a), Not\ (a'), \Box(a \to b), \Box(a' \to b)\}$ we should be able to prove P^* $\vdash_L Not(b)$.

This we cannot do unless we recognise that the computation finitely fails, because the *only* way to get b is through the clauses $a \to b$ and $a' \to b$, through asking the queries ?a or ?a'.

We thus need to read and translate the program as

$P^* = \{Not\ (a), Not\ (a'), \Box((a \lor a') \leftrightarrow b)\}$

We conclude the following third Heuristic condition:

HC3: The 'if' part in the program should be translated into the modal logic as 'iff' (as in Clarks completion).

At this stage we probably should add that since we are reading the program as 'iff', we should try to read $\neg a$ as *refutability* and hence translate Not (a) as $\Box \sim a$. This is certainly intuitive for the notion of finite failure.

Consider now the program $P = \{\neg a \to a\}$. Its matrix $E(x)$ should be, according to what we have already qualitatively analysed, something like:

$E(x) = \Box(\Box(x \to \sim a) \leftrightarrow a)$

and P^* should be the fixed point solution of

$E(x) \leftrightarrow x$.

We should expect P^* and E to be consistent in L, ie to have models. We also expect, since neither a succeeds nor $\neg a$ succeeds, that:

$P^* \nvdash_L \Box\ a$

$P^* \nvdash_L \Box \sim a$

We first check whether a solution to $E(x) \leftrightarrow x$ exists. This is a property of the modal logic. If such a solution exists, it is valid for all a. Substitute a = **truth**, in the equivalence. We get that x satisfies

$x \leftrightarrow \Box(\Box \sim x \leftrightarrow truth) \leftrightarrow \Box\Box \sim x$.

Thus the logic L must be able to solve the equation $x \leftrightarrow \Box\Box \sim x$.
We immediately draw the conclusion that L cannot be a reflexive modal logic, ie satisfy the axiom $(\Box A \to A)$ because we will get inconsistency $x \leftrightarrow \sim x$.

L can be one of two types of logics. The provability like logics, where the set of possible worlds is finite, satisfying Löbs axiom, $\Diamond A \to \Diamond (A \land \Box \sim A)$, or a temporal logic type of a system.

In the provability logic case a fixed point solution is always guaranteed, since x is always within the scope of $\Box$ in E (see appendix). The solution to the equation $x \leftrightarrow \Box\Box \sim x$ is $x = \Box\Box$ f.

In the temporal logic type case. $\Box A$ can be read as "A is true tomorrow", and $x \leftrightarrow \Box\Box \sim x$ can be understood as the specification that x changes value every third day (going on to infinity).

We see again that we are faced with the same key choice we had before. Do we choose a temporal type of modal logic or a provability type. However, at this choice junction, we would use the temporal type logic for simulating provability (ie fixed points) and not for simulating the Horn clause computation. Again heuristically I would opt for provability type logics and not for the temporal type, for the following reasons:

1   The calculations of fixed points in the provability type logic is effective. In fact, we prove a theorem later on that for any wff of the form $\Box B(x)$, the solution of $x = \Box B(x)$ is simply $x = B(t)$.
In comparison, the fixed points fo the temporal like logics involves infinities and may not be effective. I am not saying we cannot find an extension of eg S4 which is suitable, I am just following my instincts, trying to choose the best option.

2   The "temporal" approach may end up being not logic but just a modal logic "provability" doing "simulation", a metalevel description of what the program does computationally, an option which I feel less happy about and which we have already rejected. One can simulate anything in an appropriately chosen logic.

3   There are notions of failure in other extensions of Prolog, such as N-Prolog (Gabbay-Reyle), near Horn Prolog (Loveland), various modal and temporal Prologs and many more. If we work within the provability logic framework we may be able to generate and handle all of them.

The reader should note that the temporal logic type approach has been pursued by other authors (by Balbiani and by Terracini) in reaction to earlier versions to this paper.

I think that at this stage, I am allowed the choice of the modal logic **Pr** of provability as my working logic **L**. The reader is entitled to his own choice, but I think I motivated my choice as a reasonable option. The logic **Pr** is the extension of modal **K** with the axioms:

$\Box A \rightarrow \Box\Box A$

$\Diamond A \rightarrow \Diamond(A \wedge \Box\sim A)$.

Having made up our minds on what logic we want to use, let us see what happens to typical examples.

The programs we consider are:

1     $P_1 = \{\neg a \rightarrow a\}$, a typical looping program
2     $P_2 = \{\neg a \rightarrow b, \neg b \rightarrow c, a\}$, a typical simple program, and
3     $P_3 = \{\neg a \rightarrow a, a\}$

The matrices for these programs are:

$E_1(x) = \Box(\Box(x \rightarrow \sim a) \leftrightarrow a)$

$E_2(x) = \Box(\Box a \wedge (\Box(x \rightarrow \sim b) \leftrightarrow c) \wedge (\Box(x \rightarrow \sim a) \leftrightarrow b))$

$E_3(x) = \Box(t \vee \Box(x \rightarrow \sim a)) \leftrightarrow a)$

Here $\neg a$ is interpreted as refutability and therefore the "iff" reading of the progam is taken. We expect the fixed point solution of each $x \leftrightarrow E(x)$ to be consistent and satisfy $x \vdash \Box A$ if A succeeds and $x \vdash \Box\sim A$ if A finitely fails.

We know from a later theorem (theorem T3) that the fixed point solution is obtained from $E(x)$ (which satisfies $\vdash E \leftrightarrow \Box E$) by taking $x_0 = E(t)$.

Thus the three modal completions are:

$M_1 = \Box(\Box\sim a \leftrightarrow a)$

$M_2 = \Box(\Box a \wedge (\Box\sim b \leftrightarrow c) \wedge (\Box\sim a \leftrightarrow b))$

$M_3 = \Box a$

We now check model theoretically what the completions are in the logic **Pr**. We will find that the logic **Pr** is not adequate and some extension **N1** of **Pr** needs to be taken. Thus we are essentially motivating **N1** on technical grounds. Let us start with M_2. In the program P_2, a succeeds, b finitely fails and c succeeds. We thus must have:

$$M_2 \vdash^? \Box a \wedge \Box \sim b \wedge \Box c$$

The **Pr** models are finite trees. Take such a tree and assume that the tree is a model of M_2

t ◂ top point

0

we observe the following:

1   $\Box a$ is true, so this is OK.

2   Since M_2 says that $\Box(\Box \sim a \leftrightarrow b)$ holds, we get that b = t at the endpoints and b = f at all other points. This is the case because at the endpoints, any $\Box A$ is true. We thus see that we are not getting $M_2 \vdash \Box \sim b$. The endpoint "side effect" spoils it.

3   This side effect on b propagates disasterously to c. M_2 proves $\Box (c \leftrightarrow \Box \sim b)$, we get c true at the endpoints and false at all other points because b = t at endpoints which falsifies $\Box \sim b$ everywhere. We thus get $M_2 \vdash \Box(c \leftrightarrow \Box f)$ instead of $M_2 \vdash \Box c$.

Our conclusion is that all goes wrong because of the fact that any $\Box A$ is always true at endpoints.

Suppose now we modify the logic **Pr** to an extension **N1** which requires the assignments to atoms to satisfy the following condition:

If an atom is uniformly true (or false) at all non endpoints, then it must have the same value at endpoints.

This restriction on assignments, yields a *smaller* class of acceptable models and hence gives rise to a *stronger* logic. Call the logic **N1**. **N1** is semantically defined. It does have a sematically defined consequence relation, $\vDash_{N1}$. Let us now check whether for our completion we have:

$$M_2 \vDash_{N1} \Box a \wedge \Box \sim b \wedge \Box c$$

Consider any **N1** model of M_2. Since $\Box a$ must be true and we also have $\Box(\Box \sim a \leftrightarrow b)$, the only **N1** model available for b is that b is true at endpoints and false everywhere else. Thus since **N1** does not allow such a model, we get that M_2 is *not consistent*.

The trouble arises from insisting on the "iff" part of the program to hold at endpoints, ie we wanted $\Box \sim a \leftrightarrow b$ to hold at *all* points and thus we wrote $\Box(\Box \sim a \leftrightarrow b)$ into the completion matrix $E(x)$. But we can see the endpoints are trouble. Let us then require the equivalence to hold at all other points which are not endpoints and we don't care about endpoints.

Thus the new matrix is

$$E_2'(x) = \Box a \wedge \Box^0(\Box(x \to \sim a) \leftrightarrow b)$$

$$\wedge \, \Box^0(\Box(x \to \sim b) \leftrightarrow c))$$

Here $\Box^0 A$ says that A is true at all points which are not endpoints. We have:

$$\Box^0 A = \Box(\Box f \vee A).$$

The fixed point M_2' will be:

$$\Box a \wedge \Box^0(\Box \sim a \leftrightarrow b) \wedge \Box^0(\Box \sim b \leftrightarrow c).$$

In the logic N1 this completion does prove

$$\Box a \wedge \Box \sim b \wedge \Box c$$

Let us see why:

It is clear that $\Box a$ follows. From $\Box^0(\Box \sim a \leftrightarrow b)$ we know b is false at all points which are not endpoints. We have no value for b at endpoints.

But the only models allowed in N1 are the ones where b gets the same value false at the endpoints. Thus $M_2 \models \Box \sim b$ follows in N1, because it holds in all models.

Similarly since $\Box^0(\Box \sim b \leftrightarrow c)$ is in M_2, we get that c is true at all non-endpoints and must be true at the endpoints as well by the restrictions of N1.

Thus $M2 \models_{N1} \Box c$

We can now conclude that perhaps N1 is our logic and $E'(x)$ are our completions.

Let us check the other examples:

$$E_1'(x) = \Box^0(\Box(x \to \sim a) \leftrightarrow a))$$
$$M_1' = \Box^0(\Box \sim a \leftrightarrow a)$$

which is certainly N1 consistent, eg it allows for a to be $\Box\Box f$.

We are now at a stage which we almost found our logic. We need to axiomatise it, if that is possible, and prove all the relevant translation theorems systematically.

We need a few more technical observations. We translated $\neg A$ as $\Box \sim A$, ie as refutability. When A does not loop, and is indeed refutatble, we will get that the completion proves $\Box \sim A$. It turns out that even if we had taken $\neg A$ to mean non-provability (or provable non-provability) (ie $\Diamond \sim A$ or $\Box \Diamond \sim A$) then we can still get from the completion that $\Box \sim A$ is provable. To be more precise:

If $E_1(x)$ is the matrix obtained from taking all $\neg A$ as $\Box(x \to \sim A)$ and $E_2(x)$ is obtained by taking $\neg A$ as $\sim \Box(x \to A)$ and $E_3(x)$ is obtained by taking $\neg A$ as $\Box \sim \Box(x \to A)$ (provable unprovability) and if $M_1 = E_1(M_1)$ and $M_2 = E_2(M_2)$ and $M_3 = E_3(M_3)$ then $M_1 \models_{N1} \Box \sim A$ iff $M_2 \models_{N1} \Box \sim A$ and iff $M_3 \models_{N1} \Box \sim A$.

This means that we can translate $\neg A$ as non-provability, $\neg A = \sim \Box(x \to A)$ and provided we take the "iff" reading of the program, the translation will effectively be $\neg A = \Box(x \to \sim A)$ (ie refutability.) A difference might arise for looping A (eg $\neg A \to A$) where non-provability is *technically more* convenient.

We now summarise our preference in modelling negation by failure as a provability notion:

1 We read $\neg A$ as A is refutable from the (modal translation of) the program $(\Box(x \to \sim A))$.
2 Success of A means provable A $(\Box A)$.
3 Finite failure of A means provable $\sim A$ $(\Box \sim A)$.

4   The logic is essentially the logic of modal provability, modified to the extension **N1** for techncial reasons.

5   The matrix E(x) is based on the "iff" reading of the program which allows us to obtain the refutabiltiy reading.

6   We *technically*, but not conceptually replace $\Box(x \to \sim A)$ by $\sim\Box(x \to A)$ (unprovabilty) to achieve convenience for looping A's. For non looping A's (success or failure) the completion yields the same results as in the case of refutability.

7   It is also more convienient to use in the matrix E(x) the translation $G^O B = B \wedge \Box^O B$ for clauses and not just $\Box^O B$.

Thus the final version of the matrix for P_2 will be

$$E"_2(x) = a \wedge \Box a \wedge G^O (\Box(x \to \sim b) \leftrightarrow c) \wedge G^O(\Box(x \to \sim a) \leftrightarrow b))$$

where $G^O A = A \wedge \Box(\Box f \vee A)$.

We thus conclude our informal motivation.

It is now time to develop the necessary machinery in detail.

The first step is to formally define the modal logic N1 we are going to work with.

Definition D1:

Let **N1** be a modal system with the following connectives:

(1)   The classical connectives and quantifiers, $\sim$, $\wedge$, $\vee$, $\to$, $\leftrightarrow$, $\forall$, $\exists$, and the equality symbol =.

(2)   The modal unary connective $\Box$.

(3)   We allow also the constants **t** for **truth** **f** for **falsity**, and define the further connectives

$GA = $ definition $A \wedge \Box A$

$\Diamond A = $ definition $\sim\Box \sim A$

$G^O A = $ definition $G(A \vee \Box f)$.

In the propositional case especially, we write $A \equiv B$ to mean $G(A \leftrightarrow B)$.

Definition D2:

(a)   The logic N1 is defined semantically as follows:

we consider a *finite* tree $(T,<,0)$ with a first point $0 \in T$ and an irreflexive and transitive relation $<$.

Note that from the point of view of the logic all is needed in the Kripke semantics is that the converse of $<$ (ie $>$) is well founded, (ie $(T, <)$ is well capped). However, for any wff A, if A does not hold at a well capped model $(T, <)$ then A is false at some $(T, <, t_0)$ and then, of course, the points which matter are $T1 = \{t \mid t_0 < t\}$. $(T1, <, t_0)$ is now a finite model. We can thus restrict ourselves to finite $(T, <)$. .

Note: The trees are drawn upwards with the root at the bottom

(b)   A **Pr** modal *structure* (or *model*) has the form $(T,<,0,D,h)$ where $(T,<,0)$ is a finite tree with root $0 \in T$, D is a non empty domain and h is an assignment function associating with each $t \in T$ and each atomic n-place predicate Q a subset $h(t,Q) \, b \, D^n$.

Equality is always interpreted as identity and we never assigns the *same* element d∈ D to two syntactically different individual constants. If function symbols are used in the syntax then syntactically diffemt terms are assigned different elements of the domain.

Note that the above restrictions satisfy the equality axioms below:

$x = y \rightarrow G(x=y)$

$x \neq y \rightarrow G(x\neq y)$

$G(a\neq b)$, wherever a,b are syntactically distinct terms.

The domain D is the same for all the possible worlds of T. A model is called a Herbrand Model of terms if the domain D is exactly the set of all terms generated in the language.

We have further requirements on $(T,<,0,D,h)$ for it to qualify as an N1-model. These are

(c1) $\exists t_1 \; \exists t_2 \; (0<t_1 <t_2)$.

(c2) For any atomic $Q(x_1, ... ,x_n)$ and any $d_1,...,d_n \in D$ the following:

(*)   If $(d_1, ... ,d_n) \notin h(t, Q)$ for all non-endpoints t∈ T then $(d_1, ... ,d_n) \notin h(t,Q)$ for all t∈ T

(**)   If $(d_1,...,d_n) \in h(t,Q)$ for all non-endpoints t∈ T then $(d_1,...,d_n) \in h(t,Q)$ for all t∈ T

(d)   The truth value of a wff $B(x_1, ... ,x_n)$ with free variables $x_1, ... ,x_n$ at a point t∈ T under the assignment $x_1=d_1, ... ,x_n=d_n$ is defined inductively as follows:

We use the notation $\| B(d_1, ... ,d_n) \| (h,t) = $ **truth** or **falsity** (also abbreviated as **t** and **f**).

(d1)   For atomic $P(x_1, ... ,x_n)$:

$\| P(d_1, ... ,d_n) \| (h,t) = $ **truth** iff $(d_1, ... ,d_n)$ $h(t,P)$.

$\| P(d_1, ... ,d_n) \| (h,t) = $ **falsity**, otherwise.

(d2) $\| A \wedge B \| (h,t) = $ **truth** iff

$\| A \| (h,t) = $ **truth** and $\| B \| (h,t) = $ **truth**.

(d3) $\| \sim A \| (h,t) = $ **truth** iff $\| A \| (h,t) = $ **falsity**.

(d4) $\| \forall x \, B(x) \| (h,t) = $ **truth** iff for all d∈ D $\| B(d) \| (h,t) = $ **truth**.

(d5)   The truth definition of $\rightarrow, \vee, \exists$ are similar and reflect the classical definition of these connectives in terms of $\sim, \wedge, \forall$.

(d6) $\| \Box B \| (h,t) = $ **truth** iff for every s such that t<s we have $\| B \| (h,s) = $ **truth**.

(d7)   We say $Pr \models B$ iff $\| B \| (h,0) = $ **truth** for any Pr structure $(T,<,0,D,h)$.

Similarly we define $N1 \models B$, using N1-structures.

(e)   Note that the following holds:

(e1) $\Box f$ holds at t∈ T iff t is an endpoint.

(e2) $\diamond \diamond t$ always holds at 0∈ T

(e3) $\| GA \| (h,t) = $ **truth** iff $\| A \| (h,s) = $ **truth** for s ≥ t.

(e4) $\| G^0 A \| (h,t) = $ **truth** iff for all s>t which is *not an endpoint* we have $\| A \| (h,s) = $ **truth**.

(e5) For any atomic P, $G^0P = GP$ and $G^0\sim P = G\sim P$.

A further discussion of modal provability logics as well as an axiom system is given in Appendix 1. Note that N1 was defined as a logic semantically. The notion $N1 \models A$ is defined model theoretically. When we give proof procedures for N1 we will be able to write $N1 \vdash A$.

We are now ready to define the modal completion of the Prolog program P. We will start with the propositional case, because it is easier to discuss the concepts without the added complication of quantifiers. We will deal with quantifiers later. We would like to stress that contrary to the area of Pure Logic, where the main technical problems are usually resolved in the propositional level, in Logic Programming where computational aspects have more prominence among other conceptual aspects, the quantificational case is of main importance and we shall give it our full attention later on. It is only for reasons of exposition and presentation of ideas that we start with the propositional case.

Definition D3:

Let P be a propositional program. P is a set of clauses of the form:

$C_{ij} = B_{ij} \rightarrow q_i$

For each i, q_i is the head and B_{ij}, j=1, 2, ... are the various bodies for this head.

Let $H^+(P)$ be the set of all atoms appearing somewhere in P which are also heads of clauses with no bodies, i.e. which are assertions. Let $H^-(P)$ be the set of all atoms appearing in P which are *not* heads of clauses.

Let x be a new variable. For each B_{ij} let $B^*_{ij}(x)$ be the result of simultaneously replacing each occurrence of a "$\neg A$" ($\neg$ negation by failure) by $\sim \square (x \rightarrow A)$.

We now define a matrix E(P,x) (or E(x) for short) as the conjunction of the following three formulas $E_1 \wedge E_2 \wedge E_3$

where   (note that in N1, $G^0 q = Gq$ and $G^0 \sim q = G \sim q$ for atoms q):

$E_1 = \bigwedge Gq$

$\quad (q \in H^+(P))$.

$E_2 = \bigwedge G \sim q$

$\quad (q \in H^-(P))$.

$E_3 = G^0 \wedge_i (q_l \leftrightarrow \bigvee_j B^*_{ij}(x))$

$\quad = G(\square f \vee \bigwedge_i (q_i \leftrightarrow \bigvee_j B^*_{ij}(x)))$.

Notice that we basically took the Clark completion *Com*(P) and substituted $\sim \square(x \rightarrow A)$ for each $\neg A$ appearing in it, to obtain *Com*(P)*(x) and then let E(x) = G^0 *Com*(P)*(x). Also note that E_3 contains implicitly E_1 and E_2. We prefer to write them out explicitly.

Since in our logic of modal provability, $G^0 q = Gq$ and $G^0 \sim q = G \sim q$ for any atom q.

Example E1:

(a) $P = \{\neg b \rightarrow a\}$.
        Then
        $E_2 = G \sim b$

$E_3 = G^0([\sim\Box (x \to b)] \leftrightarrow a)$

$E(x) = G\sim b \wedge G^0(a \leftrightarrow \Diamond (x \wedge \sim b)))$

(b) $P = \{\neg a \to a\}$

$E(x) = G^0\{\sim\Box (x \to a) \leftrightarrow a\} = G^0(a \leftrightarrow \Diamond(x \wedge \sim a)))$

(c) $P = \{\neg b \to a, \neg a \to a\}$

$\qquad E_2 = G\sim b$

$\qquad E_3 = G^0((\sim\Box (x \to b) \vee \sim\Box (x \to a)) \leftrightarrow a)$

$E(x) = G\sim b \wedge G^0(a \leftrightarrow \Diamond (x \wedge \sim a) \vee \Diamond (x \wedge \sim b))$

(d) $P = \{a \to b, \neg a \to b, a \to a\}$

$E(x)$ is

$G^0((a \vee \sim\Box(x \to a)) \leftrightarrow b) \wedge G(a \leftrightarrow a).$

$= G(\Box f \vee (b \leftrightarrow a \vee \Diamond (x \wedge \sim a)))$

We now proceed to show that any program matrix $E(x)$ has a fixed point solution $x_0, x_0 \equiv E(x_0)$. We will investigate properties of the fixed point solution. We need some lemmas and definitions

Lemma L1:

Let P be a program. Then its matrix $E(x)$ satisfies $E(x) \to \Box E(x)$.

Proof:

By definition E is a conjunction of formulas beginning with G, and for all A, $GA \to \Box GA$.

Theorem T0:

Assume $E(x)$ is such that x occurs under the scope of $\Box$ and further assume that $E(x) \to \Box E(x)$. Let $E(t)$ be obtained by substituting t for x.

Then

$\quad E(E(t)) \equiv E(t)$

i.e. $E(t)$ is the unique fixed point solution of $x \equiv E(x)$.

Proof:

We show that at any s in any model $E(E(t))$ and $E(t)$ have the same truth values.

(1) If s is an endpoint then the value of $E(x)$ does not depend on x and so $E(t) \leftrightarrow E(E(t))$.

(2) If s is not an endpoint assume that

$E(t)$ and $E(E(t))$ have the same value at all points above s, we show that $E(t)$ and $E(E(t))$ have equal value at s. x occurs in $E(x)$ only under the scope of $\Box$ and therefore $E(x)$ depends for its truth value at s on the values of x at point above s. Since both $E(t)$ and $E(E(t))$ have the same value above s, we get that at s: $E(E(t)) \equiv E(E(E(t)))$.

we now show that $E(t) \equiv E(E(t))$ at s.

(a) $E(t) \models E(E(t))$ by lemma L2.

(b) Assume $E(E(t)$ is true at s. Hence $\Box E(E(t))$ is true at s because $\vdash E \to \Box E$. Hence $E(t)$ is true at s since from the point of view of s, $\Box (E(E(t)) \equiv t)$.

This completes the induction on the tree structure and hence proves the existence part of theorem T1. The uniqueness can be proved by the same induction on the tree model.

Definition D4:

Let P be a propositional Prolog program and let $E(x)$ be the associated provability matrix. Let **p** be the unique fixed point $p \equiv E(p)$ computed as in theorem T1. Then **p** is called the modal provability completion of P and is denoted by $m(P)$.

Theorem T1: (Gabbay - Terracini)

Let P be a program and let $E(x)$ be its matrix. Then $m(P)$, the fixed point solution to $x=E(x)$, is no other than $E(t)$.

Proof:

Follows from theorem T0 and the fact that $\vDash E \rightarrow \Box E$.

Theorems T1 give us a simple way of computing the fixed point of $E(x)$ **which carry over to predicate logic.** The proofs do not use the assumption that we are dealing with propositional logic.

Theorem T2:   (Modularity of the completion.)

Let P_i be any programs and let $E_i(x)$ be the associated matrices. Let $m(P_i)$ be the fixed point completion. i.e. we have:

$$E_i(m(P_i)) \equiv m(P_i).$$

Assume that P_i, P_j, for $i \neq j$ have no atoms in common.

Then:

$$m(\cup P_i) \equiv m(P_i)$$

Proof:

We prove a few lemmas.

Lemma L2:

Let A be such that $\vDash A \rightarrow \Box A$, and let $B(y_1,...,y_m)$ and $C_1,...,C_m$ any wffs. Then

$$A \vDash [B (\Box C_1,...,\Box C_m) = B(\Box (A \wedge C_1),..., \Box (A \wedge C_m))]$$

Proof:

If A is true then $\Box A$ is true and therefore inside $B(... \Box(A \wedge C_i) ...)$, the "A" within the scope of $\Box$ is **truth.** Hence we have really $B(... \Box (C_i \wedge truth)...)$ in the presence of the assumption A.

Lemma L3:

Let $E_1(x)$ and $E_2(x)$ be two wffs such that x occurs only under the scope of $\Box$. Let A_1 be the fixed point of $E_1(x)$ and A_2 be the fixed point of $E_2(x)$. Assume $\vDash E_1 \rightarrow \Box E_1$ and $\vDash E_2 \rightarrow \Box E_2$. Then $A_1 \wedge A_2$ is the fixed point of $E_1(x) \wedge E_2(x)$.

Proof:

From the assumptions we can represent $E_1(x)$ and $E_2(x)$ as:

$$E_1(x) = B_1(\Box C_{1,1}(x), ... , \Box C_{1,m}(x))$$
$$E_2(x) = B_2(\Box C_{2,1}(x),...,\Box C_{2,n}(x))$$

(1)   Assume $A_1 \wedge A_2$ and show

$E_1(A_1 \wedge A_2) \wedge E_2(A_1 \wedge A_2)$.

Proof of (1):

$A_1 \wedge A_2 \equiv E_1(A_1) \wedge E_2(A_2) \equiv$

$B_2(\Box C_{2,i}(A_2)) \wedge B_1(\Box C_{1,i}(A_1))$

From the previous lemma

$\equiv B_2(\Box C_{2,i}(A_1 \wedge A_2)) \wedge B_1(\Box C_{1,i}(A_1 \wedge A_2))$

$\equiv E_1(A_1 \wedge A_2) \wedge E_2(A_1 \wedge A_2)$

(2)   Assume $E_1(A_1 \wedge A_2) \wedge E_2(A_1 \wedge A_2)$ and show $A_1 \wedge A_2$

Proof of (2):

$E_1(A_1 \wedge A_2) \wedge E_2(A_1 \wedge A_2)$

   by using $A_i \equiv E(A_i)$

$\equiv E_2(E_1(A_1) \wedge A_2) \wedge E_1(A_1 \wedge E_2(A_2))$

   using the lemma L2 we get:

$\equiv E_2(E_1(A_1 \wedge A_2) \wedge A_2) \wedge E_1(E_2(A_1 \wedge A_2) \wedge A_1)$

Since $E_1(A_1 \wedge A_2) \equiv E_2(A_1 \wedge A_2) \equiv t$ as far as our assumptions are concerned we get:

$\equiv E_1(A_1) \wedge E_2(A_2) \equiv A_1 \wedge A_2$

This completes the proof of lemma L3.

We can now prove theorem T2.   Under the assumption of the theorem $E(P_1, x) \wedge E(P_2, x)$ $\equiv E(P_1 \cup P_2, x)$.   From the lemmas, again, the fixed point solution of $E(P_1 \cup P_2, x)$ is the conjunction of the fixed points of $E(P_i, x)$. Hence

   $m(P_1 \cup P_2) \equiv m(P_1) \wedge m(P_2)$.

Theorem T3: (Soundness for the case of no nested negations).

Let P be a program with negations on the atoms only and let g be an atomic goal. Then the following holds for the modal completion m(P), in N1:

$P?g = 1 \Rightarrow m(P) \vDash Gg$

$P?g = 0 \Rightarrow m(P) \vDash G(\sim g)$.

Proof:

By induction on the length of the computation of g from P. $\vDash$ means semantically follows in N1, in this proof.

Length 1:

If $P?g = 1$, then $g \in P$ as an assertion and therefore $Gg \in m(P)$ and hence $m(P) \vDash Gg$.

If $P?g = 0$, then g is not a head of any clause in P and hence $G\sim g \in m(P)$ and therefore $m(P) \vDash G(\sim g)$.

Length n:

Assume $P?g = 1$.

Then for some clause in P of the form $\bigwedge_j \neg a_j \wedge b_i \to g$

We have that

$P?b_i = 1$, for all i

$P?a_j = 0$, for all j.

Hence by the induction hypothesis, $m(P) \vDash Gb_i$, for all i and $m(P) \vDash G(\sim a_j)$, for all j.

The modal completion $m(P)$ contains the conjunct below

$$G(xf \vee [g \leftrightarrow (\bigwedge_i b_i \wedge \bigwedge_j (z \sim a_j)) \vee C]$$

where C is a disjunction of the translations of the bodies of the other clauses with the head g.

and so $m(P) \vDash G(\sim a_j) \rightarrow G(\Box f \vee \Diamond \sim a_j))$

we get

$m(P) \vDash G(g \vee \Box f)$ and hence $m(P) \vDash Gg$.

Assume $P?g = 0$.

Let for i=1,...,m

$A_i = \bigwedge_k \neg a_{i,j} \wedge \bigwedge_j b_{i,j} \rightarrow g$, be all the clauses in P with the head g.

Since g fails, for each i there exists a conjunct u_i in the body of clause A_i such that $P ? u_i = 0$.
We can assume that for some $0 \leq m_1 \leq m$

$u_i = b_{i,1}$ for $i \leq m_1$.

and

$u_i = \neg a_{i,1}$ for $i > m_1$.

We thus have

$P?b_{i,1} = 0$, for $i \leq m_1$.

$P?a_{i,1} = 1$, for $i > m_1$.

Hence by the induction hypothesis

$m(P) \vDash Ga_{i,1}, i > m_1$

$m(P) \vDash G \sim b_{i,1}, i \leq m_1$.

We want to prove

$m(P) \vDash G(\sim g \vee \Box f) \vDash G \sim g$.

$m(P)$ contains the conjunct

$$G[(g \leftrightarrow \bigvee_{i=1}^{m} ((\Diamond \sim a_{i,k} \wedge \bigwedge_j b_{i,j})) \vee \Box f]$$

which we rewrite as

$$G[(g \leftrightarrow \bigvee_{i=1}^{m} (\Diamond \sim a_{i,1}) \wedge b_{i,1} \wedge B_i) \vee \Box f]$$

where B_i denotes the rest of the i-th conjunction.

Let us check semantically when g can be true.

Take any model and any middle point s in the tree of the model (i.e. not an endpoint). $\Box f$ is false at s.

Hence from our assumptions for any $i > m_1$, $\Diamond (\sim a_{i,1} \wedge m(P))$ is false at s and for $i \leq m_1$, $b_{i,1}$ is false at

s. Thus each conjunct in the equation for g is false at s and hence g is false at s.

If s is an endpoint then g may be true or may be false.

We have proved

$m(P) \models G(\sim g \vee \Box f)$, and since our logic is N1, $m(P) \models G \sim g$.

This completes the proof of the Soundness Theorem.

Theorem T4: (Completeness).

Let P be a program with negation only on atoms and let g be an atomic goal.

Then:

$m(P) \models Gg$ in $N1 \Rightarrow P?g = 1$,

$m(P) \models G(\sim g)$ in $N1 \Rightarrow P?g = 0$,

Proof: (Due to L. Terracini)

Let $\quad Q_1 = \{q \mid P?q = 1\}$

$\qquad Q_0 = \{q \mid P?q = 0\}$

$\qquad Q_2 = \{q \mid P?q = loops\}$.

Construct a model with three points as in the diagram

$$\begin{array}{l} \ast\, c \\ \ast\, b \\ \bot\, a \end{array}$$

The root is a, i.e. a<b<c.

Let all atoms of Q_1 be true at all points. Let all atoms of Q_0 be always false.

Let all atoms of Q_2 be true at points a and c and false at point b. We claim that this is model of m(P). If we show this claim, then if $m(P) \models Gg$ then $P?g = 1$ and if $m(P) \models G\sim q$ then $P?g = 0$

To prove that we have a model of m(P) we look at E(P,x). m(P) is the solution x=E(P,x). We thus consider E(P,x) and we need only look at the conjunct

(*) $\quad G[\Box f \vee \bigwedge_i (q_i \leftrightarrow \bigvee_j B^*_{i,j})]$.

Also observe that at the top point c, $\Box f$ holds and hence (*) holds. Thus at the top point $E(x) \equiv t$ and since $x \equiv E(x)$, we get $x \equiv t$ at point c.

We now check the value of (*) at the point b. Each $B_{i,j}^*$ has the form

$$\bigwedge_k a_{i,j,k} \wedge \bigwedge_k Z(x \wedge \sim b_{i,j,k})$$

Since at c, x is t, $Z(x \wedge \sim b_{i,j,k})$ reduces to $Z \sim b_{i,j,k}$, which is true iff $\sim b_{i,j,k}$ is true at c and this holds iff $P?b_{i,j,k}=0$.

Similarly $a_{i,j,k}$ holds at b iff $P?a_{i,j,k}=1$. Thus $B_{i,j}^*$ holds at b iff $P?B_{i,j}=1$. It therefore follows that q_i holds at c iff $P?q_i=1$. Thus E(x) holds at b and hence $x \equiv t$ at b.

We now check the value of $E(x)$ at the point a. We look at $E(x)$ at a. Each $B_{i,j}{}^*$ is

$$\bigwedge_k a_{i,j,k} \wedge \bigwedge_k Z(x \wedge \sim b_{i,j,k}).$$

Since $x \equiv t$ at points b and c, $B_{i,j}{}^*$ is reduced to

$$\bigwedge_k a_{i,j,k} \wedge \bigwedge_k Z(\sim b_{i,j,k}).$$

$a_{i,j,k}$ holds at a exactly when $P?a_{i,j,k}$ loops or succeeds. $\Diamond \sim b_{i,j,k}$ holds at a again exactly when $P?b_{i,j,k}$ loops or fails i.e. $P?\neg b_{i,j,k}$ loops or succeeds. Hence $B_{i,j}{}^*$ holds at a exactly when $P?B_{i,j}$ does not finitely fail or equivalently $B_{i,j}$ is f at a iff $P?B_{i,j} = 0$. $\bigvee_j B_{i,j}{}^*$ is f at a iff all disjuncts $B_{i,j}{}^*$ are f at a which is exactly when $P?B_{i,j} = 0$ for all j.

We now show $q_i \leftrightarrow \bigvee B_{i,j}{}^*$ holds at a.

If $\bigvee B_{i,j}{}^*$ is f at a, then $P?B_{i,j}$ finitely fail for all j, hence $P?q_i$ finitely fail hence q_i is f at a by the definition of the model. If q_i is f at a, then $P?q_i = 0$ then $P?B_{i,j} = 0$ for each j and hence $\bigvee_j B_{i,j}$ is f at a because $x \equiv E(x)$ and $E(x)$ is t at a.
We thus proved our claim.

This concludes the proof of the theorem.

Remark R1 The case of nested negations:
Consider the Program P

$$P = \{\neg\neg a \rightarrow a\}$$

We have that $m(P) \equiv G(\Box f \vee (a \leftrightarrow Z\Box a))$

If we rewrite the program P as $P_1 = (a \rightarrow a)$ i.e. reducing $\neg\neg a$ to a, we get $m(P_1) \equiv (a \leftrightarrow a) \equiv$ **truth**.

The two completions are not the same.
Conceptually $\neg\neg a$ is not the same as a in the modal interpretation of $\neg$. This should not surprise us. In Peano arithmetic *not provable that not provable* a is not necessarily the same as *provable a*. Our modal provability logic is the logic of provability of Peano arithmetics as well as other systems.

Perhaps we can add more axioms to the modal logic for the special case of negation as failure. Since the problem is with nested negations, we try to check whether it matters in the calculation of $m(P)$ whether we put a or $\neg\neg a$ in P. We find that we need that $m(P) \equiv m(P_1)$ must be valid for any a. This means we need the axiom $G(\Box f \vee (a \leftrightarrow Z\Box a))$. This axiom is a "bad" axiom because $Z\Box a$ is always true because $\Box a$ is true at the end points. We thus have to make further technical changes in order to get a proper system N1* for which the translation of $\neg\neg A$ and of A are equivalent.

We observe, purely mathematically, that if we translate $\neg A$ as $\Box f \vee \sim\Box (x \rightarrow a)$, we get the following properties:

1 For programs without nested negations, the two matrices ($E(x)$ with $\neg A$ translated as $\Box f \vee \sim\Box (x \rightarrow A)$ and $E^*(x)$ with $\neg A$ translated as $\sim\Box (x \rightarrow A)$) are logically equivalent. Thus we can take the translation of $\neg A$ to be the *new* translation and all our results will still be valid. We can intuitively read the translation as: "if the modal translation of the program is consistent, then a is not provable form it",

which makes sense.

However, in case we take $\neg A$ as $\Box f \vee \sim\Box (x \rightarrow A)$, the additional axiom for making the translation of $\neg\neg A$ the same as A becomes: $\vdash z(zt \wedge \Box A) \leftrightarrow A$

This axiom is consistent, it can be added to N1 to form a consistent N1*, as shown in Appendix 1.

The reader could see that we needed the modification to overcome the problem of $\Box A$ being always true at endpoints.

The straightforward way is to eliminate nested negations as follows:

Given a clause with nested negations in it, for example the clause:

$\quad c \wedge \neg(\neg a \wedge b) \rightarrow d$

replace it by the two clauses

$\quad c\wedge a \rightarrow d$

$\quad c\wedge\neg b \rightarrow d$

If b does not exist, that is, we have $\neg\neg a$ then:

Replace $c\wedge\neg\neg a \rightarrow d$ by $c\wedge a \rightarrow d$.

Thus a program P with nested negation can be transformed to a unique program P_1 with all negations next to atoms. Since (in the propositional case, at least) we have for all g, P?g succeeds iff P_1?g succeeds, we can define m(P) as m(P1).

This approach to nested negations is simpler than modifying the modal logic.

Remark R2

The observant reader would have no doubt wondered at the simplicity of the counter model given in the proof of theorem T4. We are really using a three or four valued logic (compare Fitting 1985). Clearly all we need are three point models with assignments fff, ttt and tft. Applying negation we also get the value ftf. Thus the question is why do we need the machinery of modal provability at all.

The answer to the above question is computational. We obtain the assignment of values to the atoms by giving h(q) = ttt to q which succeed, h(q) = fff to q which finitely fails and h(q) = tft to q which loops. This assignment 'explains' semantically what the program does only *after* (or with the complete knowledge of how) the computation of program is carried out. A priori, just from the syntax of the program P, we cannot find the assignment h. However in the modal logic, we can get syntactically the completion m(P) and can use modal provability, to characterise Success or Failure.

To make my point even more strongly, I will quote one of my own theorems in Gabbay-Sergot 1985.

Theorem:

Given a program P without nested negations, let $q_1, ..., q_n$ be all the atoms appearing in P which finitely fail.

Let $P^* = P \cup \{\neg q_i\}$.

Consider P* as a theory of classical logic, reading $\neg A$ as classical negation. Then in classical logic:

1 P ? q = 1 implies $P^* \vdash q$

2 P ? q = 0 implies $P^* \vdash \neg q$

Proof: By induction on the length of the computation of q from P.

So if we know before carrying out the computation which q_i's finitely fail, we can reduce $\neg$ to classical negtion. The whole point of the completion is to do a 'syntactic analysis' using logic without carrying out the computation procedure.

1a Examples

Example E2:
Program $\neg b \to a$.
$E(x) = E_2 \wedge E_3$
$E_2 = G{\sim}b$
$E_3 = G^0 [{\sim}\square (x \to b) \leftrightarrow a] = G(\square f \vee (a \leftrightarrow \Diamond (x \wedge {\sim}b)))$

Thus in N1 the fixed point is $G{\sim}b \wedge Ga$, since in N1, $G(a \vee \square f) = Ga$, and this fixed point is the modal completion of the program $P = \{\neg b \to a\}$.
Indeed $m(P) \vdash \square{\sim}b$
$\qquad\quad m(P) \vdash \square a$
$\qquad\quad P\, ?\, b = 0$
$\qquad\quad P\, ?\, a = 1.$

Example E3:
This example shows that for a program without negations, the modal completion is essentially identical with the ordinary Clark completion.
Let P be $\{B_{i,j} \to q_j \mid i=1,\ldots,m,\; j = 1,\ldots,n\}$
$E(x)$ is not dependent on x (since no negation occurs) and it is $E \equiv E_1 \wedge E_2 \wedge E_3$ where:

$E_1 = \wedge Gq$ for any assertion clause q in P

$E_2 = \wedge G{\sim}a_k$, for any a_k occurring in P which is not a head of a clause

$E_3 = \underset{i}{\wedge}\; G^0(\underset{j}{\vee} B_{i,j} \leftrightarrow q_i).$

The fixed point of E is E itself since x does not appear in E. The modal logic acts on E the same way as classical logic, since Ga can be read as $a = t$ and $G{\sim}a$ as $a=f$. $G^0(x \leftrightarrow y)$ behaves like if and only if. Thus $m(P)$ behaves in the modal logic, like Clark's completion behaves in classical logic.

Example E4:
$P = \{\neg a \to a\}$

Translation:
$E(x) = G^0({\sim}\square (x \to a) \leftrightarrow a) = G(\square f \vee (a \leftrightarrow \Diamond ({\sim}a \wedge x)))$
Thus the modal completion of $\{\neg a \to a\}$ is $E(t) \equiv G(\square f \vee (a \leftrightarrow \Diamond {\sim}a))$
It is a consistent sentence of the modal logic.

Example E5:
P is:

$\neg b \to a$

$\neg a \to a$

We want to find $m(P)$, the fixed point. Note that b should fail and a should succeed.
$E(x) = G{\sim}b \wedge G^0[a \leftrightarrow (\Diamond (x \wedge {\sim}b) \vee \Diamond (x \wedge {\sim}a))]$
Since $E \vdash G{\sim}b$, we can simplify:

$E(x) \equiv G\sim b \wedge G^0[a \leftrightarrow (\Diamond (x \wedge \sim a) \vee \Diamond x)]$

    $\equiv G\sim b \wedge G^0[a \leftrightarrow \Diamond x]$

$E(t) \equiv G\sim b \wedge G(a \vee \Box f)$

This is indeed correct, since a succeeds and b fails, and in N1 the fixed point is equal to $G\sim b \wedge Ga$.

Example E6:

Consider the program P_1

$a \rightarrow b$

$\neg a \rightarrow b$

$a \rightarrow a$

b does not succeed from this program. However, Clark's completion is

    $b \leftrightarrow a \vee \neg a$

and it proves b.

Our completion should not prove b.

A variation of the above is the well known P_2:

$a \rightarrow b$

$\neg a \rightarrow b$

$a \rightarrow a$

$\neg b \rightarrow d.$

The ordinary Clark completion proves $\neg d$ even though d does *not* finitely fail

Let us check our modal completion of P_1.

$E(x) = G^0[(a \vee \sim \Box (x \rightarrow a)) \leftrightarrow b] \wedge G^0(a \leftrightarrow a)$

We can ignore $a \leftrightarrow a$ which is t.

$E(t) \equiv G^0[a \vee (b \vee \sim \Box a)] = G(\Box f \vee a \vee (b \leftrightarrow \Diamond \sim a)]$

It doesn't matter now what the above fixed point says exactly. What we have to check is that $m(P_1)$ does not prove Gb in N1, because b loops from the program. To see that we check that $m(P_1) \cup \{\sim Gb\}$ is consistent in N1 and this will show that the above completion does not prove Gb in N1.

The above is satisfiable in a three point model.

$$1 \quad \uparrow \quad \text{top}$$
$$2 \quad \wedge \quad \text{middle}$$
$$3 \quad | \quad \text{botton}$$

at 1 and 2 we have: $a = b = t$

at 3 we have: $a = b = f$

Notice that if $(a \rightarrow a)$ is taken out of the data then b does succeed.

Indeed, if $\{a \rightarrow a\}$ is taken out, a is no longer a head in the program

$P_0 = \{a \rightarrow b, \neg a \rightarrow b\}$ and hence $G\sim a$ should be added as a conjunct to the modal completion. In this case the completion is obtained by substituting $a = f$ in the fixed point $m(P_1)$ and we get

$m(P_0) \equiv G\sim a \wedge [m(P_1) \text{ with } a=f]$

    $\equiv G\sim a \wedge G(\Box f \vee b)$

This is equivalent in N1 to $G\sim a \wedge Gb$.

Example E7:

Let P be

   $\neg a \rightarrow b$

   $a \rightarrow b$

   $a \rightarrow a$

   $\neg b \rightarrow d$

Then E(x) is

$G^0((\Diamond (x \wedge \neg a) \vee a) \leftrightarrow b) \wedge G^0(a \leftrightarrow a) \wedge G^0([\Diamond (x \wedge \neg b)] \leftrightarrow d)$.

The modal completion m(P) is:

$m(P) \equiv E(t) \equiv G(\Box f \vee [\Diamond (\neg a) \vee a \leftrightarrow b]) \wedge$

    $\wedge G[\Box f \vee (\Diamond (\neg b) \leftrightarrow d)]$

We show a model in which m(P) is true and G(~d) is false.

Take a=b=f, d=t

Thus $m(P) \not\vdash G(\neg d)$ as indeed it should be the case since P ? d loops.

In this model also $m(P) \not\vdash Gb$.

Example E8:

Let us now check the program P_0, where

   $\neg a \rightarrow b$

   $a \rightarrow b$

and see whether indeed $m(P_0) \vdash Gb \wedge G\neg a$.

                    N1

$E(x) \equiv G\neg a \wedge G^0(b \leftrightarrow (a \vee \times (x \wedge \neg a)))$ which simplifies, since $E \vdash G\neg a$, to $G\neg a \wedge G(\Box f \vee (b \leftrightarrow \Diamond x))$

$E(t) \equiv G\neg a \wedge G(b \vee \Box f)$.

Example E9:

The Clark completion of $P \cup \{\neg c \rightarrow c\}$ is a contradiction, although c may have nothing to do with P, and all computation of goals from P still work. Our modal completion is modular in the different parts of the program.

Thus for example the completion of $(\neg b \rightarrow a)$ is $G\neg b \wedge G(a \vee \Box f)$. The completion of $\neg c \rightarrow c$ is given in example E4. Hence the completion of

   $\neg b \rightarrow a$

   $\neg c \rightarrow c$

is the conjunction, which is quite sensible.

Example E10:

Consider the program P with the following clauses:

(1)   c

(2) $\neg c \rightarrow b$

(3) $\neg b \rightarrow a$

(4) $\neg a \rightarrow d$.

From this program the goals c and a succeed and the goals b and d finitely fail.
The matrix E(x) is:

$E(x) \equiv Gc \wedge G[\Box f \vee ((b \leftrightarrow \Diamond (x \wedge \neg c)) \wedge (a \leftrightarrow \Diamond (x \wedge \neg b)) \wedge (d \leftrightarrow \Diamond (x \wedge \neg a)))]$

$\equiv Gc \wedge G(\Box f \vee (G(\Box f \vee \neg b) \wedge (a \leftrightarrow \Diamond (x \wedge \neg b)) \wedge (d \leftrightarrow \Diamond (x \wedge \neg a))))]$.

$\equiv$ Gc $\wedge$ G[$\Box$f $\vee$ ~b) $\wedge$ G($\Box$f $\vee$ ((a $\leftrightarrow$ $\Diamond$ (x $\wedge$ ~b) $\wedge$ (d $\leftrightarrow$ $\Diamond$ (x $\wedge$ ~a)))]

E(t) $\equiv$ Gc$\wedge$G~b $\wedge$ G($\Box$f $\vee$ (a $\wedge$ (d $\leftrightarrow$ $\Diamond$ ~a)))

Since we are interested only in N1 models, such models will force Ga to hold and hence also G~d. The other alternative also allowed by the above equation in **Pr** is Gc$\wedge$G~b $\wedge$ G(a$\leftrightarrow$~$\Box$f) $\wedge$ Gd.

However G(a$\leftrightarrow$~$\Box$f) is not allowed in N1 and hence only the solution Gc$\wedge$G~b $\wedge$ Ga$\wedge$G~d is allowed in N1.

Example E11:

Consider two programs P_1 = {¬b $\rightarrow$ a} and P_2 = P1 $\cup$ {b $\rightarrow$ b}., where b is not any head in P_1.

$m(P_1)$ = G~b $\wedge$ G(a $\vee$ $\Box$f) from example E2

$m(P_2)$ = G($\Box$f $\vee$ [a$\leftrightarrow$$\Diamond$ (G($\Box$f $\vee$ a) $\wedge$ ~b)])

Notice the modularity, $m(P_1)$ = $m(P_2)$ $\wedge$ G ~ b.

Indeed $m(P_2)$ $\wedge$ G~b is equivalent to

G~b $\wedge$ G($\Box$f $\vee$ (a$\leftrightarrow$$\Diamond$ G($\Box$f $\vee$ a)))

$\equiv$ G~b $\wedge$ G(a $\vee$ $\Box$f)

Example E12:

We show why we need the logic N1, rather than use **Pr**.

Take **P** to be

   a

¬a $\rightarrow$ b

then a succeeds and b fails. E(x) is:

   Ga $\wedge$ G^0(($\Diamond$ (x $\wedge$ ~a)) $\leftrightarrow$ b)

which can be simplified to

   Ga $\wedge$ G(~b $\vee$ $\Box$f)

Since x does not appear here we get that

$m(P)$ = Ga $\wedge$ G(~b $\vee$ $\Box$f).

Clearly $m(P)$ $\models$ Ga in **Pr**

          $m(P)$ $\not\models$ G~b in **Pr**

but $m(P)$ $\models$ G ($\Box$f $\vee$ ~b) $\rightarrow$ G~b in N1

1b Comparison with Fitting's Three-valued Approach

I wanted to compare our approach with the 3-valued approach introduced by Fitting in 1985, to bring out the differences and the similarities. The approach uses Kleene's 3-valued logic, with values T, F and I, I stands for non determined. Each program P has a mapping φ_P associated with it, which maps sets S of signed atomic statements to sets of signed atomic statements as follows[2]:

1   q $\in$ φ_P(S) if q $\in$ P or for some clause of the form $\wedge$ a_i $\wedge\wedge$ ¬b_j $\rightarrow$ q $\in$ P we have that a_i $\in$ S and ¬b_j $\in$ S, for all i, j.

2   ¬q $\in$ φ_P(S) if for every clause of the form $\wedge$ a_i $\wedge\wedge$ ¬b_j $\rightarrow$ q $\in$ S, either there exists an i with ¬a_i $\in$ S, or there exists a j with b_j $\in$ S.

---

[2](See page 305 of Fitting's paper.) Note that we adapted his definition for the case of no nested negations. In general, for the case with nested negations, Fitting's definitions reduce to the case of non-nested negations (Fitting, page 308). Our method is to reduce syntactically first to the non nested case and then find the modal completion.

A set S is said to be a fixed point of φ_P iff $S = \varphi_P(S)$.

Two programs P_1, P_2 are considered equivalent if the associated mappings φ_{P_1}, φ_{P_2} have the same fixed points.

I suppose in the 3-valued approach we have to say that the 'logical content' of P is what is true or false in *all* fixed points of φ_P.

We are now ready to compare the two approaches.

Examples:

1   Consider the program $\{\neg a \rightarrow a\}$. This program has $\emptyset$ as its fixed point (Fitting (1985), example II, page 307). Its modal content (Example E4 of this paper) is G ($\Box f \vee (a \leftrightarrow \Diamond \sim a)$). We give a definite answer to what this program means.

2   Consider the two programs
$P_1 = \{\neg r \rightarrow q, \neg q \rightarrow r\}$
$P_2 = \{\neg r \rightarrow q, r \rightarrow r\}$

These two programs are equivalent according to the 3-valued approach. According to us they are not. We have

$m(P_1) = G(\Box f \vee((q \leftrightarrow \Diamond \sim r) \wedge (r \leftrightarrow \Diamond \sim q)))$
$M(P_2) = G(\Box f \vee(q \leftrightarrow \Diamond \sim r))$

The two modal completions are not the same.

3   Again, according to the 3-valued approach the following two programs are not equivalent:
$P_3 = \{r \vee \neg r \rightarrow r\}$
$P_4 = \{\neg r \rightarrow r\}$

P_3 can be rewritten as
$P_3' = \{\neg r \rightarrow r, r \rightarrow r\}$
P_3 is example III of Fitting's. It has $\emptyset$ as its least fixed point and $\{r\}$ as a maximal fixed point.
P_4 has only $\emptyset$ as its fixed point.
The modal completions are also not equivalent:
$m(P_4) = G(\Box f \vee(r \leftrightarrow \Diamond \sim r))$
$m(P_3) = G(\Box f \vee(r \leftrightarrow (r \vee \Diamond \sim r)))$
       $= G(\Box f \vee(\Diamond \sim r \rightarrow r))$
However, they behave differently in the presence of integrity constraints, our next point:

Discussion (Integrity constraints)

We see that in the 3-valued approach it is difficult to see differences in 'logical content' of P_3 and P_4. Neither of the 3-valued meanings give any values to any atom. In the modal completion, we get an answer to what these programs should mean.

Having a modal formula as a completion of a program, helps us understand what integrity constraints mean.

Consider the program P_1 and the integrity constraint $I = \{q \vee r, \neg (q \wedge r)\}$. The agreed reading of integrity constraints is meta-level. For example, we do not mean that the integrity constraint $a \vee \neg b$ is to be logically added to the program or database (what would you add for $a \vee \neg a$?), but we mean that the meta-level requirement is that either a be proved (ie succeed) from the program or $\neg$ b be proved (ie b finitely fails) from the program. Similarly $\neg(a \wedge \neg b)$ as an integirty constraint means that we do not want that both a and $\neg$ b succeed from the program.

How would the 3-valued approach handle this? The most natural meaning is to say that we have an integrity constrant on the fixed point operator φ_P and we expect (in the case of the integrity constraint a $\vee$ $\neg$ b), that either a is in all fixed points or $\neg$b is in all fixed points.

This requirement does not give us any new information. We cannot use it to narrow down the possibilities.

In the modal completion method, we can add the integrity constraints to the modal completion and thus narrow the possibilities.

Let MI $(a \vee \neg b) = Ga \vee G{\sim}b$

　　MI $(\neg(a \wedge \neg b)) = \Diamond{\sim}a \vee \Diamond b$

(MI stands for 'modal completion of integrity constraints').

Thus the completion of P_1 with the integrity constraints q $\vee$ r is:

$G(\Box f \vee((q \leftrightarrow \Diamond{\sim}r) \wedge (r \leftrightarrow \Diamond{\sim}q))) \wedge (Gq \wedge G{\sim}r) \vee (G{\sim}q \wedge Gr)$.

Consider as a further example, adding the integrity constraint $r \vee \neg$ r to the program P_4. The modal completion is:

$G(\Box f \vee(r \leftrightarrow \Diamond{\sim}r)) \wedge (Gr \vee G{\sim}r) = f$

The requirements and the program are contradictory.

This does not exclude us from adding the clause r to the program and getting r to succeed. We then get a new program $\{\neg r \rightarrow r, r\}$ and its modal completion is Gr. What is contradictory is to require one of two options (ie r succeeds or finitely fails) from the program $\{\neg r \rightarrow r\}$ which has *none of these options*.

If we add the same integrity constraints $(r \vee \neg r)$ to the program P_3, we get as completion:

　　$G(\Box f \vee(\Diamond{\sim}r \rightarrow r)) \wedge (Gr \vee G{\sim}r) = Gr$

We see now that P_3 does not give us the option for r to succeed while P_4 does not. These facts are not reflected in the 3-valued approach, becuse the only fixed set of P_4 is $\emptyset$ which is less restrictive than the two fixed sets of P_3, namely $\emptyset$ and $\{r\}$.

We see that the true metalevel meaning of integrity constraints can be easily and natrually brought forward in the object level (ie using conjunction of $m(P) \wedge MI(I)$) of the modal completion logic.

2　Negation by failure in the presence of Quantifiers

We presented our modal completion for the propositional case. What about quantifiers? This presents no logical problems as long as we are careful. There are difficulties with negation by failure and variables especially in relation to instantiation. We are not concerned with these difficulties because they are not of a logical nature. Whatever solutions are found to these difficulties they will automatically transfer to our modal case. This paper solves the logical difficulties with negation as failure. If we assume that we always delay and never negate $\neg A(x)$ unless x is instantiated, then success of a goal $G(z_j)$ from a database (program) $P(x_i)$ means that for some fully instantiating substitution θ(for z_j) $\forall x_i P(x_i)$? $G(z)\theta = 1$

Let P_1 be the result of substituting all possible terms for x_i, then we get that $P_1?G(z)\theta = 1$ via a propositional computation!! If P_1 is finite then we can take $m(P)$ to be $m(P_1)$. Otherwise we must show how to compute $m(P)$ directly as a fixed point in a predicate modal provability logic. This is our task in this section. Note that we *must assume* that $\neg A(x)$ is *always* computed after full instantiation, i.e. we are reading $\neg A(x)$ as for some $x\theta$, $A(x\theta)$ fails.

Our work will probably extend to any version of negation as failure and quantifiers which makes logical sense. See the Shepherdson papers.

Example E13:
Let P be the program
R(a,b)
$\neg R(x,y) \rightarrow R(y,x)$.

The propositional reading of this program is obtained by substituting all possible terms in the rules. If there are infinitely many terms, we get an infinite database:

   R(a,b)

$\neg\ R(a,b) \rightarrow R(b,a)$

$\neg\ R(b,a) \rightarrow R(a,b)$

$\neg\ R(a,a) \rightarrow R(a,a)$

$\neg\ R(b,b) \rightarrow R(b,b)$.

The matrix for this program is:

$E(q) = GR(a,b) \wedge G(\Box f \vee A(q))$

where $A(q)$ is the conjunction of the following:

$R(b,a) \leftrightarrow \Diamond (q \wedge \sim R(a,b))$

$R(a,b) \leftrightarrow \Diamond (q \wedge \sim R(b,a))$

$R(a,a) \leftrightarrow \Diamond (q \wedge \sim R(a,a))$

$R(b,b) \leftrightarrow \Diamond (q \wedge \sim R(b,b))$

As a propositional program the fixed point solution q_0 can prove in **Pr** both GR(a,b) and G($\Box f \vee$ $\sim R(b,a)$)   and no more.   In N1 $\models$ G($\Box f \vee$ B) $\rightarrow$ GB, for B a literal, and hence $q_0 \models$ G$\sim$R(b,a) in N1.

The matrix can be written in predicate logic as:

$E(q) = GR(a,b) \wedge G(\Box f \vee \forall xy\ [R(x,y) \leftrightarrow \Diamond (q \wedge \sim R(y,x))])$

By theorem T6 of the previous section, the fixed point solution to $q=E(q)$ is $E(t)$.

Definition D5:
Let P be a Prolog program with negation by failure in the body of clauses. Let the clauses be of the form
$H_i(x)$ if $B_{i,j}(x,y) \wedge \neg D_{i,j}(x,y)$
where $H_i(x)$ is the i-th head with the variables $x = (x_1,...,x_{n,i})$ and $B_{i,j}$ and $D_{i,j}$ are conjunctions of negationless atomic wffs which may contain additional variables from $y = (y_1,...,y_{m,i,j})$. To be able to write any Program in this form we must use the equality symbol = and rewrite an assertion like R(a,b) as

   $R(x_1,x_2)$ if $x_1 = a \wedge x_2=b$.

and assertions like $R(x_1,x_3)$ as

   $R(x_1,x_3)$ if truth.

Let E(q), the matrix associated with the program P, be the following conjunction (a)∧(b)∧(c).

(a) G(uc)A, for any assertion A (uc means universal closure).

(b) $G(\Box f \vee \wedge (\forall x) \, H_i(x) \leftrightarrow (\exists y) \, _j \, (B_{i,j} \wedge \Diamond \, (q \wedge \sim D_{i,j})))$

(c) G(uc)~Q

for any atomic Q appearing in the program but is not the head of any clause or assertion.

Our matrix is essentially G($\Box$f ∨ Clark's completion).

The modal provability completion of a program P is the fixed point q_0 of its matrix equation q=E(q).

Example E14:

Consider the program P

Q(a) → B

¬Q(a) → B

Q(g(x)) → Q(x)

The matrix for P is:

$E(q) = G(\Box f \vee [B \leftrightarrow (Q(a) \vee \Diamond (q \wedge \sim Q(a)))]) \wedge \forall x[Q(x) \leftrightarrow \exists y(y=g(x) \wedge Q(y))]]$

The fixed point is $G(\Box f \vee [B \leftrightarrow (Q(a) \vee \Diamond \sim Q(a))]) \wedge G \, \forall x[Q(x) \leftrightarrow Q(g(x))]$.

Notice that the fixed point of the program

Q(a) → B

¬Q(a) → B

is the first conjunct above.

See example E6 of Section 1.

Theorem T5:

Let P be a predicate logic program without nested negations and let E(q) be the associated provability matrix. Then E(t) is the fixed point solution of q≡E(q). We have that for any atomic goal Q and substitution θ.

(a) P?Qθ=1 iff E(t) ⊨ GQθ

(b) P?Qθ=0 iff E(t) ⊨ G~Qθ

We assume Qθ is ground.

Proof:

That E(t) is the fixed point follows from theorems T6-T7. The completeness and soundness proofs carry over from the propositional case.

Let us now consider fixed point solution of infinite propositional programs. This represent another point of view at predicate logic programs, where we substitute all terms in the predicate program and get a propositional program.

Definition D6:

(a) The infinite propositional modal logic allows for infinite conjunctions and disjunctions as well as finite ones. Thus

   (1)   Any atom q is a wff

   (2)   If A is a wff, so are ~A and $\Box$A

(3) If A_i are wffs i=1,2, ... so are $\bigwedge_i A_i$, $\bigvee_i A_i$

(b) The semantical interpretation for this calculus is the same as for the finite case. We have to know that

(1) $\| \bigwedge_i A_i \| (h,t) = \textbf{truth}$ iff for all i, $\| A_i \| (h,t) = \textbf{truth}$.

(c) An infinite Program $\mathbf{P}$ is simply a program with infinite number of clauses. Each clause is finite.

Define E(P,x) in the usual way i.e.

$$E(P,x) = \bigwedge_{q \in H^+(P)} Gq \wedge \bigwedge_{q \in H^-(P)} G\sim q \wedge \bigwedge_i G^0(q_i \leftrightarrow \bigvee_j B_{i,j})$$

In this case the $\wedge$ and $\vee$ may be infinite. There may be infinite number of heads and for each head an infinite number of possible bodies in the program.

In general we are not promised a fixed point for a matrix of the form $E(x) = B(\Box C_i (x))$, where B may be infinite and the number of $\Box C_i(x)$ may be infinite. Even if there happens to be a solution $x_0 = E(x_0)$, we may not be able to compute it finitely. The method outlined for the finite case uses induction on the number of $\Box C_i(x)$ in B.

However, in our case the matrix E(x) is of special form, it satisfies $E(x) \to xE(x)$. Theorem T1 shows that E(t) is the fixed point and E(t) can be computed.

The following is a summary of the way we see the computation in predicate logic. When we write

$$P(x) ? G(y)$$

the logical meaning is:

$$\forall x \, P(x) \vdash^? \exists y \, G(y)$$

(x and y are the free variables in the program and goal respectively). We have the same meaning when negation by failure is present in P and G. So let us understand

$$P(x) ? G(y)$$

as follows:

Let $\theta_1, \theta_2, \theta_3, \ldots$ be all possible *ground* substitutions to x and $\eta_1, \eta_2, \eta_3, \ldots$ be all possible ground substitutions to y.

Then success of the above means *propositional success* of

$$\{D(x)\theta_1, D(x)\theta_2, \ldots \mid D(x) \in P(x)\} ? G(y) \eta_j \text{ for some j.}$$

In other words:

$$(*) \quad \bigwedge_{D \in P} \bigwedge_{i=1}^{\infty} D\theta_i \, ? \bigvee_{j=1}^{\infty} G\eta_j$$

succeeds propositionally.

Let us check the following example.

$D(x) = \neg q(x) \rightarrow p$

$\quad G = p$

Assume we have constants $a_1, a_2, \ldots$ The query is then

$\{ \neg q(a_1) \rightarrow p, \neg q(a_2) \rightarrow p, \ldots \}$? p

The query p should succeed. If we perform the computation in Prolog we get:

$$\neg q(x) \rightarrow p \, ? \, p$$

unify and ask

$$? \neg q\,(x)$$

In SLDNF resolution we flounder, we cannot continue and ask

$$? \, q\,(x)$$

because x is not grounded. However, in G-SLDNF resolution we are allowed to choose a substitution, and when it is grounded it will succeed. If we want to obtain all possible choices of substitution which will make it succeed, we can use anti-unification here[3].

3   What is negation by failure?   (A proposed view)

I would like to see negation by failure as a pure logical concept. To explain this point of view let us consider an arbitrary logical system L, one which may have nothing to do with computing. This system has its own notion of theoremhood and consequence. Let us denote by $\vdash$ the consequence relation of this system. Thus if P is a set of sentences of the logic and A is a well formed formula of the logic, P $\vdash$ A reads that A follows from P in the logic L.

Depending on the nature of L there may be several proof procedures for checking whether A follows in L from P. There may be Gentzen type systems, natural deduction systems, various theorem proving systems and the like. Certainly in the case of classical logic, intuitionistic logic, relevance logics and the various modal logics, there are many different systems for checking consequence.

If we consider only proof systems which are sound and complete, they would all agree in the case when $P \vdash_L A$, but may behave differently when $PO_L A$. In the latter case, some proof systems may loop, while other may finitely fail in different ways. Thus if s and s' are two proof systems then for all P, A

$$P \vdash_L A \quad \text{iff} \quad P \Vdash_s A \quad \text{iff} \quad P \Vdash_{s'} A$$

where $P \Vdash_s A$ means that the particular proof procedure s for establishing whether A follows in L from P is successful.

Thus $\Vdash$ is more than a logical consequence relation. It is a consequence relation together with a particular computational way of establishing whether it holds.

If it gives us a computation to check whether $\vdash$ holds, it is quite possible that in many occasions one can positively show for some P and A that the computation of $\Vdash$ finitely fails. We can now add a new symbol $\neg$ to the language of L, and read $P \Vdash \neg A$ as A finitely fails from P in the computation

---

[3] I stress the importance here of anti-unification when I ask ? $\neg A(x)$. I want all such η such that $\neg A\eta$
succeeds, ie $A\eta$ fails. So I can find all θ or the most general θ such that $A\theta$ *succeed* and then look for η' such that
$A\eta'$ can *never* unify with $A\theta$. This will ensure that $A\eta'$ fails. η' is the anti-unifier for θ.

procedure of $\Vdash$. Provided we can define in a natural way the basic inductive step for failure from $\Vdash$, we can form a new logic L(s), for a language with the additional $\neg$, and define its computation procedures using $\Vdash$. Different computation procedures s and s' may give rise to different logic L(s'). They may be related but they need not be the same. We may attempt to characterise s and s' in terms of the logical systems L(s) and L(s') and their relationship to L itself.

From the point of view of logic, different theorem provers s and s' for the same logic L need not necessarily be viewed as different "implementations" of the same logic, or different "practical" ways of proving theorems for L. They can be viewed as *new logics*, with possibly different notions of failure giving rise to different L(s) and L(s').

The above may not be particularly interesting to the practical logic programmer, but it does have theoretical value for the foundations of negation by failure. Here is a typical possible conjecture:

Conjecture:

Let L be a non monotonic logical system based on a propositional language with $\rightarrow$, $\wedge$, and $\neg$ only. Assume we are dealing with wffs of the form $(\bigwedge a_i \wedge\bigwedge \neg b_j) \rightarrow q$, $\bigwedge a_i \wedge\bigwedge \neg b_j \rightarrow \neg q$. Assume that the consequence relation $\Vdash_L$ is guaranteed to satisfy modus ponens, reflexivity but not necessarily any other properties. Further assume that for every theorem prover s for it we have that the following schemes holds:

$$\frac{P \Vdash_s A;\ P, B \Vdash_s \neg A}{P \Vdash_s \neg B}$$

and

$P \Vdash A \neg B$ iff ($P \Vdash A$ implies $P \Vdash B$)

and

$$\frac{P \Vdash_s \neg A;\ P, B \Vdash_s A}{P \Vdash_s \neg B}$$

$P \not\Vdash_s$ **a, for any atom a not appearing in P.**

Then L is "essentially" the usual Horn clause computational logic, with $\neg$ interpreted as negation by failure.

End of conjecture.

I don't know whether the above is true or false. It is certainly true for Horn clause Prolog with negation by failure.

There are various extensions and variations of Prolog, with their own notion of failure, for example N-Prolog. The above view of negation by failure can characterise theoretically the different negations. The

point of view shows the essential modal provability nature of negation. ¬A means finite failure in the compuatation procedure s. This is a general point of view.

We saw that for the case of Prolog programs P, the fixed point of E(P,x) can be computed easily by substituting x=t.

This means that we can take the Clark completion of P, *Com*(P); replace each "¬A" by "◇~A", put G in front and we get our modal completion. So why go through all the trouble of talking about fixed points, modal provability etc, etc.?!

The answer to that is three fold. First, as we explained above, the real notion for negation by failure is the notion of non-provability. Thus introducing the general concepts explains things better. Otherwise it looks like a logic "hack".

Second and, more importantly, there are extensions of Prolog around, N-Prolog, near-Horn Prolog, etc. They all have notions of failure and may not (in fact, certainly not, in some cases, eg N-Prolog) satisfy the nice theorem we have here. We therefore do need the general logic of modal provability and the fixed point calculations. This we leave to another part of this paper.

The third point does not concern logic programming directly but the community of logicians working on modal provability. It is worth pointing out again, that we did not in this paper just cook up a logic for explaining negation by failure and for producing a new completion. We presented a conceptual connection between two well established areas of logic, the area of Modal Provability where researchers needs to compute fixed points and the area of Logic Programming where the researchers do compute exactly that. This is a new application of Logic Programming to General Logic. It may not matter to the modal logician whether we can explicitly express fixed points in modal predicate logic. It may be quite sufficient for him to identify the fixed point implicitly via a Prolog Program!

This direction of research we also leave for another part of this paper.

The Logic Programmer should take Modal Logic seriously. Many of his day to day operations have modal meaning.

Let us pursue this point of view further. What other modal operations do we perform when we program in Prolog?
A common one is the running several programs in several windows and letting them communicate. Let P_1 and P_2 be two programs sharing some common predicates. We can ask goals of the form:

   P_1 ? A∧WB

where W sends the goal B to be asked from P_2 and brings back a successful instantiation. When we ask

   P_2 ? WB

then W sends B as a goal to P_1 and brings back any successful instantiation. (This is actually how a two window system is implemented in the Fraunhoffer Institute in Stuttgart). If we allow for W in the goal we can also put it in the body of clauses. Thus WA becomes an operator of the Prolog language just like ¬A. It is a modal operator. P_i can be thought of as a possible world, and WB sends the goal B to another world.

Example E15:
Let P_1 be the propositional program with the following clauses.

(1)   Wb → a

(2) c → a

(3) Wd → b

(4) Wc → d.

and let P2 contain:

(5) Wc ∧ b → a

(6) Wd → b

(7) Wc → d

(8) c

The computation rule for W is as indicated, namely:

Computation rule for W:

(1) P_1 ? WA = 1 iff P_2 ? A = 1

and

(2) P_2 ? WA = 1 iff P_1 ? A = 1

In case we have several programs, $P_1,...,P_n$ we have to index the W, or agree on a cycle. We can either have for example:

P_i ? W_j A =1 iff P_j ? A = 1

or possibly we can agree on:

P_i ? WA = 1 iff P_{i+1} ? A = 1 for i < n

and

P_n ? WA = 1 iff P_1 ? A = 1.

Why have we mentioned all of this? The reason is that negation by failure for *stratified* programs (i.e. where no head H depends in its computation on ¬H) is *not negation at all* but a modal operator W.

The Programs P_1 and P_2 mentioned above illustrate this point:
Rewrite P_1 by reading "W" as "¬" and get P_1* below:

(1*)   ¬b → a

(2*)   c → a

(3*)   ¬d → b

(4*)   ¬c → d.

For ¬A to succeed we need A to fail. Looking at failure from P_1* we get a positive program P_2*:
P_2*:

(5*)   fail c ∧ b → fail a

(6*)   d → fail b

(7*)   c → fail d

(8*)   fail c.

Thus to succeed with the goal A we ask P_1* ? A. To fail with the goal A we ask P_2* ? fail A i.e. we ask positively the goal "fail A". The programs P_1 and P_2 exactly do that. P_2 is the positive program describing how to fail from P_1.

This idea is not new and has been explored by several authors. In predicate program it can be done easily *when all the variables appearing in the body of any clause appear in the head of that clause.*

I brought this up simply to point out the modal nature of some actual Prolog practice.

Appendix 1   Modal Provability

The propositional modal logic of provability **Pr** is obtained by extending the propositional modal logic **K4** with the axiom schema of Löb, namely:

$$\Box(\Box q \rightarrow q) \rightarrow \Box q$$

It is complete for the class of all Kripke Models with finite irreflexive trees.

Solovay has shown that the modality $\Box$ of this logic captures exactly the syntactical provability properties of Gödel's proof predicate of Peano's Arithmetic. He has shown the following:

Let $A(q_1,...,q_n)$ be any wff of the above modal logic, **Pr**.

Let A^* be the formal translation of A obtained by formally replacing $\Box x$ by *Prov*(x) in A, where *Prov* is the proof predicate of Peano's Arithmetic. Then the following holds!

Theorem T1:

$A(q_1,...,q_n)$ is not a theorem of our modal logic if and only if for some sentences $Q_1,...,Q_n$ of Peano Arithmetic $A^*(Q_1,...,Q_n)$ is not a theorem of Peano's Arithmetic.

The above modal logic **Pr** has the further property, which is what we need for our study of negation by failure:

Theorem T2:

Let $A(x)$ be any wff of the modal logic with the property that x always appears in the scope of a modality $\Box$. Then there exists a unique (up to logical equivalence) modal wff q_0 such that modal logic $\vdash q_0 \leftrightarrow A(q_0)$.

q_0 is the fixed point of the equation $x \leftrightarrow A(x)$. It is this property which gives rise to various Gödel sentences in Arithmetic.

We need not go more into detail about this modal logic and its relation to Arithmetic. The reader can look up the references. There are several books on the subject, Boolos 1979 and Smorynski 1985.

For our purposes, the reader should note that we are not cooking up here a special modal logic for the purpose of explaining negation by failure, but we are linking two independently existing and interesting concepts, well known and well used; namely the logic of modal provability and the concept of negation by failure. We are showing an intimate connection between the two notions and we are solving some difficulties associated with negation by failure.

Let us formally define the modal logic of provability and study its properties.

Definition D0:

Consider a modal language with the classical connectives ~, ∧, ∨, →, and with the unary modal operator $\Box A$.

Let t denote **truth** and f denote **falsity**. t and f are atomic constants. Let GA be $A \wedge \square A$.

Let $\Diamond A$ be $\sim \square \sim A$.

Consider the following axiom system **Pr** for the language with $\square$.

(1) $\vdash A$ if A is substitution of a classical truth functional tautology.

(2) $\vdash \square(A \rightarrow B) \rightarrow (\square A \rightarrow \square B)$

(3) $\vdash \square A \rightarrow \square \square A$

(4) $\vdash \square(\square A \rightarrow A) \rightarrow \square A$

(5) The rules $\vdash A$

$\vdash \square A$

(6) and $\vdash A \rightarrow B, \vdash A$

$\vdash B$

Let $A \equiv B$ be $\vdash A \leftrightarrow B$.

Defnition D1:

The following is a semantical interpretation for propositional **Pr**.

(a) A model is a finite tree $(T, <, h)$ with an assignment h giving each atomic wff q a subset $h(q) \, b \, T$. T is subset of points. $<$ is transitive and irreflexive. $h(q)$ is the set of points where q is true.

(b) The truth value of a wff A at a point $t \in T$ under the assignment h is defined by induction and is denoted by $\| A \| (h,t)$.

$\|q\| (h,t) = $ **truth** iff $t \in h(q)$

$\| A \wedge B \| (h,t) = $ **truth** iff $\|A\| (h,t) = $ **truth** and $\|B\| (h,t) = $ **truth**.

(c) Similarly for $\vee$, $\rightarrow$ and $\sim$.

(d) $\| \square q \| (h,t) = $ **truth** iff $\forall y \, (t<y \rightarrow \|q\| (h,y) = $ **truth**).

Theorem T3:

For any A

Pr $\vdash A$ iff for all models $(T,<,h)$ and all $t \in T$, $\|A\| (h,t) = $ **truth**.

Proof:

See Boolos's book or Smorynsky's book.

Theorem T4: (Propositional fixed point theorem).

In the propositional case, let $E(x)$ be a propositional modal formula with the atomic variable x, and possibly other atoms. Assume that all occurrences of the letter x are within the scope of $\times$. Then there exists a unique (up to $\models$ equivalence) modal propositional formula A (not containing x) such that $\vdash A \leftrightarrow E(A)$.

Proof:

First we prove existence. From the assumption on E, $E(x)$ can be written (not necessarily uniquely) in the form:

$E(x) = B(\square C_1(x), \dots , \square C_n(x)),$

where $B(y_1, ... ,y_n)$ is another wff built up from the variables $y_1,...,y_n$, and $E(x)$ is obtained from B by substituting $y_i =\Box C_i(x)$. We prove the theorem by induction on n. For n=1 let $A_0 = B(\textbf{truth})$ (i.e. substitute **truth** for $\Box C_1(x)$ in B).

Let $A = E(A_0)$. We claim that $A=E(A)$. This follows from the fact that $\Box C_1 (E(A_0))$ and $\Box C_1(A_0)$ have the same truth value at any node $t \in T$ of any Pr modal structure (irrespective of whether it satisfies the restrictions of N1 modal structures), which can be proved by considering, in any structure, a first node from the top in which the values of $\Box C_1(A_0)$ and $\Box C_1(E(A_0)$ differ (remember our trees are drawn upwards). Assume that at all nodes above t, $\Box C_1 (E(A_0))$ and $\Box C_1 (A_0)$ have identical truth value. We show that the same holds at t.

Case 1.   Assume $\Box C_1(A_0)$ is true at t. Hence since $\vdash \Box D \to \Box\Box D$ for any D we get $\Box C_1 (A_0)$ is **truth** at all points above t.   We have by definition that $\Box C_1(E(A_0)) = \Box C_1(B(\Box C_1(A_0)))$ but since $\Box C_1 (A_0)$ is **truth** for our case we get

$\equiv \quad \Box C_1 (B(\textbf{truth}))$

$\equiv \quad \Box C_1 (A_0)$.

Case 2.   Assume$\Box C_1 (E(A_0))$ is true at t. Again since this is a necessitated statement we get that $\Box C_1 (E(A_0))$ is equivalent to **truth** at all points above t.
Hence

$\Box C_1 (A_0) \quad \equiv \Box C_1(B(\textbf{truth}))$

$\equiv \Box C_1(B(\Box C_1(E(A_0))))$

and since above t we assumed $\Box C_1(E(A_0)) \equiv \Box C_1(A_0)$, we get:

$\equiv \Box C_1(B(\Box C_1(A_0)))$

$\equiv \Box C_1 (E(A_0))$

This proves the case n=1.

For the induction step, n=m+1, let z be a new propositional letter and write $E^*(x,z)$ to be $B(\Box C_1(x), ... ,\Box C_m(x), \Box C_{m+1}(z))$. Apply the case of n=1 for the variable z. We get a formula $A^*(x)$ such that $A^*(x) \equiv E(x, A^*(x))$. The proof of the case n=1 shows that $A^*(x)$ is:

(#): $A^*(x) = B(\Box C_1(x), ... ,\Box C_m(x), \Box C_{m+1} (B(\Box C_1(x), ... ,\Box C_m(x), \textbf{truth})))$

The inductive hypotheis applies to $A^*(x)$ to produce an A with $A \equiv A^*(A)$. A is a fixed point of $E(x)$ because

$E(A) \equiv E^*(A,A) \equiv E^*(A,A^*(A)) \equiv A^*(A) \equiv A$.

The uniqueness of the fixed point is immediate by induction on the tree of the model.

This concludes the proof of theorem T4.

Theorem T4 is true only in propositional logic. In the predicate case there may be an $E(x)$ with no syntactically defined formula A such that $A\equiv E(A)$. Semantically one can always define such an A, but we need to extend the syntax of our modal logic with special fixed point operators to enable us to give a syntactical representation for the semantically definable A. See Example E2 in section 2 for more details.

Theorem T5:

(a) The unique x_0 for $E(x)$ is effectively computable (via a computer program)

(b)   The logic **Pr** is decidable

Proof:

(a)   The algorithm is given in section 1 of this paper.

(b)   Since **Pr** is both finitely axiomatizable and is characterised by finite models.

We are now ready to define the logic for expressing negation by failure. We call this logic **N1**; it is an extension of **Pr**. We first explain it semantically. **Pr** is complete for models with finite trees. Thus the following are two **Pr** models for the atomic q.

Remember we draw trees going up.

$$q = t \nwarrow \qquad \nearrow q = f$$
$$q = t$$
$$q = t$$

Diagram 1

$$q = t \nwarrow \qquad \nearrow q = f$$
$$q = t$$
$$q = f$$

Diagram 2

The models of **N1** are only some of the models of **Pr**. These are the models which satisfy the following restriction of every atom q.

(a) If q is true at all non-endpoints then q is true at all endpoints as well.

(b)   If q is false at all non-endpoints then q is false at all endpoints as well.

(c) There are at least three point $t_1 < t_2 < t_3$.

In other words, **N1** restricts the assignment h in such a way that if h assigns a constant value to any atom q at all the middle (non-end) points then h must give the same value to all endpoints. Thus Diagram 1 is not acceptable as an **N1** model but Diagram 2 is a good **N1** model.

Since the models of **N1** are only some of the models of **Pr**, **N1** proves more theorems than **Pr**. Of course all fixed point calculations done in **Pr** are also valid for **N1**. If $x \equiv E(x)$ holds in every **Pr** model it certainly holds in every **N1** model. Though since **N1** is a stronger logic, there may be more fixed points in **N1**. In **Pr**, recall, there is a unique fixed point.

To check whether $A \vdash_{N1} B$, we can check whether B holds in any **N1** model in which A holds.

This can be done semantically, but it would be nice to have an axiom system for **N1**. This we give now. The completeness proof can be found later.

Definition D2:

Let **N1** be the modal system with the following axioms and rules:

(1)   ⊢A, if A is a substitution instance of a classical truth functional tautology.

(2)   The schemas:

    (a) ⊢ □(A → B) → (□A → □B)

    (b) ⊢ □(□(A → B) → (□A → □B))

(3)   The schemas:

    (a) ⊢ □A → □□A.

    (b) ⊢ □(□A → □□A)

(4)   The schemas:

    (a) ⊢ □(□A → A) → □A

    (b) ⊢ □[□(□A → A) → □A].

(5)   For every atom q.

    (a) ⊢ □(q ∨ □f) → □q

    (b) ⊢ □(~q ∨ □f) → □~q

    (c) ⊢ ◇◇t

(6)   ⊢ A, ⊢A → B

    ⊢B

Notice that the rule of necessitation in the formulation of **Pr** was dropped and instead we added the new axioms of the form □ (old axiom) for each of the old axioms (1)-(4). Note that we do not allow closure under substitution. There is no reason to insist on axiomatising a logic with the rule of substitution. The notion of a 'logic' is understood as a 'consequence relation', ⊢ , satisfying Reflexivity, Monotonicity and Cut. ⊢$_{N1}$ certainly satisfies these requirements.

Theorem T6:
If **Pr** ⊢ A then **N1** ⊢ A.
Proof:
By induction on the length of the proof of A from the axioms. First show that if B is a **Pr** axiom then **N1** ⊢ □^{m}B for any m. This holds for m=1 and since **N1** ⊢□B → □□B we get that **N1** ⊢ □^{m}B for any m.

Lemma L1:
For any B, if **Pr** ⊢ B then **N1** ⊢ B and further **N1** ⊢ □^{m}B for all m.

Proof:
By induction on the length of the proof π of B in **Pr**.
Length 1:
Then B is an axiom of **Pr** and so B, and □^{m}B are provable in **N1** as we showed earlier.
Length n+1:
Let the proof of B be D$_1$,...,D$_{n+1}$ = B.
Then there are three cases.
(a) B is an axiom, in which case **N1** ⊢ B ∧ □^{m}B for all m.
(b)   B is obtained from two previous D$_i$, D$_j$ by modus ponens i.e. D$_j$ = D$_i$ → B.

By the induction hypothesis $N1 \vdash D_j$ and $N1 \vdash D_i$ and hence $N1 \vdash B$. Further $N1 \vdash \Box^m D_j$ = $\Box^m(D_i \to B)$ hence $N1 \vdash \Box^m D_i \to \Box^m B$ and since by the induction hypothesis $N1 \vdash \Box\Box^m Di$ we get that $N1 \vdash \Box^m B$.

(c)B is obtained from a previous D_i by necessitation.

Then $B = \Box D_i$.

By the induction hypothesis $N1 \vdash D_i \wedge \Box^m D_i$ for all m hence $N1 \vdash B \wedge \Box^m B$ for all m.

Pr can be alternatively obtained form the first four axioms and their necessitations and rule (6) (modus ponens) and **N1** is the extension of **Pr** with rule (5).

The reason we had to reformulate **Pr** without Necessitation is that the necessitation rule

$$\vdash A$$
$$\overline{\qquad\qquad}$$
$$\vdash \Box A$$

together with the axioms

   (5a) $\Box (q \vee \Box f) \to \Box q$

   (5b) $\Box (\sim q \vee \Box f) \to \Box \sim q$

would collapse the logic as $\Box f$ is provable. This means that the set of possible worlds has only one point.

In practice we check provability semantically in the models of **N1**.

Theorem T7:

N1 is complete for the suggested semantics.

Proof:

It is easy to verify that if $N1 \vdash B$ then $\|B\| (h,0) = t$ in any **N1** - model.

We want to prove the converse. Assume $N1 \nvdash B$. Let $q_1,...,q_n$ be all atoms in B. Then certainly in **Pr** we cannot have that B is provable from A where

$$A = \Diamond\Diamond t \wedge \underset{i}{\;} [G(\Box f \vee q_i) \to Gq_i] \wedge \underset{i}{\;} [G(\Box f \vee \sim q_i) \to G\sim q_i].$$

This follows from Theorem T6, and the fact that $N1 \vdash A$. Therefore by the completeness of **Pr**, there exists a **Pr** structure $(T,<,0, h)$ such that $\|A\|(h,0)=t$ and $\|B\|(h,0)=f$.

This structure is indeed an **N1**-structure because A holds at 0.

Theorem T8:

Propositional **N1** is decidable.

Proof:

Because it is both axiomatizable and characterised by finite models.

Definition D3

Let **N1*** be the extension of **N1** with the axioms:

(1) $a \leftrightarrow Z (Z t \wedge X a)$

   for a atomic.

The system N1* arose in connection with the condition $\neg\neg a = a$ for negation by failure, discussed in remark R1 of Section 1.

Lemma L2:
N1* is a consistent logic, ie it has models.

Proof:
Let K be the class of all models of the form $(T, <, o, h)$, where $T = \{0, 1, 2\}$ and h is restricted by the condition:
  $h(q) = \{1\}$ or $h(q) = \{0, 2\}$ for all atoms q. For example the model of diagram 3 satisfies this condition. It is easy to verify that in the models of K we have that for all h, and all atomic a:
$$\|A\|_{(h,o)} = \|z(zt \wedge x \; A)\|_{(h,o)}$$

The precise class of models for which N1* is complete is not important. What is important is the soundness and completeness theorem for our modal interpretation, namely theorems T3 and T4 for the case of the logic N1*. The crucial observation here is that theorem T4, (completeness) was proved using three point odels from the class K. This means that N1* can be used instead of N1 for the purpose of our modal completion.

Example E1:
We copy from Smorynski's paper an example showing that in the predicate logic of provability **QPr**, there does not always exist a fixed point to an arbitrary matrix $E(q)$. We give an $E(q)$ such that there is no syntactically definable solution $q_0 = E(q_0)$.
We are fortunate to have theorems T5 and T6 that allow us to get syntactically definable fixed points for the case of a matrix arising from a program **P**. Note that in the general case we can always compute the fixed point semantically in each model but it may not be syntactically definable.

Let $E(q)$ be
  $$\forall x[\Box\Box Q(x) \rightarrow \Box(q \rightarrow Q(x))]$$

Then there is no modal sentence q_0 such that $q_0 = E(q_0)$, and q_0 is syntactically definable using $\Box$ alone.

This means that in the general case we need a modal predicate logic of provability stronger than what we have; a provability logic with a special fixed point operator, capturing the semantic fixed point which always exists.

To show that there is no fixed point solution to Smorynski's example we present a sequence of finite Kripke models where the semantically defined fixed point solution in the model cannot be syntactically defined.

The set of possible worlds is $\{1,2,3,4,....\}$. The accessibility relation is $>$ (greater than). The elements of the domain D are $\{0,1,2,3,....\}$. The model Mn has the domain D and the set of worlds $\{1,......n\}$.
The truth values of Q at each point is as follows:
At world n, exactly $Q(n-1)$ is false. The other $Q(x)$ for $x \neq n-1$ are true.
The following diagram describes our sequence of models. It describes what is false for Q. Q is true if not mentioned as false.

The Model Mn:

World	True
1	~Q(0)
2	~Q(1)
3	~Q(2)
4	~Q(3)
.	.
.	.
.	.
n	~Q(n-1)

For any m, Q(m) is true from m+2 onwards. Thus all atomic sentences become constantly true at point n of Mn after an initial segment. By induction we can show that any wff built up using quantifiers and connectives (including □) becomes constantly true or false at n of Mn after an initial segment.

The semantically defined fixed point q0 is true at odd numbers n and false at even numbers. It therefore oscillates in its truth value in the sequence Mn and is therefore not definable syntactically from □. Note that the models Mn are Herbrand models. *D* can be generated from the constant 0 and the successor function.

Appendix 2
Computational complexity of Pr

It is of importance to examine the axiomatizability and decision procedure of predicate **Pr**. We will show that **Pr** has the same complexity as classical logic enriched with the notion of a finite set.

Theorem T0:
Propositional **Pr** is log space complete

Proof:
This follows from a result of R E Ladner 1977, who has shwon that modal K is P-space complete. **Pr** is a finite extension of K.

Theorem T1
Consider the modal logic **Pr***, defined by the class of all Herbrand Models of **Pr**, for the language with an arbitrary number of unary predicates and an arbitrary number of unary function symbols. Then the set of non-theorems of **Pr*** is enumerable.
Proof:
This follows from Rabin's Theorem (Rabin,1966) about the decidability of SωS, the monadic second order theory of ω successor functions. The models of **Pr***, for a given finite tree, can be expressed in SωS and therefore the notion of truth in any fixed finite model can also be expressed in SωS. Since SωS is decidable, we can scan the list of all finite models looking for counter models.

We now describe how the translation can be done for given modal formula φ.

Let $(T,<,0,D,h)$ be a **Pr** model. Then $(T,<,0)$ is a finite tree. For each t∈ T associate a successor function r_t of SωS. **D** is a Herbrand domain based on a finite set of constants $c_1,\ldots c_k$ and unary function symbols $f_1,\ldots f_m$. Associate with ci the elements of SωS s_0 (Λ), s_0 s_0 (Λ),........, s_0^k (Λ) and if **u** is associated with the term u then s_i (u) is associated with fi (u).

The SωS formula **D(v)** below defines the notion of "v is a term in the domain"

$$D(v) = \text{definition } [\; \bigvee_{i=1}^{k} v = s_0^i\, (\Lambda)] \;\wedge$$

$$\forall C[\; \bigwedge_{i=1}^{k} s_0^i\, (\Lambda) \in C \;\wedge\; \forall y\, (y \in C \rightarrow \bigwedge_{i=1}^{m} s_i(y) \in C) \rightarrow v \in C)]$$

C is a set variable.

Let Q_1, Q_2.......... be the unary predicates appearing in φ. We want to translate $\|Q(u)\|_t = 1$.

Translate ψ = "Q(u) is true at $t \in$ T" by $\psi^t = Q(r_t(u))$.

Where **Q** is the set variable associated with the predicate Q and u is the SøS term associated with u.

We can now translate "ψ is true at t" for any ψ and any t to ψ^t as follows:

$\|Q(u)\|_t = 1$ is translated as $Q\,(r_t\,(u))$

$\|\psi_1 \wedge \psi_2\|_t = 1$ is translated to $\psi_1^t \wedge \psi_2^t$

$\|\sim\psi\|_t = 1$ is translated to $\sim \psi_1^{\,t}$

$\|\forall v \psi\|_t = 1$ is translated to $\forall\, v(D(v) \rightarrow \psi^t)$

$\|\Box\psi\|_t = 1$ is translated into $\bigwedge_{\{s|\; t<s\}} \psi^s.$

Note that the translation of $\Box\psi$ is done by case analysis on the finite tree (T, <). For a different tree we get a different conjunction. The relation < itself cannot be translated.

We can show:

ψ is valid at all **Pr** models with tree (T,<,0) iff SωS $\vdash \forall Q_1,\ldots,Q_k\, \varphi^0$.

Where ($Q_1 \ldots Q_k$) are the predicates of ψ.

We have thus shown that for any finite tree (T,<,0) and any formula ψ of the modal logic a formula ψ of SωS can be contructed saying ψ is true in all Kripke models based on (T,<). Since ψ can be recursively decided, we get an enumeration of all non-theorems of the logic, by systematically going over all finite trees (T,<,0).

Remark:
Note that we have a similar situation in the case of satisfiability in all *finite* classical models. It is known that we can enumerate all non-theorems by systematically checking all finite models. The set of valid theorems, however, is not axiomatizable. We believe a similar situation occurs in the case of unary **Pr**.

The following formula α of **Pr**, built up using only one new unary predicate Q and equality =, can say that the domain of D of a **Pr** model is finite.

α = $\forall x \lozenge (Q(x) \wedge \forall y \ (x \approx y \rightarrow \sim Q(y)))$

Since, in **Pr**, the set of possible worlds is finite, the domain D must be finite if α is true.

The following formula ψ(x,y) can codify any binary relation R on the domain D:

$(x,y) = \lozenge((Q(x) \wedge \forall y(x \approx y \rightarrow \sim Q(y)) \wedge \Box\Box f \wedge \lozenge (Q(y) \wedge \Box \ f))$

This is the case because whenever aRb holds, we can put a possible world denoted by 'a', in which exactly Q(a) is true and another possible world, denoted by '(a, b)' accessible to it, which is an endpoint and in which exactly Q(b) is true, as shown in the diagram:

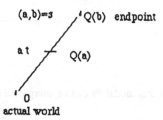

The world a is recognised because $\Box\Box f$ holds in it.
If aRb does not hold, we can avoid putting in the above constellation.

Given a classical finite model (D,R) of a binary relation R, we can define the following
Pr model $(T,<,o,D,h)$
Let $T = \{0\} \cup D \cup \{(a,b) \mid aRb\}$
Let $<$ be the transitive closure of the relation $<$o below:
$<0 = \{0\} \times D \cup \{(a,(a,b)) \mid aRb\}$
Let Q be a new atomic predicate. Let h make Q(a) true exactly at $a \in T$ and at any $(b,a) \in T$.
The following diagram illustrates what is happening.

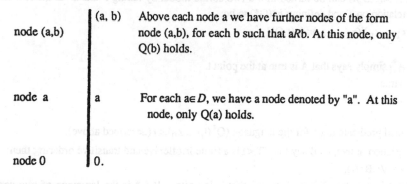

	(a, b)	Above each node a we have further nodes of the form node (a,b), for each b such that aRb. At this node, only Q(b) holds.
node (a,b)		
node a	a	For each $a \in D$, we have a node denoted by "a". At this node, only Q(a) holds.
node 0	0.	

The following holds:
$\lozenge [\ Q(a) \wedge \forall y \ (a \approx y) \rightarrow \sim Q(y)) \wedge \lozenge \ (Q(b) \wedge \forall y(b \approx y \rightarrow \sim Q(y)))]$
holds at 0 iff aRb holds.

We can show:
$\|\psi(a,b)\|_0^h = $ **truth iff aRb holds.**
$\|\varphi(a)\|_0^h = $ **truth iff $a \in D$.**

We have proved:

Theorem T2:
Any Wff B of the theory of finite models for binary relations R can be translated into a formula B^* of **Pr** such that the following holds:
$$\vdash B \text{ iff } \textbf{Pr} \vdash \exists\, x\alpha\ (x) \rightarrow B^*$$

Proof:
Translate B to B^* by induction as follows (ψ, α were defined in the previous remark):

$(xRy)^* = \psi(x,y)$

$(A \wedge B)^* = A^* \wedge B^*$

$(\sim A)^* = \sim A^*$

$(\forall xA)^* = \forall x(\alpha(x) \rightarrow A^*)$

$(\exists xA)^* = \exists x(\alpha(x) \wedge A^*)$

We now show the converse, namely that modal **Pr** can be interpreted in classical logic as follows:

Consider a two sorted predicate logic. One sort ranges over T and the other ranges over D.
Each atomic predicate $Q(x_1....,x_n)$ of **Pr**, with x_i ranging over D is translated into an atomic predicate $Q^*(t,x_1,......,x_n)$, with t ranging over T and x_i over D. Let t<s be a predicate over $T \times T$.
With every modal formula B we associate a two sorted classical formula $B^*(t)$ as follows:

1. $[Q(x_1,.....x_n)]^*_t = Q^*(t,x_1,......x_n)$, for Q atomic

2. $[A_1 \wedge A_2]^*_t = [A_1]^*_t \wedge [A_2]^*_t$

   $[\sim A]^*_t = \sim A^*_t$

3. $[xA]^*_t = \forall s(t<s \rightarrow A^*_s)$

4. $[\forall xA(x)]^*_t = \forall xA(x)^*_t$

Any **Pr** model $(T,<,0,D,h)$ can be turned into a two sorted model by taking T and D as the two sorts, taking < as the relation on T and defining $h^*(Q^*)$ to be:
$$h^*(Q^*) = \{(t,x_1,....x_n)|(x_1,....x_n) \in h\ (t,Q)\}$$

In other words A^*_t simply says that A is true at the point t.
The following is true:

Theorem T3:
Let L be two sorted predicate logic for the language $(Q^*(t,x,...x_n),<)$ (described above).
Let * be the translation above, let β say that $(T,<)$ is a finite irreflexive and transitive ordering then: **Pr** $\vdash B$ iff $L \vdash \beta \rightarrow \forall t\ B^*(t)$.
Note that β is not first order. We need to say that T is finite. If L^* is the language of two sorted predicate logic with the extra non first order predicate **Finite** (Q), saying that the extension of Q is finite, then the complexity of L^* is exactly that of **Pr**. We have seen already how **Finite** (Q) can be defined in **Pr**, using the formula α.

Theorem T4:
The complexity of **Pr** is that of predicate logic with the additional predicate **Finite** (Q), for finite sets.

Concluding Remark

From the computational point of view such a predicate as **Finite** is manageable. Therefore the complexity of **Pr** is acceptable. On going work of Fariñas del Cerro and his group is studying theorem provers which can compute fixed points.

REFERENCES

K. R. Apt and M. H. Van Emden, Contributions to the Theory of Logic Programming in *Journal of the Association for Computing Machinery 29*, 1982, pp. 841-862.

P. Balbiani, *Modal Considerations on Negation as Failure*, Technical Report, LSI, Toulouse, (1989).

P. Balbiani, Modal Logic and Negation as Failure, to apear *Journal of Logic and Computation*.

G. Boolos, *The Unprovability of Consistency*, Cambridge University Press, 1979.

K. L. Clark, Negation as Failure, in *Logic and Databases*. H. Gallaire and J. Minker (eds), Plenum, 1978, pp. 293-322.

M. Fitting, A Kripke Kleene Semantics for Logic Programs in *Journal of Logic Programming 2*, 1985, pp. 295-312 .

D. M. Gabbay, N-Prolog Part II, *Journal of Logic Programming*, 4, 1985, pp 251-283.

D. M. Gabbay, *Modal Provability Foundations for Negation by Failure*, Technical Report 86/4, Imperial College, Department of Computing, 1986.

D. M. Gabbay and U. Reyle, N-Prolog, Part 1, *Journal of Logic Programming*, 1, 1984, pp 319-355

D. M. Gabbay, What is Negation in a System in Logic Colloquium 86, F. Drake and J. Truss, (eds), North Holland, 1988, pp.95-112.

D. M. Gabbay and M. J. Sergot, Negation as inconsistency, in *Journal of Logic Programming*, 4, 1986, pp 1-35.

S. Kripke, Semantical Considerations in Modal Logic, in *Reference and Modality*, L. Linsky (ed.) Oxford University Press ,1971.

K. Kunen, Negation in Logic Programming in *Journal of Logic Programming 4*, 1987, pp. 289-308

K. Kunen, Answer Sets and Negation as Failure, in *Logic Programming*, (Proceedings of the Fourth International Conference), MIT Press 1987. J L Lassez (ed).

R. E. Ladner, The computational complexity of provability in systems of modal propositional logic, *SIAM Journal of Computation* 6, 1977, pp 467-480.

J. L. Lassez and M. J. Maher, Optimal Fixed Points of Logic Programs, in *Theoretical Computer Science 39*: 1985, pp. 15-25.

J. W. Lloyd, *Foundations of Logic Programming* (2nd edition), Springer Verlag, 1987.

D. W. Loveland, *Near Horn Prolog and Beyond*, Technical Report CS 1988-25, Duke University, 1988.

R. Milner, The Use of Machines to Assist in Rigorous Proof in *Mathematical Logic and Programming Languages*, C.A.R. Hoare and J.C. Shepherdson (eds.) Prentics-Hall 1985 pp. 77-88.

M.O Rabin, Decidability of Second Order Theories and Automata on Infinite Trees in *Transactions of the American Mathematical Society 141*, 1966, pp.1-35.

J. C. Shepherdson, Negation as Failure 1 in *Journal of Logic Programming 1* , 1984, pp. 1-48.

J. C. Shepherdson, Negation As Failure 2 in *Journal of Logic Programming 2*, 1985, pp. 185-202.

J. C.Shepherdson, Negation in Logic Programming in *Foundations of Deductive Databases and Logic Programming*, J Minker (ed), Morgan Kaufman, Los Altos, 1988, pp 19-88

C. Smorynski, Modal Logic and Self Reference in *Handbook of Philosophical Logic* vol 2, D. Gabbay and F. Guenthener (eds), D. Reidel pub. 1984, pp. 441-497.

C. Smorynski, *Quantified Modal Logic and Self Reference*, to appear.

C. Smorynski, *Self Reference and Modal Logic*, Springer Verlag 1985.

R. M. Solovay, Provability Interpretation of Modal Logic in *Israel Journal of Mathematics 25*, 1976, pp. 287-304.

L. Terracini, Private communication (1987)

L. Terracini, Modal Interpretation for Negation by Failure, in *Atti dell'Academia delle Scienze di torino*, 122, 1988, pp 81-88.

L. Terracini, A complete bi-modal system for a class of models in *Atti dell'Academia delle Scienze di torino*, 122, 1988, pp 116-125.

Extensions to Logic Programming Motivated by the Construction of a Generic Theorem Prover

Elsa L. Gunter[*]

Bell Labs, AT&T, Murray Hill, NJ, USA

Abstract

In this article, we discuss several possible extensions to traditional logic programming languages. The specific extensions proposed here fall into two categories: logical extensions and the addition of constructs to allow for increased control. There is a unifying theme to the proposed logical extensions, and that is the scoped introduction of extensions to a programming context. More specifically, these extensions are the ability to introduce variables whose scope is limited to the term in which they occur (*i.e.* λ-bound variables within λ-terms), the ability to introduce into a goal a fresh constant whose scope is limited to the derivation of that goal, and the ability to introduce into a goal a program clause whose scope is limited to the derivation of that goal. The purpose of the additions for increased control is to facilitate the raising and handling of failures.

To motivate these various extensions, we have repeatedly appealed to examples related to the construction of a generic theorem prover. It is our thesis that this problem domain is specific enough to lend focus when one is considering various language constructs, and yet complex enough to encompass many of the general difficulties found in other areas of symbolic computation.

1 Introduction

The implementation of theorem provers is a good testing ground for the appropriateness of a programming language for doing symbolic computation. Many of the needs that arise in other specific problems in symbolic computation have analogies in the design and construction of various kinds of theorem provers. Moreover, many specific problems in symbolic computation (parsing, for example) may actually be viewed as theorem proving activities themselves. In this paper, we discuss a collection of extensions to traditional logic programming

---

[*] The work reported here has been supported in part by grant NSF CCR-87-05596, while the author was at the University of Pennsylvania.

whose consideration was motivated by concerns arising from an attempt to implement in a logic programming setting an environment for the rapid construction of theorem provers. While the motivation for the consideration of each of these extensions is derived from the particular example of the construction of a generic theorem prover, we propose that they are of general interest.

Throughout this discussion, the point of the proposed extensions to traditional logic programming is not that they are fundamentally essential to implementing whatever constructs are being examined for motivation. It is never our point that we cannot carry out various tasks without some extension. Rather, our point is that the clarity of meaning of a given construct, and the ease of understanding the correctness of an implementation would be considerably enhanced by various extensions discussed here. Also, throughout this discussion we shall endeavor to motivate the various proposed extensions by appealing to concerns that arise from attempting to implement an interactive generic theorem prover. However, we shall endeavor to appeal to those concerns which have broad applicability, and to skirt those issues that seem peculiar to this particular problem. For more on the particulars of implementing a generic theorem prover, see [2, 3, 4, 15].

The particular language that was used in the building of a generic theorem prover was the higher-order logic programming language λProlog, initially designed and prototype-implemented by Nadathur and Miller [12], and subsequently reimplemented as part of the Ergo project at CMU by Pfenning and Elliot. Several of the extensions that we discuss here have been implemented in λProlog. For this reason, it proved to be a reasonable platform for the project. Throughout this paper when giving examples, we will express them using the syntax of λProlog, which differs slightly from that of more traditional logic programming languages such as Prolog.

2 Bound Variables, λ-Terms, Universal Quantification, and Implication

When implementing theorem provers for logics with quantifiers in a logic programming setting, first-order horn clauses are inadequate for a clear representation of formulas involving quantification, as was argued in [2] and [10]. To see an example of why this is the case, consider the first order formula $\exists x.\forall y.P(x) \supset P(y)$. The names of the bound variables occurring in this formula are not important, but that they are distinct variables is important. In Prolog, for example, we could choose to represent the bound variables by either constants or by logic variables. If we choose to use constants, the above term would be represented by something like `exists(x,forall(y,imp(p(x),p(y))))`. If we choose such an encoding, then we will need to implement procedures for explicitly dealing with equality up to α-conversion (*e.g.* for realizing that `exists(x,forall(y,imp(p(x),p(y))))` and `exists(y,forall(x,imp(p(y),p(x))))` are really representing the same term, whereas `exists(y,forall(y,imp(p(y),p(y))))` is not). Such a need interferes with the clarity of meaning of such expressions. These problems are not alleviated by the use of logic variables instead of constants. At first thought, it seems that α-conversion might be achieved by unification. However, one still has to deal with problems of free variable capture, as before. Moreover, if we unify the expressions `exists(X,forall(Y,imp(p(X),p(Y))))` and `exists(Y,forall(X,imp(p(Y),p(X))))` we will get the expression `exists(X,forall(X,imp(p(X),p(X))))` with the constraint `X = Y`, which clearly should not have the same meaning as the other two. An elegant solution to this problem exists if our logic programming language is extended to include bound variables and λ-terms, and unification is modulo α-conversion and, as we shall see later, at least a weak form of β-conversion. When we have such a datatype of λ-terms, then we can use the meta-language binding to represent the object-language quantified variables. Following the syntax of λProlog, if we use an infix \ to represent the binding of a logic variable in an expression, then we may represent the formula $\exists x.\forall y.p(x) \supset p(y)$ by the term `exists X \ (forall Y \ (imp (p X) (p Y)))`, which is equal in the meta-language to the term `exists Y \ (forall X \ (imp (p Y) (p X)))`, but which is not unifiable with the term `exists Y \ (forall Y \ (imp (p Y) (p Y)))`. It should be pointed out that in the previous expressions `exists` and `forall` are not binding constructs of our meta-language, but rather they are terms which are being applied to other terms, more specifically to λ-terms.

The need to be able to express variable binding is not restricted to expressing logics and implementing theorem provers. The same need arises, for example, if one wishes to implement an interpreter for a functional programming language (see [5]). The desirability of having bound variables in a meta-language has also arisen in the context of natural language parsing (see [13, 14], for example).

Once we have included a datatype of λ-terms into our language, there are two other constructs which go along with this extension in order to facilitate reasoning and programming with it. These two features are universal quantification and implication within goal formulae. Universal quantification within goals is necessary to allow one to define predicates on terms involving λ-terms. In order to be able to reason about an abstraction one needs to be able to reduce to reasoning about a generic instance. This reduction of an abstraction to a generic instance is done via universal quantification. An intentional interpretation of universal quantification within a goal says that the universally quantified goal is derivable just in case a generic instance of the goal is derivable. Thus by using universal quantification, we may decompose an abstraction within a goal by universally quantifying the goal and applying the abstraction to the variable of the universal quantification. This goal will then be reduced to the generic instance. For an actual reduction to take place it is necessary for unification to treat an application of an abstraction to a universally quantified variable as equal to the result of substituting the universally quantified variable for the bound variable of the abstraction in the body of the abstraction. Without at least this much β-conversion built into the unification of our logic programming language there would be no way at actually eliminate an abstraction. The language λProlog has unification which respects full β-conversion. However, it is possible to have a language whose unification respects only this weak form of β-conversion, as has been done in the language L_λ (see [9]).

Once we have a datatype of λ-terms and a construct for universal quantification in our language, a new difficulty is introduced. A generic instance of a goal will generally contain occurrences of the newly introduced generic constant for which information may need to be added in order to allow them to be reasoned about. We need to be able to introduce additional definite clauses that will allow us to reason about a generic constant when we are within its scope. Scoped addition of definite clauses is what implication gives us.

Formally, the language we have been talking about may be described as follows. Let A be a syntactic variable ranging over atomic formulae (by which we mean propositional terms whose heads are either variables or non-logical predicate constants (*i.e.* not $\wedge$, $\vee$, $\supset$, $\forall$, $\exists$) and which may contain λ-abstractions as subterms). We will also require that no subterm of A contain an implication. Let D be a syntactic variable ranging over definite clauses, and let G be a syntactic variable ranging over goal formulae. We may then define the classes of definite clauses and of goal formulae by the following mutual recursion:

$$D := A \mid G \supset A \mid D_1 \wedge D_2 \mid \forall x.D$$
$$G := A \mid G_1 \wedge G_2 \mid G_1 \vee G_2 \mid \exists x.G \mid D \supset G \mid \forall x.G$$

Usually, definite clauses in a program are considered to be implicitly universally quantified at the outermost level and goals are considered to be existentially quantified at the outermost level. Since we will be allowing definite clauses to occur withing goals (through implication) we wish to allow for these quantifications to be made explicit. The real extension that is being made here is the inclusion of implication and universal quantification in goals.

Not all definite clauses generated by the above recursion are consistent as program clauses. For example, from a definite clause of $\forall x.x$ we could derive any goal. From a definite clause of $\forall x.Px$, if P is a free variable we could derive any goal, whereas this is not so if P is a constant. What programs are allowable depends upon what constants are are available. Let Σ be a signature, *i.e.* a set of available constants. Then we may define which definite clauses and which goals are allowable over Σ by the following mutual recursion. For definite clauses:

1. If D is atomic then D is allowable over Σ if the head of D is in Σ.
2. If $D = G \supset A$ then D is allowable over Σ if the head of A is in Σ, and G is allowable over Σ.
3. If $D = D_1 \wedge D_2$ then D is allowable over Σ if both D_1 and D_2 are allowable over Σ.
4. If $D = \forall x.D_1$ then D is allowable over Σ if D_1 is allowable over Σ.

and for goals:

1. If G is atomic then G is allowable over Σ.
2. If $G = G_1 \wedge G_2$ or $G = G_1 \vee G_2$ then G is allowable over Σ if both G_1 and G_2 are.

3. If $G = \exists x.G_1$ then G is allowable over Σ if G_1 is.
4. If $G = D \supset G_1$ then G is allowable over Σ if both D and G_1 are.
5. If $G = \forall x.G_1$ then G is allowable over Σ if $G_1[c/x]$ is allowable over $\Sigma \cup \{c\}$ where c is a fresh constant not occurring in Σ or G.

Our notion of goal derivation needs to be with respect to not only a set of allowable definite clauses, but also with respect to a signature. Fix a signature Σ containing the constant true. A *program context* over Σ is a set closed definite clauses that are allowable over Σ. Let $T(\Sigma)$ be the set of closed terms, not involving implication, all of whose constant subterms are contained in Σ. The closure $\text{clos}_\Sigma(P)$ of a program context P relative to Σ is the smallest program context over Σ containing P and true such that

- if $D_1 \wedge D_2 \in \text{clos}_\Sigma(P)$, then $D_1 \in \text{clos}_\Sigma(P)$ and $D_2 \in \text{clos}_\Sigma(P)$, and
- if $\forall x.D \in \text{clos}_\Sigma(P)$, then for all $t \in T(\Sigma)$, we have $D[t/x] \in \text{clos}_\Sigma(P)$.

If the terms of our language are typed, then in the second condition we need to restrict to those terms t which have a type which is an instance of the type of the universally quantified variable x. Notice that, if P_1 and P_2 are program contexts, then $\text{clos}(P_1 \cup P_2) = \text{clos}(P_1) \cup \text{clos}(P_2)$.

Using these notions, we may define what it means for a closed goal G which is allowable over over a signature Σ to be non-deterministically derivable from Σ and a program context P over Σ, which we shall write as $\Sigma, P \vdash G$, by the following rules:

1. $\Sigma, P \vdash A$, if A is atomic and $A \in \text{clos}_\Sigma(P)$.
2. $\Sigma, P \vdash A$, if A is atomic and $G \supset A \in \text{clos}_\Sigma(P)$ and $\Sigma, P \vdash G$.
3. $\Sigma, P \vdash G_1 \wedge G_2$ if $\Sigma, P \vdash G_1$ and $\Sigma, P \vdash G_2$.
4. $\Sigma, P \vdash G_1 \vee G_2$ if $\Sigma, P \vdash G_1$ or $\Sigma, P \vdash G_2$.
5. $\Sigma, P \vdash \exists x.G$ if there exists some $t \in T(\Sigma)$ such that $\Sigma, P \vdash G[t/x]$.
6. $\Sigma, P \vdash \forall x.G$ if $\Sigma \cup \{c\}, P \vdash G[c/x]$ where c is a fresh constant not occurring in Σ, P or G.
7. $\Sigma, P \vdash D \supset G$ if $\Sigma, P \cup \{D\} \vdash G$.

The second to last rule allows for a scoped introduction of a new constant in our language, and the last rule allows for a scoped extension of our program context for deriving a particular goal. The reason for the requirement that atomic formulae and terms in $T(\Sigma)$ not involve implication is to insure that instances of goals are again goals. It was shown in [8] that, so long as we restrict to using only goals and definite clauses that are allowable over a signature Σ, a goal G is derivable from Σ and a program context P if and only if the sequent $\Sigma; P \to G$ is intuitionistically provable. It follows from this that it is always consistent to to augment a program context by an allowable definite clause.

To see how this all works, let us look at an example. Suppose we have an object language consisting of propositional letters p and q, the logical connectives and and imp, and the quantifiers forall and exists. (The terms p, q, and, imp, forall and exists are constants in the logic programming language.)

Further suppose that we wish to implement a procedure for counting the number of quantifications (universal or existential) occurring in a given formula. We shall follow the syntax of λProlog once again, and represent a universally quantified goal by pi c \ *goal*(c) and implication by *goal1* => *goal2*. Then we may describe a predicate numb_quant as follows:

```
numb_quant p 0.
numb_quant q 0.

numb_quant (and X Y) N :-
    numb_quant X K,
    numb_quant Y M,
    N is K + M.

numb_quant (imp X Y) N :-
    numb_quant X K,
    numb_quant Y M,
    N is K + M.

numb_quant (exists P) N :-
    pi c \ (numb_quant c 0 => numb_quant (P c) M),
    N is M + 1.

numb_quant (forall P) N :-
    pi c \ (numb_quant c 0 => numb_quant (P c) M),
    N is M + 1.
```

Now let us consider what happens with the query

```
?- numb_quant (forall X \ (exists Y \ (imp X Y))) N.
```

When we descend through the forall, we are confronted with an abstraction which we decompose by generating a fresh pi-constant, say c1, and applying the abstraction to it. This new constant is not in the original object language, and hence there is no clause of numb_quant that applies to it. After descending through the remaining exists and imp, we are confronted with the goal:

```
numb_quant c1 K
```

In order to be able to satisfy this goal we need to have previously augmented our program with a clause specifically mentioning c1 to enable us to solve it. However, clearly, such a clause should only be considered valid within the scope of c1. This is what is expressed by the goal

```
pi c \ (numb_quant c 0 => numb_quant (P c) M)
```

During the attempt to solve numb_quant (P c) M, we have access to the additional definite clause numb_quant c 0. Once the goal numb_quant (P c) M has either succeeded or failed, the clause numb_quant c 0 is discharged and we no longer have access to it.

Notice that, as was mentioned before, to be able to use universal quantification in a logic programming language to decompose an abstraction, it is necessary for unification to work modulo β-reduction, at least in the instance where an abstraction is being applied to a pi-bound constant. That is, an expression such as (X \ (imp X X)) c, where c is a pi-bound constant, must be treated as equal to (imp c c).

In the example given above, we were viewing the object language of the theorem prover as a sub-language of the meta-language. In that instance we argued that if we had abstraction in our object language that we needed abstraction in our meta-language. However, not all object languages we might wish to consider will yield to such a direct representation. It is still desirable to use the meta-language abstraction to represent object language abstraction. As an example of this, suppose we have data-constructors atom A, app X Y and abs F for the datatype of terms for the object language we looked at before, in addition to the constants p, q, and, imp, forall and exists. Then we may represent, for example, $\forall x. \exists y. x \supset y$ by

app forall (abs X \ (app exists (abs Y \ (app (app imp X) Y)))).

In this case, we would encode the procedure for counting quantifications by

```
atom p.
atom q.

quantifier forall.
quantifier exists.

connective and.
connective imp.

numb_quant (atom A) 0.

numb_quant (app Quantifier (abs Exp)) N :-
    quantifier Quantifier,
    pi c \ (numb_quant c 0 => numb_quant (Exp c) M),
    N is M + 1.

numb_quant (app (app Connective X) Y) N :-
    connective Connective,
    numb_quant X K,
    numb_quant Y M,
    N is K + M.
```

The advantage to representing object language abstractions by using abstraction in the meta-language is the same as before. The problems of α-convertibility and variable capture are pushed to the meta-level and handled by the programming language, thereby improving the conciseness and clarity of the programmers code. Moreover, when abstraction is combined with universal quantification, the problem of verifying that eigenvariable conditions are satisfied is pushed to the meta-level where they become the direct result of the eigenvariable conditions of the programming language.

3 Modules and Abstract Modules

The need for having some form of encapsulation when doing medium to large scale programming has long been recognized. This need is made quite apparent when one considers the problem of constructing a generic theorem prover. The very nature of the problem requires that the generic theorem prover form one unit, or module, which is an incomplete program until it is supplied with another user-constructed module implementing the specific logic for which the user wants a theorem prover. Therefore, one is forced to consider from the outset the questions of what a specification of a module might be, what an interface between modules might be and what form of encapsulation might be achieved. Within the logic programming setting one should also consider the logical interpretation of modules. In [7] it was argued that, in a logic programming language with implication in goals, we already have a natural notion of a module implicit in our language. This notion of module, when used in the setting of implementing a generic theorem prover, proves useful, but more restricted than one might find desirable. We wish to argue here that the particular problem of implementing a generic theorem prover motivates an extension to this notion of module, which requires a further extension of the language, but which will allow greater flexibility and clarity in the use of modules.

Let us begin to approximate the construction of an interactive generic theorem prover by considering the problem of writing a procedure that, when given a goal to be proved, repeatedly queries the user for an inference rule to be used to reduce the goal until the goal reaches some success state. If we have a fixed constant **success** to indicate the success state, and if we assume that we have a database of clauses of the form

```
rule RuleName InputGoal OutputGoal.
```

then we could implement such a procedure as follows:

```
prove Goal :- reduce Goal success, write "Goal succeeded.", nl.

reduce success success.

reduce InputGoal OutputGoal :-
    write "Current Goal = ", write InputGoal, nl,
    write "Enter Rule Name: ",
    read RuleName,
```

```
    apply RuleName InputGoal OutputGoal.

reduce InputGoal OutputGoal :-
    write "Trying again ... ", nl,
    reduce InputGoal OutputGoal.

apply RuleName InputGoal OutputGoal :-
    rule RuleName InputGoal MidGoal,
    reduce MidGoal OutputGoal.
```

Now, suppose that we wish to use this framework to build proof-objects for a specific logic, and that the goals we wish to prove contain free variables which will be instantiated to these proof-objects during the solving of the goal. Further suppose that we have two different ways of implementing the inference rules for this logic, and that we would like to develop proof-objects for a given goal using each of the two systems, and then ask if the resulting two proof-objects are equal. We would like to be able to write a procedure something like

```
test_proof Goal :-
    write "Using first set of inference rules...", nl,
    prove (pf Goal Proof1),
    write "Using second set of inference rules...", nl,
    prove (pf Goal Proof2),
    Proof1 = Proof2.
```

For this procedure to work requires that it be supplied with a database of clauses for rule. Each of the calls to the predicate prove must be able to access this database. Therefore, this database must contain all of the clauses for rule that are needed to express each of the implementations of the inference rules for our logic. This means that each of the calls to prove has access to the clauses for rule that are intended for the other implementation. Such a mixing of clauses is not what is intended, and conceivably might render the total implementation unsound, even if each implementation alone were sound. Under any circumstances, it is undesirable. Using a notion of module that is afforded us by implication, we can encapsulate each of the systems to prevent this kind of interference. To see how this is done let us review the notion of module that is given to us in the presence of implication in goals, as discussed in [7].

Let A be a syntactic variable ranging over atomic formulae (with constant head), let D be a syntactic variable ranging over definite clauses, and let G be a syntactic variable ranging over goal formulae. We may then define the classes of definite clauses and of goal formulae by the following mutual recursion:

$$D := A \mid G \supset A \mid D_1 \wedge D_1 \mid \forall x.D$$
$$G := A \mid G_1 \wedge G_2 \mid G_1 \vee G_2 \mid \exists x.G \mid D \supset G$$

In the previous section we discussed extending traditional logic programming by both implication and universal quantification in goals, together with a datatype of λ-terms. Here, we are assuming only that we are extending by implication. For the moment, we are assuming the existence of one universal signature, and so our definitions do not need to be relative to a signature. We define what it means for a goal G to be non-deterministically derivable from a program context P, written $P \vdash G$, in a manner analogous to before.

In this setting, a module may be understood as a definite clause which is introduced into a goal by implication. Using a module M in deriving a goal G means deriving the goal $M \supset G$. Importing a module M_1 into a module M_2 can be defined as follows:

- If M_2 is atomic, the result is just M_2.
- If M_2 is of the form $G \supset A$, the result is $(M_2 \supset G) \supset A$.
- If M_2 is of the form $D_3 \wedge D_4$, the result is $M_3 \wedge M_4$ where M_3 is the result of importing M_1 into D_3 and M_4 is the result of importing M_1 into D_4.
- If M_2 is of the form $\forall x.D$ where x does not occur free in M_1, then the result is $\forall x.M_3$ where M_3 is the result of importing M_1 into D.

From the above we have that, if M is the result of importing M_1 into M_2 and if M is used in deriving a goal G, then the definite clause M_1 is not directly available when we are attempting to derive G. It is only available for deriving goals which arise from reducing G by a definite clause in $\mathsf{clos}(M)$ (*i.e.* when backchaining). Given that we have the possibility of free variables occurring in a goal of the form $D(x) \supset G(x)$ which can be existentially quantified, our notion of module extends to that of a parametrized module, parametrized by the free variables occurring in it.

To facilitate the use of this notion of module we can introduce the following syntax (borrowed almost verbatim from λProlog) for creating a module:

```
module M x₁...xₖ.
import M₁...Mₘ.
A₁ :- G₁.
    ⋮
Aₙ :- Gₙ.
endmodule.
```

which stands for the definite clause

$$(\forall y_{1,1} \ldots y_{1,m_1}.(D \supset G_1) \supset A_1) \wedge \ldots \wedge (\forall y_{n,1} \ldots y_{n,m_n}.(D \supset G_n) \supset A_n)$$

where D is the definite clause corresponding to the the module $M_1 \wedge \ldots \wedge M_m$, where $y_{i,1}, \ldots, y_{i,m_i}$ are all the variables occurring free in D, G_i and A_i except for the variables $x_1, \ldots x_n$, which remain free. The result of instantiating the free variables $x_1, \ldots x_k$ with values $e_1, \ldots e_k$ will be represented by $(M \; e_1 \ldots e_k)$. To use the module M instantiated with the values $e_1, \ldots e_k$ in deriving a goal G, we will write $(M \; e_1 \ldots e_k)$ ==> G.

Using this notion of module and the above notation, we can now reimplement our procedure to compare two proofs of a goal proven in two different inference systems as follows:

```
module prover.

prove Goal :- reduce Goal success, write "Goal succeeded.", nl.

reduce success success.

reduce InputGoal OutputGoal :-
    write "Current Goal = ", write InputGoal, nl,
    write "Enter Rule Name: ",
    read RuleName,
    apply RuleName InputGoal OutputGoal.

reduce InputGoal OutputGoal :-
    write "Trying again ... ", nl,
    reduce InputGoal OutputGoal.

apply RuleName InputGoal OutputGoal :-
    rule RuleName InputGoal MidGoal,
    reduce MidGoal OutputGoal.

endmodule.


test_proof Goal :-
    prover ==>
    (write "Using first set of inference rules...", nl,
    logic1 ==> prove (pf Goal Proof1),
    write "Using second set of inference rules...", nl,
    logic2 ==> prove (pf Goal Proof2),
    Proof1 = Proof2).
```

If we use this procedure at top-level with two different modules logic1 and logic2, when prove (pf Goal Proof1) is being derived, we have both the definite clause associated with logic1 and the definite clause associated with prover in our program context, but we do not have the definite clause associated with logic2. Thus we have achieved the encapsulation that we indicated was necessary when we posed the problem, in the case that our program context consists only of the clause for test_proof.

That the use of the module logic1 is isolated from the use of logic2 depends on the assumption that logic2 is not already in out program context. However, if a subgoal test_proof Goal arises during the derivation of a goal of the form logic2 ==> G, then this assumption no longer holds. In such a situation, the definite clause associated with logic2 would already be a part of our program context, and attempts to derive the goal prove (pf Goal Proof1) could make use of the resulting extended database for rule. In writing the module prover and the clause for test_proof, we want to be able to enforce a stronger form of encapsulation. We would like to be able to specify a scope for the predicate rule in such a way as to ensure that there can be no further extensions to rule, beyond the clauses found in the logic module.

Now let us return to the logic programming language discussed in the previous section, and consider extending it by a limited form of existential quantification in definite clauses. The motivation for universal quantification in goals and a limited form of existential quantification in definite clauses is to provide lexical scoping for constants, such as rule. The connection between lexical scoping and universal quantification was discussed at length in [6]. To describe this extension more thoroughly, as before let A range over atomic formulae, let G range over goal formulae, let D range over definite clauses, and let E range over existential definite clauses. Then as before we may define these by the following mutual recursion:

$$D := A \mid G \supset A \mid D_1 \wedge D_1 \mid \forall x.D$$
$$E := D \mid \exists x.E$$
$$G := A \mid G_1 \wedge G_2 \mid G_1 \vee G_2 \mid E \exists x.G \mid \supset G \mid \forall x.G$$

As we did in Sect. 2 we wish to restrict program clauses to those definite clauses that are allowable over a given signature Σ. For this we need to extend our definition of allowable to include existentially quantified definite clauses by adding the following rule to the four given for definite clauses in Sect. 2:

5. If $E = \exists x.E_1$ then E is allowable over Σ if $E_1[c/x]$ is allowable over $\Sigma \cup \{c\}$ where c is a fresh constant not occurring in Σ or E.

Again, a program context is a set of closed definite clauses (with no outer existential quantification), and the closure of a program context with respect to a signature is defined exactly as before. To define the derivation of a goal G from a program context P and a signature Σ, we need to add an additional rule to the seven given in Sect. 2, namely

8. $\Sigma, P \vdash (\exists x.E) \supset G$ if $\Sigma \cup \{c\}, P \vdash (E[c/x] \supset G)$, where c is a fresh constant not occurring in Σ, P or G.

This last rule reflects the intuitionistic equivalence

$$(\exists x.D) \supset G \quad \equiv \quad \forall x.(D \supset G)$$

provided that x does not occur free in G. In light of this, the logical system described above is essentially that of higher-order hereditary Harrop formulae as described in [8]. This formulation of this logic is essentially that given in [6] when discussing the construction of abstract datatypes in a logic programming language. However, the purpose we have of presenting this formulation here is to allow us to give an interpretation to a more flexible notion of module. A specific instance of this notion of module is an abstract datatype.

Given these extensions to logic programming, we can now think of modules as existential definite clauses. To reflect this additional expressiveness, let us introduce the following expanded notation for modules:

module M $x_1 \ldots x_k$.

hiding $y_1 \ldots y_l$.

import $M \ldots M_m$.

A_1 :- G_1.

$\vdots$

A_n :- G_n.

endmodule.

which stands for the existential definite clause

$$\exists y_1 \ldots y_l.(\forall z_{1,1} \ldots z_{1,p_1}.(E_1 \supset \cdots \supset E_m \supset G_1) \supset A_1) \wedge \ldots$$
$$\wedge (\forall z_{n,1} \ldots z_{n,p_n}.(E_1 \supset \cdots \supset E_m \supset G_n) \supset A_n)$$

where E_j is the definite clause corresponding to the the module M_j, and $z_{i,1}, \ldots, z_{i,p_i}$ are all the variables occurring free in G_i, A_i and any E_j except for the variables $y_1, \ldots, y_m$ and $x_1, \ldots, x_n$.

There are still a difficulties with this approach. One difficulty lies with saying what the free variables in the body of a module are. Whether a symbol is a free variable or not is determined by the context in which it occurs and the signature that is present. Given that we have universal quantification in goals, we can no longer assume the presence of one universal signature which determines once and for all what our constants are. Constants have scope. However, the interpretation of a module as an existential definite clause should not depend the context in which the module is being used. In the example we gave with the interactive theorem prover, the module logic1 needs to provide clauses defining the predicate rule. Within this module, rule needs to be a constant. We cannot treat rule as free variable, for then we would have a free variable as the head of an atomic definite clause, which is not allowable. Moreover, we need to have the occurrence of rule in prover and in logic1 refer to the same entity. However, in order to be able to limit the scope of rule, we want to be able to existentially quantify it within the body of the module prover.

The problem is that we want the meaning of a module to be given by the module itself, independent of whatever signature might be present at the time the module is used, and yet we also wish to be able to have terms within the module to be the same as terms in the context in which a module is used. Moreover, we need to be able to specify that the heads of atoms be "constants" (*i.e.* not variables that are universally bound in a definite clause containing it, or existentially bound in a goal containing it). This can be solved by changing our view of what a module is. We need to view a module as a function from a signature to an existential definite clause. To use a module, we must first instantiate the module with a signature. To deal with signatures, let us begin by extending our language by a datatype of records over constants. Assume that we have a fixed countable collection of labels which are distinct from the classes of variables and constants. We will represent a signature as a record of constants over these labels. The reason for using records instead of tuples, for example, is to simplify the use of a module applied to a signature.

Once again, let us modify our notation to reflect this change of view. The new notation is the following:

> module M $x_1 \ldots x_j$.
> signature $\{s_1 \gg w_1, \ldots, s_k \gg w_k\}$
> hiding $y_1 \ldots y_l$.
> import $M_1 :: \{t_{1,1} \gg k_{1,1}, \ldots, t_{1,n_1} \gg k_{1,n_1}\}$.
> $\vdots$
> import $M_m :: \{t_{m,1} \gg k_{m,1}, \ldots, t_{m,n_m} \gg k_{m,n_m}\}$.
> $A_1 :- G_1$.
> $\vdots$
> $A_p :- G_p$.
> endmodule.

which will be interpreted by the function

$$\lambda x_1 \ldots x_j. \Lambda w_1 \ldots w_k. \exists y_1 \ldots y_l. (\forall z_{1,1} \ldots z_{1,q_1}. (E_1 \supset \cdots \supset E_m \supset G_1) \supset A_1) \wedge$$
$$\ldots \wedge (\forall z_{n,1} \ldots z_{n,q_n}. (E_1 \supset \cdots \supset E_m \supset G_n) \supset A_n)$$

where E_i is the existential definite clause corresponding to the instantiated module $M_i :: \{t_{i,1} \gg k_{i,1}, \ldots, t_{i,n_i} \gg k_{i,n_i}\}$ and where $z_{i,1}, \ldots, z_{i,q_i}$ are all the variables occurring free in $E_1 \ldots E_m$, G_i, and A_i, excluding $x_1, \ldots, x_j, y_1, \ldots, y_l$ and $w_1, \ldots, w_k$. We use the capital Λ in the abstraction of the $w_1, \ldots, w_k$ to indicate that this abstraction is only over constants, and not over arbitrary terms. We shall refer to the variables $x_1, \ldots, x_j$ as the formal parameter of the module M, and we shall refer to the record $\{s_1 \gg w_1, \ldots, s_k \gg w_k\}$ as the formal signature of M. In a formal signature $\{s_1 \gg w_1, \ldots, s_k \gg w_k\}$ the s_i's range over labels and the w_i's are required to range over variables (just as the X in X \ p X is required to range over variables). If we use a module which has been instantiated with a signature which does not contain constants for every labeled term in the formal signature, those terms will be existentially quantified, *i.e.* hidden.

There is another difficulty with this approach to modules. It is that on the one hand we would like to be able to parameterize modules by other modules, but on the other hand, variables are restricted to not being instantiated by terms involving implication, and the existential definite clause represented by a module essentially always involve implication. A solution to this difficulty is to treat modules as formally distinct from the existential definite clauses they represent, and to formalize in our logic the interpretation of modules as definite clauses.

One way of making this formal distinction is to add type to our logic, and for modules to be of a different type than propositions. The language λProlog gives an example typed logic programming language which supports most of what is mentioned here. If modules are of a different type than definite clauses, then we need to augment our language with a construct for module implication. Let M range over terms od type module (that is, instantiated modules) and let Interp be a partially definied function from modules to the existential definite clauses that provide the interpretations of modules described above. As before let A range over attomic formulae, G range over goals, D range over definite clauses and E range over existential definite clauses. Then our mutually recursive definition now becomes:

$$D := A \mid G \supset A \mid D_1 \wedge D_1 \mid \forall x.D$$
$$E := D \mid \exists x.E$$
$$G := A \mid G_1 \wedge G_2 \mid G_1 \vee G_2 \mid E \supset G \mid M \Rightarrow G \mid \exists x.G \mid \forall x.G$$

where we must add to our rules for allowability over a signature Σ the rule

7. If $G = M \Rightarrow G_1$ then G is allowable over Σ if Interp(M) exists and Interp$(M) \supset G$ is allowable over Σ.

and we must add to the rules for the derivation of an allowable goal G from program context P and signature Σ the rule

9. $\Sigma, P \vdash M \Rightarrow G$ if $\Sigma, P \vdash$ Interp$(M) \supset G$.

Once we have made these modifications, we may allow variables in the formal parameter of a module to range over modules and to be instantiated by any construct of module type. Moreover, it is not necessary to restrict terms being substituted for variables to not include module implication. As a result of the restrictions that have been placed on the heads of atomic definite clauses, it can be shown by structural induction that any substitution instance of a goal is again a goal and any substitution instance of definite clause is again a definite clause. We must, however, still keep the restriction that atomic formulae not involve regular implication and that variables not be instantiated by terms involving implication. This notion of parameterized module that we now have available yields a notion of module that is similar in functionality to the notions of structure, functor and abstraction found in the functional programming language Standard ML (see [11]).

Using this expanded logic and revised notation we may yet again reimplement our procedure to compare two proofs of a goal proven in two different inference systems as follows:

```
module prover
        (Logic : rule_name -> module)
        (RuleNameList : rule_name list).
```

```
signature {#prove >> prove : thm -> o.
           #pf >> pf : proof -> statement -> thm,
           #reduce >> reduce : thm  -> thm -> o,
           #apply >> apply : rule_name -> thm  -> thm -> o,
           #success >> success : thm}.

hiding Rule.

import (Logic RuleNameList)
       ::{#rule >> Rule, #success >> success}.


prove Goal :- reduce Goal success, write "Goal succeeded.", nl.


reduce success success.


reduce InputGoal OutputGoal :-
    write "Current Goal = ", write InputGoal, nl,
    write "Enter Rule Name: ",
    read RuleName,
    apply RuleName InputGoal OutputGoal.


reduce InputGoal OutputGoal :-
    write "Trying again ... ", nl,
    reduce InputGoal OutputGoal.


apply RuleName InputGoal OutputGoal :-
    Rule RuleName InputGoal MidGoal,
    reduce MidGoal OutputGoal.

endmodule.


test_proof Goal :-
    write "Using first set of inference rules...", nl,
    (prover logic1 [l1_rule1,l1_rule2,l1_rule3])
         :: {#prove >> first_prove, #pf >> pf}
      ==> first_prove (pf Goal Proof1),
    write "Using second set of inference rules...", nl,
    (prover logic2 [l2_rule1,l2_rule2])
         :: {#prove >> second_prove, #pf >> pf}
      ==> second_prove (pf Goal Proof2)),
    Proof1 = Proof2.
```

With this new implementation, we are guaranteed that the clauses that are introduced by the logic module for the predicate Rule cannot be augmented except as explicitly indicated within the logic module. Notice that, in addition to allowing the module **prover** to give a scope to the predicate **Rule**, the fact that the module **Logic** has **Rule** in its signature forms a weak kind of specification for the module **Logic**.

When attempting to develop a notion of modularity in a logic programming setting, implication allows for the expression of the scope of clauses, universal quantification allows for the expression of the scope of constants, and higher order variables allow for the expression of the dependencies between modules. The idea that implication gives scope to clauses and that universal quantification gives scope to constants is not new (see [7, 6]), nor is its applicability limited to defining modules. However, the considerable desirability of having a notion of module that takes advantage of all of these concepts is made quite clear when one studies the problem of what functionality is wanted from modules when one is attempting to construct a generic theorem prover.

4 Handling Different Kinds of Failure

When implementing a theorem prover which combines a degree of interaction with a degree of automation, various problems of control begin to manifest themselves. This is particularly the case when the automated aspects include a degree of search. In this setting there are several possibilities for a given portion of a computation to generate failure, and it is desirable to be able to distinguish between these different possibilities of failure and to modify how the computation continues accordingly. In a functional programming language, such as Standard ML, during a computation, one has the ability to generate an error, which then may be detected during a second computation awaiting a result from the first, and upon such detection the second computation may continue accordingly. (See [11], for instance.) If we assume a conventional left-most depth-first interpreter, then a logic programming language such as Prolog, using *or* (that is, using ;) may be viewed as having an ability to "raise" a failure and to subsequently "handle" it with the *or*. However, there is only one kind of failure that can be generated; there is no direct ability to detect information about the circumstances that generated the failure. To see the limitations of having only one kind of failure, consider a procedure for an interactive loop for proof development. In overall structure, the loop should print the current goal, query the user for the next reduction rule to be attempted, attempt the specified reduction and if it succeeds it should call itself recursively, while if the attempt fails, it should backtrack to the beginning of the loop and try the loop again. At the end of the one execution of the loop, when the user is queried again, he may wish to continue the reduction, or he may wish to have the previous reduction reinterpreted and retried (*e.g.* have a different clause executed), or he may wish to undo the previous attempt entirely and try something else. Each of the last two options requires that commitments to instantiations of variables be undone, and hence each requires a failure to be generated. The first of the two failures needs to cause backtracking to the reduction where it should be handled by causing the reduction to be retried. The second of the two failures needs to cause backtracking through the attempted reduction back to the previous level of the interactive loop. These two cases require that different kinds of failure be generated and subsequently that they be handled in different fashions.

To be able to continue in different manners based on different kinds of failure of preceding goals requires that information about the nature of the failure of a goal be returned when failure does occur. For the time-being, let us assume that these "different kinds of failure" are distinct from fail. In order to be able to "return different kinds of failure", let us extend the syntax of our logic programming language by two system predicates:

```
raise Error.
```

```
handling Error Goal1 Goal2.
```

When a goal of the form `raise Error` is encountered, the current effort should be abandoned, passing back the error `Error`, and undoing any bindings that occurred at previous levels. When a goal of the form `handling Error Goal1 Goal2` is encountered, first the goal `Goal1` is attempted, and if it succeeds, the consequences are the same as if only `Goal1` had been encountered. In particular, the `handling` should not effect the ability to backtrack and seek another solution to `Goal1`. If `Goal1` simply fails, then `handling Error Goal1 Goal2` also fails. However, if `Goal1` passes back an error, then any binding that would have been made in attempting `Goal1` will have been undone, and if the error passed back unifies with the pattern `Error`, then the result is the same as if only the goal

```
Error = error_passed_back, Goal2
```

had been encountered. In particular, if `Goal2` passes back an error, it would not be trapped by the `handling` in this goal, but rather would continue to be passed back.

Even though there is a strong similarity between the combination of `fail` and `or` on the one hand and the combination of `raise Error` and `handling Error` on the other, the first is not just a simple subcase of the other. While `or` frequently is implemented in a deterministic, left-most, depth-first fashion, it has a proper non-deterministic reading. This is not the case with `handling`. With `handling`, the first goal must be evaluated and the second goal is only evaluated in the case that the first goal passes back the right kind of error. It would simply be incorrect for `handling` to non-deterministically choose to evaluated the second goal without attempting the first. Therefore, it is appropriate that the raising of errors and the subsequent handling of them be distinct from `fail` and `or`.

To help clarify the behavior of `raise` and `handling`, let us consider the following example:

```
first closed.
first (partial Inst) :- raise (context (partial Inst)).

snd free.
```

```
snd (partial Inst) :- raise (context bad).

test1 A :- handling E (first A) (snd A).
test2 A :- handling (context A) (first A) (snd A).
```

Consider the query test1 A, snd A. Matching with the clause first closed yields the substitution A = closed, which causes snd A to fail. Upon backtracking to the second clause for first, initially A is bound to partial Inst. Then the error context (partial Inst) is raised, causing the instantiation of A to be undone. Next, the handling causes E to be unified with context (partial Inst), and the goal snd A to be tried. The result of the entire goal is that E is instantiated with context (partial Inst) and A is instantiated with free. Consider now the query test2 A, snd A. Computation proceeds in the same manner, except that the handling causes A to be unified once again with partial Inst, and hence the goal snd (partial Inst) is attempted, which results in the error context bad being passed back.

With this kind of ability to raise errors, we could modify the first interactive loop for a generic theorem prover found in Sect. 3 to allow for an ability to retry the previous reduction step (perhaps applying different clauses), and to allow for an ability to completely undo some number of previous steps of reduction as follows:

```
prove Goal :- reduce Goal success, write "Goal succeeded.", nl.

reduce success success.

reduce InputGoal OutputGoal :-
    write "Current Goal = ", write InputGoal, nl,
    write "Enter Rule Name: ",
    read RuleName,
    handling (backup N)
      (apply RuleName InputGoal OutputGoal)
      (dec_undo N).

reduce InputGoal OutputGoal :-
    write "Trying again ... ", nl,
    reduce InputGoal OutputGoal.

apply (undo N) InputGoal OutputGoal :- raise (backup N).

apply retry InputGoal OutputGoal :- raise backtrack.

apply RuleName InputGoal OutputGoal :-
    rule RuleName InputGoal MidGoal,
    handling backtrack
      (reduce MidGoal OutputGoal)
      fail.
```

```
dec_undo 0 :- fail.

dec_undo N :-
  N > 0,
  M is N - 1,
  raise (undo M).
```

In the previous example, notice that it is necessary for the error (backup N) not to be trapped by the occurrence of handling backtrack which is in the main clause for apply. Also notice that we made use of the ability to pass back values within errors, and not just the ability to pass back one of some fixed class of errors.

If our logic programming language has universal quantification within goals, then we need to understand how the ability to pass back values within errors interacts with the existence of pi constants that may occur within those values. Should an error be able to pass a pi-constant back out of the scope that introduced the pi-constant? Might that constant then enter into a computation that was intended too exclude that constant? Since all constants may be viewed as being pi-constants bound implicitly at top-level, simply barring all pi-constants from occurring in an error is unsatisfactory. It is also unnecessary.

The only way that a value contained within an error that has been passed back can enter into further computation is if it is trapped by an occurrence of handling Error where the error unifies with the pattern Error. One approach, therefore, is to say that the difficulty lies not in raising and passing back an error, but in being able to unify with the pattern given by an occurrence of handling against it. Implicit in the fourth rule of the definition of the derivation of a goal from a context and a signature, found in Sect. 3, is the fact that when searching for a derivation of a goal, we may only substitute for a variable within the goal those terms which involve only constants existing in the signature. If Goal1 raises an error which contains a value involving a pi-constant whose scope is internal to the derivation of Goal1, then any goal of the form handling Error Goal1 Goal2 will continue to pass back the error. This is because such an error involves a constant which cannot be substituted for any of the variables in Error, and hence cannot occur in any instance of Error. With this approach, the goal pi E \ (raise E) would pass back an error that could not be caught. This approach parallels closely the way in which Standard ML deals with let-bound identifiers and the raising of exceptions containing such values.

Another approach to the problem, and one which appeals to the author, is to say that a value only exists within those contexts whose signatures contain all the constants that occur in the value. Thus a goal that attempted to pass an error involving a pi-constant out of the scope of that pi-constant would fail, thus ceasing to percolate the error. Hence, the goal pi E \ (raise E) would not pass back any error, but would simply fail.

With either of these operational behaviors, if we assume that any subgoal of the form `raise E` is not derivable from any program context, then if a goal of the form `handling Goal1 Goal2` succeeds in a given program context, then there exists an instantiation of the variables in `Goal1` and `Goal2` such that the goal `Goal1; Goal2` under that instantiation is derivable from that program context. However, in general there will be many more solutions to the goal `Goal1; Goal2` than there will be to the goal `handling Goal1 Goal2`. In this way we may view either of these implementations of `raise` and `handling` as providing greater control over search. Without further practical experience in the ramifications of these two different approaches, and perhaps a logical interpretation, it remains unclear as to which approach, if either, is to be preferred.

Acknowledgements

The author is grateful to Dale Miller for many helpful discussions on topics related to work in this paper. She is also appreciative of the thoughtful comments of the reviewers.

References

1. W. F. Clocksin and C. S. Mellish. *Programming in Prolog*. Springer-Verlag, third edition, 1987.
2. A. Felty and D. Miller. Specifying theorem prover in a higher-order logic programming language. In E. Lusk and R. Overbeek, editors, *Proceedings of the Ninth International Conference on Automated Deduction*, pages 61 – 80, Springer-Verlag, May 23 – 26 1988.
3. Amy Felty. *Specifying and Implementing Theorem Provers in a Higher-Order Logic Programming Language*. PhD thesis, University of Pennsylvania, 1989.
4. Elsa L. Gunter. *The Construction and Use of a Generic Theorem Prover in λ-Prolog*. Technical Report, Dept. of Computer and Information Science, Moore School of Engineering, University of Pennsylvania, 1990.
5. John Hannan and Dale Miller. A meta language for functional programs. In H. Rogers and H. Abramson, editors, *Meta-Programming in Logic Programming*, pages 453 – 476, 1989.
6. D. Miller. Lexical scoping as universal quantification. In G. Levi and M. Martelli, editors, *Sixth International Logic Programming Conference*, pages 268 – 283, The MIT Press, 1989.
7. D. Miller. A logical analysis of modules in logic programming. *Journal of Logic Programming*, 6:79 – 108, 1989.
8. D. Miller, G. Nadathur, F. Pfenning, and A. Scedrov. Uniform proofs as a foundation for logic programming. *Annals of Pure and Applied Logic*, (to appear).
9. Dale Miller. A logic programming language with lambda abstraction, function variables and simple unification. In Peter Schoeder-Heister, editor, *Extensions of Logic Programming*, To appear.
10. Dale Miller and Gopalan Nadathur. A logic programming approach to manipulating formulas and programs. In *Proceeding of the IEEE Fourth Symposium on Logic Programming, San Francisco*, pages 379 – 388, September 1987.

11. R. Milner, M. Tofte, and R. Harper. *The Definition of Standard ML*. The MIT Press, Cambridge, Mass., 1990.

12. Gopalan Nadathur and Dale Miller. An overview of λ-Prolog. In *Proceedings of the Fifth International Logic Programming Conference and Symposium, Seattle, Wash.*, pages 810 – 827, The MIT Press, August 15 – 19 1988.

13. Remo Pareschi. *Type-driven Natural Language Analysis*. PhD thesis, University of Edinburgh, 1989.

14. Remo Pareschi and Dale Miller. Extending definite clause grammars and scoping constructs. In *The Seventh International Conference of Logic Programming, Jerusalem*, 1990.

15. Laurence C. Paulson. The foundation of a generic theorem prover. *Journal of Automated Reasoning*, 5(3):363 – 397, 1989.

A Decision Procedure for Propositional N-Prolog

Jörg Hudelmaier
CIS, Universität München
Leopoldstr. 139, D-8000 München

ABSTRACT

The purpose of this paper is to present a Gentzen style formulation for the fragment of intuitionistic propositional logic having only conjunction and implication, capturing the spirit of Gabbay's goal directed theorem prover for this logic [1], later modified into N-PROLOG (cf.[2]), which, however, does not need loop checking.

1. INTRODUCTION

In his lecture notes [1] Gabbay has proposed a backward goal directed computation procedure for intuitionistic and classical logic based on conjunction, implication and falsity. This approach was used to develop N-PROLOG in [2,3] and was further extended to intermediate logics in a paper with F. Kriwaczek [4]. The system was implemented in LPA-PROLOG by Kriwaczek as described in [4]. Gabbay's rules for the propositional case first reduce any formula w in the restricted language into an equivalent conjunction of formulas v in ready-for-computation form i.e. where $v=u\rightarrow a$, a is atomic or equal to $\perp$ and u is a conjunction of atomic formulas a_i and formulas $p_j\rightarrow c_j$ in ready-for-computation form. The formula a is called the head of v and the formulas a_i and $p_j\rightarrow c_j$ are called its components. (In the following the letters v, u, a, a_i, p_j and c_j shall always denote formulas of the type indicated here.) This is done via the intuitionistically valid equivalences $a\rightarrow(b\rightarrow c)\equiv(a\wedge b)\rightarrow c$ and $a\rightarrow(b\wedge c)\equiv(a\rightarrow b)\wedge(a\rightarrow c)$.

Now N-PROLOG is used to derive from multisets of formulas in ready-for-computation form atomic formulas: If an atomic formula a is derivable intuitionistically from a multiset Δ of such formulas, this is noted as "Δ ? a succeeds". To test for success in this sense N-PROLOG has two axioms and one rule: The axioms are:

$\Delta, \perp$? a succeeds.

Δ, a ? a succeeds .

and the rule N is

> $\Delta, v\ ?\ a$ succeeds if
> for all i $\Delta, v\ ?\ a_i$ succeeds and for all j $\Delta, v, p_j\ ?\ c_j$ succeeds.

(In the following we shall also simply call N-PROLOG the calculus N.)

That this rule suffices has been shown e.g.in [2]. Note that the premisses of this rule are at least as complex as its conclusion, whence it does not yield a simple decision procedure. Therefore a loop checker has to be invoked every time the rule is applied. In their implementation Gabbay and Kriwaczek used a historical loop checker, which, however, is costly. (Actually, with the usual depth first search strategy a loop checker is already required to obtain completeness, because looping in an unsuccessful branch will prevent backtracking.)

Examples for the use of N-PROLOG:

1. A proof that $(((p{\to}q){\to}p){\to}p){\to}q\ ?\ q$ succeeds:

$$
\begin{array}{lll}
(((p{\to}q){\to}p){\to}p){\to}q\ ,(p{\to}q){\to}p\ ,p\ ,(p{\to}q){\to}p & ? & p \\
(((p{\to}q){\to}p){\to}p){\to}q\ ,(p{\to}q){\to}p\ ,p & ? & q \\
(((p{\to}q){\to}p){\to}p){\to}q\ ,(p{\to}q){\to}p & ? & p \\
(((p{\to}q){\to}p){\to}p){\to}q & ? & q
\end{array}
$$

2. One of the eight branches of the proof that $((((p{\to}r){\to}p){\to}p)\wedge(((q{\to}r){\to}q){\to}q)){\to}r\ ?\ r$ succeeds:

$$
\begin{array}{lll}
((((p{\to}r){\to}p){\to}p)\wedge(((q{\to}r){\to}q){\to}q)){\to}r,\ (p{\to}r){\to}p,\ p,\ (q{\to}r){\to}q,\ q,\ (p{\to}r){\to}p & ? & p \\
((((p{\to}r){\to}p){\to}p)\wedge(((q{\to}r){\to}q){\to}q)){\to}r,\ (p{\to}r){\to}p,\ p,\ (q{\to}r){\to}q,\ q & ? & r \\
((((p{\to}r){\to}p){\to}p)\wedge(((q{\to}r){\to}q){\to}q)){\to}r,\ (p{\to}r){\to}p,\ p,\ (q{\to}r){\to}q & ? & q \\
((((p{\to}r){\to}p){\to}p)\wedge(((q{\to}r){\to}q){\to}q)){\to}r,\ (p{\to}r){\to}p,\ p & ? & r \\
((((p{\to}r){\to}p){\to}p)\wedge(((q{\to}r){\to}q){\to}q)){\to}r,\ (p{\to}r){\to}p & ? & p \\
((((p{\to}r){\to}p){\to}p)\wedge(((q{\to}r){\to}q){\to}q)){\to}r & ? & r
\end{array}
$$

3. A proof that $q{\to}p,\ (p{\to}q){\to}q\ ?\ p$ does not succeed :

The only possible premiss from which it could be deduced is $q{\to}p,\ (p{\to}q){\to}q\ ?\ q$, which in turn could only be deduced from $q{\to}p,\ (p{\to}q){\to}q,\ p\ ?q$, which could only be deduced from itself, thus causing a loop.

This paper presents a proof theoretical formulation of the goal directed computation rule with a modification which allows the complexity of the formulas to be tested to be reduced at each step. This dispenses with the need for a historical loop checker because every sequence of successive tests automatically breaks off. In contrast to the rule N this new rule Q is not directly PROLOG oriented in that it does not require the head of its principal formula to match the formula on the right hand side. This additional degree of freedom has to be compensated for by having an additional premiss. This means that in the worst case for a principal formula with n conjuncts, we have $n+1$ premisses instead of n. (In most cases however the number of premisses will be considerably smaller than in N.) On the other hand the new inference rule is more restrictive than N in that it requires its principle formula to have no atomic components. (We shall see how this restriction reduces the number of possible choices at each step.) Now the rule Q determining the new calculus Q says:

$\Delta, v\ ?\ q$ *succeeds if*

Simp$(\Delta, a)\ ?\ q$ *succeeds and for all j Simp*$(\Delta, p_j, c_j{\to}a)\ ?\ c_j$ *succeeds,*

where v has no atomic components and Simp(Δ) results from Δ by cancelling in all formulas v of Δ those atomic components a_i which occur in Δ.

Consider again the examples given above for N:

1. The proof for $(((p{\to}q){\to}p){\to}p){\to}q\ ?\ q$ now looks as follows:

$$
\begin{array}{cc}
 & p,q\,?\,p \qquad p,q\,?\,q \\
q\,?\,q & (p{\to}q){\to}p, p{\to}q\,?\,p \\
\multicolumn{2}{c}{(((p{\to}q){\to}p){\to}p){\to}q\,?\,q}
\end{array}
$$

(Note that $p, q = Simp(p, p{\to}q)$ and $p, q = Simp(p, q{\to}p, p{\to}q)$.)

2. The proof for $((((p{\to}r){\to}p){\to}p)\wedge(((q{\to}r){\to}q){\to}q)){\to}r\ ?\ r$ is

$$
\begin{array}{cccc}
 & p,r\,?\,p \quad p,r\,?\,r & q,r\,?\,q \quad q,r\,?\,r \\
r\,?\,r & (p{\to}r){\to}p, p{\to}r\,?\,p & (q{\to}r){\to}q, q{\to}r\,?\,q \\
\multicolumn{4}{c}{((((p{\to}r){\to}p){\to}p)\wedge(((q{\to}r){\to}q){\to}q)){\to}r\,?\,r}
\end{array}
$$

(Note that $p,r = Simp(p, p{\to}r)$ and $p,r = Simp(p, r{\to}p, p{\to}r)$ and similarly for q,r.)

3. Suppose now we had a proof of $q{\to}p, (p{\to}q){\to}q\ ?\ p$, then since $q{\to}p$ could not be the principal formula of the last inference of this proof, this principal formula must be $(p{\to}q){\to}q$, but then the second premiss of this inference would be $q{\to}p, p, q{\to}q\ ?\ q$, which is neither an axiom nor the conclusion of an instance of the rule Q.

4. Note that if Δ consists entirely of Horn clauses, i.e. formulas with only atomic components, then Δ ? q *succeeds* iff q is in $Simp(\Delta)$, hence $Simp(\Delta)$? q is an axiom.

In his "Theory of Algorithmic proof" ([1]), Gabbay proposes a different approach to avoid backtracking at least in those cases where the components of the principal formula are not atomic: Using this procedure one simply throws away every principal formula which has been used. This procedure is of course incomplete unless one compensates for it by introducing the so called Bounded Restart Rule, which allows the changing of a current right hand side formula a into another right hand side formula occurring earlier on the same branch of the computation, provided there is another a further up on this same branch. For this purpose it is convenient to keep a list of all right hand sides; this list is called *history*. It is interesting to see how the Bounded Restart Rule works for the third example above:

3. Suppose there was a proof of $q{\rightarrow}p$, $(p{\rightarrow}q){\rightarrow}q$? p with empty history, then the only possible premiss of its last inference would be $(p{\rightarrow}q){\rightarrow}q$? q with history (p). The only possible premiss leading to this conclusion would be p ? q with history (q,p). Now there is no q to the right of p in the history, so we cannot change p ? q into p ? p, hence we fail. (Note however that if we were using classical logic, then we would be allowed to do so — for classical logic unbounded restart is admissible.)

2. PROOFS

In order to prove the equivalence of N-PROLOG and the new calculus Q we introduce two intermediate calculi O and P both having the same axioms as N and one rule:
The rule O states that

Δ, v ?r succeeds if
Δ, a ? r succeeds, for all i Δ, v ? a_i succeeds and for all j Δ, v, p_j ? c_j succeeds.

and the rule P states that

Δ, a_0, ... , a_n, v ?r succeeds if
Δ, a_0, ... , a_n, a ? r succeeds and for all j Δ, a_0, ... ,a_n, p_j, $c_j{\rightarrow}a$? c_j succeeds.

Now we prove

THEOREM: $N \subseteq P \subseteq O \subseteq N$

(where "$\subseteq$" means inclusion of the corresponding sets of theorems.)

We first remark, that if Δ, Δ ? r is provable by N or O, then so is Δ ? r, and if Δ ? r is provable, then so are all Γ, Δ ? r. Below we shall tacitly apply this remark. Now we are going to prove one lemma on N and two lemmas on O:

LEMMA ON N:

    a) if N proves Γ, a ? r and Δ ? a, then it proves Γ, Δ ? r.

    b) if N proves Γ, v ? r and $\Delta, a_0, \dots ,a_m, p_0 \to c_0, \dots , p_n \to c_n$? a,

       then it proves Γ, Δ ? r.

a) is proved by induction on the length of the deduction of Γ, a ? r. If Γ, a ? r is an axiom of the first type, then $\bot$ is in Γ and Γ, Δ ? r is also an axiom. If it is an axiom of the second type, then either $r=a$ or $r \neq a$. In the first case we know that Δ ? r is provable, in the second case Γ ? r is also an axiom, hence in both cases Γ, Δ ? r is provable. If Γ, a ? r is not an axiom, then a is present in every premiss of the inference leading to Γ, a ? r. So by the induction hypothesis we may cancel it everywhere, add Δ, apply the same inference again and deduce Γ, Δ ? r.

For b) we use lexicographic induction on the pairs consisting of the degree of v and the length of the deduction of Γ, v ? r (where the degree of an atomic formula is 0 and the degree of a composite formula is 1 plus the maximum of the degrees of its components): If Γ, v ? r is an axiom, then so is Γ, Δ ? r. Otherwise if v is not the principal formula of the last inference of this deduction, then by the induction hypothesis we may cancel it from all premisses, apply the same inference again and deduce Γ, Δ ? r. Else if v is the principal formula, then $r=a$ and the last inference has premisses Γ, v ? a_i and Γ, v, p_j ? c_j and by the induction hypothesis we may again cancel all v's and add Δ everywhere. Moreover by applying a) m times to the resulting Γ, Δ ? a_i and to $\Delta, a_0, \dots , a_m, p_0 \to c_0, \dots , p_n \to c_n$? a we obtain $\Gamma, \Delta, p_0 \to c_0, \dots , p_n \to c_n$? r. Now if the degree of v is 1, then we are ready. Otherwise, since the degree of all $p_i \to c_i$ is smaller than the degree of v, we may apply the induction hypothesis n times to this sequent and to the Γ, Δ, p_j ? c_j and obtain Γ, Δ ? r.

This lemma immediately shows that the rule P is admissible for N-PROLOG, i.e. $N \subseteq P$: Suppose that N proves $\Delta, a_0, \dots , a_n, a$? r as well as all $\Delta, a_0, \dots ,a_n, p_j, c_j \to a$? c_j . Then since N proves $p_j, c_j, (p_j \to c_j) \to a$? a it also proves all $\Delta, a_0, \dots , a_n, p_j, (p_j \to c_j) \to a$? c_j, hence all $\Delta, a_0, \dots , a_n, (p_j \to c_j) \to a$? a. As N proves $((p_0 \to c_0) \to a) \to a, \dots , (p_n \to c_n) \to a) \to a, v$? a, it also proves $\Delta, a_0, \dots , a_n, v$? a and finally $\Delta, a_0, \dots , a_n, v$? r.

FIRST LEMMA ON O:

If $\Delta, v ? r$ has an O-deduction of length n, then $\Delta, a ? r$ and $\Delta, p_j, c_j \rightarrow a ? r$ have O-deductions of length smaller than or equal to n.

This lemma is proved by a straightforward induction on the length of the given deduction.

SECOND LEMMA ON O:

If $\Delta ? r$ is provable by O, then it has an O-deduction in which all premisses which are of the form $\Gamma, v ? a_i$ are axioms.

Of course it suffices to show this for deductions in which all inferences but the last one have this property. For this we use induction on the sum of the lengths of all deductions leading to one of the $\Gamma, v ? a_i$. One of these is not an axiom, hence it is the conclusion of an O-inference with principal formula $b \rightarrow c$ and first premiss $\Gamma', v, c ? a_i$. Now the preceding lemma shows that from the deductions of the $\Gamma, v ? a_k k \neq i$, of the $\Gamma, v, p_j ? c_j$ and of $\Gamma, a ? r$ we obtain deductions of the $\Gamma', v, c ? a_k$, of the $\Gamma', v, p_j, c ? c_j$ and of $\Gamma', a, c ? r$ of smaller or equal length. Hence if we apply an O-inference to all of these and to $\Gamma', v, c ? a_i$ we get a deduction of $\Gamma', v, c ? r$, which either has the required property or a smaller induction parameter. In the latter case the induction hypothesis gives us a deduction of $\Gamma', v, c ? r$ which we may take as the first premiss of the inference with principal formula $b \rightarrow c$, resulting in a deduction of $\Gamma, v ? r$ with the desired property.

Now these two lemmas yield P $\subseteq$ O as follows:
Suppose we have an O-deduction of $\Delta, v ? r$ with premisses $\Delta, a ? r$, $\Delta, v ? a_i$ and $\Delta, v, p_j ? c_j$. By the second lemma we may assume that all $\Delta, v ? a_i$ are axioms, hence that $\Delta = \Gamma, a_0, \dots, a_n$. Furthermore the first lemma shows that from the deductions of the $\Delta, v, p_j ? c_j$ we obtain deductions of all $\Delta, p_j, c_j \rightarrow a ? c_j$ of smaller or equal length. Hence by the induction hypothesis all premisses necessary for an application of a P-inference with conclusion $\Delta, v ? r$ are provable by P.

Since the inclusion O $\subseteq$ N is trivial this completes the proof of the theorem.

LEMMA ON P:

P proves $\Delta ? r$ iff it proves $Simp(\Delta) ? r$.

If P proves Δ ? r then a straightforward induction on the length of its deduction shows that P also proves $Simp(\Delta)$? r. On the other hand if P proves $Simp(\Delta)$? r then by the theorem we may apply the lemma on N sufficiently often to $Simp(\Delta)$? r and to expressions of the type q, $(q\wedge u)\to a$, u ? a and obtain a deduction of Δ ? r.

This lemma and the theorem immediately show:

COROLLARY:

N-PROLOG proves Δ ? r iff the calculus Q proves $Simp(\Delta)$? r

ACKNOWLEDGEMENT

I am grateful to Prof. D.M. Gabbay for his encouragement, for making me available his papers, and for pointing out to me his alternative approach to avoiding loop checking and his elegant connection between classical and intuitionistic logic.

REFERENCES

[1] Gabbay, D.M.: Theory of Algorithmic Proof. In: *Handbook of Logic in Theoretical Computer Science*, vol.1, ed. by Gabbay, D.M. & T.S.E. Maibaum, Oxford, to appear
[2] Gabbay, D.M. & U. Reyle: N-Prolog. Part 1. In: *Journal of Logic Programming* 1 (1984), p.319–355
[3] Gabbay, D.M.: N-Prolog. Part 2. In: *Journal of Logic Programming* 2 (1985), p.251–285
[4] Gabbay, D.M. & F. Kriwaczek: A Goal Directed Theorem Prover for Intuitionistic and Intermediate Logics, Based on Conjunctions and Implications. To appear in *Journal of Automated Reasoning*
[5] Gabbay, D.M. & U. Reyle: *N-Prolog. Part 3 — Computation with Run Time Skolemization*. Technical report, Imperial College 1987

A Logic Programming Language with Lambda-Abstraction, Function Variables, and Simple Unification

Dale Miller
Department of Computer and Information Science
University of Pennsylvania
Philadelphia, PA 19104–6389 USA
dale@cis.upenn.edu

Abstract: It has been argued elsewhere that a logic programming language with function variables and λ-abstractions within terms makes a very good meta-programming language, especially when an object language contains notions of bound variables and scope. The λProlog logic programming language and the closely related Elf and Isabelle systems provide meta-programs with both function variables and λ-abstractions by containing implementations of higher-order unification. In this paper, we present a logic programming language, called L_λ, that also contains both function variables and λ-abstractions, but certain restriction are placed on occurrences of function variables. As a result, an implementation of L_λ does not need to implement full higher-order unification. Instead, an extension to first-order unification that respects bound variable names and scopes is all that is required. Such unification problems are shown to be decidable and to possess most general unifiers when unifiers exist. A unification algorithm and logic programming interpreter are described and proved correct. Several examples of using L_λ as a meta-programming language are presented.

1. Introduction

A meta-programming language must be able to represent and manipulate such syntactic structures as programs, formulas, types, and proofs. A common characteristic of all these structures is that they involve notions of abstractions, scope, bound and free variables, substitution instances, and equality up to alphabetic changes of bound variables. Although the data types available in most computer programming languages are, of course, rich enough to represent all these kinds of structures, such data types do not have direct support for these common characteristics. For example, although it is trivial to represent first-order formulas in Lisp, it is a more complex matter to write Lisp programs that correctly substitute a term into a formulas (being careful not to capture bound variables), to test for the equality of formulas up to alphabetic variation, and to determine if a certain variable's occurrence is free or bound. This situation is the same when structures like programs or (natural deduction) proofs are to be manipulated and if other programming languages, such as Pascal, Prolog, and ML, replace Lisp.

It is desirable for a meta-programming language to have language-level support for these various aspects of formulas, proofs, types, and programs. What is a common framework for representing these structures? Early work by Church, Curry, Howard, Martin-Löf, Scott, Strachey, Tait, and others concluded that typed and untyped λ-calculi provide a common syntactic representation for all these structures. Thus a meta-programming language that is able to represent terms in such λ-calculi directly could be used to represent these structures using the techniques described by these authors.

One problem with designing a data type for λ-terms is that methods for destructuring them should be invariant under the intended notions of equality of λ-terms, which usually include α-conversion. Thus, destructuring the λ-term $\lambda x.fxx$ into its bound variable x and body fxx is not invariant under α-conversion: this term is α-convertible to $\lambda y.fyy$ but the results of destructuring this equal term does not yield equal answers. Although the use of nameless dummies [1] can help simplify this one problem since both of these terms are represented by the same structure $\lambda(f11)$, that representation still requires fairly complex manipulations to represent the full range of desired operations on λ-terms. A more high-level approach to the manipulation of λ-terms modulo α and β-conversion has been the use of unification of simply typed λ-terms [9, 15, 24, 26]. Huet and Lang [10] describe how such a technique, when restricted to second-order matching, could be used to analyze and manipulate simple functional and imperative programs. Their reliance on unification, which solved equations up to α, β, and η-conversion, made their meta programs elegant, simple to write, and easy to prove correct. They chose second-order matching because it was strong enough to implement a certain collection of template matching program transformations and it was decidable. The general problem of the unification of simply typed λ-terms of order 2 and higher is undecidable [11].

This use of unification on λ-terms has been extended in several recent papers. In [4, 5, 6, 16] various meta programs, including theorem provers and program transformers, were written in the logic programming language λProlog [18] that contains unification of simply typed λ-terms. Paulson [20, 21] exploits such unification in the theorem proving system Isabelle. Pfenning and Elliot [22] argue that product types are also of use. Elliot [3] has studied unification in a dependent type framework and Pfenning [23] developed a logic programming language, Elf, that incorporates that unification process. That programming language can be used to provide a direct implementation of signatures written in the LF type specification language [7].

In this paper, we shall focus on a particularly simple logic programming language, called L_λ, that is completely contained within λProlog and admits a very natural implementation of the data type of λ-terms. The term language of L_λ is the simply typed λ-calculus with equality modulo α, β, and η-conversion. The "β-aspects" of L_λ are, however, greatly restricted and, as a result, unification in this language will resemble first-order unification – the main difference being that λ-abstractions are handled directly.

The structure of L_λ is motivated in Section 2 and formally defined in Section 3. An interperter and unification algorithm for L_λ are presented in Sections 4 and 5, respectively. The unification algorithm is proved correct in Section 6 and the interpreter is proved correct in Section 7. Finally, several examples of L_λ programs are presented in Section 8.

2. Two motivations

There are at least two motivations for studying the logic L_λ. The first is based on experience with using stronger logics for the specification of meta-programs. The second is based on seeing how L_λ can be thought of as a kind of "closure" of a first-order logic programming language.

2.1. Past experience. Both the Isabelle theorem prover and λProlog contain simply typed λ-terms, β-conversion, and quantification of variables at all functional orders. These systems have been used to specify and implement a large number of meta-programming tasks, including theorem proving, type checking, and program transformation, interpretation, and compilation. An examination of the structure of those specifications and implementations revealed two interesting facts. First, free or "logic" variables of functional type were often applied only to distinct λ-bound variables. For example, the free functional variable M might appear in the following context:

$$\lambda x \ldots \lambda y \ldots (Myx) \ldots .$$

When such free variables were instantiated, the only new β-redexes that arise are those involving distinct λ-bound variables. For example, if M above is instantiated with a λ-terms, say $\lambda u \lambda v.t$, then the only new β-redex formed is $((\lambda u \lambda v.t)yx)$. This is reduced to normal form simply by renaming the variables u and v to y and x — a very simple computation. Second, in the cases where free variables of functional type were applied to general terms, meta-level β-reduction was invoked to simply perform object-level substitution.

The logic L_λ is designed to permit the first kind of β-redex but not the second. As a result, implementations of this logic can make use of a very simple kind of unification. The fact that object-level substitution is not automatically available can be fixed, however, since object-level substitution can be written very simply as L_λ programs. We illustrate this for a simple, first-order, object logic in Section 8. Thus, L_λ requires that some of the functionality of β-conversion be moved from the term level to the logic level. The result can be more complex logic programs but with simpler unification problems. This seems like a trade-off worth investigating.

Another characteristic of most meta programs written in Isabelle and λProlog is that they quantify over at most second-order functional types. Despite this observation, we shall present an ω-order version of L_λ here. As we shall see, however, in Section 5, the unification procedure of L_λ is not dependent on types and, hence, not on order.

2.2. Discharging constants from terms. Consider a first-order logic whose logical connectives are $\wedge$ (conjunction), $\supset$ (implication), and $\forall$ (universal quantification). Let A be a syntactic variable that ranges over atomic formulas, and let D and G range over formulas defined by the following grammar:

$$G ::= A \mid G_1 \wedge G_2 \mid D \supset G \mid \forall x.G$$
$$D ::= A \mid G \supset A \mid \forall x.D.$$

It has been argued in various places (for example, [14, 17]) that the intuitionistic theory of these formulas provides a foundation for logic programming if we permit D-formulas to be program clauses and G-formulas as goals or queries asked of them. As a logic programming language, it forms a rich extension to Horn clauses and still retains several important properties that make it suitable for program specification and implementation.

One of those important properties is that a theorem prover having a simple operational description is sound and non-deterministically complete with respect to intuitionistic logic. This operational behavior can be described as follows. Let Σ be a first-order signature (set of constants), let $\mathcal{P}$ be a finite set of closed D-formulas, and let G be a closed G-formula, both over Σ (*i.e.*, all of whose constants are from Σ). Intuitionistic provability of G from Σ and $\mathcal{P}$, written as $\Sigma; \mathcal{P} \vdash_I B$ can be characterized using the following search operations:

AND: $\Sigma; \mathcal{P} \vdash_I G_1 \wedge G_2$ if $\Sigma; \mathcal{P} \vdash_I G_1$ and $\Sigma; \mathcal{P} \vdash_I G_2$.

AUGMENT: $\Sigma; \mathcal{P} \vdash_I D \supset G$ if $\Sigma; \mathcal{P} \cup \{D\} \vdash_I G$.

GENERIC: $\Sigma; \mathcal{P} \vdash_I \forall x.G$ if $\Sigma \cup \{c\}; \mathcal{P} \vdash_I [x \mapsto c]G$, provided that c is not in Σ.

BACKCHAIN: $\Sigma; \mathcal{P} \vdash_I A$ if there is a formula $D \in \mathcal{P}$ whose universal instantiation with closed terms over Σ is A or is $G \supset A$ and $\Sigma; \mathcal{P} \vdash_I G$.

Clearly, this characterization of intuitionistic provability can be molded into a simple theorem proving mechanism. Such a mechanism using unification and a depth-first searching discipline can be used to give a logic programming interpretation to this logic. Notice that both components to the left of the turnstile may vary within the search for a proof. For example, the terms used to instantiate the universal quantifiers mentioned in the BACKCHAIN rule can be taken from different signatures at different parts of a proof.

While this logic has its uses (for example, see [12, 13, 14]), there is a kind of incompleteness in its space of values. Consider the following example. Let Σ_0 be a signature containing at least the constants *append, cons, nil, a, b* and let $\mathcal{P}_0$ contain just the two clauses

$$\forall x \forall l \forall k \forall m(append\ l\ k\ m \supset append\ (cons\ x\ l)\ k\ (cons\ x\ m))$$

$$\forall k(append\ nil\ k\ k).$$

Now, consider the problem of finding a substitution term over Σ_0 for the free variable X so that the goal formula $\forall y(append\ (cons\ a\ (cons\ b\ nil))\ y\ X)$ is provable. Proving this goal can be reduced to finding an instantiation of X so that

$$(append\ (cons\ a\ (cons\ b\ nil))\ k\ X)$$

is provable, where k is not a member of Σ_0. Using BACKCHAIN twice, this goal is provable if and only if X can be instantiated with $(cons\ a\ (cons\ b\ k))$. This is not possible, however, since X can be instantiated with terms over Σ_0 but not over $\Sigma_0 \cup \{k\}$. Such a failure here is quite sensible since the value of X should be independent of the choice of the constant used to instantiate $\forall y$. It might be very desirable, however, to have this computation succeed if we could, in some sense, abstract away this particular choice of constant. That is, an interesting value is computed here, but it cannot be used since it is not well defined. If we are willing to admit some forms of λ-abstraction into our logic, this value can be represented.

Consider, for example, proving the goal $\forall y\ (append\ (cons\ a\ (cons\ b\ nil))\ y\ (H\ y))$ where H is a functional variable that may be instantiated with a λ-term whose constants are again from the set Σ_0. Assume that we instantiate $\forall y$ again with the constant k. This time we need $(H\ k)$ to be equal to $(cons\ a\ (cons\ b\ k))$. There are two simply-typed λ-terms (up to λ-conversion) that when substituted for H into $(H\ k)$ and then λ-normalized yield $(cons\ a\ (cons\ b\ k))$, namely, the terms $\lambda w\ (cons\ a\ (cons\ b\ k))$ and $\lambda w\ (cons\ a\ (cons\ b\ w))$. Since H cannot contain k free, only the second of these possible substitutions will succeed in being a legal solution for this goal. Notice that the choice of constant to instantiate the universal quantifier in this goal is not reflected in this answer substitution since λ-terms obey α-conversion. In a sense, the λ-term $\lambda w\ (cons\ a\ (cons\ b\ w))$ is the result of *discharging* the constant k from the term $(cons\ a\ (cons\ b\ k))$. Notice, however, that discharging a first-order constant from a first-order term is now a "second-order" term: it can be used to instantiate a function variable.

The higher-order variable H in the above example is restricted in such a way that when it is involved in a unification problem, there is a single, most general unifier for it. We shall define L_λ in such a way that this is the only kind of "higher-order" unification problem that can occur. All such uses of a higher-order variable will be associated with discharging a constant from a term. Term models for β-reduction of the simply typed λ-calculus interpret a λ-term, say $\lambda x.t$ of type $\tau \to \sigma$, as a mapping from λ-equivalence classes of type τ to such equivalence classes of type σ. In L_λ, this functional interpretation must be restricted greatly: $\lambda x.t$ can be though of as a function that carries an increment in a signature to a term over that signature.

The reader who is comfortable with the above discussion and who is familiar with basic notions of logic programming and simply typed λ-terms may wish to read next Section 8 where several examples of L_λ programs are given and discussed. The following five sections are rather formal and address technical aspects of a unification algorithm and interpreter for L_λ.

3. Definition of L_λ

We assume that the reader is familiar with the basic properties of λ-terms and λ-conversion. Below we review some definitions and properties. See [8] for a more complete presentation.

Let S be a fixed, finite set of *primitive types* (also called *sorts*). The set of *types* is the smallest set of expressions that contains the primitive types and is closed under the construction of function types, denoted by the binary, infix symbol $\to$. This arrow associates to the right: read $\tau_1 \to \tau_2 \to \tau_3$ as $\tau_1 \to (\tau_2 \to \tau_3)$. The Greek letters τ and σ are used as syntactic variables ranging over types.

Let τ be the type $\tau_1 \to \cdots \to \tau_n \to \tau_0$ where $\tau_0 \in S$ and $n \geq 0$. (By convention, if $n = 0$ then τ is simply the type τ_0.) The types $\tau_1, \ldots, \tau_n$ are the *argument types of* τ while the type τ_0 is the *target type of* τ. The order of a type τ is defined as follows: If $\tau \in S$ then τ has order 0; otherwise, the order of τ is one greater than the maximum order of the argument types of τ. Thus, τ has order 1 exactly when τ is of the form $\tau_1 \to \cdots \to \tau_n \to \tau_0$ where $n \geq 1$ and $\{\tau_0, \tau_1, \ldots, \tau_n\} \subseteq S$.

A *signature (over S)* is a (possibly infinite) set Σ of pairs of tokens and types that satisfies the usual functionality condition: a given token is associated with at most one type in a given signature. We shall also assume that there are denumerably many tokens that are not mentioned in a given signature. We often enumerate signatures by listing their pairs as $a : \tau$. A signature is of order n if all its tokens have types of order n or less. The expression $\Sigma + c : \tau$ is legal if c is not assigned by Σ, in which case, it is equal to $\Sigma \cup \{c : \tau\}$.

A Σ-*term of type* τ is defined by the proof system in Figure 1. If the sequent $\Sigma \xrightarrow{stt} t : \tau$ is provable from those rules, we write $\Sigma \vdash_{stt} t : \tau$ and say that t is a Σ-term of type τ.

$$\Sigma + c : \tau \xrightarrow{stt} c : \tau$$

$$\frac{\Sigma \xrightarrow{stt} t : \tau \to \sigma \qquad \Sigma \xrightarrow{stt} s : \tau}{\Sigma \xrightarrow{stt} (ts) : \sigma}$$

$$\frac{\Sigma + d : \tau \xrightarrow{stt} [c \mapsto d]t : \sigma}{\Sigma \xrightarrow{stt} \lambda c.t : \tau \to \sigma}$$

Figure 1: Proof rules for the syntax of simply typed λ-terms

The proof rules of Figure 1 show that tokens can change status from being a constant (*i.e.* a member of signature) to being a bound variable. Context will make it clear when a given token is considered a constant or a bound variable.

Substitution and the rules of α, β, and η conversion are defined as usual. Expressions of the form $\lambda x\,(t\,x)$ are called η-redexes (provided x is not free in t) while expressions of the form $(\lambda x\,t)s$ are called β-redexes. A term is λ-*normal* if it contains no β or η-redexes. The binary relation $\lambda conv$, denoting λ-*conversion*, is defined so that $t\,\lambda conv\,s$ if there is a list of terms $t_1, \ldots, t_n$, with $n \geq 1$, t equal to t_1, s equal to t_n, and for $i = 1, \ldots, n-1$, either t_i converts to t_{i+1} or t_{i+1} converts to t_i by α, β, or η. Every term can be converted to a λ-normal term, and that normal term is unique up to the name of bound variables. We shall consider two terms, say t and s, identical if they are α-convertible to one another and in such a case we shall write $t = s$. The operator $[x_1 \mapsto s_1, \ldots, x_n \mapsto s_n]$ denotes the operation of simultaneous substitution, systematically changing bound variables in order to avoid variable capture, and then returning the λ-normalized result.

Following Church [2], we introduce logic over these terms by assuming that the primitive type o, meant to denote propositions, is always given as a member of S. Predicate types are type expressions of the form

$$\tau_1 \to \cdots \to \tau_n \to o \quad (n \geq 0)$$

where the type expressions $\tau_1, \ldots, \tau_n$ do not contain o. Signatures are constrained so that if a type in it contains o, that type must be a predicate type. If Σ assigns a token a predicate type, that token is called a predicate (via Σ). Equality can be admitted as a special predicate, but it shall not be used in this paper. The following defines the class of Σ-*formulas*.

o If A is a λ-normal Σ-term of type o then A is an atomic Σ-formula.

o If B and C are Σ-formulas then $B \wedge C$ and $B \supset C$ are Σ-formulas.

o If $[c \mapsto d]B$ is a $\Sigma+d{:}\tau$-formula then $\forall_\tau c.B$ is a Σ-formula. In this paper we shall also assume the additional restriction that the type τ does not contain the primitive type o. Thus, predicate quantification is not permitted in this logic. There are various ways to allow forms of predicate quantification in this setting: one approach is described in [17, 19] and another is described in [13]. The kinds of meta-programs that we discuss here do not require any forms of predicate quantification.

These formulas will now be restricted using the proof system in Figure 2. Let $\mathcal{Q}$ denote a list of universal and existential quantifiers in which the quantified variables are all distinct. We write $\mathcal{Q} \vdash_T t : \tau$ if the sequent $\mathcal{Q} \xrightarrow{T} t : \tau$ is provable, $\mathcal{Q} \vdash_D B$ if the sequent $\mathcal{Q} \xrightarrow{D} B$ is provable, and $\mathcal{Q} \vdash_G B$ if the sequent $\mathcal{Q} \xrightarrow{G} B$ is provable. This proof system has four provisos. The first two, (α) and $(\dagger)$, deal with only bound variable names and hence are not significant restrictions. The remaining two restrictions are of more consequence.

(α) The terms t and t' are related by α-conversion.

($\dagger$) The variable x does not occur in $\mathcal{Q}$.

($\ddagger$) The quantifier prefix $\mathcal{Q}$ contains $\forall h$ where the type on the quantifier is $\tau_1 \to \cdots \to \tau_n \to \tau$ ($n \geq 0$).

($\sharp$) The variable y is existentially quantified in $\mathcal{Q}$ with type $\tau_1 \to \cdots \to \tau_n \to \tau$ to the left of where the distinct variables $x_1, \ldots, x_n$ are universally quantified with types $\tau_1, \ldots, \tau_n$, respectively ($n \geq 0$).

Let Σ be a given signature and let $\mathcal{Q}_\Sigma$ be the prefix that is an enumeration of the quantifiers $\forall_\tau x$, for each pair $x{:}\tau \in \Sigma$, in some arbitrary but fixed order. A *goal formula* of L_λ is a Σ-formula G so that $\mathcal{Q}_\Sigma \vdash_G G$. A *definite clause* (or *program clause*) of L_λ is a Σ-formula D so that $\mathcal{Q}_\Sigma \vdash_D D$.

The restrictions that these additional syntax rules provide are of two kinds. First is the mild restriction that if a definite clause is an implication, its consequence must be atomic. Given the intuitionistic equivalences

$$B_1 \supset (B_2 \wedge B_3) \equiv (B_1 \supset B_2) \wedge (B_1 \supset B_3)$$
$$B_1 \supset (B_2 \supset B_3) \equiv (B_1 \wedge B_2) \supset B_3$$
$$B_1 \supset \forall_\tau x B_2 \equiv \forall_\tau x (B_1 \supset B_2),$$

(provided in the last case that x is not free in B_1) such a restriction is largely superficial: proofs involving formulas on either side of $\equiv$ differ only trivially. Much more restrictive are the kinds of applications that can be formed using variables bound at the top-level of a definite clause. In particular, if $\forall_\tau y D$ is a definite formula, then the only occurrences of y in D are in subterms of the form $y x_1 \cdots x_n$, where $n \geq 0$ and $x_1, \ldots, x_n$ are distinct tokens bound by either negative universal quantifiers occurrences in D or by internal λ-abstractions.

$$\frac{Q \xrightarrow{T} t : \tau}{Q \xrightarrow{T} t' : \tau}\; \alpha \qquad\qquad \frac{Q \xrightarrow{G} t}{Q \xrightarrow{G} t'}\; \alpha \qquad\qquad \frac{Q \xrightarrow{D} t}{Q \xrightarrow{D} t'}\; \alpha$$

$$\frac{Q \forall_\tau x \xrightarrow{T} t : \sigma}{Q \xrightarrow{T} \lambda x.t : \tau \to \sigma}\; \dagger \qquad \frac{}{Q \xrightarrow{T} y x_1 \cdots x_n : \tau}\; \sharp \qquad \frac{Q \xrightarrow{T} t_1 : \tau_1 \quad \cdots \quad Q \xrightarrow{T} t_n : \tau_n}{Q \xrightarrow{T} h t_1 \cdots t_n : \tau}\; \ddagger$$

$$\frac{Q \forall_\tau x \xrightarrow{G} G}{Q \xrightarrow{G} \forall_\tau x.G}\; \dagger \qquad \frac{Q \xrightarrow{G} G_1 \quad Q \xrightarrow{G} G_2}{Q \xrightarrow{G} G_1 \wedge G_2} \qquad \frac{Q \xrightarrow{D} D \quad Q \xrightarrow{G} G}{Q \xrightarrow{G} D \supset G} \qquad \frac{Q \xrightarrow{T} A : o}{Q \xrightarrow{G} A}$$

$$\frac{Q \exists_\tau x \xrightarrow{D} D}{Q \xrightarrow{D} \forall_\tau x.D}\; \dagger \qquad \frac{Q \xrightarrow{D} D_1 \quad Q \xrightarrow{D} D_2}{Q \xrightarrow{D} D_1 \wedge D_2} \qquad \frac{Q \xrightarrow{G} G \quad Q \xrightarrow{T} A : o}{Q \xrightarrow{D} G \supset A} \qquad \frac{Q \xrightarrow{T} A : o}{Q \xrightarrow{D} A}$$

Figure 2: Proof rules for the syntax of L_λ

All first-order positive Horn clauses are legal definite clauses and goal formulas. Let Σ_1 be the signature $\{p : (i \to i) \to i \to i \to o, f : (i \to i) \to i\}$. The following Σ_1-formula is an example of a definite clause:

$$\forall_i t \forall_{i \to i} n \forall_{i \to i \to i} m [\forall_i y (p\,(\lambda x.y)\, t\, y \supset p\,(\lambda x.m\, x\, y)\, t\, (n\, y)) \supset p\,(\lambda x.f(m\, x))\, t\, (f\, n)].$$

Section 8 contains several examples of L_λ programs.

Before we present a proof system for L_λ, we need the following *elaboration* function that maps definite formulas to slightly more restricted definite formulas:

o elab$(A) = \{A\}$,
o elab$(G \supset A) = \{G \supset A\}$,
o elab$(D_1 \wedge D_2) = $ elab$(D_1) \cup$ elab(D_2), and
o elab$(\forall x.D) = \{\forall x.D' \mid D' \in$ elab$(D)\}$.

Elaboration essentially breaks a D-formula into its conjuncts. If a conjunction occurs in a formula of elab(D), that occurrence is in the scope of an implication. The conjunction of all the formulas in elab(D) is intuitionistically equivalent to D.

A sequent (for L_λ) is a triple $\Sigma\,;\,\mathcal{P} \longrightarrow G$ where $Q_\Sigma \vdash_G G$ and for all $D \in \mathcal{P}$, $Q_\Sigma \vdash_D D$ and all occurrences of conjunctions in D are in the scope of an implication. A sequent-style proof system for L_λ is given in Figure 3. The proviso $\dagger$ states that there must be some formula

$$\forall_{\tau_1} x_1 \ldots \forall_{\tau_n} x_n (G' \supset A') \in \mathcal{P} \quad (n \geq 0)$$

and terms t_i so that $Q_\Sigma \vdash_T t_i : \tau_i \ (i = 1, \ldots, n)$ and $[x_1 \mapsto t_1, \ldots, x_n \mapsto t_n]G' = G$ and $[x_1 \mapsto t_1, \ldots, x_n \mapsto t_n]A' = A$. A sequent is *initial* if it is of the form $\Sigma\,;\,\mathcal{P} \longrightarrow A$ for atomic A such that there is some formula $\forall_{\tau_1} x_1 \ldots \forall_{\tau_n} x_n.A' \in \mathcal{P}$ and terms t_i so that $\Sigma \vdash_T t_i : \tau_i$ and $[x_1 \mapsto t_1, \ldots, x_n \mapsto t_n]A' = A$. Proof trees built in the usual way from these initial sequents using the rules in Figure 3 will be called *goal-directed* proofs. As the following theorem states, restricting to goal-directed proofs for L_λ yields a logic that is sound and complete for intuitionistic logic (formulated to permit empty types).

$$\frac{\Sigma\,;\,\mathcal{P} \longrightarrow G_1 \qquad \Sigma\,;\,\mathcal{P} \longrightarrow G_2}{\Sigma\,;\,\mathcal{P} \longrightarrow G_1 \wedge G_2}\; \wedge\text{-R}$$

$$\frac{\Sigma\,;\,\text{elab}(D),\mathcal{P} \longrightarrow G}{\Sigma\,;\,\mathcal{P} \longrightarrow D \supset G}\; \supset\text{-R} \qquad\qquad \frac{\Sigma + c:\tau\,;\,\mathcal{P} \longrightarrow [x \mapsto c]B}{\Sigma\,;\,\mathcal{P} \longrightarrow \forall_\tau x\, B}\; \forall\text{-R}$$

$$\frac{\Sigma\,;\,\mathcal{P} \longrightarrow G}{\Sigma\,;\,\mathcal{P} \longrightarrow A}\; \text{BC}^\dagger$$

Figure 3: Proof rules for L_λ

Theorem 3.1. *Let* $\Sigma\,;\,\mathcal{P} \longrightarrow G$ *be a sequent. The formula* G *follows from* Σ *and* $\mathcal{P}$ *intuitionistically if and only if this sequent has a goal-directed proof.*
Proof. Proofs in [12] and in [17] can be easily modified to prove this theorem. It can be proved directly by transforming a given cut-free proof into a goal-directed proof by permuting inference rules in a straightforward fashion. QED

As a result of this theorem, the operational interpretation of provability presented in the previous section can be applied to L_λ.

4. An interpreter for L_λ

An interpreter for L_λ can be implemented to search for goal-directed proofs by attempting to build them in a bottom-up fashion. The BACKCHAIN step is, of course, the most difficult since it requires chosing a clause and terms to substitute into that clause. We shall present a standard technique using "free" variables and unification to help in chosing such substitution terms.

In such an interpreter, it is necessary, in some fashion, to keep track of notions such as the "current goal," the "current program," the "current set of constants," and restrictions on free variables. Interpreters for Horn clauses need to keep track of only the first of these: there the current program and set of constants remains unchanged during a computation, and restrictions on free variables do not need to be made. In the description of interpreter for L_λ given below, a *quantifier prefix* is used to encode both the current set of constants and the restrictions on free variables, and a *sequent* is used to connect a program to a goal.

Let $\mathcal{Q}$ be a quantifier prefix, *i.e.* a list of universally and existentially quantified distinct tokens, and let Σ be a signature. Signatures and prefixes are similar in their use below, although quantifier prefixes have more structure. In particular, we have already defined Q_Σ as a way to map a signature into a prefix. Similarly, we define Σ_Q to be the signature that contains the pair $x : \tau$ if $\forall_\tau x$ is in Q (existential quantifiers are ignored).

A *Q-substitution* is a substitution that contains a substitution term for precisely the existentially quantified variables in Q. Furthermore, if Q is of the form $Q'\exists_\tau x Q''$ and the pair $x \mapsto t$ is in such a substitution, then t is λ-normal and $\Sigma, \Sigma_{Q'} \vdash_{stt} t : \tau$. In other words, the only tokens free in t are either in Σ or are universally quantified to the left of x. In this sense, a Q-substitution is a closed substitution; that is, substitution terms do not contain existentially quantified variables. Two Q-substitutions, say φ and ψ, are equal if for each $\exists x$ in Q, $\varphi x = \psi x$. In that case, we write $\varphi = \psi$.

It is possible that for a given Σ and Q, there may not be any Q-substitutions. For example, if Σ is the signature $\{f : i \to i, g : i \to i \to i\}$ and Q is the prefix $\exists_i x$, there is no Q-substitution since there is no λ-term whose only free tokens are f and g and which has type i. That is, the type i is, in a sense, empty. Since the problem of determining if there is a Q-substitution for a given Q and Σ reduces to proving theorems in the implicational fragment of intuitionistic logic, this problem is decidable [25] (this assumes that there is only a finite set of distinct types in Σ).

A *Q-sequent* is a pair $\mathcal{P} \longrightarrow G$ where $Q_\Sigma Q \vdash_G G$ and where for every D in the finite set $\mathcal{P}$, $Q_\Sigma Q \vdash_D D$. Furthermore, we assume that D is the result of an elaboration; that is, every occurrence of a conjunction in D is in the scope of an implication. A *state* (of the interpreter) is a triple $\langle \theta, Q, S \rangle$ where θ is a substitution, Q is a quantifier prefix, and S is a finite set of Q-sequents. These sequents specify what remains to be proved for the interpretation to be successful. A *success state* is a state in which the set of sequents is empty.

A substitution φ *satisfies* a prefix Q and a set of Q-sequents S if φ is a Q-substitution such that for every sequent $\mathcal{P} \longrightarrow G$ in S it is the case that $\Sigma \cup \Sigma_Q, \varphi \mathcal{P} \vdash_I \varphi G$. If the set S is empty, this condition reduces to requiring that φ is just a Q-substitution. The purpose of an interpreter is to search for the existence of satisfying substitutions for the prefix and sequents of its state. Checking satisfiability is, of course, not decidable.

The following transition rules describe the heart of a non-deterministic interpreter. The operation $\uplus$ denotes disjoint union.

AND: Given the state $\langle \theta, Q, \{\mathcal{P} \longrightarrow G_1 \wedge G_2\} \uplus S \rangle$, change to the state

$$\langle \theta, Q, \{\mathcal{P} \longrightarrow G_1, \mathcal{P} \longrightarrow G_2\} \cup S \rangle.$$

This transition simply translates the logical connective $\wedge$ into an AND-node in the interpreter's search space.

AUGMENT: Given the state $\langle \theta, Q, \{\mathcal{P} \longrightarrow D \supset G\} \uplus S \rangle$, change to the state

$$\langle \theta, Q, \{\mathrm{elab}(D) \cup \mathcal{P} \longrightarrow G\} \cup S \rangle.$$

An implication in a goal is thus an instruction to augment the program with the (elaboration of the) antecedent of the implication.

GENERIC: Given the state $\langle \theta, Q, \{\mathcal{P} \longrightarrow \forall_\tau x.G\} \uplus S \rangle$, change to the state

$$\langle \theta, Q \forall_\tau y, \{\mathcal{P} \longrightarrow [x \mapsto y]G\} \cup S \rangle,$$

where y is a token not bound in $Q_\Sigma Q$. A universal quantifier in a goal causes a new constant to be added to the current signature.

The following two transitions assume the existence of a unification algorithm. This will be described in the next section. The algorithm is called by unify(θ, QP), where θ is a substitution that is being accumulated, Q is a quantifier prefix, and P is a list of typed equations between terms. The algorithm returns either *fail* or a pair, $\langle \theta', Q' \rangle$, where Q' is a quantifier prefix and θ' is the new accumulated substitution. The symbol $\emptyset$ will denote the empty substitution.

BACKCHAIN: Consider the state $\langle \theta, Q, \{ P \longrightarrow A' \} \uplus S \rangle$ where

$$\forall x_1 \ldots \forall x_n (G \supset A) \in P \quad (n \geq 0)$$

and A and A' are atomic formulas. Using α-conversion, we may assume that $x_1, \ldots, x_n$ are not bound in $Q_\Sigma Q$. If unify$(\emptyset, Q \exists x_1 \ldots \exists x_n [A \overset{\circ}{=} A']) = \langle \rho, Q' \rangle$ then the interpreter can make a transition to the state

$$\langle \theta \circ \rho, Q', \rho(\{ P \longrightarrow G \} \cup S') \rangle.$$

(Composition is defined as $(\theta \circ \rho)(x) = \rho(\theta(x))$. The application of ρ to a set of sequents is the set of sequents resulting from applying ρ to all formulas in all the sequents.)

CLOSE: Consider the state $\langle \theta, Q, S \rangle$ where S is the set

$$\{ \{ \forall x_1 \ldots \forall x_n . A \} \cup P \longrightarrow A' \} \uplus S'$$

for some set S' and for $n \geq 0$ and for atomic formulas A and A'. Using α-conversion, we may assume that $x_1, \ldots, x_n$ are not bound in $Q_\Sigma Q$. If

$$\text{unify}(\emptyset, Q \exists x_1 \ldots \exists x_n [A \overset{\circ}{=} A']) = \langle \rho, Q' \rangle$$

then the interpreter can make a transition to the state $\langle \theta \circ \rho, Q', \rho S' \rangle$.

No transition can be applied to a success state.

The formal correctness properties for this interpreter will be proved in Section 7. We can now describe a simple, depth-first, deterministic interpreter for L_λ. First, we must consider the third component of a state and the antecedent of sequents as lists instead of sets. AUGMENT concatenates elaborated clauses to the front of an antecedent. When given a non-success state, the first sequent is used to determine which transition to consider. If the succedent of that sequent is an implication, apply AUGMENT; if it is a conjunction, apply AND; if it is universally quantified, apply GENERIC. The choice of new token used in GENERIC is immaterial. Finally, if the succedent is an atom, then we need to use BACKCHAIN or CLOSE. Here, we select a D-formula from the antecedent in a left-to-right order and see if either of these transitions can be applied. The only backtrack points we must store are those involved with the selection of this clause: these backtrack points will be returned to in a depth-first fashion. This style of search, although incomplete, is similar to the ones used in Prolog and λProlog. In this paper, we shall be mostly interested in the non-deterministic version of this interpreter.

5. A unification algorithm for L_λ

In order to complete the interpreter for L_λ, we need to describe a unification algorithm. That is, given a quantifier prefix $\mathcal{Q}$ and a finite collection of typed equalities, $t_1 \stackrel{\tau_1}{=} s_1, \ldots, t_n \stackrel{\tau_n}{=} s_n$, so that $\mathcal{Q}_\Sigma \mathcal{Q} \vdash_T t_i : \tau_i$ and $\mathcal{Q}_\Sigma \mathcal{Q} \vdash_T s_i : \tau_i$ for each $i = 1, \ldots, n$, we wish to determine whether or not there is a $\mathcal{Q}$-substitution φ such that for $i = 1, \ldots, n$, $\varphi t_i = \varphi s_i$. Furthermore, we shall need to characterize all such φ if they exist. The BACKCHAIN and CLOSE transitions will call this algorithm with an initial quantifier prefix and a single, typed equation $A \stackrel{o}{=} A'$.

Let Σ be a fixed signature. A *unification problem* is a quantified list of equations, written

$$\mathcal{Q}[t_1 \stackrel{\tau_1}{=} s_1, \ldots, t_n \stackrel{\tau_n}{=} s_n], \quad (n \geq 0) \qquad (*)$$

where $\mathcal{Q}$ is a quantifier prefix, and $\mathcal{Q}_\Sigma \mathcal{Q} \vdash_T t_i : \tau_i$ and $\mathcal{Q}_\Sigma \mathcal{Q} \vdash_T s_i : \tau_i$ for each $i = 1, \ldots, n$. (These unification problems are examples of the *variable-defining* unification problems described in [15].) If n is zero, we shall write [] to denote the empty list. A *solution* to $(*)$ is a $\mathcal{Q}$-substitution φ such that for $i = 1, \ldots, n$, φt_i and φs_i are λ-convertible.

In describing a unification algorithm below, we shall drop most mentioning of types since the equations we need to unify can be solved over λ-normal, untyped terms. That is, if we delete all references to types in $(*)$ above, we can decide whether or not that unification problem has a solution. We can also produce a substitution, which is unique up to λ-conversion and variable renamings, so that all instances of it that are $\mathcal{Q}$-substitutions are precisely the set of solutions. This substitution essentially corresponds to a *most general unifier*, a technical term we shall not need here. In this setting, the untyped and typed calculus differ only on the typing restriction in η-conversion. The only care that we must exercise below is to use η-expansion only in situations where, in the typed setting, the expansion is performed on a term that would have to have functional type. Otherwise, types play no role in this unification algorithm, something that is not true for the problem of unifying unrestricted simply typed λ-terms [9].

Types do play a role, however, in the interpretation of the results of the unification algorithm. If $\text{unify}(\emptyset, \mathcal{Q}P) = \langle \theta, \mathcal{Q}' \rangle$ then (as stated in Proposition 6.4) $\mathcal{Q}'$-substitutions and the solutions to $\mathcal{Q}P$ can be placed in a one-to-one correspondence. While this is true of both the typed and untyped cases, in the untyped case, there are always $\mathcal{Q}'$-substitutions for all $\mathcal{Q}'$ while in the typed case, there may not be $\mathcal{Q}'$-substitutions. Thus, in the typed case, the unification algorithm may return a non-failure value and there still may not be solutions to the given unification problem.

In the remainder of this paper, the expression $t = s$ can mean either the proposition that t and s are α-convertible or the pair of terms t and s is a member of a unification problem. The choice of these two interpretations should always be clear from context. The use of a bar over a letter, *e.g.* $\bar{x}$, will be used as shorthand to refer to some list, such as $x_1, \ldots, x_n$, for some index n that is determined from context or whose value is not needed.

The state of the unification algorithm is a pair, $\langle \theta, \mathcal{Q}P \rangle$, where θ is a substitution that is being accumulated and $\mathcal{Q}P$ is a unification problem that needs to be solved. The algorithm is a loop out of which it is possible to fail. In that case, the algorithm returns the keyword *fail*. Otherwise, the algorithm returns a pair, such as $\langle \theta', \mathcal{Q}' \rangle$, where θ' is a substitution and $\mathcal{Q}'$ is a quantifier prefix. The expression $\text{unify}(\theta, \mathcal{Q}P)$ denotes the value the unification algorithm returns when applied to the state $\langle \theta, \mathcal{Q}P \rangle$. The algorithm's description is given below. There is an initial check for an immediate, successful termination. If that is not possible, then three preprocessing steps — simplification, raising, and pruning — are applied to the first equation in the unification problem. After that preprocessing, the first equation of the processed unification problem is either solved completely or causes a failure. The algorithm then repeats all these steps. It is convenient to introduce the following two terms: if t is a term in a unification problem with prefix $\mathcal{Q}$, t is *flexible* if its head is existentially quantified in $\mathcal{Q}_\Sigma \mathcal{Q}$ and is *rigid* otherwise, *i.e.* its head is universally quantified in $\mathcal{Q}_\Sigma \mathcal{Q}$.

Successful termination. Given a state of the form $\langle \theta, \mathcal{Q}[] \rangle$ return $\langle \theta, \mathcal{Q} \rangle$.

If this step is not applicable, then the state is of the form $\langle \theta, \mathcal{Q}[t = s, P] \rangle$, where P is a list of all the equations after the first (P may be empty). There are two kinds of simplifications that are applied to this state. Repeatedly apply both of these two simplifications to the state until they return a failure or are both no longer applicable.

Simplification step 1. We can write t as $\lambda \bar{x}.t'$ and s as $\lambda \bar{y}.s'$, where t' and s' are not themselves abstractions. If the lists of binders $\lambda \bar{x}$ and $\lambda \bar{y}$ are not of equal length, then use η-expansions to increase the length of the shorter binder until they are of the same length. Notice that in the typed case, if it is $\lambda \bar{x}$ that is the shorter, then t' would be of functional type, and such an η-expansion would be permitted. Using α-conversion, we may assume that these two binders are the same, that is, $t = s$ can be written as $\lambda \bar{w}.t'' = \lambda \bar{w}.s''$, and that the variables in $\bar{w}$ are not bound in $\mathcal{Q}_\Sigma \mathcal{Q}$. Then change to the state $\langle \theta, \mathcal{Q} \forall \bar{w}[t'' = s'', P] \rangle$.

Simplification step 2. If the first equation $t = s$ has the form $h t_1 \ldots t_n = h s_1 \ldots s_n$, where h is universally quantified in $\mathcal{Q}_\Sigma \mathcal{Q}$, replace the equation $t = s$ with the equations $t_1 = s_1, \ldots t_n = s_n$. If the first equation $t = s$ has the form $h t_1 \ldots t_n = k s_1 \ldots s_m$, where h and k are different universally quantified variables in $\mathcal{Q}_\Sigma \mathcal{Q}$, then return *fail*.

If we have reached this point and neither of these rules are applicable, then at least one of the terms in the first equation is flexible. We may assume, therefore, that the first term is flexible, since otherwise we simply switch around the equation. Thus, the unification algorithm has a state of the form

$$\langle \theta, \mathcal{Q}[v y_1 \ldots y_n = t, P] \rangle, \qquad (**)$$

where v is existentially quantified in $\mathcal{Q}$, the distinct variables $y_1, \ldots, y_n$ are universally quantified to the right of v in $\mathcal{Q}$, and t is some term (either flexible or rigid). We next perform the raising and pruning steps. These steps test for and simplify the interdependencies of universally and existentially quantified variables.

Raising step. Is there an existential variable u free in t and such that the prefix is of the form $\mathcal{Q}_1 \exists v \mathcal{Q}_2 \exists u \mathcal{Q}_3$ where $\mathcal{Q}_2$ has at least one universally quantified variable? If not, go to the next step. Otherwise, let $\bar{w}$ be the list of universally quantified tokens that occur in $\mathcal{Q}_2$. Set $\rho = [u \mapsto u'\bar{w}]$, where u' is not bound in $\mathcal{Q}_\Sigma \mathcal{Q}$, and change state to $\langle \theta \circ \rho, \mathcal{Q}_1 \exists v \exists u' \mathcal{Q}_2 \mathcal{Q}_3[v\bar{y} = \rho t, \rho P] \rangle$. Repeat this step until it no longer applies. Notice that the fact that the tokens in $\bar{w}$ may appear in substitution terms for u is made explicit by replacing u with a "higher-type" token u', which may not be instantiated with a term containing those tokens, applied explicitly to $\bar{w}$. Repeat this step until it is no longer applicable.

Pruning step. Is there a universal variable z of Q that has a free occurrence in t, is to the right of v, and is not in the list $\bar{y}$? If not, go to the next step. If so and if that occurrence in t is not in the scope of an existentially quantified variable, then return *fail*. Otherwise, z occurs in a subformula occurrence of the form $u\bar{w}_1 z\bar{w}_2$ of t where u is existentially quantified in Q and $\bar{w}_1$ and $\bar{w}_2$ are lists of universally quantified variables to the right of u. We must prune away u's dependency on the argument occupied by z. This is done by setting ρ to the substitution $[u \mapsto \lambda\bar{w}_1\lambda z\lambda\bar{w}_2.u'\bar{w}_1\bar{w}_2]$, where u' is not bound in $Q_\Sigma Q$. Update the state to be

$$\langle \theta \circ \rho, Q'[\rho(vy_1 \cdots y_n) = \rho t, \rho P]\rangle,$$

where Q' is the same as Q except that $\exists u'$ replaces $\exists u$. Repeat this step until it is no longer applicable.

If we reach here, it must be the case that the unification problem is still of the form (**) and that all the universally quantified tokens to the right of v that are free in t are in the list $\bar{y}$, and that a universally quantified token to the left of an existentially quantified variable free in t is also to the left of v.

Flexible-flexible step. First, we deal with the case that the term t is also flexible; that is, it has the form $uz_1 \ldots z_p$ where $z_1, \ldots, z_p$ are distinct universally quantified variables bound to the right of where u is existentially bound. It must be the case that the variables in $\bar{z}$ are contained in the list $\bar{y}$ and that there are no universal quantifiers to the right of $\exists v$ which are also to the left of $\exists u$ in the prefix. We distinguish two cases.

Case 1. Assume that v and u are different. Set ρ to the substitution $[v \mapsto \lambda\bar{y}.u\bar{z}]$. Change state to $\langle \theta \circ \rho, Q'\rho P\rangle$, where Q' is the result of deleting $\exists v$ from Q.

Case 2. Assume that v and u are equal. Then the pair is of the form $vy_1 \ldots y_n = vz_1 \ldots z_n$ where $y_1 \ldots y_n$ is a permutation of $z_1 \ldots z_n$. Let $\bar{w}$ be the enumeration of the set $\{y_i \mid y_i = z_i, i \in \{1, \ldots, n\}\}$ which orders variables the same as they are ordered in $\bar{y}$ (the choice of this particular ordering is not important). Set ρ to the substitution $[v \mapsto \lambda\bar{y}.v'\bar{w}]$ (notice that this is the same via α-conversion to $[v \mapsto \lambda\bar{z}.v'\bar{w}]$), where v' is not quantified in $Q_\Sigma Q$. Change state to $\langle \theta \circ \rho, Q'\rho P\rangle$, where Q' is the result of replacing $\exists v$ with $\exists v'$.

Occurrence check step. The only remaining case occurs when the term t is rigid. If the variable v occurs free in t then return *fail*. Otherwise, set ρ to the substitution $[v \mapsto \lambda\bar{y}.t]$ and set the state to $\langle \theta \circ \rho, Q'\rho P\rangle$, where Q' is the result of deleting $\exists v$ from Q.

This completes the description of the unification algorithm. In the next section we prove its formal correctness. It is worth making the following simple observations about this unification algorithm here.

(1) The cases above are exhaustive. That is, no matter what equation occurs first in the given unification problem, some step of the algorithm can be applied to it.

(2) There are four places where this unification algorithm is nondeterministic: the choice of the name of binders in the first simplification step; the choice of which order to raise existential variables; the choice of which order to prune existential variables; and the choice of what name to give the new variables. In each case, the resulting unification problems differ either up to α-conversion or in the order of existential variables within a sequence of existential variables. Neither difference is significant for our purposes here, and we shall assume that unification problems

are equal modulo such differences. Thus, if the unification algorithm terminates, its value is uniquely determined.

(3) The substitutions ρ that are constructed and applied to terms in unification problems are such that one existentially quantified variable is substituted with a term and the result of performing that substitution and subsequent λ-normalization yields another unification problem; that is, occurrences of existentially quantified variables in the resulting problem are properly restricted.

(4) When a substitution is applied, the only new β-redexes are those of the form $(\lambda x.t)y$ where y is a token that is either universally quantified or is λ-bound and is such that y is not free in $\lambda x.t$. That is, full β-conversion is not required. In particular, let β_0 be the equation $(\lambda x.t)x = t$; that is, we can only perform a β-reduction if it involves a token that is not free in the abstraction. The restrictions on terms in L_λ are such that the equality theory that is being considered is only that of α, β_0, and η.

(5) The unification procedure described in [9] can be applied to unification problems with unrestricted function variable application and with purely existentially quantified prefixes. As described in [15], it is straightforward to extend Huet's procedure to the mixed quantifier prefix case described here. The process in [9], however, computes pre-unifiers instead of unifiers; that is, it finds substitutions that reduce unification problems into just problems that contain flexible-flexible equations. In the general, unrestricted setting, computing unifiers for flexible-flexible equations is a very unconstrained and undirected procedure, so it is often best avoided. In the L_λ case, however, flexible-flexible equations are so simple that their solutions can be completely characterized. Thus, if Huet's procedure is modified to handle a mixed quantifier prefix and to solve those flexible-flexible equations as describe above, then it would also serve as a complete unification procedure for L_λ.

6. Correctness of the unification algorithm

We first show that the unification algorithm terminates. For this, we need some measures on unification problems. If t is a λ-normal term all of whose free variables are contained in the quantifier prefix Q, the measure $|t|$ counts the number of occurrences of applications in t that are not in the scope of existentially quantified variables of Q. (Of course, $|t|$ also has Q as an argument, but its value will always be clear from context.) That is, $|t|$ is defined by

$$|\lambda \bar{x}(ht_1 \ldots t_n)| = \begin{cases} 0 & \text{if } h \text{ is existentially quantified in } Q \\ n + \sum_{i=1}^n |t_i| & \text{if } h \text{ is universally quantified in } Q \end{cases} \quad (n \geq 0).$$

Let QP be a unification problem where P is the list $[t_1 = s_1, \ldots, t_n = s_n]$ and Q contains m existentially quantified variables. The measure associated to this unification problem is defined by the triple

$$|QP| = \langle m, \sum_{i=1}^n |t_i| + |s_i|, n \rangle.$$

Triples are ordered lexicographically.

Theorem 6.1. *The unification algorithm always terminates.*

Proof. The unification algorithm is a looping program that first applies the simplification, raising, and pruning steps, and then attempts to construct a substitution that solves the first equation in a most general fashion. We shall show that the measure of a unification problem does not rise during the simplification, raising, and pruning steps, while it decreases when an equation is removed.

The simplification step must terminate since it decreases the total number of applications and abstractions that occur in the unification problem. If $Q'P'$ arises from applying either simplification step to QP, then $|Q'P'| \leq |QP|$.

The raising step terminates since there are only a finite number of existential quantifiers and these can only be moved a finite number of times to the left. Raising may cause the number of applications in a unification problem to increase, but all new occurrences of applications are in the scope of an existentially quantified variable. Hence, if $Q'P'$ arises from applying the raising step to QP, then $|Q'P'| = |QP|$.

The pruning step terminates since there are only a finite number of universal quantifiers that can be pruned. Pruning will cause the number of applications in a unification problem to decrease, but all deleted occurrences of applications are in the scope of an existentially quantified variable. Hence, if $Q'P'$ arises from applying the pruning step to QP, then $|Q'P'| = |QP|$.

We shall now show that after every successful application of a remaining step, the resulting unification problem has a measure strictly less than the original unification problem.

In the first flexible-flexible step, the number of existentially quantified variables decreases by one. Hence, the overall measure decreases. In the second case, the number of existentially quantified variables and the number of occurrences of applications not in the scope of existentially quantified variables remain the same. Since the number of equations decrease, the overall measure decreases.

Finally, in the flexible-rigid case, if the occurrence check succeeds, then the number of existentially quantified variables decreases by one so the overall measure decreases.

Thus, the main loop of the unification algorithm either returns *fail* or decreases the measure on a unification problem. As a result, the algorithm must terminate. QED

The following series of propositions and lemmas show that the unification algorithm can be used to determine whether or not solutions exist and to characterize all of them if they do exists.

Lemma 6.2. *Assume that the unification algorithm makes a single transition from the state $\langle \theta, QP \rangle$ to the state $\langle \theta \circ \rho, Q'P' \rangle$. The solutions to QP can be put into one-to-one correspondence with the solution to $Q'P'$ so that if the solution φ for QP corresponds to the solution φ' for $Q'P'$ then $\rho \circ \varphi' = \varphi$.*

Proof. We consider each case in which a transition can occur. The result is immediate if the transition was caused by either simplification step. In those two steps, ρ is the empty substitution and the set of solutions do not change.

Assume that the transition was caused by the raising step. That is, the state changed from $\langle \theta, Q_1 \exists v Q_2 \exists u Q_3, [v\bar{y} = t, P] \rangle$ to the state $\langle \theta \circ \rho, Q_1 \exists v \exists u' Q_2 Q_3, [v\bar{y} = \rho t, \rho P] \rangle$, where ρ is the substitution $[u \mapsto u'\bar{w}]$ and where $\bar{w}$ is the list of universally quantified variables in Q_2. The correspondence of solutions is given by either letting φ'

be the result of replacing $u \mapsto s$ in φ with $u' \mapsto \lambda \bar{w}.s$, or conversely, letting φ be the result of replacing $u' \mapsto r$ in φ' with $u \mapsto r\bar{w}$. Via the rules of λ-conversion, these two descriptions are inverses. The fact that the resulting φ and φ' are substitution for their respective prefixes is easy to check. Since φ and φ' differ only on u and u' and since $(\rho \circ \varphi')u = \varphi'(u'\bar{w}) = (\lambda \bar{w}.s)\bar{w} \; \lambda\mathrm{conv} \; s = \varphi u$, it follows that $\rho \circ \varphi' = \varphi$. Notice that raising is a general transition for unification problems: it is dependent only on the prefix of unification problems and not on the actual list of equality pairs. A fuller description of this transition is presented in [15].

Assume that the transition was caused by the pruning step. That is, the state changed from $\langle \theta, Q_1 \exists u Q_2, [v\bar{y} = t, P] \rangle$ to the state $\langle \theta \circ \rho, Q_1 \exists u' Q_2, [\rho(v\bar{y}) = \rho t, \rho P] \rangle$, where ρ is the substitution $[u \mapsto \lambda \bar{w}_1 \lambda z \lambda \bar{w}_2.u'\bar{w}_1\bar{w}_2]$ and where z is a universal variable in Q that has a free occurrence in t, is to the right of v, and is not in the list $\bar{y}$, and where $u\bar{w}_1 z\bar{w}_2$ is a subterm of t. Thus z is not free in $\varphi(v\bar{y})$ for any solution φ to the first unification problem. Hence, if we write φu as $\lambda \bar{w}_1 \lambda z \lambda \bar{w}_2.s$ it must be the case that z is also not free in s, since otherwise, it would be free in φt and hence in $\varphi(v\bar{y})$. Thus, the correspondence of solutions is given by either letting φ' be the result of replacing $u \mapsto \lambda \bar{w}_1 \lambda z \lambda \bar{w}_2.s$ in φ with $u' \mapsto \lambda \bar{w}_1 \lambda \bar{w}_2.s$, or conversely, letting φ be the result of replacing $u' \mapsto \lambda \bar{w}_1 \lambda \bar{w}_2.s$ in φ' with $u \mapsto \lambda \bar{w}_1 \lambda z \lambda \bar{w}_2.s$. Since φ and φ' differ only on u and u' and since $(\rho \circ \varphi')u = \varphi'(\lambda \bar{w}_1 \lambda z \lambda \bar{w}_2.u'\bar{w}_1\bar{w}_2) = (\lambda \bar{w}_1 \lambda z \lambda \bar{w}_2.(\lambda \bar{w}_1 \lambda \bar{w}_2.s)\bar{w}_1\bar{w}_2) \; \lambda\mathrm{conv} \; \lambda \bar{w}_1 \lambda z \lambda \bar{w}_2.s = \varphi u$, it follows that $\rho \circ \varphi' = \varphi$.

Assume that the transition was caused by the first of the flexible-flexible steps. That is, there is a transition from the state $\langle \theta, Q_1 \exists v Q_2, [v\bar{y} = u\bar{z}, P] \rangle$ to the state $\langle \theta \circ \rho, Q_1 Q_2, \rho P \rangle$, where the variables of $\bar{z}$ are contained in the list $\bar{y}$, where there are no universal quantifiers to the right of $\exists v$ which are also to the left of $\exists u$ in the prefix, and where ρ is the substitution $[v \mapsto \lambda \bar{y}.u\bar{z}]$. Let φ be a solution to the unification problem in the first state. Then φv is $\lambda \bar{y}.t$ and φu is $\lambda \bar{z}.t$ for some t. Let φ' be the result of deleting the substitution pair for v from φ. (Conversely, from φ' we can insert the substitution term $\lambda \bar{y}.t$ for v given that $\varphi'u$ is $\lambda \bar{z}.t$.) Since $(\rho \circ \varphi')v = \varphi'(\lambda \bar{y}.u\bar{z}) = \lambda \bar{y}.(\lambda \bar{z}.t)\bar{z} \; \lambda\mathrm{conv} \; \lambda \bar{y}.t = \varphi v$, we have $\rho \circ \varphi' = \varphi$.

Assume that the transition was caused by the second of the flexible-flexible steps. That is, there is a transition from the state $\langle \theta, Q_1 \exists v Q_2, [v\bar{y} = v\bar{z}, P] \rangle$ to the state $\langle \theta \circ \rho, Q_1 \exists v' Q_2, \rho P \rangle$, where $\bar{y}$ is a permutation of $\bar{z}$, ρ is the substitution $[v \mapsto \lambda \bar{y}.v'\bar{w}]$, and $\bar{w}$ is the enumeration of the set $\{y_i \mid y_i = z_i, i = 1, \ldots, n\}$. Let φ be a solution to the unification problem in the first state and let φv be $\lambda \bar{y}.t$, for some term t. Thus, applying φ to the first equation, we have $t = (\lambda \bar{y}.t)\bar{z}$. It is easy to show by induction on the structure of t that if y_i and z_i are not the same token, then y_i cannot be free in t. Thus, only the variables in $\bar{w}$ can be free in t: the others can be pruned. Hence, set φ' to the result of replacing $v \mapsto \lambda \bar{y}.t$ with $v' \mapsto \lambda \bar{w}.t$. (The reverse construction of φ from φ' is immediate.) Given $(\rho \circ \varphi')v = \varphi'(\lambda \bar{y}.v'\bar{w}) = \lambda \bar{y}.(\lambda \bar{w}.t)\bar{w} \; \lambda\mathrm{conv} \; \lambda \bar{y}.t = \varphi v$, we again have $\rho \circ \varphi' = \varphi$.

The final case to consider is the flexible-rigid case, that is, the unification algorithm makes a transition from the state $\langle \theta, Q_1 \exists v Q_2, [v\bar{y} = t, P] \rangle$ to the state $\langle \theta \circ \rho, Q_1 Q_2, \rho P \rangle$, where v is not free in t and ρ is $[v \mapsto \lambda \bar{y}.t]$. Let φ be a solution to the unification problem in the first state. Thus, φv is some term $\lambda \bar{y}.s$ where s is φt. Let φ' be the substitution resulting from deleting the substitution term for v in φ. Then $(\rho \circ \varphi')v = \varphi'(\lambda \bar{y}.t)$. Since v is not free in t, this latter term is also equal to $\varphi(\lambda \bar{y}.t)$. As a result of raising, φ

does not substitute into any existentially quantified tokens in t terms containing tokens in $\bar{y}$. Thus, $\varphi(\lambda\bar{y}.t)$ is also equal to $\lambda\bar{y}.\varphi t = \lambda\bar{y}.s = \varphi v$. Again we have $\rho \circ \varphi' = \varphi$. QED

Proposition 6.3. *If* $\mathit{unify}(\theta, QP) = \mathit{fail}$ *then* QP *has no solution.*

Proof. There are three places where the unification algorithm can return *fail*: step 2 of simplification, pruning, and the occurrence check. We show that in each of these cases, the unification problem that caused the problem had no solution.

In the second step of simplification, a failure occurs if the first term is of the form $ht_1 \ldots t_n = ks_1 \ldots s_m$, where h and k are different universally quantified variables in $Q_\Sigma Q$. Since instances of these two terms will always have different top-level structure, they can never be made equal and hence a unification problem containing them cannot have a solution.

In the pruning step, assume that the first equation is of the form $v\bar{y} = t$ and that there is a universal variable z of Q that has a free occurrence in t, is to the right of v in Q, is not in the list $\bar{y}$, and it has an occurrence in t that is not in the scope of an existentially quantified variable. Thus, z occurs free in t and in every substitution instance of t. However, z will not have an occurrence in $\varphi(v\bar{y})$ for any Q-substitution φ. Thus, there can be no solution.

Finally, in the occurrence check step, the first equation is $v\bar{y} = t$ where v occurs in t. Assume that φ is a solution and let φv be $\lambda\bar{y}.s$. Clearly, $|\varphi t| > |s|$ since φt contains a proper subterm that is an alphabetic variant of s. Thus, no occurrence of $v\bar{y}$ can be equal to the same instance of t. QED

Proposition 6.4. *If* $\mathit{unify}(\emptyset, QP) = \langle\theta, Q'\rangle$ *then the solutions to* QP *can be put into one-to-one correspondence with* Q'-*substitutions so that if the solution* φ *for* QP *corresponds to the* Q'-*substitution* φ' *then* $\theta \circ \varphi' = \varphi$.

Proof. Assume that the unification algorithm makes a series of transitions through the states

$$\langle\emptyset, Q_0 P_0\rangle, \langle\rho_1, Q_1 P_1\rangle, \langle\rho_1 \circ \rho_2, Q_2 P_2\rangle, \ldots, \langle\rho_1 \circ \cdots \circ \rho_n, Q_n P_n\rangle,$$

where $n \geq 1$. Using Lemma 6.2, it is possible to place solutions of $Q_i P_i$ $(i = 1, \ldots, n)$ in one-to-one correspondence so that, if for $i = 1, \ldots, n$, the selection φ_i as a solution for $Q_i P_i$ is in such a correspondence, we have

$$\varphi_0 = \rho_1 \circ \varphi_1, \quad \ldots, \quad \varphi_{n-1} = \rho_n \circ \varphi_n.$$

Thus, $\varphi_0 = \rho_1 \circ \cdots \circ \rho_n \circ \varphi_n$. If $\mathit{unify}(\emptyset, QP) = \langle\theta, Q'\rangle$ then a series of transitions were made where $Q_0 P_0$ is equal to QP, $\theta = \rho_1 \circ \cdots \circ \rho_n$, the prefix Q' is equal to Q_n, and P_n is the empty list. Thus Q'-substitutions, since they are solutions to $Q_n P_n$, can be placed in one-to-one correspondence with solutions to QP. If φ' is a Q'-substitution and φ is the corresponding solution to QP, then $\varphi = \theta \circ \varphi'$. QED

The following proposition follows immediately from the previous propositions.

Proposition 6.5. *The unification problem* QP *has no solution if and only if either* $\mathit{unify}(\emptyset, QP) = \mathit{fail}$ *or* $\mathit{unify}(\emptyset, QP) = \langle\theta, Q'\rangle$ *and there are no* Q'-*substitutions.*

As we mentioned earlier, one difference between the typed and untyped versions of the unification problems is in determining whether or not there is a Q-substitution for a given prefix Q. For the untyped case, such substitutions always exist. For the typed case, this is not always the case. Hence, in the typed case the fact that the unification algorithm does not return *fail* is not enough to guarantee that there exist solutions.

7. Correctness of interpretation

We can now prove the correctness of the interpreter described in Section 4.

If QQ' is a quantifier prefix and if φ is a QQ'-substitution, then $\varphi \downarrow Q$ is the Q-substitution that results from deleting from φ those pairs $x \mapsto t$ where x is existentially quantified in Q'.

Lemma 7.1. *If the interpreter makes a single transition from the state $\langle \theta, Q, S \rangle$ to the state $\langle \theta \circ \rho, Q', S' \rangle$ and if φ satisfies Q' and S' then $(\rho \circ \varphi) \downarrow Q$ satisfies Q and S.*
Proof. We proceed by considering the cases that can cause a transition in the interpreter.

Assume that the transition was caused by BACKCHAIN. That is, the state changed from $\langle \theta, Q, \{P \longrightarrow A'\} \uplus S \rangle$ to the state $\langle \theta \circ \rho, Q', \rho(\{P \longrightarrow G\} \cup S)\rangle$, where P contains $\forall \bar{x}(G \supset A)$ (and $\bar{x}$ are tokens not bound in $Q_\Sigma Q$), and

$$(\rho, Q') = \text{unify}(\emptyset, Q \exists \bar{x}[A \stackrel{\circ}{=} A']).$$

Also assume that φ satisfies Q' and $\rho(\{P \longrightarrow G\} \cup S)$. Thus, there is a goal-directed proof of the sequent

$$\Sigma, \Sigma_{Q'} ; (\rho \circ \varphi)P \longrightarrow (\rho \circ \varphi)G.$$

By Proposition 6.4, $\rho \circ \varphi$ is a $Q \exists \bar{x}$-substitution such that $(\rho \circ \varphi)A = (\rho \circ \varphi)A'$. Let ψ be $(\rho \circ \varphi) \downarrow Q$. Since the tokens in $\bar{x}$ are not free in P or in A', and since Σ_Q and $\Sigma_{Q'}$ are the same, $(\rho \circ \varphi)A = \psi A'$ and this sequent can be written as simply

$$\Sigma, \Sigma_Q ; \psi P \longrightarrow (\rho \circ \varphi)G$$

Using the BC inference rule, we can build a proof of the sequent $\Sigma, \Sigma_Q ; \psi P \longrightarrow \psi A'$. Since the tokens in $\bar{x}$ are not free in the sequents in S, it then follows that ψ satisfies Q and $\{P \longrightarrow A'\} \uplus S$.

The case when the transition was caused by CLOSE is similar and simpler.

Assume that the transition was caused by GENERIC. That is, the state changed from $\langle \theta, Q, \{P \longrightarrow \forall_\tau x G\} \uplus S \rangle$ to the state $\langle \theta \circ \rho, Q\forall_\tau x, \{P \longrightarrow G\} \cup S \rangle$, where x is not bound in $Q_\Sigma Q$ and where ρ is the empty substitution. Also assume that φ satisfies $Q\forall_\tau x$ and $\{P \longrightarrow G\} \cup S$. Thus, $\rho \circ \varphi = \varphi$ and this is also a Q-substitution. Since $\Sigma, \Sigma_Q, y : \tau ; \varphi P \longrightarrow \varphi G$ has a sequent proof and since y is not free in φP, using $\forall$-R we can build a proof for $\Sigma, \Sigma_Q ; \varphi P \longrightarrow \forall_\tau y.\varphi G$. Since no term in the range of φ contains y free, this sequent is the same as $\Sigma, \Sigma_Q ; \varphi P \longrightarrow \varphi(\forall_\tau y.G)$. Thus, φ satisfies Q and S.

If the transition was the result of AND, the result is immediate: simply use $\wedge$-R to put the two proofs guaranteed by induction together. If the transition was the result of AUGMENT, build the new proof using the $\supset$-R rule. QED

Theorem 7.2. *There is a substitution φ that satisfies Q and S if and only if there is a series of transitions that carries the state $\langle \emptyset, Q, S \rangle$ to the success state $\langle \theta, Q', \emptyset \rangle$ such that there is a Q'-substitution φ' so that $\varphi = (\theta \circ \varphi') \downarrow Q$.*

Proof. Assume that the interpreter makes a series of transitions

$$\langle \emptyset, \mathcal{Q}_0, \mathcal{S}_0 \rangle, \langle \rho_1, \mathcal{Q}_1, \mathcal{S}_1 \rangle, \langle \rho_1 \circ \rho_2, \mathcal{Q}_2, \mathcal{S}_2 \rangle, \ldots, \langle \rho_1 \circ \cdots \circ \rho_n, \mathcal{Q}_n, \mathcal{S}_n \rangle,$$

where $n \geq 1$. Let φ_n satisfy $\mathcal{Q}_n$ and $\mathcal{S}_n$. Using Lemma 7.1, there is a sequence of substitutions $\varphi_1, \ldots, \varphi_{n-1}$ such that for $i = 1, \ldots, n-1$, φ_i satisfies $\mathcal{Q}_i$ and $\mathcal{S}_i$ and $\varphi_i = (\rho_{i+1} \circ \varphi_{i+1}) \downarrow \mathcal{Q}_i$. Thus, $(\rho_1 \circ \cdots \circ \rho_n \circ \varphi_n) \downarrow \mathcal{Q}_0$ satisfies $\mathcal{Q}_0$ and $\mathcal{S}_0$. If $\mathcal{S}_n$ is empty, $\mathcal{Q}_n$ is $\mathcal{Q}'$, and $\varphi' = \varphi_n$ then setting θ to the substitution $\rho_1 \circ \cdots \circ \rho_n$ completes this part of the proof.

Now assume that the interpreter's state is $\langle \theta, \mathcal{Q}, \mathcal{S} \rangle$ and that there is a φ that satisfies $\mathcal{Q}$ and $\mathcal{S}$. Thus, every sequent in $\varphi \mathcal{S}$ has a goal-directed proof. We proceed by induction on the sum of the number of inference rule occurrences in those goal-directed proofs. If this number is zero, then $\mathcal{S}$ is empty and we are finished. Otherwise, let $\mathcal{S}$ be written as $\{\mathcal{P} \longrightarrow G\} \uplus \mathcal{S}'$. The structure of a goal-directed proof of $\Sigma_{\mathcal{Q}} ; \varphi \mathcal{P} \longrightarrow \varphi G$ dictates which transition can be performed. In particular, if the proof is an initial sequent, then use CLOSE. Otherwise, if the last inference rule in that proof is $\wedge$-R, use AND; if it is $\supset$-R, use AUGMENT; if it is $\forall$-L, use GENERIC; if it is BC, use BACKCHAIN. We illustrate this final case in more detail since it is the hardest.

Since the last rule is BC, there is a $\forall \bar{x}(G' \supset A') \in \varphi \mathcal{P}$ and a list of $\Sigma, \Sigma_{\mathcal{Q}}$-terms $\bar{t}$ so that $[\bar{x} \mapsto \bar{t}]A' = \varphi A$ and the sequent $\Sigma, \Sigma_{\mathcal{Q}} ; \varphi \mathcal{P} \longrightarrow [\bar{x} \mapsto \bar{t}]G'$ is provable ($[\bar{x} \mapsto \bar{t}]$ is an abbreviation for $[x_1 \mapsto t_1, \ldots, x_n \mapsto t_n]$). Since the variables in $\bar{x}$ can be picked to be new, there is a $\forall \bar{x}(G'' \supset A'') \in \mathcal{P}$ so that $\varphi G'' = G'$ and $\varphi A'' = A'$. Set ψ to be the substitution $\varphi \circ [\bar{x} \mapsto \bar{t}]$. Thus, ψ is a $\mathcal{Q} \exists \bar{x}$-substitution that unifies A and A'' and is such that $\Sigma, \Sigma_{\mathcal{Q}} ; \psi \mathcal{P} \longrightarrow \psi G''$ is provable. Set $\langle \mathcal{Q}', \rho \rangle = \mathrm{unify}(\emptyset, \mathcal{Q} \exists \bar{x}[A = A''])$. Since unification does not delete universal quantifiers, $\Sigma_{\mathcal{Q}} \subseteq \Sigma_{\mathcal{Q}'}$. The result of the BACKCHAIN transition is then the state $\langle \theta \circ \rho, \mathcal{Q}', \rho(\{\mathcal{P} \longrightarrow G''\} \cup \mathcal{S}') \rangle$. By Lemma 6.4, there is a $\mathcal{Q}'$-substitution φ' so that $\psi = \rho \circ \varphi'$. Thus, φ' satisfies $\mathcal{Q}'$ and $\rho(\{\mathcal{P} \longrightarrow G\} \cup \mathcal{S}')$, and the proof of the inductive case is complete. QED

The nondeterministic interpreter for L_λ described above can be thought of doing computation in the following fashion. Let $\mathcal{Q}$ be a purely existential prefix and let $\mathcal{P} \longrightarrow G$ be a $\mathcal{Q}$-sequent. Here, $\mathcal{P}$ is considered to be a logic program and G a query to be proved. The existential variables in $\mathcal{Q}$ are essentially *logic variables* that the interpreter can instantiate as it needs in order to find a proof. If the interpreter makes a transition from the initial state $\langle \emptyset, \mathcal{Q}, \{\mathcal{P} \longrightarrow G\} \rangle$ to a success state $\langle \theta, \mathcal{Q}', \emptyset \rangle$, then for every $\mathcal{Q}'$-substitution φ', the substitution $\theta \circ \varphi'$ restricted to the variables in $\mathcal{Q}$ is a solution or answer to this computation.

8. Examples of L_λ programs

Below we present several examples of programs written using L_λ. Since the logic programming language λProlog [18] fully implements L_λ (and more), we shall use the syntax of λProlog to present L_λ programs. The symbol => denotes ⊃, :- denotes its converse, a comma denotes conjunction, an infix occurrence of backslash \ denotes λ-abstraction, and pi along with a λ-abstraction denotes universal quantification. Tokens with an uppercase initial letter are assumed to be universally quantified variables with outermost scope. The piece of syntax

```
kind i          type.

type sterile    i -> o.

type bug        i -> o.

type in         i -> i -> o.

type dead       i -> o.

sterile J :- pi b\((bug b, in b J) => dead b).
```

declares i to be a primitive type, declares the type for four predicate constants, and presents one definite clause, which could be written as

$$\forall J(\forall b((bug\ b \wedge in\ b\ J) \supset dead\ b) \supset sterile\ J).$$

In all the examples given in this section, once types are given for tokens that are to be taken as constants, the type of bound variables can easily be inferred from their context.

8.1. Specifying an object logic.

Three meta-programs — substitution, Horn clause interpretation, and the computation of prenex normal forms — are presented in this section. All there programs will compute with the same first-order, object logic, which contains universal and existential quantification and implication and conjunction. These are introduced by the syntax

```
kind   term     type.
kind   form     type.

type   all      (term -> form) -> form.
type   some     (term -> form) -> form.

type   and      form -> form -> form.

type   imp      form -> form -> form.
```

The first two lines declare the tokens term and form as primitive types.

The object logic will contain just five non-logical constants: an individual constant, a function symbol of one argument and another of two arguments, and a predicate symbol of one argument and another of two arguments. Their types are declared with the following lines.

```
type   a        term.

type   f        term -> term.

type   g        term -> term -> term.

type   p        term -> form.

type   q        term -> term -> form.
```

Terms over this signature of type `form` denote object logic formulas and of type `term` denote object logic terms. We shall need to lift this typing information more directly into the meta language by introducing the following two meta-level predicates and clauses. These clauses are obviously derived directly from the above signature. (The token `term` is used as both predicate symbol and type symbol.)

```
type term    term -> o.
type atom    form -> o.

term a.
term (f X)    :- term X.
term (g X Y) :- term X, term Y.
atom (p X)    :- term X.
atom (q X Y) :- term X, term Y.
```

Various other meta-predicates over object formulas are easy to write. For example, the following defines a predicate that determines whether or not its argument is a quantifier-free object-level formula.

```
type    quant_free        form -> o.

quant_free A :- atom A.
quant_free (and B C) :- quant_free B, quant_free C.
quant_free (imp B C) :- quant_free B, quant_free C.
```

This predicate is used in the definition of prenex normal formulas below. The following code describes how to determine if a term of type `form` encodes a Horn clause or a conjunction of atomic formulas.

```
type  hornc  form -> o.
type  conj   form -> o.

hornc (all C) :- pi x\(term x => hornc (C x)).
hornc (imp G A) :- atom A, conj G.
hornc A :- atom A.

conj (and B C) :- conj B, conj C.
conj A :- atom A.
```

Notice the structure of the first of the `hornc` clauses above. It involves a second-order variable `C` of type `term -> form` as well as an implication and universal quantifier in the clause's body. The variable `C` will get bound to an abstraction over an object-level formula. For example, if the goal

$$\texttt{hornc (all u\\(all v\\(imp (p u) (and (q v a) (q a u)))))}$$

is attempted, the variable `C` will get bound to the λ-abstraction

$$\texttt{u\\(all v\\(imp (p u) (and (q v a) (q a u)))).}$$

The intended processing of this λ-abstraction can be described by the following set of operations. Via the universally quantified goal, a new constants is picked. This new constant will play the role of a name for the bound variable x. Since this new constant is now temporarily part of the object logic, program clauses that were determined from the signature of the object logic may need to be extended. Thus, the definition of the term predicate needs to be extended with the fact that this new constant is a term. Thus, when hornc subsequently calls atom, the latter predicate will succeed for formulas containing this new constant. Finally, the application (c x) represents the body of the object-level abstraction with the new constant substituted for the abstracted variable. Thus, if the new constant picked by an L_λ interpreter is d, then the next goal to be attempted will be

```
hornc (all v\(imp (p d) (and (q v a) (q a d))))
```

with the additional assumption (term d) added to the program.

8.2. Implementing object-level substitution.

Substitution at the object-level can be implemented by first specifying the following copy-clauses.

```
type     copyterm    term -> term -> o.
type     copyform    form -> form -> o.

copyterm a a.
copyterm (f X) (f U)       :- copyterm X U.
copyterm (g X Y) (g U V) :- copyterm X U, copyterm Y V.
copyform (p X) (p U)       :- copyterm X U.
copyform (q X Y) (q U V) :- copyterm X U, copyterm Y V.
copyform (and X Y) (and U V) :- copyform X U, copyform Y V.
copyform (imp X Y) (imp U V) :- copyform X U, copyform Y V.
copyform (all X) (all U)    :-
   pi y\(pi z\(copyterm y z => copyform (X y) (U z))).
copyform (some X) (some U)   :-
   pi y\(pi z\(copyterm y z => copyform (X y) (U z))).
```

These clauses can be derived directly from the signature of the constants they are based on by using the following function. Let $[\![t, s : \tau]\!]$ be a formula defined by recursion on the structure of the type τ, which is assumed to be built only from the base types term and form, with the following clauses:

$$[\![t, s : \text{term}]\!] = \text{copyterm } t\ s$$
$$[\![t, s : \text{form}]\!] = \text{copyform } t\ s$$
$$[\![t, s : \tau \to \sigma]\!] = \forall x \forall y ([\![x, y : \tau]\!] \supset [\![t\ x, s\ y : \sigma]\!])$$

The copy-clauses displayed above are essentially those clauses that are equal to $[\![c, c : \tau]\!]$ where the signature for representing the object logic contains $c : \tau$.

The extension of these copy-clauses is exactly the same as that for equality. That is, (copyterm $t\ s$) is provable from these clauses if and only if t and s are the same term. A similar statement is true for copyform. Now consider adding a new constant, say c, of type term, and adding the clause (copy c (f a)). Given this extended set of copy-clauses, (copyterm *t* *s*) is provable if and only if *s* is the result of replacing every occurrence of c in *t* with (f a); that is, *s* is [c ↦ (f a)]*t*. This can be formalized using the following code.

```
type subst   (term -> form) -> term -> form -> o.

subst M T N :- pi c\(copyterm c T => copyform (M c) N).
```

Here, the first argument of subst is an abstraction over formulas. The second argument is then substituted into that abstraction to get the third argument. To instantiate a universal quantifier with a given term, the following code could be used.

```
type uni_instan  form -> term -> form -> o.

uni_instan (all B) T C :- subst B T C.
```

Consider the somewhat simpler clause for implementing subst:

```
    subst M T (M T).
```

This clause is not a legal L_λ D-formula since the second occurrence of M is applied to another positively quantified universally variable. This clause correctly specifies substitution if the meta-level contains the full theory of β-conversion for simply typed λ-terms. Such a clause is available in λProlog and the higher-order logic programming languages described in [17] and [19]. These languages have a much richer unification problem than L_λ.

8.3. Implementing a simple higher-order unification problem.

The restriction on functional variables in L_λ ensures that it is never the case that a term, such as (F a) (for function variable F) is unified with a term such as (g a a) (here, g and a are as declared in Subsection 8.1). Such a unification problem, however, is permitted in the more general setting explored in [9]. While this is not a permissible unification problem in L_λ, it is very easy to solve this problem in L_λ using the subst program written above. In particular, the set of substitutions for F that unify (F a) and (g a a) is exactly the set of substitutions for F that makes the goal

$$\text{subst F a (g a a)}$$

provable. In particular, an L_λ interpreter should return the following four substitutions for F:

$$\text{w\textbackslash(g w w)} \quad \text{w\textbackslash(g w a)} \quad \text{w\textbackslash(g a w)} \quad \text{w\textbackslash(g a a)}.$$

These are exactly the unifiers for this more general unification problem. Arbitrary higher-order unification problems can be encoded into L_λ using various calls to predicates like subst defined above, although the translation is often more complex than the simple example illustrated here.

8.4. Interpretation of first-order Horn clauses.

Since object-level logic programs will be denoted by lists of formulas, we first specify the data type of formula lists and a simple membership program. These are supplied by the following code.

```
kind  lst      type.

type  nil      lst.
type  cons     form -> lst -> lst.
type  memb     form -> lst -> o.

memb X (cons X L).
memb X (cons Y L) :- memb X L.
```

It is possible in λProlog to specify lists and list operations that are polymorphic; such lists, however, are not required for this example.

The following code describes the interpreter for Horn clauses.

```
type    interp       lst -> form -> o.
type    instan       form -> form -> o.
type    backchain     lst -> form -> form -> o.

interp Cs (and B C) :- interp Cs B, interp Cs C.
interp Cs A :- memb D Cs, instan D E, backchain Cs E A.

instan (all A) B :- pi x\(copyterm x T => instan (A x) B).
instan B C :- copyform B C.

backchain Cs A A.
backchain Cs (imp G A) A :- interp Cs G.
```

The `backchain` clause preforms operations similar to those called BACKCHAIN and CLOSE in Section 4. The `instan` predicate implements substitution as describe above. Operationally, its function can be thought of as stripping off the universal quantifiers on a Horn clause by instantiating them with unspecified terms. Subsequent actions of the `interp` program and meta-level unification will further specify those terms.

8.5. Computing prenex-normal forms.

Our last example of a meta-program on our small object logic is the computation of prenex-normal forms. Our goal is to write a set of clauses so that the formula (prenex B C) is provable if and only if C is a prenex-normal form of B. This relationship is not functional: there are possibly many prenex-normal formulas that can arise from moving embedded quantifiers into a prefix. The following code correctly captures this full relation. To define `prenex`, an auxillary predicate `merge` is used.

```
type    prenex       form -> form -> o.
type    merge        form -> form -> o.

prenex B B :- atom B.
prenex (and B C) D :- prenex B U, prenex C V, merge (and U V) D.
prenex (imp B C) D :- prenex B U, prenex C V, merge (imp U V) D.
prenex (all B) (all D)  :- pi x\(term x => prenex (B x) (D x)).
```

```
prenex (some B) (some D) :- pi x\(term x => prenex (B x) (D x)).
merge (and (all B) (all C)) (all D) :-
  pi x\(term x => merge (and (B x) (C x)) (D x)).
merge (and (all B) C) (all D) :-
  pi x\(term x => merge (and (B x) C) (D x)).
merge (and B (all C)) (all D) :-
  pi x\(term x => merge (and B (C x)) (D x)).
merge (and (some B) C) (some D) :-
  pi x\(term x => merge (and (B x) C) (D x)).
merge (and B (some C)) (some D) :-
  pi x\(term x => merge (and B (C x)) (D x)).
merge (imp (all B) (some C)) (some D) :-
  pi x\(term x => merge (imp (B x) (C x)) (D x)).
merge (imp (all B) C) (some D) :-
  pi x\(term x => merge (imp (B x) C) (D x)).
merge (imp B (some C)) (some D) :-
  pi x\(term x => merge (imp B (C x)) (D x)).
merge (imp (some B) C) (all D) :-
  pi x\(term x => merge (imp (B x) C) (D x)).
merge (imp B (all C)) (all D) :-
  pi x\(term x => merge (imp B (C x)) (D x)).
merge B B :- quant_free B.
```

The merge predicate is used to bring together two prenex normal formulas into a single prenex normal formula. Notice the nondeterminism in merge: there are three clauses that can be employed to solve a merge-goal whose first argument is of the form (and (all B) (all C)). These clauses represent the fact that the universal quantifiers can be jointly moved into the prefix or that one can be moved out before the other.

Given these clauses, there is a unique prenex-normal form for the formula

```
imp (all x\(and (p x) (and (all y\(q x y)) (p (f x))))) (p a),
```

which is the formula

```
some x\(some y\(imp (and (p x) (and (q x y) (p (f x)))) (p a))).
```

The formula (and (all x\(q x x)) (all z\(all y\(q z y)))), however, has the following five prenex-normal forms:

```
all z\(all y\(and (q z z) (q z y)))
all x\(all z\(all y\(and (q x x) (q z y))))
all z\(all x\(and (q x x) (q z x)))
all z\(all x\(all y\(and (q x x) (q z y))))
all z\(all y\(all x\(and (q x x) (q z y)))).
```

These results can be computed on a depth-first implementation of L_λ, such as λProlog, in the following fashion. Given the clauses presented above, λProlog can be asked to search for substitution instances of the variable P so that the atom

```
prenex (and (all x\(q x x)) (all z\(all y\(q z y)))) P
```

is provable. Using its depth-first search stradegy, λProlog will find five different proofs of this atom, each with a different instance of P (the five terms listed above, in that order). As written, however, the depth-first interpretation of this code cannot be used to determine the converse relation, namely, compute those formulas which have a given prenex-normal form, since it would start to generate object-level formulas in an undirected fashion and would not, in general, terminate. A breath-first search could, however, compute this converse.

9. Conclusion

Meta-programming systems need to be able to treat various structures that naturally contain notions of scope and bound variable. Conventional programming languages do not contain language-level support for such structures. Computation systems such as λProlog, Elf, and Isabelle do have such support since they contain typed λ-terms and implement the equations of α, β, and η. Such a treatment of λ-terms is, however, a complex operation since the unification of λ-terms modulo those equations is undecidable in general. Many uses of function variables and λ-terms in meta-programs can, however, be restricted to the point where unification over these same equations is a simple extension of first-order unification. Much of what is lost in restricting function variables can be regained by writing logic programs. This restriction on functional variables is integrated into logic programming yielding a language called L_λ. Unification for L_λ is decidable and generalizes first-order unification. A nondeterministic interpretation of L_λ is easily described by merging unification with a sequent-style theorem prover.

Acknowledgements. I am grateful to Amy Felty, Elsa Gunter, John Hannan, and Frank Pfenning for discussions related to the paper. An anonymous reviewer also made several helpful comments on an earlier draft of this paper. The work reported here has been supported in part by grants ONR N00014-88-K-0633, NSF CCR-87-05596, and DARPA N00014-85-K-0018.

10. References

[1]   de Bruijn, N. (1972), Lambda Calculus Notation with Nameless Dummies, a Tool for Automatic Formula Manipulation, with Application to the Church-Rosser Theorem, Indag. Math. (34:5), 381 – 392.

[2]   Church, A. (1940), A Formulation of the Simple Theory of Types, Journal of Symbolic Logic 5, 56 – 68.

[3]   Elliott, C. (1989), Higher-Order Unification with Dependent Types, Proceedings of the 1989 Rewriting Techniques and Applications, Springer-Verlag LNCS.

[4]   Felty, A. and Miller, D. (1988), Specifying Theorem Provers in a Higher-Order Logic Programming Language, Proceedings of the Ninth International Conference

on Automated Deduction, Argonne, IL, 23 – 26, eds. E. Lusk and R. Overbeek, Springer-Verlag Lecture Notes in Computer Science, Vol. 310, 61 – 80.

[5]   Hannan, J. and Miller, D. (1988), Uses of Higher-Order Unification for Implementing Program Transformers, Fifth International Conference and Symposium on Logic Programming, ed. K. Bowen and R. Kowalski, MIT Press, 942 – 959.

[6]   Hannan, J. and Miller, D. (1989), A Meta Language for Functional Programs, Chapter 24 of *Meta-Programming in Logic Programming*, eds. H. Rogers and H. Abramson, MIT Press, 453–476.

[7]   Harper, R., Honsell, F. and Plotkin, G. (1987), A Framework for Defining Logics, Second Annual Symposium on Logic in Computer Science, Ithaca, NY, 194 – 204.

[8]   Hindley, J. and Seldin, J. (1986), *Introduction to Combinators and λ-calculus*, Cambridge University Press.

[9]   Huet, G. (1975), A Unification Algorithm for Typed λ-Calculus, Theoretical Computer Science **1**, 27 – 57.

[10] Huet, G. and Lang, B. (1978), Proving and Applying Program Transformations Expressed with Second-Order Logic, Acta Informatica **11**, 31 – 55.

[11] Goldfarb, W. (1981), The Undecidability of the Second-Order Unification Problem, Theoretical Computer Science **13**, 225 – 230.

[12] Miller, D. (1989), A Logical Analysis of Modules in Logic Programming, Journal of Logic Programming **6**, 79 – 108.

[13] Miller, D. (1989), Lexical Scoping as Universal Quantification, Sixth International Logic Programming Conference, Lisbon, eds. G. Levi and M. Martelli, MIT Press, 268 – 283.

[14] Miller, D. (1990), Abstractions in logic programming, in *Logic and Computer Science* edited by P. Odifreddi, Academic Press, 329 – 359.

[15] Miller, D., Unification under a Mixed Prefix, Journal of Symbolic Computation (to appear).

[16] Miller, D. and Nadathur, G. (1987), A Logic Programming Approach to Manipulating Formulas and Programs, Proceedings of the IEEE Fourth Symposium on Logic Programming, IEEE Press, 379 – 388.

[17] Miller, D., Nadathur, G., Pfenning, F., and Scedrov, A., Uniform Proofs as a Foundation for Logic Programming, Annals of Pure and Applied Logic (to appear).

[18] Nadathur, G. and Miller, D. (1988), An Overview of λProlog, Fifth International Conference on Logic Programming, eds. R. Kowlaski and K. Bowen, MIT Press, 810 – 827.

[19] Nadathur, G. and Miller, D., Higher-Order Horn Clauses, Journal of the ACM (to appear).

[20] Paulson, L. (1986), Natural Deduction as Higher-Order Resolution, Journal of Logic Programming **3**, 237 – 258.

[21] Pauslon, L. (1989), The Foundation of a Generic Theorem Prover, Journal of Automated Reasoning **5**, 363 – 397.

[22] Pfenning, F. and Elliot, C. (1988), Higher-Order Abstract Syntax, Proceedings of the ACM-SIGPLAN Conference on Programming Language Design and Implementation, ACM Press, 199 – 208.

[23] Pfenning, F. (1989), Elf: A Language for Logic Definition and Verified Metaprogramming, Fourth Annual Symposium on Logic in Computer Science, Monterey, CA, 313 – 321.

[24] Pietrzykowski, T. and Jensen, D. (1976), Mechanizing ω-Order Type Theory Through Unification, Theoretical Computer Science 3, 123 – 171.

[25] Statman, R. (1979), Intuitionistic Propositional Logic is Polynomial-Space Complete, Theoretical Computer Science 9, 67 – 72.

[26] Snyder, W. and Gallier, J. (1989), Higher-Order Unification Revisited: Complete Sets of Transformations, Journal of Symbolic Computation 8, 101 – 140.

Logic Programming, Functional Programming, and Inductive Definitions

Lawrence C. Paulson [1] *and Andrew W. Smith* [2]

1 Computer Laboratory, University of Cambridge, Cambridge CB2 3QG, England
2 Harlequin Limited, Barrington, Cambridge CB2 5RG, England

1 Introduction

The unification of logic and functional programming, like the Holy Grail, is sought by countless people [6, 14]. In reporting our attempt, we first discuss the motivation. We argue that logic programming is still immature, compared with functional programming, because few logic programs are both useful and pure. Functions can help to purify logic programming, for they can eliminate certain uses of the cut and can express certain negations positively.

More generally, we suggest that the traditional paradigm — logic programming as first-order logic — is seriously out of step with practice. We offer an alternative paradigm. We view the logic program as an *inductive definition* of sets and relations. This view explains certain uses of Negation as Failure, and explains why most attempts to extend PROLOG to larger fragments of first-order logic have not been successful. It suggests a logic language with functions, incorporating equational unification.

We have implemented a prototype of this language. It is very slow, but complete, and appear to be faster than some earlier implementations of narrowing. Our experiments illustrate the programming style and shed light on the further development of such languages.

2 Declarative programmers: realists versus purists

Logic Programming and Functional Programming are often lumped together under the heading 'Declarative Programming'. Ideally, a declarative program simply specifies the problem — what we want — and the computer works out how to do it.

Of course this is an oversimplification. For the declarative languages that exist now, the problem description really is a program: not for any physical machine, but for an abstract machine. A functional program defines a system of rewriting rules that can evaluate a desired function. A logic program defines a search space of problem reductions that can solve all instances of the desired goal. The declarative program expresses the algorithm more abstractly than, say, a Pascal program, but the means of expression are restrictive when regarded as a specification language: even more so if we care about efficiency.

Users of declarative languages can be described as *realists* or *purists*:

– Realists set out to write useful programs. While they value the declarative reading, they are prepared to compromise it if necessary.
– Purists set out to demonstrate their declarative paradigm, and perhaps its application to program correctness and synthesis. Their programs are completely pure, regardless of the consequences for efficiency.

Realists and purists are equally worthy; they simply have different priorities. Note that an impure program can be more readable than a pure one, while a pure program can be more efficient than an impure one.

Let us compare functional programming and logic programming through these concepts. For the purist view we can compare the presentations by David Turner and Robert Kowalski at a special meeting of the Royal Society in London.

2.1 Functional programming

A purist functional programmer might use Miranda, Lazy ML, or Haskell: lazy functional languages with no side-effects whatever. David Turner's presentation to the Royal Society includes quick sort, a topological sort, and a program to find a Knight's tour of the chess board [42]. He also gives some simple proofs and program derivations. Bird and Wadler [7] give a fuller account of the purist approach; they derive functional programs from formal specifications.

Purists avoid LISP because of its imperative features. David Turner says [42, page 53]:

> It needs to be said very firmly that LISP, at least as represented by the dialects in common use, is not a functional language at all.

LISP has been impure from the very start. Assignments and go to's feature prominently in the LISP *1.5 Programmer's Manual* [32]. But that same book devotes a chapter to a program for the propositional calculus (Wang's Algorithm). This is a substantial, purely functional program — probably the first ever — and it is written in LISP.

A realist functional programmer might use LISP or ML. These languages support a functional style but do not enforce it. Abelson and Sussman [1] illustrate the realist approach using Scheme, a dialect of LISP. Many of their examples are purely functional.

The realists and the purists share some common ground. Many LISP and ML programmers strive for a pure style, while many pure functional programs can be executed with reasonable efficiency.

2.2 Logic programming

Kowalski illustrates the purist approach. His presentation to the Royal Society emphasises the relationship between logic programs and specifications [28, page 11]:

> The only difference between a complete specification and a program is one of efficiency.

As an example, Kowalski gives a specification of sorting. He then gives the following sorting program:

```
sort(X,X) :- ordered(X).
sort(X,Y) :- I<J, X[I] > X[J], interchange(X,I,J,Z), sort(Z,Y).
```

Given X, the program computes the sorted version Y by repeatedly exchanging some X[I] and X[J] that are out of order. The program is highly nondeterministic: the condition X[I] > X[J] is the only constraint on I and J.[3] To regard this as a useful sorting program we must further constrain I and J, to reduce the search drastically. We also must find a compiler clever enough to execute interchange(X,I,J,Z) without copying.

Perhaps it is unfair to bear down on this little example. But the literature offers few others. Hogger [26] writes at length about pure logic programs, typically to reverse a list or test for list membership. By comparison, the pure functional programs in Bird and Wadler [7] perform α-β search, construct Huffman coding trees, and print calendars.

Clocksin and Mellish [13] illustrate the realist approach. They teach PROLOG style using a wide variety of programs, with applications such as parsing. But many of these involve logically meaningless (or 'extralogical') predicates.

For logic programming, the realists and purists are far apart. Programming in a pure style is difficult. Existing PROLOG systems do not even provide pure PROLOG as a subset. They use depth-first search (which is incomplete) and they omit the occurs check (which can create circular data structures).

Pure logic programs can be written by translating functional programs into clauses. But this is hardly logic programming: key aspects like backtracking are lost. Logic programming is far more ambitious than functional programming, which is why it has not reached a similar stage of maturity.

---

3 The subscripting in X[I] > X[J] abbreviates contains(X,I,U), contains(X,J,V), U>V

The widespread interest in extending PROLOG stems mainly from purist principles. Kowalski again [28, page 22]:

> In the longer term, we need to develop improved logic programming languages, which do not rely on extralogical features for the sake of efficiency.

3 Logic programs: first-order theories or inductive definitions?

We need an improved logic programming paradigm, not just an improved language, if pure logic programming is to become practical. So let us consider what logic programming really means. We begin with the orthodox view and then propose an alternative.

3.1 Logic programs as first-order theories

PROLOG is descended from Robinson's resolution principle for proving theorems in first-order logic [37]. Every clause in a pure PROLOG program stands for a first-order formula; we are PROgramming in LOGic. To illustrate this orthodox view, consider the traditional 'family relationships' example:

```
grandparent(X,Z) :- parent(X,Y), parent(Y,Z).
cousin(X,Y) :- grandparent(Z,X), grandparent(Z,Y).
parent(elizabeth,charles).
parent(elizabeth,andrew).
parent(charles,william).
parent(charles,henry).
parent(andrew,beatrice).
```

We can regard this PROLOG program as a first-order theory. The first clause corresponds to the logical axiom

$$(\forall x)(\forall y)(\forall z)\, \mathrm{parent}(x,y) \wedge \mathrm{parent}(y,z) \to \mathrm{grandparent}(x,z)$$

If we pose the query

```
?- cousin(henry,beatrice).
```

then PROLOG answers yes, for the query has an obvious proof from the axioms.
If we ask

```
?- cousin(elizabeth,asterix).
```

disproved, for it is true in some models, false in others. The answer **no** conveys less information than **yes**.

Now imagine we pose the negative query

```
?- not cousin(elizabeth,asterix).
```

A typical PROLOG system will answer **yes** because there is no proof of

```
cousin(elizabeth,asterix).
```

This treatment of negation is called *Negation as Failure*; it differs from logical negation, since the query is not a logical consequence of the axioms. Some people think that Negation as Failure is a cheap hack, and that researchers should aim to implement logical negation. Logical negation would answer **no** to our query — but this is often undesirable. PROLOG programmers recognise that our database *defines relations* such as 'cousin-of', where cousin(elizabeth,asterix) does not hold. Negation as Failure is a natural way to test whether a relation holds. This point of view is hard to justify under the orthodox paradigm for logic programming.

3.2 Logic programs as inductive definitions

Here is an alternative paradigm for logic programming. A set of clauses is not a first-order theory, but the definition of a new logic. The meaning of a logic program is the set of theorems in this 'private' logic: all derivable ground atoms. This is a monotone inductive definition of a family of sets, one for each predicate.

Inductive definitions appear in all branches of mathematics. The natural numbers are the least set containing 0 and closed under successor. The Boolean expressions are the least set containing propositional letters and closed under $\land$, $\lor$, $\neg$. Most importantly: the set of *theorems* in a logical system is the least set containing all axioms and closed under all applications of inference rules. As Aczel explains, this is the general form of an inductive definition [2].

What has this to do with logic programming? We can regard a logic program as an inductive definition by taking its clauses as axioms and inference rules. We regard our family relationships database as a new logic with rules like

$$\frac{\text{parent}(x,y) \quad \text{parent}(y,z)}{\text{grandparent}(x,z)} \qquad \frac{\text{grandparent}(z,x) \quad \text{grandparent}(z,y)}{\text{cousin}(x,y)}$$

This inductively defines various sets. The 'grandparent of' relation is the set of all pairs $\langle x, y \rangle$ such that grandparent(x, y) follows from the database. Similarly the derivable instances of cousin(x, y) define the 'cousin of' relation.

Aczel [2] gives the semantics of an inductive definition as follows.

- A *rule* has the form $p \leftarrow P$, where P is the set of premises and p is the conclusion.
- Let Φ be a set of rules. A set A is Φ-*closed* provided that for each rule $p \leftarrow P$ in Φ, if $P \subseteq A$ then $p \in A$. (Thus if the premises are in A then so is the conclusion.)
- The set $I(\Phi)$ *inductively defined* by Φ is given by

$$I(\Phi) = \bigcap \{A \mid A \text{ is } \Phi\text{-closed}\}$$

The inductively defined set $I(\Phi)$ can also be expressed as the least fixed point of a monotone operator. A set of rules Φ defines a universe or assertion language A, namely the set of all premises and conclusions of rules:

$$A = \bigcup \{P \cup \{p\} \mid \text{rule } p \leftarrow P \text{ is in } \Phi\}$$

Note that A corresponds to the Herbrand base of a set of clauses. Now Φ defines a monotone operator ϕ over A, corresponding to all possible rule applications in a set Y of assertions. Precisely, if $Y \subseteq A$ then

$$\phi(Y) = \{p \in A \mid \text{rule } p \leftarrow P \text{ is in } \Phi \text{ and } P \subseteq Y\}$$

The iterates of ϕ are defined as usual:

$$\phi^0 = \emptyset$$
$$\phi^{n+1} = \phi^n \cup \phi(\phi^n)$$
$$\phi^\omega = \bigcup_{n \in \omega} \phi^n$$

If all rules in Φ have a finite number of premises then $\phi^\omega = I(\Phi)$ and ϕ^ω is the least fixed point of ϕ.

The full theory of inductive definitions is complicated, but much of it need not concern us. A rule $p \leftarrow P$ could have an infinite number of premises, unlike rules in logic programs. The rules in an inductive definition contain no variables. A schematic rule (like the rule for **cousin**) abbreviates an infinite set of rules: all ground instances under the Herbrand universe.

In the semantics of logic programming, such theory has long been used as a technical device. We suggest, rather, that an inductive definition is a logic program's intrinsic declarative content. Clauses should not be viewed as assertions in first-order logic, but as rules generating a set.

For a concrete example, consider how a formal grammar generates the strings of a language. Grammars are inductive definitions. This may explain why logic programming works so well at natural language processing.

3.3 Least models and the Closed World Assumption

Definite clauses are a fragment of first-order logic enjoying remarkable qualities. Any set of definite clauses is consistent. In the greatest model, each predicate is universally true; in the unique least model, each predicate holds just when it must. The least model is the interesting one, for it corresponds to our intuition that our logic program defines a set of relationships.

Van Emden and Kowalski [43] observed that the model-theoretic semantics of a logic program is best given by the least Herbrand model, which is the intersection of all Herbrand models. This coincides with the operational and fixed point semantics. Their fixed point semantics is precisely our inductively defined set $I(\Phi)$.

The least model can be formalized in first-order logic as the Closed World Assumption, augmenting the database with the negations of all ground atoms that do not hold in the least model. Shepherdson shows how this leads to difficulties [40]. First-order logic is simply too weak to characterize the least model.[4] Horn clause logic is even weaker. But the least model can be directly expressed by an inductive definition.

Negation as Failure is investigated by Apt and van Emden [3] and Lloyd [29]. Essentially, they develop the theory of inductive definitions so as to distinguish divergent computations from finite failures. Negation goes beyond monotone inductive definitions: with negated subgoals, the function ϕ above may not be monotone. However, perhaps the database can be partitioned into several inductive definitions, so that each negation refers to a set that has already been defined (the dependency graph must be acyclic). The database can then be interpreted as an iterated inductive definition (via some treatment of finite failure.) Such databases are called *stratified* or *free from recursive negation* [44]. The main stream of (sound) research into negation [34] uses the mathematics of fixedpoints, ordinals, and inductive definitions, not that of classical first-order logic.

In different situations, either view of logic programming — inductive definitions or first-order logic — could be more useful. Where the Closed World Assumption is wrong, so is the inductive view. Below we contrast these views with respect to several aspects of logic programming.

3.4 Specification and verification of logic programs

A key selling point for 'programming in logic' is that programs can be viewed as specifications. Programs can be derived from specifications, and these programs

---

4 By the Skolem-Löwenheim Theorem, no set of first-order axioms can even fix the cardinality of its models, let alone fix a single model.

are guaranteed to be correct. Can we verify logic programs when regarding them as inductive definitions?

Given a specification, a logic program is *correct* if it is sound and complete. *Sound* (or partially correct) means that each successful goal in an execution is permitted by the specification. *Complete* means that each permitted goal will succeed during execution. Specifications are still written in some sort of logical formalism even when we regard programs as inductive definitions.

Every inductive definition gives rise to a principle of inductive proof. In simple cases, this principle resembles structural induction or mathematical induction (on the natural numbers). The general principle is induction over derivations in our 'private' logic. It is used to prove soundness of logic programs, basically by showing that each rule is individually sound. Completeness proofs typically involve some form of induction over the data, showing that the rules suffice for all the necessary derivations.

Fitting gives examples of correctness proofs [17, pages 49–53]. His book is a unique treatment of computability theory in the context of logic programming. He presents logic programs not as first-order theories, but as 'elementary formal systems', which are a restricted case of inductive definitions.

Kowalski [28, page 19] says that a program is totally correct provided it is logically equivalent to its specification. That is nice and simple. But Hogger notes [26, page 141]

> In practice, though, this is rarely possible: logic procedure sets usually have less information content than the specifications to which they conform, even though they may be complete.

Hogger goes on to demonstrate a more general method called *definiens transformation*. Each predicate is defined as logically equivalent to some formula. These definitions are transformed by replacing formulae by equivalent formulae. Finally each 'if-and-only-if' is replaced by 'if' when this results in a set of definite clauses. Hogger states [26, page 153]

> If this is accomplished successfully then the program (P,G) is thereby proven to be totally correct. Its partial correctness is directly established .... Its completeness is established by the fact that each definiens transformation preserves equivalence ...

Let us illustrate this method by deriving a predicate $nat(X)$ meaning 'X is a natural number'. Informally, let us say that X is a natural number if and only if X has the form $s(s(\cdots s(0) \cdots))$.

The specification is

$$nat(X) \leftrightarrow X \text{ is a natural number.}$$

Now X is a natural number if and only if $X = 0$ or X is the successor $s(Y)$ of some natural number Y. Therefore we may transform the specification to

$$\text{nat}(X) \leftrightarrow X = 0 \vee (\exists Y)(X = s(Y) \wedge Y \text{ is a natural number}).$$

Substituting back the original specification introduces a recursive call:

$$\text{nat}(X) \leftrightarrow X = 0 \vee (\exists Y)(X = s(Y) \wedge \text{nat}(Y))$$

Each disjunct has the form of a clause body, so replace $\leftrightarrow$ by $\leftarrow$:

$$\text{nat}(X) \leftarrow X = 0 \vee (\exists Y)(X = s(Y) \wedge \text{nat}(Y))$$

Simplification yields two clauses, a correct program:

$$\text{nat}(0) \qquad \text{nat}(s(Y)) \leftarrow \text{nat}(Y)$$

But here is another derivation. Note that X is a natural number if and only if $s(X)$ is a natural numer. Therefore the specification is equivalent to

$$\text{nat}(X) \leftrightarrow s(X) \text{ is a natural number}.$$

Substituting back the original specification introduces a recursive call:

$$\text{nat}(X) \leftrightarrow \text{nat}(s(X))$$

Dropping the $\leftrightarrow$ gives the clause

$$\text{nat}(X) \leftarrow \text{nat}(s(X)).$$

How did we get such a useless program? Hogger's verification method requires a separate termination proof, which must be performed with respect to a given computational strategy [26, page 143–150]. So the connection between 'logic program' and 'logic specification' is not as simple as commonly thought.

When the above programs are viewed as inductive definitions, it is obvious that the first defines the natural numbers and the second defines the empty set. We can understand the 'definiens transformations' as equational reasoning on sets. If a set satisfies a recursive equation like $S = f(S)$, then S is some fixedpoint of f. Replacing $\leftrightarrow$ by $\leftarrow$ picks out the least fixedpoint. These fixedpoints could differ, as they did above. The theory of inductive definitions could lead to better techniques [16].

4 Extended logic programming languages

Many extended logic programming languages aim to increase the power of pure declarative programming. Most extensions adopt the first-order logic viewpoint, but several are best understood from the viewpoint of inductive definition. While surveying other work, this section also discusses the design of our logic language with functions.

4.1 Larger fragments of first-order logic

If our goal is to program in logic then we should go beyond Horn clauses, aiming ultimately at programming in full first-order logic. Bowen [10] proposed a complete theorem-prover where programs consist of sequents of the form $A_1, \ldots, A_m \vdash B_1, \ldots, B_n$; a standard PROLOG interpreter handles the case where these resemble definite clauses. Many similar proposals have appeared since.

Stickel's Prolog Technology Theorem Prover [41] exploits the sophistication of current PROLOG implementations. He extends them to full first-order logic using sound unification with occurs check, the model-elimination inference rule, and depth-first iterative deepening for completeness. Stickel's stated aim is high-performance theorem proving; he specifically de-emphasises its potential for logic programming [41, page 375].

Applications of a full first-order logic programming language are hard to visualize. Perhaps the problem is that first-order logic destroys that vital property, the least model property. The disjunction $p \lor q$ has two minimal models, where either p or q is true. Therefore, disjunctive axioms destroy the least model property. So do negative goals and nested implication, for $p \leftarrow \neg q$ and $q \leftarrow (q \leftarrow p)$ are classically equivalent to $p \lor q$. Makowsky has formalized the least model property in terms of initial structures and generic examples. He shows that Horn clauses are the largest fragment of first-order logic enjoying this property [30]. By regarding logic programs as inductive definitions, we come to the same conclusion at once. Makowsky's work is rigorous confirmation of our intuitive idea.

4.2 Other work concerning inductive definitions

Hagiya and Sakurai [23] present a formal system for logic programming, based on the theory of iterative inductive definitions. This system captures the least fixedpoint semantics of a set of clauses and formally justifies Negation as Failure. They envisage programs consisting of several levels, each defined inductively in terms of its predecessor. The formal system is given as a foundation for PROLOG, with applications to program specification, verification, and synthesis. Hagiya and Sakurai take the traditional first-order view of logic programming, but at times appear to question this paradigm [23, page 71]:

> PROLOG usually explained as being based on SLD-resolution. It is more natural, however, to regard a PROLOG program and its execution as a set of productions and generation of a normal proof than to regard them as a set of Horn clauses and SLD-resolution, since it more faithfully reflects the procedural interpretation of predicate logic ... Some resolution procedures are more clearly understood in terms of deduction, even if deduction and refutation are equivalent.

Hallnäs and Schroeder-Heister [25] advance a view of logic programming based on inductive definitions. Calling the traditional view 'clauses-as-formulae', they advocate instead 'clauses-as-rules': the clauses are a system of inference rules. Their approach is inspired by natural deduction proof theory and defines the semantics of programs as inductively defined sets. They model non-ground answer substitutions directly, not as the set of ground instances.

Their language of Generalized Horn Clauses resembles earlier proposals for permitting nested implications in clause bodies [20, 33], but they obtain a much simpler treatment of free variables by distinguishing assumptions from program clauses. Nested implication falls outside the framework of *monotone* inductive definitions (as remarked above) but programs can be understood as *partial* inductive definitions [24].

Their approach includes a new idea, similar to elimination rules in natural deduction. A predicate p is inductively defined by its set of introduction rules, namely the clauses with head p. If we then are told that p happens to be true, then the body of some introduction rule must also be true. This gives a form of Negation as Failure and non-monotonic reasoning. Aronsson et al. [4] describe the language in more detail and discuss a prototype implementation.

4.3 The language LOGLISP

LOGLISP, by Robinson and Sibert, is one of the earlist attempts to combine logic and functional programming [39, page 400]:

> Our own early attempts (as devoted users of LISP) to use PROLOG convinced us that it would be worth the effort to create *within* LISP a faithful implementation of Kowalski's logic programming idea. ... We set out to honor the principle of the separation of logic from control (no CUT, no preferred ordering of assertions within procedures nor of atomic sentences within hypotheses of assertions) by making the logic programming engine 'purely denotative'.

LOGLISP is not completely pure. The LOGIC component can invoke arbitrary LISP functions. A more fundamental problem is the treatment of uninstantiated variables in function calls. LOGLISP leaves such variables unchanged during expression reduction, so the result can depend on the order in which goals are solved. Dincbas and van Hentenryck show how this leads to anomalies [15].

But LOGLISP's Horn clause interpreter — thanks to a form of *best-first search* — is complete. Although PROLOG's depth-first search strategy is incomplete, this only matters if the search space is infinite, when we must be prepared to give up after a finite time. So a call to the LOGIC interpreter specifies how many solutions to find before stopping. We could say that LOGLISP views the clauses as an inductive definition of solution sets; the LISP half operates on lists of solutions from the LOGIC half. This resembles PROLOG's **setof** predicate.

Robinson's later work [38] aims to integrate the functional and logic components using a single reduction semantics for both.

4.4 A logic language with functions

Though many combined languages have appeared since LOGLISP, few tackle the problem of uninstantiated variables. Equational unification, although not completely understood, seems to be the solution. Equational unification treats functions in a natural way, retaining PROLOG's bidirectionality: functions can be inverted. We have implemented such a language; a similar one is IDEAL [9].

An inductive view of functions in clauses Viewing logic programs as inductive definitions gives a framework for a logic language with functions. Recall that the inference rules in an inductive definition contain no variables. A rule containing variables is merely an abbreviation for the set of its ground instances. We extend this means of abbreviation by permitting clauses to invoke functions defined in a functional language. Such a rule abbreviates the set of its ground instances where all functions have been evaluated.

Terms may contain *constructors* and defined *functions*. Constructors, such as constants, the pairing operator, and list CONS, generate what amounts to a Herbrand universe. Functions denote operations over this universe. Computable values are elements of this universe. Solution terms need not be ground, but should contain no defined functions. (Henceforth we shall just say 'function', not 'defined function'.)

For example, suppose f and g are functions. The clause

$$p(f(X), Y) \leftarrow p(X, g(Y))$$

stands for the set of instances

$$p(u, y) \leftarrow p(x, v)$$

where u, v, x, and y are values such that u is the value of $f(x)$ and v is the value of $g(y)$, provided the function calls terminate.

In the first-order logic view of logic programming, programs in this kind of language are viewed as theories in Horn Clause logic plus equality. Severe restrictions are imposed on equality so that programs can be executed. The equalities must form a term rewriting system with strong properties: they must be confluent, left-linear, and terminating. In short, the equalities must take the form of function definitions. The model theory of Horn Clauses with equality, as developed by Goguen and Meseguer [22], conveys no clear picture of what their programs compute.

An inductive definition has an intuitive reading as a process generating a set of results using some rules. The function definitions help to generate the set of ground rules. An alternative picture: function evaluation is interleaved with rule application. An implementation must 'guess' suitable instances using some sort of unification. Resolving the goal $p(a, g(b))$ against $p(f(X), Y)$, requires solving the equations $a = f(X)$ and $g(b) = Y$ by unification in the equational theory of the functions f and g.

The unification process can be seen as symbolic evaluation of the defined functions. Suppose that the list append is defined as follows:

$$\text{app}([], V) \rightarrow V$$
$$\text{app}([X \mid U], V) \rightarrow [X \mid \text{app}(U, V)]$$

The goal $\text{app}(U, V) = [a, b]$ calls the function app with uninstantiated arguments. Solving the goal requires unifying $[a, b]$ with $\text{app}(U, V)$. The list $[a, b]$ is already a construction; but $\text{app}(U, V)$ must be rewritten, and this instantiates U.

- $U = []$, the first rewrite reduces $\text{app}(U, V)$ to V, giving the solution $V = [a, b]$.
- $U = [X_1 \mid U_1]$, for new variables X_1 and U_1, reduces $\text{app}(U, V)$ to $[X_1 \mid \text{app}(U_1, V)]$. Unification sets $X_1 = a$ and leaves the problem of unifying $[b]$ with $\text{app}(U_1, V)$. There are two subcases.
  - $U_1 = []$ gives the solution $U = [a]$ and $V = [b]$.
  - $U_1 = [X_2 \mid U_2]$ sets $X_2 = b$, where we must unify $[]$ with $\text{app}(U_2, V)$.
    - $U_2 = []$ gives the solution $U = [a, b]$ and $V = []$.
    - $U_2 = [X_3 \mid U_3]$ terminates the search because $[]$ and $[X_3 \mid \text{app}(U_3, V)]$ cannot be unified.

This is essentially *narrowing*, a special case of the paramodulation rule used in unification algorithms for suitable equational theories [46]. There are several implementations [19, 27] and many variations. We have chosen a form of *lazy narrowing* — where a function's arguments are evaluated only when necessary — in the hope of postponing the discovery that a variable is uninstantiated. Fribourg has dealt with the strict case [18].

Treatments of negation and 'cut' The *cut*, written (!), curtails backtracking. Cuts can speed the search exponentially by pruning redundant parts of the search space. Cuts also compensate for implementation deficiencies, preventing the 'trail' of choice points from using up too much store. Cuts are by far the commonest impurity, and are often used needlessly. How can we do without them?

Negation as Failure can be defined through cut [13]:

```
not(P) :- call(P), !, fail.
not(P).
```

Conversely, Clocksin and Mellish recommend replacing cuts by negations whenever possible. So a pure language must include a clean treatment of Negation as Failure. This line of research is orthogonal to our own; see Minker [34].

Cuts are often used when expressing functional dependence, forcing the non-deterministic PROLOG machine to behave deterministically. By having functions in our language, we reduce the need for cuts; indeed, our prototype interpreter dynamically inserts cuts when evaluating functions.

Predicates should not be confused with boolean-valued functions. Although predicates can be represented by their characteristic functions, few logical systems formally identify them.[5] The booleans true and false are symmetric while success and failure are not. Whether a boolean function returns true or false, it has terminated successfully. But failure conveys less information than success, and may not happen in finite time.

Simple tests, such as arithmetic comparisons, should be boolean functions rather than predicates. Testing whether a boolean expression equals false gives a kind of negation. Our language does not allow conditional equations. The conditional rewrite rule

$$a = b \text{ if } p$$

where the condition p is a predicate, says nothing about a when p does not hold. Instead we prefer a conditional expression controlled by a boolean expression c:

$$a = \text{if } c \text{ then } b_1 \text{ else } b_2$$

5 A Prototype of the language

This implementation was developed (by A. W. Smith) to investigate what was possible and what was desirable in such a language. It was written as an interpreter in PROLOG to carry over such features as the parser and backtracking mechanism. We have not investigated how low-level techniques for logic and functional languages might be integrated.

A program file contains clauses, function rewrite rules, type declarations, operator declarations and comments. The system is similar to a simple PROLOG interpreter but uses a lazy semantic unification algorithm. The syntax of definite clauses follows that of Edinburgh PROLOG. Built in predicates include true, which always succeeds; fail, which always fails; and $A = B$, which succeeds if A and B unify semantically. PROLOG's (extralogical!) output predicates nl and write are also provided.[6]

---

5 The main formal system that does is classical higher-order logic. Intuitionistic higher-order logic identifies predicates with propositional functions, but the corresponding set of truth values is not a Boolean algebra.

6 Because of iterative deepening, the search may pass through the same point several times and will repeat the output on each occasion.

5.1 Rewrite Rules

Function definitions are given as a series of rewrite rules of the form

$$f(expr_1, expr_2, \ldots) \;\texttt{-->}\; expr \;.$$

For example, the append function for list is

```
app([], V)     ->> V.
app([X|U], V)  ->> [X | app(U,V)].
```

Answers to queries are returned as in PROLOG. When a solution is found, the system returns bindings for the variables. Further answers may be elicited using the ';' key. Example:

```
| ?- solve(app(U,V)=[1,2]).
    U=[]
    V=[1,2] ;

    U=[1]
    V=[2] ;

    U=[1,2]
    V=[] ;
no
```

To ensure that the rewrite rules form a confluent system, certain restrictions are imposed. Though these are not necessary conditions, they are sufficient and are, furthermore, not unreasonable for a functional language:

The Constructor Discipline. The names are divided into two disjoint classes — *functions* and *constructors* — depending on whether there are rewrite rules for that name. No function should appear in the arguments of the left side of any rule.

Left Linearity. No variable should appear more than once in the left side of a rule.

Term Rewriting. All the variables appearing in the right side of a rule should also appear in the left side of the rule.

Non-overlapping. No two rule left sides should be unifiable with each other. (The rules should be mutually exclusive.)

If any condition is broken, the offending rewrite rule is identified in a warning. The system does not prevent the user defining and using non-confluent rules, but it contains optimisations based on the assumption that the conditions are obeyed. The interpreter assumes the constructor discipline holds, so defined functions within the left side of a rule are treated like constructors. Left linearity enables the interpreter to omit the occurs check when it unifies the function with the left side of a rule in the application of that rule. Rules which are not left linear may cause the system to loop or crash.

Finally, the assumption that rules do not overlap allows the interpreter to reduce the search space. If a function application is rewritten without instantiating any variables, then no other rule can be applicable unless it overlaps with the first. The effect is like cut — upon backtracking, no other rules need be tried.[7]

The system also checks whether the rewrite rules exhaust all possible values for the arguments. This check is rather involved. The approach is to consider the tuples formed by the arguments of the left sides of the rules. A tuple of variables is then successively instantiated (to terms of the appropriate type) so that it does not unify with each of the rule tuples taken in turn.

5.2 Type Declarations

The built-in types include int and bool. Type operators such as list can be declared, permitting types such as list(int) and list(list(bool)). Polymorphic types like list(A) are permitted, as well as function types with the following syntax:

$[type_1, type_2, \ldots]$ =>> $type$

Type declarations must be given for all predicates, constructors and functions. Predicate type declarations take the form

pred $p(type_1, type_2, \ldots)$.

where $type_1, type_2, \ldots$ are the types of the arguments. The type may be polymorphic: a general list appending predicate could be declared by

pred append(list(A), list(A), list(A)).

The types of constructors are declared by

constructors $type$ => $con_1, con_2, \ldots$.

Here $con_1, con_2, \ldots$ are made up from a constructor for the given $type$, applied to type arguments. For example, the constructors for the natural numbers (type nat) are zero and s, where s must be applied to an argument of type nat.

constructors nat => zero, s(nat).

---

7 A clever user could make use of this final optimisation to provide a default case for a function. This would work only for ground arguments.

The constructors for the polymorphic type list(A) are given as follows (we can use standard PROLOG list syntax, denoting PROLOG's list constructors):

```
constructors list(A) => [], [A|list(A)].
```

The type of a function is declared as follows:

function f ($type_1, type_2, \ldots$) =>> $type$.

For example:

```
function mult(nat,nat) =>> nat.
function app(list(A),list(A)) =>> list(A).
```

The type checking scheme follows Mycroft and O'Keefe [35] with a straightforward extension to include function rewrite rules.

A typeless version of the language could be envisaged. Type information is required by the built in equality function.

5.3 The equality function 'eq'

The equality function eq returns true or false. It behaves something like a set of rewrite rules, testing all possible combinations of constructors for a given type. The equality test is defined for each (non-function) type.

For example, the equality test for lists behaves something like the following function:

```
       [] listeq []        ->> true.
       [] listeq [A|As]  ->> false.
    [A|As] listeq []        ->> false.
    [A|As] listeq [B|Bs] ->> (A eq B) and (As listeq Bs).
```

Here and denotes Boolean conjunction, while eq is an equality test for the list's element type.

The test is more efficient than suggested above, for X eq t gives true while instantiating X to t. When returning false, the equality test instantiates its arguments to all possible pairs of different constructors.

5.4 Other features

Arithmetic To perform integer arithmetic there are built in integer valued functions +, -, *, div, mod, and abs with the obvious meanings. These use the arithmetic routines of the host language but behave as if they are defined by an infinite collection of rewrite rules such as 0+0->>0, 0+1->>1, -1+0->>-1, etc.

For example, the goal 15=X+Y succeeds infinitely often, finding all pairs of numbers that sum to 15. This may seem odd, but the implementation aims to be complete. The PROLOG goal 15 is X+Y typically results in an error message.

The relations >, <, >=, and =< are boolean valued functions — not predicates — since they are decidable.

Integers have type int; booleans have type bool.

Higher-order functions The built in function apply returns the value obtained by applying the function contained in its first argument to the list of arguments contained in its second argument. Thus apply(+,[1,2]) returns 3. Since there is no higher-order unification, when apply is rewritten, the first argument must be normalisable to a function or a λ-expression.

The user can define higher-order functions:

```
map(F, [])      ->> []
map(F, [H|T]) ->> [apply(F,[H]) | map(F,T)]
```

The value of map(lambda([X],X * X),[1,2,3]) is [1,4,9].

The justification of higher-order functions requires extending the theory of narrowing to allow function variables in rewrite rules. This appears straightforward if function variables are not allowed in goals. The full incorporation of function variables would require higher-order equational unification. Our experience with higher-order unification shows that it can be effective in simple cases [36], but it also suggests that ambitious applications are impractical.

Descriptions Descriptions, or η-terms, call the predicate level from the function level. The term eta(X,G) means 'some X such that G', and returns some value of variable X that makes goal G succeed. Remaining values are found on backtracking. IDEAL has a similar feature [9, page 90].

Descriptions cause expressions to be nondeterministic, violating the separation of concerns into functions (deterministic) and predicates (nondeterministic). They pose interesting but very difficult semantic questions.

6 Operation of the prototype

The interpreter is essentially PROLOG with a modified unification algorithm to allow defined functions within terms. The unification algorithm is similar to that given by Martelli, Moiso and Rossi [31]. It effectively uses a selection strategy for narrowing described as 'outer narrowing' by You [45, 46]. You describes a matching algorithm; we have extended this to a unification algorithm but have not attempted a proof of correctness. The occurs check during unification could perhaps be omitted by allowing cyclic expressions to denote fixedpoints.

6.1 Unification

The effect of the unification algorithm can be described as follows. In unifying two terms A and B

1. If either term is a variable, then instantiate that variable if permitted by occurs check (see below). Unification is lazy: the other term may contain function terms which are not rewritten now (maybe never).
2. If both are constructor terms, then if they have different principal constructors the unification fails, otherwise the two sets of arguments are unified.
3. Otherwise one term must be a function application. It is rewritten by narrowing (see later) to some new term, which must unify with the other term.

Only (3) distinguishes this from ordinary unification.

Rewriting A function application is rewritten using a rewrite rule from the function's definition. In a functional language this is achieved by matching the term with the left side of the rule. In a logic language, however, there may well be logic variables within the term; some instance of these variables might be needed to apply the rule. A narrowing step consists of unifying a term with the left side of a rule and replacing it with the right side.

If there are nested function applications, which should be chosen for narrowing? The brute-force approach would be to try every possible occurrence. This will certainly find all possible solutions but could produce the same solution many times. A practical selection strategy would chose a single occurrence. The obvious choices are the innermost or outermost occurrence.

The innermost strategy can be shown to be complete provided the rewrite system is confluent and terminating and the functions are exhaustively defined [18]. However, an innermost strategy is eager and one of the design objectives of the language was that it should be lazy.

The outermost strategy is incomplete (see also You [46]):

$$f(W, a) \rightarrow a \qquad f(a, b) \rightarrow b$$

Given the term $f(f(X, Y), Z)$, the innermost strategy can produce both a and b, while the outermost strategy only produces a. The problem arises because $f(X, Y)$ can only be unified syntactically with the variable W in the first rule. However if it were rewritten first to a the second rule could be used as well — in other words a and $f(X, Y)$ unify semantically when applying the second rule.

The solution is to use an outermost selection strategy (allowing laziness), but when narrowing, the unification between the term and rewrite rule should be semantic rather than syntactic. This differs from the usual definition of narrowing.

An advantage of using PROLOG as the host language is that the logic variables can be used as pointers. When a variable is instantiated, that value is propagated with no need to make substitutions explicitly. However the value of the pointer cannot be reassigned when a function application is rewritten. The same term could be evaluated repeatedly, giving call-by-name. To get call-by-need, function applications are represented by a structure containing a new variable to point to the rewritten value.

The unification algorithm is lazy and so only performs rewriting when required. However, the user requires answers in normal form. Thus after the system has found a solution it normalises the answer substitutions by repeatedly rewriting any defined function terms in the substitutions. The same rewriting algorithm is used as in unification. (This normalisation is too eager; in consequence, infinite data structures cannot be displayed as results, although they may take part in computations.)

The occurs check When a variable is to be unified with a term, it must be checked not to occur within the term. In the presence of rewrite rules an occurrence within a defined function might disappear: thus X and $0 + X$ unify semantically.

The occurs check does not fail just because there is a syntactic occurrence of the variable within the term. Instead, it copies the term, replacing by a new variable each function application containing an occurrence, adding these as new disagreement pairs to (eventually) solve. If an occurrence of the variable is encountered other than in a function application, then the check fails. The new term built in this way will not contain any occurrences of the variable.

Without this extended occurs check, cases involving occurrence would have to be solved using the full unification algorithm, which would be slower.

Search strategy The search for a solution uses *depth-first iterative deepening* [41]. During each iteration the search is cut off if it exceeds the given limit. At the end of the iteration, if the search has been cut off at any point, then the limit is increased and the next iteration started. When a solution is found, its depth is checked to be within the range of the current iteration — to prevent a solution being returned several times.

The depth is incremented when either rewrites or clauses are applied. Thus the search is complete at both the function and clause level.

Iterative deepening is complete, straightforward to implement, and gives a sensible compromise between time and space efficiency. Perhaps some more sophisticated strategy would be more efficient, while retaining completeness.

6.2 Example: An Eight Queens Program

This eight queens program begins by introducing the type `list`. Predicate `upto` generates a range of numbers, while `queens` generates boards of non-attacking queens. The membership test is a function (`mem`) since its negation is used. Predicate `safe` could also be a boolean function.

```
constructors list(A) => [],[A|list(A)].

pred queens(int,list(int)).
queens(N,[Q|B]) :- (N>0)=true, queens(N-1,B), upto(1,8,Q),
                   mem(Q,B)=false, safe(1,Q,B).
queens(0, []).

pred upto(int,int,int).
upto(M,N,M) :- (M=<N)=true.
upto(M,N,K) :- (M<N)=true, upto(M+1,N,K).

function mem(A,list(A)) =>> bool.
mem(X,[]) ->> false.
mem(X,[Y|Ys]) ->> (X eq Y) or mem(X,Ys).

pred safe(int,int,list(int)).
safe(_,_,[]).
safe(I,Q,[Q1|B]) :- (I eq abs(Q-Q1))=false, safe(I+1,Q,B).
```

Our interpreter is slow, taking six minutes to find the first three solutions.

```
| ?- solve(queens(8,B)).
    B=[4,2,7,3,6,8,5,1] ;

    B=[5,2,4,7,3,8,6,1] ;

    B=[3,5,2,8,6,4,7,1]
yes
```

6.3 Example: A Propositional calculus theorem prover

Wang's Algorithm for the propositional calculus [32] works by constructing a backwards proof using the rules of the sequent calculus [21]. The following program also constructs a proof tree. Each label names some sequent calculus rule, such as `andl` for ∧ left. The subtrees represent proofs of the premises of the rule.

This program demonstrates function inversion. The function `sizeof` computes the size of proof trees. In PROLOG this function must be coded by two different predicates, depending on whether it is used to compute the size or (backwards) to generate trees of a given size.

The program begins with PROLOG infix declarations. Types of formulæ, labels, and trees are declared. Note that a tree node contains a label and a list of subtrees. The remainder of the program is basically PROLOG. The program appears in Figure 1.

The first sample execution demonstrates programming with non-ground data. Here we construct non-ground trees of size 5, then instantiate them to valid proof trees. This generates theorems whose proofs have size 5. A similar program in PROLOG crashed due to a cycle (no occurs check).

The output has been beautified by indenting and by shortening internal variable names.

```
?- solve((5=sizeof(T), proof([],[B],T))).
    T=node(andr,[node(impr,[node(basic(_1),[])]),
                 node(impr,[node(basic(_2),[])])])
    B=(_1-->_1)&(_2-->_2) ;

    T=node(impr,[node(andr,[node(basic(_1),[]),
                            node(impr,[node(basic(_2),[])])])])
    B=_1-->_1&(_2-->_2) ;

    T=node(impr,[node(andr,[node(basic(_1),[]),
                            node(impr,[node(basic(_1),[])])])])
    B=_1-->_1&(_2-->_1) ;

    T=node(impr,[node(andr,[node(basic(_1&_2),[]),
                            node(andl,[node(basic(_1),[])])])])
    B=_1&_2-->(_1&_2)&_1
yes
```

The program can also prove theorems and report the size of the proof.

```
?- solve((proof([],[p & (q & r)  -->  (p & q) & r],T), N=sizeof(T))).
    T=node(impr,[node(andl,[node(andl,
        [node(andr,[node(andr,[node(basic(p),[]),
                               node(basic(q),[])]),
                    node(basic(r),[])])])])])
    N=8
yes
```

7 Conclusions

We have criticised logic programming as a declarative paradigm. What can be done to make pure logic programming practical?

To justify the Closed World Assumption, we propose that logic programs should be viewed as inductive definitions, not as first-order theories. Some people

Fig. 1. A Program for Wang's Algorithm

```
/*logical connectives are constructors of type form. */
op(5,fy,~). op(10,xfy,&). op(20,xfy,\/). op(30,xfy,-->).
constructors form => &(form,form), \/(form,form), ~(form),
                     -->(form,form), p,q,r.


/*labels of proof trees*/
constructors label => basic(form),andl,andr,orl,orr,notl,notr,
        impl,impr,iffl,iffr.
constructors tree => node(label, list(tree)).

function sizeof(tree) =>> int.
function sizeoflist(list(tree)) =>> int.
sizeof(node(L,Ts)) ->> sizeoflist(Ts) + 1.
sizeoflist([]) ->> 0.
sizeoflist([T|Ts]) ->> sizeof(T) + sizeoflist(Ts).

/*delmem(X,Ys,Zs) finds and removes X from Ys giving Zs */
pred delmem(A,list(A),list(A)).
delmem(X,[X|Xs],Xs).
delmem(X,[Y|Ys],[Y|Zs]) :- delmem(X,Ys,Zs).

/*common(As,Bs,B) when B is a common element of As and Bs*/
pred common(list(A),list(A),A).
common(As,[B|_],B) :- delmem(B,As,_).
common(As,[_|Bs],B) :- common(As,Bs,B).

/*proof(left formulae,right formulae,proof tree) */
pred proof(list(form), list(form), tree).

proof(As,Bs,node(basic(B),[])) :- common(As,Bs,B). /*0 subproofs*/

/*1 subproof*/
proof(As,Bs,node(notr,[T])) :- delmem(~B,Bs,Ds),proof([B|As],Ds,T).
proof(As,Bs,node(andl,[T])) :- delmem(A1&A2,As,Cs), proof([A1,A2|Cs],Bs,T).
proof(As,Bs,node(orr,[T]))  :- delmem(B1\/B2,Bs,Ds),proof(As,[B1,B2|Ds],T).
proof(As,Bs,node(notl,[T])) :- delmem(~A,As,Cs), proof(Cs,[A|Bs],T).
proof(As,Bs,node(impr,[T])) :- delmem(B1-->B2,Bs,Ds),
        proof([B1|As],[B2|Ds],T).

/*2 subproofs*/
proof(As,Bs,node(andr,[T1,T2])) :- delmem(B1&B2,Bs,Ds),
        proof(As,[B1|Ds],T1), proof(As,[B2|Ds],T2).
proof(As,Bs,node(orl,[T1,T2])) :- delmem(A1\/A2,As,Cs),
        proof([A1|Cs],Bs,T1), proof([A2|Cs],Bs,T2).
```

refuse to abandon the dream of programming in first-order logic. But we have to ask whether this dream is possible — even whether it is desirable. The first-order paradigm does not deal adequately with negation in databases, and seems to be an unreliable guide in research on program correctness and language design. Inductive definitions are more fundamental than first-order logic, and perhaps easier to understand.

Uses of PROLOG's cut can be largely eliminated by providing functions and negation. Two forms of negation can be mathematically justified: testing whether a boolean expression returns `false`, and restricted forms of Negation as Failure. Concepts such as 'stratified program' are best understood from the perspective of inductive definition. Future languages should provide means for organizing a program into a suite of inductive definitions, since stratification will not hold by accident.

The PROLOG goal `var(X)` tests whether or not the variable `X` is bound. This clearly has no logical meaning. Some uses of `var` can be eliminated by allowing functions to accept non-ground arguments. But there are some difficult examples, such as writing a polymorphic type checker [11]. This is natural to write in PROLOG, since it uses unification and search. When the type has been inferred, certain of its variables must be labelled as 'generic', and such manipulation of logical variables must use `var`.

Such uses of `var` serve not to make up for language deficiencies, but to exploit global properties of the program. Similarly, it is hard to eliminate certain instances of cut. We must either retain such impurities in our languages, or be prepared to tolerate some inconvenience.

Input/output is the greatest challenge. Pure approaches to input/output constitute much of the research in functional programming, and perhaps could be applied to the functional part of our language. Most approaches involve continuations, so our extended logic languages must provide higher-order functions.

Our prototype is far too slow for programmers. But the authors of IDEAL, a similar language, claim outstanding efficiency [5, 8]. Their system translates functions into PROLOG clauses, and then into a modified Warren Abstract Machine. It is incomplete due to depth-first search, but presumably there could be a version using iterative deepening. An OR-parallel machine such as DelPhi [12] could support such languages in future. Functions make explicit the granularity for OR-parallelism: evaluation is deterministic while search is not.

Acknowledgements. This work was supported by the Alvey Diamond project: SERC grants GR/E/02369 and GR/F/10811. William Clocksin, Martin Hyland, Tobias Nipkow, Andrew Pitts, Peter Schroeder-Heister, Lincoln Wallen, David Wolfram, and the referees commented on drafts of this paper.

References

1. Harold Abelson and Gerald J. Sussman. *Structure and Interpretation of Computer Programs*. MIT Press, 1985.

2. Peter Aczel. An introduction to inductive definitions. In J. Barwise, editor, *Handbook of Mathematical Logic*, pages 739–782. North-Holland, 1977.

3. K. R. Apt and M. H. van Emden. Contributions to the theory of logic programming. *Journal of the ACM*, 29:841–862, 1982.

4. Martin Aronsson, Lars-Henrik Eriksson, Anette Gäredal, Lars Hallnäs, and Peter Olin. The programming language GCLA — a definitional approach to logic programming. *New Generation Computing*, 7:381–404, 1990.

5. M. Bellia, P. G. Bosco, E. Giovannetti, G. Levi, C. Moiso, and C. Palamidessi. A two-level approach to logic plus functional programming integration. In J. W. de Bakker, A. J. Nijman, and P. C. Treleaven, editors, *PARLE: Parallel Architectures and Languages Europe*, volume I, pages 374–393. Springer-Verlag, 1987. LNCS 258.

6. Marco Bellia and Giorgio Levi. The relation between logic and functional languages: A survey. *Journal of Logic Programming*, 3:217–236, 1986.

7. Richard Bird and Philip Wadler. *Introduction to Functional Programming*. Prentice-Hall International, 1988.

8. P. G. Bosco, C. Cecchi, and C. Moiso. IDEAL & K-LEAF implementation: A progress report. In E. Odijk, M. Rem, and J.-C. Syre, editors, *PARLE: Parallel Architectures and Languages Europe*, volume I, pages 413–432. Springer-Verlag, 1989. LNCS 365.

9. P. G. Bosco and E. Giovannetti. Ideal: An Ideal DEductive Applicative Language. In *Symposium on Logic Programming*, pages 89–94. IEEE Computer Society Press, 1986.

10. K. A. Bowen. Programming with full first-order logic. In J. E. Hayes, D. Michie, and Y.-H. Pao, editors, *Machine Intelligence 10*, pages 421–440. Ellis Horwood Ltd, 1982.

11. D. Clément, J. Despeyroux, Th. Despeyroux, L. Hascoet, and G. Kahn. Natural semantics on the computer. Technical Report Research Report 416, INRIA Sophia-Antipolis, 1985.

12. W. F. Clocksin. Principles of the DelPhi parallel inference machine. *Computer Journal*, 30:386–392, 1987.

13. W. F. Clocksin and C. S. Mellish. *Programming in Prolog*. Springer-Verlag, 3rd edition, 1987.

14. Doug DeGroot and Gary Lindstrom, editors. *Logic Programming: Functions, Relations and Equations*. Prentice-Hall International, 1986.

15. Mehmet Dincbas and Pascal van Hentenryck. Extended unification algorithms for the integration of functional programming into logic programming. *Journal of Logic Programming*, 4:199–227, 1987.

16. Lars-Henrik Eriksson and Lars Hallnäs. A programming calculus based on partial inductive definitions, with an introduction to the theory of partial inductive definitions. Technical Report R88013, Swedish Institute of Computer Science, 1988.

17. Melvin Fitting. *Computability Theory, Semantics, and Logic Programming.* Oxford University Press, 1987.

18. Laurent Fribourg. SLOG: A logic programming language interpreter based on clausal superposition and rewriting. In *Symposium on Logic Programming,* pages 172–184. IEEE Computer Society Press, 1985.

19. Laurent Fribourg. Prolog with simplification. In K. Fuchi and M. Nivat, editors, *Programming of Future Generation Computers,* pages 161–183. Elsevier Science Publishers, 1988.

20. D. M. Gabbay and U. Reyle. N-PROLOG: An extension of PROLOG with hypothetical implications. I. *Journal of Logic Programming,* 4:319–355, 1984.

21. J. H. Gallier. *Logic for Computer Science: Foundations of Automatic Theorem Proving.* Harper & Row, 1986.

22. Joseph A. Goguen and José Meseguer. Eqlog: Equality, types, and generic modules for logic programming. In Doug DeGroot and Gary Lindstrom, editors, *Logic Programming: Functions, Relations and Equations,* pages 295–364. Prentice-Hall International, 1986.

23. Masami Hagiya and Takafumi Sakurai. Foundation of logic programming based on inductive definition. *New Generation Computing,* 2:59–77, 1984.

24. Lars Hallnäs. Partial inductive definitions. *Theoretical Computer Science.* in press.

25. Lars Hallnäs and Peter Schroeder-Heister. A proof-theoretic approach to logic programming I. Generalized Horn clauses. Technical Report R88005, Swedish Institute of Computer Science, 1988.

26. C. J. Hogger. *Introduction to Logic Programming.* Academic Press, 1984.

27. Heinrich Hussmann. Rapid prototyping for algebraic specifications — R A P system user's manual. Technical Report MIP-8504, Fakultät für Mathematik und Informatik, Universität Passau, Germany, March 1985.

28. R. Kowalski. The relation between logic programming and logic specification. In C. A. R. Hoare and J. C. Shepherdson, editors, *Mathematical Logic and Programming Languages,* pages 11–27. Prentice-Hall International, 1985.

29. J. W. Lloyd. *Foundations of Logic Programming.* Springer-Verlag, 1984.

30. J. A. Makowsky. Why Horn formulas matter in computer science: Initial structures and generic examples. *Journal of Computer and System Sciences,* 34:266–292, 1987.

31. A. Martelli, C. Moiso, and G. F. Rossi. An algorithm for unification in equational theories. In *Symposium on Logic Programming,* pages 180–186. IEEE Computer Society Press, 1986.

32. John McCarthy, Paul W. Abrahams, Daniel J. Edwards, Timothy P. Hart, and Michael I. Levin. *LISP 1.5 Programmer's Manual.* MIT Press, 1962.

33. Dale Miller. A theory of modules for logic programming. In *Symposium on Logic Programming,* pages 106–114. IEEE Computer Society Press, 1986.

34. Jack Minker, editor. *Foundations of Deductive Databases and Logic Programming.* Morgan Kaufmann, 1988.

35. Alan Mycroft and Richard A. O'Keefe. A polymorphic type system for Prolog. *Artificial Intelligence,* 23:295–307, 1984.

36. Lawrence C. Paulson. Natural deduction as higher-order resolution. *Journal of Logic Programming*, 3:237–258, 1986.
37. J. A. Robinson. A machine-oriented logic based on the resolution principle. *Journal of the ACM*, 12:23–41, 1965.
38. J. A. Robinson. Beyond loglisp: combining functional and relational programming in a reduction setting. Technical report, Syracuse University, 1985.
39. J. A. Robinson and E. E. Sibert. LOGLISP: an alternative to PROLOG. In J. E. Hayes, D. Michie, and Y.-H. Pao, editors, *Machine Intelligence 10*, pages 399–419. Ellis Horwood Ltd, 1982.
40. John C. Shepherson. Negation in logic programming. In Jack Minker, editor, *Foundations of Deductive Databases and Logic Programming*, pages 19–88. Morgan Kaufmann, 1988.
41. Mark E. Stickel. A Prolog technology theorem prover: Implementation by an extended Prolog compiler. *Journal of Automated Reasoning*, 4:353–380, 1988.
42. D. A. Turner. Functional programs as executable specifications. In C. A. R. Hoare and J. C. Shepherdson, editors, *Mathematical Logic and Programming Languages*, pages 29–54. Prentice-Hall International, 1985.
43. M. H. van Emden and R. A. Kowalski. The semantics of predicate logic as a programming language. *Journal of the ACM*, 23:733–742, 1976.
44. Allen Van Gelder. Negation as failure using tight derivations for general logic programs. In Jack Minker, editor, *Foundations of Deductive Databases and Logic Programming*, pages 149–176. Morgan Kaufmann, 1988.
45. Jia-Huai You. Solving equations in an equational language. In J. Grabowski, P. Lescanne, and W. Wechler, editors, *Algebraic and Logic Programming*, pages 245–254. Springer-Verlag, 1988. LNCS 343.
46. Jia-Huai You. Enumerating outer narrowing derivations for constructor-based term rewriting systems. *Journal of Symbolic Computation*, 7:319–342, 1989.

Logic Programming with Strong Negation

David Pearce   Gerd Wagner

Gruppe für Logik, Wissenstheorie und Information

Freie Universität Berlin

Abstract

We show how a negation operation which allows for the possibility to represent explicit negative information can be added to Prolog without essentially altering its computational structure.

1   Background and Aims

In [Pearce & Wagner 1989] we have outlined a general approach to the representation and processing of negative information which we believe should have promising applications in AI. We also sketched there an application of our ideas to logic programming, by showing (for the propositional case) how standard Prolog can be extended by adding strong negation. In this paper we elaborate further on our idea of logic programming with strong negation and generalise our earlier results.

According to the standard view, a logic program is a set of definite Horn clauses. Thus, logic programs are regarded as syntactically restricted first order theories within the framework of classical logic. Correspondingly, the proof-theory of logic programs is considered as the specialised version of classical resolution, known as SLD-resolution. This view, however, neglects the fact that a program clause, $a_0 \leftarrow a_1, a_2, \ldots, a_n$, is an expression of a fragment of positive logic[1] rather than an implicational formula of classical logic. The classical interpretation of logic programs, therefore, seems to be a semantical overkill.

It should be clear that in order to explain the deduction mechanism of Prolog one does not have to refer to the indirect method of SLD-resolution which checks for the refutability of the contrary. It is certainly more natural to view Prolog's proof procedure as a kind of natural deduction, as, e.g., in [Hallnäs & Schroeder-Heister 1987] and [Miller 1989]. This also is more in line with the intuitions of a Prolog programmer. Since Prolog is the paradigm, logic programming semantics should take it as a point of departure.

---

[1] a subsystem of intuitionistic logic

With this in mind, we present here a system extending Prolog by adding strong negation which, in essential respects, is already known from constructive logic, and, in a limited form, from 3-valued, and from partial logic, respectively. Our system is a conservative extension: it respects the top-down query evaluation procedure and the Herbrand fixed point semantics of Prolog. It can additionally be equipped with a negation as failure operator in the same way (creating the same problems) as positive standard Prolog.[2] Below, we outlie a model theory and proof theory for this system and discuss possible applications as well as its relation to other systems. We begin, however, with some remarks to motivate the use of strong negation in logic programs.

2 Motivation

Most research on negation in logic programming has concetrated on the handling of implicit negative information, as embodied in negation-as-failure and related notions like Reiter's Closed-World Assumption and Clark's Completed Database. Moreover, relatively little work has been devoted to extending the expressive power of Prolog by allowing for the use of negative facts and rules (some notable exceptions will be mentioned below). However, as Gabbay and Sergot [1986] have noted, the logical landscape of negation is considerably richer than often supposed, and much of it remains to be explored. In particular, they discuss five different, logical types of negation, including strong negation (to be studied here) and negation as inconsistency (the central concept of their paper). Favouring the latter notion, they pass over the topic of strong negation with little comment, despite the fact that the absence of a strong negation in standard logic programming has sometimes been lamented by AI-researchers, notably Sergot, Sadri, Kowalski et al. [1986].

In fact, strong negation is the only stable or persistent form of negation appearing on Gabbay and Sergot's list. All the other types of negation are fragile in the sense that knowledge of what is not the case may change in time. Moreover, it is worth noting, that negation as inconsistency, a form of which is also treated by Miller [1989], is less fundamental, since it can be defined by means of strong negation. In contrast to negation as inconsistency, strong negation is a local notion. Consequently, it is computationally cheap. Additionally, strong negation expresses constructible falsity which is established directly, whereas falsity in classical, intuitionistic and minimal logic is not a constructive notion and is typically established by an indirect proof. As Gabbay and Sergot concede, their negation as inconsistency is even less efficient computationally than negation as failure.[3]

---

[2]The second-named author will present a partial logic semantics for logic programs with both forms of negations in a future paper.

[3]It is also interesting to note, as Gabbay has pointed out to us in discussion, that some

The concept of strong negation dates back to the constructive logic of [Nelson 1949], though it has its roots in the 3-valued systems of Lukasiewicz and Kleene. The AI community seems hardly to be aware of it, and one can often find confusion in the treatment of negation in the literature. For example, the weak negation operation not in Prolog is sometimes semantically treated as strong negation. Or one can find ad-hoc treatments of problems where strong negation would be needed. For example, in [Levesque 1986] it is suggested to transform a negative literal like ¬married(Jack,Jan) to an atom like not_married(Jack,Jan) in order to avoid the computational difficulties of classical negation. While this transformation is justified to a certain extent by a theorem on the eliminability of strong negation (see Sect. 6), it destroys the contradiction relationship between a literal and its contrary in the object language. As a consequence of this, we lose all reasoning capabilities based on inconsistency handling.

The alternative we suggest is to express explicit negative information by means of strong negation. So, the negative fact ~married(Jack,Jan) can simply be added to our program. If we then were told that Jack is married either to Jan or Jill we could express this as two clauses, namely,

$$married(Jack,Jan) \leftarrow {\sim}married(Jack,Jill)$$
$$married(Jack,Jill) \leftarrow {\sim}married(Jack,Jan)$$

We would then obtain the direct conclusion that Jack is married to Jill.

There seems to be no clear attitude towards the role of falsity, negative information and negation among AI researchers. For example, Przymusinski [1989, p.660] states that logic programs and deductive databases should be "free from excessive amounts of explicit negative information and as close to natural discourse as possible". This is obviously questionable. First, logic programs and deductive databases do not usually permit one to represent explicit negative information at all. Secondly, explicit negative information clearly plays an important role in natural discourse[4], and hence, should be taken into consideration in vivid knowledge bases, deductive databases and logic programs.

Additionally, many empirical predicates which are to be represented e.g. in Prolog-based expert systems for diagnostic reasoning have to be considered as *inexact predicates*. This notion was suggested by Körner [1966] for the analysis of the relation between empirical and theoretical affairs. It turns out that our semantical treatment of logic programs with strong negation is capable of handling inexact as well as exact predicates.[5] This seems to emphasise the

---

systems of strong negation do not satisfy his criteria of what negation is or should be in a system ([Gabbay 1988]). This is because Gabbay's criteria are based roughly on the idea that ¬A means something like "A is to be excluded because it leads to undesirable consequences (like inconsistency)". This is not the basic idea underlying strong negation, however, and in our view there are good grounds for adjusting his criteria to embrace such strong negation systems.

[4] see [Pearce & Wagner 1989]

[5] This topic is explored further in [Wagner 1990a].

practical significance of our suggestions.

Summarising, the following features of strong negation as conceived here seem in particular to underline its usefulness:

- It is the only genuinely stable and persistent negation, and is thus adequate for handling explicit, unrevisable negative information.

- The strong negation of a proposition A is directly verifiable (equivalently, A is constructively falsifiable), without having to check for contradictions, etc. This makes it computationally tractable.

- Intuitionistic and related forms of negation are definable from it.

- To take account of implicit negative information, weaker forms of negation, like negation as failure, can easily be added to a system including strong negation.

- It is well-suited for handling the problem of inexact predicates.

3   The Language of Logic Programs

The language of logic programs with strong negation consists of the logical operator symbols $\wedge, \vee, \sim$ and 1 standing for conjunction, disjunction, strong negation and the verum, respectively, predicate symbols, constant symbols, function symbols and variables. Notice that there are no explicit quantifiers.

A *literal* is either 1 or an atom or a strongly negated atom (if it is not 1 it is called *proper*). We use a, l and F, G, H as metavariables for atoms, literals and formulas, respectively; formulas being built-up in the usual way, allowing eg. for iterations of $\sim$. A variable-free expression is called *ground*. A program **P** consists of clauses of the form $l \leftarrow F$. We consider such clauses as specific *inference rules* and not as implicational formulas[6]. A rule with premise 1 is also called a *fact*, and we abbreviate $l \leftarrow 1$ by l. Examples of clauses are $\sim \text{flies}(x) \leftarrow \text{emu}(x) \vee \text{penguin}(x)$ or switch_on_light $\leftarrow$ dark $\wedge \sim$ illuminated. In Sect. 6 we shall mention a method by means of which a clause in our sense can be transformed to expressions $a_0 \leftarrow a_1 \wedge \ldots \wedge a_n$ which are usually called 'definite Horn clauses'.[7]

We consider a program **P** containing non-ground clauses as a dynamic representation of the corresponding set of ground clauses formed by means of the current domain of individuals U and denoted by $[\mathbf{P}]_U$. Formally,

---

[6]Of course, one can view inference rules of this form as first-degree implications.

[7]Notice that it was already suggested in [Lloyd & Topor 1984] to make Prolog more expressive by allowing general formulas instead of a conjunction of atoms in the premise of a program clause. Some authors, like Fitting [1986] and Miller [1989], adopt this syntactical generalization, while many others stick to the (unnecessarily) restricted notion of a program clause.

$$[\mathbf{P}]_U = \{l\sigma \leftarrow F\sigma : l \leftarrow F \in \mathbf{P} \text{ and } \sigma : \text{Var}(l, F) \rightarrow U\}$$

where σ ranges over all mappings from the set of variables of l and F into the Herbrand universe U. We call σ a *ground substitution* for $l \leftarrow F$ and $[\mathbf{P}]_U$ the *Herbrand expansion* of $\mathbf{P}$ with respect to a certain Herbrand universe U. We shall write $[\mathbf{P}]$ for the Herbrand expansion of $\mathbf{P}$ with respect to the Herbrand universe U_P of $\mathbf{P}$.

Example: For $\mathbf{P} = \{\sim\text{flies}(x) \leftarrow \text{emu}(x) \vee \text{penguin}(x), \text{emu}(\text{molly})\}$ and $U = \{\text{molly}, \text{tweety}\}$ we obtain

$$[\mathbf{P}]_U = \left\{ \begin{array}{l} \sim\text{flies}(\text{molly}) \leftarrow \text{emu}(\text{molly}) \vee \text{penguin}(\text{molly}) \\ \sim\text{flies}(\text{tweety}) \leftarrow \text{emu}(\text{tweety}) \vee \text{penguin}(\text{tweety}) \\ \text{emu}(\text{molly}) \end{array} \right.$$

Notice that the head of a program clause may consist of a negative literal. This is essential for expressing explicit negative information or, logically speaking, constructible falsity. It corresponds to the fact that Sergot, Sadri, Kowalski et al. "did expect to need negative conclusions" [1986, p.379] in order to represent negative knowledge in a legal reasoning system.

4 Model Theory

Let $\mathcal{M} = \langle M^+, M^- \rangle$ be a partial Herbrand interpretation, in our case this is to mean that M^+ contains the positive facts (ground atoms) which are believed to be true, whereas M^- contains the negative facts (ground atoms) which are believed to be false. Such an interpretation gives rise to a model as well as to a countermodel relation, inductively defined as follows:

$$\begin{array}{lll} \mathcal{M} \models a & \text{iff} & a \in M^+ \\ \mathcal{M} \models F \wedge G & \text{iff} & \mathcal{M} \models F \text{ and } \mathcal{M} \models G \\ \mathcal{M} \models F \vee G & \text{iff} & \mathcal{M} \models F \text{ or } \mathcal{M} \models G \\ \\ \mathcal{M} \models \sim F & \text{iff} & \mathcal{M} =\!\!\mid F \\ \mathcal{M} =\!\!\mid a & \text{iff} & a \in M^- \\ \mathcal{M} =\!\!\mid F \wedge G & \text{iff} & \mathcal{M} =\!\!\mid F \text{ or } \mathcal{M} =\!\!\mid G \\ \mathcal{M} =\!\!\mid F \vee G & \text{iff} & \mathcal{M} =\!\!\mid F \text{ and } \mathcal{M} =\!\!\mid G \\ \mathcal{M} =\!\!\mid \sim F & \text{iff} & \mathcal{M} \models F \end{array}$$

where a, F and G are ground, and the model relation holds for a non-ground formula if it holds for some ground instance of it[8],

$$\mathcal{M} \models F(x) \quad \text{iff} \quad \mathcal{M} \models F(t) \text{ for some ground term } t$$

---

[8]We shall not define here a countermodel relation for non-ground formulas.

We also stipulate that $\mathcal{M} \models 1$ and $\mathcal{M} \not\models \sim 1$. Because of

$$\mathcal{M} \models F \wedge G \quad \text{iff} \quad \mathcal{M} \models \sim(\sim F \vee \sim G)$$
$$\mathcal{M} \models F \vee G \quad \text{iff} \quad \mathcal{M} \models \sim(\sim F \wedge \sim G)$$

conjunction and disjunction are interdefinable and we can restrict definitions and proofs to the cases without $\vee$.

We call $\mathcal{M}'$ an *extension* of $\mathcal{M}$, symbolically $\mathcal{M}' \geq \mathcal{M}$, if $M^+ \subseteq M'^+$ and $M^- \subseteq M'^-$. An extension of a model represents a growth of information since it assigns truth or falsity to formerly undetermined sentences. We could also consider total extensions of a model which then determine the truth or falsity of all sentences.

Observation 1 *Let $\mathcal{M}' \geq \mathcal{M}$, then*

(i) *For all formulas F, $\mathcal{M} \models F \Rightarrow \mathcal{M}' \models F$*

(ii) *For all ground formulas F, $\mathcal{M} \not\models F \Rightarrow \mathcal{M}' \not\models F$*

Proof: by straightforward induction on the complexity of F.

In [Körner 1966] this is called the *permanence principle*. It can also be regarded as expressing the monotonicity of truth and falsity with respect to model extensions.

We say that $\mathcal{M}$ is a *partial model* of **P**, symbolically $\mathcal{M} \models \mathbf{P}$, if for all $l \leftarrow F \in \mathbf{P}$, and any ground instance $F\sigma$ of F, $\mathcal{M} \models F\sigma$ implies $\mathcal{M} \models l\sigma$ (we shall assume, throughout the paper, that all variables occuring in l also occur in F, which implies that $l\sigma$ is ground). In the sequel, when we speak of a 'model' we mean just this notion.

In order to simplify notation we shall also represent a model $\mathcal{M}$ as the set M of all ground literals supported by it,

$$M = \{l\sigma \,:\, \sigma \text{ is a ground substitution for } l \text{ and } \mathcal{M} \models l\sigma\}.$$

M is also called the *diagram* of $\mathcal{M}$. Let $\text{Mod}(\mathbf{P}) = \{M \,:\, \mathcal{M} \models \mathbf{P}\}$ and $M_P = \bigcap \text{Mod}(\mathbf{P})$.

Claim 1 *Every program **P** has a least model, viz. M_P.*

Proof: Obviously, if M_P is a model of **P**, it is the least one. Assume that it is not a model of **P**. Then there is some ground clause $l \leftarrow F \in [\mathbf{P}]$ such that $M_P \models F$, but $l \notin M_P$. Since M_P is the meet of all models of **P**, there exists $M' \in \text{Mod}(\mathbf{P})$ with $l \notin M'$. But $\mathcal{M}' \models F$ (as a consequence of $\mathcal{M}' \geq M_P$ and the permanence principle). So, $\mathcal{M}' \models l$, i.e. $l \in M'$, which is a contradiction. $\square$

We say that F is a *logical consequence* of **P**, symbolically $\mathbf{P} \models F$, if every model of **P** is also a model of F.

Claim 2 $\mathbf{P} \models F$ iff $\mathcal{M}_P \models F$

This is a straightforward consequence of the previous claim and the permanence principle. It states that the model-theoretic consequence relation between a program and a formula is completely characterized by the least model of the program, and is the analogue of the well-known least Herbrand model characterization of positive logic programs.

4.1 Three-Valued Truth Tables

A partial model $\mathcal{M}$ for which we assume that $M^+ \cap M^- = \emptyset$ determines a three-valued assignment v_M on ground atoms a in the following way:

$$v_M(a) = \begin{cases} 1 & \text{if } a \in M^+ \\ 0 & \text{if } a \in M^- \\ u & \text{otherwise} \end{cases}$$

The recursive truth and falsity definitions above correspond to the following truth tables:

$\wedge$	0	u	1		$\vee$	0	u	1		$\sim$	
0	0	0	0		0	0	u	1		0	1
u	0	u	u		u	u	u	1		u	u
1	0	u	1		1	u	1	1		1	0

If $\bar{v}_M$ is the valuation extending v_M according to these tables in the usual way, i.e. as a homomorphism from the free algebra of formulas into the DeMorgan algebra of truth values, $\langle \{0, u, 1\}, \wedge, \vee, \sim \rangle$, for ground formulas F we can make the following

Observation 2   *1.* $\mathcal{M} \models F$ iff $\bar{v}_M(F) = 1$

    2. $\mathcal{M} =\!\!| F$ iff $\bar{v}_M(F) = 0$

    3. $\mathcal{M} \not\models F$ & $\mathcal{M} \not=\!\!| F$ iff $\bar{v}_M(F) = u$

The connectives $\wedge, \vee, \sim$ given by the above truth tables were first investigated by Łukasiewicz [1920] and are nowadays often called 'strong Kleene connectives'.

4.2 Tautologies and Constructive Properties

A tautology is a formula F which is valid in any model $\mathcal{M}$, $\mathcal{M} \models F$. An antitautology is a formula F which is invalid in any model $\mathcal{M}$, $\mathcal{M} =\!\!| F$.

There are no tautologies in our logic: neither $F \vee \sim F$ nor $\sim (F \wedge \sim F)$ is a tautology. Nor are there anti-tautologies, eg. of the form $F \wedge \sim F$. Since there is no implication in the object language, implication relations between formulas cannot be expressed by respective tautologies. They are, however, reflected in the deduction rules in Sect. 5.

Let X be a set of literals, and let $\models$ denote the consequence relation of a given logic. There are at least two constructivity principles a logic can satisfy (with respect to a negation operation $\neg$ and the underlying notion of falsity):

1. Constructible Truth: $X \models F \vee G \Rightarrow X \models F$ or $X \models G$

2. Constructible Falsity: $X \models \neg(F \wedge G) \Rightarrow X \models \neg F$ or $X \models \neg G$

In our logic both principles are valid, whereas neither the principle of constructible truth nor the principle of constructible falsity hold in classical logic, and furthermore, only the former but not the latter holds for intuitionistic negation.

5 Proof Theory

We define a derivability relation between a program and a well-formed formula in the style of a natural deduction system by means of the introduction rules $(l),(\wedge),(\sim \wedge), (\sim\sim)$ and $(\exists)$[9]. Since we are interested in an operational proof theory which amounts to a procedural semantics we have to take care of the handling of autodependency loops. One way to do so is to exclude them by requiring the program to be in an appropriate sense well-founded. Another way is to give bottom-up procedures for constructing the hierarchy of derivable facts. These procedures are robust with respect to autodependency loops.

We now present the deduction rules for complex formulas. We write "$\mathbf{P} \vdash F, G$" as an abbreviation of "$\mathbf{P} \vdash F$ and $\mathbf{P} \vdash G$".

$$(\wedge) \quad \frac{\mathbf{P} \vdash F, G}{\mathbf{P} \vdash F \wedge G} \qquad (\sim\vee) \quad \frac{\mathbf{P} \vdash \sim F, \sim G}{\mathbf{P} \vdash \sim(F \vee G)}$$

$$(\vee) \quad \frac{\mathbf{P} \vdash F}{\mathbf{P} \vdash F \vee G} \qquad \frac{\mathbf{P} \vdash G}{\mathbf{P} \vdash F \vee G}$$

$$(\sim\wedge) \quad \frac{\mathbf{P} \vdash \sim F}{\mathbf{P} \vdash \sim(F \wedge G)} \qquad \frac{\mathbf{P} \vdash \sim G}{\mathbf{P} \vdash \sim(F \wedge G)}$$

$$(\sim\sim) \quad \frac{\mathbf{P} \vdash F}{\mathbf{P} \vdash \sim\sim F}$$

where F and G are ground formulas, and a non-ground formula is provable if some ground instance of it is,

$$(\exists) \quad \frac{\mathbf{P} \vdash F(t) \quad \text{for some ground term } t}{\mathbf{P} \vdash F(x)}$$

---

[9]There is no need for elimination rules because $\vdash$ does not allow for arbitrary formulas in the premise.

We also stipulate that $\mathbf{P} \vdash 1$. Alternatively, we could state all these rules in the form of iff-sentences, as e.g.

$(\sim\wedge)$ $\quad \mathbf{P} \vdash \sim(F \wedge G)$ $\quad$ iff $\quad \mathbf{P} \vdash \sim F$ or $\mathbf{P} \vdash \sim G$

In order to complete this definition of derivability relative to a program $\mathbf{P}$ we have to say what it means for a ground literal to be derivable[10]. This we shall do below.

Notice that we do not have a 'trivialization rule' yet, so as to conclude anything from a contradiction. The principle *ex contradictione sequitur quodlibet*,

$$\frac{\mathbf{P} \vdash F, \sim F}{\mathbf{P} \vdash G}$$

which is fundamental in classical and intuitionistic logic, should only be assumed if one wants the effect of a single contradiction to be globally destructive, i.e. a single contradiction causes the loss of the entire information content of the data base.

Alternatively, we might want to validate certain conclusions while invalidating others even in the presence of a contradiction. Of course, the admission of contradictions in the data base gives rise to at least two questions:

- What is the logical status of a contradictory piece of information? Can it count as true or false anyway?

- How does a contradiction affect the manner of deriving further information possibly relying on the contradictory piece?

For a short discussion of these questions and possible solutions see Sect. 7.

Concerning the recursive structure of a program, the most straightforward way to define derivability for ground literals is the following

(l) $\quad \mathbf{P} \vdash l$ $\quad$ iff $\quad \exists(l \leftarrow F) \in [\mathbf{P}] : \mathbf{P} \vdash F$

However, this definition only works for 'well-behaved' programs which we call *well-founded*. In other cases it enters a loop. This problem does not arise in standard logic where the notion of derivability is not operational but simply requires the existence of a proof. It does not provide any effective method, though, to find the proof if it exists, or to find out that none exists, respectively. So, in the standard setting we would add the following deduction rule to the ones stated above:

$$\frac{\mathbf{P} \vdash F}{\mathbf{P} \vdash l} \quad \text{(provided that } l\sigma \leftarrow F \in [\mathbf{P}])$$

---

[10]It is clear, however, that at least all literals l explicitly declared as true by a program $\mathbf{P}$, $l \leftarrow 1 \in \mathbf{P}$, have to be derivable.

A literal l, then, is derivable from **P** if there is a derivation (i.e. a sequence of justified deduction-rule applications starting from '**P** ⊢ 1') for the sequent '**P** ⊢ l'.

In the case of a well-founded program one can use a complexity measure based on the length of dependency chains in order to prove by induction that for any well-founded program **P**,

Claim 3 (Adequacy) [11] **P** ⊢ F iff **P** ⊨ F.

Our derivability relation between a program and a formula models the query evaluation procedure of Prolog, as is shown by the following example:

$$\mathbf{P} \quad = \quad \begin{cases} \text{on}(a, b) \\ \text{on}(b, c) \\ \text{above}(x, y) \leftarrow \text{on}(x, y) \vee (\text{on}(\text{x}, \text{z}) \wedge \text{above}(z, y)) \\ \sim\text{above}(x, y) \leftarrow \text{above}(y, x) \end{cases}$$

Clearly, **P** ⊢ above(a, c), according to the above rules. The query

$$\text{above}(a, x) \wedge \sim\text{above}(y, x)$$

succeeds with the answer $x = b$ and $y = c$. If we had used negation as failure instead of strong negation the same query would fail because of a floundering subgoal. As a matter of fact, there is no floundering query problem for logic programs with strong negation.

6 Relation to Other Logics

6.1 Reducibility to Positive Logic

We define a reductive translation of a formula $F \in L(\wedge, \vee, \sim, 1)$ to a formula $F^+ \in L(\wedge, \vee, 1)$:

$$\begin{aligned}
(F \wedge G)^+ &= F^+ \wedge G^+ \\
(F \vee G)^+ &= F^+ \vee G^+ \\
(\sim(F \wedge G))^+ &= (\sim F)^+ \vee (\sim G)^+ \\
(\sim(F \vee G))^+ &= (\sim F)^+ \wedge (\sim G)^+ \\
(\sim\sim F)^+ &= F^+ \\
(\sim a)^+ &= \text{not\_}a \\
a^+ &= a \\
1^+ &= 1 \\
\mathbf{P}^+ &= \{l^+ \leftarrow F^+ : l \leftarrow F \in \mathbf{P}\}
\end{aligned}$$

---

[11]A precise formulation and proof of this result as well as a complete proof theory for non-well-founded programs appears in [Wagner 1990a]. For the remainder of the present paper we shall assume wherever needed that ⊢ is the derivability relation for arbitrary programs.

where not a is an ad-hoc newly introduced atom.

Claim 4 $\mathbf{P} \vdash F$ iff $\mathbf{P}^+ \vdash F^+$

A reduction of the above kind seems to be a feature peculiar to strong negation. At least no analogous result appears to hold for systems of eg. classical, intuitionistic and minimal negation, or negation-as-failure, which define a stronger semantical link between an atomic formula and its negation.

Furthermore, let us define the *disjunctive normal set*, $DNS(F)$, of a formula F to be the set of all sets collecting conjuncts belonging to the disjunctive normal form of F (cf. [Wagner 1990a]). Then, the following can be shown:

Observation 3   *A program clause, $l \leftarrow F$, can be translated to a set of definite Horn clauses $\{l^+ \leftarrow a_1, \ldots, a_n : \{a_1, \ldots, a_n\} \in \mathrm{DNS}(F^+)\}$ such that a formula G is derivable from $\mathbf{P}$ iff G^+ is derivable from the definite Horn clause translation of $\mathbf{P}$.*

6.2   Relation to Classical Logic

We define a ternary derivability relation between a program, a premise formula and a conclusion formula (both of which are ground):

$$\mathbf{P}, F \vdash G \quad \text{iff} \quad \text{for every } K \in \mathrm{DNS}(F) : \mathbf{P} \cup K \vdash G$$

We call this relation *conditional derivability*. It captures the notion of positive implication between (implication-free) formulas in the sense of the metalogical implication $\mathbf{P} \vdash F \Rightarrow \mathbf{P} \vdash G$. Indeed, as is shown in [Wagner 1989], we obtain the *cut rule*: if $\mathbf{P} \vdash F$ and $\mathbf{P}, F \vdash G$ then $\mathbf{P} \vdash G$.

Claim 5   *A ground formula G is derivable from $P = \bigwedge\{\forall \overline{x}(F \to l) : l \leftarrow F \in \mathbf{P}\}$ in classical logic iff $\mathbf{P}, \bigwedge\{a \vee \sim a : a \in A\} \vdash G$, where A is the Herbrand base of $\{\mathbf{P}, G\}$.*

A similar result for his logic of inexact predicates was proved by Cleave [1974].

6.3   Relation to Constructive Logics

Since our use of strong negation is inspired by the system of constructive logic N of [Nelson 1949], we should expect that there is a close connection between the derivability of a formula G from a program $\mathbf{P}$ in the above sense and its derivability in N, given the clauses of $\mathbf{P}$ as a set of implicational premises. This is indeed the case, as we show now.[12]

---

[12]For a concise survey of the proof and model theory of N, see [van Dalen, 1986].

For any program $\mathbf{P}$, let $\mathbf{P}^*$ be the set of sentences of the form $\forall \overline{x}(F\overline{x} \rightarrow l\overline{x})$ obtained from clauses $l \leftarrow F \in \mathbf{P}$, where $\overline{x}$ is the (possibly empty) set of variables of $l \leftarrow F$. Until further notice, let $\mathbf{P}$ be any consistent program in the sense that for no ground formula G we have both $\mathbf{P} \vdash G$ and $\mathbf{P} \vdash \sim G$. Let $\vdash_N$ denote derivability in N. For any formula G with the (possibly empty) set of variables $\overline{x}$, we have

Claim 6 $\mathbf{P} \vdash G$ iff $\mathbf{P}^* \vdash_N \exists \overline{x} G \overline{x}$.

Proof sketch: Suppose that $\mathbf{P} \vdash G$. Then, by completeness, G is true in every model of $\mathbf{P}$. Let $\mathcal{M}$ be any Kripke model of $\mathbf{P}^*$ in the sense of [van Dalen, 1986, p.302]. In particular, $\mathcal{M}$ comprises a partially-ordered set I of nodes α, and can be represented by assigning to each node two sets of ground atoms M_α^+, M_α^- which are verified (resp. falsified) at that node. It follows that for each $\alpha \in I$, $M_\alpha = \langle M_\alpha^+, M_\alpha^- \rangle$ is a partial model of $\mathbf{P}$ in the sense of Sect. 4 above, since the truth-conditions for the Kripke semantics ensure that for all $l \leftarrow F \in \mathbf{P}$ and ground substitutions σ of F, $M_\alpha \models F\sigma \Rightarrow M_\alpha \models l\sigma$. So $M_\alpha \models G$, which means (if G is non-ground) that there is a ground term t for which $M_\alpha \models Gt$. By the truth-conditions again, this implies that $\exists \overline{x} G \overline{x}$ is true in $\mathcal{M}$ at α, for all $\alpha \in I$. So, for all models $\mathcal{M}$ of $\mathbf{P}^*$, $\mathcal{M} \models \exists \overline{x} G \overline{x}$. By the completeness of the Kripke semantics wrt N, we have that $\mathbf{P}^* \vdash_N \exists \overline{x} G \overline{x}$.

For the converse direction, suppose that $\mathbf{P}^* \vdash_N \exists \overline{x} G \overline{x}$, but that $\mathbf{P} \nvdash G$. By completeness, there is a model $\mathcal{M}$ of $\mathbf{P}$ such that $\mathcal{M} \nvDash G$. Regarding $\mathcal{M}$ as a set of literals, it is equivalent to a single-node Kripke model in which (for all $l \leftarrow F \in \mathbf{P}$) the truth of $F\sigma$ implies the truth of $l\sigma$, for all ground substitutions σ. It is therefore a Kripke model of $\forall \overline{x}(F\overline{x} \rightarrow l\overline{x})$ and hence of $\mathbf{P}^*$. But since there is no t for which $\mathcal{M} \models Gt$, $\mathcal{M}$ is not in the Kripke sense a model of $\exists \overline{x} G \overline{x}$, contradicting our initial assumption. $\square$

An analogous argument goes through for arbitrary (ie. possibly inconsistent) programs, but in the above claim N should be replaced by the weaker logic N^- of [Almukdad and Nelson, 1984]. This logic contains no *ex contradictione sequitur quodlibet* principle, and is complete for Kripke models for which the sets of verified and falsified atoms at any node are not required to be disjoint. We now turn briefly to the topic of inconsistency in general.

7 Inconsistency Handling

There are at least three general strategies for dealing with inconsistency in our system.

- In mathematical logic (classical as well as intuitionistic), the occurence of a contradiction is usually considered a devastating event causing the immediate loss of all meaning of the theory in question (it becomes *trivial* according to the principle *ex contradictione sequitur quodlibet*). We have the same option for logic programs with strong negation: we could postulate that as soon as a contradiction is derivable from a program, every formula is derivable from it. We would then have three-valued models of a program only if it is consistent, but there would be no model for it, if it is not. In this framework we could add intuitionistic negation $\neg$ by defining

$$(\neg) \quad \frac{\mathbf{P} \vdash F \rightarrow a \wedge \sim a \quad \text{for some atom } a}{\mathbf{P} \vdash \neg F}$$

Of course, before that, we have to add intuitionistic implication by defining

$$(\rightarrow) \quad \frac{\mathbf{P}, F \vdash G}{\mathbf{P} \vdash F \rightarrow G}$$

We shall study the properties of this in a future paper.

- In terms of a logical semantics for information processing it seems to be inadequate and over-restrictive to consider a single contradiction as being globally destructive. Rather one should either not bother at all about contradictions, or, one should maintain their effect locally, ie. consider the specific pieces of information which are contradictory as useless, and regard all remaining information as unaffected by it. In [Wagner 1990] the former approach is called *liberal* and the latter one *conservative*. Both approaches lead to an extended partial semantics where every program, even an inconsistent one, has a model.

The liberal approach leads to the 4-valued logic of DeMorgan algebras described in [Rasiowa 1974] (a closely related version of which is discussed in [Belnap 1977]). The conservative approach leads to a nonmonotonic 6-valued logic which, to our knowledge, has not yet been studied in the literature. In [Wagner 1990] the principles of this logic were described, and its close relation to Reiter's logic of normal defaults was discussed. We hope to present more on it in a future paper.

8 Related Work

As we noted earlier, logic programming languages which generalise Horn clause programming have been presented by several authors. Generalising his earlier semantics for logic programs,[13] [Fitting 88] considers programs whose formulas take truth values in a topological bilattice. However, Fitting allows negations

---

[13]In [Fitting 86], see also [Pearce & Wagner 89] for discussion

in the bodies but not in the heads of program clauses (definitions in his terminology). Moreover, although Fitting's semantics generalises the usual Kripke semantics for intuitionistic logic and (in one version) tollerates inconsistencies, his negation operator is interpreted along intuitionistic lines. Falsity is an 'indirect' notion in his system, being preserved 'backwards' along the accessibility relation on possible worlds.

[Gabbay & Sergot 86] have added to Prolog a negation as inconsistency, which under suitable circumstances contains negation as failure as a special case. Their claim that it "allows (effectively) for putting negative facts and negative rules in the database" [1986, p.2] needs to be interpreted with some caution, however. They handle negative information by allowing for the presence of goals which are supposed to fail. But their program *clauses* are all of the form $a \leftarrow F$, for atomic a; therefore inference to falsity is not directly expressible in their system.

[Miller 89a, b] allows the falsity constant $\perp$ to appear in (generalised) program clauses and goals. The resulting negation in his framework, defined by $\sim F :=$ $F \rightarrow \perp$, coincides with that of minimal logic or, with an added proof rule, intuitionistic logic. As in the case of the above-mentioned systems, it is therefore an 'indirect', 'nonconstructive' notion.

In [Blair & Subrahmanian 89] a logic programming language allowing for negative literals in the head of a clause is presented. To be more precise, in their language, atoms have so-called annotations, ie. they have an explicit truth value attribute. Thus, for an atom a, there are the four expressions, $a : f, a : \perp, a : \top$ and $a : t$ standing for 'a is false', 'a is undetermined', 'a is overdetermined' and 'a is true', respectively. Clauses of *paraconsistent programs* have the form

$$l_0 : \mu_0 \leftarrow l_1 : \mu_1, \ldots, l_n : \mu_n$$

where l_i is a literal and μ_i is its annotation, i.e. one of the four truth-values.

We shall now sketch a translation from a paraconsistent program to a program with strong negation.

1. Replace all negative literals $\neg a : \mu$ by $a : \bar{\mu}$ where $\bar{f} = t, \bar{\perp} = \perp, \bar{\top} = \top$ and $\bar{t} = f$ everywhere in the program.

2. Replace everywhere in the program $a : t$ by a and $a : f$ by $\sim a$.

3. Replace all clauses $a : \top \leftarrow X$ by the two clauses $a \leftarrow X$ and $\sim a \leftarrow X$.

4. Delete all clauses $a : \perp \leftarrow X$.

5. Lastly, replace everywhere in the program the annotated atoms which remained in the body of clauses namely $a : \perp$ by $not\, a \wedge not \sim a$, and $a : \top$ by $a \wedge \sim a$.

325

The translated program, then, has the same set of consequences as the paraconsistent version. It seems clear, however, that our language is much more natural, and that it is more elegant to express the undeterminacy and the overdeterminacy of some piece of information by the usual logical expressions (containing the weak negation not if necessary).

References

[Almukdad & Nelson 1984] A. Almukdad and D. Nelson: Constructible falsity and inexact predicates, *JSL 49/1* (1984), 231–233

[Belnap 1977] N.D. Belnap: A Useful Four-valued Logic, in G. Epstein and J.M. Dunn (eds.), *Modern Uses of Many-valued Logic*, Reidel, 1977, 8–37

[Blair & Subrahmanian 1989] H. Blair and V.S. Subrahmanian: Paraconsistent Logic Programming, *Theoretical Computer Science* 68 (1989), 135–154

[Cleave 1974] J.P. Cleave: The notion of logical consequence in the logic of inexact predicates, *Zeitschrift für mathematische Logik und Grundlagen der Mathematik 20* (1974), 307–324

[van Dalen 1986] D. van Dalen: Intuitionistic Logic, in D. Gabbay & F. Guenthner (eds.), *Handbook of Philosophical Logic, Vol. III*, Kluwer, Dordrecht, 1986.

[Fitting 1986] M. Fitting: A Kripke-Kleene Semantics for Logic Programs, *J. Logic Programming* 3 (1986), 75-88.

[Fitting 1988] M. Fitting: Logic Programming on a Topological Bilattice, *Fund. Inf.* 11 (1988), 209-218.

[Gabbay 1988] D. Gabbay: What is Negation in a System?, in F.R. Drake & J.K. Truss (eds.), *Logic Colloquium '86*, Elsevier, Amsterdam, 1988.

[Gabbay & Sergot 1986] D. Gabbay and M.J. Sergot: Negation as Inconsistency I, *J. Logic Programming* 3 (1986), 1-35.

[Hallnäs & Schroeder-Heister 1987] L. Hallnäs and P. Schroeder-Heister: A Proof-Theoretic Approach to Logic Programming I: Generalized Horn Clauses, SICS Research Report, 1987; forthcoming in *J. Logic and Computation*.

[Kleene 1952] S. Kleene: *Introduction to Metamathematics*, Van Nostrand, 1952

[Körner 1966] S. Körner: *Experience and theory*, Kegan Paul, London 1966

[Lloyd & Topor 1984] J.W. Lloyd and R.W. Topor: Making Prolog More Expressive, *JLP* 1984:3, 225–240

[Lukasiewicz 1920] J. Łukasiewicz: On 3-valued logic, in S. McCall (ed.): *Polish Logic*, Oxford University Press, 1967

[Miller 1989] D. Miller: A Logical Analysis of Modules in Logic Programming, *J. Logic Programming* 6 (1989), 79-108.

[Nelson 1949] D. Nelson: Constructible falsity, *JSL 14* (1949), 16–26

[Pearce & Wagner 1989] D. Pearce and G. Wagner: *Reasoning with Negative Information I - Strong Negation in Logic Programs*, Technical Report, Gruppe für Logik, Wissenstheorie und Information, Freie Universität Berlin, 1989

[Przymusinksi 1989] T.C. Przymusinski: Non-Monotonic Formalisms and Logic Programming, in *Proc. Conf. on Logic Programming 1989*, MIT 1989

[Rasiowa 1974] H. Rasiowa, *An Algebraic Approach to Non-classical Logics*, North-Holland, 1974

[Reiter 1978] R. Reiter: On Closed-World Databases, in J. Minker and H. Gallaire (eds.): *Logic and Databases*, Plenum Press, 1978

[Sergot, Sadri, Kowalski et al.] M.J. Sergot, F. Sadri, R.A. Kowalski, F. Kriwaczek, P. Hammond and H.T. Cory: The British Nationality Act as a Logic Program, *Communications of the ACM* 29/5 (1986), 370–386

[Wagner 1989] G. Wagner: *Algebraic Semantics of Propositional Logic Programs*, Technical Report, Gruppe für Logik, Wissenstheorie und Information, Freie Universität Berlin, 1989

[Wagner 1990] G. Wagner: The Two Sources of Nonmonotonicity in Vivid Logic - Inconsistency Handling and Weak Falsity, in G. Brewka and H. Freitag (eds.), *Proceedings of the GMD Workshop on Nonmonotonic Reasoning 1989*, Gesellschaft für Mathematik und Datenverarbeitung, Bonn - St. Augustin, 1990

[Wagner 1990a] G. Wagner: Logic Programming with Strong Negation and Inexact Predicates, Technical Report, Gruppe für Logik, Wissenstheorie und Information, Freie Universität Berlin, 1990.

Hypothetical Reasoning and Definitional Reflection in Logic Programming

Peter Schroeder-Heister *

Universität Tübingen/SNS
Biesingerstr. 10, 7400 Tübingen, Germany

This paper describes the logical and philosophical background of an extension of logic programming which uses a general schema for introducing assumptions and thus presents a new view of hypothetical reasoning. The detailed proof theory of this system is given in [7], matters of implementation and control of the corresponding programming language GCLA with detailed examples can be found in [1, 2]. In Section 1 we consider the local rule-based approach to a notion of atomic consequence as opposed to the global logical approach. Section 2 describes our system and characterises the inference schema of definitional reflection which is central for our approach. In Section 3 we motivate the computational interpretation of this system. Finally, Section 4 relates our approach to the idea of logical frameworks and the way elimination inferences for logical constants are treated therein, and thus to the notions of logic and structure. It shows that from a certain perspective, logical reasoning is nothing but a special case of reasoning in our system.

1 Local and global consequence

If one poses an atom A as a query with respect to a definite Horn clause program P, this is normally understood as asking whether there is a substitution θ such that $A\theta$ can be inferred from P, and for which substitutions this holds. Symbolically, we may represent this as

$$(?\theta)\ P \models A\theta, \tag{1}$$

where $\models$ denotes first-order logical consequence. Because first-order logic is complete, we may alternatively write

$$(?\theta)\ P \vdash_L A\theta, \tag{2}$$

where $\vdash_L$ denotes derivability in some formalization of first-order logic. Expression (1) would represent a model-theoretic interpretation, (2) a proof-theoretic

---

* I would like to thank Michael Morreau for helpful suggestions.

interpretation of definite Horn clause programming. In both cases, the program P is considered a collection of formulae of a certain form, viz.

$$(\forall)(A_1 \wedge \ldots \wedge A_n \supset A) \tag{3}$$

for atoms $A_1, \ldots, A_n, A$, or some equivalent of it (here $\forall$ denotes universal closure). We call this the *clauses-as-formulae* view of logic programs. Since program clauses are considered hypotheses or axioms with respect to which something is proved, we may also speak of the *clauses-as-axioms* view. If one wants to apply proof-theoretic methods to prove, e.g., the soundness and completeness of SLD-resolution, one might consider for L a system which is proof-theoretically easily tractable such as Gentzen's sequent calculus LK or some appropriate subsystem thereof. This is the way the theory of logic programming is presented in Beeson [3] and completeness is proved.

It is then easy to extend logic programming to cover hypothetical queries posing A with respect to a hypothesis H and asking for which substitution θ the atom $A\theta$ can be inferred from $H\theta$ with respect to P, symbolically

$$(?\theta)\ H\theta, P \vdash_L A\theta. \tag{4}$$

The hypothesis $H\theta$ is simply put on the left side of the turnstile in addition to the program P. Extensions of logic programing, which treat hypothetical reasoning in that way, have been developed by Gabbay and Reyle [5], and, in a sequent-style framework, by Miller [11] and Beeson [3].

We propose a different approach to hypothetical reasoning, considering a program P to be a set of rules rather than a set of axioms. As rules, which may be written as

$$A_1, \ldots, A_n \Rightarrow A \tag{5}$$

instead of (3), clauses define themselves a notion of consequence $\vdash_P$. According to this *clauses-as-rules* view, instead of (2) we now interpret a query posing A as asking

$$(?\theta)\ \vdash_P A\theta,$$

and instead of (4), a hypothetical query is now interpreted as asking

$$(?\theta)\ H\theta \vdash_P A\theta. \tag{6}$$

If we consider $\vdash_P$ to be a local notion of consequence and $\vdash_L$ to be a global one, we may say that according to (4) program clauses are axioms with respect to a global notion of consequence whereas according to (6) they are rules defining a local notion of consequence. Concerning hypotheses, we may say that in (4) they are formally treated in the same way as program clauses (namely as assumptions with respect to global deducibility), whereas in (6) they are treated differently from clauses: The hypotheses as *assumptions* with respect to global deducibility, and the program clauses as *defining* local deducibility.

Unter a certain interpretation of $\vdash_P$ (see below), these two approaches are intertranslatable:

$$\ldots, P \vdash_L \ldots \quad (derivability\ from\ P\ in\ L) \tag{7}$$

and

$$\ldots \vdash_P \ldots \quad (derivability\ in\ P) \qquad (8)$$

are equivalent (if rules of the form (5) are appropriately translated into formulae of the form (3) and vice versa). From this point of view, the difference between the clauses-as-axioms view and the clauses-as-rules view is analogous to that between Hilbert-style and Gentzen-style formalizations of logic, now appearing at the level of atoms rather than logical constants. The (global) derivability *from* P in L corresponds to the derivability *from* logical axioms using only the global rule of modus ponens (in the propositional case), whereas the (local) derivability *in* P corresponds to the derivability *using* logical rules which are specific for every logical constant. This leads to an important shift in perspective on logic programming, corresponding to the conceptual shift from Hilbert- to Gentzen-style calculi. In particular, it allows one to prove standard results of the theory of logic programming (such as the completeness of SLD-resolution) in a straightforward way, since derivations in the sense of $\vdash_P$ are closely related to SLD-derivations (such a proof is given in [7]).

Proof-theoretically, this means that logic programming basically belongs to the theory of atomic systems. According to this view logic programming is, literally speaking, not *logic* programming but programming with *atomic* rules. These rules can be translated into logical language, but this translation is conceptually secondary.

2 Definitional reflection

However, we propose an even stronger reading of $\vdash_P$, according to which

$$\ldots, P \vdash_L \ldots$$

and

$$\ldots \vdash_P \ldots$$

are no longer equivalent. This reading is based on a definitional view of logic programs. We look upon the clauses of a program as *definitions* of their heads. In contradistinction to program clauses, assumptions appearing to the left of the turnstile are not considered as contributing anything to the meaning of atoms. Whereas as a definition the program fixes the "world" one is dealing with in a particular context, assumptions are just hypotheses about what is the case in this world without changing it.

This idea will be captured by defining a consequence relation $\vdash_P$ by means of a sequent calculus.[1] The definitional reading of programs is determined by a specific inference schema of definitional reflection. This schema allows one to assume an atom A by reference to the program rules defining (= permitting to infer) A. If one uses this schema with respect to A, one refers in a specific

---

[1] Here "consequence relation" is not understood in Tarski's sense but quite unspecifically as a relation between assumptions and assertions.

way to what the *program* (definition) says about A and not to anything else we *assume* about A. For example, suppose $B{\Rightarrow}A$ is the only program rule by means of which A can be inferred, and we have derived

$$B{\rightarrow}A, B{\vdash}C,$$

then by definitional reflection we may pass to

$$B{\rightarrow}A, A{\vdash}C.$$

If there is no such program sule, we cannot perform this step, although the assumption $B{\rightarrow}A$ seems to say the same about A as does the program rule $B{\Rightarrow}A$ (the precise inference schemata for definitional reflection and for $\rightarrow$ are given below). The basic difference is that as a program rule $B{\Rightarrow}A$ is considered as defining A whereas as an assumption $B{\rightarrow}A$ is not so considered, and the inference schema of definitional reflection only refers to the definitional aspects (the meaning) of A.

The (local) consequence relation $\vdash_P$ generated by the program P is formally defined as follows:

We use A, B, C for atoms, F and G for implicational formulae built up from atoms by means of implication $\rightarrow$ (including atoms as a limiting case), and X, Y, Z for finite sets of implicational formulae. All letters may have subcripts. A *sequent* has the form

$$X{\vdash}F,$$

a *clause* or *program rule* the form

$$X{\Rightarrow}A.$$

Expressions like $X,Y{\vdash}F$ or $X,F{\Rightarrow}A$ are understood in the obvious way. A program P is a finite set of clauses. We write $X{\vdash}_P F$ to express that the sequent $X{\vdash}F$ is derivable in the sequent calculus with respect to a fixed program P.

The sequent system has the following three program-independent inference schemata:

$$(I) \quad \frac{}{X, A{\vdash}A}$$

$$({\vdash}{\rightarrow}) \quad \frac{X, F_1{\vdash}F_2}{X{\vdash}F_1{\rightarrow}F_2}$$

$$({\rightarrow}{\vdash}) \quad \frac{X{\vdash}F_1 \quad X, F_2{\vdash}F}{X, F_1{\rightarrow}F_2{\vdash}F}.$$

These inference schemata constitute a Gentzen sequent-style implicational calculus. One also could give schemata for other operators such as conjunction or universal quantification. For simplicity (as regards the computational interpretation of the system) we restrict ourselves to implication. These operators need not be read as logical constants in the narrower sense, since they can be used in bodies of rules to *define* logical constants. We would rather prefer to speak of "structural" operators or connectives as opposed to logical ones. So we call $\rightarrow$ a "structural implication" to be distinguished from "logical implication" $\supset$. The reason for introducing $\rightarrow$ at all is that implications in the bodies of rules strongly increase the expressive power of logic programming, especially in connection with definitional reflection. Without $\rightarrow$ one would lose the power that one has in logical rules which allow discharge of assumptions. (For the relationship between logic programming and logical rules and generally between rules and structure see §4 below.)

There are two schemata referring to the program P. The first one is the following:

$$(\vdash P) \quad \frac{(X \vdash F\sigma)_{F \in Y}}{X \vdash A\sigma}$$

for any clause $Y \Rightarrow A$ in P. It simply says that from a substitution instance of the premisses of a clause one may pass over to the corresponding substitution instance of its conclusion, i.e., it expresses closure under program rules. Since we look at programs as definitions, it may be called the schema of *definitional closure*. It is what one would normally expect as a schema for rule application. We use the label "$(\vdash P)$", since it operates on the right side of the turnstile.

The schema of *definitional reflection* $(P\vdash)$, which is characteristic of our approach to hypothetical reasoning, permits the introduction of an atom on the left side of the turnstile. It is a natural counterpart of the schema of closure under program rules and is defined as follows: Let for any atom A,

$$\mathbf{D}_P(A) := \{Y\sigma : A = B\sigma \text{ for a clause } Y \Rightarrow B \text{ in } P\}.$$

Here $\mathbf{D}_P(A)$ is to be read as "the definiens of A according to P". Then

$$(P\vdash) \quad \frac{(X, Z \vdash F)_{Z \in \mathbf{D}_P(A)}}{X, A \vdash F} \text{ provided } \mathbf{D}_P(A\tau) = (\mathbf{D}_P(A))\tau \text{ for all substitutions } \tau$$

This inference schema can informally be read as follows: If F follows from X and the definiens of A, then F follows from X and A itself. It may be motivated in the following way: Since P is considered a definition, the clauses $Y \Rightarrow B$ in P whose heads have A as a substitution instance (i.e., $A = B\sigma$ for some σ), define A. The $Y\sigma$ in $\mathbf{D}_P(A)$ then exhaust all possibilities of inferring A according to the program and thus represent the "meaning" of A. Therefore everything one obtains from every $Y\sigma$ is obtained from A itself.

The proviso for the application of $(P\vdash)$ is an invariance condition. What should not happen is that by further specializing A by means of substitution the definiens of A is enlarged. This guarantees that the inference schema $(P\vdash)$ is closed under substitution.

The schema $(P\vdash)$ is a natural counterpart of the schema $(\vdash P)$ and thus fits in a very natural way into the schemata of Right- and Left- introductions in sequent style systems. To give a deeper understanding of this duality it might be useful to formulate $(\vdash P)$ and $(P\vdash)$ in natural deduction style as introduction and elimination schemata for A. The schema $(\vdash P)$ then reads

$$(A - I) \quad \frac{Y\sigma}{A} \quad Y \Rightarrow B \in P \text{ and } A = B\sigma$$

and $(P\vdash)$ reads

$$(A-E) \quad \cfrac{A \quad \begin{pmatrix} Y\sigma \\ \vdots \\ F \end{pmatrix} \quad (Y\Rightarrow B) \in P \text{ and } A=B\sigma}{F},$$

where $\begin{pmatrix} Y\sigma \\ \vdots \\ F \end{pmatrix}_{...}$ means that there are derivations of F from $Y\sigma$ for every $Y\sigma$

fulfilling the given condition. It is obvious that this inference schema is modelled according to the schema of $\lor$-elimination in natural deduction. It is furthermore obvious that $(A-I)$ and $(A-E)$ represent introduction and elimination schemata for an atom A and not for the predicate p, if A is $p(t)$ for some term t. The minor premisses of $(A-E)$ may change completely if one changes from $p(t)$ to some $p(t')$, if t' is not a substitution instance of t. Thus $(A-E)$ is not specific for p but for the whole atom $p(t)$. This makes our schema differ fundamentally from Martin-Löfs elimination principle for predicates in his theory of iterated inductive definitions ([10]), where the minor premisses are only dependent on the predicate being eliminated and not on a particular instance thereof. In this sense our principle of definitional reflection is local and not a global induction principle as Martin-Löf's. It is more closely related to Lorenzen's inversion principle (see [9, 8]).[2] Obviously the natural deduction schema $(A-E)$ is not very useful from a computational point of view (i.e., for backward reasoning), since the major premiss A does not occur below the line.

To illustrate $(P\vdash)$ by an example, consider the following propositional program as an example: $P = \{p\Rightarrow s, \ q\Rightarrow s\}$. Then we have the following derivation:

$$\cfrac{\cfrac{p,q\to r\vdash p \quad r,p,q\to r\vdash r}{p,p\to r,q\to r\vdash r}(\to\vdash) \quad \cfrac{q,p\to r\vdash q \quad r,q,p\to r\vdash r}{q,p\to r,q\to r\vdash r}(\to\vdash)}{s,p\to r,q\to r\vdash r}(P\vdash),$$

which corresponds to $\lor$-elimination if s is $p\lor q$. (For the relationship of the schema of definitional reflection to elimination inferences in natural deduction see §4.)

Another example: Let $\bot$ be a 0-ary predicate which in P is given no definition, i.e., there is no clause with head $\bot$ in P (otherwise P is arbitrary). Then $\mathbf{D}_P(\bot) = \emptyset$, thus the set of premisses of $(P\vdash)$ is empty, so that we can trivially derive

$$\overline{X, \bot \vdash F}$$

for any X and F. This means that we have an intrinsic notion of falsity built into the system with the *ex falso quodlibet* as its characteristic feature.

---

[2] If the set $\mathbf{D}_P(A)$ is just a singleton $\{Y\sigma\}$, the schema $(P\vdash)$ actually allows to invert the clause $Y\Rightarrow B$ (with $B\sigma = A$) in the sense that $A\vdash Y\sigma$ becomes derivable.

If one takes away from the system the schema $(P\vdash)$ one obtains a system which is extensionally equivalent to the system QN-Prolog of Gabbay & Reyle [5], and to a certain subsystem of systems by Miller and by Beeson ([11, 3]). Conceptually, however, it is still different from them, since they are all based on the clauses-as-formulae view. It is the clauses-as-rules view and its different treatment of assumptions and programs, which makes definitional reflection possible and thus the full symmetry in the inference schemata of the sequent calculus.

3 Computational interpretation

We now give a computational interpretation of the sequent system we have described so far. This computational interpretation may be viewed as an operational semantics of a programming language. A description of such a language GCLA is given in [1, 2].

A *goal* is defined to be a finite set of sequents. Goals are denoted by capital Greek letters $\Delta, \Gamma, \Sigma, \Pi$. We say that Σ is *valid* with respect to the program P if for each sequent $X\vdash F$ in Σ, $X\vdash_P F$ holds. When proving a goal Σ as a query with respect to P, we ask for substitutions θ such that $\Sigma\theta$ is valid with respect to P. In the following, we describe in abstract terms a method of how to compute, given Σ, substitutions θ such that $\Sigma\theta$ is valid with respect to P. This method is partly based on a generalization of SLD-resolution. The abstract description is given by an inductive definition of the relation "σ is computable for Σ with respect to P", in short: $\langle \Sigma, \sigma, P \rangle$ or $\langle \Sigma, \sigma \rangle$ (since P is assumed to be fixed).[3] We give this inductive definition in terms of a formal system; i.e., if one has derived $\langle \Sigma, \sigma \rangle$ in this system, this is to mean that σ is computable for Σ with respect to P. We throughout use the fact that the inference schemata of the sequent calculus introduced in the previous section are closed under substitution.

In the following we state inference schemata and give in each case an intuitive motivation telling why the schema reflects a computation step with respect to the consequence relation $\vdash_P$. In each case, a step

$$\frac{\langle \Sigma_1, \sigma_1 \rangle}{\langle \Sigma_2, \sigma_2 \rangle}$$

corresponds to a computation step leading from a goal Σ_2 to a subsequent goal Σ_1, expressing that if σ_1 is computable for the goal Σ_1 then σ_2 is computable for the goal Σ_2. In steps where no bindings to variables are created during computation, σ_1 equals σ_2. If a substitution σ is computed at that step, then σ_2 is $\sigma\sigma_1$. This corresponds to the fact that during evaluation of a query, substitutions are created stepwise and are then composed.

Axioms are of the form

$$\langle \emptyset, \sigma \rangle$$

---

[3] The third component P may be important for a concrete programming language, where one allows one to change the program P in addition to adding or deleting assumptions. This is actually the case in GCLA.

for any substitution σ.

Motivation: If the goal is empty then for any substitution σ, nothing needs to be computed, so every substitution is correct.

The remaining inference schemata correspond to those given for the relation $\vdash_P$:

$$\frac{\langle \Sigma\sigma, \theta \rangle}{\langle \Sigma \mathbin{\dot{\cup}} \{X, A\vdash B\}, \sigma\theta \rangle} \quad if \ A\sigma = B\sigma.$$

Motivation: Suppose the sequent $X, A\vdash B$ occurs as a subgoal of the considered goal $\Sigma \mathbin{\dot{\cup}} \{X, A\vdash B\}$, and A unifies with B. This means that by applying the substitution σ to the goal $\Sigma \mathbin{\dot{\cup}} \{X, A\vdash B\}$ one obtains $\Sigma\sigma \mathbin{\dot{\cup}} \{X\sigma, A\sigma\vdash A\sigma\}$. Since $X\sigma, A\sigma\vdash A\sigma$ can be obtained by (I), one may omit this sequent from the goal and continue with $\Sigma\sigma$ as the subsequent goal. Therefore, if some θ is computable for the subsequent goal $\Sigma\sigma$, $\sigma\theta$ is computable for the original goal $\Sigma \mathbin{\dot{\cup}} \{X, A\vdash B\}$, since σ is the additional substitution computed at this step.

$$\frac{\langle \Sigma \cup \{X, F_1\vdash F_2\}, \theta \rangle}{\langle \Sigma \mathbin{\dot{\cup}} \{X\vdash F_1 \rightarrow F_2\}, \theta \rangle}$$

$$\frac{\langle \Sigma \cup \{X\vdash F_1\} \cup \{X, F_1\vdash F\}, \theta \rangle}{\langle \Sigma \mathbin{\dot{\cup}} \{X, F_1 \rightarrow F_2\vdash F\}, \theta \rangle}$$

Motivation: Obvious from $(\vdash\rightarrow)$ and $(\rightarrow\vdash)$. No substitution is computed at these steps.

$$\frac{\langle \Sigma\sigma \cup \{X\sigma\vdash F\sigma : F \in Y\}, \theta \rangle}{\langle \Sigma \mathbin{\dot{\cup}} \{X\vdash B\}, \sigma\theta \rangle} \quad if \ Y \Rightarrow A \ is \ in \ P \ and \ A\sigma = B\sigma$$

Motivation: Suppose $X\vdash B$ occurs as a subgoal of the considered goal $\Sigma \mathbin{\dot{\cup}} \{X\vdash B\}$ and B unifies with the head A of a program clause $Y \Rightarrow A$. Then by applying the substitution σ to this goal one obtains $\Sigma\sigma \mathbin{\dot{\cup}} \{X\sigma\vdash A\sigma\}$. Since the sequent $X\sigma\vdash A\sigma$ can be obtained from $\{X\sigma\vdash F\sigma : F \in Y\}$ by $(\vdash P)$, one may replace it by $\{X\sigma\vdash F\sigma : F \in Y\}$ and continue with $\Sigma\sigma \cup \{X\sigma\vdash F\sigma : F \in Y\}$ as the subsequent goal. Therefore, if θ is computable for this subsequent goal, $\sigma\theta$ is computable for the original goal, since σ is the additional substitution computed at this step.

$$\frac{\langle \Sigma\sigma \cup \{Y, X\sigma\vdash F\sigma : Y \in \mathbf{D}_P(A\sigma)\}, \theta \rangle}{\langle \Sigma \mathbin{\dot{\cup}} \{A, X\vdash F\}, \sigma\theta \rangle} \quad if \ \mathbf{D}_P(A\sigma\tau) = (\mathbf{D}_P(A\sigma))\tau \ for \ all \ \tau$$

If the proviso (i.e., $\mathbf{D}_P(A\sigma\tau) = (\mathbf{D}_P(A\sigma))\tau \ for \ all \ \tau$) is fulfilled for σ, we also say that σ is *A-sufficient*.

Motivation: Suppose $A, X\vdash F$ occurs as a subgoal of the considered goal $\Sigma \mathbin{\dot{\cup}} \{A, X\vdash F\}$ and σ is A-sufficient. Then by applying the substitution σ to this goal one obtains $\Sigma\sigma \mathbin{\dot{\cup}} \{A\sigma, X\sigma\vdash F\sigma\}$. Since σ is A-sufficient, the proviso for the application of $(P\vdash)$ with respect to $A\sigma$ is fulfilled, i.e., $A\sigma, X\sigma\vdash F\sigma$ can be obtained from $\{Y, X\sigma\vdash F\sigma : Y \in \mathbf{D}_P(A\sigma)\}$ by $(P\vdash)$. Thus we may replace it by $\{Y, X\sigma\vdash F\sigma : Y \in \mathbf{D}_P(A\sigma)\}$ and continue with $\Sigma\sigma\cup\{Y, X\sigma\vdash F\sigma : Y \in \mathbf{D}_P(A\sigma)\}$

as the subsequent goal. Therefore, if θ is computable for this subsequent goal, $\sigma\theta$ is computable for the original goal, since σ is the additional substitution computed at this step.

If one considers only definite Horn clause programs, i.e., programs with only atoms in bodies of clauses, and allows only goals of the form $\{\vdash A_1, \ldots, \vdash A_n\}$, then one only needs ($\vdash P$) and the corresponding schema in the definition of computability (and axioms $\langle \emptyset, \sigma \rangle$, of course). This corresponds exactly to SLD-resolution, showing that computability in our sense extends SLD-resolution in a certain way. In our case bindings are created at two new places: In the evaluation of (I) and of ($P\vdash$). In the case of (I) this is just unification of the succedent with one antecedent of a sequent. In the case of ($P\vdash$) it means the computation of an A-sufficient substitution. A feasible algorithm for the computation of A-sufficient substitutions is decribed in [7]. It must be noted, however, that there is no unique minimal (that is, most general) A-sufficient substitution for every A.

It can be shown that computability is *sound* and *complete* in the following sense:

Completeness of computability: For any substitution σ, $\Sigma\sigma$ is valid with respect to P iff there is a τ which assigns the same terms to variables occurring in Σ as σ and which is computable for Σ with respect to P.

The proof (see [7]) proceeds by stepwise comparing the inductive definitions of $\vdash_P$ and of computability with respect ot P. Since the inference schemata in these inductive definitions can be completely separated, it also contains proofs of the completeness of standard SLD-resolution for definite Horn clause programs and of an extended notion of computability for the system without ($P\vdash$). Of course, this is only the abstract, nondeterministic notion of completeness, as it is normally considered in the theory of logic programming.[4]

4 Definitional Reflection and Structural Frameworks

It was basic for the described approach to logic programming that programs as sets of rules are conceptually kept apart from inference schemata handling these rules. In this way certain inferences, particularly definitional reflection ($P\vdash$), can specifically refer to these rules as a separate sort of objects. This makes our approach differ from proof-theoretic approaches where program clauses are treated as special initial sequents or as sets of assumption formulae.

The conceptual division between rules and inference schemata is fundamental for the idea of structural frameworks, too. A structural framework (see [15]) is characterized by a concept of "rule" and a set of inference schemata that describe which inferences can be performed given a database of rules. Following Gentzen's terminology, these inference schemata are called "structural", since they do not contain logical content. When dealing with logics, the logical content is given

---

[4] For soundness and completeness results of the notion of falsity in our systems with respect to finite failure see [7].

through the database of rules. However, the inference schemata of a structural framework go much beyond what Gentzen called "structural". They do not only regulate the way formulae in a sequent may be associated (such as Thinning or Contraction), but also the way rules are treated. Furthermore, they may contain schemata concerning a sort (or sorts) of implication which is then not considered logical but structural implication, i.e., some analogue to logical implication at the strutural level (corresponding to the comma, which is a structural analogue of logical conjunction at the structural level, i.e., a structural conjunction). They may also contain a structural generalization corresponding to universal quantification in logic. So a structural framework is a kind of "structural logic" which particularly describes the handling of a database of rules. Therefore the picture is the following:

> Principles for structural conjunction
> and implication
>
> Principles for handling the database   Database of rules

whereas in Gentzen's approach we have

> Principles for structural conjunction
>
> Principles for logical constants

In Gentzen the content which is now in the database is part of specific inference schemata dealing with logical constants.

Structural frameworks are particularly well-suited for the treatment of logics with restricted structural postulates. In permitting different families of conjunction-like connectives with different structural postulates assumed for them they are similar to Belnap's display logic (see [4]). However, the consideration of structural implication(s) in combination with the treatment of databases of rules which may contain such structural implications in their bodies extends this approach considerably. It allows us a uniform treatment of logical constants in varying structural environments (see [12]).

More important in the present context, however, is that this approach is entirely independent of whether the content of the database is logical or not. It works for specific logical rules as well as for rules dealing with atoms. Moreover, it can be made plausible that the inference schema $(P\vdash)$ of definitional reflection is a reasonable ingredient of a structural framework which is not specific for the reasoning with atoms, but treats logically compound formulae as well. In this sense the sequent calculus presented in §2 represents a structural framework.

To demonstrate this universal character of our system let us use it as a structural framework for intuitionistic propositional logic, taking as the database the following introduction rules for propositional operators:

$$p, q \Rightarrow p \wedge q \qquad p \Rightarrow p \vee q \qquad q \Rightarrow p \vee q \qquad p \rightarrow q \Rightarrow p \supset q.$$

Here p and q are variables for formulae built up from certain sentential letters by means of the operators $\wedge$, $\vee$, $\supset$ and $\perp$. (Remember that $\rightarrow$ is a structural implication to be distinguished from $\supset$.) These formulae are viewed as atoms in the sense of the sequent calculus of §2 - we just consider the propositional operators as functors transforming atoms into atoms, without requiring that atoms start with predicates. It is then obvious that by using $(\vdash P)$ the following inference schemata can be derived:

$$\frac{X \vdash p \quad X \vdash q}{X \vdash p \wedge q} \qquad \frac{X \vdash p}{X \vdash p \vee q} \qquad \frac{X \vdash q}{X \vdash p \vee q} \qquad \frac{X \vdash p \rightarrow q}{X \vdash p \supset q} \,,$$

where the last one is interadmissible with

$$\frac{X, p \vdash q}{X \vdash p \supset q} \,.$$

By using $(P \vdash)$ the following inference schemata are immediately obtained:

$$\frac{X, p, q \vdash F}{X, p \wedge q \vdash F} \qquad \frac{X, p \vdash F \quad X, q \vdash F}{X, p \vee q \vdash F} \qquad \frac{X, p \rightarrow q \vdash F}{X, p \supset q \vdash F} \,,$$

where the last one is interadmissible with

$$\frac{X \vdash p \quad X, q \vdash F}{X, p \supset q \vdash F} \,.$$

Together with the fact that

$$\frac{X \vdash \perp}{X \vdash F}$$

is admissible (one has again to use $(P \vdash)$, if $X \vdash \perp$ is an axiom), this yields with $\neg p$ as $p \supset \perp$ an intuitionistic sequent calculus.

Its remarkable feature is that it was obtained by just taking a database of introduction rules, which by $(\vdash P)$ generated the right-introduction inferences and by $(P \vdash)$ the left-introduction inferences. A natural deduction version with elimination inferences instead of left-introduction inferences can also be obtained:

$$\frac{X \vdash p \wedge q \quad Y, p, q \vdash F}{Y, X \vdash F} \qquad \frac{X \vdash p \vee q \quad Y, p \vdash F \quad Y, q \vdash F}{Y, X \vdash F} \qquad \frac{X \vdash p \supset q \quad Y, p \rightarrow q \vdash F}{Y, X \vdash F} \,.$$

Here the first schema is equivalent to

$$\frac{X \vdash p \wedge q}{X \vdash p} \qquad \frac{X \vdash p \wedge q}{X \vdash q}$$

and the third one to

$$\frac{X \vdash p \supset q \quad Y \vdash p}{Y, X \vdash q} \,.$$

This shows that the schema of definitional reflection is very closely related to the uniform pattern for elimination inferences for natural deduction proposed in [13]. However, whereas there a general metalinguistic schema was proposed to generate explicit rules like

$$p \vee q, p \rightarrow r, q \rightarrow r \Rightarrow r$$

$$p \supset q, (p \to q) \to r \Rightarrow r,$$

$(P\vdash)$ works at the object level, so that elimination inferences are intrinsically available. This seems to be a good explication of Gentzen's dictum that "the introductions represent, as it were, the 'definitions' of the symbols concerned, and the eliminations are no more, in the final analysis, than the consequences of these definitions" ([6]). Our definitional reading of logic programming may be viewed as a generalization of Gentzen's definitional view of logical introduction rules. It expresses the computational reading of logic according to which introduction rules are the computationally basic production rules whereas elimination inferences just make explicit what is contained in the introduction rules read as definitions.

Apart from that, consideration of systems with weaker structural postulates suggests that this is the only way to deal with elimination inferences. As shown in [12], explicit rules like those just mentioned for $\vee$ or $\supset$ do not work in that context. This has to do with the fact that assumptions discharged in elimination inferences may be embedded in an arbitrary structural context and cannot in general be moved out if certain structural postulates (such as Exchange or Thinning) are not available. An intrinsic schema like $(P\vdash)$ seems to be the only way of treating these logics in a structural framework and obtaining a uniform picture of them. This supports definitional reflection from a completely different point of view. Definitional reflection is a principle that is neither specific to logic nor to logic programming but applies to the whole area of a computational approach to inference and hypothetical reasoning - logical or extra-logical. This view extends to all structural postulates, not just to definitional reflection. Any framework with restricted structural postulates naturally gives a declarative semantics of a logic programming language. Properly understood, it is not just a framework for, e.g., contraction-free, linear or relevant *logic*, but for any database of rules (see [12]).

It should be mentioned that when generalizing structural frameworks to permit arbitrary databases of rules one loses Cut as a general principle.[5] Cut holds, if rules are restricted in such a way that they obey certain well-foundedness principles. This is the case for introduction rules for logical operators where only subformulae of the conclusion occur in the premisses. It is also the case if the database is a definite Horn clause program (i.e., without $\to$ in the premiss of a rule), but it may fail, if one goes beyond that. The reason is that, when (structural) implication is available, the premiss of a program rule may be of higher complexity than its conclusion, which destroys induction over the complexity of the Cut-formula. However, this should not to be seen as a disadvantage, but as reflecting the generality of our approach. That Cut holds is a property of programs that one is lucky to obtain in many cases, and not a restriction on permissible programs which has to be checked in advance.

---

[5] If one takes a natural deduction version of the structural framework, with $(A - E)$ instead of $(P\vdash)$ (see §2) and Modus Ponens instead of $(\to\vdash)$ (or a corresponding formulation in sequent-style natural deduction), one loses normalizability.

1. Aronsson, M., Eriksson, L.-H., Gäredal, A., Hallnäs, L. & Olin, P. The programming language GCLA: A definitional approach to logic programming. *New Generation Computing*, 7 (1990), 381-404.

2. Aronsson, M., Eriksson, L.-H., Hallnäs, L. & Kreuger, P. A survey of GCLA: A definitional approach to logic programming (this volume).

3. Beeson, M. Some applications of Gentzen's proof theory in automated deduction (this volume).

4. Belnap, N. D. Display logic. *Journal of Philosophical Logic*, 11 (1982), 375-417.

5. Gabbay, D.M. & Reyle, U. N-PROLOG: An extension of PROLOG with hypothetical implications: I., *Journal of Logic Programming*, 1 (1984), 319-355.

6. Gentzen, G. Untersuchungen über das logische Schließen. *Mathematische Zeitschrift*, 39 (1935), 176-210, 405-431, English translation in: M.E. Szabo (ed.), *The Collected Papers of Gerhard Gentzen*, Amsterdam: North Holland, 1969, 68-131.

7. Hallnäs, L. & Schroeder-Heister, P. A proof-theoretic approach to logic programming. *SICS Research Report*, no. 88005, 1988. To appear in revised form in *Journal of Logic and Computation*.

8. Hermes, H. Zum Inversionsprinzip der operativen Logik. In: A. Heyting (ed.), *Constructivity in Mathematics*, Amsterdam: North-Holland, 1961, 62-68.

9. Lorenzen, P. *Einführung in die operative Logik und Mathematik*, Berlin: Springer, 1955.

10. Martin-Löf, P. Hauptsatz for the intuitionistic theory of iterated inductive definitions. In: J. E. Fenstad (ed.), *Proceedings of the Second Scandinavian Logic Symposium*, Amsterdam: North Holland, 1971, 179-216.

11. Miller, D. A theory of modules for logic programming. In: *Proceedings of the 1986 Symposium on Logic Programming (Salt Lake City Utah)*, IEEE Computer Society Press, Washington, 1986.

12. Schroeder-Heister, P. The role of elimination inferences in a structural framework. In: G. Huet (ed.), *Proceedings of the Esprit BRA Logical Frameworks Workshop, Sophia Antipolis 1990*.

13. Schroeder-Heister, P. A natural extension of natural deduction. *Journal of Symbolic Logic*, 49 (1984), 1284-1300.

14. Schroeder-Heister, P. Logic programming with weak structural rules. In preparation.

15. Schroeder-Heister, P. *Structural Frameworks with Higher-Level Rules: Proof-Theoretic Investigations.* Habilitationsschrift. Universität Konstanz, 1987.

Non-Monotonicity and Conditionals in Dialogue Logic

Toine van Hoof[1]   *Jaap Hoepelman*[2]

[1] Fraunhofer Institut für Arbeitswirtschaft und Organisation, Stuttgart
[2] IBM Institut für wissensbasierte Systeme, Heidelberg

1 Introduction

In this paper we will present some results of our work in the area of so-called dialogue logic. This is an approach to the study of logics that treats the concepts of inference and proof not as pure grammatical or semantic notions — like the axiomatic and model-theoretic approach — but as inherently pragmatic notions. It is an overt, externalized *argumentation* that is counted as a proof by a company of language users. This idea is formalized by treating inferences as idealized formal *dialogues* between two parties taking up the roles of *Opponent* and *Proponent* of the issue at stake, called the principal *Thesis* of the dialogue. The Proponent has to try to defend the Thesis against all possible allowed criticism of the Opponent, thereby being allowed to use eventual statements that the Opponent has made at the outset of the dialogue (the initial *Concessions*). An inference of the formula T from a set of premisses Con is a *proof* of T from Con if and only if a Proponent with initial Thesis T succeeds in defending T against all possible allowed criticism of any Opponent that initially admits Con. In the jargon of game-theory: the Proponent has a *winning strategy* for T relative to Con.

A series of rules specifying the initial positions, the allowed moves during the exchange and the end positions define what exactly is to be counted as a formal dialogue. Of special interest are the so-called *striprules* that define the *meaning in use* of the logical connectives. They specify what is to be counted as an allowed attack and possible defense of a statement containing these connectives. Table 1 presents these rules for the standard connectives. Using the rule for implication as an example, the table is to be read as follows. If a party N — i.e. either Opponent or Proponent — utters the sentence $U \to V$ then the other party, $\bar{N}$, is allowed to attack the sentence by stating $(?)U$ ("okay, let us suppose that U"). The former party then has the right, indicated by the square brackets, to defend itself by stating the sentence V ("all right, if you have accepted U for the sake of argument, then I will continue with V").

It is possible to construct rule systems for dialogues in such a way that they are provably equivalent to standard classical, intuitionistic and minimal logic.

Table 1. Striprules for standard logical connectives

Sentence N	Attack $\tilde{N}$	Defense N
$U \to V$ (implication)	(?)U	$[V]$
$\neg U$ (negation)	(?)U	$[\,]$
$U \wedge V$ (conjunction)	?L(eft) ?R(ight)	$[U]$ $[V]$
$U \vee V$ (disjunction)	?	$[U, V]$
$\forall x R(x)$ (universal)	m? (parameter)	$[R(m)]$
$\exists x R(x)$ (existential)	?	$[R(m)]$ (m parameter)

The formal apparatus used to describe such dialogue systems is structurally similar to the techniques used in semantic and deductive tableaux. Here we refer to the work of Barth and Krabbe [BK82].

What we are going to do in the following is to extend these standard dialogue systems to non-standard systems in that we will introduce a new logical operator, **F**, into the language. Its dialogue rules are sketched in Sect. 2. We will show in Sect. 3 how this fail-operator can be used to model indicative conditionals and counterfactuals. Finally, in Sect. 4 we will present a particular subsystem of the newly developed logics that makes maximal use of the inferential features of PROLOG. As such we expect this subsystem to be efficiently implementable as an extended PROLOG system.

2 A Dialogical Failure Operator

In this section we will introduce a new operator, **F**, into the standard logical languages and present its dialogical meaning. The sentence **F**α is to be interpreted as "α is not winnable relative to the concessions in this dialogue". Thus, sentences with fail-operator say something about the dialogue in which they themselves are contained. To make the meaning of **F** more precise we need some extra formalization. We will limit our explanation to the case of dialogues with propositional languages. The extension to predicate-logical languages is straightforward.

In traditional dialogue logics the concept of a winning strategy is defined relative to the dialogical *roles* of Opponent and Proponent. For the introduction of the fail-operator we have to redefine this concept in terms of the actual parties that play these roles. We will call them *Black* and *White*. As a convention we will start all dialogues with Black playing the role of Opponent and White the role of Proponent. A formula T will be called provable, or winnable, relative to a set of premisses or concessions, Con, if and only if White has a winning strategy for T relative to Con. That is, if and only if White, starting as Proponent of T, succeeds in defending T against all possible allowed criticism of any other party, called Black, that initially starts as Opponent and admits Con. Given our standard language without fail-operator this change of the formalism doesn't bring about anything new. The old and new provability/winnability concepts are in this case equivalent. This changes as soon as we introduce **F** into the language.

OPPONENT	PROPONENT
N	$\bar{N}$
Con_i	$F\alpha$
?	[check!]
	check!

$\bar{N}$	N
Con_i^*	$[\alpha]$
$\vdots$	$\vdots$
($\bar{N}$ loses)	(N wins)

(N wins)   ($\bar{N}$ loses)

(or the other way around)

OPPONENT	PROPONENT
N	$\bar{N}$
$\vdots$	$\vdots$
$F\alpha$	
[check!]	?
check!	

N	$\bar{N}$
Con_0^*	$[\alpha]$
$\vdots$	$\vdots$
(N wins)	($\bar{N}$ loses)

(N wins)   ($\bar{N}$ loses)

(or the other way around)

Fig. 1. Treatment of the fail-operator on the Proponent and on the Opponent side

The *meaning in use* of statements containing the operator **F** is presented pictorially in Fig. 1. This is to be understood as follows. An attack on a fail-statement, $F\alpha$, gives the party[3] that uttered the statement the right to carry out a so-called *checking dialogue* on α. If this party makes use of its right then this checking dialogue is carried out relative to a certain set of concessions. The

---

[3] As already said before, the parties are named "Black" and "White". In Fig. 1 we use N and $\bar{N}$. If N therefore designates one of either Black or White, then $\bar{N}$ designates the other.

checking dialogues are indicated in the figure by the fully framed subdiscussions, headed with the indication which party plays what role. As the figure shows, we have to distinguish between fail-statements on the Proponent and the Opponent side.

In the case of a fail-statement on the Proponent side, the parties N and $\bar{N}$ *have to change roles* in the checking dialogue. Intuitively, the motivation for this role-change is the following observation. In a dialogue each party has an interest in winning. After the Proponent-playing party has stated $F\alpha$, saying in effect that α is not winnable, it loses its interest in finding a way to win α and, to the contrary, now has an interest in showing that α is *not* winnable. Moreover, the opposing party now *has* an interest in showing that α is winnable, because that would make this party winner. We therefore let the opposing party play Proponent of α in the checking dialogue. The set of initial concessions of this checking dialogue is in principle the set of concessions as present at the stage in the original ("superordinate") dialogue at which the fail-statement was attacked. This is indicated in the figure by using the same subscript i as in the superordinate dialogue.

In the case of a fail-statement on the Opponent side, there is no role-change. Neither is it intuitively necessary. The Proponent-playing party criticises the statement that α is not winnable. Therefore this party effectively has an interest in finding a way to win α. So this party can itself play the role of Proponent of α in the checking Dialogue. The set of initial concessions in the checking dialogue is in principle the set of initial concessions of the superordinate dialogue. Hence we use the subscript 0.

We have said that the sets of initial concessions of the checking dialogues are *in principle* equal to the sets Con_i and Con_0. The asterisk superscripts on the initial concessions of the checking dialogue indicate that there is a restriction on the selected concessions. In order to avoid infinite repetitions of checking dialogues, there is a marking convention for concessions which have already been used in the dialogue. Such 'used' concessions do not carry over into the checking dialogues[4].

This definition of the fail-operator has been our first deviation from the role-neutral definition of the meaning in use of connectives. As the reader can see from Table 1 the standard connectives have been defined in a role-neutral way. Apart from the fact that role-neutrality provides a neat and concise way to define the connectives, there is nothing special about it. Moreover, the asymmetric definition of connectives is not completely new. In [Fe85] one can find an asymmetric treatment of the quantifiers. In the following sections we will introduce more asymetric connectives.

All checking dialogues are started by the party that plays the role of Proponent. As such it can decide to attack some of the concessions before it states the original thesis of the checking dialogue. This can be formalized by putting down the thesis as a defense right, indicated by the square brackets. We will also let the Proponent start the main dialogue in the same manner. Following [Kr82] we

---

[4] The details can be read in [HH91].

will call theses in such dialogues *provocative theses*. The dialogues themselves will be called provocative dialogues[5].

The dialogue systems thus obtained are non-monotonic. For example, White has a winning strategy for a thesis V relative to the singleton set of initial concessions $\{(FU) \to V\}$[6]. But it does *not* have a winning strategy for V anymore if the set of initial concessions is being extended to become $\{FU \to V, U\}$. For these dialogue systems we have been able to prove (in [HH91]) that they have a fixpoint and that they satisfy so-called Makinson-cumulativity[7] and cut-elimination.

3 Treatment of Conditionals

In dialogue systems with fail-operator we can deal with a number of interesting problems some of which are also relevant for natural language semantics. In [HH88] we showed how one can use the fail-operator to treat negative questions, the paradox of the small number[8], and natural language indicative conditionals. In this section we will delve more deeply into the subject of natural language conditionals in general.

It has often been noticed, that the source of paradox in the paradox of the small number[9] might be found in the role of the indicative conditional, and efforts to resolve the paradox have been concentrated on the treatment of the conditional[10]. Let us first discuss this paradox, which runs as follows:

> 1 is a small number,
> but there exists a number that is not small.
> if n is a small number so is n+1.
> ――――――――――――
> there exists a number that is both small and not small,
> which is absurd.

Given the representation in predicate logic of this inference it can be shown that the following is a valid inference:

―――――――――――――

[5] The question of who starts a dialogue is an interesting one from a formal point of view. In the case of standard *monotonic* logics it does not matter who starts; one obtains the same logical results. This does not hold any more for the case of so-called *non-monotonic* logics. To obtain intuitive results and to prove mathematical properties for those one has to set up the dialogues in such a way that the Proponent begins. This has already been noted by Krabbe in [Kr85].

[6] The fail-operator binds stronger than the other connectives. The parentheses around the antecedent of the implication are therefore unnecessary. In the following we will omit them where unnecessary.

[7] Intuitively, cumulativity says that adding a theorem of a set of premisses to these premisses does not change the derivable formulas. More formally, cumulativity can be expressed as the condition: If $\Gamma \vdash \alpha$ then ($\Gamma \vdash \beta$ if and only if $\Gamma \cup \{\alpha\} \vdash \beta$).

[8] Also known as Wang's Paradox.

[9] And related paradoxes, like "the bald man" and "the heap".

[10] See [Ho86] and the references therein.

$$small(1)$$
$$\exists n \neg small(n)$$
$$\forall n(small(n) \rightarrow small(n+1))$$
$$\exists n(small(n) \land \neg small(n)) \ .$$

Clearly the paradox is generated in the last premiss which allows for the generation of small numbers that get larger and larger, thereby reaching the number which is supposed not to be small[11] and collapsing into inconsistency. The conclusion follows from the premisses because, taken together, they are inconsistent. And from an inconsistency anything follows.

The fail operator leads to an elegant solution of this problem. One of its merits is that it allows us to do a "pre-check" on the consistency of a set of concessions/premisses. If we build this pre-check into the last premiss we can prevent the paradoxical inference:

$$small(1)$$
$$\exists n \neg small(n)$$
$$\forall n(small(n) \rightarrow (\mathbf{F} \neg small(n+1) \rightarrow small(n+1)))$$
$$(*) \ \exists n(small(n) \land \neg small(n)) \ .$$

Now the contradiction is no longer provable. For no number larger than 1, that satisfies the second premiss by being not small, can one prove that it is small as well, using the last premiss, *because one cannot succeed in proving that the number is not not small:* the number was chosen as an instantiation for the second premiss in the first place *because* it is not small.

Interpreted as a concession in a dialogue game, the last premiss can be read as: "For all n, if I, the Opponent, have already conceded that n is small, then I will also concede that $n+1$ is small, as long as (of course) it has not been established that $n + 1$ is not small". At any rate, the paradox fits more closely in the garb of dialogue logics then in the garb of axiomatic systems. Imagine a sophist (Proponent of the absurd thesis), who lures the innocent debater (Opponent) into conceding sentences:

  – "Do you admit that 1 is a small number?"
  – "Yes, I grant you that."
  – "Do you admit that there exist numbers
    that are not small?"
  – "Yes, I agree with that as well."
  – "Do you admit then that if some number is
    considered to be small, the direct successor of
    that number is also small?"
  – "Yes, I suppose that that is correct."
  – ...

Thus a set of seeming concessions is established, from which the sophist sets out to show absurdity. The opponent is not given the opportunity to amend his

---

[11] That such a number exists is guaranteed by the second premiss.

last concession by making a provision like "unless, of course, this successor is not already agreed to be not small" — which everybody tacitly understands.

Notice, that this way of looking at the paradox is independent of the vagueness of the adjective "small". The vagueness of the adjective rests in the fact, that there is no fixed criterium to distinguish sharply between the small and the not-small. The point of the paradox is to force a partner in a discussion to introduce such a sharp distinction in a step-by-step way. And the point of the solution is, that under a reasonable interpretation of the function of a conceded conditional this partner is not thereby forced to contradict herself.

It is even possible to give a range of vagueness in the definition of small number by widening the pre-check, e.g.

$$\forall n(small(n) \rightarrow (\mathbf{F}(\neg small(n+1) \vee \ldots \vee \neg small(n+k)) \rightarrow small(n+1))) \ .$$

In this way there will always be a range of k numbers between the provably small numbers and the numbers that are provably not small, of which one can neither prove that they are small nor that they are not. One can also extend the example by adding a definition of large number in an analogous way and make the connection between both definitions in an obvious way. Starting from definitely small on the one end and definitely large on the other end, there are several distinct results in which numbers can be called small or large or "neither small nor large" depending on the exact applications of the recursive part of the definitions, i.e. it depends on how a proponent would go about attacking these concessions.

Looking at it in a somewhat different way, the solution to the paradox of the small number rests on a modification of the function of the conditional in concessions. In conceding a conditional, you indicate that you are prepared to admit the consequent, given that you have already conceded the antecedent. But as a human being with limited resources, not being able to oversee all effects of such a concession, you make a proviso; namely, that the counterpart of the consequent has not been (or will not be) established.

This treatment of conceded conditionals seems to be applicable beyond the paradox of the small number. We will therefore introduce a connective "$\gg$" (called provisional implication), which will function as a new conditional with the above-mentioned pre-check behaviour.

3.1 Indicative Conditionals

It is our contention that there is a difference in the way people use "if...then..." sentences that corresponds to the distinction made in dialogue logical theory between putting a sentence forward as a (possible) thesis and stating it as a concession. This distinction originates from the fundamental asymmetry of the roles of Proponent and Opponent. In normal life we do not normally encounter such clear-cut asymmetric discussions, because, at different times during such discussion, both parties have some opinions to which they strongly oppose or that they want to defend. This asymmetrical idealization in dialogue logical theory however, has proved to be fruitful in the past, and we will show how it can bring some new insights in the semantics of conditionals.

As already indicated above, we will use the symbol $\gg$ as connective for indicative "if... then..." sentences. We propose that the "meaning in use" of an indicative conditional statement, as stated by an Opponent, can be defined thus:[12]

$$\phi \gg \psi \quad =_{\mathrm{def}} \quad \phi \to (\mathbf{F}\neg\psi \to \psi) .$$

This is the same interpretation as the one we have already presented in Sect. 3 for the paradox of the small number. The Opponent concedes that ψ will be the case if ϕ is *unless, of course, ...* Given this non-monotonic interpretation of indicative conditionals some standard properties of inferences do not hold *as a general rule* any more: antecedent strengthening, transitivity, contraposition. They hold per default, but can be "overruled" by the actual context of the inference. For example, if I concede that putting sugar in my coffee does not negatively affect its suitability for human consumption, then I might (per default) also be willing to accept that putting sugar and milk in my coffee does not negatively affect it either. However, since I know, or concede, that consumption of mineral oil is not healthy for humans, I cannot really be expected to accept that putting sugar and oil in my coffee does not negatively affect its suitability for human consumption.

Still, this definition for the conditional on the Opponent side does not account for another feature present in the use of natural language conditionals. We will call it the 'relevance of the most specific conditional'. Suppose an Opponent has stated following conditionals:

- 'if α then ω.'
- 'if α and β then $\neg\omega$.'
- 'if α and β and γ then ω.'
- 'if α and β and γ and δ then $\neg\omega$.'
- ....

If in a dialogue the Opponent has also stated that α and β and γ *are* the case, then the first and second conditional are not relevant for the discussion about ω anymore. Especially the second conditional is not allowed to be used to argue against ω to be the case, because somehow the third conditional whose antecedent is satisfied by the conjunction of α, β and *gamma*, 'subsumes' the second conditional. The third conditional is in the context of the present dialogue 'more specific' than the second.

The present dialogue systems do not account for this 'relevance of the most specific conditional'. Given the above dialogue in which apart from the conditionals all of α and β and γ have been conceded, the second and third conditional would cancel each other out. A Proponent would neither be able to prove ω nor $\neg\omega$[13]. To implement the 'relevance of the most specific conditional' into

---

[12] It is straightforward to provide a direct striprule for the connective on the Opponent side.

[13] We call such a database hermetic with respect to ω.

our dialogues we propose to add an extra condition to discussions on a conditional: if there is another conditional in the concessions, that has a consequent that is the negation of the consequent of the conditional under discussion, and if the antecedents of both conditionals are provable, then the first conditional under discussion is used legally only if its antecedent does not follow from the antecedent of the second conditional.

This condition forbids the use of the second conditional in our above example as a counterproof for ω because (α and β) follows from (α and β and γ). In Sect. 4.3 we will present a quantificational example of this condition.

We now turn to the indicative conditional on the Proponent side. The same definition of "$\gg$" on the Proponent side would not do. The party playing the Proponent role would be able to win $\phi \gg \psi$ from any Opponent player that merely has stated $\neg\psi$! We believe that "if...then..." here needs to have a strong sense of consequence. In practice this means that there are at least two conditions of relevance that have to be met for accepting that a Proponent has won a thesis $\phi \gg \psi$. The first is that the antecedent has to be consistent with what the Opponent has already conceded. One cannot really say that ψ is a consequence of ϕ, if adding ϕ to the stock of concessions makes them inconsistent, because from this anything follows. The second condition is that ϕ has to be a necessary addition to the stock of concessions; without it one would not have a winning strategy for ψ. These conditions are met by the following definition of $\gg$ on the Proponent side:

$$\phi \gg \psi \quad =_{\text{def}} \quad \mathbf{F}\neg\phi \land \mathbf{F}\psi \land (\phi \to \psi) \ .^{14}$$

The first conjunct provides the Opponent with the opportunity to check the consistency of ϕ relative to the concessions. If one cannot prove $\neg\phi$ from them then obviously ϕ can be added consistently. The second conjunct gives him the opportunity to check whether it is possible to infer ψ from the concessions without the use of ϕ. If both are satisfied, then the conditional can further be treated as a material implication.

Given such an interpretation one can successfully object with "does not follow" to, for example, the thesis "if $2 + 2 \neq 4$ then it will rain tomorrow". Or to the thesis "if it will rain tomorrow then $2 + 2 = 4$".

Our system also provides an explanation of the fact that conditional theses cannot always be upheld under expanding knowledge (expansion of the set of concessions). I.e. it is able to support cases of non-monotonic reasoning. As an example of this, consider the following scenario[15].

Imagine you are walking along a long beach. It is a beautiful night. Still you feel somewhat uncomfortable. You are hungry. But you know that at the end of the beach there are two restaurants, one of them run by Annie, the other by Ben. Now, you are still far away from the restaurants but you happen to perceive a shimmering light coming from that direction. So you believe that

---

[14] The connective "$\to$" is to be interpreted as material implication here, as in the rest of the article.

[15] This example is from Hans Rott in his [Ro89].

either Annie's or Ben's restaurant is open. And consequently, you are willing to accept the conditional "If Annie's restaurant is not open, then Ben's restaurant is open". Approaching the promising end of the beach, you realize that it is Annie's restaurant that has its lights shining brightly. Ben's restaurant is dark. You just learned something new, nothing at all causes any contradiction. Nevertheless, you lose the conditional. You no longer believe that if Annie's restaurant is not open then Bill's is.

Our formal representation of these two knowledge states is as follows:

state t_0: $open(Annie) \lor open(Ben)$
state t_n: $open(Annie) \lor open(Ben), open(Annie), \neg open(Ben)$

Now, from state t_0 one can infer $\neg open(Annie) \gg open(Ben)$, but not so any more from state t_n. In the last state the first conjunct of our definition of "$\gg$" is not provable any more: because we have $open(Annie)$ in the last state, of course $\neg\neg open(Annie)$ is provable, but, because of this, not so $\mathbf{F}\neg\neg open(Annie)$.

Indeed, people are no longer prepared to accept the indicative conditional "if Annie's is not open then Ben's is" given state t_n. But they are willing to accept the *subjunctive* conditional "If Annie's had not been open then Ben's would have". This sentence is a so-called counterfactual. So not surprisingly, there is a difference between indicative and subjunctive conditionals. We therefore need a different analysis for counterfactual conditionals which we will present in Sect. 3.2.

It is interesting to note that there are some close connections between our analysis of indicative conditionals and so-called relevance logics. Famous is the work of Anderson and Belnap presented in their [AB72]. Our "$\gg$" can be shown to be equivalent, minus uniform substitution, to the relevant implication in Anderson and Belnap's system $\mathbf{R}^{\rightarrow}$ — the implicational fragment of relevance logic. Another researcher in the field of relevance logics, Richard M. Diaz, has argued that it is, amongst others, unifor substitution that disqualifies $\mathbf{R}^{\rightarrow}$ and the full fragment R as systems that implement the natural intuitions about relevance. In his [Di81] Diaz presents a new calculus, $\mathbf{OR}$, in which uniform substitution is not valid. It seems that our dialogue system with "$\gg$" is equivalent to his system.

3.2 Counterfactuals

We now turn to the treatment of sentences of the form: "If it were the case that A, then it would be the case that C". These sentences are usually called counterfactuals because the antecedent is pretended not to have the truth value it "really" has. In [Ti84] one can find an overview of some of the most prominent theories on counterfactuals. What Tichý shows is that none of the theories discussed — those of Goodman, Chisholm, Lewis, Pollock, Blue and Kratzer[16] — is successful on all members of a set of mostly very plausible test cases. Tichý remarks:

---

[16] [Go47], [Ch55], [Le73], [Po81], [Bl81], [Kz81].

If world similarity or world-partitioning are what the truth-value of a subjunctive conditional turns upon, how is it that disputes about conditional statements are never settled by reference to such matters? ... Those who think the conditional is true will typically invoke some facts ... and physical laws (or what they believe to be such). ... Their opponents, on their part, are likely to try and cast doubt on the alleged facts, or on the alleged laws, or on their adversaries logic... [17]

Unfortunately, not much of this insight, that counterfactuals should be studied in connection with their roles in disputes, can be found in the proposal which is put forward by Tichý himself. A main obstacle in this respect is the effort to deal with counterfactuals in terms of truth and falsehood, instead of in terms of what can be defended and what must be admitted given a set of overtly stated concessions in a dispute.

Now, what kind of discussional behaviour do people who make counterfactual statements have to satisfy? As in the case of the indicative conditionals, one has to distinguish in the answer to this question between the roles those people take up in such a discussion.

If the speaker is an Opponent and the counterfactual statement therefore a concession, we think that such a statement only is to signal that the speaker is prepared to concede the corresponding indicative conditional in such dialogues where the antecedent of the counterfactual is supposed to be really the case. The subjunctive mood of the conditional merely indicates that the speaker has not (yet) conceded the antecedent. Our proposal therefore is to treat counterfactual statements on the Opponent side in the same way as indicative conditionals are treated.

It is only when counterfactuals are put forward as theses by a Proponent that their treatment really has to differ from those of indicative conditionals, as the following is intended to show. One thing which simply is "not done" when discussing a counterfactual is the following: Suppose you forward the thesis "if kangaroos had no tails, they would topple over" for discussion to somebody who has already admitted that kangaroos do have tails[18]. Suppose that your adversary accepts the invitation to discuss and takes the antecedent of the counterfactual as a temporary additional concession. Then it would be completely out of order for you to claim to have won the discussion on the ground that your adversary has contradicted himself because he has now stated both the antecedent and its negation.

This phenomenon shows similarity to the treatment of negation in so-called minimal calculus, a logic that is even weaker than intuitionistic logic. The difference between these logics lies in the treatment of negation. This is most easily explained in dialogue logic by defining negation as material implication of some absurd statement[19]. Now the difference between minimal and intuitionistic dialogues consists in the absence of the "absurdum dixisti" rule in minimal

---

[17] [Ti84], p. 164.

[18] This, of course, is David Lewis' famous example from [Le73]

[19] We will use the sign $\perp$ for absurd

dialogues. In dialogues for intuitionistic logic (and also for classical logic) this rule allows the proponent to state "*absurdum dixisti!*" in case the opponent has stated the absurd $\perp$. This closes the discussion with the proponent being the winner. So minimal logic permits contradictions *without becoming necessarily inconsistent*!

Not surprisingly however, as the following examples show, counterfactuals cannot simply be treated as implication in minimal calculus. Let the concessions be: "Jones is alive" (ϕ) and "Jones has stepped on the brake" (ψ), and nothing more — in particular there is no concession that relates the two propositions to each other[20]. We would not like the counterfactual "If Jones had not stepped on the brake, then Jones would not be alive" to be winnable under these circumstances. But it is, if the counterfactual conditional would simply be interpreted as minimal implication, because of the validity in minimal calculus of: $\phi, \psi \vdash_{min} \neg\psi \rightarrow \neg\phi$.

To take another case: Suppose you have a dog (Dg), it is healthy (Hl) and you step on its tail (Stp). You concede all this. You also concede that the dog yelps (Ylp). Moreover, you concede that if one steps on the tail of this healthy dog, then, provided there are no contrary reasons, it yelps $(Dg \wedge Hl \wedge Stp \gg Ylp)$[21]. Under these circumstances, the counterfactual "If you had not stepped on the tail of the dog, it would have yelped" should be winnable. After all, it has been conceded that the dog, for whatever reasons, yelps. The reason may be the stepping on its tail, and the concessions speak for it. But there may be other reasons, and nothing in the concessions precludes it. As long as the Opponent[22] has not given any reason to the effect that stepping on its tail is the only reason for the dog's yelping, the proponent should win[23]. However, even if we were to add a concession to the effect that stepping on the tail of the dog is — other things being equal — the only reason for its yelping, the Opponent would still lose, if we were to treat the counterfactual as minimal implication. In fact, in minimal calculus we have the validity of $\Gamma, \psi \vdash_{min} \phi \rightarrow \psi$. If an opponent has already stated ψ he will always immediately lose the discussion, and no adding of reasons can help him to prevent this.

On the other hand, if you concede that you have a dog (Dg), that it is healthy (Hl), that you definitely do not step on its tail ($\neg Stp$) and that, in the absence of contrary reasons, healthy dogs with stepped-on tails do yelp $(Dg \wedge Hl \wedge Stp \gg Ylp)$, the counterfactual "If you had stepped on the tail of the dog it would yelp" should be winnable.

So we should look for ways to carry on dialogues on counterfactuals that give an opponent a better chance to defend himself, e.g. by giving him an opportunity

---

[20] This and other examples have been adapted from [Ti84]

[21] This is the indicative conditional explained in Sect. 3.1.

[22] In this context "Opponent" should be interpreted as "the party that plays the role of Opponent". The same holds for "Proponent".

[23] The example has again been taken from [Ti84], p. 153, "The inverse Bowser test". Tichý's opinion on this case is, that it should not hold. To us it seems that he has forgotten to take into account the hidden premiss we describe in the text, namely that stepping on the dog's tail provisionally is the only reason for its yelping.

to make use of the reasons he has given for the presence or absence of certain concessions. In our first dog example, the proponent playing party can choose to ignore such reasons and will win, simply because Ylp "is there". However, if we change roles, things will be different. If the former Opponent now plays the Proponent part, it has the opportunity of bringing into play its reasons for Ylp being there, by attacking the further relevant concessions.

Changing of roles can be induced by the fail operator, as we have presented in Sect. 2. It should be clear, however, that discussing a counterfactual statement of the form "If ϕ were the case, then ψ would be the case" after *one* change of roles will not lead to the desired result. Therefore, after having given the original Opponent the opportunity to make use of his own concessions (by putting them into play as temporary Proponent), we should return to the order of roles as it was before the checking dialogue took place. In order to achieve this, we will place another F-operator in front of the consequent of the counterfactual, and obtain formulae of the form $F(\phi \rightarrow F\psi)$ as a definition for counterfactuals on the Proponent side.

What we have now are formulae which, intuitively, say : "You (the Opponent) will fail in showing that ψ fails, after ϕ has provisionally been added to the concessions". As it turns out, playing the checking game on the consequent under the rules for negation of minimal calculus still leads to undesirable results. This happens when the consequent of the counterfactual is a negated formula as in the example of the Brake above. This means that, concerning negation in counterfactuals, we must look for rules which are even stricter than those of minimal calculus.

It is common practice to translate negation as implication of some absurdum. In doing so, we in fact consider negation as a function taking formulae to formulae. By accepting the definition we implicitly accept:

MAN. $\qquad (\phi \rightarrow \neg\phi) \rightarrow \neg\phi$.

In [Va89] Valerius, who calls it the "meaning axiom for negation", considers MAN to be the minimal requirement that can be posed upon any logic possessing an operator, $\neg$, which deserves to be called "negation". The family of logics that satisfy the axioms of negationless intuitionistic logic and, as for negation, solely possess the axiom MAN are called "Most Minimal Calculus" (MM) by Valerius; "Most Minimal" because they can be shown to be weaker than minimal calculus (M). In fact, it is easy to show that MM + EXTN = M, where

EXTN. $\qquad (\phi \leftrightarrow \psi) \leftrightarrow (\neg\phi \leftrightarrow \neg\psi)$

is the axiom for the extensionality of negation. In addition, it can be shown that accepting EXTN in addition to MAN is equivalent to accepting just one absurdum. In other words, we define negation as a many to one function: we pair each formula ϕ with a counterpart $\perp(\phi)$, and state that $\perp(\phi) = \perp(\psi)$ for any ϕ and ψ[24].

---

[24] These results can be found in [Va89].

In this sense, Minimal Calculus actually is a strong logic, since there is no a priori need to assume that there should be just one absurd statement. On the contrary, in practical argumentation — as the case of counterfactuals shows — there may be very good reasons to consider several non-equivalent absurd statements. For example, in daily practice it often happens that two consistent sets of data , data1 and data2, are put together. Their union may be inconsistent in the classical sense. But taking into account that data1 and data2 may be related to different theoretical and/or conceptual backgrounds, it may be rational to introduce two absurdi, $\perp 1$ and $\perp 2$, in order to get reliable answers from the union.

As it turns out, playing the checking dialogues connected with counterfactual theses in most minimal calculus gives the results we would intuitively like to have, at least for the set of examples of [Ti84], i.e. we could interpret "If ϕ, then would ψ" as $F(\phi \rightarrow F\psi)$ and get results we find appealing.

However, it also appears that the difference between minimal calculus rules and classical rules other than those for negation seems to play no role in our discussions about counterfactuals, at least not for Tichý's examples. Therefore, in our practical implementation we took the rules of what we call "classical logic with interpreted negation" (KIN), for which we now briefly present the dialogue logical rules:

1. attack and defense rules for all connectives other than negation, but including the fail operator, are those of classical logic;
2. the usual definition of a "literal" is extended in the following way:
   (a) any atomic formula α is a literal;
   (b) if L is a literal, then $\neg L$ is a literal;
3. the attack and defense rules for negated formulae that are not literals are those of classical logic;
4. a negated literal in the concessions can only be attacked by the Proponent, if the Proponent itself has stated the same literal and this literal was attacked by the Opponent;
5. all further rules are those for classical logic.

In the following we will use the connective "$=\gg$" to indicate the counter-facual. If we attach a subscript to the fail-operators, indicating the use of KIN logic in the checking dialogue, then we can present our final dialogue logical analysis of counterfactuals thus:

- definition for the Opponent side:

$$\phi =\gg \psi \quad =_{\text{def}} \quad \phi \rightarrow (F\neg\psi \rightarrow \psi) \; ;$$

- definition for the Proponent side:

$$\phi =\gg \psi \quad =_{\text{def}} \quad F_{kin}(\phi \rightarrow F_{kin}\psi) \; .$$

We stress the fact that there is no deep principle involved in the choice of KIN as opposed to MM — at least not that we are aware of. Rather, these rules fit best into our PROLOG implementation, that we will describe in Sect. 4. Moreover, they seem to work well for the sample test cases in [Ti84]. Among these are such well-known examples as Nelson Goodman's wet match and Kit Fine's holocaust example. Also the so-called Nixon Diamond and Double Nixon Diamond examples behave well in our thus defined dialogue logic.

4 A PROLOG Subsystem

In this part of the paper we will present an actual implementation of the theoretical work presented in the previous sections. It concerns a PROLOG metainterpreter for dialogue logic. For reasons of efficiency this implementation only covers part of the fully-fledged dialogue logical system. We start in Sect. 4.1 with a definition of the language the meta-interpreter can deal with. In Sect. 4.2 the architecture of the meta-interpreter is sketched. Finally, in Sect. 4.3 the reader can find some examples that the system deals with satisfactorily.

4.1 Definition of the Language

As in standard PROLOG, one can distinguish between the syntax of data in the database and the syntax of queries. As for the syntax of data, the program accepts *facts* and *rules*. They are defined by the following Backus-Naur definitions.

fact	::	atomic-statement.	neg(atomic-statement).
rule	::	*monotonic-rule*	*provisional-rule*
monotonic-rule	::	head <- body	
provisional-rule	::	head << body	
head	::	atomic-statement	neg(atomic-statement)
body	::	*fact*	*head*, *body*	*head*; *body*

There are a few remarks to be made concerning these definitions. Firstly, we did not yet say what we mean by atomic statement. We have opted for the standard PROLOG definition of atomic statement, thereby obtaining a language with quantification. The interpretation and scoping of quantifiers in our language follows the same conventions as those of standard PROLOG.

Secondly, the above definitions allow for standard PROLOG data. It is straighthforward to see that PROLOG facts are also facts in our language, and that PROLOG rules can be identified with the so-called *monotonic* rules. Moreover, these definitions extend the definition of standard PROLOG data. Apart from positive facts and positive heads of rules do we allow for negative ones as well. The atomic negation, 'neg()', is to be interpreted by the meta-interpreter as proper (intuitionistic) negation. Furthermore, we introduced *provisional* rules. The provisional rule *fact << body* is to be interpreted as the meta-interpreter variant of *body ≫ fact*, the provisional implication used in previous sections.

The following rules define the syntax of queries.

query   ::   *body* | *counterfactual*
counterfactual   ::   *restr-body* =>> *body*
restr-body   ::   *head* | *head, restr-body*

The syntax of queries is also defined in such a way as to extend standard PROLOG queries. In this language there is the possibility to ask counterfactual queries. For efficiency reasons the antecedent of a counterfactual is only allowed to be a conjunction of atomic statements or their negations.

4.2 Architecture of the Meta-Interpreter

The implementation of the meta-interpreter makes use of several tables. These tables are stored in the present implementation in so-called PROLOG internal databases. Upon reading an input file the data that have to be interpreted are stored in six tables:

literal/pos   contains the positive atomic facts;
literal/neg   contains the negative atomic facts (neg(_).);
if/pos   contains the monotonic rules with positive heads;
if/neg   contains the monotonic rules with negative heads;
provif/pos   contains the non-monotonic rules with positive heads;
provif/neg   contains the non-monotonic rules with negative heads.

If, for example, a file to be loaded into the meta-interpreter contains the following code:

```
small_number(1).
neg(small_number(10)).
small_number( X) << Y is X - 1, small_number(Y).
```

then following tables will be updated with the following entries:

```
literal/pos:
    small_number(1)
```

```
literal/neg:
    small_number(10)
```

```
provif/pos:
    small_number(X),( Y is X - 1, small_number(Y) )
```

Entries in literal/pos and literal/neg only have one element, whereas the if- and provif-tables always have two elements, corresponding to head and body of the corresponding monotonic and provisional clauses.

The user can make use of PROLOG built-in predicates and operators in his code, as the above example shows (use of the built-ins 'is' and '-'). Built-ins are not meta-interpreted but given for immediate execution to the standard PROLOG interpreter. The user can declare any predicate written by herself to be a built-in, thereby circumventing meta-interpretation. For this she has to add the clause is_builtin(*pred*, *n*). to the database, where *pred* is the name of the predicate and *n* the number of arguments it has.

The meta-interpreter is called by the predicates success/1 and success/2. The argument of success/1 has to be a query. The result is **yes** if the call was successful. If the query contained any variables their instantiation is given. If the call to success was not successful the result is **no**.

In success/2 the first argument has to be a query. The second argument has to be a list. In the list the user can put additional *facts* that can be used in the proof of the query — in addition to the data stored in the database. The meta-interpreter behaves as if these additional facts were actually present in the database. The result of success/2 is the same as that of success/1. Both predicates can backtrack through all solutions.

To prove complex queries (queries not consisting of a single fact) the meta-interpreter follows the same strategy as the PROLOG-interpreter. To prove 'a, b.' it has to prove both 'a' and 'b'. To prove 'a; b.' it has to prove either 'a' or 'b'[25]. Eventually we reach simple goals (atomic statements and their negations) and counterfactual goals.

To satisfy a simple goal the meta-interpreter has the following strategy. It first determines whether the goal is declared to be a built-in. If so, the goal is handed over directly to the standard PROLOG interpreter. Meta-interpretation continues as soon as the control is back. If the goal is not a built-in, the meta-interpreter searches through the six tables in a PROLOG-like head-matching search. It first determines whether it has to match a positive or negative head. Then it searches for the first matching clause through the corresponding tables in the following order: facts, monotonic rules, non-monotonic rules.

The strategy followed after a successful match with facts and monotonic rules is standard. The meta-interpreter behaves basically the same as the PROLOG interpreter. If a simple goal matches with the head of a non-monotonic rule, then the meta-interpreter has to prove two separate subgoals. First, it has to prove that the dual of the simple goal is *not provable*. Second, it has to prove that the body of the matched clause is provable. The bare bones PROLOG code for this meta-interpreter strategy is as follows[26].

```
satisfy( Polarity, Atomic, Logic) :-
    find_match( provif, Polarity, Atomic, NewSubGoals),
    negation( Logic, Polarity, NegPolarity),
    not satisfy( NegPolarity, Atomic, Logic),
    prove_complex( NewSubGoals, Logic).
```

---

[25] Notice that this last strategy makes that the meta-interpreter, like the PROLOG interpreter, is non-classical in inferential strength. We rather obtain intuitionistic logic.

[26] The actual code is, of course, much more complex, to account for, amongst others, information needed for loop-checking and keeping track of counterfactual sub-proofs.

```
negation( _, pos, neg).
negation( intuitionistic, neg, pos).
negation( interpreted_neg, neg, neg(neg)).
```

The arguments Polarity and Atomic together make up the simple goal to be satisfied. The argument Logic can be either the atom intuitionistic or interpreted_neg, indicating which logical strategies the meta-interpreter is allowed to follow. The latter atom indicates an intuitionistic system with interpreted negation in the sense of Sect. 3.2[27]. The predicate find_match defines the actual table look-up.

The predicate negation decides what the negation of the simple goal looks like. This is different for intuitionistic negation and interpreted negation, as discussed in Sect. 3.2. Because $\phi \rightarrow \neg\neg\psi$ is an intuitionistic tautology, we have proved the double negation of a formula if we succeed in proving the formula itself[28]. The same does not hold for interpreted negation.

The predicate prove_complex is the actual meta-interpreter top-level call. It is called by the success-predicates after they have done some administrative work.

The important thing to notice in this code is the use of the PROLOG-operator not. Since a << b is intended to implement the logical statement '$a \gg b$', that can be paraphrased here as '$a \wedge \mathbf{F}\neg b \rightarrow b$', there seems to be a very close correspondence between our failure operator on the Proponent side in dialogues and PROLOGs operator for finite failure. Both lead to a sub-proof procedure on their argument and invert the result. The important difference between both lies in the database usable for the sub-proof. In pure PROLOG this database is the original one from which the main query started. In the meta-interpreter that implements a dialogue system this is not the case. At least the provisional rule that gave rise to the sub-proof will not be usable anymore in all cases[29]. So the difference between lies in the overall structure of the proof-systems.

Contrary to the PROLOG interpreter the meta-interpreter performs loop-checking. A further feature is a consistency check; if required, the meta-interpreter performs additionally to the goal directed search a further search for such facts or heads that occur both positive and negative in the six tables. If it finds such a formula then it tries to prove both the atomic fact and its negation. If it is successful then we have obtained, of course, a proof by inconsistency. When the meta-interpreter is in 'intuitionistic mode' this inconsistency proof mechanism is used per default.

The treatment of counterfactual queries now turns out to be fairly simple. The antecedent of the counterfactual consists of facts that are treated by the

---

[27] But in this case we end up with IIN (Intuitionistic logic with Interpreted Negation) instead of KIN.

[28] And that is the only option open to us, because the definition of our language does not allow double negated facts or heads of rules.

[29] In the case of a fully ground rule this rule is not to be considered at all anymore in the sub-proof. In other cases the rule can only be used if the variable instantiation is not unifiable with a previous instantiation of the rule.

meta-interpreter as if they are part of the database. The meta-interpreter now has to prove the consequent in 'interpreted negation mode'. There are two differences between this mode and the intuitionistic one: the result of the **negation** predicate is different in the case of negation and the inconsistency proof mechanism cannot be used. This makes the interpreted negation proof weaker than the intuitionistic proof, in fact weak enough to use it for counterfactual proofs in a way as discussed in Sect. 3.2.

4.3 Some Examples

In this section we list some examples run by the program. Every example starts with a printout of the relevant data in the database. Then follow the queries and their answers.

```
% EXAMPLE 1

small_number(1).
neg(small_number(10)).
small_number( X) << Y is X - 1, small_number(Y).

?- success(small_number(5)).
        yes
?- success(small_number(10)).
        no
?- success(small_number(15)).
        no
```

Example 1 is the PROLOG version of the paradox of the small number. Since PROLOG does not allow for existential quantification in facts[30] we took the number 10 as an instantiation of a non-small number (One could consider it as an appropriate skolem constant). The third clause says that every number that has a predecessor that is small can be provisionally considered to be small itself.

Given these three clauses the meta-interpreter can prove that 5 is a small number: `success(small_number(5)).` returns with **yes**. But it can prove neither that 10 is a small number nor any number larger than 10, for example 15. The meta-interpreter returns with no in those cases, indicating failure of the proof.

```
% EXAMPLE 2

sugar.
drink << sugar.
neg(drink) <- oil.
```

---

[30] All variables in facts and in the head of a rule are treated as universally quantified in PROLOG.

```
?- success( drink).
        yes
?- success( drink, [milk]).
        yes
?- success( drink, [oil]).
        no
?- success( neg(drink)).
        no
?- success( neg(drink), [milk]).
        no
?- success( neg(drink), [oil]).
        yes
```

Example 2 is an elaboration of Stalnaker's example on the drinkability of coffee. The first clause in the database states that one has put sugar in some cup of coffee. the second clause states that if one puts sugar in a cup of coffee then it 'normally' is (still) fit for consumption by humans. The last clause states that putting oil in coffee makes it definitively unfit for consumption by humans, hence the monotonic implication.

The first query amounts to asking whether the cup of coffee in question is fit for consumption by humans. The answer to this is affirmative. The second query is to be interpreted as follows: "We also put milk into the cup of coffee. Is it (still) fit for consumption?". The meta-interpreter's answer is affirmative. If we play the same game with putting oil in, however, the answer is negative, as it should be. The meta-interpreter cannot prove **drink** from the provisional rule because **neg(drink)** will *not* fail. The query whether the coffee will definitively be not drinkable if milk is added is not successful, but the same question with oil instead of milk of course is. The last follows directly from the monotonic rule together with the additional fact **oil**.

% EXAMPLE 3

```
married(X) << adult(X).
neg(married(X)) << student(X).
adult(X) <- student(X).
student(john).

?- success(married(john)).
        no
?- success(neg(married(john))).
        yes
```

Example 3 is a quantificational example of the 'relevance of the most specific conditional' discussed in Sect. 3.1. Student john can successfully be assumed to be unmarried. The fact that he is also an adult and therefore possibly married (the first clause in the database) cannot be used as a counterargument, because the fact that he is an adult follows from the fact that he is a student.

```
% EXAMPLE 4:   COUNTERFACTUAL

yelp << dog, healthy, step.
dog.
healthy.
neg(step).

?- success(step =>> yelp).
        yes

% to show that there is no inconsistency:
?- success(step =>> any_formula_you_like).
        no
```

Example 4 shows the treatment of counterfactuals. The database states that if one steps on the tail of a healthy dog it 'normally' yelps (first clause). Further it is stated that we have a healthy dog present, but we did definitely not step on its tail. The meta-interpreter provides an affirmative answer to the query 'if we had stepped on the tail of this dog it would have yelped'. The second query in the example shows that the meta-interpreter does not find a proof by inconsistency, although both step and neg(step) are assumed to be in the database.

```
% EXAMPLE 5:   THE DOUBLE NIXON DIAMOND

tt << aa.
pp << aa.
ss << tt.
neg(ss) << pp.
qq << pp.
rr << ss.
neg(rr) << qq.
aa.

?- success(tt).
        yes
?- success(pp).
        yes
?- success(ss).
        no
?- success(neg(ss)).
        no
?- success(qq).
        yes
?- success(rr).
        no
?- success(neg(rr)).
        no
```

```
?- success((neg(pp) =>> rr)).
        yes
?- success((neg(pp) =>> neg(rr))).
        no
?- success((neg(tt) =>> rr)).
        no
?- success((neg(tt) =>> neg(rr))).
        yes
```

The database in example 5 presents a logical description of the so-called double Nixon diamond, an example well-known in the community of non-monotonic logicians. As the queries show, the database is hermetic with respect to rr and ss: neither the positive formula nor its negation are provable, because in both cases there are provisional rules that cancel each other out in a legal way (The condition 'relevance of the most specific conditional' does not apply here). The counterfactual queries show that assuming either neg(pp) or neg(tt) changes this situation. rr is provable if we assume neg(pp), and its negation is provable if we assume neg(tt). This is exactly the behaviour one would expect.

```
% EXAMPLE 6: THE YALE SHOOTING PROBLEM

holds(alive,s0).
holds(loaded,SS) <- result(load,S,SS).
neg(holds(alive,SS)) <- result(shoot,S,SS), holds(loaded,S).
holds(F,SS) << result(E,S,SS), holds(F,S).


result(load,s0,s1).
result(wait,s1,s2).
result(shoot,s2,s3).


?- success(neg(holds(alive,s3))).
        yes
?- success((holds(alive,s3) =>> neg(holds(loaded,s2)))).
        no
```

We conclude our examples with another famous example from the non-monotonic literature, first presented in [HM86]. It describes the development of three successive states. In the first, s0, in which a gun is loaded, some person is alive. This loading of the gun brings us to the following state, s1, in which nothing happens but waiting. From there we get into a state, s2, in which the gun is aimed at the person and fired, which brings us to state s3. The connecting of states is achieved by the result statements. The two monotonic rules in the database state that as a result of loading a gun, that gun is loaded in the next state, and that the result of firing a loaded gun pointed to a person will definitely assure that this person will not be alive in the following state. The provisional rule is the statement of the so-called 'frame axiom'. It says that facts normally carry over from one state into the next one. Given this database one can predict that the person in the description will not be alive in state s3, which is as one would expect. The first query shows this. Now, the problem that is adressed in [HM86] is, that if we additionally assume that the person will still be alive at s3 most non-monotonic logics derive from the database plus this assumption that the gun was not loaded at s2. This does not seem to be intuitively correct, according to [HM86]. The second query in our example shows that our meta-interpreter does not come to this intuitively incorrect conclusion, but deals with it properly.

References

[AB72]   Anderson, A. R., Belnap, N. D.: *Entailment*, Vol. 1, Princeton, 1972.

[BK82]   Barth, E. M., Krabbe, E. C. W.: *From Axiom to Dialogue. A Philosophical Study of Logics and Argumentation*, Berlin, New York, 1982.

[Bl81]   Blue, N. A.: A Metalinguistic Interpretation of Counterfactual Conditionals, in: *Journal of Philosophical Logic* 10, 1981, pp. 179–200.

[Ch55]   Chisholm, R. M.: Law Statements and Counterfactua Inference, in: *Analysis* 15, 1955, pp. 97–105.

[Di81]   Diaz, R. M.: *Topics in the Logic of Relevance*, München, 1981.

[Fe85]   Felscher, W.: Dialogues as a Foundation for Intuitionistic Logic, in: Gabbay, D., Guenthner, F. (Eds.), *Handbook of Philosophical Logic, Vol. III*, Dordrecht, 1985.

[Go47]   Goodman, N.: The Problem of Counterfactual Conditionals, in: *Journal of Philosophy* 44, 1947, pp. 113–128.

[HM86]   Hanks, S., McDermott, D.: Default Reasoning, Nonmonotonic Logics and the Frame Problem, in: *Proceedings of the Fifth National Conference on Artificial Intelligence*, 1986, pp. 328–333.

[Ho86]   Hoepelman, J. Ph.: *Action, Comparison and Change. A Study in the Semantics of Verbs and Adjectives*, Tübingen, 1986.

[HH88]   Hoepelman, J. Ph., van Hoof, A. J. M.: The Success of Failure. The Concept of Failure in Dialogue Logics and its Relevance for Natural Language Semantics, in *Proceedings of COLING Budapest*, Budapest, 1988, pp. 250–255.

[HH91]   Hoepelman, J. Ph., van Hoof, A. J. M.: *Two-Role Two-Party Semantics: Knowledge Representation, Conditionals and Non-Monotonicity*, Oxford, to appear.

[Kr82]   Krabbe, E. C. W.: *Studies in Dialogical Logic*, dissertation, University of Groningen, 1982.

[Kr85]   Krabbe, E. C. W.: Noncumulative Dialectical Models and Formal Dialectics, in: *Journal of Philosophical Logic* 14, 1985, pp. 129–168.

[Kz81]   Kratzer, A.: Partition and Revision: the Semantics of Counterfactuals, in: *Journal of Philosophical Logic* 10, 1981, pp. 201–216.

[Le73]   Lewis, D.: *Counterfactuals*, Oxford, 1973.

[Po81]   Pollock, J. L.: A Refined Theory of Counterfactuals, in *Journal of Philosophical Logic* 10, 1981, pp. 239–266.

[Ro89]   Rott, H.: A Nonmonotonic Conditional Logic for Belief Revision. Part I: Semantics and Logic, in: *Proceedings of the Workshop on Nonmonotonic Reasoning 1989, GMD Arbeitspapier 443*, 1990, pp. 45–51.

[Ti84]   Tichý, P.: Subjunctive Conditionals: Two Parameters vs Three, in: *Philosophical Studies* 45, 1984, pp. 147–174.
[Va89]   Valerius, R.: The Logic of Frame– and Stoprules in Lorenzen Games, FhG-IAO Internal Paper, 1989.

Lecture Notes in Computer Science